FROM THE SECRET ARCHIVES OF THE
HITLER SS, THE COMPLETE STORY IS TOLD.

Heinz Höhne, the distinguished German journalist,
discloses the private files and documents of the Nazi
SS along with the confidential diaries of German ambassadors. With these secret papers never before
available and hundreds of personal interviews, Höhne
has fashioned a superbly detailed and documented
book that will long stand as the definitive work on
Hitler's SS.

THE ORDER OF
THE DEATH'S HEAD

Absorbing. Terrifying. And true.

"THE FASCINATION OF A NIGHTMARE."
Los Angeles Times

Also by Heinz Höhne
Published by Ballantine Books:

CODEWORD: DIREKTOR

THE ORDER
OF THE
DEATH'S HEAD

The Story of Hitler's S.S.

Heinz Höhne

Translated from the German by
Richard Barry

BALLANTINE BOOKS • NEW YORK

Library of Congress Catalog Card Number: 69-19032

ISBN 0-345-34504-5

This edition published by arrangement with
Coward, McCann & Geoghegan, Inc.

Manufactured in the United States of America

First Ballantine Books Edition: October 1971
Eighth Printing: October 1989

Cover photo: Courtesy of United Press International, Inc.

Contents

	AUTHOR'S ACKNOWLEDGMENTS	vii
	TRANSLATOR'S NOTE	viii
	CALENDAR OF EVENTS	ix-xiii
1	INTRODUCTION	1
2	THE FORMATION OF THE SS	16
3	HEINRICH HIMMLER	33
4	FROM BODYGUARD TO PARTY POLICE FORCE	58
5	SEIZURE OF POWER	87
6	THE RÖHM PUTSCH	106
7	THE ORDER OF THE SS	150
8	HEYDRICH AND THE GESTAPO	182
9	THE SD	221
10	THE RSHA	255
11	THE SS AND FOREIGN POLICY	293
12	RACIAL POLICY IN THE EAST	332
13	THE JEWISH QUESTION	367
14	THE "FINAL SOLUTION"	400
15	THE IMPOTENCE OF POWER	454
16	THE WAFFEN–SS	493
17	THE SS AND GERMAN RESISTANCE	546
18	THE END	610

Appendixes

1	*Notes*	659
2	*Glossary*	731
3	*Table of SS Ranks*	744
4	*Partition of Poland 1939–1942*	745
5	*The Fate of German Jewry*	746
6	*Einsatzgruppen in Occupied Russia*	747
7	*The Destruction of European Jewry*	748
8	*The Victims of the "Final Solution"*	749
9	*The Military Situation at the End of January 1945*	750
10	*Bibliography*	751
	INDEX	769

Author's Acknowledgments

I would like to take this opportunity of thanking all those persons and institutions without whose active assistance this book could not have been written. My thanks go: first to Herr Rudolf Augstein, the editor of *Der Spiegel*, whose patient criticism both facilitated and improved my work; secondly to Herr Hans Detlev Becker, the publication director of *Der Spiegel*, who initiated the SS Series, took immense interest and was always ready with advice. I equally feel under an obligation to all those men and women—former members, opponents and victims of the SS—who were prepared, time and again, to provide information; they are too numerous to be mentioned individually. They have contributed much to this book but they carry not the smallest responsibility for any errors or misinterpretations of which I may have been guilty.

Translator's Note

In most cases German technical terms, titles and ranks have been retained in this book. On the first occasion when such words appear, a literal translation is given in brackets. A glossary of German words regularly used in the book is at Appendix 2. A table of SS ranks with their approximate equivalents in the British and American Armies is at Appendix 3.

Calendar of Events

1889

    20 April   Birth of Adolf Hitler

1900

    7 October   Birth of Heinrich Himmler

1923

    9 November   Hitler "putsch" in Munich

1925

    February   Reconstitution of National-Socialist Party

    Summer   Formation of first SS units

1929

    6 January   Himmler becomes "Reichsführer-SS"

1930

    Late autumn   The SS in practice becomes independent of the SA

1931

    Autumn   SS Security Service set up under Reinhard Heydrich

31 December	SS "Race and Resettlement" Office set up under Walter Darré

1933

30 January	Hitler becomes Reich Chancellor
27 February	The Reichstag fire
28 February	The "Ordinance for the Protection of People and State" lays the foundation for National-Socialist dictatorship
9 March	Himmler becomes Police President of Munich
17 March	Formation of the "Leibstandarte Adolf Hitler" under Sepp Dietrich
20 March	Dachau Concentration Camp set up
1 April	Himmler becomes Commander of the Bavarian Political Police
26 April	Formation of the Gestapo, Berlin

1934

20 April	Himmler becomes Inspector of the Prussian Gestapo
22 April	Heydrich becomes Head of the Gestapo
9 June	The SD constituted sole political intelligence and counter-espionage service of the Nazi Party
30 June	The "Röhm putsch". Formation of armed SS units begins. All concentration camps placed under the SS
20 July	The SS formally constituted as a force independent of the SA
2 August	Death of Hindenburg. Hitler becomes Führer and Chancellor

of the Reich and Supreme Commander of the Wehrmacht

1935

16 March   Introduction of universal military service

1936

Early March   Formation of VOMI (Volksdeutsche Mittelstelle)

7 March   Reoccupation of the Rhineland

29 March   SS Guard formations renamed "SS Totenkopfverbände" and expanded to 3,500 men

17 June   Himmler nominated Reichsführer-SS and Chief of the German Police

1938

2 February   The Blomberg-Fritsch crisis

13 March   The Austrian Anschluss

28 September/
1 October   The Munich Agreement. Germany occupies the Sudetenland

9 November   Anti-Jewish pogrom ("Kristallnacht")

1939

15 March   Occupation of the "remainder of Czechoslovakia"; formation of the "Protectorate of Bohemia and Moravia"

22 May   The "Pact of Steel" between Germany and Italy

23 August   Non-Aggression Pact between Germany and the Soviet Union

1 September   Outbreak of war. SS "Verfügungstruppe" raised from 8,000 to 9,000, SS "Totenkopfver-

	bände" to 6,500. Security Police and SD "Einsatzgruppen" commence activity in Poland
22 September	Formation of the RSHA under Heydrich
October	Formation of the SS division "Das Reich" and of one SS "Totenkopf" division.
7 October	Himmler becomes "Reich Commissar for the strengthening of Germanism" (RKF)

1940

January	Introduction of the title "Waffen-SS"
9 April	Invasion of Denmark and Norway
10 May	Attack on Holland, Belgium and France
1 June	Strength of Waffen-SS 100,000 (raised to 150,000 by end of year)
27 September	Three-Power Pact between Germany, Italy and Japan

1941

22 June	German attack on Russia. Four "Einsatzgruppen" of the Security Police and SD move into the Soviet Union
Summer	Beginning of the "Final Solution of the Jewish question"
7/11 December	Japanese attack on Pearl Harbour. Hitler declares war on USA.
19 December	Hitler takes over as Commander-in-Chief of the Army
End year	Overall strength of SS troops 230,000

1942

1 February	Formation of SS Economic and Administrative "Hauptamt" (WVHA)
16 March	All concentration camps placed under the WVHA
6 June	Assassination of Heydrich
8 November	Anglo-American landing in North Africa

1943

31 January/ 1 February	Surrender of Stalingrad
13 May	End of the war in North Africa
25 August	Himmler becomes Minister of the Interior
8 September	Surrender of Italy
12 September	Rescue of Mussolini by Skorzeny

1944

6 June	D-Day
30 June	Overall strength of the Waffen-SS 594,000, "Allgemeine SS" 200,000, concentration camp guards 24,000
20 July	Bomb attack on Hitler
21 July	Himmler becomes C-in-C Replacement Army
25 August	Allies enter Paris
October	Peak of Waffen-SS manpower 910,000. Total of 38 SS divisions
16 December	Ardennes offensive

1945

2 February	Yalta Conference
30 April	Suicide of Hitler
23 May	Suicide of Himmler

1
Introduction

THEIR uniform was black and they were the terror of a nation. Their badge was the death's head and they swore eternal allegiance to the Führer. Their flash was the runic double-S and they murdered men in millions. Hardly an aspect of the nation's life seemed safe from their interference; they were in charge of the police and the secret service; they provided the sentries on the Reich Chancellery and the guards in the concentration camps; they manned the divisions which carried the death's-head symbol to Europe; they occupied key positions in agriculture, the health service, racial policy and scientific affairs; they crushed their way into traditional diplomatic festivities; they had their watchdogs among the ministerial bureaucrats.

They called themselves the "Schutzstaffel" [guard echelon SS] of the National-Socialist Party and in the words of SS-Hauptsturmführer [Captain] Dieter Wisliceny they considered themselves a "new form of religious sect with its own rites and customs."

No layman was allowed a glimpse of the inner working of this secret society; the Führer's SS was intended to be mysterious, sinister and incomprehensible to the ordinary citizen, like the Order of Jesuits which the SS officially abominated but actually imitated down to the smallest detail. The lords of this black-uniformed secret Order deliberately cultivated the fear evoked by their mere existence. SS-Obergruppenführer [General] Reinhard Heydrich, head of the Sicherheitspolizei [Security Police], boasted: "The Gestapo, the Kriminalpolizei [Criminal Police] and the security services are enveloped in the mysterious aura of the political detective story."[1] Heinrich Himmler, the Reichsführer-SS [Reich SS leader] and Grand Master of the Order said with some satisfaction: "I know that there are many in Germany who feel uncomfortable when they see this black tunic; we understand that and do not expect to be beloved by overmany people."[2] The German people sensed that the SS had enveloped the Reich in a fine-spun web, whose individual threads they could not see. The Germans merely heard the tramp of the black columns resounding on the cobbles of their towns and villages; they simply heard hundreds of thousands of masculine voices roar:

"SS marschiert, die Strasse frei!	Clear the streets, the SS marches
Die Sturmkolonnen stehen!	The storm-columns stand at the ready.
Sie werden aus der Tyrannei Den Weg zur Freiheit gehen.	They will take the road From tyranny to freedom.
Drum auf bereit zum letzten Stoss!	So we are ready to give our all
Wie's unsere Väter waren!	As did our fathers before us.
Der Tod sei unser Kampfgenoss!	Let death be our battle companion.
Wir sind die schwarzen Scharen.	We are the Black Band.[3]

Thousands upon thousands of unseen eyes seemed to watch every step taken by every German. The tentacles of the police octopus wrapped themselves round the community; any trace of anti-Nazi sentiment was duly noted by 45,000 officials and employees of the Gestapo distributed over 20 Leitstellen [regional offices] and 39 Stellen [sub-regional offices] fed by so-called "antennae" in a further 300 Leitstellen and 850 Frontier Police "Commissariats."[4] The security of the state was guarded by 64,000 men in the Sicherheitspolizei and 2,800,000 men in the Ordnungspolizei [regular police] headed by 30 HSSPF [Höhere SS- and Polizeiführer—senior SS and Police Commanders].[5] 40,000 guards terrorised hundreds of thousands of actual or supposed enemies of the regime in 20 concentration camps and 160 affiliated labour camps.[6] Alongside the Wehrmacht, and eyeing their military rivals,[7] stood 950,000 soldiers of the Waffen-SS [Armed SS] including 310,000 "racial Germans" and 200,-000 foreigners. A shadowy army of 100,000 SD [Sicherheitsdienst—the SS security service] informers kept a continuous check on the population's thinking.[8] Whatever the source—universities, businesses, farms or local authorities —every detail of any significance was sucked in and pumped to the Berlin central office.

But the outer world was never allowed to know anything of what went on inside the SS; nothing was allowed to emerge which might indicate the thinking within Heinrich Himmler's empire. Himmler took care to ensure that no member of his Order came in too close contact with laymen; SS leaders were not allowed to go to law with ordinary people lest the courts gain an insight into SS internal affairs;[9] the Reich Ministry of Economics was refused information on SS industrial concerns.[10] An order from Himmler to the concentration-camp guards, the Totenkopfverbände [Death's-Head formations—TV] laid down that: 1. No unit was to be located in its home area; a Pomeranian Sturm [SS unit equivalent to a company] would therefore never serve in Pomerania, for instance. 2. Units were to be moved every three months. 3. Individual men were never to be employed on street duties.[11] Even the most exalted dignitaries of the Third Reich did not know what went on in the SS; in 1945 Göring said: "I had no insight into the SS. No outsider knew anything of Himmler's organisation."[12]

Not until the collapse of the Third Reich was the curtain concealing the SS empire removed. Then the men who had commanded the SS over the years appeared in the dock at Nuremberg accused of instigating war and other almost inconceivable crimes.

The allied military courts set out in detail all that the SS safety curtain had so carefully concealed. From the statements of the witnesses and the documents brought in evidence by the prosecution emerged an apocalyptic picture of racial mania, the grisly story of the SS as the guillotine used by a gang of psychopaths obsessed with racial purity. The bill of horror showed: 4–5 million Jews murdered, 2,500,000 Poles liquidated, 520,000 gipsies eliminated, 473,000 Russian prisoners of war executed, 100,000 incurables gassed under the euthanasia pro-

gramme.[13] On 30 September 1946 the allied judges pronounced sentence on Himmler's SS, declaring it to be a
criminal organisation on the grounds that: "The SS was
used for purposes which were criminal, involving the persecution and extermination of the Jews, brutalities and
killings in concentration camps, excesses in the administration of occupied territories, the administration of the slave
labour programme and the maltreatment and murder of
prisoners of war."[14] As a result, the judgment continued,
suspicion of crime attached to all persons "who had been
officially accepted as members of the SS . . . who became or remained members of the organisation with
knowledge that it was being used for the commission of
acts declared criminal by Article 6 of the [London War
Crimes] Charter."[15]

By this judgement of the Nuremberg court the badge of
the SS became the sign of a criminal political organisation, a mark of Cain henceforth branded upon anyone who
had ever worn the black uniform. Once the breeding-
ground of a self-styled élite, the SS became the "army of
outlaws," in the self-pitying words of SS General Felix
Steiner.[16] Nevertheless the Allied judgement suffered
from a serious defect; it did not explain why more than a
million men had turned, collectively and almost overnight,
into mass murderers; it did not explain the source of the
power which enabled the SS to turn the racial fantasies of
the National-Socialist regime into dreadful fact.

Ex-members of the SS either could not or would not
explain the mystery. They evaded the issue, either pretending that they knew nothing about it, or off-loading
the responsibility upon others who were dead. In 1948
came a somewhat timid effort at self-criticism from ex-SS-
Untersturmführer [Lieutenant] Erich Kernmayr, alias
Kern, with his book *Der Grosse Rausch* (The Great
Frenzy);[17] but then West Germany, with its atmosphere
of rehabilitation, provided a kind of protective twilight
from which emerged a body of exculpatory literature
written by ex-SS-commanders who clearly believed that
memories are short. At Nuremberg, for instance, Oberstgruppenführer [Colonel-General] Hausser, the senior
Waffen-SS general, referred to Himmler as "completely
unmilitary" and could hardly ever remember having seen
him with troops;[18] SS-Sturmbannführer [Lieutenant-

Colonel] Brill described the Allgemeine SS [General SS] as "a voluntary organisation entirely distinct from the Waffen-SS";[19] SS men invariably stated that they had never been taught racial hatred."[20]

But then came the ex-inmates of the concentration camps, the survivors of the SS terror, and the explanation of the mystery which they gave to the German nation was this:

The SS was a monolithic organisation directed by the demoniac will of one man; it was composed of fanatical ideologists and unscrupulous power-hungry functionaries; the SS had gradually laid hands upon every position of power in the Third Reich, until finally it had constructed a "super-organised master and slave system, every part at all times controllable."[21] These are the words of Eugen Kogon, an ex-inmate of Buchenwald and now Professor of Politics at the Darmstadt Political High School, in his well-known book *Die SS Staat*; Kogon has an analytical mind and in his book he pictures the SS leaders as a homogeneous clique "pursuing a plan consistently step by step at any cost. Each partial step was sought with a degree of ruthlessness completely transcending ordinary concepts."[22] Kogon concluded that only by such methods could the "well-built structure of the SS State" have arisen "which permeated first the Nazi Party, next Germany and finally the whole of Europe."[23] In other words the concentration camps were a "scale model"[24] of the SS state and the SS the real rulers in Adolf Hitler's Germany.

Kogon thus produced a striking theory, apparently the first to give a comprehensible explanation of the SS phenomenon. In 1948 Otto Ohlendorf himself wrote in his death-cell: "We must take a man like Kogon seriously."[25] Kogon, to give him his due, did make certain small reservations and introduce some minor nuances, but others soon followed to paint an even blacker picture of SS omnipotence.

Gerald Reitlinger in *The Final Solution* described Himmler's empire as "a state within a state . . . the only thing with which it could be compared was the Russian NKVD";[26] Comer Clarke, Eichmann's biographer, saw the SS carrying "the shadow of the Nazi terror into nearly every home on the continent";[27] in the eyes of the French

writer Joseph Kessel, the whole of Europe lay under the
SS jackboot—"from the Arctic Ocean to the Mediterranean, from the Atlantic to the Volga and the Caucasus, all
were at his [Himmler's] mercy."[28]

The greater the power ascribed to the SS, the clearer
and more horrifying became the picture of the SS man
painted both by German and foreign writers. Rudolf
Pechel, editor of the *Deutsche Rundschau* and a former
inmate of Sachsenhausen, thought that "with their dull
cold-fish stare, betraying the absence of any spiritual life
within, the eyes were the SS mens' common denominator"
and he believed that he could spot an SD informer "simply
from the look in his eye."[29] Kogon described SS men as
"maladjusted and frustrated, men whom circumstances had
deprived of success, whose innate endowment was slight,
who often enough were total social failures."[30] The
lower-level Gestapo officials he called "a catch-all of down-
and-outs";[31] SD informers were "the worst scum collected
from the aristocracy and the bourgeoisie, the working
and white-collar classes."[32]

Having exhausted the stock of derogatory adjectives, the
supporters of the SS-state theory then turned to the
formulae of modern psychoanalysis. Elie Cohen, an ex-
inmate of Auschwitz, considered that "SS men (apart from
certain exceptions) consisted of normal individuals who,
because of their criminal super-ego, had become normal
criminals."[33] Another psychologist, Leo Alexander, regarded the SS as a completely ordinary collection of
gangsters, who collectively behaved exactly as criminal
cliques usually do: "If a member did anything which put
his loyalty to the organisation in a questionable light, he
was either liquidated—killed—or he had to undertake a
criminal act which definitely and irrevocably tied him to
the organisation. According to the age-old custom of criminal gangs, this act had to include murder."[34]

Meanwhile, however, other voices were raised to dispute
the theories of the Kogon school. In a sociological study
published in 1954, Karl O. Paetel questioned whether collectively the SS could be written down so far. He considered that the SS did not consist of a "single type of man;
there were criminals and idealists, blockheads and intellectuals."[35] In 1956 Dr Ermenhild Neusüss-Hunkel published
a book on the SS in which she stated that the difference in

function between the numerous branches of Himmler's organisation meant that "an unequivocal estimate of the character of the SS membership as a whole was not possible."[36] She calculated that no more than 15% of SS members had actively contributed to the National-Socialist system of tyranny: in 1944 there were 800,000 enrolled members of the SS,[37] of whom 39,415 were serving in the SS central offices, 26,000 in the so-called "police reinforcements," 19,294 in Sicherheitspolizei and SD units in occupied territory, less than 6,000 with the Sicherheits- and Ordnungspolizei in Germany and 2,000 as concentration-camp guards.[38]

At about this time the SS files were released by the Allies and study of these led to further alterations in the post-war picture of the SS. The first result was to throw doubt on Kogon's book; the files showed numerous inaccuracies in his dates, statistics and descriptions of personalities, when not based on his personal experiences in Buchenwald; moreover it had already become noticeable that each fresh edition of Kogon's book contained numerous amendments.

Remarkably enough the Germans practically ignored the new picture of the SS presented by the realist historians—and for good reason—the historians were threatening to destroy the alibi of a nation, the theory of SS omnipotence.

The Germans had been both horrified and relieved by the revelations of SS crimes—horrified because the reputation of their country would be besmirched for years to come in the eyes of the world, relieved because, at least for the older generation, the news of the terrifying power of the SS offered a tiny loophole for escape from a past with which they had not been able to come to terms. If, they said to themselves, the SS had really been so all-powerful, if it had really held the country in an unassailable iron grip, then for the ordinary citizen of the Third Reich criticism of the regime's policy or active opposition to the misdeeds of the Nazi state was simply tantamount to suicide.

Exposure of the SS crimes was no unwelcome development for many Germans; these horrors formed the great alibi, a nation's excuse to itself and to the world. Compared to the activities of Himmler's corps of thugs, the

failings of so many other Germans under the Third Reich
paled into insignificance. As early as 1946 Laternser, the
Defence Counsel for OKW [Oberkommando der Wehrmacht—Armed Forces Defence Staff] said in Nuremberg
that the SS commanders would have to die anyway and
therefore everything should be laid at their door—the
Wehrmacht [regular armed forces] escutcheon must remain clean.[39] When it later became known from American sources that Himmler himself had temporarily flirted
with the 20 July 1944 conspiracy to kill Hitler, Hans
Rothfels adjured his German fellow-historians not to attach
too much weight to this theory, saying that: "there is
in fact no chapter entitled 'Himmler' in the history of the
German underground movement."[40]

For the general run of German historians the subject
of the SS was taboo. The intellectual descendants of Ranke
and Treitschke carefully concealed their thoughts regarding the most horrifying organisation ever invented by
Germans—they wrote no book on the SS, no major work
on Himmler's Eastern policy, no study of the National-
Socialist police machine. The German historians left the
field wide open to their foreign colleagues, who began, with
varying degrees of sympathy, realism and intensity of research, to study the most recent period of German history
with the SS as the centrepiece. One or two standard works
were produced, such as Raul Hilberg's *The Destruction
of the European Jews*[41] and Alexander Dallin's *German
Rule in Russia*[42] (both authors were American); many
other books were translated and published by reputable
German firms but the majority of their authors lacked
adequate source material and so they contributed little to
the formation of a more factual picture of the SS.

The Frenchman Jacques Delarue, for instance, produced a *History of the Gestapo* without even having examined the most important source for his subject, the
files of Himmler's private office.[43] In his history of the
Gestapo the British journalist Edward Crankshaw seems
unable to distinguish between the duties of the Gestapo
and those of the Einsatzgruppen [Action Groups—SS
liquidation squads];[44] another Frenchman, Benoist-
Méchin, produced a 10-volume *History of the German
Army*, in which he passes over the whole Röhm affair with

a couple of Hitler speeches and some out-of-date newspaper quotations.[45] The result was, of course, fatal. The book simply confirmed what the Nazis had always been saying. When history is written with such levity, the experts are bound to discover mistakes.

The first serious work was that of Hannah Arendt, the German sociologist who emigrated to America. Her book *Eichmann in Jerusalem* published in 1963, was the first to produce a credible picture of an SS commander as a human being.[46] In the same year Enno Georg, in his book on the SS economic concerns, showed how diverse were the components which went to make up the SS.[47] Shortly thereafter, led by Hans Buchheim with his *SS und Polizei im NS-Staat* (SS and Police in the National Socialist State) the historians of the Institut für Zeitgeschichte (Institute for Contemporary History), Munich, attacked the problem and produced *Anatomy of the SS State*[48] as a "counterweight to the widespread habit of painting a highly emotionalised picture of the past in order to highlight certain major truths but at the price of historical exactitude regarding facts and circumstances"—as their foreword puts it.[49] From America came the first real history of the Waffen-SS written by George H. Stein.[50] Stein summarises the matter: "The doctrine of criminal conspiracy and collective guilt formulated during the Nuremberg era no longer satisfies serious investigators. Without minimising the extent of the staggering crimes committed by Himmler's minions, recent research has shown that the SS was in fact more varied and complex than the monolithic criminal organisation indicted before the International Military Tribunal."[51]

Nevertheless the investigators are still only in the early stages. Many are still unable to put their false picture of the SS State entirely out of their mind; many still believe with Karl Paetel that at any rate in the final phases of the Third Reich "only two men mattered—Adolf Hitler and Heinrich Himmler."[52] For a long time now many historians have supported the mistaken notion that the SS was the sole undisputed source of authority under the National-Socialist dictatorship; they can hardly be expected to abandon their favourite theory too quickly.

The Third Reich has been pictured as a totalitarian

state, "super-organised" (Kogon's phrase),[53] all-embracing, encompassing every individual citizen and subjecting him to a single co-ordinated central directing force. The National-Socialists seemed to have made the age-old dream of the Germans come true: a strong state in which only one man's will prevailed—that of the Führer, in which only one political ideology was authoritative—that of the National-Socialist Party, in which only one force ruled over law and order—that of the SS/Police.

But the dream of the strong state remained a figment of the imagination. The Third Reich was not a totalitarian state; it was a caricature of one—a caricature reflecting all the dreams, hopes and ideas of the early Nazi leaders as they constructed their authoritarian state. Hans Buchheim concluded that the totalitarian Führer state was "not a machine perfected down to the smallest detail; it was no super-rationalised system; it was a jumble of vested interests and political strings, spheres of authority and plenary powers, and ultimately a free-for-all referred to at the time as 'National-Socialist war games.' "[54] Professor Trevor-Roper exclaimed: "How many people in the past years were unconsciously seduced by Nazi propaganda into believing that Nazi Germany was organised as a 'totalitarian' state—totally integrated, totally mobilised, centrally controlled! . . . But in fact the totalitarianism of Germany was something quite different from this."[55]

In Nazi Germany nothing was total except the will of Hitler; that, with its "Führer decrees" and "Führer orders," was what ruled 80 million people. When the Führer's intentions were laid down in black and white, the SS, as the most important instrument of the Führer dictatorship, had absolute power. In SS eyes, however, the ever-suspicious Führer had one failing—his orders did not always explain what he wanted, nor did they necessarily cover every sphere of the nation's life. Since the Reich cabinet had ceased to sit and Hitler in his field headquarters became ever more distant from his Ministers, the outcome of a Führer order was frequently the product of chance.

Moreover part of Hitler's cunning as a leader was his ability to keep the centre of political power permanently shifting among his closest collaborators, thereby preventing the emergence of unwelcome rivals. It was an unwritten law of the Führer's dictatorship that no official or legal structure should be allowed to arise which might inhibit Hitler's freedom of action. The hallmark of the National-Socialist regime was not monolithic unity but the "anarchy of authority," in the words of Hans Frank, the disillusioned Nazi legal adviser.[56] Hitler had no wish to be tied to any hierarchical system and so he passed his orders to the largest possible number of minor authorities. A system of multiplicity, instinctive rather than deliberate, ensured that no subordinate could combine with one of his rivals to act against Hitler.

The result was a curious system of "permanent self-frustration," as Hannah Arendt puts it;[57] by entrusting the solution of any one problem to a number of authorities simultaneously, the dictator assured his independence from his own subordinates; at the same time, however, the state became the arena of a power struggle more injurious to the efficiency of the official machine than the democratic party strife which the Nazis so much despised. The state was down-graded to a non-political administrative machine, to a façade behind which the regime's warlords carried on their struggle for power. Ulrich von Hassell, later one of the leaders of the 20 July 1944 plot, said: "These people have no conception of what a State is."[58] The more intelligent of the SS leaders, such as Otto Ohlendorf, criticised Hitler because "the strange thing is that, theoretically speaking, an absolute Führer State existed but, in particular during the war, a pluralist anarchy developed."[59] In 1947 Ohlendorf admitted at Nuremberg: "The Führer not only denied the State as a purpose in itself but totally destroyed it, so that it was no longer available to him as an instrument; the State was superseded by arbitrary action on the part of a multiplicity of authorities."[60] In this "confusion of private empires, private armies and private intelligence services"[61] there was no place for an SS monopoly. Unless they could quote a Hitler decree, the SS became one among many second-level power groups struggling for influence.

Unless the SS was carrying out a direct order from Hitler it was without the protective screen of Hitler's authority, and Himmler had to reach agreement with the other Reich authorities. The SS was frequently forced to act in the area not covered by clearly defined Führer orders, where there were no rules and victory went, not to the most orthodox National-Socialist but to whoever had the strongest private army or the greatest personal influence. This too was in accordance with the Führer's wishes; the persistent gang warfare and internal struggles of the Nazi Party spilled over into the machinery of the State—and the quarrels of his subordinates guaranteed Hitler his undisputed position both in the Party and in the State.

Like medieval feudal barons, Hitler's minions coalesced, split and came together again. They even made formal alliances among themselves; in 1936, for instance, the Sicherheitspolizei concluded a 10-point agreement with the Abwehr [military intelligence] which became known as the "Ten Commandments";[62] von Ribbentrop, the Foreign Minister, accepted a number of SS Commanders into his Ministry as the price of a short armistice in the battle between the SS and the Foreign Ministry;[63] Rosenberg, the Minister for the East, negotiated with SS-Gruppenführer Berger to protect himself against the intrigues of his theoretical subordinate Koch, the Reich Commissar for the Ukraine.[64]

Progress through this jungle of competing authorities was so laborious that the SS hardly had time or energy to grab the dominant position in Germany. They did, indeed, seize one position of power after another, but there were two authorities they could never overcome—The Party and The Wehrmacht. The SS had to swallow a man-hunt by the Party Labour Front and SA after the SD's secret informers;[65] they had to accept the suppression of the SD's "Reports from the Reich";[66] they had to look on, powerless, while Frank, the Governor-General of Poland, supported by the Wehrmacht and the SA, manoeuvred SS-Obergruppenführer Krüger, the most powerful man in German-occupied Poland, out of office.[67]

Although more and more SS uniforms were to be seen among Hitler's immediate entourage, the mistrustful dictator never allowed the SS to reach the final decisive position of power in the State. Hitler left the SS leaders in no doubt that they were his minions. The police in the new Germany were just as bad as those in the old, he

grumbled,[68] and when, contrary to his wishes, the SS meddled in German policy in Rumania, he shouted that he
would "smoke out the black plague!"[69] Himmler, the
Reichsführer-SS, was always in a cold panic when summoned by his Chief, and Hitler seldom treated him other
than as an industrious, but not particularly intelligent,
pupil. Hitler never regarded him as his successor and in
March 1945, he gave his reasons—Himmler would be rejected by the Party and, in addition, he was unacceptable
because of his lack of artistic feeling.[70]

   One of the rules of this free-for-all, of course, was that
no one was likely to oppose the SS unless he knew that
he had the bigger battalions on his side. In Adolf Hitler's
Reich, however, there was one helpless group of human
beings completely without protection—the Jews. They were
easy meat for the SS concentration camps and crematoria;
none of the Party bosses would stand up for them. So the
one place where the SS state was to be seen, the only
place where it really existed, was the secluded world of the
concentration camps. The inmates of Himmler's camps
really were slaves, victims of an inexorable process. And
yet the history of the destruction of the Jews shows that
some men who wore the brown shirt, some of the older
Nazis, prominent figures in the SS and founder members of
the Third Reich, managed to defy Himmler's death
machine.

   Ex-Gauleiter Kube, the Commissar-General in White
Ruthenia, for instance, accused police officers of anti-
Jewish excesses, took under his protection Jews being
transported to Minsk for extermination, and conducted a
one-man campaign against the SS and SD until Soviet
partisans blew him up with a bomb.[71] SS-Obergruppenführer Dr Werner Best sabotaged Himmler's Jew-murder
programme and enabled thousands of Danish Jews to
escape to neutral Sweden.[72] Felix Kersten the masseur,
Himmler's personal physician, "my only friend, my
Buddha",[73] used his capacity to relieve his master of his
stomach pains to save thousands of Jewish lives, first the
Jews of Finland, then thousands of others who were
permitted to emigrate to Sweden.[74] Finally an assortment
of Italian generals, Balkan politicians and French collaborators wove a web of deception and lies round hundreds

of thousands of European Jews and blocked Eichmann's
executioners for long enough to get them to safety.

Werner Best's attitude alone shows that the SS-State
theory does not hold water. The SS was never a monolithic
organisation; of all the manifestations of the Third Reich
the SS was the most random and the most self-contradic-
tory. There was hardly an informer who was not at
loggerheads with another of his ilk, hardly a practical
political problem upon which any two senior SS leaders
thought alike. In Nuremberg SS-Oberführer [Brigadier]
Reinecke lamented that the SS had been "infiltrated by
persons and organisations completely alien to the character of the SS."[75]

The SS secret files show the internal conflict only too
clearly. Himmler, for instance, accused SS-Gruppenführer
Reeder of sabotaging the SS policy of Germanisation in
Belgium;[76] the Nuremberg Waffen-SS Garrison Command-
er refused to work with the Allgemeine SS or the SD;[77]
an SS-Untersturmführer collected evidence against SS-
Gruppenführer Berger,[78] while Berger was accusing other
SS Commanders of working for the Catholic Church.[79]
Ohlendorf ridiculed Himmler's "blood and soil" fanta-
sies;[80] the RSHA [Reichssicherheitshauptamt—Reich Se-
curity Department] and the WVHA [Wirtschafts- und
Verwaltungshauptamt—SS Economic and Administrative
Department] quarrelled over whether Jews should be kept
as slave labour or murdered;[81] the Gestapo shot down
Soviet deserters whom the SD wished to use as a Russian
counter-revolutionary army.[82] Even non-members of the
order contributed to the internal conflicts within the SS;
Dr Richard Korherr, a devout Catholic, was appointed
Himmler's Inspector of Statistics;[83] Hans Hohberg, an accountant, became the power behind the throne in the SS
economic concerns;[84] Kammler, a civil servant from the
Works Department of the Air Ministry, rose rapidly to the
rank of SS General as builder of the famous concentration
camps.[85]

In fact the SS world was a bizarre nonsensical affair,
devoid of all logic. The theories hitherto advanced to
explain the SS phenomenon have been equally bizarre,
though superficially logical. In fact, history shows that the
SS was anything but an organisation constructed and
directed on some diabolically efficient system; it was a

product of accident and automatism. The real history of the SS is a story of idealists and criminals, of place-seekers and romantics: it is the history of the most fantastic association of men imaginable.

2

The Formation of the SS

THE history of the SS, like that of the National-Socialist Movement, starts in the turbulent post-war spring of 1919 when the Free Corps and the Reichswehr had driven the Red "Soldiers and Workers Councils" out of Bavaria.

An unwitting midwife at the birth of the National-Socialist Movement was the Munich historian, Karl Alexander von Müller. He was in close touch with the young nationalist officers who were calling the tune in Munich at the time and at a soldiers' rally he was impressed by a man who seemed to have an extraordinarily compelling power of oratory. He says: "Below locks of hair hanging down in a most unmilitary fashion, I saw a pale thin face with a close-cropped moustache and strikingly large light-blue eyes with a cold fanatical stare."[1] Müller nudged his school-friend Mayr, who was sitting next him: "Do you know you have got a 'natural' orator among your pupils?"

Captain Karl Mayr was head of Abteilung Ib/P (Press and Propaganda) in Reichswehr Group Headquarters No. 4 (Bavaria). He knew the man: "That's Hitler from the List Regiment. You, Hitler, come here a moment." Müller remembers that Hitler "did as he was told, moving awkwardly, half defiant, half embarrassed." The scene typifies Adolf Hitler's dependence upon the officers of the Bavarian Reichswehr and the sense of inferiority which the future Führer of the Great German Reich took years to overcome.

Mayr was quick to recognise Corporal Hitler's propagandist ability. In July 1919 Mayr's section in the Bavarian

War Ministry drew up a confidential list of their contact men in individual units: the list included one "Hittler, Adolf."[2] Mayr found Hitler only too ready to use his oratory wherever the ideological front was threatened.

The corporal gradually proved himself so useful that Mayr dropped his parade-ground manner, and began to address his letters politely "Dear Herr Hitler."[3] Hitler was a frequent visitor to the War Ministry and ranked as a member of Mayr's political staff. One day in the demobilisation camp at Lechfeld it looked as if the officers were losing control of their men; Hitler moved in at once and restored the situation. Another contact man, Lorenz Frank, reported on 23 August 1919: "Hitler particularly is a born demagogue; at a meeting his fanaticism and popular appeal compel his audience to listen to him."[4]

Mayr decided to use his discovery for greater things. One of his duties was to watch political parties in Bavaria; in September 1919 he accordingly despatched Hitler to a meeting of the German Workers Party (Deutsche Arbeiter Partei—DAP)[5]—a collection of nationalist sectarians who, in addition to hatred of the Jews and the Republic, preached an emotional lower-middle-class socialism using such phrases as "breaking the yoke of the usurer." Hitler soon became the star speaker at the DAP meetings and had little difficulty in shouting down the more discreet among his competitors in the beer cellars. In January 1920, the party, then 64 strong, elected him Head of Propaganda and accepted the party programme which he drew up. It later re-named itself National-Socialist German Workers Party (NSDAP).[6]

At this point Mayr was retired, and his place was taken by a little snub-nosed man with a crew cut whose battered, florid face gave evidence of unbounded energy. This was Captain Ernst Röhm, who, more than any other one man, was responsible for launching Hitler, now demobilised, into German politics. Röhm was a curious mixture of military reformer and Bavarian crook, an irrepressible conspirator, a homosexual, coarse and uncouth; nevertheless his comrades regarded him as a real soldier and he had a remarkable degree of moral courage.

Röhm was a contradictory character—a staunch Bavarian monarchist, ex-Company Commander in No. 10 Bavarian Infantry Regiment, "The Kings" with Ludwig

III as its Colonel-in-Chief; when the monarchy fell in 1918 Röhm had been ready to "honour his oath unto death."[7] On the other hand he now regarded Bavaria as an "orderly corner" in which the nationalists could gather their strength for the assault on that revolutionary tower of Babel, Berlin.

The 1919 Munich *condottieri* consisted primarily of the extremists from a generation of disillusioned embittered officers who, with the war lost and the monarchy fallen, found themselves condemned to a drab, humdrum existence. They had lost their social status and, so they said, their honour as well; they were vainly searching for a new form of society to which their experiences at the front had seemed to point the way. So democracy and the "November Republic," which was weak and precarious anyway, became the target for the officers' wrath and were held responsible for all their miseries. Germany's military men were determined to regain their social position and to restore to their country the capacity to defend itself, which the victors of 1918 had removed.

Chance came to their assistance. For a short while, and primarily in Bavaria, the struggle against the Communists and the Spartacists placed the officers in power; on the fall of the Red Republic no one counted who could not boast a uniform. Until constitutional government was restored, Bavarian politics were dominated by the officers, to some extent opposed by the Social Democrats and to some extent supported by the right-wing Catholic Bavarian Peoples Party. Captain Mayr kept watch on the political parties; Dr Roth was in charge of the judiciary; Lieutenant Ernst Pöhner became Police President of Munich;[8] Rohm, then 32, was initially Chief of Staff to the Munich Garrison Commander, then head of Section Ib (Arms and Equipment) on the staff of Colonel Ritter von Epp's Infantry Brigade and finally was given the most delicate task imaginable for a German officer at the time, the formation and equipment of the Bavarian Home Guard [Einwohnerwehr].[9]

The Versailles Treaty had placed strict limits on the strength and equipment of the Reichswehr. Germany was allowed 7 infantry and 2 cavalry divisions[10] but there were no reserves for use in emergency. The officers could see only one way out—formation of a second ("black")

Reichswehr. Röhm conceived this reserve as a sort of
national militia, a "Citizen army with its rifles in the cupboard," in Konrad Heiden's words. He found a resource-
ful ally in Escherich, a forestry official and member of the
Bavarian Peoples Party. Together they formed the most
powerful militia Germany has ever known—The Bavarian
Home Guard.[11]

Röhm worked tirelessly collecting weapons and forming
secret ammunition dumps; the Allies became suspicious
but he covered his tracks well. In Munich alone he
amassed 169 light and 11 heavy guns, 760 machine guns,
21,351 rifles, carbines and revolvers, 300,000 hand grenades and 8,000,000 rounds of ammunition;[12] when the
army was expanded in the mid 1930s, one-third of the additional weapons required by the Wehrmacht came from
Röhm's secret arsenals.[13]

In the summer of 1921, however, the Bavarian Home
Guard was brought abruptly to an end. The Berlin Central
Government kept its promise to the Allies and insisted
upon the disbandment of the Munich defence formations.[14]
Röhm had lost his main ally, and was left with nothing
but a little collection of extreme right-wing defence organisations, remnants of the Free Corps leading a useless
shadowy existence, playing at soldiers and pursuing their
blood feuds. Although they despised democracy, the officers suddenly realised that the masses were indispensible
and that they had no following to give them political
weight; Bogislaw von Selchow's poem was coming true:

Ich hasse	I hate
die Masse,	The crowd
die Kleine,	The little men
gemeine,	The mean men
den Nacken gebeugt,	Who bow their heads
die isst und schläft und Kinder zeugt.	And eat, sleep and beget children
Ich hasse	I hate
die Masse,	The crowd
die lahme,	The impotent crowd
die zahme	The pliable crowd
die heut' an mich glaubt	Which believes in me today
und die mir morgen mein Herzblut raubt.	And tomorrow will tear my heart out.[15]

Röhm, however, thought he knew a man who could draw the crowd. He had met Hitler of the NSDAP at a meeting of a Munich Nationalist circle known as the "Iron Fist."[16] Röhm saw in Hitler the demagogue he required to mobilise mass support for his secret army. In July 1921 Hitler became first President of the NSDAP[17] and Röhm's mind was made up—with Hitler he would march to power. The Austrian agitator went the rounds of the beer cellars, stirring up feeling among the lower-middle class and the victims of inflation against the "November criminals." Meanwhile Röhm formed the first mobile squads to protect his orator. Men of No. 19 Trench Mortar Company under Captain Streck were employed to beat up any disturbers of the peace at NSDAP meetings.[18] From this military body developed the Party's strong-arm organisation, which turned into the "Gymnastics and Sport" Section and finally gave birth to the most characteristic of all the National-Socialist Movement's formations, the SA [Sturmabteilung—Storm Detachment].[19]

Röhm had selected his first recruits and he now began to look for SA commanders. He found them among the wreckage of No. 2 Naval Brigade commanded by the ultra-conservative Captain Ehrhardt. The organisation had been scattered to the four winds after the failure of the attempt to instal Dr Kapp as Chancellor in March 1920[20] and some of the fugitives had taken refuge in Munich, calling themselves the "Consul Organisation."[21] Ehrhardt, a crusty sea-captain and an eccentric character totally unsuited to conspiratorial ways, initially refused to have anything to do with Hitler, saying: "Good God, what will the fool do next?"[22] Röhm, however, pointed out to him that his officers must have some organisation to command and Ehrhardt eventually agreed. He lent Röhm some of his best men; Lieutenant Johann Ulrich Klintzsch took over the training and co-ordination of the SA;[23] Lieutenant-Commander Hoffmann became Chief of Staff[24] and Lieutenant-Commander Manfred Freiherr von Killinger, though still wanted for his part in the assassination of Erzberger, joined them later.[25] The "Ehrhardt Brigade" simply turned into "Sturmabteilung Hitler"; even the sailors' battle song required little alteration:

Hakenkreuz am Stahlhelm	The Swastika on our helmet
Schwarzweissrotes Band,	Black-white-red armband
Sturmabteilung Hitler	Storm Detachment Hitler
Werden wir genannt.	Is our name.[26]

On 3 August 1921, according to the proclamation constituting the SA, these men undertook to serve the NSDAP "as an iron organisation" and to "render willing obedience to its leader."[27] But it was soon made clear to Hitler that, as far as the SA was concerned, he was an outsider. He did not call the tune: the men who gave the orders were Röhm's and Ehrhardt's officers.

Hitler regarded the SA as an instrument of political propaganda, a force to stick up election posters, use its knuckle-dusters in meeting-hall fights and impress the discipline-loving Germans by propaganda marches. In the eyes of its leaders, however, the SA was a genuine military force[28] and, in fact, it figured as a regular formation in the Reichswehr's mobilisation plans; No. 7 Pioneer Battalion and No. 19 Infantry Regiment of the Bavarian Reichswehr were responsible for the military training of the SA; the Munich SA regiment, at a strength of 1,150 in 1923, included an artillery company and cavalry platoons and used army ranks such as corporal and bombardier.[29]

As a counterweight to the Ehrhardt officers, Hitler recruited Captain Hermann Göring, a wearer of the *Pour-le-Mérite* [the German equivalent of the Victoria Cross], and placed him at the head of the SA; early in 1923 Göring formed an SA headquarters[30] on the lines of a divisional staff with infantry and artillery commanders.[31] Hitler sensed instinctively that within the Party a force was taking shape which would look elsewhere for its orders. There were a number of danger signals; the NSDAP, together with other extreme right-wing groups, had affiliated itself to the Arbeitsgemeinschaft der vaterländischen Kampfverbände [Working Association of Patriotic Fighting Formations] whose military commander was Lieutenant-Colonel (Retired) Kriebel; he said flatly that: "The politicians must keep their mouths shut."[32] News-sheet No. 2 from SA headquarters stated that local group leaders [Ortsgruppenführer] could "best serve" their commander by assuming the role of "tub-thumper."[33] An

instruction from Hoffmann, the Chief of Staff, stated that
the SA was "a specialist organisation within the National-
Socialist movement to be dealt with as a separate force
by local groups and Party headquarters";[34] this made
ominous reading for Hitler.

Here were the first signs of the conflict which was
later to plague the Movement right up to Röhm's death
—the murderous strife between the SA and the political
leadership. Hitler was quick to see the danger, so, to free
himself from the pressure of unruly SA officers, he surrounded himself with a praetorian guard.

What later proved to be the germ of the SS appeared
in March 1923; a few of the "old fighters" swore to protect
Hitler from all internal and external enemies if necessary
at the risk of their lives; they called themselves the
Stabswache [headquarters guard].[35] The black uniform
later adopted by the SS was seen for the first time; to distinguish themselves from the SA the "headquarters guard"
wore field-grey overcoats and jackets, black ski-caps
with a silver death's-head button, and black-bordered
swastika armbands.[36]

This bodyguard did not last long. Two months later
Ehrhardt broke with Hitler and recalled his men from the
SA.[37] Hitler thereupon formed a new bodyguard to which
he gave the name "Stosstrupp Adolf Hitler" [Assault
Squard].[38] Its leaders were an SA man named Julius
Schreck and a diminutive man called Joseph Berchtold
who ran a stationery business and was Number Two in
the NSDAP Treasury; its normal meeting place was the
Torbräu in Munich, near the Isartor.[39] Here, in the skittle
alley, the assault squad's first assignments were discussed.
Though all were members of the Party, the men of the
assault squad came from a social background very different from that of the followers of Ehrhardt and Röhm;
they were mostly labourers from the lower-middle or
working classes of Munich and the few officers among
them carried ranks no higher than second lieutenant on
the reserve.

Ulrich Graf, for instance, Hitler's first and leading
bodyguard, was a butcher who had made quite a name
for himself as an amateur boxer.[40] Emil Maurice, Hitler's
bosom companion, was a watchmaker who had been convicted for embezzlement;[41] Christian Weber had been a

groom and was now earning a pittance in the Blaue Bock in Munich.[42] The bond which held them all together was their great task of guarding the lives of Hitler and the other National-Socialist leaders. Hitler merely had to say the word and they would wade in with their "indiarubbers" and "matchboxes" (as they called their rubber trunchons and pistols)[43] to protect their Führer from tiresome opponents. Even in 1942 Hitler would still talk of the "men who were ready for revolution and knew that some day things would come to hard knocks."[44]

That day came in November 1923. The head of the Government in Bavaria was Gustav Ritter von Kahr, the Commissar General, a Bavarian separatist and monarchist; the Reichswehr Commander was Major General Otto Hermann Lossow. Both were at such loggerheads with Berlin that Bavaria seemed likely to secede from the Reich at any moment. For years all the forces opposed to democracy and progress had been collecting in that "orderly corner," the Bavarian military state, and now they were girding their loins for the decisive blow. Hitler thought that he could make good use of this turn in Bavarian politics.

Von Kahr had summoned a meeting of all the Bavarian dignitaries in the Munich Bürgerbräukeller in the Rosenheimer Strasse for the evening of 8 November,[45] and Hitler decided to use this occasion for his own coup. He suspected that Kahr intended to announce Bavaria's independence and was determined to force Kahr to overreach himself and march on Berlin to depose the "November Republic."[46] Hitler hastily alerted his allies and persuaded them to support his surprise action;[47] they included the ex-Quarter-Master General, Ludendorff, who was hurriedly brought into line;[48] he arrived for the putsch totally unaware that he was cast for the star role. Hitler collected the fifty men of his assault squad and he was ready; he put on a black overcoat, pinned to it his Iron Cross First Class and set off.[49] By 8 p.m. he was at the entrance to the Bürgerbräukeller, waiting for his moment.[50]

Three-quarters of an hour later Berchtold, the assault squad commander, brought along a machine gun and set it up at the entrance.[51] Hitler and his bodyguard thereupon forced their way into the crowded hall; drawing a revolver Hitler fired into the air and then jumped onto a table[52] shouting; "The national revolution has begun. The hall is surrounded by six hundred heavily armed men and no one may leave. The Bavarian Government and the Reich Government have been deposed and a provisional Reich Government will be formed."[53] Bavaria's surprised officers and politicians allowed this apparent madman to proceed and declared themselves ready to come to terms with Hitler.[54] The next day, however, Kahr and Lossow disowned him and mobilised against him.[55] As if paralysed, Hitler remained in the Bürgerbräukeller waiting for good news which did not come. There was only one favourable report and this finally drove Hitler on to the streets; Röhm with his defence organisation, "Reichskriegsflagge," had forced his way into the War Ministry and was holding it in face of increasing military and police pressure.[56]

About mid-day on 9 November Hitler and his followers and allies marched off, eight abreast, down the narrow Residenzstrasse[57] to relieve Röhm in the War Ministry. On the Odeonsplatz they were faced by about a hundred police in position on the steps of the Feldherrnhalle, barring the procession's way.[58] When the putschists continued to move on, Hitler and Ludendorff marching in step, a second police unit moved in.[59] Ulrich Graf, Hitler's bodyguard, rushed up to the muzzles of the police rifles, shouting: "Don't shoot! It is His Excellency Ludendorff and Hitler!"[60] The police opened fire; sixteen National-Socialists, including five members of the assault squad, and three policemen were killed; practically all the leaders of the Nazi movement were arrested.[61] Berchtold, the leader of the assault squad, and Göring, Commander of the SA, though severely wounded, escaped to Austria.[62]

Hitler's act of lunacy wrecked the NSDAP. The Party Organisation, the SA and the Assault Squad were banned, leaving only a collection of Nazis quarrelling among themselves; initially they tried to take refuge under Ludendorff's banner but later split into an increasing number of small groups and cliques.[63] The only man who still worked away was Röhm; he had been cashiered from the army and released on probation after a short period under arrest;[64] he believed that he could continue as before and, while still in prison in Landsberg, Hitler nominated him head of the SA, now an illegal organisation.[65]

Röhm soon realised, however, that the Bavarian Government had no intention of lifting the ban on the SA. Assisted by Ritter von Epp, Röhm's former master, Kahr had brought all the defence formations under control, combining them in a "Notbann" [Emergency Formation].[66] Röhm thereupon formed a new defence organisation from the remnants of the SA and placed it under the patronage of General Ludendorff. It was called "Frontbann."[67]

The formation of the Frontbann brought Röhm and Hitler their first recruits from outside Bavaria. Until the November putsch Hitler's movement had hardly penetrated outside the Munich city limits, but now the survivors of the old Free Corps and the leaderless North German National-Socialists streamed into the Frontbann.[68] Röhm was joined by a series of ruthless desperadoes, the Free Corps officers, nationalist extremists who later made thuggery the hallmark of the SA; such were Captain von Heydebreck and Graf Helldorff.[69] There was also Lieutenant Edmund Heines, a roughneck highly qualified in all sorts of vice. (Röhm, who was always interested in male relationships, says in his memoirs that Heines "approached him for the first time."[70])

At their peak as an armed force Hitler's SA had numbered at the most 2,000 men;[71] Röhm's Frontbann now had 30,000.[72] In his Landsberg cell Hitler became somewhat uneasy at the growth of Röhm's army; Röhm had been heard to say "I am still a soldier and nothing but a soldier."[73] and he was still insisting upon the autonomy of the defence organisations. "The political and defence movements are entirely independent one of another," he wrote to Ludendorff.[74] When, in December 1924, Hitler was released[75] and charged Röhm with the reconstitution of the SA, the two clashed openly. Hitler was determined never to have an independent SA on the lines of the Ehrhardt Brigade; Röhm, however, insisted that the Party bosses had no business giving orders to the soldiers and that Hitler was no more than the rabble-rouser for the defence formations.[76] A memorandum from Röhm gave the ex-corporal to understand that: "Party politics will not be tolerated either in the Frontbann or in the SA"; it ended with the blunt statement: "I categorically refuse to allow the SA to become involved in Party matters; equally

I categorically refuse to allow SA commanders to accept instructions from Party political leaders."[77]

Röhm did not realise that Hitler had already made up his mind; he was not going to let the SA revive until he could be sure that there would be no outsiders in SA uniform to dictate to him. So Hitler split with Röhm, leaving him no choice by bidding him farewell on 30 April 1925: "In memory of glorious and difficult days which we have survived together. With heartfelt thanks for your comradeship and in the hope that you will not refuse me your personal friendship in future."[78] Barely a month later Hitler gave some indication of his plans; his Secretariat announced: "Herr Hitler has no intention of setting up a new defence formation. That he once did so was due to the activities of a certain gentleman who left him in the lurch. All he needs today are men to keep order at meetings, as in the days before 1923."[79] The birth of the SS was now not far off. Hiter was determined to have a force which, wherever he might be, would guarantee his authority in the Party and would be prepared to carry out his orders without question and at all times. This the old SA under Röhm and Ehrhardt had not been prepared to do, and so the SS was now to undertake it. In 1942 Hitler said: "I told myself then that I needed a bodyguard, even a very restricted one, but made up of men who would be enlisted unconditionally, ready even to march against their own brothers. Rather a mere twenty men to a city (on condition that one could count on them absolutely) than an unreliable mass."[80]

(The Party at large, and later the Third Reich as a whole, was given an entirely different version of the formation of the SS. As the SA was still banned, the story ran, when the Party was reformed in February 1925, a protective organisation had to be constituted against the increasing terrorism of its political opponents.[81] This statement concealed the facts that Hitler deliberately postponed reconstitution of the SA, that the ban on the SA did not extend to all German Länder [States], and that, primarily in North and West Germany, the SA increased considerably in size but refused to subordinate itself to the Munich party leader, who was still a controversial figure.[82])

Hitler now set about forming his own bodyguard. In April 1925 he ordered Julius Schreck, who had been a member of the Assault Squad and was now his chauffeur, to form a new headquarters guard. A fortnight later this headquarters guard was re-christened "Schutzstaffel" (SS).[83] Schreck's first men were recruited from the same source as the headquarters guard and the Assault Squad— the Torbräu beer cellar near the Isartor, Munich. Initially, there were only eight men,[84] almost all from the Adolf Hitler Assault Squad. They wore the old Assault Squad uniform, unchanged except that the field-grey tunic had given way to the brown shirt* (now the official party uniform) with a black tie.[85]

Schreck now set about forming SS units in other cities. On 21 September 1925 he sent out "Circular No. 1" urging all local Party Groups to set up an SS.[87] They were to be small, efficient, elite groups, at the most a commander and ten men; Berlin alone was allowed two commanders and twenty men.[88] Schreck was insistent that, in accordance with the Nazi elite theory, only specially selected men should enter the SS. SS Headquarters only accepted applicants between 23 and 35 years of age; they had to name two sponsors, be registered by the police as residents of five years' standing, and be "strong and healthy."[89]

The SS "guidelines" stated: "Habitual drunkards, gossip-mongers and other delinquents will not be considered."[90] In November 1925 Schreck discovered from the *Völkischer Beobachter* that in Munich-Neuhausen a Party member named Daub had formed 15 ex-SA men into an SS unit and was styling himself SS commander;[91] on 27 November Schreck protested to Party Headquarters: "This new formation is no more than the old SA rechristened SS. SS Headquarters therefore requests the Party leadership to do what it can to bring to the notice of these gentlemen that the name SS may not be used by these detachments. The SS is an organization laboriously built up upon sound foundations and its image must not be tarnished by imitation copies."[92]

Schreck worked hard to collect "the best and most re-

* The brown shirt had become the official Party uniform by accident. A certain SA commander named Rossbach had been in Austria and there received a large consignment of brown shirts, originally intended for German troops in East Africa; Rossbach took them back to Germany in 1924. With the brown shirt the SA wore a brown tie, the SS a black one.[86]

liable Party members to protect the movement and work selflessly and tirelessly for it"; he listed the tasks of the SS as: "Protection of meetings in their area, recruitment of subscribers and advertisers for the *Völkischer Beobachter*, and recruitment of party members."[93] Alois Rosenwink, a section head and the real organiser of SS headquarters, said with typical Nazi bombast: "We carry the death's head on our black cap as a warning to our enemies and an indication to our Führer that we will sacrifice our lives for his concept."[94]

The first success stories began to arrive in Munich. In Dresden SS men had forestalled an attempt by fifty Communists to break up a Nazi meeting;[95] from Saxony "in the Marble Palace, Chemnitz, the combined SS of Dresden, Plauen, Zwickau and Chemnitz gave the Communists a fearful beating-up, throwing some of them out of the windows, since when no Communist has dared to disturb our meetings."[96] By Christmas 1925 SS headquarters could record that "We have available a properly constituted defence organisation of about a thousand men."[97] Shortly thereafter the number of genuine SS men had sunk to about 200.[98] Nevertheless as the first nation-wide Nazi organisation, the SS was now firmly established.

In April 1926 Berchtold, the old leader of the assault squad, returned from exile in Austria and took over command of the SS from Schreck.[99] As the men of November 1923 returned, Hitler publicly proclaimed the SS as his elite organisation; at the second Party Rally in Weimar on 4 July 1926 he handed to the SS the "blood banner," the flag which had led the procession down the Residenzstrasse on 9 November 1923.[100] Now that the SS was established and growing, Hitler could once more try his luck with the SA. He knew only too well that he must have some mass formation as his link to the people, that in a Germany ruled by Party armies and political processions he must have his own army to hoist him into power.

The non-Bavarian SA leaders, however, were still suspicious of Hitler, who after all was still only an Austrian, and he had to find someone to act as his contact man with the numerous scattered SA groups. He chose Captain Franz Pfeffer von Salomon, a North German Free Corps commander.[101] Goebbels' diary of 27 July 1926 records: "With the Chief at midday. Serious discussion. Pfeffer be-

comes Reich SA leader."[102] From Hitler's point of view the
position was serious, for as the contact man from the
North German National-Socialist leaders, Pfeffer had to
be given a place in the party hierarchy—he was to be a
watchdog as well.

Hitler had to give Pfeffer considerable power. With effect from 1 November 1926 he was entitled "Supreme
SA leader" [Oberste SA Führer—OSAF] and placed in
command of all SA in Germany; although he was bound
to follow the basic directives of Hitler as party leader, he
was allowed to build up the SA organisation as he saw
fit.[103] In Hitler's view, however, the alliance with the
North German National-Socialists was worth some concessions over the power of the SS. So the SS was also
paced under Pfeffer, its commander, Berchtold, being
given only a small crumb of comfort in being permitted
to call himself Reichsführer-SS [Reich SS leader].[104]
Berchtold soon became discouraged, fearing that his little elite force would be entirely subordinated to the SA
and the Party functionaries—exactly what he had been put
into office to prevent; his predecessor, Schreck, had been
voted down by the members of SS headquarters as too
easy-going and likely to become a tool of crafty Party
bureaucrats such as Philip Bouhler and Franz Xaver
Schwarz.[105] Ernst Wagner wrote to Hitler saying that
Schreck had had to go because he "had insufficient command and organising ability, nor did he carry sufficient
weight to ensure that the SS remained the movement's elite
force."[106]

So the more dynamic Berchtold had been appointed but
even he was now finding it difficult to keep the Party
organisers at bay. One of his instructions ran: "Neither
the headquarters of the local group nor of the Gau [Nazi
Party Territorial District] is to interfere in the internal
organisational problems of the local SS."[107] Another order
stated: "The SS is a completely independent organisation
within the Movement."[108] But Berchtold did not gain his
point versus the party functionaries; here was the first
indication of that latent strife between the SS aristocrats
and the party bosses which was to rage right up to the
end of the Third Reich. (At an internal party meeting on
11 May 1926, for instance, Wagner, a member of the
SS, shouted that "The bosses must be smoked out"; Bouh-

ler and Schwarz thereupon forbade him entry into SS
headquarters. Berchtold, the Reichsführer, was compelled
to put the ban in writing; Wagner protested to Hitler
indignantly: "Berchtold told me that he had been compelled to do so by Bouhler and Schwarz."[109])

When in addition to these vexations the SA was allowed
to increase its strength once more, Berchtold resigned. In
March 1927 his deputy, Erhard Heiden, was appointed
Reichsführer-SS[110] but he too found it difficult to compete
with the growing size and influence of the SA; Pfeffer,
for instance, forbade the SS to form units in towns where
the SA was still below strength.[111]

In each locality [Gemeinde] the SS was not allowed to
exceed ten per cent of the strength of the SA,[112] so by
1928 it had only reached the miserable figure of 280
men.[113] The SS elite frequently had to allow themselves
to be ordered about by SA commanders and do the
chores, such as delivering orders of the day, distributing
propaganda material and selling the *Völkischer Beobachter*.[114] The scale of their achievements can be judged by
the following report from the year 1926: "During October
the SS recruited throughout the Reich: 249 new members
for the NSDAP, 54 new readers for the *Völkischer
Beobachter*, 169 new readers for the *Stürmer*, 82 new
readers for the *Nationalsozialist*, 140 new readers for the
Südwestdeutscher Beobachter, 475 new readers for the
Westdeutscher Beobachter, 189 new readers for the remaining National-Socialist newspapers. In addition 2000
copies of the *Illustrierte Beobachter* were sold." The report was headed sarcastically: "So this is what we do!"[115]

This force, which in Heiden's words was "perhaps super-
efficient but certainly arrogant," was held together only
by its belief in its own selectivity.[116] Its slogan was: "The
aristocracy keeps its mouth shut."[117] It became a silent
appendage to the SA marching columns, but it kept alive
its elite concept by ever stricter conditions of entry and
ever more severe service regulations. "Order No. 1" for
instance of 13 September 1927 from the Reichsführer,
Erhard Heiden, laid down that: "The SS will never take
part in discussions at members' meetings. SS men will
attend discussion evenings for the purpose of political instruction only; no SS man will smoke during the address
and no one will be allowed to leave the room. The SS

man and SS commander will remain silent and will never become involved in matters (concerning the local political leadership and SA) which do not concern him".[118] Orders laid down that before entering a meeting each unit was to parade "sized in two ranks"; dress and passes were to be checked; the SS man was always to carry his NSDAP membership book, his SS pass and the SS songbook.[119] Special attention was paid to the contents of Order No. 8 forbidding the carrying of arms; Hitler had decided to seize power by ostensibly legal methods and part of his scheme was that the Party must officially keep itself aloof from all defence organisations and illegal military bodies. Before going on duty, SS commanders had to search men of their unit for arms and confiscate any weapons found.[120]

Even their political opponents were impressed by the iron discipline of the SS. In a secret report of 7 May 1929 Munich police headquarters noted: "Strict discipline is demanded from SS men. Even the smallest infraction of regulations set out in the current SS orders is punished by a fine, temporary withdrawal of the right to wear the armband, or suspension from duty. Particular stress is laid upon bearing and turnout."[121] Their strict rules were supposed to demonstrate that the SS formed a Party aristocracy. "The SS man is the most exemplary party member conceivable" an SS instruction stated.[122] The SS song, sung at the end of every SS meeting, showed the organisation's fanatical belief in its mission:

Wenn alle untreu werden	When all are disloyal
So bleiben wir doch treu	Then we remain loyal
Dass immer noch auf Erden	So that always upon this earth
Fur Euch ein Fähnlein sei	There may be a banner in front of you.[123]

"The SA is the infantry of the line, the SS the Guards. There has always been a guard; the Persians had one, the Greeks, Caesar and Napoleon, Frederick the Great, right up to the world war; the SS will be the imperial guard of the new Germany.[124] These words were spoken by the man who was determined to make the SS the masters of the Reich. From this point the story of the SS becomes his story, the history of their deeds his history, the list of their crimes his crimes. On 6 January 1929 Hitler placed him at the head of the SS as the new Reichsführer: his name was Heinrich Himmler.[125]

3

Heinrich Himmler

AS the train rumbled steadily northwards, the passenger looked increasingly bored. Albert Krebs, the first National-Socialist Gauleiter [the senior Nazi party representative in a Gau] of Hamburg, had been listening for hours to the chatter of the man opposite, who had boarded the train with him at Elberfeld.[1]

The man was of medium height, well built with a rather puffy, commonplace, face. The small, slightly receding chin betrayed a certain weakness, but the blue-grey eyes behind the pince-nez seemed to indicate considerable strength of will. His somewhat blunt manner, too, hardly seemed to accord with his small, well-manicured, almost feminine hands.

At the time—spring 1929—Gauleiter Krebs took no particular notice of these inconsistencies in his fellow-passenger's outward appearance. He was merely noting with increasing distaste what the new Reichsführer-SS, Heinrich Himmler, had to say about the political situation. Himmler was lecturing him: in politics, he said, people's private affairs were what mattered; for instance, it was particularly important to know how a certain SA commander, Conn, had come by his curious name—it sounded rather like the Jewish name Cohen; Gauleiter Lohse had been a bank official and so his possible dependence upon Jewish capital should be investigated. Krebs shook his head.[2] Even thirty years later Krebs could still remember Himmler's disquisition as "terrifying," "a remarkable mixture of martial bombast, lower-middle-class beer-hall gossip and the impassioned prophesyings of a non conformist preacher."[3]

Himmler was only 29 and was on his first inspection trip to the SS; Krebs wrote him off as a loud-mouthed, dubious and somewhat provincial henchman of Adolf Hitler; many National-Socialists who had tried to preserve some freedom of judgment thought the same way. Later, instead of this picture of the preacher and beer-hall gossip, the man was painted as a sinister diabolical figure. As Himmler's power increased, the figure of the Reichsführer-SS appeared more unreal, ghostly and inhuman to the Germans. Himmler soon became a depersonalised abstraction, the inanimate embodiment of the National-Socialist police state, a monster divorced from all humanity, waiting only to annihilate any dissentients. No detail of his private life revealed what sort of a man the Reichsführer-SS was —we still do not really know today.

Those who knew him in the flesh were incapable of giving an intelligible description of Himmler as a man. Any coherent picture contained so many discordant features that his contemporaries and biographers have presented him in a number of different lights. There is Himmler the hangman, Himmler the good companion, Himmler the fanatical racial ideologist, Himmler the incorruptible apostle of rectitude, Himmler the willing tool of his Führer; finally there is a pensive Himmler deliberating with the German resistance.

General Friedrich Hossbach, Hitler's ex-Military Assistant, said: "This man, Hitler's evil spirit, cold, calculating and ambitious, was undoubtedly the most purposeful and most unscrupulous figure in the Third Reich."[4] General Guderian says: "He seemed like a man from another planet."[5] Burckhardt, the Swiss, League of Nations High Commissioner in Danzig, wrote: "What made him sinister was his capacity to concentrate upon little things, his pettifogging conscientiousness and his inhuman methodology; he had a touch of the robot.[6] Looking at a photograph of Himmler, Alfred Rosenberg, the Nazi ideologist, was struck by the fact that "I had never been able to look Heinrich Himmler straight in the eye. His eyes were always hooded, blinking behind his pince-nez. Now, however, I could see them gazing at me from the photograph and I thought I could detect one thing in them—malice."[7]

General Walter Dornberger, on the other hand, who was in charge of the V2 programme, thought him "like an intelligent schoolmaster, certainly not a man of violence"; Himmler, he said, had "the rare gift of listening attentively" and his manner was "quiet and unemotional—a man without nerves."[8]

Count Bernadotte, who negotiated with Himmler in 1945, found him surprising: "Certainly there was nothing diabolical in his appearance." According to Bernadotte he had been extremely affable and was always ready with a joke when conversation threatened to flag.[9] Many diplomats described him as a man of sober judgment; both German and foreign resistance movements at one time thought that Himmler was the only National-Socialist leader who could be used to bring Hitler down. Trevor-Roper says: "In this monster there were many curious qualities which have made him, to some, an incredible, enigmatical figure."[10]

Himmler's biographers eventually contrived a theory to give some sort of explanation to the existence of so many differing characters in one man. The key to the Himmler riddle, they said, lay in his boyhood and youth; he was the lonely son of a middle-class family, overshadowed by a pedantic father and an unsympathetic mother; in the post-war period he had wandered about, unrecognised by society, until the National-Socialist Movement gave him the security which his home had failed to provide.[11]

This makes a plausible theory and is typical of the present-day tendency to invent some psychoanalytical explanation for the inexplicable. Unfortunately it is not true. Himmler came from the most normal of Bavarian middle-class families; he had two brothers, Gebhard, born in 1898, two years before Heinrich, and Ernst, born in 1905;[12] there was nothing particular to upset the family relationship. As Himmler rose in the ranks of the SS and became increasingly imbued with a sense of mission, family harmony did suffer to a degree; his wife Margarete, a nervous and plaintive individual, did not fit into the family—"I always have to take a deep breath when I think of your parents," she once said.[13] Nevertheless, the Reichsführer never broke with his family. When his mother died, although unwell himself, Himmler kept watch at her bedside for a whole night; at her funeral he linked hands across the coffin with his two brothers,[14] saying in his somewhat pompous manner; "We will always stay together."[15]

Himmler was the self-appointed family mentor. In 1921, when still a student, he wrote to: "Dearest Mummy"[16]— "Daddy should not work so hard; during the week he should go for a walk more often to ensure that he does not overwork." To his brothers he adopted the attitude of a pedantic schoolmaster. "Little Ernst," although only five years his junior, was told on 14 November 1920: "I am very pleased with your good report. But do not rest on your laurels. Moreover, I expect you to do well in history. Do not become unbalanced. Be a good, brave boy and do not vex Daddy and Mummy."[17]

Himmler's brother Gebhard had an even worse time. He had the misfortune to become engaged to Paula Stölzle, the daughter of a Weilheim banker, and Heinrich did not approve. He was quick to put his objections on paper, writing to Paula on 18 April 1923: "If your union is to be a happy one for the two of you and salutary for our people, the very foundation of which must be healthy, clean-living families, you will have to be ridden on a tight rein and with the utmost severity. Since your own code of behaviour is not a strict one and your future husband is too kind-hearted, someone else must perform this function. I feel it my duty to do so."[18] Determination to ensure that twentieth-century women adopted the same code of morals as the heroines of the old German sagas was one of Himmler's obsessions; he regarded any extra-marital relations as an offence against his code of purity; accordingly he instructed Max Blüml, a Munich detective agency, to investigate Paula's past.[19] Blüml reported on 14 March 1924.[20] But Himmler had already instituted other enquiries; on 12 March he wrote to an official named Rössner; "May I request you to inform me by return of all you know about Fräulein Stölzle and particularly about her relationship with your colleague, Daffner?"[21] Brother Gebhard capitulated and broke off the engagement.[22]

The incident shows that Himmler, unlike most other Nazi leaders, had been brought up in the security of a true middle-class civil servant milieu. Hitler had his nightmare memories of a Vienna workhouse; Joseph Goebbels was the son of a works foreman; Alfred Rosenberg was an embittered émigré Balt; but Himmler was a true offspring of middle-class officialdom, simply the second son of Gebhard Himmler, a private tutor.

Heinrich was born on 7 October 1900 on the second floor of 2 Hildegardstrasse, Munich.[23] His social position was already assured, for one of the great figures of the Bavarian Kingdom, Prince Heinrich of Wittelsbach, who had been old Himmler's pupil, was godfather to the baby.[24] On being informed in an obsequious letter that it weighed 7 lb 3 oz, the Prince gave permission for it to be named after him.[25] With such a name and such a godfather, Heinrich was clearly destined for the ranks of the loyal citizenry.

While at school it never crossed Heinrich's mind to question the authority of his parents or the order of society of his time.[26] From his father he learnt that the ancient Germans had been good people, and the foundation was laid for that romantic interpretation of history characteristic of the late Wagnerian era when the world was peopled by Germanic heroes and glorious women—so easily transformable into the Nordic German master race to meet the requirements of the Nazi regime. Himmler quickly learned to treat those around him with proper respect. While at school he kept an impeccable diary in which anyone he met was invariably given his correct title.[27]

For anyone who had a prince of the Royal House as his godfather, the natural career was that of an officer, and here lies a key to Himmler's character; he was always dreaming of leading his troops to victory, but could never quite make the picture come true. First he wanted to join the Navy,[28] but he had weak eyes and the Navy would not accept men who wore glasses. He then decided on the Army. On 26 June 1917 his father wrote: "My son Heinrich earnestly desires to become a career infantry officer."[29] Himmler could hardly wait to get into the war. When his brother Gebhard entered the Landsturm in 1915, Heinrich wrote: "Oh how I wish to be as old as that and so able to go to the front."[30] He transcribed the news bulletins from general headquarters word for word and reproached the people of Landshut, where his family had moved, with lack of enthusiasm for the war.[31]

Heinrich was so persistent that his father asked some

friends at court to allow the young man to enter the army early,[82] and the friends pulled the necessary strings. About the same time Heinrich had his last present from his royal godfather, who had meanwhile been killed in action. Himmler's father received a letter from the court informing him that: "The J.N. Oberndörffer Bank, 18 Salvatorstrasse, Munich, has been instructed to send you 1,000 5% German War Loan. Please accept this sum as a gift for your son Heinrich from his late godfather, Weiland, his Royal Highness Prince Heinrich."[83]

In late 1917 Himmler joined 11 Bavarian Infantry Regiment, the "Von der Tann."[84] But his military career ended before it had really begun. Shortly before his death Himmler told Count Bernadotte that he had "gone to war" with his men[35] and other sources refer to his participation in a battle on the Western Front;[36] but in fact Himmler was never more than a cadet and never reached the front. The war went too quickly for him; he spent six months in Regensburg doing basic infantry training; from 15 June to 15 September 1918 he attended a cadets' course in Freising; from 15 September to 1 October 1918 he did a machine-gun course with No. 17 Machine Gun Company in Bayreuth.[87] Two months later he was demobilised from No. 4 Company of the Reserve Battalion of 11 Infantry Regiment.[88]

In the turbulent post-war period it seemed for a while that Himmler would be able to continue his military career. In February 1919 Kurt Eisner, Bavaria's left-wing socialist Minister-President, was murdered by an officer,[39] whereupon the Communists and their revolutionary supporters set up a red republic.[40] The constitutional Social Democratic Government of Bavaria fled to Bamberg and was compelled, much against its will, to raise troops; they consisted primarily of ex-soldiers and volunteers and called themselves Free Corps.[41]

Berlin set the Reichswehr on the move, and in April 1919 the Free Corps prepared to march on Munich.[42] Himmler joined a small Free Corps commanded by Lieutenant Lautenbacher[43] but once more he missed the battle. The unit never entered Munich[44] and Himmler remained a barrack-square soldier. But he did not give up. On 17 June 1919 he wrote to the depot of II Infantry Regiment asking for his military papers, "since I am transferring to the Reichswehr in a few days' time."[45]

Nothing came of this, however, for his father had meanwhile decided that, being no longer protected by the King and in view of the rising inflation it was high time that Heinrich qualified in some more secure profession than that of war; he wanted him to become a farmer.[46] Heinrich agreed: next to soldiering farming had always interested him. As a boy he had kept a large collection of plants,[47] and he developed a strange addiction to gardens of herbs. (Later this was to provide an added burden for the inmates of the concentration camps; each camp had to produce a collection of every conceivable type of herb, since Himmler considered them far more efficacious than medicines in curing diseases.[48])

But with farming also ill luck continued to dog him. He went to a farm near Ingolstadt to learn the business but had hardly begun when he was laid low by a typhus epidemic.[49] A certain Dr Grünstadt decided: "Must interrupt for a year and study."[50] So on 18 October 1919 Himmler enrolled as a student of agriculture at the Technical High School, Munich University.[51] It would hardly have been surprising had he emerged from these misfortunes in a state of depression and become a "lone wolf," the unwanted outsider on the fringe of society, as the Himmler legend would have it, but not at all—in Munich he entered upon a gay period of his career which presents many problems to the biographers.

He was friendly, helpful, studious and something of a bore. He appeared at fancy-dress parties as "Abdul Hamid, the Sultan of Trukey." He had an unfortunate love affair with a girl named Maja Loritz; he developed a passion for sweetmeats.[52] No one would have suspected that here was the later mass murderer.

Nevertheless he was still fascinated by politics and soldiering. A receipt of 16 May 1920 shows that he enrolled in the Munich Home Guard [Einwohnerwehr] receiving from No. 21 Rifle Brigade "1 rifle and 50 rounds, 1 steel helmet, 2 ammunition pouches, 1 haversack (old type)."[53] 1 December 1921 was a great day in his life—the Reichswehr informed him that he could henceforth call himself "Fähnrich" [Ensign].[54] Together with other nationalist students and officers he was preparing a plot to liberate Eisner's murderer, Count Arco-Valley. When the Count's sentence of death was commuted to life imprisonment the conspirators abandoned their plan, but Himmler was not downcast, simply noting in his diary: "Well then, some other time."[55]

He had far more serious worries. In November 1919 he had joined a students' association named "Apollo"[56] and was now cudgelling his brains over the problem of reconciling his new existence with his strict Catholic family upbringing and the weakness of his stomach—the Church forbade duelling and his doctor prohibited the customary drinking in the beer cellars. The beer problem was quickly solved; he managed to obtain special dispensation from the fraternity, excusing him from beer-drinking.[57] The members of "Apollo," however, did not take Himmler very seriously and at the next elections for membership he was dropped.[58] He also had difficulty in finding a duelling partner—most of his fellow students evidently considered him unworthy. Not until his last term, in June 1922, was an opponent found to give Himmler the facial scars which the future Reichsführer-SS considered any true teutonic student must be able to display.[59]

The church's ban on duelling was a much more agonising problem than the beer. The Himmlers had always been Catholics; a cousin, August Wilhelm Patin, was even a Canon of Munich Cathedral.[60] Himmler was a practising Catholic and Sunday Mass was more than an outward ritual for him; it was a spiritual experience. He always noted in his diary when he went to Church, frequently saying: "I like being in this Church."[61] When he learnt that a girl whom he was shyly courting went to Communion daily, he commented: "This was the greatest joy which I have experienced these past eight days."[62]

His entry into the students' fraternity cast a shadow over Himmler's relationship with the Church. There was no sudden break but his separation from the Church gradually became more definite. Personally averse to duelling, Himmler initially tried to follow the Church's dictates but eventually the urge to conform to his social environment (a heritage from his parents) overcame his religious scruples. On 15 December 1919 he noted "I believe that I have come into conflict with my religion,"[63] but he continued: "Come what may, I shall always love God, shall pray to him and shall remain faithful to the Catholic Church and shall defend it even if I should be expelled from it."[64] (Yet this was the man who later compelled tens of thousands of SS men to leave the Church and advocated a public execution of the Pope.)[65]

His relationship to the Church left him worried but unshaken. He was more interested in worldly matters, more concerned with the gay society of Munich, meals in Frau Loritz's house and a student's sexual problems than with religion and politics.

Anna Loritz, widow of a professional singer, was a distant relative of the Himmlers. She kept a boarding-house at 9 Jägerstrasse, Munich. Himmler fell in love with her daughter, Maria, known as Maja, but found that his rival, Hans Knipp, who later became a leather merchant in Stuttgart, stood higher in her affections.[66] The whole Himmler family would sometimes meet in the Loritz house. Knipp recalled that "there were always great greetings in the Loritz house when the five Himmlers arrived. The Himmler family knew that the food was always good at Auntie Loritz's."[67] Himmler enjoyed the parties in the Loritz home. While he was still in Landshut, Robert Kistler, a regimental friend, had written to him: "Are you taking dancing lessons?"[68] and in Munich he immediately took lessons in the hope of improving his standing with Maja. By January 1920 he had already learnt "the Boston."[69] With his friend Ludwig, nicknamed "Lu," he was a regular attendant at Munich Festivities.[70] Every detail went down in his diary; he describes one of the Loritz parties: "The room decked out as a harem, lanterns, a tent near the oven in the corner for Lu and myself . . . Frau Loritz served enormously much food, first cocoa, which I spilled over my pants."[71] So occupied was he with his social life that the National-Socialist Party Rally, held in Munich at about this time, passed him by.[72] The American historians, Werner Angress and Bradley Smith, describe him as: "a young man who thought in conventional terms, cherished Bavarian middle-class values and who seems to have been eminently good-natured, colourless and normal."[73]

He was full of good works. During the Christmas vacation he read to a blind man, fetched a cake for an old pauper woman and took part in a charity play for the poor children of Vienna; he rushed from one meeting to another,[74] for he was a member of numerous societies —cultural, farming, humanist, rifle-shooting, ex-servicemen, mountain-climbing, touring, gymnastics, regimental old comrades.[75] A member of so many societies had little difficulty in adapting himself to his environment. His political ideas were mere reflections of the views and prejudices of the society in which he moved—normal middle-class nationalist ideas with no trace of National-Socialist ideological fanaticism or of its spectral creed.

In fact at this period Himmler was a typical Bavarian conservative. He borrowed a top hat and frock coat to attend the funeral of ex-King Ludwig III; he was proud of being a Bavarian. At the elections for Asta, the student government at the University, he voted for the Nationalists.[76] Even his comments on the Jews at this stage were moderate. When he heard of the murder of Rathenau, the Foreign Minister, he noted: "I am glad" but nevertheless considered him "an able man."[77] He referred good-humouredly to Wolfgang Hallgarten, with whom he had been at school, as "a Jewish louse";[78] when he met the Jewish cabaret artist, Inge Barco, in the Reichsadler Bar, he found her "a girl who deserves respect," although she had been turned out of home for having an affair with a student.[79]

Only on one point do his diaries show the aggressive spirit characteristic of the later Himmler: he could not accept the fact that his military career was over. When Maja Loritz refused her gauche suitor, soldiering and war seemed to him the surest way to escape from the pangs of love. On 28 November 1919 he noted: "If I only could face dangers now, could risk my life, could fight, it would be a relief to me."[80] On 22 November 1921 the style of the latter-day Himmler showed through for the first time; he wrote: "If there is another campaign in the East I will go along. The East is most important for us. The West will die easily. In the East we must fight and colonise."[81] From time to time his longing for war and a military career would get the better of him; on 19 February 1922 he wrote: "If only there would he fighting again, war, departing troops!"[82] And on 11 June: "Perhaps I will join up in one way or another. For basically I am a soldier. But first I am going to take my exams."[83]

In July 1922 Himmler told his parents: "So far I think all is going reasonably well with my exams."[84] But then there entered Heinrich Himmler's life the man with whom his association was to end in such bloody and dramatic circumstances—Captain Ernst Röhm—and he offered the unrequited lover some prospect of satisfying his military ambitions.

It is impossible to establish with any accuracy when the two men first met. Their paths had crossed on several occasions: in late 1918 Röhm was serving on the staff of 12 Bavarian Infantry Division located in Landshut, Himmler's home town;[85] then he had been Armaments and Equipment Officer of 21 Rifle Brigade in Munich,[86] the unit from which Himmler had recieved his weapons in May 1920; now in 1922 Röhm was acting as secret quartermaster to the quasi-legal defence organisations accepted by the Reichswehr as a type of militia. Himmler met Röhm in January 1922 in the Arzberger Keller, Munich, at a meeting of one of these formations; he noted: "Captain Röhm and Major Angerer [Himmler's late Company Commander] were also there; very friendly. Röhm pessimistic as to Bolshevism."[87] Himmler was impressed by Röhm; he became the barrack-square cadet once more, unable to forget that Röhm stood several rungs higher on the military ladder; whenever Himmler met Röhm, he instinctively tended to click his heels. They were an ill-assorted pair—the much-decorated First World War Company Commander and the frustrated warrior, the homosexual freebooter and the prim son of a middle-class family. Yet Röhm knew how to rouse the young man's enthusiasm—Himmler was prepared to stake his all for Röhm.

Himmler passed his examination on 5 August 1922[88] and took a job as agricultural assistant at a chemical factory in Schleissheim;[89] immediately thereafter, on Röhm's advice, he joined a nationalist organisation called "Reichsflagge."[90] He was glad to be entitled at last to wear uniform again, even if only the gaiters and light grey windcheater of the "Reichsflagge." He was only too ready to shoulder his rifle on Saturday evenings and train with others of his ilk for the street fighting which the imminent civil war would bring.

He soon had a chance to give practical expression to

his admiration for Röhm. At the end of August 1923 he gave up his job in Schleissheim and returned to Munich;[91] shortly thereafter Hitler's November putsch gave him his first opportunity of appearing in the forefront of the nationalist movement. After considerable internal intrigue Reichsflagge had been rechristened "Reichskriegsflagge" and placed itself under the leadership of Röhm and Hitler.[92] Röhm had long been a member of Hitler's Party and he knew how to persuade his friends to join the NSDAP; Himmler did so.[93] But this did not mean that he was a Nazi; he saw Röhm, not Hitler, as the coming man; for him the flag of the monarchy, not the swastika, was the standard of the future.

On the evening of 8 November 1923 Himmler appeared at a meeting of the Reichskriegsflagge in the Löwenbräukeller, Munich, carrying the Imperial war flag; during the meeting the news arrived that Hitler, brandishing his revolver, had at last persuaded Bavaria's leading politicians and military personalities assembled in the Bürgerbräukeller to strike against the Berlin "November Criminals."[94] Röhm has described the scene, saying that in their enthusiasm "people leapt on to chairs and embraced each other, many were weeping from joy and emotion. The Reichswehr soldiers tore the yellow cockades from their caps. At last! Those were the words of relief which burst from every throat."[95] Röhm handed Himmler the old Reich war flag to which the unit had just sworn its oath, and called his men out on to the streets. A few minutes later they were formed up in column and moved off in step towards the Bürgerbräukeller where Hitler was discussing the "National Revolution" with the great men of Bavaria, Ritter von Kahr the Bavarian Nationalist Commissar-General, and General von Lossow, the Reichswehr Commander in Bavaria. When it reached the Briennerstrasse, Röhm's column was stopped by a messenger from the Bürgerbräukeller with an order to occupy the War Ministry in the Schönfeld strasse, which contained the headquarters of Wehrkreis [Military District] VII (Bavaria).[96] Röhm did as he was told and barely an hour later he was in possession of the War Ministry.[97] He had 400 men; the muzzles of their machine guns poked menacingly out of the windows,[98] for even Röhm was gradually beginning to realise that something had gone wrong—after their initial surprise Bavaria's politicians and generals were striking back.

Early on the morning of 9 November the intruders in the War Ministry were left in no doubt that things had indeed gone wrong; the noise of approaching tanks was heard; Reichswehr and police units moved forward and cordoned off each house, brought machine guns and artillery into position and waited for the order to fire.[99] An ominous silence ensued. On the Ludwigstrasse, where friend and foe were separated by a barbed-wire entanglement, Himmler still clutched the Reich war flag. Hitler's lunatic miscalculation had brought together a curious concourse of men—future friends and enemies, future murderers and victims; next to Himmler stood Röhm, the future head of the SA, who eleven years later was to be struck down by the SS myrmidons of the man now carrying his standard; next to Röhm was Count du Moulin-Eckardt, the future SA Intelligence Chief, who was to end in one of Himmler's concentration camps.[100] Opposite them, on the other side of the barbed wire, was Reichswehr Lieutenant Hermann Höfle, Röhm's ex-aide and a secret member of Reichskriegsflagge, who in the summer of 1934 was to warn his old chief of impending danger and later be a thorn in Himmler's flesh as a Waffen-SS general.[101]

Today's enemies are tomorrow's friends, today's comrades tomorrow's murderers; von Kahr and Röhm, the enemies of 1923, met a similar fate at the hands of the SS thugs on 30 June 1934.[102] The only actors on the 1923 stage whom the SS allowed to survive were those who tried to mediate between Kahr and the putschists—Röhm's form commander, Ritter von Epp and Hörauf, later an SA Commander.[103] But their attempt at mediation failed. Röhm had to capitulate to the Reichswehr and the police, handing over his weapons; the men of Reichskriegsflagge were only allowed through the cordon when disarmed.[104] Hitler's and Röhm's movement had apparently collapsed. Rohm was imprisoned in Stadelheim.[105]

So Himmler was alone again—no uniform, no idol, no creed. He was facing a crisis; he had lost his job and in spite of numerous applications could not find another. Maja Loritz had definitely turned him down and politics had proved a disappointment. His only consolation was the worship of his female admirers, who seriously

thought that Himmler had done something historic by
carrying the flag on 9 November 1923. One of them wrote
emotionally: "Troops of the Reichskriegsflagge in front
of the War Ministry. Heinrich Himmler at their head carrying the flag; one could see how secure the flag felt in his
hands and how proud he was of it. I go up to him incapable of speaking a word but ringing in my ears is:

> Be proud I carry the flag
> Have no cares I carry the flag
> Love me I carry the flag."[106]

This letter from an unknown admirer was forwarded
to Himmler by his friend "Maria R." (probably Mariele
Rauschmeier) with a note: "This letter is for my friend
Heinrich. Let it be a small indication of our fervent gratitude and faithful memory of that deed which gave us a
few moments when we learnt to hope once more."[107]

In spite of the failure of the beer-cellar putsch,
Himmler decided to stay in politics. When the NSDAP
was banned, the movement split into two warring "Völkisch" groups:[108] Himmler joined the National-Socialist
Freedom Movement headed by General Ludendorff.[109]
Another member was Gregor Strasser,[110] a chemist from
Landshut and a passing acquaintance of Himmler's; he was
an aggressive, energetic, shrewd National-Socialist, regarded
as the real brains of the Movement, and he soon recognised
Himmler's organising ability; he began to make use of
him forthwith.

In May 1924 there were to be elections for the Reichstag and the enemies of the Republic decided to seize
the opportunity to use democracy's weapons and virtues
—to bring democracy down. Strasser wished to cash in on
the nation-wide publicity evoked by the Hitler putsch to
get his Nazis into the Reichstag at last. Bavaria thought of
little else but its first election campaign, and a feature
of it was a Swedish motorcycle carrying a heavily muffled
propagandist who rushed from one Lower Bavarian village
to another spreading Gregor Strasser's message.

With his motor-cycle Himmler beat all records of National Socialist demagogy. He raged against Jews and
Freemasons; he whipped up the peasants against the
capitalists; he painted a picture of a world peopled only

by noble peasants; he thundered against Bolshevism; he decried democracy and all forms of rational policy.[111] He travelled indefatigably; in one week his diary shows: "23 February 1924, speeches in Eggmuhl, Lanwaid and Birnbach. 24 February, discussions in Kelheim and Saal followed by 'individual enlightenment.' 25 February, one and a half hour's lecture in Rohr."[112] On 22 August 1924 he told his friend Kistler: "I have a terrible amount to do; I have to direct and build up the organisation in the whole of Lower Bavaria—and that in every sense."[113] His industry was rewarded, for Strasser's movement captured nearly two million votes and entered the Reichstag with 32 deputies.[114] But this success brought no joy to Himmler; he was beginning to wonder whether the Movement he had joined really offered prospects for the future. In a letter to Kistler he referred to "the unselfish efforts we Völkische are making, efforts which will apparently never bear fruit in the immediate future," adding that he felt he was supporting "a potentially lost cause."[115]

A weak character like Himmler was discouraged by the quarrelling between the Völkische and the National-Socialists and by the intrigues between the supporters and opponents of Hitler. He just stood bewildered, a member of the extremist right-wing gang, searching for an idol who would once more give him something to conform to. He was ready to be a slave but could not find a master. He was determined to believe in something but did not know what. He was longing to play some role in history and could already see himself as a martyr, writing:

"Although they may pierce you
Fight, resist, stand by
You yourself may perish
But keep the banner high.
Others may win victory
When you're laid to rest
And shall gain that glory
To which you aspired."[116]

The problem was—what was this banner to be, what was the sacred cause it was worth dying for? Himmler knew only too well that he was no saviour, was not born to greatness. His self-confidence was always sapped by a

nagging doubt; he could never quite convince himself that
he was cut out to be a commanding figure. Faithfully he
recorded in his diary what he thought of himself and
decided that he lacked self-assurance, talked too much and
was inclined to make too many silly jokes: "What a miserable creature is man," he wrote on 7 November 1919,[117]
and on 29 January 1922: "I am a phrasemonger and chatter box and without energy. Got nothing done . . . they
think of me as a gay fellow who is amusing and takes
care of everything: 'Heini will see to it.' "[118] He knew better.

He was so unsure of himself that he seriously toyed
with the idea of leaving Germany. He learnt Russian and
thought of settling and farming somewhere in the East;
on another occasion his future seemed to him to lie in
Turkey or Peru; between 1919 and 1924 his diary contains no fewer than fourteen references to plans for
emigrating.[119] Yet this insecure and superstitious being became convinced that he was destined for some terrible
fate. (Years later he wrote to his wife: "We soldiers of
fortune are doomed to remain lonely outlaws," to which
she replied: "Don't always look on the black side; let
the future take care of itself."[120] A few days later she was
even more explicit: "Here you are again saying that this
New Year is going to be horrible. Have you joined the
astrologers and become convinced that Mars is in the ascendant and that therefore there will be horror upon
horror? Do please stop it."[121]) He did not master his self-
torturing doubts until he came into the orbit of the man
who at once became his demi-god—Adolf Hitler. Hitler
was released from Landsberg prison in December 1924.[122]
He at once set about reforming the proscribed and divided
NSDAP and within a year had swept away all that
Himmler had found distasteful in the Völkisch camp. On
27 February 1925 he united under his leadership the main
body of Bavaria's Völkisch and National-Socialist Parties
to form a new NSDAP; two months later he founded
the SS, and by the end of 1926 he had eliminated all his
Party rivals and could form his own Party army, the
SA.[123] With his instinct for subordinating himself to someone, Himmler sensed that he had found his idol. In August
1925 he received his membership card for the reconstituted Nazi Party;[124] shortly thereafter he was installed in

a sparsely furnished room near St Martin's church in Landshut as secretary to Gregor Strasser, at a salary of 120 marks a month.[125] Strasser, who was in charge of Party propaganda in Lower Bavaria, had plenty for his amanuensis to do. Himmler maintained contact with the most remote local Nazi groups; for the Nazi backwoodsmen he and his motorcycle became the outward and visible sign of the Nazi Party. Soon he was nominated local organiser for Lower Bavaria.[126]

It had been held that, like Goebbels, Himmler was an ideological disciple of Strasser, who later opposed Hitler. In fact Himmler always considered himself a Party headquarters employee rather than a follower of Strasser.[127] When Strasser moved to Berlin and became the North German counterweight to Hitler, Himmler moved closer to his Leader. It is not known when the two first met, but Himmler never overcame his shyness when in personal contact with the "greatest brain of all times," as he called Hitler.

While still in Strasser's office in Landshut, Himmler developed a schoolboyish adulation for his Führer. A friend of Himmler's told the writer Willi Frischauer that on the wall of his office was a picture of Hitler with which Himmler would hold murmured conversations.[128] Even when speaking to Hitler on the telephone Himmler would click his heels; on one occasion during the war his masseur, Felix Kersten, took a call from Hitler and Himmler could hardly contain himself at his good fortune: "Herr Kersten, do you know whom you have been talking to? You have heard the voice of the Führer. What luck! Put that in a letter to your wife straight away! How happy she will be that you should have had such a unique opportunity."[129]

The "time of struggle" when he was at Hitler's side was the high spot of Himmler's career. Even in 1945 he could still enthuse over it: "Those were glorious days. We members of the Movement were in constant danger of our lives, but we were not afraid. Adolf Hitler led us and held us together. They were the most wonderful years of my life."[130] He was always rushing about on his motorcycle in the service of his Führer, riddled with inhibitions, burning with ambition, plagued by stomach pains which often brought him near to fainting. "It is incredible what

you do," one of his Berlin female admirers told him at the
end of 1927: "You ask too much of yourself and your
stomach pays you back. Not surprising, since your stomach's right."[131] His future wife wrote to him in desperation: "So you're on the road again; I was only thinking
today that your life is one long rush."[132]

Hitler gave him his deserts and Himmler rose in the
Party hierarchy. In 1925 he became Deputy Gauleiter of
Upper Bavaria-Swabia, in the same year Deputy Reich
Propaganda Chief, in 1927 Deputy Reichsführer-SS.[133] In
the course of a few years the diffident, aimless student
developed into a fanatical disciple of Hitler, appreciated
by his Führer for his outstanding organising ability. But
good organisation alone did not satisfy Himmler; he
wished to be the trainer and teacher of those around him;
he saw himself leading Party and people back to the true
springs of life.

His long stay in the Lower Bavarian farm country had
left him strangely obsessed with the philosophy of "blood
and soil." From his earliest days his romantic historical
notions had led him to regard the peasantry as the main-
spring of the nation. "The yeoman on his own acre," he
opined, "is the backbone of the German people's strength
and character."[134] Later he maintained that by "origin,
blood and character" he was a peasant himself.[135] He
imagined all great men to be sons of peasants, and he
referred to his favourite hero, Heinrich I, "The Fowler"
(876–936), King of Saxony and conqueror of the Slavs,
as a "noble peasant of his people."[136] In his post-student
period, he was already under the spell of popular propaganda and he drew a picture for himself of a society
built around the peasantry. An undated memorandum by
Himmler envisages the farmers' shcool as the core of the
"back-to-the-land" State; its teachers and pupils were to
present the "true picture of the German character" and
be the forerunners of the new society.[137]

The teachers in this school, and for the peasant population of which he dreamed, were to be "masters" and
"companions," both male and female. The men must have
qualities of leadership and be conscious of this world's
"lies and frauds"; the schoolmistresses must be "lively,
clean-living women, with true maternal instincts, free from
the diseases of today's degenerate city women, strong and

gracious, leaving the last word to the man in the every-day things of life." This spring of life for Himmler's peas-antry was to be "decorated with homely taste" and be open at all times to "German citizens, poets and artists," thus forming a "spiritual and cultural centre" where the in-tellectual workers could "create, free from the intellectual currents of delusion." Here was clearly the origin of the National-Socialist and SS sociological Utopia. "But value will be placed upon character, rather than knowledge." Himmler went on; the products of his school were to be "men of healthy bodies, strong nerves and strong wills" who "in permanent and close contact with their school would rise to be leaders of the people."

Himmler even found friends prepared to take steps to put this nonsense into practice. They bought a farm in Lower Bavaria and made it available to Himmler. He hoped that there might be "a further set of generous people with the means and the will to set up a foundation." But he was disappointed;[138] the peasant school remained a figment of the imagination. Nevertheless Himmler did not abandon his idea of the peasants' Utopia; his father, after all, had been a tutor, and he thought he had dis-covered in himself a genius for teaching; he thought he had been born to be the great educator, ever ready to draw the useful lesson from events and circumstances.

Those around him were continually subjected to lectures on the doings of their ancestors in this case or that; he could always quote some historical example to illustrate the present and enlighten his contemporaries. Even during the war he longed for peace "when people could be educated again." Kersten, his masseur and perhaps most intimate friend, seriously thought that in his heart of hearts Himmler would have preferred to educate rather than exterminate the subject peoples of the East.[139] Himm-ler drew a conclusion even from the failure of his peasant school project but it was an unrealistic partisan conclusion. For the first time he had first-hand knowledge of the economic straits in which the farming population was placed—but his resultant reasoning was crazy.

Himmler, the peasant mystic, was oblivious to the fact that German agriculture was passing through a structural crisis dating from the abolition of Bismarck's protec-tionist policy, if not earlier; he was equally oblivious to the

pressing necessity for rationalisation and the elimination
of unproductive smallholdings. His picture was quite different; he saw a multi-coloured web of evil labelled "International Jewry." The countryman's "worst enemy," he
wrote in 1924, was "international Jewish capital" because
it "set the townsman against the countryman." This was
how it was done: "By speculation and playing the markets,
the Jews ensure that production prices are low and con-
sumer prices high. The farmer is supposed to earn little,
the townsman to pay much. The Jews and their hangers-
on grab the middleman's inflated profits."[140] Up to the
putsch of November 1923 the Jews pictured in Himmler's
diaries had, at least, been individuals; now, however, the
Jew became a stereotyped generalised caricature and
every "non-Aryan" a partisan of the supposed world-wide
menace of Jewry. From this point, the Jews in Himmler's
scheme of things became simply a target for collective
vilification. The future Reichsführer-SS had found his enemy.

In this same memorandum Himmler referred to another
equally indispensable arch-enemy—the Slavs. The German
peasantry, he argued, could only be proved and strength-
ened in battle against the Slavs, since the only future lay
in the East. "Particularly in the East," he said, "there are,
today, great masses of land available for purchase; they
are now held by the great estates. The sons of farmers
and farm-workers must be settled there to prevent the
second and third sons of the German farmer being forced
into the towns, as has been the case hitherto. The countryman can only regain decisive influence in Germany by
widespread resettlement." This re-settlement, moreover,
was a factor in German nationalist policy: "Increase of
our peasant population is the only effective defence
against the influx of the Slav working-class masses from
the East. As six hundred years ago, the German peasant's
destiny must be to preserve and increase the German people's patrimony in their holy mother earth in battle
against the Slav race."[141]

In this memorandum Heinrich Himmler had unconsciously formulated two of the central points of the later
SS programme, theories which lay at the root of the Third
Reich's anti-Jewish and anti-Slav policies. Battle against
the Slav "sub-human" and against "international Jewry"

became an *idée fixe*. The programme, of course, still lacked its fanatical overtones, its pseudo-religious frenzy but, in the case of Himmler, here is definitely the point at which the development of political fantasy began.

At this stage, of course, the Nazi Party was in no position to offer Himmler any hope of putting his peasant theories into practice. He accordingly joined a group known as the "Artamans," which seemed to be prepared to do something serious about the back-to-the-land idea. The Artamans originated from the Völkisch wing of the German Youth Movement. They were nationalist idealists obsessed with the notion of the owner-settler. Most of them did not belong to the NSDAP (although their leader Georg Kenstler did); they were a collection of youths who swore by "blood and soil" and suffered from an anti-Slav complex; one of the points in their programme was to force Polish farmworkers in the eastern provinces to return to Poland.[142]

In 1924 the first Artaman group set off for an estate in Saxony to do what they thought was their duty both to the economy and to the nation (Himmler's dream of an estate in Lower Bavaria was undoubtedly inspired by the Artamans); 2,000 youths rushed off to farms in East Germany and formed themselves up to defend Germany against the Slavs.[143] Himmler was fast becoming one of the leaders of the movement; he was made "Gauführer" of Bavaria[144] and maintained contact with other Artaman groups in Germany (including one in Brandenburg, a member of which was a certain Rudolf Höss,[145] later to become one of Himmler's most sinister minions as commandant of Auschwitz).

In the ranks of the Artamans Himmler met a man who gave an ideological veneer to his own ideas on peasant policy and incorporated them into a body of racial doctrine, that of the superiority of the nordic race. This was Richard Walther Darré, an Argentine German, born in 1895, educated at King's College School, Wimbledon, ex-official in the Prussian Ministry of Agriculture and future Nazi Party agrarian expert; Himmler was five years his junior, and Darré took him under his wing.[146] He taught Himmler what he had been preaching for years; the agricultural problem was not primarily one of economics but one "of the blood." According to Darré the peasantry had "always formed the only reliable basis for our people from the point of view of blood";[147] it was therefore the duty of the state to expand this peasant basis, and this must be done by settlement schemes, raising the birthrate and curbing the drift to the towns. It was imperative, so Darré said, "to bind the best blood among our people irrevocably and as quickly as possible to the soil."[148] The best source of blood, according to Darré, was that mythical concept with which the Völkisch Youth Movement was already wrestling—The Nordic Race. Darré claimed to have discovered that historically the world had been fashioned by "men with nordic blood in their veins." "We know," he went on, "that almost all great empires in the history of the world and all the greatest cultures have been founded and maintained by men of nordic blood. We know also that these great empires and cultures have fallen into ruins because the men of nordic blood who had constructed them, did not keep their blood pure."[149]

The practical present-day consequences of this theory were that all influences inimical to the nordic blood myth must be held at bay, all international humanist organisations must be suppressed—and these ranged from freemasonry, endowed by National-Socialist propagandists with the attributes of a dominant world power, to Christainity, which preached reconciliation between peoples and among men. Fascinated, Himmler saw opening up before him a world whose existence he had dimly suspected but which he had never been able to visualise clearly. Darré, with his doctrine of blood and soil, opened Himmler's eyes, and what he saw was wonderful—the Völkisch élite of the future, the lords of the new Germanic tribes, the men of his SS Order.

The Artamans disappeared into the quicksands of history; the idealism of the Youth Movement yielded to the egoism of the great eastern landowners who were quick to turn the townee dreamers to good use.[150] But for a long time Himmler did not forget his debt to Darré and the Artamans. Later he recruited Darré into the SS, and put him in charge of his new "Rasse-und Siedlungsamt" [Race and Re-Settlement Office],[151] which Darré used as a stepping stone to the Reich Ministry of Agriculture. Himmler himself now began to teach this "blood and soil" mythology to his own organisation, the Lower Bavarian SS. The peasant theorist in SS uniform caught the eye of the senior Party members and Himmler saw before him the possibility of becoming head of the entire SS. Even so, he was still uncertain whether his future lay on the land or with the SS. He thought he had found someone with whom to share his life as a peasant settler.

In 1926, to escape a sudden shower, he dashed into the foyer of a hotel in Bad Reichenhall and almost ran into a lady to whom he swept off his dripping hat with such gallantry that she was soaked.[152] When Himmler looked up in embarrassment, he saw before him the Germanic goddess of his dreams—blonde and blue-eyed, like one of the Valkyries. She was Margarete Boden, daughter of a German landowner in Goncerzewo, West Prussia.[153] She had worked as a nurse during the First World War, and then moved to Berlin where, after a short-lived marriage, she had used her father's money to found a private clinic.[154]

Himmler fell in love at first sight, but his parents were less than pleased with their son's choice. Marga, as she was called, was eight years older than Heinrich and, to make matters worse, a Protestant *and* divorced.[155] Himmler hesitated for a long time before producing Marga to his parents. He said to his brother Gebhard, "I would rather clear a hall of a thousand Communists single-handed,"[156] but the parents eventually gave way and abandoned the two to their illusions. Heinrich and Marga were married on 3 July 1928[157] and planned to set up on a farm together. Marga sold her private clinic, and with the proceeds the two bought a piece of land at Waldt-rudering near Munich, on which they built a small wooden house—three up and two down. Heinrich insisted upon putting up a chicken-house himself, for they planned to run a large chicken farm.[158]

Months before they were married Marga wrote: "Darling I think so often of that little bit of land which we shall eventually own," and then continued in the bantering style she initially used to Himmler: "Darling, I believe the wicked husband always has to worry about the savings, for you know that the bad wife always spends all the money she's got."[159] They collected 50 laying hens[160] but the farming project failed owing to lack of money and the

calls of Heinrich's Party career. As an NSDAP employee
Himmler earned 200 marks a month[161] but this proved inadequate to run a chicken farm. On 6 May 1929 Marga
wrote to her husband: "The hens are laying frightfully
badly—two eggs a day. I worry so much about what we're
going to live on and how we're going to save for Whitsun.
Something's always going wrong. I save so hard, but the
money's like everything else."[162] Money was a continual
worry; another letter said: "You have not written; that's
naughty. Now the money won't come tomorrow morning and so Berta [the maid] won't be able to get your
shoes."[163]

In addition to their financial troubles the marriage now
began to break up—far more rapidly than either of them
had thought possible. Marga was cold, nervous and anything but cheerful; she irked her sensitive husband so
much that he began to stay away from home more often.
After the birth of their only child, a daughter named
Gudrun,[164] the Himmlers lived apart.

Vainly Marga hoped that one day National-Socialist politics would allow her husband to return to her: "When
the elections are over, then we could at least have a few
years of peace. And you, you will be with me all the
time."[165] In another letter: "You naughty soldier of fortune; you must come to this part of the world sometimes."[166] And again: "Even if you're only coming for two
days, at least you're coming."[167] Gradually, however,
Marga realised that she had lost him. "Sometimes it makes
me sad that I just have to sit at home here all the
time. Only today I was thinking how we could celebrate
your birthday. My dear, let's go to some exhibition together. We've never done that."[168] And in another letter: "Things are not good with me. What is going to
become of me. One is continually wondering that. Oh
my dear, what is going to become of me?"[169]

Heinrich Himmler did not know what *was* going to become of her. He was under the spell of the Führer, who
on 6 January 1929 had called him to head of the SS
in which he was member No. 168.[170] Now he could show
what he had learned from Strasser and Walther Darré.
The SS was waiting, Himmler thought, only for the
master's hand to turn it into an order of chivalry, the
elite of National-Socialism. In fact, the new Reichsführer-

SS soon found out that ideological purism was not what his Führer demanded of him. Hitler wanted no order of faithful Germanic knights, but a blindly obedient body-guard as an instrument of his personal power. The National-Socialist Party had reached a crossroads. The economic crisis of the late 1920s was driving an increasing number of embittered Germans into the Nazi camp, both reinforcing and endangering Hitler's position as Party Leader. That position had to be safeguarded in face of all opposition: the most murderous chapter in the history of German party politics was about to open.

4

From Bodyguard to
Party Police Force

DURING the Nazi "struggle period," Ludolf Haase, the local Nazi leader for Hanover South, wrote a memorandum to Party Headquarters in which he suggested that the NSDAP had disintegrated after the November 1923 putsch because the Party had no corps of leaders, and the leaders had no instrument of power. What the reconstituted Party needed was: "A National Socialist Order within the Party," a secret society, ready at all times to provide the leadership with guards and henchmen. It should be a secret Order within the Party to hold the movement together in an iron grip. The men of this Order would "cleanse the organisation including, if necessary, affiliated formations and authorities"; at the same time "by observation, etc." they should obtain "the indispensable knowledge concerning the enemy's plans, actions and circumstances." Within the "general ruck of the NSDAP" the future National-Socialist Order must form an organisation "to provide the instrument which a senior leader must have, if he is successfully to pursue any popular power policy."[1]

This was a prophetic description of the basic SS concept which was later to throw its shadow over the whole Party. But Haase's memorandum produced no action from Party Headquarters; it was pigeon-holed, and its author forgotten.

In January 1929, however, in an annexe to the Party Headquarters building (50 Schellingstrasse, Munich) a man arrived who thought the same way as Haase and in whose personal files Haase's memorandum was later found. This was Heinrich Himmler, the new Reichsführer-SS, and he had every intention of forming his own organisation "within the general ruck of the NSDAP." Initially, however, he fared little better than Haase. The Party greeted his ambitions with pitying condescension.

Many regarded Himmler as an eccentric. People said that he was a fanatic who had produced this curious elite concept by applying his professional knowledge of animal breeding to the official racial doctrine of the Party. Moreover, his exorbitant ambition was out of all proportion to the minute size of the Party organisation for which he was responsible. The strength of the SS at the time was 280 men; it was under Franz Pfeffer von Salomon, the "SA Supreme Commander" [OSAF] who regarded it with little favour, and it had difficulty in making headway against the view current in the NSDAP that it was a sort of canvassing organisation for the Party Press.

But Himmler was undeterred by the Party's scorn. He drew up an ambitious expansion programme envisaging a rapid numerical increase in the SS and official acceptance of its status as an elite. In April 1929 he submitted to Hitler and von Salomon a draft of regulations which, in effect, constituted the Order of the SS.[2] Henceforth no one was to be accepted into the SS who did not satisfy the strictest selection conditions; Darré, the "blood and soil" mystic, was of course behind it and his only criterion was race, his ideal human being the romanticised picture of the nordic warrior hero.

In a wartime speech Himmler said: "We went about it like a nursery gardener trying to reproduce a good old strain which has been adulterated and debased; we started from the principles of plant selection and then proceeded, quite unashamedly, to weed out the men whom we did not think we could use for the build-up of the SS."[3] Had such lofty principles been strictly applied, Himmler would have had to dismiss the best part of half his SS, for they were mostly simple middle-class citizens, bearing little resemblance to Walther Darré's picture of glorious Germanic man. But Himmler had no intention of carrying out so self-destructive an exercise. His orders stated that the new regulations did not apply to old SS

members who had served in the First World War.[4] He
tightened his selection programme only by degrees: "I
started with a minimum height requirement of 5 ft 8 in,"[5]
adding with the pride of the visionary: "I knew that
men of a certain height must somewhere possess the blood
I desired."[6]

Every applicant had to submit a photograph, at which
Himmler would gaze through a magnifying glass until he
was convinced that the man possessed what, in his vocabulary of racial purity, was termed "good blood."[7] He once
told his officers: "I used to think: are there any definite
indications of foreign blood in this man—prominent cheek
bones, for instance, which might cause people to say 'he
has a Mongolian or Slav look about him'? Why did I
do that? Let me draw your attention to the lessons of
experience. Think of the types who were members of
the soldiers' councils in 1918 and 1919."[8]

This remark shows that Himmler's insistence on biological criteria, primarily that of "good blood," did not
stem solely from racist fantasy, He was also appealing
to the idaas and emotions of the ex-officers and Free
Corps commanders for whom the "soldiers' councils"
epitomised their own degradation. At the end of the war
left-wing soldier extremists had torn off their officers'
badges of rank, and the officers had never recovered
from this traumatic experience; but on the other side
of the coin, the soldiers' councils had found these same
officers unwilling to lift a finger to protect their imperial
supreme commander against revolution. Himmler had only
been a cadet at the time, and so had no personal experience of the soldiers' councils—what Röhm called "this
ignoble capitulation to the red mob";[9] nevertheless, he
would frequently remind ex-officers of that unhappy
period; "every one of you who was an officer at the time
has personal experience of a large number of these people. You will therefore be able to confirm that, in general,
they were people who somehow looked odd to Germans,
who had some peculiar feature showing that there was
foreign blood somewhere."[10]

Such arguments were well calculated to appeal to the
emotions of the section of society from which Himmler
drew his first SS men. They were a lonely collection of
ex-soldiers, academics whose careers had been ruined by

inflation, and unemployed professional men; after drifting through the Free Corps and the Nationalist Defence Formations, they were now looking for a new form of community existence and Himmler's notion of a racial elite fascinated them. He could promise them a home and release from the constrictions imposed by life as an uprooted member of a society whose social prestige had vanished.

Hitherto the word "elite" had had a social connotation; entry into the elite postulated possessions, education and good breeding, but the lost generation which had grown up at the front found that door closed; the difficulties of re-adaptation and their romanticised "soldier-of-fortune" theories had driven them into society's no-man's land. Instead of the social elite, Himmler now held out to them the prospect of a quite different elite—a racial aristocracy, an ideological nobility. The notion of the "good blood" elite was propounded in sufficiently broad and nebulous terms to offer a refuge to all this lost collection of humanity—provided they satisfied Himmler. They were soon presenting themselves in droves.

The original founders of the SS had come from lower-middle-class suburbia, men like Ulrich Graf, who worked in a butcher's shop, and Josef Berchtold, who kept a small stationery business. Now men from another level of society were flooding into the SS—the lost souls of the middle and upper-middle classes. The SS attracted these newcomers by its philosophy of "hardness" and its attitude of bellicosity per se, basically unconnected with ideology. The newcomers' background was obvious; they were the left-overs from the Free Corps, people whom Ernst von Salomon, the Free Corps minstrel and one of Rathenau's murderers, referred to in 1930 as "the men whom war will never let go, who will always have war in their blood."[11]

The men of the Free Corps were an example, only too typically German, of a generation which despised culture and civilisation. They had looked to the world war they had longed for as the means of sweeping away all the evils of bourgeois hypocrisy and complacency; they had hoped to "lose their selves," in the words of their British idol, T. E. Lawrence.[12] The war was now over but, to their annoyance, bourgeois society was still in existence.

The men who had survived the trenches hoped that they had fought the war to end all wars, but the generation which had grown up during the war still hoped that the bourgeois world they despised could be brought down by force.

Contempt for the pre-war world turned into loathing for the post-war order of society; to the wartime generation, force and savagery were justified, even in peacetime, in order to destroy the ill-gotten gains of bourgeois civilisation; to make matters worse, among them were poets, the beauty of whose language inhibited clear thinking. Perhaps the greatest mouthpiece of this lost generation was Ernst Jünger, who had risen to the rank of captain and won the *Pour-le-Mérite;* he proclaimed that for all time war would remain "like a rocky mountain within us, from which we shall stride down into the valley below to seek the promised land. And so long as the wheel of life turns within us, this war will always be the axle around which it revolves. The war may be at an end, its battlefields deserted and condemned as torture chambers and Calvaries, but in its acolytes its spirit lives on; it will never allow them to leave its service."[13]

In the confused post-war period in Germany there was plenty of opportunity for life to revolve around the axle of war. The State needed fighting men to defend itself against Communist insurrection and Polish insurgents; the wartime generation was only too glad to take up arms once more; had not Jünger told them: "What can be more sacred than the fighting man?" But these new-type soldiers were very different from the old. They called their units Free Corps to emphasise that they had entered government service voluntarily—and that equally voluntarily they could leave it again. Their loyalty was not to the government, but to whatever flag they happened to be following and to the particular commander in whose unit they served.

This collection of bellicose political adventurers who constituted the Free Corps of 1919 and 1920 can hardly be paralleled in German military history. Second Lieutenants commanded units calling themselves regiments; orders from far-distant headquarters were obeyed or disobeyed as the recipients thought fit. They were soldiers of fortune and proud to admit it. Like the old soldiers of fortune, their unit was their home, their fellow-soldiers their family. There were 70,000 of them and, like the old mercenaries, they were possessed with an "insatiable restlessness, a determination to burn themselves out; they felt the primeval male urge permanently to court danger. As soldiers of fortune, they accepted the disdain of the corpulent sedentary bourgeoisie and returned it in full measure round their camp fires and in their quarters, in battle or on the march. They denied both the ideas and the values of that other respectable half of the world."[14]

These men were ripe material for a doctrine of uninhibited use of force. The traditions and norms of the old-style military discipline had been swept away and their place was taken by a drum-head courtmartial system, euphemistically termed "judicial self-help." Anyone the Free Corps thought guilty they shot. Human life, either their own or that of others, counted little; their watchword, like that of the later Waffen-SS, was to deal out or to accept death.[15] In 1930 Ernst von Salomon extolled the Free Corps for their "ruthless action against armed or unarmed enemy masses, their limitless contempt for the so-called sanctity of life and their marked disinclination to take prisoners under any circumstances."[16] Ten years later these were the hallmarks of Himmler's soldiers.

When the Free Corps came to an end, the use of force infected politics like a cancer, the victims being the democrats and the republicans; terror was the watchword of the nationalist parties and defence formations. Even so, however, the men of the Free Corps were still without a home. Some of them took refuge in the SA, where they rose to senior positions. But meanwhile, driven by the economic depression, countless thousands of unemployed were streaming into the SA and the ex-Free Corps men began to realise that the SA was no home either. The SA men recruited from the queues of the labour exchanges were simply rebelling against the circumstances of the time; they were merely expecting Adolf Hitler to give them jobs so that they could return to their wives and children. The men of the Free Corps, on the other hand, although they might wear brown shirts, despised the bourgeois world to which even the toughest SA thug in his heart of hearts wished to return.[17]

Himmler's elitist Order offered these men a real home.

From 1929 onwards men of the Free Corps began to stream into the SS. They came in two waves; first appeared the veterans who had neither wished nor been able to reintegrate themselves into society. They included some well-known names: Erich von dem Bach-Zelewski, a Reichswehr officer from Pomerania, who had had to resign from his Infantry Regiment for indulging in National-Socialist intrigue; from 1931 he was the SS organiser in the Austrian frontier zone.[18] Then there was Friedrich Karl Freiherr von Eberstein, a First World War Lieutenant who became aide to Graf Helldorf when a Free Corps Commander; he later took over the SS in Saxony.[19] Finally there was Udo von Woyrsch, another First World War Lieutenant and an officer of the Frontier Protection Service; he organised the SS in Silesia.[20]

The economic crisis produced a second wave of applicants for the SS. This time they were men who had managed to get a foot in the door of everyday life, but had lost their positions in the pitiless competition of a free economy. The spur which drove them into SS uniform was bankruptcy. Friedrich-Wilhelm Krüger, for instance, a colonel's son and ex-Lieutenant in Lutzow's Free Corps, had been a freelance salesman;[21] Karl Wolff, the son of a country solicitor and ex-Lieutenant in the Grand Duke of Hesse's Regiment of Lifeguards, had run an advertising agency;[22] Dr Carl-Albrecht Oberg, a doctor's son and ex-Lieutenant on the western front, had been director of a banana import firm.[23]

With so many dynamic ex-Free Corps men entering the SS, Himmler could snap his fingers at the Party's objections to his expansion campaign. He travelled tirelessly through Germany recruiting his elite. When he announced in Hamburg that he intended to raise an SS unit of 500 men, Krebs, the Gauleiter, objected that Hamburg could hardly produce 500 National-Socialists in all; Himmler replied haughtily that the circumstances were unimportant and all that mattered was to get the men.[24]

Röhm, his former guide and counsellor, had meanwhile quarrelled with Hitler and gone off as German military instructor to Bolivia. On 29 January 1930 Himmler wrote to him that: "The SS is growing and by the end of this quarter should have reached 2,000";[25] he added that his Standartenführer [Colonels] were "splendid fellows" and that "as each month passed, service regulations and conditions of entry were being tightened."[26] SS numbers rose steadily; in January 1929 there were 280 SS men, in December 1929, 1,000, and, in December 1930, 2,717.[27] The SS grew so rapidly that Himmler finally felt himself strong enough to tap a source hitherto closed to SS recruiting—the SA.

Ever since the Frontbann period under Röhm, the SA had included certain ex-members of the Free Corps who were now only too anxious to transfer to the SS. However, Pfeffer, the head of the SA, took care that none of his subordinates should go over to Himmler; late in 1926 he had laid down that the SS was to act only in closest accord with SA Headquarters.[28] As a matter of principle the SS was forbidden to act on its own; when SA and SS were used together, the SS was always placed under the SA commander.[29] Pfeffer was particularly careful to keep control of SS recruiting, insisting on being consulted for fear lest the SS "syphon off all potential commanders and thereby involuntarily strangle the development of the SA."[30]

But Himmler was undeterred by Pfeffer's restrictions. He began quietly to sing the praises of his SS Order among the SA, and succeeded in weaning many of them away. This did not pass unnoticed by the SA commanders; early in 1931 Stennes, the SA commander in East Germany, wrote to Röhm: "It is most serious that these newly formed SS units should be carrying on their recruiting by underhand means and, in addition, trying to break up the SA."[31] In Berlin the indignant SA produced anonymous leaflets protesting against "the build-up, at the expense of the SA, of our civilian bosses' bodyguard, the SS."[32]

In an attempt to restrain the growing enmity between his two Party armies Hitler handed Himmler his first great success; late in 1930 he made the SS independent of the SA. Though still formally under the command of the OSAF, SS independence of the SA as a whole was confirmed. Hitler laid down that "No SA commander is entitled to give orders to the SS."[33] To underline its independence, the SS was now given its own uniform, black instead of the SA brown—black cap, black tie, black breeches and black-bordered swastika armband. A black

stripe, two inches above the left cuff, carried an Arabic
numeral indicating the number of the SS Sturm [an SS
formation equivalent to a company].[34]

The SS had won its first war of independence. More
important still, Hitler permitted it to adopt a new organisation. It had originally been formed on a "ten-man"
system—the SS unit in any one locality was limited to
a commander and ten men. This was now abolished and
instead a new structure appeared with ranks and units
exactly modelled upon those of the SA. The smallest SS
unit was now to be the "Schar" of eight men under a
"Scharführer" [Corporal]. Three "Scharen" formed a
"Trupp" of twenty to sixty men under a "Truppführer"
[Sergeant], equivalent to a military platoon. Three
"Trupps" formed a "Sturm," the most important SS unit;
it consisted of 70–120 men, was commanded by a
"Sturmführer" [Captain] and corresponded to a company.
Three "Stürme" made up a "Sturmbann" of 250–600
men, commanded by a "Sturmbannführer" [Major] and
corresponding to a battalion. Three or four "Sturmbanne"
formed a "standarte" of 1,000–3,000 men under a "stan-
dartenführer" [Colonel] corresponding to a regiment.
Several "Standarten" formed an "Untergruppe" (later
"Abschnitt"—Region) similar to a brigade and commanded by an "Oberführer" [Brigadier]. Later several
"Untergruppen" or "Abschnitte" formed a "Gruppe" or
"Oberabschnitt" [Major Region], a unit corresponding to
a division and commanded by a "Gruppenführer" [Lieu-
tenant-General].[35]

This new SS army, of course, existed only on paper;
Himmler still lacked the men to give real body to his
organisation, but here Hitler gave the SS an opportunity
of showing their self-assurance. He forbade the SS to
canvass the SA for recruits in future but, on the other
hand, he ordered the SA to make men available for
newly formed SS units—up to 50% of the proposed SS
unit in any one locality. The provision that they should
send only "selected personnel" to the SS was particularly
distasteful to the SA; moreover the SS Sturmbannführer
concerned was authorised to reject unsuitable SA men.[36]

The SA leaders tried to convince themselves that at
least any further SS interference in their affairs would
now be stopped. August Schneidhuber, Pfeffer's Deputy,

stated hopefully that: "The SA is now entitled to forbid SS commanders and men to canvass within our ranks, even when off duty."[67] But Schneidhuber was wrong. He had clearly missed the vital sentence in Hitler's order of 7 November 1930, the real reason for the sudden agreement to so striking an increase in the SS. This sentence ran: "The task of the SS is primarily to carry out police duties within the Party."[38] Haase's dream had come true— a secret Order now stood sentinel within the Party.

Just at this moment Adolf Hitler had good reason to call upon his bodyguard to be the maid of all work. According to the Party grapevine his position was shakier than ever. The National-Socialist Movement was degenerating into an arena for intrigue and dissimulation, murder and political long knives. The SS was intended by Hitler to hold the Party firmly together and to beat down any insubordination, and there was a great deal of insubordination in the NSDAP—it had never been a homogeneous party.

The Party, after all, had started as a lower-middle-class pan-German society; it had then been given a doctrinal top-dressing of nationalistic socialism originating in the Sudetenland; shortly thereafter it had been debased into a political appendage of the Bavarian defence formations and a nest of warring politicians from the Völkisch camp; later it had become the proving-ground for a Völkisch socialism with a proletarian twist, a refuge for the SA rabble and an inviting field for reactionary party leaders and captains of industry. So heterogeneous a party could have no real unity; it lived on activism, noise and agitation for agitation's sake. It was held together only by its hatred of progress and democracy and its determination to capture the State at all costs. Hardly an article of the NSDAP creed was undisputed by its members, hardly one of its senior functionaries was approved of by any other.

Hermann Esser, one of Hitler's closest associates, thought the North German Völkisch party "an association of visionaries, worshippers of Wotan";[39] Goebbels, who was a Rhinelander, proposed that "the petty bourgeois Adolf Hitler" should be expelled from the Party;[40] at almost every Party rally someone demanded that Julius Streicher, the Jew-baiter, should have his membership card withdrawn.[41] Goebbels stated that "The future belongs to the dictatorship of the socialist ideal within the State," and then had to admit that the sentence came from *Red Flag*, not the National-Socialist Press.[42] Gregor Strasser demanded an alliance with the Soviet Union, because Moscow would be an ally in the fight against the "Versailles Peace Settlement," and found himself in head-on collision with the anti-Soviet crusader Alfred Rosenberg, in whose view the Party was liable to fall prey to the Red enemy.[43] Not all Nazis were united even about the persecution of the Jews; every shade of anti-Semitism was to be found within the Party. Even Goebbels said: "The Jewish question is more complicated than one thinks. It may well be that the capitalist Jew is not the same thing as the bolshevist Jew."[44]

The Party was so divided that a full-time investigation and arbitration committee had to be set up under ex-Major Walter Buch, the SA Commander, Nuremberg, to deal with petty disputes between members.[45]

Hitler, however, knew how to use these intrigues to strengthen his own position. He had a flair for mediation between conflicting points of view and so was able not only to hold the Party cliques together, but to work his way to the top at the same time. Increasingly he emerged as the only man capable of keeping the Party intact but in fact he took every opportunity to fan the flames— the more violent the quarrels, the more acceptable did the arbitrator from Munich appear. Before being executed at Nuremberg, Rosenberg admitted: "Hitler deliberately allowed opposing groups to exist within the Party in order that he might then play the role of arbiter and leader."[46] When the Party was re-formed in February 1925, Hitler's authority hardly extended beyond the borders of Bavaria, but he made good use of every crisis and every difference of opinion; internal Party differences were his ladder to the leadership.

Initially Hitler made little progress with the Völkisch and National-Socialist groups of North and West Germany, because three men stood in his way; Gregor Strasser, the Landshut chemist and a gifted organiser, Strasser's eccentric doctrinaire brother Otto, and Joseph Goebbels, his propaganda chief. These three controlled the National-Socialist organisation in the north. Ideologically they were at variance with Hitler; he was steering a cautious course between restoration of the monarchy and revolution, while they believed in Völkisch socialism, nationalisation of industry and a Russo-German proletarian alliance.[47] In February 1926, however, Hitler got the better of them; at a meeting in Bamberg packed with his supporters, he had his opponents' social revolutionary programme put to the vote and carried the day.[48] Goebbels at once went over to Hitler; even Gregor Strasser concluded a half-hearted truce and entered the Munich Party Headquarters as Reich organiser.[49]

Only Otto Strasser continued to conduct open warfare against Hitler from Berlin. He was editor of the *Berliner Arbeiter Zeitung*, the most influential National-Socialist newspaper in the North, and head of a group of intellectuals who were trying to give National-Socialism a definite left-wing bias; Berlin became the main centre of internal opposition.[50] But then a third party took a hand in the game—the Berlin SA marched.

Their leader was a giant of a man named Kurt Daluege. He was a Berlin sanitary engineer, had been a member of the Free Corps which had liberated Annaberg in Upper Silesia from Polish insurgents in 1921, and was considered one of the most pugnacious rough-necks in Berlin;[51] his limited intelligence had earned him the nickname "Dummi-Dummi" ["Thicky"] in the Berlin underworld. After the 1923 putsch, he had joined the Frontbann, Röhm's substitute SA, and later formed the first Berlin SA unit, using Free Corps veterans, work-shy toughs and the gymnastic sections of the Völkisch groups.[52] Early in 1926 his unit was 500 strong, more than the whole Berlin membership of the NSDAP.[53]

The SA men made good use of their numerical superiority. They thought that the Berlin Gauführer, a civil servant named Ernst Schlange, one of Otto Strasser's men, was too weak; they accordingly demanded his resignation and put forward their own candidate, the ex-Frontbann Commander, Hauenstein.[54] The change was to take place on 25 August 1926. When Strasser defended Schlange at a combined meeting of National-Socialist and SA leaders, Hauenstein boxed his ears and the SA went away happy.[55] The change of regime seemed complete.

Hitler now weighed in, however, and once more showed his gift for playing off warring factions against each other.

In November 1926, he dispatched the renegade Goebbels to Berlin as the new Gauleiter.[56] Goebbels had every reason to stick rigidly to Hitler's line, for he had no other standing in Berlin—the Strasser camp considered him a detestable traitor and in the eyes of the Berlin SA his name was coupled with ignominious defeat. Hitler's scheme was to involve the emergent SA in the internal Party game. The SA's natural rival was Gregor Strasser's "political organisation," abbreviated PO and referred to by the SA as "P Zero."[57] Hitler calculated that the Party sleuths and the SA would neutralise each other, leaving him still in overall control of the NSDAP.

But this was not Hitler's only reason for pushing the SA into the forefront; it was certainly not the most important. He regarded the SA as the force which would bring him to power and only the history of the SA, the history of Hitler's hopes for it and disappointments with it, can really explain why, finally, it was the SS which emerged as the decisive instrument of the Führer dictatorship. In Hitler's eyes the SA was the organisation which would give to his political ideas the essential backing of force; the SA marching columns were intended to conduct "a sort of permanent electoral campaign using terrorist methods" (as the historian Wolfgang Sauer puts it), and so weaken the already somewhat feeble resistance of his democratic opponents.[58]

Like Hitler, Pfeffer von Salomon, the head of the SA, was an enthusiast for marching columns. Both believed that the tramp of marching feet, and the well-drilled advance of a body of disciplined men in column of fours, exerted a compelling psychological fascination over the masses. Von Pfeffer gave perhaps the most revealing description of National-Socialist methods of mass hypnosis: "The sight of a large number of men, disciplined and co-ordinated both mentally and physically, with a patent or potential will to fight to the limit, makes the greatest impression upon every German; the language of the message which it carries to his heart is more convincing and compelling than any writing, speech or logic."[59] In Pfeffer's eyes, the essential was "an impression of might, the might of the marching column and the might of the cause for which they march. The Germans are emotionally susceptible and the inherent might of any cause will make them believe in its justice. When whole bodies of men are to be seen deliberately staking life and limb for a cause, that cause must be great and good."[60]

Pfeffer was an ex-army Captain and so in his eyes ex-officers were the best drill sergeants for his marching columns. They knew their drill books and the majority of SA men, who had been in the army already, knew the words of command; so Pfeffer placed a number of ex-officers at the head of his army. In 1928 he created seven Oberführer [Brigadiers] commands, all under ex-regular officers;[61] Captain (Police—retired) Walther Stennes became SA-Oberführer East (Berlin), Major (Retired) Paul Dincklage SA-Oberführer North (Hanover), Lieutenant-Colonel (Retired) Curt von Ulrich SA-Oberführer West (Kassel), Commander (Navy—Retired) Manfred Freiherr von Killinger SA-Oberführer Centre (Dresden), Major (Retired), August Shneidhuber SA-Oberführer South (Munich), Lieutenant (Retired) Viktor Lutze SA-Oberführer Ruhr (Elberfeld); Captain (Retired) Hermann Reschny was held ready to take over in Austria (Vienna).[62]

Early in 1929, Pfeffer wound his ex-officers even tighter into his organisation; he appointed Stennes, Dincklage, Ulrich and Schneidhuber as his deputies and Ulrich additionally as Inspector General of SA training.[63] The cadre of the Party army was now ready to accept the mass of recruits which streamed into the SA when the economic crisis broke in autumn 1929. The increasing misery of the unemployed produced a dramatic expansion of the SA; by 1930 its strength was fluctuating between 60,000 and 100,000.[64]

Expansion increased the SA's self-confidence and its commanders were less and less prepared to accept orders from the political functionaries. The SA was making itself largely independent of the Political Organisation and Hitler became suspicious. His suspicions deepened as messages began to arrive from Berlin showing that his crafty balance-of-power game was in danger. Economic distress was producing growing criticism that Hitler's policy was insufficiently revolutionary; Otto Strasser's intellectuals and the SA commanders were drawing closer together; even Hitler's watchdog, Goebbels, was beginning to waver.[65]

Before the two groups could really coalesce, however, Hitler stamped out the threatened conflagration. On 21 May 1930 he appeared, unannounced, in Berlin and lured Strasser into an ideological argument which ended in deliberate disagreement. Hitler then disowned Otto Strasser, used Goebbels to expel all Strasser supporters from the Party, and capped his triumph with the receipt of a telegram of devotion from Gregor Strasser.[66] He thought that he had silenced the Berlin opposition; the SS began to shadow its leaders, Hitler setting increasing store on the detective instincts of Kurt Daluege, who had meanwhile left the SA and by spring 1929 had risen to be head of the Berlin SS.[67]

Daluege was now so strong that he was largely independent of the Reichsführer-SS in Munich. He was only too well aware that the Party internecine strife had placed him in a key position and he more or less refused to do business with anyone other than Hitler and the OSAF.[68] On Hitler's instructions he watched every move by the Berlin SA leaders. Not far from the Sports Palace, where the Berlin SA foregathered, he set up what one of his staff called "a meeting place for specially reliable SS men and those who aspired to be so. Only comparatively few Berliners knew of the existence of this SS headquarters and those who did were ignorant of its true purpose—and even at this stage that purpose was far wider than mere command of the Berlin SS."[69]

One of Daluege's retainers was his old friend Herbert Packebusch, a carpenter's son who had been a faithful follower of Daluege ever since the Free Corps days; as commander of Sturm No. 21 he had a desk in Berlin SA headquarters and faithfully recorded everything he noticed.[70] Unfortunately he noticed practically nothing. He did not perceive that an SA leaders' conspiracy was forming round Stennes, Pfeffer's deputy, or that the SA was planning nothing less than the deposition of the Munich Party leader. Otto Strasser had not been unseated for nothing; the Berlin SA was still under the spell of his revolutionary socialist harangues.

Mere economics drove the SA leaders into opposition against their political rivals and against Hitler. The unemployed were streaming into the SA, attracted both by its extremist slogans and by its standard of cooking; SA funds were gradually running out.[71] Stennes reported to Munich:[72] "In some Berlin Standarten 67% of the men are unemployed. There is a Sturm in Breslau which cannot parade for inspection—at least not in frost or snow—because it has no footwear." By this time (the end of 1930) there were already 3,000,000 unemployed in Germany.[73]

Alongside the unemployed, criminal elements infiltrated into the SA and, as a result, the perennial underground struggle between the SA and the Red Front took on a gang-warfare character reminiscent of Chicago. Fighting raged round the bars and speakeasies and the nicknames used showed the type of men involved; one SA Sturm in Neukölln, for instance, called itself "The Pimps Brigade" and another in Wedding, "The Robbers"; an SA commander known for his street-clearing ability was nicknamed "Rubberleg" and his henchmen "King of the Boozers," "Revolver Snout" and "The Bulletmiller."[74] The SA commanders, unwilling to lose their new recruits, were clamouring for more money, for the line between Nazis and Communists was thin indeed; but the Gauleiter, who had the money, kept the purse-strings tight. The politicals had no intention of pandering to the SA's urge for expenditure.[75]

This miserliness gave rise to a nasty suspicion on the part of the SA—suppose the Party leadership was deliberately keeping the SA small; worse still—suppose that the Party leaders were finding the SA an obstacle to their climb to power and respectability. Inflammatory cries were to be heard, such as: "Adolf is betraying us, the proletariat."[76] Anonymous pamphlets decrying the Party leaders began to appear: "We, the proletarian section of the Movement, are of course delighted! We are quite happy to starve in order that our dear 'leaders' can enjoy themselves on their salaries of 2,000–5,000 marks a month. We were also overjoyed to hear that at the Berlin Motor Show our Adolf Hitler had spent 40,000 marks on a large new Mercedes."[77]

The rumour went round Berlin that, to assist his projected coalition with the German Nationalists, Hitler was proposing gradually to cut down the SA. Stennes, the senior SA commander in eastern Germany, accordingly decided to take the bull by the horns. He had been assured of support from Pfeffer's other deputies and so his demands to Munich were stiff—authorisation for SA commanders to enter Parliament, reduction of the influence of the Gauleiter, the SA to be paid for keeping order at Party demonstrations.[78] Stennes had chosen his moment cleverly; in September 1930 new Reichstag elections were due and, for the first time, the NSDAP had an opportunity of cashing in on the discontent of the unemployed and the have-nots. The SA therefore occupied a key position in the electoral campaign.

So a delegation from the Berlin SA went to Munich to lay their demands before the Party leaders, but Hitler refused to see them.[79] Shortly thereafter the new list of Nazi candidates for the Reichstag elections was published, and it was found that Stennes and another Berlin SA leader had again been excluded. Indignation exploded; at the end of August the Berlin SA commanders resigned and their men went on strike during the electoral campaign.[80] Goebbels, for instance, had planned an election demonstration in the Sports Palace but the SA refused to keep order; in the middle of the proceedings the SA chuckers-out withdrew, leaving the Nazi speakers to be heckled by their opponents.[81] As they went they recited in chorus:

Wenn mich die Reichstagsgeister rufen	When the Reichstag gentlemen call me
Ich folge nicht.	I do not obey
Tapeten muss ich suchen	I look on the posters
Beim lampenlicht.	By lamplight
Ich sitz' auf meine Kiste,	I sit on my backside
Maltriere mein Gehirn,	And cudgel my brain
Studier' die Professorenliste	And look through the list of professors
Ob Hakenkreuz oder weiche birn'.	Whether swastika man or nincompoop.[82]

The SA men then moved off to the Wittenbergplatz and conducted an anti-Goebbels demonstration. The *Münchner Post* reported:[83] "There were loud cries of 'Let Dr Goebbels come out and give an account of himself' "; others threatened to march to the Sports Palace and take the whole "Goebbels rabble" apart. Goebbels hurriedly called in the Berlin SS. Daluege's men took over main-

tenance of order in the Sports Palace and posted guards
at the Berlin Gau Headquarters (10 Hedemannstrasse).
Goebbels feared an SA attack at any moment[84] and during the night of 30 August it came. Stennes' men
moved in, clubbed down the SS guards at Gau Headquarters and broke up the furniture.[85] In desperation the
Gauleiter had to ask the despised State Police to intervene and a police detachment arrested 25 SA men and
took them away.[86] Goebbels rushed off to Munich by train
to report the catastrophe to his Führer.[87] Though near a
nervous breakdown, Hitler kept his head.

The next day an agitated Hitler presented himself to
Stennes and begged him not to leave the Party. The
Leader trailed from one bar to another, urging the SA
to continue to trust him.[88] On the evening of 1 September
1930 reconciliation was celebrated in the Berlin Ex-
Servicemen's Building, when Hitler promised to meet the
more important of Stennes' demands and the contestants
parted peaceably.[89]

Nevertheless for the first time the SS had stood up
for their Führer against their SA comrades and Hitler
now decided on ruthless use of the SS as an internal
Party police force. A warning that Stennes might strike
again at any moment came from Dr Leonardo Conti,
Senior Medical Officer at Stennes' Headquarters, later an
SS-Obergruppenführer and the Reich Health Leader.[90] On
8 September 1930 Conti reported: "Under his [Stennes']
leadership, the SA is turning into a force owing no real
allegiance to the Movement or its ideals. Stennes himself takes no stock of National-Socialist ideology and deliberately refuses to study it; he is capable of letting
his troops loose at any moment."[91]

Hitler had long since realised that his position was in
deadly danger. He dismissed Pfeffer from his post as
head of the SA (Pfeffer was only too ready to go) and
announced that he himself would take over as Supreme
Commander of the SA.[92] He then remembered his old
friend Röhm's parting words: "You have only to give me
the word—'Be at the Siegestor at 6 a.m. on such and
such a day with your men'—and I shall be there."[93] Hitler
recalled Röhm from Bolivia.

Before the summons to return as Chief of Staff of the
SA had even reached Röhm, however, Hitler had staged

a scene which foreshadowed things to come. This was
the point at which he introduced the Party to the cult
of the charismatic Führer. Every SA man had to swear
blind, eternal loyalty to the man who claimed to unite
in his own person the Party and its leadership. On 3
September 1930 Wagner, acting Chief of Staff of the
SA, informed all OSAF deputies that they must swear
an unconditional oath of allegiance to the person of the
Party leader and Supreme Commander of the SA, Adolf
Hitler.[94] Every member of the SA had to swear "to
carry out all orders assiduously and conscientiously, in
the knowledge that my commanders will never demand
from me anything unlawful,"[95]—and, according to the
official statement, those commanders were to be appointed by Hitler in person.

The Führer, Adolf Hitler, had now assumed sole authority within the National-Socialist Party and he had installed the SS as his Party police. They were needed sooner than they thought, for National-Socialists still existed
who refused to be blinded by the Führer cult.

Conti's forecast came true and Stennes prepared to
strike once more. Hitler and Röhm had ordered more rigid
centralisation of the SA, a measure which met with immediate resistance from Stennes and his people.[96] This
time, however, Daluege's friend Packebusch was paying attention; Daluege admitted later that Packebusch kept him
continuously informed of Stennes' preparations.[97] Whatever was planned in SA Headquarters East, Daluege was
always able to take the necessary counter-measures.
Packebusch now reported that Stennes was planning a
major coup against the Munich leaders and was only
waiting for the right moment. It came during the night
of 31 March 1931.

Early on the morning of 1 April Daluege reported
to Röhm: "I have just (3.45 a.m.) received a telephone
call from the aide to a certain Standartenführer to the
effect that between midnight and 3 o'clock a highly secret
meeting of Berlin SA commanders was held under the
chairmanship of Jahn, aide to Gruppenführer East. Jahn
informed the meeting that, at a conference to be held
in Weimar at midday on 1 April, Stennes, the Gruppenführer East, was to be dismissed by our Führer, Adolf Hitler. It was made quite clear that Hitler's orders would

not be obeyed. During the meeting all the commanders present declared themselves in favour of Stennes and against Hitler."[98]

Once more SS men went into action against SA men and once more they had to yield to force of numbers. Stennes' supporters occupied the offices of the Gau Headquarters and the National-Socialist newspaper *Der Angriff*.[99] The revolt spread quickly through northern and eastern Germany. In a matter of hours Hitler's writ no longer ran beyond the Elbe. The majority of senior SA commanders in Brandenburg, Silesia, Pomerania and Mecklenburg joined the battle against Hitler[100]—Wetzel, Veltiens, Jahn, Pustrow, Lustig, Kremser[101]—all the important names were there. The only absentee was Manfred von Killinger, supposedly a close friend of Stennes;[102] elsewhere in Germany too some senior commanders refused to support him.[103]

For a short moment the democrats, depressed by Hitler's electoral success, could rejoice over the spectacle of Nazi leaders sacking each other. Stennes dismissed Goebbels from the post of Gauleiter and Goebbels replied by releasing SA men from their oath of loyalty to Stennes; the East German SA "took over" the Party and the Party promptly expelled them.[104] But the Stennes putsch rapidly lost momentum; the fire went out of the revolt as soon as the SA coffers were empty and Hitler then began to pick up the pieces. Paul Schulz, an ex-Lieutenant from Stettin, one of the heroes of the black Reichswehr period and a follower of Gregor Strasser,[105] was brought in to reconstitute the SA Group East and Hermann Göring combed the SA for Stennes supporters.[106]

Hitler let the entire Party know that he owed his victory over Stennes solely to the vigilance of his SS. The new SA Gruppenführer East was an SS man, Untersturmführer Friedrich-Wilhelm Krüger;[107] in a letter to Daluege Hitler produced the sentence which, in one form or another, the SS carried on their caps right up to the end: "SS-Mann, deine Ehre heisst Treue." (SS man, thy loyalty is thine honour).[108] The SS was now firmly in the saddle. Wherever Hitler saw his authority imperilled, whenever brown-shirted non-conformists revolted against the Führer cult, the SS was always at hand. At an SS leaders' conference Himmler shouted exultantly:

"We are not loved everywhere; when we have done our duty we may be stood in the corner; we should expect no thanks. But our Führer knows the value of the SS. We are his favourite and most valuable organisation because we have never let him down."[109]

Himmler's new instructions were designed to ensure that the SS could act rapidly and silently on Hitler's orders. SS units in any one locality were divided into sections of three to five men, each responsible for a street or area of the town; the section had to meet half an hour before the unit's time of parade to allow the section leader to check that all his members were present and to fetch any absentees.[110] Unauthorised absence was severely punished. SS regulations stated: "Punishment for the first unauthorised absence will be a reprimand in writing from the SS commander; for the second unauthorised absence the man will be warned in writing that he may be expelled from the SS and will be reprimanded in front of the entire unit; punishment for a third unauthorised absence will be expulsion from the SS."[111]

Unit commanders had to ensure that their men were mobile and ready for duty at all times. They had to make efforts to increase the numbers of motorcycles and bicycles held by their unit, arrange long-distance rides and practise the transmission of messages over distances of twenty to thirty miles.[112]

At the same time a veil of secrecy descended over the activities of the SS. No one, not even a member of the Party or an SA man, was allowed to know what the SS was doing; Himmler's Order began to withdraw into a twilight of mystery. One of Daluege's orders laid down that: "even in face of unjustified criticism, SS men and SS commanders are strictly forbidden to converse with SA men and commanders or with civilian members of the Party other than as necessary for the purposes of duty. Should criticism be voiced in a small gathering, members of the SS will immediately and silently leave the room with the curt comment that the SS carries out Adolf Hitler's orders."[113]

Wagner, the Acting Chief of Staff of the SA, issued an order explaining to the Party why the SS was necessarily a law unto itself: "The SS is a protective organisation, the duty of which is first to carry out police duties within the Movement, and secondly to ensure that no breaches of official regulations or laws are committed by members of the Movement. If it is to do its duty, the SS must be completely independent, in other words independent both of the politcal leadership and of SA Headquarters."[114] With this sort of blanket cover the SS was free to devote all its energy to the task which it had always placed first, investigation of anti-Hitler factions and Party enemies.

As early as 1925 the SS had begun collecting confidential information on the private affairs of controversial Party members. The earliest of these SS reports carries the date 24 September 1925; it is headed "U to Party Headquarters" and was forwarded by Schreck, the founder of the SS. It runs: "At yesterday's evening meeting of the local group in Neubiberg, a certain gentleman named Herzer gave the following information: 'In the Spring of this year, the *Völkischer Kurier* carried an article accusing Esser [Hermann Esser—a friend of Hitler] of accepting 30,000 marks from a Jew named Landauer. Since this statement has so far not been denied, I had to assume, and still do, that it is true. This is all the more likely, moreover, since Esser was at one time a Communist.' "[115]

Such reports were initially the product of chance but later a regular system was established. Local SS units had to submit reports to SS Headquarters on opposition groups such as the Reichsbanner and the Communist Party, on freemasons and prominent Jews and on all political events.[116] Most of them were fit only for the wastepaper basket and only with the arrival of Himmler was some order brought into SS information activities. In June 1931 Himmler ordered: "Our enemies' efforts to bolshevise Germany are increasing. Our information and intelligence service must aim to discover, and then to suppress, our Jewish and Freemason enemies; this is the most important task of the SS today."[117] In all SS Abschnitte [Districts] Himmler set up secret intelligence sections to keep a watch on the enemies of the Party, both internal and external.[118]

Himmler reported all sorts of things to the Führer. On 10 October 1931, for instance: "In certain towns the Communist Party has been expelling some of its Antifa League men [Communist activists] in order to infiltrate them as spies into SS formations." "Captain Ehrhardt,

Commander of the officially disbanded Viking Corps, has recently become very active once more. In close co-operation with Government circles and under nationalist cover, he is preparing to form a Free Corps; to judge from the manner in which it is being recruited and in view of Captain Ehrhardt's former attitude, its object must be to destroy the NSDAP."[119]

A few months earlier an ex-Lieutenant from the Navy, Reinhard Heydrich, had joined the Party and the SS. With his help Himmler proceeded to build up a so-called Ic Service [Intelligence Service] which later developed into into National-Socialism's greatest informer organisa-tion—the Sicherheitsdienst [SS Security Service—SD].[120]

Sturmführer Heydrich proved to be so gifted a collec-tor of intelligence that the SS rapidly turned into the Party's main secret service. Hitler came to regard his per-sonal security as dependent solely upon the SS. On 25 January 1932 he nominated Himmler head of security in the Brown House, the Party Headquarters at 45 Brienner-strasse, Munich (the former Barlow Palace).[121] An order issued by SA Headquarters stated: "Control of the security service throughout Party Headquarters (The Brown House and adjacent building) is hereby transferred to the Reichsführer-SS. The SA Oberführer of the Munich/ Upper Bavaria Untergruppe [Sub-Group] and the SS-Standartenführer of No. 1 SS-Standarte, Munich will for-ward to the Reichsführer-SS a list of the SA and SS men selected."[122] The order continued that Himmler was now responsible for measures to "repel Marxist/Communist at-tacks and prevent police interference."[123] Himmler had hardly completed his preparations before the Brown House was shaken by a murder story—and the clues led not to the Headquarters of the Party's enemies, but to the offices of the Brown House itself.

In its own way this affair was further proof that Hitler's one-man leadership was still by no means undisputed inside the Party. The Stennes upheaval had raised the problem of the extent to which Hitler could ride roughshod over the views of his SA commanders; the new scandal posed the question whether Hitler was strong enough to disregard the Party's remaining moral scruples. The background to the whole business was that in Ernst Röhm, the new Chief of Staff of the SA, Hitler was keeping a man who was running the SA through a ring of blatant homosexuals and turning the National-Socialist revolutionary army into a perverts' playground.

Röhm had never made any secret of his tendencies saying "I admit straightaway that I do not belong to the goody-goodies, and have no desire to do so." Any attempt by the State "to regulate human instincts by law or divert them into other channels" he countered with a quotation from Richard Wagner: "Folly, folly, everywhere folly."[124] He rejected with scorn protests by leading National-Socialists. He told the Berlin Doctor Heinsoth, for instance: "I am quarrelling violently with that blockheaded moralist, Alfred Rosenberg. His articles are aimed primarily at me since I have never made any mystery of my views. That is obvious since in my case 'people' have had to get used to these criminal goings-on in National-Socialist circles."[125]

Röhm's abnormal leanings had been common knowledge since he had taken a Berlin gigolo, Hermann Siegesmund, to court for theft of a suitcase.[126] On the evening of 13 January 1925 Röhm had invited Siegesmund to a glass of beer in the Berlin Marienkasino followed by the usual sequel to such an encounter. Siegesmund stated in evidence: "While we were still sitting fully clothed in the room of the hotel, Herr Röhm took a cigarette case from his pocket; I noticed that a slip of paper fell out and I picked it up. About half an hour later I left the hotel room because Herr Röhm expected me to take part in a form of sexual intercourse which was abhorrent to me and to which I would not agree. Out in the street I found that the slip of paper which I had taken while up in the room was a luggage ticket belonging to Herr Röhm."[127] Siegesmund collected the suitcase, which proved to contain a bundle of compromising letters.

Hitler knew all about Röhm's tendencies but insisted that they were his own affair. When Röhm took on his job as Chief of Staff of the SA, Hitler, who was still officially head of the SA, issued a parting order that the SA was "not a girls' finishing school, but a tough fighting formation." Complaints about people's private habits he rejected "indignantly and on principle" as "supposition" and "entirely private matters."[128]

Röhm's amorous adventures, however, were anything

but "an entirely private matter." He used the SA for ends
other than the purely political. SA contact men kept their
Chief of Staff supplied with suitable partners and at the
first sign of infidelity on the part of a Röhm favourite, he
would be bludgeoned down by one of the SA mobile
squads.[129] The head pimp was a shop assistant named
Peter Granninger, who had been one of Röhm's partners
since 1928 and was now given cover in the SA Intelligence
Section.[130] For a monthly salary of 200 marks he kept
Röhm supplied with new friends, his main hunting ground
being Gisela High School Munich; from this school he recruited no fewer than eleven boys, whom he first tried out
and then took to Röhm.[131] Meanwhile some of Röhm's
more dubious friends had occupied senior SA positions
left vacant as a result of the Stennes revolt.

The general meeting-point for the Granninger circle and
the SA homosexuals was Röhm's reserved table in the
Bratwurstglöckl, Munich. The proprietor, Karl Zehnter,
was a homosexual himself whom Granninger had
"assisted" at his home.[132] Another homosexual and long-
standing habitué of Röhm's table was the new Berlin
Commander, Edmund Heines;[133] he had even been expelled from the SA in 1927 for homosexual practices.
Karl Ernst, the new SA Chief of Staff, Berlin, had been a
partner of Captain Rohrbein, ex-Frontbann, who had also
frequently been seen with Röhm in Berlin homosexual
dives such as the Kleist-Kasino and Silhouette.[134] This ring
of perverted SA commanders seemed unbreakable. When
asked about the goings-on in Röhm's circle, Hitler took
refuge in the excuse that the Chief of Staff was not a
proven homosexual; if anyone could give him cast-iron
proof, he would draw the necessary conclusions.

Röhm and his highly organised squad of informers
generally succeeded in covering their tracks. In March
1932, however, Röhm's letters began to leak, several being
published in the Social-Democrat *Münchner Post*.[135]
Röhm's friends panicked. Any more-or-less normal SA
commander was suspected of having filched the letters and
passed them to some anti-Hitler National-Socialist like Dr
Helmut Klotz, an ex-Reichstag Deputy.[136] Röhm was so
agitated that he dispatched his confidant, the adventurer
journalist Georg Bell, on a curious expedition for a National-Socialist. Bell was being paid 300 marks by the

Social Democrats for information about the Nazis;[137] he was now sent to ex-Major Karl Mayr, the man who, together with Röhm, had "discovered" Hitler in 1919 and had since gone over to the Social Democrats.[138] Mayr was now one of the leaders of the Reichsbanner which was loyal to the Republic and determined, even at this late hour, to prevent the Nazis' rise to power. Bell met Mayr in the Reichsbanner offices in Magdeburg and transmitted to him Röhm's demand for a guarantee that no more of his letters would be published in the Social-Democrat newspapers.[139] "Mayr knew all about it," Bell said later, adding that Röhm "told me that it was true that these swine wished to bring us down."[140] Whoever the "swine" may have been who had leaked Röhm's letters to the press, his National-Socialist enemies now determined to solve the problem after their own fashion. When Hitler once more refused to dismiss Röhm, Buch, the Senior Nazi Judge and apostle of National-Socialist rectitude, formed a plan to murder the SA Chief of Staff together with four of his principal associates.

Buch proceeded with caution. His mind turned to an old friend from the early Party days with whom he had built up the NSDAP in Baden——Emil Traugott Danzeisen, an ex-SA-Standartenführer, now running a bandage factory.[141] Buch told Danzeisen that there was treachery abroad in the Party: Standartenführer Uhl had given the police full information about the SA informer network; moreover a "German Nationalist" clique was forming around Röhm's cronies, the Counts du Moulin-Eckart and Spreti; this gang was determined to seize power and, in addition, was ruining the Party by their homosexual practices.[142] Danzeisen got the message and had little difficulty in thinking of one or two toughs whose line was murder. He formed a murder squad headed by Karl Horn, a bankrupt architect.[143] To secure his alibi Danzeisen moved to Austria, whence he issued orders in writing, using the pseudonym "Wieland II." On 16 March 1932 Horn received his detailed orders as follows: "Facts; Count du M who works in Room 50 is a para 175 man [paragraph 175 of the criminal code dealt with homosexual offences]. As such he has great influence with his superior R. An old story. Both are being blackmailed by a Herr Bell from Grottenmühl am Chiemsee. Stabsführer

Uhl, who lives in the same house, to be dealt with similarly."[144] Horn proposed that an SA bandsman named Grinsch with eight men should lie in wait for Bell, slug him with a hammer and string him up with a swastika pinned on him. Then it would be Röhm's turn. Danzeisen's orders to Grinsch ended: "Do your duty; don't forget the Chief of Staff. Heil and good luck. W.II."[145] Horn then received another order: "Room 50 drives a large Opel 10/50. It is parked every day in front of the house. Wheel nuts."[146] The occupant of Room 50 in the Brown House was Karl Leonhardt Graf du Moulin-Eckart, head of the SA Intelligence Service, and he went to work every day by car; this message therefore meant that Horn was to liquidate him by engineering a road accident. When Horn, however, began observing the Brown House, he suddenly had his doubts. Instead of loosening a wheel of the Opel, he presented himself to du Moulin and told him everything. The Count, who in any case was not a homosexual,[147] had an idea. Supposing Horn would assist to unravel the murder plot right back to its real organisers? Horn said he would.[148]

Horn then laid a trap. He found Buch's private number in Munich-Solln and called him up. "Horn here, Karlsruhe. I must speak to you urgently."

Buch: "Come to the Holzkirchner Station at 4.15 today."

Horn: "But I don't know you."

Buch: "I shall be wearing brown shorts, brown shirt, brown jacket, grey overcoat, grey hat and I shall wear the overcoat open."[149]

When they met at the Station, however, Buch was clearly sharper than Horn had thought and obviously saw through Horn's game, telling him that the matter had been settled, since the information about du Moulin had proved to be inexact. He asked Horn to send a telegram forthwith to Danzeisen as follows: "Helen's engagement broken off."[150] The next day Horn received proof in the shape of three revolver shots that Buch had not, in fact, abandoned his plans. Horn was fired on as he was about to enter Danzeisen's house in Munich-Laim about 11 p.m.[151] It was easy to guess who had fired them. Count Spreti, Röhm's aide, knew only too well; that morning Buch had observed Horn leaving the Chief of Staff's room in the Brown House. SA Headquarters thereupon took Horn under their protection.[152]

At this point Himmler put his oar in. Being in charge of security at the Brown House, he felt he should protect Röhm against Buch's people. On 24 March 1932 Horn learnt that (in his words) Himmler had "had up Major B [Buchs] and asked him to explain himself, as a result of which the whole matter is finally at an end."[153] But Röhm was not so sure. He and Bell flew to Berlin to see what their political opponents thought. On 1 April Röhm met Mayr and asked him for evidence against Paul Schulz, who was in charge of SA reorganisation and whom Röhm wrongly thought to be behind the murder plot.[154] A week later Bell wandered through the editorial office of the Social-Democrat newspaper Vorwärts and once more told the whole story.[155] Friedrich Stampfer, the editor, noted: "They were, in fact, running away because they thought that they would be executed by their own people. He [Bell] was instructed to tell us of the plan so that, in the event of his death, the world should know who was responsible."[156]

Himmler now reappears in the story once more, this time in Röhm's Berlin hideout, but what role he played is not clear. In any case he succeeded in persuading Röhm to return to Munich.[157] He could not, of course, prevent the Party scandal from coming out into the open; the two SA counts, du Moulin and Spreti, had lost their nerve and gone to the police, accusing Buch and his associates. In October 1932 Danzeisen was sentenced to six months imprisonment for instigation to murder; Buch and the Horn gang went scot-free.[158]

The Danzeisen case and the subsequent action for libel brought by the Party against the Münchner Post uncovered an incredible sink of iniquity. The whole situation could not have been more ironical—the SA perverts had had to appeal for help to Mayr, the champion of democracy, in order to save themselves from the murderous intentions of one of their own judges. Martin Bormann, Buch's son-in-law and confidant, was incensed; "this beats the band," he wrote, "one of the leading members of the Party reviles another leading member as his bitterest enemy and insults our Party leaders, calling them swine."[159] The greater the stench rising from the brown-shirted morass, however, the more desirable Himmler's Order became in the eyes of the Party. On 5 October 1932 Bormann wrote to Rudolf Hess, Hitler's personal assistant: "Look at the SS. After all they know Himmler and they know his capabilities."[160]

Outside the Party too, people began to realise that in the 50,000 men of the SS[161] there existed an uncompromising army of puritans ready to cry halt to the wild, dissolute mob of SA homosexuals. They remembered that Himmler had said to his SS commanders on 13 June 1931: "Perhaps it will be months or perhaps only days before the decision comes. We shall stand where our Führer stations us."[162] The SS had not long to wait; 30 January 1933 was not far off. The scene was set for the Night of the Long Knives but it was not yet clear who would be wielding them—the SA or the SS.

5
Seizure of Power

FOR Heinrich Himmler the Third Reich opened in disappointment. On 30 January 1933 the "National Revolution" took charge of Germany; bustle and dynamism became the order of the day. But no one summoned the
Reichsführer-SS to assume any key post; the SA was let
loose, dominating the streets and terrorising the dissentients; Adolf Hitler's lieutenants moved into official positions. But Himmler and his SS were not among the major
participants in the new regime.

Many indeed thought that Himmler was among the "also-
rans" in the National-Socialist assumption of power. Germany's new Chancellor had refused his faithful Heinrich
any important assignment in the new Third Reich.
Himmler had risked his health, tearing about on his motorcycle in wind and rain, his SS had secured Hitler's position
in the Party—but his master had clearly forgotten him.
Göring, Goebbels, Frick and the rest had all been rewarded with the spoils of office, but Himmler, the colourless assiduous factotum, was ignored.

Even on 9 March 1933, when the SA and SS overwhelmed the legal Bavarian Government led by the right-
wing Catholic Dr Heinrich Held, Himmler played no major
part. The putsch was led by Röhm's old divisional commander, Franz Ritter von Epp, whom SS men ridiculed
as "the mother-goddess general" because of his religious
views.[1] And it was this reactionary general, rather than
Himmler, whom Hitler installed as Reichsstatthalter [State
Governor] of Bavaria.[2] Himmler was still left with no
position of any importance; he was only allowed to ad-

vance one small step, becoming Acting Police President of Munich.[3]

Even more vexatious was the fact that in far-off Prussia, under the protection of Göring, who was initially Minister of the Interior and later Minister-President, Gruppen-führer Kurt Daluege, Himmler's bitterest rival, rose to the highest offices of state. Göring cordially loathed the prim, servile "Reichs-Heini" and was only too ready to play off Himmler against his theoretical subordinate, the ambitious Daluege. He included Daluege in the Government as State Commissar without Portfolio, he placed him at the head of the Prussian Ordnungspolizei, nominated him Ministerial Director, and even promoted him to Lieu-tenant-General of Police.[4] Daluege lost no time in work-ing out that he was the youngest general since Napoleon[5] and now saw no reason why he should take orders from the Reichsführer-SS. The last ties between Daluege and Himmler were severed.

To bring the renegade Daluege to heel, Himmler dis-patched to Berlin his best man, Reinhard Heydrich (who had meanwhile been promoted SS-Standartenführer[6]) with orders to set up a secret information service and keep Himmler continuously posted on Daluege's manoeuvres. Heydrich packed his bags and went off to Berlin with his wife, Lina, who was pregnant. He rented a house in the city's West End, and set about getting in touch with Göring's pseudo-Napoleon.[7]

The pompous Daluege, however, would not allow this tiresome visitor from Munich to get further than his outer office; Heydrich was told that the General could not receive the Standartenführer, since he was otherwise en-gaged.[8] Heydrich tried other avenues but was invariably rebuffed. When he persisted, Göring's Gestapo threatened to take proceedings against him. Lina Heydrich recalled: "My husband knew that Göring had an arrest warrant out for him."[9] Heydrich realised that his mission was doomed to failure and departed. His wife waited until the birth of her first child (a boy) and then also returned to Munich.[10]

Himmler and Heydrich now knew that power was not going to fall into their hands for the asking. The Third Reich bore not the remotest resemblance to the totalitarian state pictured by the theoreticians. Since 30 January 1933

the German State machine had been overlaid by a thick
tangled web of rivalries and competing authorities: anyone
wishing to amass power in Adolf Hitler's Germany had
to fight his way through this web.

Like many others, Himmler's picture of a National-
Socialist takeover had been a very hazy one before the
event. The majority had simply assumed that in some way
National-Socialists would take over the machinery of Government of the Weimar Republic and do away with
democracy, Hitler being responsible for all details and
the provision of wise counsel. Anyone who thought more
deeply considered that the National-Socialist Movement and
the State must be completely fused—inevitable since the
Nazi leaders would be occupying all important positions in
the State. Anything inhibiting development of the national
energy, the Nazis thought, would be swallowed up in this
great entity; all other interests must give way to the
totalitarian State. Goebbels declared: "The aim of the
National Revolution must be a totalitarian state, which will
permeate all aspects of public life."[11] Hitler proclaimed
the "establishment of the totality of the State."[12] Frick
foresaw "a strong Government, unhampered by individual
persons, groups, classes, privileges, parties or parlia-
ments."[13]

But the actual situation after 30 January 1933 was very
different. Instead of the democratic parties there appeared
the heterogeneous cliques of the National-Socialist Party
State; instead of the Reichstag with its unstable majorities,
there appeared a new form of parliamentary life—the
struggle for authority between the satraps and vested interests of National-Socialism.

With the advent of the Nazis the State came under the
control of a Party which, though apparently monolithic,
was in fact the most contradictory in the history of German party politics. Held together only by the charismatic
leadership of Hitler, a peculiar collection of factions and
splinter groups milled around—a faithful reflection of
German society in the aftermath of defeat, inflation, unemployment and the disintegration of democracy.

According to the American historian, Robert L. Koehl,
Hitler's party was divided into four groups; around the
Party leader was ranged a "group of old fighters," the
"hard core" of Nazism,[14] the fanatical survivors of the old

Party days; closely allied to them was a second group of
extreme right-wing individualists, mostly doctrinaire racists
who had joined the Party between 1925 and 1929, when
the Nazis were still socially unacceptable. The third group
was what Koehl called a "combination of Völkisch nationalism and petty-bourgeois Socialism", formed in the
years of economic depression (1930–33) when shop-
keepers, professional workers and farmers were all attracted by the dynamism of the "National Revolution."
Finally the fourth group consisted of solid citizens who
had turned to the "Party of National Revival," loyalists
from the army, the bureaucracy and the business world,
who seriously believed that, with Hitler as their demagogue, they could re-create their pre-war world.[15]

Even when in opposition, so heterogeneous a Party
had had difficulty in finding a common denominator; after
30 January 1933, however, the internal diversity of the
Party became reflected in the State. The much-trumpeted
totalitarian State degenerated into a farce, particularly
since the peculiar circumstances of Hitler's take-over
forced him initially to include bourgeois right-wing politicians and Conservative officials in his Government.

National-Socialist shadow organisations grew up along-
side the traditional offices of State. Practically every
authority had its brown-shirted watchdog; the Foreign
Ministry, for example, had its counterpart in the external
offices of the NSDAP, later paralleled by the so-called
Ribbentrop Bureau;[16] Kerrl, as Reich Commissar for the
Administration of Justice in Prussia, and Frank as Reich
Commissar for Justice, were ambitious rivals to the Reich
Ministry of Justice;[17] Wagner, the ex-Chief of Staff of
the SA, as Reich Commissar for the Economy, kept an
eye on the Reich Ministry of Economics.[18] Super-
imposed upon and overlapping this dual structure were
new political satrapies created by the leaders of the Nazi
groups and cliques. New states sprang up within the State.
Baldur von Schirach, the Reich Youth Leader, wanted
what he called a "Youth State within the State"[19]; Lasch,
the SA Gruppenführer in Thuringia, demanded the formation of an SA State as the purest expression of National-
Socialist ideology;[20] Himmler dreamed of an SS State and
Konstantin Hierl, ex-Colonel and later Reich Labour
Leader, thought up a special form of Defence State.[21]

These swashbucklers did not bother about theory; they simply grabbed every official position they could lay their hands on. Göring, who was anyway Prussian Minister President and Reich Minister for Air, lopped the Forestry Section off the Ministry of Agriculture and proclaimed himself Reich Forester.[22] Goebbels, the Minister of Propaganda—an office created for him—set up his own Reich Chamber of Culture, encroaching upon the preserves of Bernhard Rust.[23]

Hitler's viceroys spent their time building up their private empires and laying claim to their neighbours' prerogatives. Robert Ley, for instance, chief organiser of the Nazi Political Office and head of the German Labour Front, wished to turn his staff into a National-Socialist Order;[24] Himmler, however, insisted that the SS was the true elite and destined to be the Nazi Order.[25] Then Rosenberg, the Party ideologist, laid claim to the National-Socialist Order, maintaining that his own organisation, the Office for National-Socialist Ideological Training, provided the best foundation.[26] Finally there was Röhm, the Chief of Staff of the SA, who considered that the ideal of a National-Socialist Order had already been achieved in the form of his SA with its alleged unit socialism.[27]

Over and above this layer of personal intrigue lay a third level of conflict, striking deep into the roots of the National-Socialist State. This brought out into the open the controversy between State and Party, together with a new version of the old clash between the Reich and the Länder. Under Dr Wilhelm Frick the Reich Ministry of the Interior now included National-Socialists who took Hitler's dictum about the totalitarian State in deadly earnest. They produced a blueprint of an all-embracing state machine on the Prussian model and wished to restrict the Party to pure propaganda functions.[28] But the Party bureaucracy would have none of it, nor of Frick's proposed reform visualising complete centralisation of the administration under the Reich Ministry of the Interior; any administrative streamlining, after all, was bound to cut through that jungle of authorities and prerogatives which allowed the Gauleiters to act like feudal barons. Led by Göring, moreover, the proposed reform was sabotaged by the largest German State—Prussia. Göring foresaw that his administration would be increasingly subjected to the

authority of the Reich Ministry and therefore hived off
sections of the Prussian Administration, placing them
under his personal orders—to all intents and purposes out
of reach of Frick's reformers.[29]

So this was what Adolf Hitler's totalitarian State with
the strong Government unhampered by groups, classes
and parties, looked like in practice. In this jungle of a
governmental system, in Professor Trevor-Roper's words
"as incalculable . . . as any Oriental Sultanate,"[30] what
place was there for Himmler's SS? In Spring 1933, after
the failure of Heydrich's mission, the Reichsführer himself
can hardly have known the answer.

He could do nothing other than wait for his moment,
nothing other than continue to do what he had always
done—guard the life of his demi-god, Adolf Hitler, and
safeguard his predominant position in the Party. He pursued his self-appointed task with his usual conscientiousness. Being Police President in the "Capital of the Movement," Himmler had plenty of opportunity to prove to his
Führer how wrong he had been to treat the best-behaved
of all his followers so scurvily in the distribution of the
spoils of office. Himmler was not averse to publicity and
he kept his name in the headlines by numerous prophecies
of gloom.

In mid-March Himmler arrested Count Arco-Valley, the
murderer of Eisner and the man whom, as a student, he
had plotted to liberate from prison. According to Himmler
the reason was that the Count had "on his own admission
planned a coup against the Reich Chancellor, Adolf
Hitler."[31] A fortnight later Himmler gave further proof
of his vigilance; this time he had "discovered a planned
hand-grenade attack on the Reich Chancellor." Three
Soviet agents, he announced, had "placed three hand-
grenades near the Richard Wagner memorial where Adolf
Hitler's car was bound to pass."[32] The ubiquitous Police
President then warned his Führer and the populace against
further terrible dangers: "Through information from
Switzerland we have, for several days, been aware that
attacks on the Reich Chancellor, Adolf Hitler, and on
leading personalities of the new State, have been planned
by the Communists."[33]

Himmler's assassination claptrap touched Hitler on a
particularly sensitive spot. Ever since 27 February 1933,

when, according to the Nazi version of the story, the
lunatic Dutchman, van der Lubbe, had set fire to the
Reichstag, Hitler had been terrified of plots and explosions; he had convinced himself that assassins were continually slinking around. Hardly a meeting of the cabinet
went by without the Führer tilting at this windmill. "The
effect upon the public of a successful attack on me would
be fearful," he declared in Cabinet on 7 March;[34] a week
later the Cabinet minutes recorded: "The Chancellor indicated that a time-limit should be set for the surrender of
explosives. During recent years 150 tons of explosive had
been stolen, of which only 15 tons had so far been recovered."[35] Nothing could convince him that adequate
precautions were being taken for his personal safety. His
imaginary assassins appeared in every conceivable guise
—for instance: "One day a perfectly innocent-looking
fellow will instal himself in an attic somewhere in the
Wilhelmstrasse. He will look like a retired schoolmaster.
A perfectly ordinary citizen, horn-rimmed spectacles, ill-
shaven, with a little beard. No one will ever be allowed
to see his shabby little room. There he will quietly instal
some weapon and will gaze through his telescopic sight at
the balcony of the Reich Chancellery hour after hour and
day after day with sinister pertinacity—and then one
day he'll pull the trigger!"[36]

Even in his office Hitler did not feel secure. At Cabinet
meetings he sat with three members of his Party (Göring,
Goebbels, Frick) facing a majority of bourgeois ministers;[37] the sentries on the Reich Chancellery were provided by the Reichswehr and it was by no means impossible that the Generals might one day decide to mount a
putsch against him. So who more suitable to assist than
the faithful Himmler, who was so obviously preoccupied
with his Führer's security? Hitler ordered SS Headquarters to form a "Headquarters Guard" (the third in the
history of the SS) for his personal protection. As Commander, Hitler and Himmler selected a hefty Bavarian,
SS-Gruppenführer Josef (Sepp) Dietrich.[38]

Dietrich collected 120 SS men, most of whom had
carried out similar functions in the Brown House. They
formed around Hitler a triple cordon any visitor must
pass through before he could reach the Chancellor.[39] At
the Nuremberg Party Rally of September 1933, Hitler

christened the unit "Leibstandarte-SS Adolf Hitler" [Adolf Hitler's Bodyguard].[40] Unwittingly he had laid the foundation of a second Wehrmacht.

The example of the Leibstandarte inspired Himmler to form further similar units known as SS-Sonderkommandos [Special Detachments] and later Politische Bereitschaften [Political Alarm Squads].[41] Pseudo-police units appeared in many German Länder to protect Germany's new masters and terrorise political opponents. Himmler's force made its first appearance in the summer of 1933; in Ellwangen and Reutlingen the SS formed Politische Bereitschaften (800 strong in 1934)[42] to harry the democrats on behalf of the Württemberg Political Police;[43] in Dresden Sonderkommando 3 was formed of volunteers from the Hessian SS; similar units were to be found in Munich and Arolsen.[44] At one stroke Himmler had succeeded in gaining a foothold in the police machine outside Bavaria. Since he could provide the most highly disciplined force in the Party, the Police Chiefs of many German Länder, still new and unsure of themselves, went to him for advice and support. Himmler's grandfather, Konrad Himmler, had been Commissioner of the Munich Gendarmerie[45] and his grandson now realised that his future lay with the police —only through the police machine could he hope to secure a place in the National-Socialist hierarchy.

Meanwhile Himmler had also advanced in Bavaria. On 1 April 1933 he was placed in charge of the entire Bavarian Political Police together with a special section of the Bavarian Ministry of the Interior, and assumed the title Political Police Commander.[46] He soon gave practical proof of his concept of National-Socialist police work. With cold bureaucratic attention to detail, he hounded the Nazis' political enemies; he put a stop to the wilder excesses of the local SA leaders who had been venting their wrath on their less well-armed rivals; he forbade the arrest of Catholic priests unless personally authorised by him.[47] But at the same time he brought system into the political terror. Around a couple of old stone huts in the precincts of a disused powder factory near Dachau, Himmler set up a camp in which arrested Communists and Social Democrats were held.[48] The Germans learnt a new expression—"Concentration Camp": it became the watchword of Heinrich Himmler's police.

Hardly a soul realised the significance of Himmler's concentration camp; the police chiefs of the new Germany were mesmerised by the bureaucratic efficiency and superlative organisation of Himmler's machine. For the first time people sensed that Himmler was the coming Police Chief of all Germany. He was already drafting plans for an integrated nation-wide police force, since in his doctrinaire manner he found the existing police force "a complete shambles. A police force in which the best sections had become demoralised, in which the officer had had his sabre removed and the man was given only a rubber truncheon, a police force infested with ex-criminals and Marxists."[49]

Himmler was determined to abolish the democratic State's established police force, saying: "I wish in the end to create a real Reich police force from these sixteen disparate Länder Forces; for a nationwide police force is the strongest lynch-pin which a State can have."[50] In summer 1933 he told Dr Werner Best, head of the Police Division in the Hesse State Ministry, that the police must be removed from the authority of the local Party barons but that it must be done carefully and patiently.[51] He then asked Best whether he would like to assist in the formation of a Reich police force, and Best volunteered;[52] he was one of the few police officials whom Himmler kept in reserve, pending the extension of his power to Berlin. Himmler's *alter ego*, Heydrich, was meanwhile keeping a list of candidates for the proposed Reich police force; its attraction increased when it was found to include many officials of the old school, such as the Munich detective quartet, Flach, Müller, Meisinger and Huber.[53]

There was, however, one apparently insuperable obstacle to Himmler's ambitions; more than half the total area of Germany was closed to him. Göring, as Minister-President of Prussia, was quite prepared to use his own police force against the intruder from Munich. Göring and Himmler shared the same ambition—both wished to control the Third Reich's police machine, but Göring had one advantage over his rival—he already controlled the Prussian police, and they must inevitably form the core of any nation-wide police structure.

Göring had laid hands on the police as soon as he took over in Prussia. He created his own bodyguard, known as the "Special Duty Police Squad" under a Major Wecke, chairman of a National-Socialist Association of Police Officials;[54] he dismissed from the police all opponents of the regime, 1,457 in all.[55] The focal point of Göring's system of control was an unobtrusive section, Abteilung IA, in Berlin Police Headquarters; even under the Weimar Republic and in spite of the official ban on an all German secret police, it had been a kind of political-police intelligence centre for the whole Reich;[56] it was now to give birth to Prussia's fearsome political police.

As head of Abteilung IA, Göring appointed Dr Rudolf Diels, a civil servant from the political-police branch of the Prussian Ministry of the Interior.[57] He was a *bon viveur* but proved to be an outstandingly subtle official, always ready with new proposals to satisfy Göring's childishly naïve acquisitive tendencies. Diels was no Nazi, but he promised Göring, to whom he later became related (in 1943 he married Ilse Göring, widow of Goring's younger brother, Karl), that he would construct an instrument of power such as had never been seen in Prussian history. He recruited more and more criminal police officers and the strength of Abteilung IA rose from 60 to 250:[58] Göring passed the necessary laws, gradually divorcing Diels' police from the State administration; he set up a Prussian central political intelligence agency[59] and gave it independent executive authority;[60] he exempted the new organisation, later to be known as Geheime Staatspolizei [Secret State Police] from Paragraph 14 of the Prussian Administrative Police Law[61] which laid down that the police should act only "within the framework of current laws"—in other words observing basic human rights.[62] The political police office was, moreover, physically divorced from the remainder of the police force, moving away from police headquarters in the Alexanderplatz; a new "special section for suppression of Bolshevism" occupied the ex-Communist "Karl-Liebknecht" house,[63] while the main body of Diels' organisation moved to a disused Arts and Crafts School in Prinz-Albrecht-Strasse, not far from Göring's office in the Leipzigerstrasse.[64] At the end of April Göring signed a law giving Diels' office the title: "Geheimes Staatspolizeiamt" [Secret State Police Office] and constituting it an independent Land Police Authority responsible only to the Minister President, Göring.[65] An unknown post-office official, faced with designing a franking stamp, invented an abbreviation for this new institution—Gestapa.[66] Popular slang turned it into the most sinister word in the German language over a period of twelve years—Gestapo.

Even though buttressed by this new police machine, however, Göring's position was not unassailable. A rival was on the move; Göring was left in no doubt on this score in spring 1933 when he proclaimed the SA an auxiliary police force[67] and launched both it and the police into a major "Gleichschaltung" and terror campaign against the last islands of democratic resistance. He called for "the severest methods to drive out anti-State organisations, including, if necessary, ruthless use of armed force"[68]; he told the SA: "in this case I have no obligation to abide by the law; my job is simply to annihilate and exterminate—nothing more!"[69] As time went on, his expressions became more violent and his voice more hoarse; the fight against Communism, he screamed, could not be conducted solely by police methods; "I will carry on this fight to the death with those people down there, the brownshirts! I will make clear to the people that the people must defend itself."[70]

But when the men in the brown shirts, the SA, went into action against these imaginary enemies of the State, Göring was appalled by the violence of the forces he had let loose. All the SA's basest instincts, all its pent-up social discontent, all that inflammatory orators and propagandists had been dinning into it for years, was given free rein—and Prussia turned into a terrorists' witch's cauldron. Mobile squads of SA swept through the streets of the towns, the worst thugs being in Berlin. Section Ic of SA headquarters, Berlin–Brandenburg, for instance, drove so-called enemies of the State in front of it, dragged them into huts, shelters, cellars and other out-of-the-way places, beat them up and tortured them.[71] In Berlin alone the SA set up 50 impromptu concentration camps.[72] In the General-Pape-Strasse, in the Kantstrasse, in the Hedemannstrasse, in the Fürstenfeldstrasse—in all of these there were bunkers where the SA maltreated their prisoners. This state of affairs was not confined to Berlin; terror reigned in the provinces too; tales of horror came from Sonnenburg, Bornim, Königswusterhausen and Kemna.[73]

Göring realised that he had lost control of the SA, but unhappily he was surrounded by SA men—many of Prussia's Police Presidents wore SA uniform[74] and, in addition, so-called SA advisers were attached to all Regierungspräsidenten [Government Presidents].[75] There could be no doubt that Göring's authority in Germany's largest State was being undermined.

Diels kept urging his master to come out into the open against the SA but Göring was hesitant. Diels, however, had long since begun to take action on his own; information from the Berlin Herrenklub had put him on the track of the SA torturers.[76] Heller, one of his staff, soon reported that there was a secret SA torture chamber on the fourth floor of 10 Hedemannstrasse, the headquarters of the Berlin SA Gau. Diels thereupon collected some men of the Police Emergency Duty Battalion and surrounded the place with machine guns. After a long drawn-out palaver, he persuaded the SA to hand over their prisoners;[77] "The victims whom we found," he wrote, "were half dead from starvation. In order to extort confessions from them, they had been kept standing for days in narrow cupboards. 'Interrogation' consisted simply of beating up, a dozen or so thugs being employed in fifteen-minute shifts to belabour their victims with iron bars, rubber truncheons and whips. When we entered, these living skeletons were lying in rows on filthy straw with festoring wounds."[78]

Diels continued his campaign. He mobilised his Secret Police and began to smoke out one SA shelter after another. Only half-heartedly supported by Göring, he made it his business to deal with the SA thugs and was himself frequently in danger of being beaten up by the SA underworld. By the end of May there were no more impromptu SA concentration camps in Prussia.[79] But Diels still continued; he joined forces with a group of courageous lawyers from the Prussian Ministry of Justice led by Werner von Haacke and Dr Joel, to hunt out the SA gangsters and bring them to court.[80]

As the struggle against the SA increased in severity Diels began to sense that he was conducting too single-handed a war—the hotter the battle against the SA, the greater the opportunity for Heinrich Himmler's people to infiltrate unobtrusively into Göring's Prussian preserve.

Diels began to suspect that the SS was the greater menace to Göring's position in Prussia. "There was longer-range planning," he said, "and greater logic behind the SS moves than behind those of the happy-go-lucky SA."[81] He had good reason to know; he had crossed swords with the SS on several occasions.

The SS had never forgiven Diels for robbing them of a prisoner who had become almost a symbol of their efficiency—Captain Walther Stennes, the SA mutineer of 1931; his death had seemed a foregone conclusion.[82] Diels, however, had persuaded Göring to take an interest in Stennes and demand that he be handed over to the Gestapo prison.[83] Stennes, after all, was involved in one of Göring's setbacks of the pre-Nazi period; in 1931 Göring, who had once commanded the SA, had been only too anxious to regain his position and had intrigued with Stennes against the SA leadership;[84] he had promised the Berlin SA that he would plead their cause in Munich.

Even at that time Stennes felt that the main enemy was Himmler's SS. On 10 October 1931 his newspaper the *Wahrheiten der Woche* reported: "Göring declared spontaneously that he would henceforth do all in his power to bring these goings-on to an end. He assured us, moreover, that . . . he would not shrink from relieving the Reichsführer-SS Himmler of his post."[85] Even after this, the SA opposition still considered Göring to be one of Himmler's enemies; after the Stennes putsch, the *Wahrheiten der Woche* reported: "Göring was genuinely determined to push this matter through, but had not the power to do so."[86] He was now willing to make amends for his 1931 failure and he ordered Diels to rescue Stennes from the SS.[87] In the autumn of 1933, assisted by Stennes' wife and a German training officer attached to the Chinese Army, Diels managed to slip him across the Dutch frontier.[88] Stennes ended up as commander of Chiang-Kai-Shek's bodyguard.[89]

But such victories over the SS were rare. In most cases Diels was worsted. He never cracked Columbia House, the SS torture chamber in Berlin,[90] and the illegal SS concentration camp, Papenburg, another objective in his anti-beating-up campaign, was closed down only by an order from Hitler. An interview with Diels left the dictator so incensed that he ordered the camp, together with its unruly complement of SS men, to be "ruthlessly shot to pieces" by army artillery.[91]

Diels was particularly irritated by the undeniable fact that SS members had a foot in both Göring's and Himmler's camps. How long, he wondered, would they remain loyal to Göring's Prussia? SS-Gruppenführer Daluege, the Chief of the Prussian Police, might have personal reasons for keeping aloof from Himmler's circus, but behind him stood men who were finding their way blocked by Göring-nominated officials. Diels was particularly suspicious of the sallow-faced Arthur Nebe, one of the few Nazis in the Gestapo, and of his *éminence grise*, an official named Hans-Bernd Gisevius.[92]

Nebe's ambition was well known; he was Executive Head of the Gestapo and Liebermann von Sonnenberg, a Criminal Police Commissioner, prophesied: "He will either become a really great man one day or be hanged."[93] Nebe's favourite story was that which attributed to him the remark: "There are no such things as principles, only circumstances."[94] A literary friend objected: "Herr Nebe, what sort of a quotation is that! That was said by Balzac's Vautrin, the prisoner from the Bagno," to which Nebe is said to have retorted: "But you will remember that that prisoner later became Police Chief of Paris."[95]

Nebe now found Diels blocking his way to promotion and Gisevius, a deserter from the German nationalist camp,[96] added fuel to the fire; Nebe was State-educated and Diels had everything he had not—education, upper-middle-class background, self-assurance in society and a nonchalance which occasionally took even Göring aback. Göring once said to him: "I warn you, Diels, you're trying to sit on both sides of the fence"; Diels merely chuckled: "Herr Minister President, the Head of the Secret Police has to sit on all sides of the fence at once."[97]

Nebe took this "lack of character," as he described it, as an indication that Diels was in reality a disguised Communist, a suspicion which Gisevius took care to foster. "I could very well venture combat with Diels, the unstable playboy," he wrote.[98] Nebe and Gisevius collected incriminating evidence against Diels and even persuaded the gullible Daluege to believe in their Communist story.[99] Nevertheless Daluege, Himmler's rival, with a flash of perspicacity said to Nebe and Gisevius: "You're jumping out of the frying pan into the fire."[100] Little did he know that Nebe, and presumably also Gisevius, had been playing with fire for a long time. Himmler was informed of every move made by his adversary Göring. In early October he considered Göring's position so weak that he advanced to the assault of the Prussian fortress.

SS Headquarters requested Hitler's permission to move the SD and SS offices from Munich to Berlin;[101] at the same time, led by Herbert Packebusch, Daluege's old crony, SS men entered Diels' apartment. His wife was locked into the bedroom and Packebusch then broke open Diels' desk.[102] Frau Diels, however, managed to get her husband on the telephone in time, and in a few minutes Diels, with a squad of police from the Tiergarten Division, arrived at his home in the Potsdamer Strasse. Packebusch looked up as if he had seen a ghost, but before he could grab his revolver, the police had seized him and led him off.[103]

Diels' triumph, however, was short-lived. Daluege appeared in order to explain Packebusch's "indiscipline" to Göring; there had been considerable suspicion, he said, that Diels was intriguing against the Berlin SS.[104] Göring began to wonder about his Chief of Police, who seemed to him altogether too inscrutable and he released Packebusch from arrest.[105] Diels saw the drift; Göring was unwilling to act too forcibly against the SS. When, a fortnight later, he learnt that on Göring's instructions police and SS had searched his office, he panicked. He fled to Karlsbad in Bohemia and awaited his moment.[106] Meanwhile, however, Göring had survived the SS assault. Hitler refused to sanction transfer of the SS offices from Munich to Berlin, though as a small crumb of comfort the Reichsführer was allowed to instal an SD outpost in the capital.[107]

Accordingly a certain Dr Hermann Behrends set up an office in the Eichenallee, Berlin; he was an old friend of Heydrich, son of an innkeeper in Kiel where Heydrich had often stayed as a naval lieutenant.[108] Behrends formed SD Oberabschnitt [Region] East, while another of Heydrich's confidants, SS-Hauptsturmführer Heinz Jost, was appointed Himmler's representative with the Gestapa.

Himmler could make no further inroads into Göring's empire, however. Göring recalled Diels saying: "Himmler and Heydrich shall never come to Berlin."[109] So Himmler had to stage a reconciliation with Göring and placate his enemy Diels. From 9 November 1933 Diels was accorded the honour of appearing in the uniform of an SS-Standartenführer. In his personal file, however, his SS masters noted what they really thought of this remarkable recruit to the SS—he was slippery as an eel, insincere and self-seeking.[110]

So Himmler's second assault on Göring's police empire had failed. Now, however, he found an unexpected ally in the shape of Dr Wilhelm Frick's Ministry of the Interior. After the Reichstag elections of 12 November 1933 Frick had decided to abolish the last remnants of the German Länder's sovereign rights. The Länder were to be left merely as administrative units under a Government centrally directed from Berlin.[111] Nicolai, an ex-Regierungspräsident and Medicus, a civil servant, the leading centralisers in the Ministry of the Interior, drew up a constitution under which the centre would have authority to issue instructions to the Länder Governments.[112] And the thorniest problem in this reform was that of authority over the police. Hitherto police authority had rested with the Governments of the sixteen German Länder; they alone were in charge of the police and they controlled police organisation, duties and administrative law. The Reich Minister of the Interior was allowed to exercise only general supervision, although he could bring some influence to bear through the allocation of grants to the Länder police.[113]

The main feature of the draft submitted by Frick's centralisers was the transfer to the Reich Government of the sovereign rights of the Länder, including, of course, police authority. In other words the Reich Minister was claiming control over all German police forces. Henceforth no police regulations were to be issued, no changes of location planned, no promotions or appointments (to Major and upwards) made, without prior agreement from the Reich Minister of the Interior.[114] Frick's reformers were in fact trying to put into practice the programme Himmler had outlined to Dr Best—to remove command of the police from the local barons. But there was one local baron who had no intention of yielding to the Ministry of the Interior.

Though no one outside the Ministry knew of the Nicolai/Medicus plan, Göring was too quick for the centralisers. On 30 November 1933 he issued a law raising the Prussian Secret Police to the status of an independent branch in the internal administration; matters hitherto dealt with by the Prussian Ministry of the Interior were transferred to the Gestapo, and it was placed directly under the Minister-President. Göring nominated an inspector to supervise the Gestapo on his behalf and to be responsible for appointing the head of the Gestapo.[115] At one stroke, before it had even been put in legal form, Göring had dealt a deadly blow to the Reich reform. As far as the police were concerned, the largest German Land had escaped Frick's clutches.

In face of Göring, Frick was powerless; he had no private army and as he had once been a follower of Gregor Strasser his standing with Hitler was low. So the Ministry of the Interior centralisers turned to the man who had already announced that he was going to remove control of the police from the local barons. Heinrich Himmler looked to them like a saviour; he was in control of the internal Party police; his Politische Bereitschaften already existed in many German Länder, and he had long been preaching the formation of a centralised police force.

Frick's officials were now in league with Himmler's police centralisers against Prussian separatism—undoubtedly not without Hitler's agreement.[116] With the connivance of the Ministry of the Interior, Himmler took over command of the political police in one Land after another —November 1933: Hamburg, Lübeck and Mecklenburg-Schwerin; December 1933: Anhalt, Baden, Bremen, Hesse, Thuringia and Württemberg; January 1934; Brunswick, Oldenburg and Saxony.[117] When, in January 1934, Frick submitted to the Reichstag yes-men his "Law for the Reconstruction of the Reich,"[118] Himmler was already in control of the political police in all German Länder except Prussia and Schaumburg-Lippe. Göring, of course, did not submit. On the contrary he prepared to strike back.

On 19 February 1934, Frick issued a decree to all Reichsstatthalter stating that he had "direct command authority over all Land police forces in the German Reich."[119] On 9 March Göring countered with a decree of his own; he himself took over direction of the Prussian police, making the head of the police section in the Prussian Ministry of the Interior directly responsbile to him for all police matters.[120] Once more Göring had disarmed his adversary.

Drug addict though he was, Göring had played his cards well; his opponents were downcast and in despair. At this juncture, however, Göring realised that he was fighting a lost cause. He thought he could see signs of a threat to his authority far more deadly than the pressure of Frick and Himmler. The terror foreshadowed by events in Prussia in the spring of 1933 now spilled over into Germany as a whole. The tramp of the brown-shirted columns, with their thundering drums and blaring trumpets, echoed louder and louder; the battle-cry of four million SA men with nothing to do, hungry for power and thirsting for revolution, was heard everywhere.

Göring sensed that the time had come to make peace with Frick and Himmler. At the end of March he opened negotiations with the Reich Ministry of the Interior,[121] haggling for the best price for a takeover by the Central Government of the Prussian Ministries. Apart from the Minister-President's office, only the Prussian Finance Ministry remained independent; internal affairs were transferred to the Reich Ministry of the Interior whither Daluege was posted and placed in command of the entire uniformed police of the Reich.[122] As far as the political police were concerned, Göring had to accept a somewhat disadvantageous compromise; although he avoided complete acceptance of the Reich Ministry of the Interior's authority, he had to allow Himmler the post of Inspector of the Gestapo. Heydrich became head of the Gestapo and Nebe took over the Prussian Criminal Police Office.[123]

Himmler had reached a turning-point in his career. For the first time the SS was now in charge of the German police. But this was no time for rejoicing; the pact between Himmler and Göring proved inconclusive and the shotgun marriage was followed by a bloody honeymoon. On 10 April 1934 Göring inducted the new masters of Prinz-Albrecht-Strasse with the words: "No point in tripping over every corpse."[124] He sent Diels to safety as Regierungspräsident in Cologne.[125] Hardly had he done so, however, than the Gestapo began to receive messages

which admitted of only one conclusion: Adolf Hitler's
state was sliding toward the severest crisis in its short
history.

The reports painted a picture of seething discontent in
the SA; its ill-assorted corps of leaders was agreed upon
only one thing—they disliked the entire trend of "Adolf's"
policy ever since his assumption of power on 30 January
1933.

6

The Röhm Putsch

IN the bars frequented by the SA anti-Hitler sentiment
was rife. As before the Stennes putsch of 1931, the word
was going round: "Adolf is betraying us." Even the lowli-
est SA leader sensed that since the advent of the National-
Socialist State the SA, the much-trumpeted National-
Socialist revolutionary army, had become a foreign body.

For years the Party leaders had been instilling revolutionary ardour into the SA, preparing it for the great day
of the seizure of power; but when that day arrived, peacefully and (ostensibly) constitutionally, the Party did not
know what to do with the SA. Eventually it had been
given the innocent task of "toughening" German youth
and, allied to the Reichswehr, turning itself into the great
National-Socialist Peoples' Army.

Ever since the SA was formed, its Chief of Staff, Ernst
Röhm, had regarded it as the seed of a new German
army. "I am the new army's Scharnhorst," he would brag[1]
—to conceal the fact that he still smarted under the arrogance and distaste with which the regular officers
treated him. President von Hindenburg had refused to
shake his hand; to the old Field-Marshal he was an object
of suspicion as both a homosexual and military rebel.[2]
As a company commander in the trenches of the Western
Front, Röhm had seen that the old Prussian barrack-
square system was no longer adequate to meet the realities
of modern war. Dimly he felt that: "We've got to produce
something new, don't you see? A new discipline. A new
principle of organisation. The generals are a lot of old
fogeys. They never have a new idea."[3] He thought he

had that idea—a militia, the people's army, his SA. The
SA had only to be made militarily competent, to be
trained for modern revolutionary war, and then the moment would come when it would take over from the
Reichswehr and he, Ernst Röhm, the reformer, would
emerge as the leader of the new Germany's new Wehrmacht.

The cadres for the new People's Army were already
available. Röhm had under his command a force of
500,000 men, numerically five times the size of the Reichswehr; the Party army was organised in five SA-Obergruppen (corresponding to armies) and eighteen Gruppen
(corresponding to Corps).[4] He had an operational staff
in which all important positions were held by ex-officers.[5]
Röhm had copied the military even down to the smallest
detail; SA units had "orderly officers"; SA standing orders
followed the lines of Army Regulations; the SA Standarten
carried the numbers of the old Imperial Army regiments.[6]

The more firmly SA Headquarters became established
in command of its vast brown-shirted army, the more did
the Reichswehr cast covetous eyes upon Röhm's military
acquisitions. The professional soldiers regarded the SA as
the ideal source of potential recruits against the day when
the Reichswehr, freed from the fetters of the Versailles
armaments restrictions, would reintroduce universal military service. Hitler's order brought the two forces together.[7] But instead of the "old fogey" he had anticipated,
Röhm found a counter-schemer standing in his way—
and he was one of the most progressive and unscrupulous
officers in the Reichswehr.

Major-General Walter von Reichenau was a sporting ar-
tilleryman in charge of the Ministeramt [Ministerial Of-
fice] of the Reichswehr Ministry; in spite of the monocle
in his right eye, he ridiculed many of the ideas sacred to
the Prussian-German military tradition. Many of his conservative fellow-officers regarded him as a showman and
a careerist; some even thought that he was a Nazi because, together with his Minister, Colonel-General Werner
von Blomberg, he had been the first senior Reichswehr
officer in whom Hitler had confided before 1933.[8] Nevertheless from the outset General von Reichenau had a plan
clear in his mind; the valuable military potential of the
SA must be brought under the Reichswehr umbrella and

Röhm's ambitions, which were a danger to the army, must be neutralised.[9] The only way to ensure that Röhm would play his game was to meet the SA man halfway.

Reichenau's proposal was to broaden the national defence base by introducing a militia element and in this context the SA could play an important part. There were serious gaps in the Reichswehr's defensive dispositions, particularly in the east. A so-called "Frontier Protection Service East" was therefore to be formed, planned as a type of militia; here, Reichenau explained, was the place for the SA army. In addition, assisted by the Reichswehr, the SA should undertake pre-military training of all organisations outside the armed forces.[10]

In May 1933 SA and Reichswehr concluded an agreement whereby the SA, the SS and the nationalist ex-soldiers association "Stahlhelm" were brought under the Reichswehr Ministry.[11] Obergruppenführer Friedrich-Wilhelm Krüger became SA Director of Training; with the assistance of a training staff from the Reichswehr, he was to train 250,000 SA men a year for subsequent entry into the Reichswehr.[12] Simultaneously Röhm was to absorb into the SA the right-wing defence formations, primarily the numerically strong and disciplined Stahlhelm.[13] As regards the latter, however, Reichenau had a special card up his sleeve.

The General urged Theodor Duesterberg, the Stahlhelm leader, to send as many of his men as possible into the SA. Reichenau's plan was that if a million or so men form the Stahlhelm entered the SA as a body, the Röhm section would then be outnumbered; if, in addition, the more important posts in the training organisation and the Frontier Protection Service were occupied by Reichswehr personnel, Röhm would have been out-manoeuvred.[14] On the surface the plan started auspiciously. The key positions in Krüger's organisation and in the Frontier Protection Service East were occupied by serving or retired officers.[15] But the Stahlhelm invasion went wrong. Röhm parried cleverly, dividing the SA into three groups of differing size, in the most important of which—the so-called active SA—he placed all his own 500,000 men and only 314,000 from the Stahlhelm.[16]

Röhm could now lay claim to a following of 4,500,-000[17] and he promptly went over to the counter-offensive.

He demanded greater influence and genuine command positions in the Frontier Protection Service East; worse still —he demanded control of the East German armaments depots, the thorniest problem of all in the eyes of the Reichswehr.[18] Röhm was in fact challenging the firm determination of the German Generals never to allow any organisation other than the Reichswehr to constitute the nation's armed force. The Reichswehr Ministry accordingly decided to have no further truck with Röhm's militia ideas. From December 1933 it refused to recognise the possibility of any basis for national defence other than universal military service.[19]

But Röhm was not to be deterred. On 1 December 1933 he had been made Reich Minister without Portfolio[20] and he now allowed the SA Obergruppen to form armed "headquarters guards."[21] He even brought the outside world into the game; at the Geneva Disarmament Conference France had been prepared to allow Germany an increased militia army and so Röhm initiated discussions on his own account with the French Military Attaché in Berlin.[22] In early February 1934 he presented the Reichswehr with his demands in writing;[23] the memorandum was so sharply worded that, speaking at a Commander-in-Chiefs' Conference, Blomberg could only conclude that Röhm was claiming the entire national defence field as an "SA domain," leaving the Reichswehr with training functions only.[24]

Colonel-General von Blomberg thereupon called for a ruling from Hitler, thus facing the Chancellor with the decision which he had hitherto managed to avoid.[25] Basically, Hitler was attracted by Röhm's ideas; he knew, however, that without the military experts he could never carry out his foreign-policy programme. Nevertheless, nothing was more painful to Hitler than to confront his friend Röhm with a flat "No." He therefore tried a compromise; on 28 February 1934 he invited the Reichswehr and SA leaders to the marble-pillared lecture hall of the Reichswehr Ministry, where he implored them in a "moving, gripping" speech to keep the peace.[26] In his presence Blomberg and Röhm had to conclude an agreement whereby the Reichswehr was recognised as the sole bearer of arms in the Third Reich and the SA was given sole responsibility for pre- and post-military training.[27] A state luncheon was then held in Röhm's headquarters in the Standartenstrasse when the SA and Reichswehr leaders ostentatiously shook hands.[28]

Hardly had the officers left the room, however, than Röhm bellowed: "What that ridiculous Corporal says means nothing to us . . . I have not the slightest intention of keeping this agreement. Hitler is a traitor and at the very least must go on leave . . . If we can't get there with him, we'll get there without him."[29] At Röhm's table sat an SA-Obergruppenführer who listened transfixed to this tipsy tirade against his revered Führer: Viktor Lutze, Lieutenant (Retired) and Commander of SA Obergruppe [Region] Hannover, felt that high treason was in the air.[30] He hurried off to do what he could to stop it.

Early in March 1934 he presented himself to Rudolf Hess, the "Führer's Deputy," and accused Röhm of making monstrous anti-Hitler speeches; but Hess did not know what to do,[31] so Lutze went further. He travelled to Berchtesgaden where he had an interview with Hitler, telling him of the discontent with the leadership of the Third Reich now rife in the SA. But Hitler gave him short shrift, merely saying: "We must let the matter develop."[32] Since Hitler was evidently unwilling to take action against his friend Röhm, Lutze confided in yet a third person; during an exercise in Braunfels he showed General von Reichenau a letter which he had written to Röhm, warning him against his anti-Reichswehr campaign.[33] Reichenau thanked him for this valuable information and, as soon as he was out of earshot, remarked sarcastically: "That Lutze is harmless. He'll be the Chief of Staff."[34]

Lutze did not know that for some days von Reichenau had been negotiating with an SS-Brigadeführer [Major-General] who had very precise ideas on a radical solution of the Röhm problem. Reinhard Heydrich, head of the Gestapa and SD, was determined to liquidate the entire Röhm clique. It had taken time to win Himmler over to his plan. The Reichsführer-SS was hesitant, perhaps due to a gloomy presentiment that the decision to liquidate Röhm would open a Pandora's Box, whose deadly contents would never again leave the SS and SA in peace.

As if oppressed by some presentiment of forthcoming developments, Himmler had held himself aloof from

Röhm's enemies.[35] He could not forget the years when, as a mere cadet, he had been thrown together with Captain Röhm. In the early months of the National-Socialist era, Himmler had been a constant member of Röhm's immediate retinue. Together they had made inflammatory speeches; together they had dined in Röhm's Berlin apartment.[36] They had planned crime together—Heydrich and SA-Standartenführer Uhl had both been responsible for dispatching the SA flying squad which had slipped across to Austria on 3 April 1933 and murdered Georg Bell, Röhm's renegade confidant, in an inn near Durchholzen.[37] On Röhm's last birthday (28 November 1933) Himmler had wished him "all that true loyalty as a soldier and a friend can offer. It was and is our greatest pride still to be one of your most faithful followers."[38] Himmler and Röhm together were godfathers to Heydrich's first child.[39] Even after the 28 February explosion and Röhm's anti-Hitler tirade in the Standartenstrasse, Himmler had tried to protect Röhm from over-hasty action on the part of Hitler and the Reichswehr.[40]

In spring 1934, however, Himmler's sense of opportunism proved stronger than his much-vaunted loyalty to Röhm; the new alliance with Göring seemed more important than his relations with his former master. Upon that alliance, after all, depended the capture by the SS of the Prussian Gestapo—whence the train of thought led direct to Heydrich's assassination plan: without Göring he would not get the Gestapo; unless he broke with Röhm he would get no co-operation from Göring. And of all the National-Socialist potentates Göring had most to fear from Röhm's SA. With his network of SA police presidents and SA advisers to the Regierungspräsidenten, Röhm was a threat to Göring's authority in Prussia; moreover he was also a threat to Göring's ultimate aim—to be Commander-in-Chief of the Wehrmacht.[41]

Himmler therefore changed course. This came all the easier in that the imprudent Röhm had now fallen out with practically every power group in the regime. Everyone had some interest in seeing the Röhm gang go under; everyone could draw some profit from the break-up of the SA. The Reichswehr and Göring would be rid of a tiresome rival; the Party organisation men and the guardians of morality would be rid of a vicious, depraved mischief-maker; the SS would finally free themselves from their last ties to the SA.

So Reinhard Heydrich's deadly game began—and deadly it had to be. In a Party like the NSDAP, which had grown up in the days of the Free Corps and the drumhead court martial, and had itself brought crime into politics, there was no answer to insoluble internal differences other than that of force. Georg Bell once remarked: "For us there is nothing very tragic in running a man round the corner. That procedure is inherent in our organisation. We call it self-defence; you call it murder. On moral grounds I find nothing extraordinary in doing away with a man if it is in the interests of the Party."[42] (His SA murderers were later to demonstrate to him how right he had been.)

Applying the argument to Röhm's case, this meant that only through his death could the lords of the regime guarantee their security against the SA. He was the most notorious homosexual in the country; he was one of Hitler's few old friends; he knew more Party secrets than anyone else. So neither a formal dismissal nor a faked trial could satisfy the Nazi leaders. Röhm had to die.

Heydrich set to work at the end of April 1934. Himmler toured SS units, priming them to strike against their SA comrades;[43] meanwhile, Heydrich set the trap which was to topple Röhm from his pedestal. His first requirement was some cast-iron case to justify action against the SA leaders. Heydrich spent May collecting material to convince Hitler and the Reichswehr of Röhm's supposedly highly treasonable activities.[44]

He did not lack for sources. SS-Untersturmführer Friedrich Wilhelm Krüger was now wearing the uniform of an SA-Obergruppenführer and, as Director of Training, had "mobilisation representatives" with SA-Obergruppen and Gruppen; his intelligence network provided some incriminating material.[45] Friedrich Graf von der Schulenburg, a First World War General and an enthusiastic supporter of the SS, was an honorary SA commander; he was also in the game.[46] Heydrich even made use of Lieutenant-General Wilhelm Adam, Commander of the 7th Division, Munich; though an anti-Nazi of the Schleicher school, he provided SS-Gruppenführer Schmauser with information on the SA.[47] Any information derogatory to the SA, and anyone willing to help bring Röhm down, was welcome.

But the results were meagre in the extreme. Apart from one or two reports of SA arms dumps in Berlin, Munich and Silesia,[48] Heydrich's informers had nothing to offer except bloodthirsty revolutionary wafflings by certain SA commanders—quite inadequate to support an accusation of high treason. In fact there were certain indications that nothing was further from the SA's thoughts than a plot against Hitler. Early in May Colonel von Rabenau, the Garrison Commander, Breslau, rated the likelihood of an SA rising as low;[49] when Heines, the SA Commander in Silesia, learnt from Göring that, contrary to his fears, the Reichswehr had no intention of taking any action against the SA, he promptly sent half his "headquarters guard" on leave.[50]

Rather than plotting against the regime, Röhm felt it his duty to urge the police and the Reichswehr to act against its enemies. He despatched SA-Brigadeführer Jüttner to the Reichswehr Ministry with a warning against the anti-regime intrigues of the ex-Chancellor, General Kurt von Schleicher[51]—whom the official story of the so-called putsch turned into one of Röhm's accomplices! When the writer Ernst von Salomon made some sarcastic remarks about Himmler, the one-armed Hans Peter von Heydebreck, an SA Commander, shouted: "I live for my Führer. The thought of him is the one thing which keeps me going. If I could no longer believe in my Führer, I would rather die."[52] A few days later his idol had him shot. But even when facing the firing squad Heydebreck called out: "Long live the Führer! Heil Hitler!"[53]

The SA was not, in fact, thinking high treason. It was not plotting a putsch or other act of insubordination. It simply wanted to force Hitler into according it that position in the State and among the military which had so long been denied it. But the tactics Röhm employed to achieve this end were dangerous. He did not believe that Hitler could do other than gradually conform to the wishes of the SA and so he initiated a carefully calculated war of nerves on Hitler. He travelled from one SA Gruppe to another; he made rumbustious speeches announcing the "second National-Socialist revolution."[54] He believed that his Brownshirts' mass marches must eventually soften

Hitler up. Röhm was oblivious to the fact that such goings-on inevitably made even the most unsuspecting of Germans apprehensive lest the SA army was preparing to seize power in Germany. Equally inevitably the military began to regard Röhm as a deadly enemy—and so became ready to participate in Heydrich's game. Captain (Navy) Conrad Patzig, Head of Counter-Espionage in the Reichswehr Ministry considered it "simply hair-raising" that "such unstable characters" should make "criminal plans" to elbow the Reichswehr out of its rightful place.[55] From this it was only a step to the cry "away with the SA!" The majority of officers thought like the Garrison Commander Breslau, who said quite openly that, although the SA was not planning a putsch, it was high time that that "Augean Stable" was cleaned up.[56]

Von Reichenau, the Reichswehr Ministry's chief political strategist, was equally uncompromising. He had found Heydrich a congenial partner and was often to be seen in the Gestapa; he provided barracks, weapons and transport for the great coup.[57] After all, as early as 1932, he had told Captain Felix Steiner (later to become the Waffen-SS General): "I tell you they [the SA] will eat out of our hand one day."[58]

Heydrich's execution squads were now getting ready to fulfil the General's prophecy—after their own fashion.

Early in June SS-Oberführer Theodor Eicke, Commandant of the Dachau Concentration Camp, held large-scale exercises when his troops practised surprise action against Munich Lechfeld and Bad Wiessee—in fact the plan of action against Röhm's SA.[59] Almost simultaneously the Munich SS formations took their precautions; SS-Untersturmführer Max Müller of SS Motor Sturm No. 3 was ordered to prepare his unit for rapid action and await a code word; on D-day it was to assemble at the Turk Barracks in Munich near the Headquarters of the Bavarian Political Police.[60] The Headquarters of SD-Oberabschnitt South at No. 10 Leopoldstrasse was placed on preparatory alert.[61]

From all directions Heydrich mobilised his forces; he reckoned upon four areas of violent resistance: Bavaria, Berlin, Silesia and Saxony.[62] The net closed ever tighter around the unsuspecting SA and the indefatigable Heydrich now opened phase two of his preparations. Who

were to be the victims? His minions were ordered to track
down Röhm's closest friends and draw up a list of candidates for execution.

As early as the end of April, Eicke had prepared a so-
called nationwide list of "unwanted persons" to be
liquidated on D-Day.[63] Naturally it consisted almost exclusively of SA leaders. Shortly thereafter, however,
Heydrich had a new idea; if a clean-up was the order of
the day, the more dangerous enemies of the regime might
as well be liquidated at the same time. His death list grew
longer and longer as the weeks went by; practically every
SD-Oberabschnitt had a register of candidates for the
firing squad, to which the SS and Gestapo were continually
adding.[64] SS-Obersturmführer [Lieutenant] Ilges of the
SD Hauptamt [Department] who kept the list, told an
acquaintance: "Do you know the meaning of the word
bloodlust? I feel as if I was going to wade in blood."[65]

Drafting death lists became a grisly sport for those in
the know. Everyone had his own list; Göring drew one
up;[66] Wagner, the Gauleiter of Bavaria, drew one up;[67]
the SS, the SD and the Gestapo competed in their choice
of candidates. Soon they were quarrelling over whether
this man or that really merited shooting. Werner Best,
Head of the Bavarian SD, wished to take the "decent,
loyal" SA-Obergruppenführer Schneidhuber off the list,
whereas Heydrich thought him "just as dangerous as the
rest."[68] Göring crossed out the name of his former Gestapo Chief, Diels, when it appeared on someone else's
list.[69]

At this point the Gestapo received information which
threatened to cut across all Heydrich's plans. Hitler and
Röhm had unexpectedly agreed to postpone solution of
the SA/Reichswehr problem; on 4 June the two had met
for four hours and agreed to send the SA on a month's
leave from 1 July.[70] Moreover on 8 June 1934 the
Völkischer Beobachter published an SA Headquarters press
office communiqué which made people prick up their ears.
On the advice of his doctor, the communiqué stated,
Röhm, the Chief of Staff, had had to take several weeks
sick leave (an iodine course in Bad Wiessee). Then followed a curious sentence: "In order to avoid any mis-
interpretation of this announcement, the Chief of Staff

would have it known that on recovery of his health he will continue to carry out in full the duties of his office."[71]

The Reichswehr breathed a sigh of relief; it seemed to the Generals that Röhm had lost a battle. Captain Hermann Höfle, Rohm's old "struggle period" companion, now at the Staff College, wrote to him "the prevailing view in influential army circles" was that "the first press announcement [of Röhm's illness] was the clearest proof that the Chief of Staff's position was shaky. Subsequent statements would not be able to remove this impression."[72]

The army was relieved but Heydrich was appalled. This new development left him short of time, for an SA on leave could hardly be accused of preparing a coup d'état. Ernst, Commander of the Berlin SA, was already thinking of taking a cruise to the Canaries;[73] Gruppenführer Georg von Detten, Head of the Political Office in SA Headquarters, was preparing to go off on holiday to Bad Wildungen[74]—so what would remain of the much-feared SA putsch? Heydrich had to act quickly if he was not to be too late for his SA drama. The plans were ready; the murder squads had been formed; Hitler's reaction was the only remaining uncertainty—and he had now agreed to disagree with Röhm.

Hitler had always recoiled from a head-on collision with the SA. He had long been playing a double game, a reflection of weakness rather than rational thinking; on the one hand he whipped up his brown-shirted army, primarily as a counter-weight to the Reichswehr; on the other, he toyed with the idea of disbanding the SA altogether. But he did not feel strong enough simply to invite the SA to commit suicide. He had hardly the courage to resist the more outrageous of Röhm's demands. In the anterooms of the Reich Chancellery a despairing voice had been heard from his office shouting: "No, no, I cannot do that. You are asking too much."[75] He frequently took refuge in the hope that other people would solve this tiresome problem for him. On occasions he would agree to one of Röhm's demands, and send him off to the Reich Minister of Finance in the knowledge that the hard-headed Schwerin von Krosigk would be man enough to demolish Röhm's plans with technical budgetary arguments.[76] On one occasion Hitler thought that he could get rid of the

SA through a disarmament agreement. When Anthony
Eden, the Lord Privy Seal, visited Berlin on 21 February
1934, Hitler proposed that, in return for armaments concessions by the Western Powers, he should demobilise two-
thirds of the SA and submit the remaining third to League
of Nations inspection.[77]

Now, however, Hitler was faced with three men, Heydrich, Himmler and Göring, who had a plan and knew
exactly how to solve the SA problem. Hitler agreed,
though not without hesitation. He was still only half-con-
vinced when a spectacular speech rocked him back on his
heels. On 17 June Franz von Papen, a Centre Party renegade and Hitler's Vice-Chancellor, ascended the rostrum
of Marburg University and declaimed against "all the self-
seeking characterlessness, untruthfulness, vulgarity and
arrogance hiding under the cloak of the German Revolution."[78] Applauded by the students, Papen proceeded:
". . . confusion between vitality and brutality. No nation
can live in a state of permanent revolution from below
. . . terroristic methods in the field of law . . . decision
whether the new German Reich is to be a Christian State
or lose its way in sectarianism and semi-religious materialism."[79]

The speech evoked a "roar of applause"
(Papen's words)[80] throughout the country, leaving the
Nazi rulers in no doubt that a conservative opposition had
survived the Gleichschaltung steamroller and was still in
existence. Although the Propaganda Ministry immediately banned publication of Papen's speech,[81] its repercussions
were clear enough. An uncomfortable suspicion began to
grow in Hitler's mind; what would happen if the SA and
bourgeois malcontents joined forces? Gestapo observers
had already detected the first indications of a connection
between the two.

The links all seemed to point to the SA showpiece
prince, SA-Gruppenführer Prince August Wilhelm of
Prussia, the ex-Kaiser's son, nicknamed Auwi. In practice
he had a foot in both camps; the Papen circle, which
looked for the restoration of the monarchy, regarded him
as the natural candidate for Reich Regent when Field-
Marshal von Hindenburg, the 86-year-old President, finally
died.[82] The Prince was also tipped as a winner by Werner
von Alvensleben, a shady tycoon masquerading as Director

of the ultra-conservative "League for the Protection of Culture." In the pre-1933 days he had arranged the contacts between Schleicher and Hitler and he had a photograph of Hitler with the inscription: "To my most faithful friend."[83] After 30 June 1934 he was to learn from the *Völkischer Beobachter* that he was "an obscure Berlin personality to whom Adolf Hitler had the greatest aversion."[84]

Von Alvensleben told everybody, whether he wished to hear it or not, that: "Auwi would be the next Kaiser." One day in May 1934 Martin Sommerfeldt, Head of Göring's Press Department, was dining with a conservative politician, von Gleichen-Russwurm, when Alvensleben came up looking important and conspiratorial. Gleichen remarked sarcastically that Alvensleben presumably had the new Cabinet list in his pocket. Alvensleben nodded and, bending over the table, whispered: "Reich Chancellor —Adolf Hitler; Vice Chancellor—Kurt von Schleicher; Reichswehr—Ernst Röhm; Reich Regent—Prince August Wilhelm of Prussia." When he was gone, Sommerfeldt asked what truth there was in this gossip. Gleichen replied: "Fifty-fifty."[85]

Hitler undoubtedly knew that this sort of talk was going round. He realised that the showdown with the opposition must come at the latest when Hindenburg died. His bourgeois opponents all had their eyes on the presidency which, in their view, must be occupied by a Hohenzollern Prince as figurehead for a monarchist restoration; with the support of the Reichswehr he would be able to bring National-Socialist dynamism under control. Hitler clearly had to strike first. So he took a sudden decision to visit Hindenburg on his estate Neudeck, East Prussia. He wished personally to check the old man's state of health, so that he could judge how much elbow-room he had; he too had an ambitious plan which was dependent upon Hindenburg's death. From the outset Hitler had been determined to make himself Dictator of Germany. As long as Hindenburg was alive, however, that goal was out of reach; both the Field-Marshal's prestige and the fact that the Reichswehr Generals were sworn to him by oath blocked Hitler's way to total power. Once Hindenburg was dead, however, the road would lie open; Hitler could then combine the offices of Chancellor and President into a new dictatorial office, "Führer and Reich Chancellor"—provided, and only provided, that the Reichswehr would go along. The Reichswehr must say yes; Hitler's plan stood or fell by the Reichswehr.

As if to remind him of the key role played by the Generals, when the Chancellor arrived at Neudeck on 21 June 1934 in sweltering heat, the first person who met him on the steps was the Reichswehr Minister, Colonel-General Werner von Blomberg.[86] As soon as he heard of the uproar caused by Papen's speech, Hindenburg had summoned Blomberg and, at the meeting which now followed, he left most of the talking to him.[87] Blomberg's theme was that re-establishment of peace at home was an urgent necessity; radical revolutionaries were out of place in the new Germany.[88] Hitler grasped the point. If he wished to have the Reichswehr on his side for his post-Hindenburg regime, he must sacrifice the Reichswehr's rival, Röhm's SA. According to Sir John Wheeler-Bennett, during the flight back to Berlin Hitler decided upon the action which, by the irony of history, is known as the Röhm Putsch—but was in fact the Hitler regime's putsch against Röhm.[89]

The next day Viktor Lutze in Hanover was called to the telephone to find Hitler on the line.[90] He was ordered to report to the Reich Chancellery forthwith. Lutze noted in his diary that on arrival "the Führer received me at once. He led me into his study and, taking me by the hand, swore me to secrecy until the whole matter was settled." Hitler then explained what "the whole matter" was; Röhm must be removed, since numerous SA Commanders' Conferences had been held under his chairmanship at which the decision had been taken to arm the SA and let it loose against the Reichswehr in order to liberate him, the Führer, from the military whose prisoner he was supposed to be. Lutze's diary continues: "The Führer said that he had always known that I would be no party to such matters. Henceforth I was to accept no orders from Munich and take instructions only from him."[91]

By 25 June at the latest, von Blomberg knew that Hitler was determined to relieve the army of the SA threat. Hitler told him that he intended to call all SA commanders to a meeting at Bad Wiessee where Röhm was taking his cure, that he would arrest them himself and

"square accounts" with them.[92] Two days later Sepp
Dietrich, the Commander of the Leibstandarte, appeared
in the Reichswehr Ministry and asked the head of the
Army Organisation Section to make weapons available
for a "secret and most important mission ordered by the
Führer." Blomberg had known what this secret mission
was ever since 25 June.[93]

When the so-called Röhm putsch took place, Dietrich
was to be responsible for the main action. With two
companies of the Leibstandarte he was to move to
Southern Bavaria, where he was to join with Eicke's units
from the Dachau Concentration Camp and move against
Bad Wiessee to take Röhm's more important followers by
surprise.[94] The Leibstandarte, however, was short of
transport and practically unarmed. Dietrich and the army
agreed that the two companies should move by rail to a
country station near Landsberg am Lech, whence army
transport would take them to Bad Wiessee; they were also
to draw additional equipment from Reichswehr
barracks.[95]

Reichenau, Heydrich and Himmler discussed the final
details of the combined Reichswehr/SS campaign against
Röhm. Preparatory moves began. On 22 June Himmler
summoned to Berlin Freiherr von Eberstein, Commander
of SS-Oberabschnitt Centre, and revealed to him that
Röhm was planning a coup d'état. Eberstein was to main-
tain contact with Wehrkreis [Military District] Commanders, place his men on "unobtrusive alert" and concentrate
them in barracks when the alarm was given.[96] On 23
June Colonel Fromm, Head of the Allgemeine Heeresamt
[General Army Office—AHA] informed his officers that a
Röhm putsch was imminent; the SS was on the side of the
Reichswehr and was to be given such weapons as it required.[97] On 24 June the Commander-in-Chief of the
Army, General Freiherr von Fritsch, warned all Wehrkreis
Commanders to take precautions against a threatened SA
putsch and quietly to concentrate their troops.[98] On 27
June Himmler summoned all SD-Oberabschnitt Command-
ers, ordering them to shadow SA leaders and to report
forthwith to SD Headquarters any suspicious move on
the part of the SA.[99]

So the regiments and the Standarten were in position,
the alarm bells were ringing in the barracks and the offi-

cers of the Reichswehr Ministry[100] kept loaded revolvers in their desks; yet—in spite of it all there was still an air of unreality and phantasmagoria about Heydrich's and Himmler's operation. Hardly anyone really believed that the SA was planning a putsch. The greatest sceptics were the officers of the Reichswehr.

After the end of the Thousand-Year Reich, when everyone was clearing themselves of responsibility for the bloodbath, the soldiers found that the risk of a Röhm putsch had been enormous. General Siegfried Westphal knew that "rumours were rife of an intended putsch by Röhm";[101] "from personal experience" Lieutenant-General Fretter-Pico considered that there was "still every justification to-day for believing in the imminence of a Röhm putsch";[102] even Colonel-General Halder "knew" that Röhm had "worked out a plan for an SA putsch against the Reichswehr."[103]

At the time however, the soldiers thought quite differently. Even in 1958 Colonel Gotthard Heinrici, a Section Head in the AHA at the time, could still remember that two or three days before the Röhm drama none of his fellow officers really feared that a putsch was imminent; no reports of SA preparations ever reached him.[104] He continued: "When someone placed a rifle by my desk so that, if necessary, I could defend myself (against the SA), I said: 'Boys don't make fools of yourselves.'" Colonel Fromm, the Head of the AHA, merely remarked laconically: "Insufficient determination in the SA."[105] The story of the SA planning a putsch seemed so improbable to General Ewald von Kleist, the Wehrkreis Commander in Silesia, that he spontaneously took a step which nearly ruined the plans of Reichenau and Heydrich. On receiving a flood of alarming reports about the SA's revolutionary intentions, Kleist summoned Heines, Head of the SA in Silesia, and asked him point-blank what anti-military game he was up to. Heines gave him his word of honour that the SA had never even dreamt of taking action against the Reichswehr. The General suddenly began to wonder whether "We—the Reichswehr and the SA—were being pitted against each other by a third party; I was thinking of Himmler." He went to Berlin and told General von Fritsch of his suspicions. Fritsch summoned Reichenau, who was entirely unruffled; he gazed at the two Generals through his eyeglass and said: "That may be, but it's too late now."[106]

To silence the sceptics such as Heinrici and von Kleist, however, Heydrich now unleashed an avalanche of rumours, false reports and doctored documents, calculated to remove all doubts. Every Reichswehr officer was to be made to believe in the putsch. Sepp Dietrich showed the Reichswehr Ministry what purported to be SA Head-quarters' firing-squad list; it showed that Röhm intended to liquidate all senior Wehrmacht officers starting with Generals Beck and von Fritsch;[107] other SS representa-tives submitted to Wehrkreis and Garrison Commanders SA lists showing that the dismissal of practically all senior officers had been decided upon.[108] An SA Ober-gruppenführer presented himself to Colonel Franz Halder, Chief of Staff Wehrkreis VI (Münster), and asked for in-formation on Halder's official business, saying that SA Headquarters would shortly be taking over the Reichs-wehr. Halder refused and made enquiries of the Reichswehr Ministry. The whole affair seemed odd to him; his SA visitor had not given his name and had departed hurriedly. He never reappeared. Halder suspected that the ostensible Obergruppenführer was not in fact an SA man at all, but an *agent provacateur* sent by interested parties.[109] Another of Heydrich's tricks was the distribu-tion of orders purporting to come from Röhm and in most cases taken at their face value by the Reichswehr. Whenever one of these forgeries was discovered by some SA Commander, the SS managed to lie their way out.

One day Karl Ernst, Commander of the SA Gruppe Berlin-Brandenburg, poured out his heart to SS-Gruppen-führer Daluege, who after all had originally been an SA man. The craziest rumours were going round in Berlin, he said, of the imminence of an SA putsch; he asked Daluege to arrange an interview for him with Frick, the Minister of the Interior, so that he might protest against this slander on the SA. Daluege, who was then a Director in the Ministry, saw to it that Frick's door remained firmly closed. Instead he went to the Reichswehr Ministry and told the Deputy Head of Counter-Espionage that he had just been speaking to an SA leader who had been present at a conference on preparations for an SA putsch; the SA

man had had second thoughts and now wished to warn
the Reichswehr against this imminent danger.[110]

General von Reichenau faithfully backed up Heydrich's
document gambit. One day Patzig, the Head of Counter-
Espionage, found that an order to the SA to arm, pur-
portedly signed by Röhm, had been spirited on to his
desk; he could only conclude that the SA was planning a
surprise attack on the Reichswehr and so he took the
document to von Reichenau, who put on an expression of
indignation and cried: "Now it is high time!"[111]

But Heydrich's false reports were not aimed at the
Reichswehr officers alone; there is much to show that
Hitler was also their target. He could hardly avoid seeing
them, since Blomberg never let a meeting with the
Chancellor go by without complaining that the SA was
arming. Hitler was, and remained, the Achilles' heel of
the anti-Röhm clique. He had, indeed, given his agreement to the proposed action, but now he repeatedly gave
signs of hesitation. Perhaps it was some last spark of
loyalty towards his oldest "struggle period companion";
perhaps he was unwilling to deprive himself of a counter-
weight to the Reichswehr and an important factor in the
regime's balance of power. Whatever the reason, from
time to time Adolf Hitler relapsed into sullen indecision.

As late as 28 June the officers of Wehrkreis Headquarters VII (Bavaria) were not sure whether Hitler was
on the side of the Reichswehr or the SA.[112] Had they
known of Hitler's conversation with Ritter von Krausser,
an SA-Obergruppenführer and one of Röhm's deputies,
they would have been even less sure. Shortly before his
execution Krausser told SA-Gruppenführer Karl
Schreyer, who was also under arrest, of a conversation he
had had with Hitler on 29 June. Schreyer records it as
follows: "Hitler had assured him [Krausser] that he would
use the occasion of the SA Leaders' Conference in
Wiessee to talk matters out with Röhm and all the
Gruppenführer and remove all differences and misunder-
standings. He realised, and regretted, that he had neglected
the old SA men. Hitler had been most conciliatory in his
references to his faithful fellow soldier, Ernst Röhm, who,
he said, would remain at his post."[113]

So during the vital days immediately preceding the
bloodbath, Hitler had given three differing versions of the

fate awaiting Röhm. He had told Blomberg that he would
arrest Röhm and "square accounts with him"; he had told
Lutze that Röhm would be dismissed; to von Krausser he
had forecast reconciliation. Such vacillation on the part
of the Führer did not suit Himmler, Göring and Heydrich
at all. Before the opening of the final scene, Hitler's hand
had to be removed from the levers of power.

Here chance came to the conspirators' assistance. Early
on 28 June Hitler, accompanied by Göring, left by air to
attend the wedding of Josef Terboven, the Gauleiter of
Westphalia.[114] The *National-Socialistische Korrespondenz*
later reported that Hitler had gone to Western Germany
"to give an outward impression of complete calm and
avoid warning the traitors."[115] The majority of historians
have accepted this story, believing that Hitler made this
journey to allow Röhm's enemies to get to work less
obtrusively.[116]

It does not, so far, seem to have occurred to anybody
that this supposed deception manoeuvre on Hitler's part
ran completely counter to the tactics of the anti-Röhm
campaign. He had no interest in covering up the quarrel
with Röhm. On the contrary—Röhm was to be challenged
in a spectacular campaign using maximum publicity, in
order to prepare the public for the forthcoming bloodbath. On 25 June in a speech over all German radio
networks Rudolf Hess threatened: "Woe to him who
breaks faith in the belief that he can serve the revolution
by revolt! Adolf Hitler is the revolution's great strategist.
Woe to him who plants his flat feet among the fine
threads of the Führer's strategic plans, thinking to force
the pace. He is an enemy of the revolution."[117] On 25
June Reichenau had Captain Ernst Röhm expelled from
the German Officers Association for unbecoming behaviour[118]—in Wheeler-Bennett's words "a measure
which smacked of the handing over of a victim by the
Holy Office to the civil arm for execution."[119] On the
same day Göring thundered: "Anyone who erodes this
confidence [in Hitler] is guilty of high treason. Anyone
who wishes to destroy this confidence is a destroyer of
Germany. Anyone who offends against this confidence will
pay with his head."[120]

The challenge to Röhm could not have been clearer.
So what could be the point of this deception manoeuvre

which Hitler's journey to West Germany was supposed to be? In fact the stage managers of the Röhm drama were only too glad to see the vacillating Chancellor leave Berlin —dependent henceforth on their messages, their suppositions and their rumours. Röhm's rival, Lutze, who was present at Terboven's wedding, said with a sudden flash of perspicacity: "I had a feeling that it suited certain circles to aggravate and accelerate 'the affair' just at this moment when the Führer was absent from Berlin and could therefore neither see nor hear things for himself, but was dependent upon the telephone."[121]

Hitler had hardly reached the wedding reception in Essen when he was called urgently to the telephone; Himmler was on the line from Berlin.[122] The cast was well distributed. Himmler had remained in Berlin and was now reading to Hitler increasingly ominous reports of SA machinations; meanwhile, at Hitler's side, the faithful Göring stood ready to confirm the least detail of Himmler's reports. Hitler was so incensed that he left the wedding breakfast and returned to his suite in the Kaiserhof Hotel, Essen. Shortly thereafter he summoned his closest collaborators, among them Göring and Lutze.[123] Lutze's diary continues: "Here in the hotel room the telephone was going almost uninterruptedly. The Führer was deep in thought but was apparently clear that he would now have to take action."[124] Another confidant of the conspirators now took a hand in Hitler's discussion; Paul (nicknamed Pilli) Körner, Göring's factotum and a Secretary in the Prussian State Ministry, had just arrived by air from Berlin with further news from Himmler.[125] Throughout Germany, apparently, the SA was arming for revolt.

Suddenly Hitler got up and proclaimed: "I've had enough. I shall make an example of them."[126] The final ultimate decision had been taken. Hitler ordered Göring and Körner to return to Berlin and be ready to act on receipt of a code word which Hitler would issue—and to act not only against the SA but also against the bourgeois opposition. Göring lost no time; early on 29 June, back in Berlin, he alerted the Leibstandarte "Adolf Hitler" and the Prussian Police unit "General Göring."[127]

Göring now drafted a letter, which was handed under seal to Heydrich. Heydrich passed it to SS-Untersturm-

führer Ernst Müller of the SD Hauptamt, instructing him
to give it to the Commander of SS-Oberabschnitt South
East.[128] The purport of this letter was that the Chancellor
had declared a state of emergency and given Göring, as
Minister-President, plenary powers in Prussia; he, Göring,
now delegated all executive authority in the province of
Silesia to the commander of SS-Oberabschnitt South East,
SS-Gruppenführer Udo von Woyrsch. Göring then or-
dered von Woyrsch to arrest certain SA leaders, to disarm
all SA "headquarters guards," to occupy Breslau Police
Headquarters and get in touch with the commander of the
Land Police.[129]

Meanwhile, in the Kaiserhof Hotel, Essen, Hitler was
thinking how he could take the SA leaders by surprise.
Eventually he fell back on his original plan as explained
to von Blomberg—to lure them to Bad Wiessee and arrest
them there. On the evening of 28 June Hitler put through
a call to Bad Wiessee and told Röhm that SA men had
insulted a foreign diplomat in the Rhineland; this could
not go on, he said, and they must have a discussion. Then
he gave his instructions; all SA-Obergruppenführer, Gruppenführer and Inspectors were to present themselves at
Röhm's holiday resort for a discussion with the Führer at
11 a.m. on Saturday 30 June 1934.[130]

Hitler then waited for his opponent to react. But on 29
June Röhm was entirely carefree; he went for long walks
in Bad Wiessee with his aide, Bergmann; he expressed
pleasure at the prospect of a discussion with Hitler and he
greeted old friends as they arrived at the Hanselbauer
Pension.[131] Meanwhile the other side was acting. The
Commander-in-Chief of the Army issued a general
alert.[132] SS Headquarters called their units into barracks
and armed them.[133] Hitler, who was inspecting a Voluntary Labour Service Camp, sent a radio message to the
Reichswehr Ministry at 3 p.m., ordering Sepp Dietrich to
come to the Hotel Dreesen in Bad Godesberg, whither he
had now moved.[134]

Dietrich arrived about 8 p.m. Hitler was in conference
with fifteen Nazi functionaries, including Lutze, Goebbels
and the three of the Führer's aides, Bruckner, Schaub and
Schreck.[135] Shortly thereafter Dietrich had to leave the
glass of beer he had ordered in the hotel lounge and
present himself to his Führer.[136] Hitler's order was a

short one: "Fly to Munich and call me from there."[137]
Dietrich flew to Munich with two Criminal Police officers
—destination: The Brown House.[138] Shortly before midnight he once more reported to Hitler by telephone and
was given a new order: proceed to Kaufering, a small
railway station near Landsberg am Lech, there take over
two companies of the Leibstandarte and move to Bad
Wiessee.[139]

About the same time (between midnight and 1 a.m.)
the Leibstandarte in the ex-Cadet College, Berlin-Lichter-
feld was alerted by a call from the Reichswehr Ministry.[140] The Duty Officer hunted 220 men out of bed and
shortly thereafter two companies were on their way to
Kaufering by train.[141] Sepp Dietrich was on the way by
road and the Leibstandarte units were already assembled
when two messages put Hitler in a towering rage and
made him alter his plans.[142]

The first was from Himmler in Berlin: the Berlin SA
had completed its putsch preparations and action was
planned for the next day, 30 June; the SA had been
alerted for 4 p.m. and, as Hitler later told the Reichstag,
"sharp at 5 p.m. action was to begin with the surprise
occupation of the Government buildings."[143] Hitler in
Bad Godesberg did not know that most of the Berlin SA
had long since gone on leave. Even on 13 July he apparently still believed that, instead of journeying to Bad
Wiessee, Karl Ernst, Head of the Berlin SA, had "remained behind in Berlin to conduct the action in person";[144] In fact Ernst left Berlin with his wife on 29
June en route to Bremen to board a ship for Tenerife.[145]

The second report bore little better relation to the
truth. It was from Adolf Wagner, the Gauleiter and Minister of the Interior, Bavaria—in Munich the SA had
come out on to the streets and were demonstrating against
the Führer and the Reichswehr.[146]

Late on the evening of 29 June certain Munich SA
units had marched through the Isar quarter with the cry
"The Reichswehr is against us." Handwritten leaflets of
unknown authorship had lured them out of the bars and,
in addition, they were aware of the alert measures taken
by the Reichswehr.[147] When Obergruppenführer August
Schneidhuber, head of the Munich and Upper Bavarian
SA, and Gruppenführer Wilhelm Schmid heard that their

units were on the march, they intervened and ordered them back home.[148] Schmid laid hands on two copies of the anonymous orders; all he knew about them was that neither he nor Schneidhuber had either drafted them or issued them.[149]

Colonel Küchler, Chief of Staff in the Munich Wehrkreis Headquarters, heard that an SA column was on the move towards the Oberwiesenfeld airfield. He summoned Major Hans Doerr, his Transport Officer, and ordered him to go out in mufti and discover what was happening.[150] Doerr drove off about 1 a.m. on 30 June and soon met an SA unit about 300 strong. At Oberwiesenfeld, however, he found no one. On the Königsplatz he observed another group of SA whose Commanders were sending their men home with the words: "Go quietly home and wait for the decision of your Führer. Whatever may happen, whether Adolf Hitler sends you on leave or whether he forbids you to wear uniform or not, we stand unreservedly behind him."[151]

In face of these two midnight messages from Berlin and Munich, Hitler, whose information was abysmally poor, panicked. Now he really knew, he thought: the traitors had dropped the mask and Röhm had come out in his true colours. Now he was determined to exterminate this "nest of traitors." Obsessed with these illusions, he took a sudden decision which left his entourage gasping; off to Munich at once, off to Bad Wiessee at once.[152] At 2 a.m. shaken, fatigued and quivering with agitation, he stumped across the Bonn airfield at Hangelar and clambered with his following into a three-engined Ju 52.[153] He slumped down into the front seat of the cabin, gazing silently out into the misty night sky. Gradually the mist gave way to the pale pink of a new day, the most murderous day of pre-war German history. Germany was headed for an orgy of blood, brutality and barbarism. Lutze thought of Röhm and hummed to himself:

Morgenrot, Morgenrot,	Red of the morning, red of the morning
Leuchtest uns zu frühem Tod.	Thou lightest us to early death.
Gestern noch auf stolzem Rossen,	Yesterday mounted on a proud steed,

| Heute durch die Brust ge-schossen | Today a bullet through the breast.[154] |

As soon as the aircraft landed at Oberwiesenfeld, Munich, Hitler leapt out, stalking through the assembled Party and SA dignitaries as if in a trance. He stopped for a moment in front of two Reichswehr officers whom he had ordered up by radio, saying: "This is the blackest day of my life. But I shall go to Bad Wiessee and pass severe judgment. Tell that to General Adam."[155] He then drove to the Bavarian Ministry of the Interior.

Shortly after 4 a.m. Gruppenführer Schmid was woken by the telephone. The Ministry of the Interior informed him that Hitler was awaiting him.[156] "Before he went," his wife stated, "he searched desperately round the bedroom for two white leaflets saying: 'They might prove that I have had nothing to do with the entire business'." But the sheets had disappeared.[157] Schmid had little chance of explaining himself to Hitler, however; the Chancellor had hardly set eyes on him when he rushed up, tore off his badges of rank, cursed him for a traitor and screamed: "You are under arrest and will be shot." Schmid was led off to Stadelheim Prison; he was only a few minutes behind Obergruppenführer Schneidhuber.[158] Leaving Gauleiter Wagner to despatch squads of SS and Bavarian Political Police to arrest named SA leaders and prominent opponents of National-Socialism,[159] Hitler rushed off to Bad Wiessee with two escort cars.

By now it was 6.30 a.m.[160] The SA leaders were still sleeping in the Hanselbauer Pension. The landlady murmured something about being honoured by so illustrious a visitor, but Hitler and his men stormed past her and took up positions at the bedroom door, revolvers in hand.[161] Lutze remained behind for a moment and thumbed through the visitors' list to see where the victims were. He arrived just in time to witness the arrest of Röhm.[162]

Lutze's diary records that he met Hitler "at Röhm's door. A detective had knocked, calling out that something urgent had arrived. There was a pause before the door opened and it was then pushed wide. The Führer stood in the doorway, revolver in hand. He called Röhm a traitor, which Röhm energetically denied; he then told him to get dressed since he was under arrest. The detectives remained behind."[163]

Hitler hurried on. He banged on the opposite door from which, shortly afterwards, appeared Obergruppenführer Edmund Heines; a male sleeping partner could be seen behind him. In a sudden access of rage against National-Socialist homosexuals, Goebbels later described the scene as "revolting—almost nauseating."[164] Hitler rushed off to the next room while Lutze went into Heines' room and searched the wardrobe for weapons. Heines shouted "Lutze, I've done nothing. Can't you help me?" In some embarrassment Hitler's man turned to him saying: "I can do nothing . . . I can do nothing."[165] The entire "nest of conspirators" had soon been cleared. The arrested SA men were marched down and locked in the cellar of the Pension, guarded by two detectives; they were soon on the way to Stadelheim.[166] Before Hitler could leave, however, a lorry arrived from which emerged, fully armed, Röhm's "Headquarters Guard" summoned from Munich.[167] The situation was critical; Standartenführer Julius Uhl, the Headquarters Guard Commander, was languishing in the Pension cellar and his men were in an ugly mood.

Hitler went forward, barked out an order and then turned on his usual charm. The SA men did as they were told and allowed their Führer to order them back to Munich. They drove off northwards.[168] But on leaving Bad Wiessee they had second thoughts. The lorry stopped and Röhm's Headquarters Guard took up what Bruckner, Hitler's aide, described as an "ambiguous position."[169] They looked so menacing that Hitler thought it better to leave Bad Wiessee in a southerly direction and return to Munich by a wide detour via Rottach-Egern and Tegernsee.[170] At about this time Dr Robert Koch, the Governor of Stadelheim Prison, strolled in through the main entrance.[171] He found on his desk a report to the effect that senior SA Commanders had been arriving uninterruptedly since 7 a.m.[172] The SS had surrounded the main station and Political Police officials held up every SA leader as he arrived; some they let go and some they arrested—more often the latter.[173]

When SA Brigadeführer Max Jüttner arrived at the station to meet his Chief, Ritter von Krausser, off the overnight train from Berlin, he found him being escorted by two plain-clothes men, clearly police officials. Krausser told Jüttner that he had just been arrested. Krausser's chauffeur, Vollmer, tried to get his master away and was also arrested.[174] One after another the SA leaders were taken off to Stadelheim—Manfred von Killinger, Hans Peter von Heydebreck, Hans Hayn, Georg von Detten, Hans Joachim von Falkenhausen[175]—the list included practically every well-known SA name.

Anyone who escaped the political police, however, and dutifully took the road to Bad Wiessee, was stopped on the way by a wildly gesticulating figure. Hitler told each SA leader that he had a new Chief, Viktor Lutze.[176] He shouted: "I have just come from Wiessee, where I have arrested Röhm. He and Schleicher had planned a putsch against me and the leaders of the State. All SA leaders involved will be shot." He ordered those he met to follow his car and hold themselves ready for a conference in the Brown House.[177]

At 10 a.m. Hitler reached Party Headquarters in the Briennerstrasse; it had meanwhile been cordoned off by the Reichswehr. He gave Goebbels the go-ahead; the Propaganda Minister rushed to the telephone and put through to Göring the agreed code word: "Kolibri."[178] Now, at last, Heydrich and Himmler really could let the SS loose, and terror stormed through the Reich. SD-Oberabschnitt Commanders opened the sealed envelopes containing their secret orders and then sent the murder squads on their way.

Bavaria provided the first SS victims. Ritter von Kahr, who had checkmated Hitler's 1923 putsch, was carried off by SS men[179] and his mutilated body was found later on Dachau Heath; he had apparently been killed with a pick-axe. Father Bernhard Stempfle, who knew too many of Hitler's secrets, ended with three bullets through his heart and a broken spine.[180]

SS men searched for the Munich doctor, Ludwig Schmitt, who had worked with Otto Strasser, one of Hitler's main enemies. They failed to find him because, unknown to them, one of the Stadelheim warders had hidden him in a woodshed.[181] Failing to find the right man, they laid hands on the wrong one, a music critic named Dr Wilhelm Eduard Schmid; he lived in a different street, he spelt his name differently, and he was a doctor of philosophy, not medicine—all the same the SS carted him away. His family knew no more until Dachau Concentration Camp delivered them a coffin which they were forbidden to open.[182]

From this point on, the most fanatical apostle of political terror was Adolf Hitler. The Reichsstatthalter, Ritter von Epp, presented himself to demand court-martial procedure for his former subordinate, Röhm; Hitler stormed at him saying that Röhm's treachery was proven and that he had forfeited his life. Von Epp was so taken aback by Hitler's bloodthirsty outburst that, as he left, he gazed tongue-tied at his aide, Prince zu Ysenburg and murmured: "Crazy!"[183] The SA Commanders who had not been arrested were equally taken aback, when at 11.30 Hitler swung open the door of the Brown House Council Chamber and approached them.[184]

Describing the scene, Gruppenführer Schreyer recalled that as he opened his mouth to speak "a gob of foam shot out of his mouth such as I have never seen before or since. In a voice frequently choked with emotion, he described what had happened: Röhm and his followers had been guilty of the greatest act of disloyalty in world history. Röhm, to whom he had always been faithful through every difficulty, possible or impossible, had committed high treason against him; Röhm had planned to arrest and kill him in order to hand Germany over to her enemies. The principal figure on the other side had been François-Poncet [the French Ambassador]; he had given Röhm, who was always in financial difficulties, a bribe of 12,000,-000 marks." Then came the decisive piece of news: "Exemplary punishment would be meted out to Röhm and his conspirators; he would have them all shot; the first group—Röhm, Schneidhuber, Schmid, Heines, Hayn, Heydebreck and Count Spreti—would be shot that very evening. He had already given the order."[185] This information was in fact somewhat premature. Röhm was not shot "that very evening" and Hitler had not given the order to execute the others on the list. He was waiting for his executioner, Sepp Dietrich. The Leibstandarte Commander did not appear until 12.30 a.m.[186]

Hitler received him in a bad temper, and wanted to know where he had been all this time. Dietrich had his excuses. The roads to Bad Wiessee were wet and the tyres of the Reichswehr lorries carrying his men were worn; in addition he had had to take on petrol at the artillery barracks in Landsberg. The Führer's order to turn back to Munich had therefore only reached him between Bad Tölz and Bad Wiessee.[187] Where were the troops now, Hitler asked. Dietrich replied that they were on the Munich Karolinerplatz. Hitler thereupon ordered him to install his two companies in the Pioneer Barracks and report back again as soon as possible.[188]

Dietrich returned at 2.30 p.m. He was kept waiting for three hours in the Brown House outer office while loud, but unintelligible, discussion was audible through the double doors of the meeting room.[189] Hitler and his immediate associates were debating the fate of the SA leaders. This was the great moment for Buch, the Party Judge, who clearly wished to make good his failure to murder the Röhm gang in 1932. Rudolf Hess and Max Amann, the Party publisher, competed for the pleasure of carrying out the murders, Hess shouting: "My Führer, the duty to shoot Röhm is mine."[190] The new SA Chief of Staff, Lutze, sat there dumbfounded, listening to the others' murderous talk. He had never imagined that a clean-up of the SA would be like this. When Hitler asked him who should be shot, Lutze was evasive, saying that he did not know who was to blame or who were Röhm's accomplices and could not quote any names. He then silently left the room.[191] About 5 p.m. the door opened and Buch's son-in-law, Martin Bormann, came out. He took Dietrich in to Hitler who said: "Go back to the barracks; select an officer and six men and have the SA leaders shot for high treason."[192] Bormann then handed Dietrich a list of prisoners sent over to the Brown House that morning by Koch, the Prison Governor; it gave the names of all the SA leaders incarcerated in Stadelheim.[193] Hitler had ticked six names in green pencil; August Schneidhuber, SA-Obergruppenführer and Police President of Munich (Cell 504); Wilhelm Schmid, SA-Gruppenführer Munich (Cell 497); Hans Peter von Heydebreck, SA-Gruppenführer Stettin (Cell 502); Hans Hayn, SA-Gruppenführer Dresden (Cell 503); Hans Joachim Graf von Spreti-Weilbach, SA-Standartenführer Munich (Cell 501) and Ed-

mund Heines, SA-Obergruppenführer and Police President Breslau (Cell 483).[194]

Röhm's name had not been ticked. Hitler drove out to
Oberwiesenfeld airfield on his way back to Berlin; he was
accompanied by von Epp and on the way Prince zu
Ysenburg heard him say: "I have pardoned Röhm because
of his services and Krausser because of his decorations."[195] Perhaps Hitler could not yet quite bring himself to murder his old friend.

Sepp Dietrich had no such scruples. He just took the
list of the condemned, sent SS-Gruppenführer Prince zu
Waldeck und Pyrmont on ahead to Stadelheim to select
a suitable execution spot[196] and himself looked out "six
good shots to ensure that nothing messy happened."[197]
At 6 p.m. he presented himself to the Prison Governor
and requested him to hand over the condemned men.[198]
But Koch was a prudent official and he had covered himself. Warned by Prince zu Waldeck's visit, he had alerted
the Bavarian Ministry of Justice. The Minister, Dr Hans
Frank, was already on the road, so Koch played for
time.[199]

He pointed out to the simple-minded Dietrich that his
list carried no signature and argued so stubbornly that
Dietrich went back to the Brown House for fresh instructions. The only high-level official he could find was Wagner, the Minister of the Interior, who wrote on Dietrich's
list:

> "By command of the Führer the men whom
SS-Gruppenführer Dietrich indicates, are to be handed
over to him.
>
> Adolf Wagner, State Minister"[200]

Meanwhile Frank, the National-Socialist legal expert,
had arrived in Stadelheim and had made one or two half-
hearted attempts to stop the murders.[201] He called Rudolf Hess, but Hess refused to become involved and insisted that the Führer's order be carried out.[202] Frank
thought that at least the proper procedure should be observed and so informed Schneidhuber that he had been
condemned to death; Schneidhuber, however, reacted so
forcefully and incredulously that Frank brought the interview to an end.[203] So Dietrich was now free to do his
duty.

Koch ordered the six SA leaders to be led out into the prison courtyard, each guarded by two policemen.[204] Seeing Dietrich approach, Schneidhuber shouted: "Sepp, my friend, what on earth's happening? We are completely innocent!"[205] In Dietrich's surly, bucolic face not a muscle moved. He clicked his heels and announced: "You have been condemned to death by the Führer. Heil Hitler!" One after another the SA leaders were led out and into the courtyard.[206] They were received by an SS officer with the words: "The Führer and Reich Chancellor has condemned you to death. The sentence will be carried out forthwith." The courtyard's walls echoed to the crack of the rifles.[207]

Even Dietrich's nerve gave way before the end and he left before all six had been shot. He said later: "Before it was Schneidhuber's turn, I was off. I had had enough."[208] He waited until mid-day next day, when he entrained his men for Berlin. He then flew back to the capital,[209] where since 10 a.m. on 30 June the Göring–Himmler version of this German Saint Bartholomew's Night had been in progress.

As soon as Goebbels had telephoned through the code word "Kolibri," the mechanism of terror had begun to operate in Göring's kingdom. The news was brought to Franz von Papen, the Vice-Chancellor, when Major Bodenschatz, Göring's aide, invited him to appear at the office of the Prussian Minister-President in the Leipziger Platz. Papen records: "Göring was in his study with Himmler. He told me that he himself had been given powers to deal with the insurgents in the capital." Von Papen felt that, as Vice-Chancellor, he had been bypassed and he protested. While the two were arguing, Himmler went out into the ante-room where Fritz-Gunther von Tschirschky, Papen's assistant was waiting. Himmler went to a telephone and Tschirschky heard him say: "You can go ahead now." The hunt for enemies of the regime was on.[210]

Police cars and lorries full of SS men roared through the streets. The Tiergarten quarter, where the most important SA Headquarters were, was cordoned off. Such SA Commanders as were found on duty allowed themselves to be carted off without demur.[211] At the same time SS and police surrounded the Vice-Chancellor's office, shot von Bose, Papen's Press Officer, and arrested certain other members of his staff.[212] The "reactionary" enemy of the State was to be put in his place.

Meanwhile in the Lichterfeld Barracks the Leibstandarte had been placed on general alert. The Battalion Commander, SS-Sturmbannführer Wagner, was ordered by SS Headquarters to prepare a number of Einsatzkommandos [Action Commandos].[213] To command the more important of these, Wagner detailed Hauptsturmführer Kurt Gildisch, who was known to be prepared to carry out any order.[214] Gildisch paraded eighteen men of his company and moved off with them. He reported to Heydrich. There were eight men already waiting in the anteroom, some in mufti and some in SS uniform.[215]

Shortly thereafter Heydrich emerged from his office and snapped out words he was to repeat very often that day: "Putsch by Röhm—state of emergency—order from the Führer—immediate action." He then withdrew into his office and summoned each of the waiting men individually. The Gestapo plain-clothes men were each given a list of names of victims. One Gestapo official, together with Gildisch's men, was to arrest so-called enemies of the State. Gildisch himself was given a special mission: "You will be responsible for the Klausener Case; you will shoot him personally. Go forthwith to the Reich Ministry of Transport." As an afterthought Heydrich asked whether Gildisch knew Klausener; when Gildisch said that he did not, Heydrich simply raised his hand in the Hitler salute, said "Heil Hitler" and Gildisch was dismissed.[216]

On the way to the Ministry of Transport in the Wilhelmstrasse Gildisch mulled over methods of shooting his victim. On his belt he carried a 9 mm "Parabellum" service pistol, but concealed in his right trouser pocket was a loaded 7.65 mm Mauser. This was the weapon he planned to use for his surprise attack.[217] One wonders whether this was all that Gildisch was thinking, and the answer is that it was. Dr Erich Klausener was a Director in the Reich Ministry of Transport, President of Catholic Action and ex-Head of the Police Section in the Prussian Ministry of the Interior, yet not for one moment did Gildisch wonder what crime Klausener might have committed to deserve to be shot without trial and without the slightest opportunity to defend himself.[218]

It was now 1 p.m. and Klausener was just coming out of his office to wash his hands when he saw the steel-helmeted SS man in front of him. He went back into his office and asked Gildisch in. When the latter told him that he was under arrest, Klausener turned and went to a cupboard to get his jacket. Gildisch thereupon drew his automatic and shot Klausener through the head; he fell to the floor dead. Gildisch seized the desk telephone and dialled Heydrich's number. The unnaturally high-pitched voice from the Prinz Albrecht-Strasse ordered him to fake a suicide, so he placed the Mauser near Klausener's limp right hand and put a double guard on the door. As far as the Third Reich was concerned, the Klausener Case was settled.[219]

Gildisch was back with Heydrich by 1.15 and only then did he learn whom he had shot—"a dangerous Catholic leader." He was forthwith dispatched on another mission—to fly to Bremen, arrest Karl Ernst, Head of the Berlin SA, and bring him to the Lichterfeld Barracks. Gildisch was responsible for a number of other victims that day, including the SA Medical Officer, Standartenführer, Dr Erwin Villain.[220]

Gildisch with his eighteen thugs, however, was nothing out of the ordinary on 30 June 1934. Everywhere in Göring's Prussia, the SS robots were hunting down supposed enemies of the State. They did not think; they simply obeyed. They did not grumble; they simply acted. Without a word they carried out the duty assigned to them. Himmler's human automata asked no questions. All they wanted to know were the names of their victims.

Escape necessitated bold and instant action. Gottfried Treviranus, for instance, a retired Minister of the Reich, heard Himmler's minions ringing his doorbell; though dressed only for tennis, he climbed his garden wall and fled abroad.[221] Captain Ehrhardt, Hitler's reluctant ally in 1923, withdrew into the woods of his own estate, taking a couple of shotguns with him and, as soon as the Gestapo had left his house, got some friends to smuggle him across into Austria.[222]

Major General Ferdinand von Bredow, Reichenau's predecessor in the Reichswehr Ministry, was suspected by the Nazis of having written Diary of a Reichswehr General which had appeared in emigré circles in Paris. Since he

was in obvious danger, a foreign Military Attaché invited
him to spend the night in his embassy, but Bredow refused.
A few hours later a Gestapo car delivered his body to the
Lichterfeld Barracks: he had been shot through the
head.[223] The SS thirst for blood increased hourly. They
soon ceased to be content with the official victims, the
mutineers and enemies of the State, and turned over to a
campaign of personal vengeance. Erich von dem Bach-
Zelewski, an SS-Oberabschnitt Commander, sent two SS
men to deal with his rival, the SS Cavalry leader, Anton
Freiherr von Hohberg und Buchwald; they shot him down
from behind in his own smokingroom on his estate. When
his seventeen-year-old son rushed in, one of them said
casually: "We have just shot your father"—and calmly
went away.[224]

The settlement of private SS scores was particularly
savage in Silesia. There the Oberabschnitt Commander,
Udo von Woyrsch, lost control of his men. SA-Sturm-
bannführer Engels, Acting Police President of Breslau, was
driven out into the woods by SS men and killed with a
shotgun.[225] Sembach, who had been a member of SS
Headquarters Silesia, was drowned in a reservoir near
Brieg and his murderer was then murdered in his turn.[226]
Vengeance for anything was the order of the day; Dr
Förster, a lawyer from Hirschberg, was killed because he
had taken part in legal proceedings against National-
Socialists;[227] Kamphausen, the Waldenburg Municipal
Engineer, was murdered for being un-co-operative over
the issue of building licences.[228] Many of Göring's and
Himmler's actions were governed by personal spite. For
instance they hunted down Gregor Strasser because, more
than any other National-Socialist leader, he had seen
through them both. Until 1932, when he had split with
Hitler on a tactical disagreement, he had been ranked
second in the Party; he had once described "the Himmlers
and Anhimmlers" (a pun meaning "Hitler's adorers")[229]
as the greatest threat ot the Führer and the Movement;
of Göring he had said: "Goring is a brutal egoist who
does not give a damn about Germany as long as he can
amount to something."[230]

For Himmler and Göring such a man was all the more
dangerous in that they could not discount the possibility
of a reconciliation between him and Hitler one day. They

knew that Hitler had toyed with the idea of appointing
Strasser Minister of the Interior.[231] There had already
been danger signals; Hitler and Strasser had had a conciliatory talk; on 23 June Hitler had invested Strasser
with the Golden Party Badge carrying the membership
number 9.[232] So if 30 June 1934 was to mean anything
for Göring and Himmler, Gregor Strasser had to die. In
the early afternoon he was arrested by two Gestapo men
and a couple of hours later an SS man shot him from
behind in Cell 16 in the Gestapo prison. His death was
officially announced as "suicide."[233]

Meanwhile, where was the fearful SA mutiny? Where
were the master-minds behind the "greatest act of disloyalty in world history" which Hitler had announced to
the SA survivors in the Brown House? The master-minds
were in fact enjoying a sunny weekend. They were at
home; they were preparing to go on leave. General Kurt
von Schleicher was sitting at his desk in his house in the
Griebnitzstrasse, Neu-Babelsberg; his cook, Marie Guntel,
ushered two men into his study and one of them asked
whether the man at the desk was the General. Marie
Guntel later stated in evidence: "On hearing the question
he [von Schleicher] looked up and said 'Yes.' At that
very instant the shots rang out." The General's wife, who
was in the room listening to the radio, ran towards him
—and was shot down too.[234]

But in the murdered man's papers the Gestapo found
nothing to indicate any collusion by Schleicher with either
Röhm or Strasser or François-Poncet. He had not met
Röhm since June 1933; as far as François-Poncet was
concerned he has said that Schleicher "at no time said
anything indicating . . . that he was involved in any sort
of plot . . . Whenever he uttered Röhm's name it was with
contempt and disgust."[235] The tale of a Schleicher–
Röhm putsch was so improbable that even the Reich
Propaganda Ministry did not believe it. That afternoon
the Ministry held a press conference and a journalist
asked whether General von Schleicher's death was in any
way connected with the action against Röhm's SA. The
Ministry's spokesman answered: "That is not the case."[236]

Göring and Himmler were uneasy, wondering whether
the Reichswehr would strike, now that its most prominent
political General had, for no good reason, been shot down

by the SS murderers. But not at all. General von Reichenau was not the man to allow a complete scheme to be
upset by one tiresome corpse. That afternoon he dictated
a communiqué: "In recent weeks it has been established
that the ex-Reichswehr Minister, General (Retired) von
Schleicher has maintained treasonable relationships with
foreign powers and with SA leadership circles inimical to
the State. It has therefore been proved that both in word
and deed he had been acting against the State and its
leaders. This meant that in connection with the general
purge now in progress, his arrest was essential. When police officers came to arrest him, General (Retired) von
Schleicher offered armed resistance. There was an exchange of shots as a result of which both he and his wife,
who placed herself in the line of fire, were mortally
wounded."[237]

As a result of the murder of von Schleicher, however, a
rift appeared between the executioners. Göring said later
that he had intended only to arrest the General but the
Gestapo squad had arrived before his policemen and had
forthwith carried out the murder.[238] In fact Göring now
felt that it was time to check this orgy of blood. The
news from the country made it clear that the SS units
were becoming increasingly violent and his policemen
were losing control; at the same time he had no wish to
spoil the picture of bonhomie and conservatism which he
liked to present to the nation.

One of the first to realise that the rift existed was von
Papen, the Vice Chancellor. On attempting to leave Göring's office in the Leipziger Platz, he was stopped at the
door by two SS guards. Bodenschatz, Göring's aide,
stormed past, shouting: "We'll see who is in command
here, Ministerpresident Göring or the SS!"[239] The victims
soon realised that they could turn the disagreement between Göring and Himmler to good account. SA-Gruppenführer Siegfried Kasche, who was clearly facing death,
held forth to Göring at such length that the latter released him;[240] Göring also took von Bülow, an Under-
Secretary in the Foreign Ministry, off the list;[241] in the
same way he saved the ex-Crown Prince, who was also
in some danger.[242]

Göring soon dropped the role of jovial saviour, however, when Hitler returned from Munich[243] at 10 p.m.

bringing the news that Röhm was not to die. Hitler had given his word to Ritter von Epp. Göring and Himmler were appalled: the slaughter would be meaningless to them if Röhm lived. As early as the evening of 29 June Himmler had told Frau von Ribbentrop: "Röhm is as good as dead";[244] and thus it had to be. Hitler may well suddenly have thought that it might be in his own interests to save Röhm from Goring and Himmler; he had no wish to scc his two henchmen become over-powerful. On 30 June 1934 Hitler was not yet the totalitarian dictator (that he would only become through the succession to Hindenburg and the elimination of the Wehrmacht as a power factor as a result of the Blomberg-Fritsch crisis). If Röhm disappeared altogether, the delicate balance-of-power system, upon which Hitler's leadership depended, would be upset.

Hitler now began to play a highly sophisticated game. He had been entirely unmoved by the shooting of the most important SA leaders in Stadelheim; he had used the word "exterminate" continuously. Back in Berlin, however, he assumed the role of the moderate, thoughtful Führer, who did not necessarily approve all that his subordinates did. He told the Cabinet that he took responsibility for the shooting of the "traitors—even though the measure of their guilt had not been proved in every case and certain of the summary shootings had not been ordered by him personally."[245] He told Jüttner that he had wished to have a legal investigation, but had been overtaken by events.[246]

Out of loyalty the SA survivors, led by Viktor Lutze, the new Chief of Staff, took their Führer at his word. In fact Hitler brought off a psychological masterstroke; the more the survivors raged against Himmler and Göring, the more shining an example of rectitude did Adolf Hitler become. "There is no question about the shootings ordered by the Führer. They are not a subject of discussion," Lutze wrote.[247] He genuinely believed that Hitler had ordered the shooting of only seven SA leaders and "subsequently recognised" ten further murders committed without his permission.[248]

Whatever Hitler's purpose may have been in playing the man of moderation, Himmler and Göring now brought pressure on him to sacrifice Röhm. Even during the night 30 June/1 July they had begun to argue—and Hitler had always been one to fight on the side of the big battalions. That night anyone whose life depended upon a promise from Hitler found that he had miscalculated. Lieutenant (Retired) Paul Schulz, who had reorganised the SA after the Stennes putsch and was a friend of Gregor Strasser, was one of them. He was running for his life through the woods near Potsdam, covered in blood, gasping, stumbling over tree roots, getting up and running again.[249]

The crazy logic of 30 June had turned Schulz, one of Röhm's bitterest enemies, into one of his accomplices. The Gestapo was after him. Later he described what happened: he had been arrested at dinner by "five young toughs in plain clothes, some without collars and ties, but with pistols at the ready." An hour later he was incarcerated in Room 10 in the Gestapa.[250] Three men had then pushed him into a grey convertible and the death ride began. They roared towards Potsdam, looking for some quiet spot where an "escaper" could be shot. But it was Saturday evening and every road was brightly lit by the headlights of approaching cars, so they had to go on.

They took the Leipzig road and at last they found a suitable spot. Schulz was made to get out and turn his back on one of the escort. He made a dash for it and, although he was hit, the range was too great for the bullet to kill him. With considerable presence of mind he pretended to be dead and his escort went back to the car to get a sheet in which to wrap the supposed corpse. Schulz's account goes on: "At that instant I jumped up and ran as fast as I could into the wood, keeping an eye on my murderers over my shoulder. They stood staring, as if transfixed."[251]

Schulz ran on. His back was hurting from the bullet which grazed his spine "but, to my relief, I noticed that I was not bleeding from the mouth." On and on he ran, determined not to faint and after the first few hundred yards he doubled back. He reached a village named Seddin, but there he saw cars with searchlights lighting every inch of the road. He dived behind a hedge—where his followers later discovered the trail of blood.[252] He crept to a stream, the Nuthe, where he hid in the reeds. By the light of the moon he washed off the blood and began to think how he could escape his pursuers.

Then a name occurred to him; he knew a certain

retired Rear-Admiral named Lübbert, who had only recently moved to Berlin and consequently was hardly known to the police; this was where he would hide. The plan worked. The Admiral took the fugitive in, while a vast posse of police and SS searched the neighbourhood of Potsdam, urging people to look for Schulz and, if necessary, to kill him. Schulz knew that he must "work quicker than those who were trying to kill me."[253]

He had a friend who had access to Hitler, and he now alerted him. Via a contact man, who was not allowed to know where Schulz was hiding, a pencilled note was smuggled through; the address given was misleading: "In a cornfield."[254] The friend rushed off to Hitler, who promised that Schulz's life should be spared and that he had nothing to fear. Another friend appeared in the hideout with the message: "You are under the Führer's protection. Hitler has said 'The past is forgiven; Schulz is under my personal protection.'"[255] But Schulz knew Hitler too well to trust him completely. For some days he refused to give away his hiding place and his friends took some time to persuade him to leave it. He had not been far wrong; as the days went by Hitler's promise became increasingly fragile and eventually Schulz had to settle for banishment from Germany—all that remained of Hitler's great promises.[256]

Like Paul Schulz, the last surviving SA leader was soon to find what Adolf Hitler's word was worth. On the morning of 1 July Hitler was still determined to save the life of his old friend Röhm, but by midday Göring and Himmler had won and SS-Brigadeführer Theodor Eicke was ordered to shoot him.[257] Hitler still hoped that Röhm would relieve him of the necessity to issue the final order and Eicke was instructed to give Röhm a chance to commit suicide. Eicke loaded a pistol with one bullet, summoned his deputy, SS-Sturmbannführer Michael Lippert, and drove out to Stadelheim. With them was SS-Gruppenführer Schmauser, the SS Liaison Officer with the Reichswehr.[258]

At 3 p.m. the trio presented themselves to Koch, the Prison Governor. Once more he made difficulties; he was not prepared to hand Röhm over simply on a verbal order, and he muttered something about the usual channels. He followed his usual procedure in such cases and alerted Frank, the Minister of Justice. When, speaking over the telephone the Minister seemed to be taking, Koch's side, Eicke snatched the receiver out of his hand and roared into it that the case had nothing to do with the Minister; he, Eicke, had an order from the Führer and that was enough.[259] Koch gave way. He summoned a warder named Lechler and ordered him to take Eicke, Lippert and Schmauser to cell 474 in the new prison block.[260] Röhm was squatting on an iron bedstead, stripped to the waist and sweating profusely. He looked up as the door grated and Eicke came into the cell. Eicke said: "You have forfeited your life. The Führer gives you one more chance to draw the conclusions."[261] He then laid the pistol on the table together with the latest edition of the *Völkischer Beobachter* carrying the banner headline: "Röhm arrested and dismissed—far-reaching purge in the SA."[262] As he went out Eicke remarked that Röhm had ten minutes, by which time all must be over. The door closed.

The three SS men waited for a quarter of an hour in the narrow passage outside the cell. No sound came from within. Eicke looked at his watch. He and Lippert drew their revolvers. Eicke pushed open the door and shouted: "Chief of Staff, get ready!" Looking sideways, he saw the revolver in Lippert's hand quivering and he hissed: "Aim slowly and calmly." There were two shots. Röhm fell to the ground, gasping: "My Führer, my Führer," to which Eicke replied: "You should have thought of that earlier; it's too late now." Röhm was still breathing; one of the two SS men (it is not clear which) shot him once more through the chest. Ernst Röhm, founder of the SA, Hilter's only friend and the rival of the Reichswehr, was dead. He died at 6 p.m. on 1 July 1934.[263]

The death of Röhm was the signal for the resumption of shooting. SA-Gruppenführer Karl Schreyer was in Columbia House, the second largest SS torture chamber. He heard the bangings of cell doors, the staccato commands and the echo of the shots getting closer and closer. Dawn was breaking on 2 July but the shooting still went on; from his cell, Schreyer could count the victims; SA-Oberführer von Falkenhausen at 2 a.m., Gruppenführer von Detten at 2.30, and at 3 a.m. Ritter von Krausser, the man to whom Hitler had granted a pardon.[264]

Half an hour later it was Schreyer's turn. The cell door

swung open and an SS-Truppführer straddled the doorway;
behind him were two SS men with fixed bayonets.
"Schreyer out!" the NCO shouted. "You will now be shot
on the Führer's orders." Schreyer said: "I demand a preliminary investigation." The SS man replied: "That would
be nice for you, you traitor. You will be taken out and
shot. Put your head under the tap like the others, so that
you look fresh and make a good impression."[265]

A little later they returned to fetch Schreyer but then
he was taken back to his cell once more; he was to be
taken to Lichterfeld to be shot but the car had not yet
arrived. It came a few minutes later; Schreyer describes
what then happened: "I was led down the stairs. A small
sports car stood before the door of the prison; two men
got in and I was preparing to follow them when a large
Mercedes roared up and a Standartenführer from the
Leibstandarte jumped out, signalling violently and shouting: 'Stop! Stop!' He then told us: 'Nothing more is to
happen; the Führer has given Hindenburg his word that
the shooting is now finally over.' "[266]

It was exactly 4 a.m. on 2 July 1934. The Third
Reich's first mass murder had happened. Eighty-three men
had been done to death[267]—without trial, without a chance
to defend themselves, victims of a brutal Party and gang
intrigue. Hitler stated: "In this hour, I was the supreme
judge of the German people."[268] The Cabinet hastened to
give legal coverage to these crimes. On 3 July the Ministers passed a law submitted by Adolf Hitler; it consisted
of the single sentence: "The measures taken on 30 June,
1 and 2 July to suppress treasonable activities, are legally considered to have been taken in emergency defence
of the State."[269]

In the Reichswehr barracks there was jubilation; champagne glasses clinked in the officers messes. When the last
SA leaders had been shot, General von Reichenau telegraphed to Patzig, his head of counter-espionage, in er-
ratic English: *"All catched."*[270] Major-General von Witzleben rubbed his hands saying: "What a pity. I ought to
have been there."[271] Blomberg, the Defence Minister, issued an order of the day praising the "soldierly decision"
and "exemplary courage" with which the Führer had
"attacked and crushed the traitors and murderers."[272] The
only discordant voice was that of Captain (Retired)

Erwin Planck, previously a Secretary in the Reich Chancellery; he warned General von Fritsch: "If you look on without lifting a finger, you will meet the same fate sooner or later."[273]

It was a prophetic remark; von Fritsch fell as the result of a similar intrigue; von Witzleben ended on a meat hook, condemned by the Peoples' Court. Even Lieutenant Schenk Graf von Stauffenberg, who reaped the bitter fruit of youthful enthusiasm in 1944, regarded 30 June 1934 as no more than the "lancing of a boil."[274] But Blomberg soon found his officers' jubilation to be somewhat sinister. Colonel Heinrici observed that Blomberg's notes for a speech to section heads in the Reichswehr Ministry included: "Troops have not adopted the attitude which one has a right to expect. Unseemly to rejoice over the victims and talk in the mess."[275]

Blomberg had already realised that the Reichswehr were not the victors of 30 June. Heinrich Himmler's SS had conquered all along the line; they were now free of SA tutelage and their power within the Party was assured. As early as 9 June Party Headquarters had announced that the SD was the sole political intelligence organisation of the NSDAP;[276] on 20 July Hitler decreed: "In view of the great services rendered by the SS, particularly in connection with the events of 30 June 1934, I hereby promote the SS to the status of independent organisation within the framework of the NSDAP."[277] Hitler also permitted the SS to form armed units,[278] thereby invalidating the Reichswehr's hallowed concept—the whole reason for its feud with the SA—the claim to be the sole bearer of arms within the State. 30 June 1934 marked a decisive phase in the history of the Third Reich. The SA murders accelerated Hitler's move towards a one-man dictatorship founded on terror; they were the basis of the Göring–Himmler axis, the decisive factor in Nazi gang warfare up to the outbreak of war;[279] they foreshadowed a development which was to be seen in the future in all its frightfulness; the SS had shown that it was prepared to carry out any, literally any, order from Adolf Hitler. At the same time, however, these murders opened a deep rift within the structure of the Party—the deadly enmity between SS and SA.

Thousands of SA men never forgot this day of shame

and humiliation when the SA was, in fact, demoted to the status of a prisoner of the SS. Nothing could have been more symbolic than the fact that on Hitler's orders Lutze had to charge SS-Gruppenführer Daluege, of all people, with purging and re-organising the entire East German SA.[280]

All sections of any political significance in SA Headquarters (the political office and the ministerial office) were abolished and Lutze was forced to issue a decree: "I charge SS-Gruppenführer Daluege with the execution of this disbandment, including responsibility for all property belonging to SA Supreme Headquarters (office furniture and equipment, cars, etc.)."[281]

Not until early August was the SA master in its own house once more. It was then allowed to carry out its own purge. SA-Gruppenführer Böchenhauer formed a special SA court, with investigation commissions accredited to each Gruppe; its task was to discover so-called accomplices of Röhm and, in the words of Hitler's order of 9 August 1934, to investigate "all circumstances by which SA leaders have rendered themselves unworthy of membership of the SA corps of leaders, such as mode of life, immorality, place-seeking materialism, embezzlement, drunkenness, snobbery and debauchery."[282] This inquisition got to work but the nature of its enquiries soon changed; instead of an organisation for hunting out Röhm's accomplices it found itself turning into a collecting centre for reports on SS behaviour on and after 30 June.

A stream of complaints testified to SA indignation, rage, hatred and revulsion. Sturmführer Hermann Baecke, who had belonged to the SA since 1925, stated: "I have, after all, always fought for justice and honesty; now I am threatened with arrest. We, the longstanding SA men, are now no longer thought worthy to be called an elite, although for years we have battled with the Communists and the Reichsbanner, been spat upon, had our clothes torn off us by the police and been thrown out of our jobs; and now we have reached the stage where we are being threatened all over again."[283] On 28 July, the Commander of SA Standarte 168 reported: "I issued strict orders to my people to comply with the orders of the SS under all circumstances. The treatment of the older SA men by the SS, many of whom were mere boys, was shattering."[284]

Scharführer Felten of Offenbach reported indignantly: "My men complain to me of the behaviour of SS patrols passing up and down the Kaiserstrasse . . . an SS probationer passed me on a bicycle calling out: 'Can't you salute—you've not woken up yet!' When I ordered him to get off his bicycle, he took no notice and rode off as quickly as he could. Had he got off, I would have made it clear to the young fellow in no uncertain terms how to behave to a war-time comrade of Adolf Hitler, longstanding Party member and an SA man entitled to the badge of honour."[285]

The SS had earned itself the undying hatred of the SA. The two Nazi Party armies were never to be reconciled. From now on SA and SS were embattled against one another in a silent, unseen war. During the night of 17—18 August 1935 Viktor Lutze threw down the challenge and declared war on the SS. He was in the restaurant of the Preussenhof Hotel, Stettin, with twenty of his SA comrades, three SS Commanders and innumerable glasses of beer.[286]

"One of these days," Lutze shouted "the unjust and arbitrary action of 30 June will be avenged. The German is a fair-minded being and this violation of justice will one day rebound upon those responsible and their end will be a bitter one." SS-Standartenführer Robert Schulz of SD-Oberabschnitt North could barely conceal his rage and he hissed back: "Unfortunately we did not exterminate them root and branch. We were far too indulgent. Some people who escaped and are still in the SA, knew perfectly well what Röhm was up to."

Lutze threw back that the SS were in no position to play the moralist, for they were living in a glass house themselves. The three SS men flew into a rage but Lutze rode through their protest shouting: "Who was always urging Röhm to live it up? Who was always swearing loyalty to him? Was it some old SA Commander or any SA Commander at all? Shall I tell you who it was?" (The subsequent report to Berlin from SD-Oberabschnitt North stated: "If Standartenführer Schulz had not once more intervened at this point, we should have had the painful experience of hearing Lutze say: 'The Reichsführer-SS!'") But Lutze was not to be stopped; he went on: "Who has been up to their necks in what Röhm was supposed to have done? Was it the SA? These bestialities were not the SA's work or, at least, not the SA alone; the other side was much worse. Shall I give you names? I can produce names straightaway!"

Schulz interjected hurriedly: "Chief of Staff, it's nearly two o'clock. We'd better go to bed." He summoned the waiter and called for the bill. The party broke up. Viktor Lutze swayed out but he had the last word and it was loud enough for everyone to hear: "I shall go on saying this, even if I am dismissed tomorrow and sent to a concentration camp."[287]

7

The Order of the SS

A NUMBER of officers, industrialists, scholars and land-owners in Munich suddenly received an invitation to an address by the Reinchsführer-SS: they attended, some curious, some hesitant and some suspicious. In recent months Germany's upper classes had become used to hearing the Nazi leaders revile them as decadent and Jew-ridden, but on this occasion no word of criticism came from Himmler. Instead of the anticipated offensive, the head of the SS called upon his audience to "assist in directing into the SS all the various currents of tradition."

Every state, he argued, required an elite. In National-Socialist Germany that elite was the SS, but it could only fulfil this function if "its members brought to the social requirements of the present day the genuine military tradition, the distinctive outlook, bearing and breeding of the German nobility, and the creative efficiency of the industrialist, on a basis of racial selection." One of the audience later told Felix Kersten, Himmler's masseur, that the address had "evoked general astonishment." This was an unusual line for a Nazi to take, and as a result practically the entire audience joined the SS.[1]

This incident, which occurred in Year One of the National-Socialist era, showed that Himmler had no lack of ability in presenting his SS to the outside world. More than any other National-Socialist organisation the SS reputedly stood on a higher level than that of the plebeian brown-shirted foot-soldiers. Walter Schellenberg later recalled that "the better type of people" preferred to join the SS rather than one of the other Party formations;[2]

in 1946 Dr Grober, the Catholic Archbishop of Freiburg, admitted that "we in Freiburg considered the SS to be the most respectable of the Party organisations."[3]

Many Germans could see nothing wrong in the SS claim to be an elite; every period had had its elite and in the long run no state, whether democracy or dictatorship, could do without one; looking at the Anglo-Saxon democratic "establishments" and the Soviet system's party hierarchy, the Germans were convinced that the more firmly a regime was based on a governing social class, the more crisis-proof it would be.

The Weimar Republic had just demonstrated the fate awaiting a state in which selectivity was not recognised. The SS elitist propaganda therefore sounded attractive, particularly when Himmler presented it in the conservative romanticist terms so dear to Germans. Even in 1934 Hitler's biographer Konrad Heiden, who was certainly no Nazi, thought that in contrast to the "revolutionary SA" the SS stood for conservatism.[4] Even the murders of 30 June 1934 did not affect the respect in which Himmler's Order was held by the man in the street. Relief at the disappearance of the SA informer, who had ruled the streets since the Nazi seizure of power, was more potent than the traditional sense of right and wrong.

"Liberation of our people from the rule of second-raters is a prize worth considerable sacrifice," announced the *Frankfurter Zeitung*,[5] echoing the thoughts of practically every German. The murders of the regime's bourgeois opponents and the slaughter of the SA leaders were forgotten. The nation lived in hope that the ordinary citizen's peace and quiet would never again be disturbed by the brown-shirted thugs. The Germans did not yet recognise the "devil's masquerade";[6] they did not yet realise that on the road to absolute dictatorship maintenance of law and order can conceal an assault on civil liberties and historical necessity can be used as cover for the "plausible crime."

Moreover this so-called crime of necessity of summer 1934 masqueraded in the costume dearest to the German heart, a uniform—and a becoming one too. Discreetly suppressing the plebeian brown, the SS was now arrayed from head to foot in black—black cap with black chin-strap and silver death's-head, black tunic over a brown shirt with black leather buttons and black tie, black Sam Browne belt, black breeches and black jackboots.[7]

The designers of this uniform had left no stone unturned to tickle the imagination of the hierarchically-minded Germans, introducing all sorts of mysterious marks and badges. An "old fighter" wore an aluminium chevron on his right forearm, a member of the notorious Sicherheitsdienst a diamond enclosing the letters "SD." The shoulder tabs had subtle distinctions. Officers of the rank of Hauptsturmführer and below carried six parallel silvered threads on the shoulder tab; from Sturmbann-führer to Standartenführer three plaited silver threads and from Oberführer upwards three double-plaited silver threads. The collar patches were even more complicated; senior officers carried the badges of their rank on both collar patches—for a Standartenführer one oak leaf, for an Oberführer two oak leaves, for a Brigadeführer two oak leaves and a star, for a Gruppenführer three oak leaves, for an Obergruppenführer three oak leaves and a star, and finally for the Reichsführer three oak leaves enclosed in an oak-leaf wreath.[8]

All this external flummery was intended to demonstrate that in the SS an elite was forming, an Imperial Guard of strict puritans, guardians of the welfare of the State; the purpose was to symbolise their spirit of obedience, which in Himmler's words "hesitates not for a single instant, but executes unquestioningly any order coming from the Führer."[9]

To admit such members of the upper classes as were willing to conform, Himmler opened the doors of his SS wide. The primary requirements in the SS, particularly in the special branches such as the SD, the Totenkopfver-bände [Death's Head Formations] and the Verfügungs-truppe [General Service SS Troops], were money and officer material, and they could come only from one source—the old-established ruling-class elite—the nobility, the world of commerce and the financiers. Himmler threw himself so wholeheartedly into the business of creating a reserve of personnel for the various branches of his growing empire that initially he hardly perceived that he was contradicting himself. For years the Imperial Guard of National-Socialism had preached the law of selection on racial and biological grounds; now, however, the SS began to lure into its ranks sections of the population possessing qualities which appeared in no dictionary of Nazi racial philosophy—prestige, money and an aptitude for command born of generations spent in positions of authority.

From the social point of view the SS picture now changed radically; men of an entirely new class of society streamed in. The original SS had consisted primarily of ex-Free Corps men, intellectuals whose careers had been cut short by the economic crisis, and the lower-middle-class Party veterans. Of this pre-1933 SS only a tiny band of leaders remained, though admittedly they occupied the decisive posts right up to the end of the Third Reich. By the outbreak of World War II, however, 90 per cent of the old SS had been pensioned off.[10]

Only 10 per cent of the old hands survived the influx of newcomers which poured into Himmler's organisation from March 1933 onwards (they were greeted with suspicion by the veterans who referred to them as "March Violets"). The first arrivals were from the aristocracy. Even before the Nazi seizure of power certain great names had been added to the SS list; they included the hereditary Grand Duke of Mecklenburg, the hereditary Prince zu Waldeck und Pyrmont, Prince Christof and Prince Wilhelm of Hesse, Count Bassewitz-Behr und von Pfeil-Burghauss, Reichsfreiherr von Tüngen and Freiherren von Geyr, von Reitzenstein and von Malsen-Ponickau.[11]

In spring 1933 came a further infusion of blue blood. Prinz von Hohenzollern-Emden of the House of Sigmaringen and Count von der Schulenburg joined the SS; its seniority list began to resemble a series of pages from the Almanach de Gotha. Hardly one of the famous names in Prussian/German military history was missing; they were all there—von Daniels, Count von Rödern, Count Strachwitz, Freiherr von der Goltz, von der Planitz, von Keudell, von Alvensleben, von Podbielski, von Treuenfeld, von Nathusius and so on and so on.[12] Many of the senior SS posts were occupied by the nobility (in 1938 18.7 per cent of SS-Obergruppenführer, 9.8 per cent of SS-Gruppenführer, 14.3 per cent of SS-Brigadeführer, 8.8 per cent of SS-Oberführer and 8.4 per cent of SS-Standartenführer[13] were from this social group).

After the artistocracy came the sons of the upper middle class. In contrast to their predecessors they were men of the twentieth century, mostly intellectuals who had completed their academic training (the majority in law); emotionally and intellectually the vast majority were products of the German Youth Movement. Almost all of them drifted into the SD, giving it a legalistic and intellectual atmosphere foreign both to the front-line-soldier socialism of the SS veterans and the vulgar lower-middle-class National Socialism of the early days. Men like Walter Schellenberg, Reinhard Höhn, Franz Six and Otto Ohlendorf were all university-trained with an educated upper-middle-class background; they were typical of the hard-boiled SS technocrats, the "social engineers" who provided the Führer dictatorship with the necessary veneer of legality and organisation; they were astute realists with no ideology other than that of power, but they were also spiritually rootless and uninhibited by any of the generally accepted norms of conduct.

Allied to the SD intellectuals was a group of young upper-middle-class economists, who manned the staffs of the SS economic enterprises. They were barely distinguishable from the technocrats to be found today in the management of West German industry. They were even less interested in SS ideology than their SD counterparts; in Himmler's economic undertakings they saw simply the prospect of an exceptionally secure career. The personal file of Standartenführer Dr Walter Salpeter, one of the up-and-coming men in the SS economic empire, contains a report by his superiors to the effect that he would do well "to temper his ambition with National-Socialist ideology";[14] the comment was equally applicable to the majority of these people.

A further group of newcomers came from the middle-class section of the Reichswehr officer corps, bringing further shades of difference into the personnel pattern of an already heterogeneous SS. These officers mostly joined the Verfügungstruppe (VT) which had been formed in 1934. They very soon overshadowed the original SS soldiers, who were mostly sergeant-major types like Sepp Dietrich. It is difficult to generalise on the subject of these new professional officers; Paul Hausser, for instance, the Inspector of the VT, had been a Reichswehr Lieutenant-General and a leader of the Stahlhelm; he was a dyed-in-the-wool monarchist and so naturally gave the VT a marked conservative twist;[15] on the other hand reformers like Major Felix Steiner from East Prussia and the ex-Air-Force Lieutenant Wilhelm Bittrich looked upon the VT as a suitable field for military experimentation.[16]

The farming community also provided its SS men. The rank and file of the Totenkopfverbände, which provided the guards for the concentration camps, were mostly drawn from the younger generation of the peasantry who could see no future on the land. The more intelligent farmers' sons, on the other hand, could try their luck in the SS Cadet Schools in Bad Tölz and Braunschweig; they offered what the Reichswehr did not—an officer's career for those without educational qualifications.[17]

As if the SS was not heterogeneous enough already, Himmler now produced a new form of SS membership, the honorary commander. Influential officials, Party functionaries, scientists and diplomats were given SS ranks and the right to wear the corresponding SS uniform; these honorary commanders were mostly carried on the strength of the Reichsführer's staff; they did not have to do a single hour's duty and had no powers of command. Himmler clearly hoped that such honorary titles would make the SS socially acceptable and influence the recipients in its favour—a fantastic notion believed in by no one except Himmler, the post-1945 de-Nazifiers and one or two historians.[18]

The fact that an anti-Nazi diplomat like Ernst Freiherr von Weizsäcker, the Permanent Secretary in the Foreign Ministry, carried the rank of an SS-Brigadeführer[19] and bitter enemies of Hitler, such as Gauleiter Forster, that of an SS-Obergruppenführer,[20] has led certain of the less perspicacious historians to see a concealed member of Himmler's State and Party fifth column in everyone who wore the black uniform. In fact the honorary commanders were no more supporters of Himmler than was Signora Ciano, the wife of the Italian Foreign Minister,[21] on whom Himmler also bestowed honorary SS membership.

The honorary rank of SS-Oberführer did not prevent Rudolf Diels, the Regierungspräsident of Cologne, from resisting any interference by the Gestapo in his internal administration;[22] in 1943 Himmler even attempted disciplinary action against another honorary commander, the military administrator SS-Gruppenführer Eggert Reeder, who openly refused to allow the SS to interfere in his business in any way.[23] SS uniform covered a number of curiosities: Konrad Henlein, the Sudeten German Party Leader, was made an SS-Gruppenführer because the SD had failed to unseat him;[24] Martin Bormann, another SS honorary commander, put many spokes in the wheel of the Inland-SD [Internal Affairs Section of the SD].[25]

Nevertheless Himmler continued to canvass for new recruits for his empire. At times he even incorporated entire organisations into the SS if he thought that they would give him the entrée to established society. He already had a foot in the door of rural society, for instance —via the Equestrian Association.

Himmler was determined to capture this stronghold of German conservatism. Some of the Equestrian Associations did indeed join the SA, but by far the greater number reinsured via the SS; all the Equestrian Associations in the main breeding areas—East Prussia, Holstein, Oldenburg, Hanover and Westphalia—put on SS uniform.[26] Himmler owed many social successes to his SS horsemen; in 1937 SS riders won all the German horse championships.[27]

Himmler had to pay dearly for these victories. He had promised the Equestrian Associations that he would accept any of their members into the SS regardless of their political views.[28] This led to grumbling on the part of the SS "old fighters" who said that, in spite of their SS uniform, the horsemen were still reactionary German nationalists. *Das Schwarze Korps,* the SS newspaper, adopted a menacing tone towards these newcomers: "In the first place, they must cultivate the National-Socialist spirit. In other words all those . . . qualities which the SS has cultivated over the years since its formation and by which it has proved itself—loyalty to the Führer, readiness to obey, and discipline."[29] The majority of the SS riders knuckled under but a few had other ideas; in 1933 eleven of them refused to take the SS oath and were dispatched to a concentration camp.[30] Anton Freiherr von Hohberg und Buchwald, the leading SS horseman in East Prussia, was shot by SS men on 2 July 1934 for giving away SS secrets to the Reichswehr;[31] ten years later Himmler had the head of his remount office, SS-Sturmbannführer Hans-Viktor Graf von Salviati, another show-ring rider, executed for plotting against Hitler.[32]

The pact with the Equestrian Associations had given Himmler the entrée to rural society. It was followed by an alliance with the leaders of the semi-monarchist ex-servicemen's association "Kyffhäuser" and this allowed him to tap the reservoir of ex-soldiers. The Central Council and local leaders of Kyffhäuser joined the SS as a body.[33] But when the "old fighters" saw General Wilhelm Reinhard, who was still loyal to the Kaiser, joining the SS at the head of the Kyffhäuser leaders,[34] they felt they could understand Himmler no longer; for Reinhard was one of those reactionary military men stigmatised by the *Schwarze Korps* in 1935 as typifying that "middle-class nationalist arrogance which excludes the worker from society and must give him the impression that he is regarded as a third-class citizen."[35]

The height of irony was reached when the ultra-conservative General Rüdiger Graf von der Goltz, a friend of Reinhard's who had fought with him in the Kapp Putsch of 1920, was accepted as an SS-Obergruppenführer just after being reviled by the *Schwarze Korps* as the worst type of reactionary.[36] Even as late as 1941 Franz Xaver Schwarz, the Reich Party Treasurer and an SS man of long standing, could not bear to see a monarchist like Reinhard in SS uniform; he said: "I regret that such a man should be an SS-Gruppenführer, should wear this fine uniform and yet basically remain exactly his old self."[37]

The SS veterans reacted similarly to the survivors of Ehrhardt's Naval Brigade, whom Himmler also lured into the SS. They thought back to SS Order No. 53 of 10 October 1931 when Himmler had warned against Ehrhardt's sinister machinations, saying that he was "trying to disrupt the NSDAP" by infiltrating his supporters into Party organisations."[38] Now Himmler wished to accept the Ehrhardt Brigade into the SS as a body. Details of the arrangement had already been worked out when the headstrong Captain torpedoed the whole project by making the strangest speech ever delivered by an SS candidate.

The Brigade was drawn up for its last parade with a number of Nazi dignitaries present. In his farewell address Ehrhardt shouted: "Men of my Brigade, you know that only rather late in the day and after numerous and prolonged battles have we declared ourselves ready to join a formation of the new Reich. And I welcome that. For only in battle does one learn to know one's enemy and respect or despise him. And thus we shall continue in future." The Nazi leaders were so put out that Himmler abandoned the Ehrhardt Brigade and only individual members joined the SS; they included Hartmuth Plaas, Ehrhardt's ex-aide, who became an SS-Sturmbannführer but in 1944 landed in a concentration camp as an accomplice of the 20 July plot.[39]

New recruits for the SS, however, were not the only objects of Himmler's canvassing; he was equally short of money for the increasingly expensive SS formations. Germany's captains of industry and managerial class, however, were only too ready to support the Reichsführer. They formed themselves into a club known as the "Friends of the Reichsführer-SS," whose members, for a variety of reasons, thought it best to be on Heinrich Himmler's side. The club included opportunists such as Dr Heinrich Bütefisch from the Board of IG Farben, convinced Nazis like the Propaganda Ministry Secretary Dr Werner Naumann, worried businessmen such as Freidrich Flick and disguised anti-Nazis such as Hans Walz, a Director of Robert Bosch; but they all had one thing in common—they gave money to the SS.[40]

The "Friends" were an offshoot of the "Planning Committee for Economic Problems" formed by Wilhelm Keppler, Hitler's Economic Adviser, in summer 1932; the committee was intended to give expert advice to Germany's future masters and it included prominent economists and financiers, among them Schacht, the President of the Reichsbank, Albert Vögler, Chairman of Vereinigte Stahlwerke and Kurt Freiherr von Schröder, a Cologne banker.[41] The economic advice idea came to nothing, but Keppler's young assistant, SS-Hauptsturmführer Fritz Kranefuss, persuaded Himmler to take an interest in the Club and it came under the Reichsführer's wing from mid-1934.[42]

Schacht and Vögler resigned[43] but in their place many firms joined the "Friends of the Reichsführer-SS." Practically every major concern lived in the hope that by sending a member of their Board to the "Friends" meetings and paying contributions to the SS, they might protect their own interests from Nazi encroachment. The membership list of the "Friends" read like an extract from the business register. It included representatives from: the Deutsche Bank, the Dresdner Bank, the Commerz und Privat Bank, the Reichsbank and the J.H. Stein Bank, Norddeutscher Lloyd and Hamburg-America Shipping Companies, German-American Petroleum and Continental Oil Companies, the Dr August Oetker Food Production Company and great concerns such as IG Farben, the Mitteldeutsche Stahlwerke, Siemens-Schuckert, Portland Cement, Rheinmetall-Borsig and the Reichswerke "Hermann Göring."[144]

Kranefuss, the Secretary of the "Friends," called regular meetings at which senior SS leaders were always present. Initially the club met twice a year, at the Party Rally in Nuremberg and the oath-taking ceremony for the Verfügungstruppe in Munich; later, however, members met monthly at the "Haus der Flieger" in Berlin.[45] From 1936 onwards Himmler required regular financial contributions from all these gentlemen. He pointed out to Schröder, the "Friends" banker, that money should be made available "for the cultural, social and charitable activities of the SS"[46] and the banker rushed off to do his bidding.[47]

The firms concerned agreed and shortly thereafter contributions began to flow into General Account S in the J.H. Stein Bank in which Schröder was a member of the Board. Total annual contributions were 1,000,000 marks. These were paid into a special SS Account R at the Dresdner Bank on which Karl Wolff, Himmler's senior aide, was authorised to draw cheques.[48] Himmler gave proof of his gratitude. A shower of SS titles descended on the members of the "Friends;" of the thirty-two non-SS members fifteen were nominated honorary SS commanders.[49]

To those averse to wearing the death's-head uniform, the SS offered an even less onerous and cheaper form of membership. The rapacious SS was the only Party formation permitted by Hitler to run its own finances and recruit "sponsoring members" [Fördernde Mitglieder —FM].[50] They were merely sympathisers who gave financial support to the SS but did not join it. They did not have to take an oath to Hitler and were not subject to SS orders.[51] Every SS-Standarte had a sponsoring mem-

bers' organisation and it was the duty of each SS man
to recruit at least one member. On 1 March 1933 Kurt
Wittje, an SS Commander, explained: "The sponsoring
members' organisation is the only sure source of SS in-
come and must constitute the guarantee for further expansion of the SS economy."[52] After the seizure of power,
the SS laid even greater emphasis on its propaganda to
sponsoring members, calculating that many Germans
would rather join this amorphous organisation than any
other Party formation. The letters FM protected the wearer from many Nazi impositions; moreover a sponsoring
member did not necessarily have to belong to the Party
and could fix the amount of his financial contribution himself; the minimum was one mark per year.[53]

In addition Himmler developed other gimmicks to attract members. He designed a silver FM badge, not obtainable on the open market; it consisted of an oval
containing the swastika, the runic double-S and the letters FM. He started an FM periodical which reached a
circulation of 365,000 by the outbreak of war; to every
citizen interested in becoming a sponsoring member, he
dispatched the motto:

Es ist eine Ehre, SS-Mann zu sein,	It is an honour to be an SS man
Es ist eine Ehre, Förderndes Mitglied zu sein;	It is an honour to be an honorary member;
Tue jeder weiter seine Pflicht,	Let each continue to do his duty
Wir SS-Männer und ihr Fördernder Mitglieder,	We SS men and their honorary members
Jeder an seiner Stelle;	Each in his appointed place
Und Deutschland wird wieder gross werden.	And Germany will be great once more.[54]

The propaganda drive was unexpectedly successful.
Soon Himmler's shadowy army of sponsoring members outnumbered the active SS and money came pouring into
the empty SS coffers; in 1932 there were 13,217 honorary
members contributing 17,000 marks, in 1933 167,272
members contributing 357,000 marks and in 1934 342,492
members contributing 581,000 marks.[55]
Nevertheless there could be no real solidarity in an SS
composed of such heterogeneous elements. The SS vet-

erans suddenly saw in SS uniform men who clearly did not know the ABC of National-Socialism. The SS idea had become all things to all men. Schwarz, the Party Treasurer, no longer liked wearing his SS uniform because, according to Gruppenführer Berger, "Too many people were in SS uniform and, still worse, many SS Commanders had neither moral nor actual right to it."[56] The uniform and badges of rank by no means meant that a man was an SS member at heart. Heinrich Müller, for instance, the future Head of the Gestapo, wore the "old fighter" chevron on his sleeve,[57] but on 4 January 1937 the Munich/Upper Bavaria Party Headquarters labelled him "ambitious and self-seeking," "no Party Comrade," a man who had "never worked actively within the Party" and therefore "had rendered no services to the National Revival."[58]

The Reichssicherheitshauptamt [Central Security Department—RSHA] personnel section noted that Dr Heinrich Bütefisch was an ex-freemason and "the complete businessman." His "whole mentality was geared to international co-operation; he therefore naturally looked upon his firm as a state within the State, with its own rules and privileges."[59] An SS internal report dated August 1937 stated that Oberführer Freiherr von Schröder, the banker, had been connected with the Rhineland separatists, was a friend of Konrad Adenauer and therefore was "certainly no activist in the SS sense."[60]

Himmler himself gradually began to see the danger threatening the internal unity of the SS. In 1937 he admitted that "numbers presented a danger" since a vast number of men had entered the SS "who were neither sincere nor idealistic."[61] Himmler thought that he had overcome this danger but in fact it persisted to the very end of the SS.

In mid-1933, however, he called a temporary halt to SS recruiting: "I said, 'No one else will be accepted' and then from 1933 to 1935 we combed all the useless material out from among the newcomers."[62] In these two years 60,000 SS men were expelled.[63] The primary victims of Himmler's clean-up were the patent opportunists, alcoholics, homosexuals and men of uncertain Aryan background; even some of the old thugs went by the board—they may have been good enough to clout down opponents during the "struggle period" but now they did not fit into the Praetorian Guard picture. In addition Himmler would no longer tolerate the professional unemployed, saying: "A man who, without valid reason, changes his job for the third time, we shall expel. We have no use for loafers."[64]

Himmler dealt particularly severely with homosexuality, which he regarded as a personal insult. In his eyes it was a crime worthy of death and no SS homosexual escaped his wrath—not even "old fighters" like Gruppenführer Kurt Wittje, the first head of the SS-Hauptamt [SS Head Department].[65] On 22 May 1935 the *Schwarze Korps* reported that Wittje had been relieved of his post "because of illness"; Himmler said in a speech that he had released Wittje "to his regret" and "with a heavy heart" and that he hoped Wittje "would be fully available again in the foreseeable future."[66] The SA Commanders, with the SS homilies about Röhm's homosexuality still ringing in their ears, knew what Wittje's real disease was. Lutze, the Head of the SA, remarked sneeringly: "It has taken time enough and pressure from all sides to get rid of Wittje."[67] In 1937 Himmler insisted that every SS homosexual be expelled and handed over to the courts; after serving his prison sentence "he will be sent on my instructions to a concentration camp and shot while attempting to escape."[68]

The discovery of any drop of non-Aryan blood in SS veins invariably excited Himmler. From 1 June 1935, every SS Commander from the rank of Sturmführer upwards had to show proof that neither he nor his wife had Jewish ancestors; from 1 October 1935 the requirement was extended to include Oberscharführer and Hauptscharführer [Warrant Officers] and shortly thereafter every SS man.[69] Everyone had to be able to produce an "Aryan" family tree going back, in the case of other ranks to 1800 and in the case of officers or officer cadets to 1750;[70] the SS men, including even old war-time comrades of Himmler, spread far and wide searching, often for years, through Church registers and other old documents. If Himmler detected any trace of Jewish origin in a man's family tree, he acted ruthlessly—at least in so far as the lower ranks were concerned. Anyone who found that he had a drop of Jewish blood in his

veins had to report to his superior officer forthwith and
request release from the SS; if he did not, the SS Court
took action and decreed expulsion.[71]

Himmler was much more lenient, however, in the
case of the senior ranks. The wife of a certain Obersturmführer M (as he is referred to in the SS files) had
a Jewish grand-parent; M was allowed to remain in the
SS provided his wife agreed to have no more children
and he undertook not to send his sons into the SS.[72]
As time went on Himmler's caution increased with the
rank of the evil-doer. Gruppenführer Walter Krüger was
treated even better than Obersturmführer M. During the
war Krüger's daughter became engaged to SS-Sturmbannführer Klingenberg; it was then suddenly discovered that
on Frau Krüger's side there was, in Himmler's words, "a
full-Jewish ancestor in 1711." Klingenberg was forbidden
to marry the daughter but Krüger's son was allowed to
join the Leibstandarte.[73]

Nevertheless the expulsion of 60,000 men could not
in itself guarantee the SS the necessary internal solidarity. Himmler realised that what the SS lacked was a
corps spirit to hold it together; it must also have rigid
organisation, stricter conditions of entry and a code of
honour to which every SS man would feel himself bound.
Hitherto the SS had been no more than an organisation;
now it was to become an Order. Himmler had discovered
from history an example on which he proposed to model
his Order—the Jesuits. It was no accident that Karl Ernst,
the murdered SA leader, had frequently ridiculed him
as the "Black Jesuit"; even Hitler referred to the Head
of the SS as "my Ignatius Loyola."[74] In the Jesuits Himmler
had found what he regarded as the central feature of
any Order's mentality—the doctrine of obedience and the
cult of organisation. Schellenberg confirms that Himmler
had built up the SS organisation "on the principles of
the Order of Jesuits."[75]

The similarity between the two was in fact astounding;
each was an Order conferring enormous privileges on its
members, subject to no temporal jurisdiction, protected
by the strictest conditions of entry and held together
by an oath of absolute blind obedience to its lord and
master—Pope or Führer. The history of the two organisations showed equally remarkable parallels; in the seven-

teenth century the Jesuits founded their own state among
the Paraguay Indians—it recognised no temporal sovereignty; during the second World War the SS dreamed
of an SS State outside the borders of the Greater German
Reich—the SS State of Burgundy with its own Government, Army, Administration and Legation in Berlin.[76] Even
the crises which each faced were similar. There were
always enemies of the Jesuits within the Catholic Church
and enemies of the SS within the Party. The Jesuits
debated whether they should be the sword of the counter-
reformation or an example of monastic piety; the SS
never made up its mind whether to be National-Socialism's
ideological leavening or the regime's policeman.

The higher organisation of the SS Order was also
reminiscent of that of the Jesuits. Ignatius Loyola (1491-
1566), the founder of the Jesuits, organised a kind of
Government of his Order with a General at its head,
advised by four assistants.[77] Himmler followed the same
system when he set about organising a central command
structure for the SS. In place of the Jesuit General's four
assistants, the Reichsführer-SS was assisted by a number
of Hauptämter [Departments]; first came the Private
Office under Brigadeführer Karl Wolff, the highest SS
operational staff, re-named "Personal Staff Reichsführer-
SS" in 1936 and raised to Hauptamt status in 1939;
next came the SD-Hauptamt under Gruppenführer Reinhard Heydrich, the directing organisation for the Security
Service; third came the "Rasse- und Siedlungshauptamt"
[Race and Resettlement Office—RuSHA] under Obergruppenführer Walther Darré, who was also Reich Minister
of Agriculture (it was the guardian of the ideological
and racial purity of all SS members); fourth came the
head of the SS-Gericht [SS Court], Brigadeführer Paul
Scharfe, responsible for special SS jurisdiction—also raised
to Hauptamt status in 1939; finally, there was the SS-
Hauptamt under Wittje's successor, August Heissmeyer,
the administrative centre for all SS units with the exception of the SD.[78]

The latter, the SS-Hauptamt, later developed into an
over-organised colossus, dealing not only with the old SS
(re-named "Allgemeine SS" in mid-1934 to distinguish
it from the special formations)[79] but also with the Totenkopfverbände and the Verfügungstruppe. When the SS-

Hauptamt additionally became responsible for the Cavalry Standarten and the entire financial administration of the SS, it was reorganised.

By 1942, four new Hauptämter had come into being, three of them taking over certain reponsibilities from the SS-Hauptamt which, in its reduced form, was placed under Gruppenführer Gottlob Berger.[80] The new offices were: The Führungshauptamt [Operational Department] under Gruppenführer Hans Jüttner, the headquarters of the Waffen-SS; the Personalhauptamt [Personnel Department] under Gruppenführer Maximilian von Herff, dealing with all SS Commanders' personal details and with appointments in the Allgemeine SS; the Wirtschafts- und Verwaltungshauptamt [Economic and Administrative Department—WVHA] under Gruppenführer Oswald Pohl, dealing with all SS economic undertakings and the administration of the concentration camps; finally, also of Hauptamt status, there was the "Office of SS-Obergruppenführer Heissmeyer," the controlling authority for the political education institutions.[81]

These central authorities supervised the closely coordinated structure—Oberabschnitte, Abschnitte, Standarten, Sturmbanne and Stürme—which comprised the great SS army. Hauptamt representatives were continually checking the discipline and efficiency of SS units. The emissaries of the Reichsführer-SS arrived unannounced: during interviews, frequently of a highly embarrassing nature, they enquired into individual commanders' knowledge of regulations, checked unit diaries and reported on the energy and enthusiasm of even the most senior officers.[82]

Guppenführer Zech of the SS-Hauptamt, for instance, commented adversely: "On my inspections I have noted that in almost every case Sturmbannführer and Standartenführer do not attend their troops' normal duty periods with sufficient frequency." He continued that the official diaries must "show exactly what the SS Commander has done with and for his troops each day" and "must be written up exactly as the regulations lay down."[83] SS units frequently regarded the arrival of one of these spies from Berlin with unconcealed apprehension, as an office note by Zech shows: "The word supervise should not be used. Our Commanders do not supervise our Stürme; they inspect them."[84]

Himmler was now free to turn to a further point in his programme. Instead of the heterogeneous types of mankind now composing the SS he wished to concentrate on the standardised SS man, the nordicised master-race type who, in Himmler's scheme of things, was to be typical of the SS. The RuSHA was ordered to work out new and stricter conditions for acceptance into the SS.[85] Hauptsturmführer Professor Bruno K. Schultz submitted a set of criteria to the RuSHA Racial Commission, before which all SS applicants had to appear for their final acceptance test.[86]

The Professor listed his criteria under three headings—racial appearance, physical condition and general bearing (there was no mention of intellectual attainments). Since Himmler was a believer in the theory developed by the National-Socialist demographic policy experts that the master race must consist solely of blond, blue-eyed Nordic beings and the SS must gradually be purged of representatives of other races, Schultz angled his scale of values on the Nordic type of mankind. He listed five racial groupings: "pure Nordic," "predominantly Nordic or Phalic," harmonious bastard with "slight Alpine, Dinaric or Mediterranean characteristics," bastards of predominantly East-Baltic or Alpine origin and bastards of extra-European origin.[87]

Only men falling into the first three categories were considered worthy of acceptance into the SS. Even this involved some concession on Himmler's part, for he considered that in a few years all important posts in the State should be held only by blond men and in a maximum of 120 years the entire German people should once more be pure-blooded Nordic Germans in appearance.[88] Nevertheless even racial background was not everything. Schultz drew up a list of nine headings as a guide for the physical examination of SS candidates to ensure that they were well-proportioned, for the Reichsführer had an aversion to "people who might be tall but were in some way disproportioned."[89]

With the fastidious precision of the expert poultry breeder Himmler insisted that the SS man must be "of well-proportioned build; for instance there must be no disproportion between the lower leg and the thigh or between the legs and the body; otherwise an exceptional bodily effort is required to carry out long marches."⁹⁰

Schultz therefore only accepted applicants who fell into the first four categories of his nine-point schedule ("ideal stature," "excellent," "very good," "good"); the bottom three categories were rejected but those in categories five and six were given another chance. In spite of their "inadequate" physique they were allowed to prove by their bearing that they were true Nordic men. Himmler laid down: "The point is that in his attitude to discipline the man should not behave like an underling, that his gait, his hands, everything, should correspond to the ideal which we set ourselves."⁹¹

Once the candidate had successfully surmounted the hurdle of the racial commission, he entered upon a phase of prolonged examination and testing. Here again Himmler had copied the Jesuits; just as the Jesuit novices had to undergo two years of severe tests and exercises before taking the three vows of poverty, chastity and obedience and entering the ranks of the scholastics, so the SS candidate had to undergo manifold tests before he was allowed to swear the "kith and kin oath" [Sippeneid] and call himself an SS man.

The various phases of the SS novitiate were geared to the great festivals of the National-Socialist calendar. On 9 November, the anniversary of the Munich Beer Cellar Putsch, the SS candidate, aged 18, was accepted as an applicant and allowed to wear an SS uniform without collar patches. On 30 January, the day of the Nazi seizure of power, the candidate became a cadet and was given a provisional SS pass. The culminating point was 20 April, Hitler's birthday, when the cadet received his collar patches and his permanent SS pass and when he swore his oath to his Führer:

Ich schwöre Dir, Adolf Hitler, Als Führer und Kanzler des Deutschen Reiches Treue und Tapferkeit. Ich gelobe Dir und den von Dir bestimmten Vorgesetzten

I swear to thee Adolf Hitler, As Führer and Chancellor of the German Reich Loyalty and Bravery. I vow to thee and to the superiors whom thou shalt appoint

Gehorsam bis in den Tod,	Obedience unto death
So wahr mir Gott helfe.	So help me God.[92]

The oath-taking ceremony was intended to give the newcomer a taste of that mystic bond uniting the charismatic Führer with his black-uniformed acolytes. Special ceremony attended the oath-swearing by the Verfügungstruppe; unlike the Allgemeine-SS, the VT took the oath at 10 p.m. every 9 November in Hitler's presence and at the National-Socialist shrine in Munich. Emil Helfferich, a member of the "Friends of the Reichsführer-SS," still remembers with emotion "the midnight oath-taking ceremony before the Feldherrnhalle in Munich. Splendid young men, serious of face, exemplary in bearing and turnout. An elite. Tears came to my eyes when, by the light of the torches, thousands of voices repeated the oath in chorus. It was like a prayer."[93]

For the Allgemeine-SS candidate, even this did not end the test. Between the oath-taking ceremony on 20 April and entry into service on 1 October, he had to obtain the Reich Sport Badge and learn the SS catechism[94] which, with its interplay of question and answer, was intended to initiate the candidate further into the SS Hitler cult. For instance: "Why do we believe in Germany and the Führer?" Answer: "Because we believe in God, we believe in Germany which He created in His world and in the Führer, Adolf Hitler, whom He has sent us." Question: "Whom must we primarily serve?" Answer: "Our people and our Führer, Adolf Hitler." Question: "Why do you obey?" Answer: "From inner conviction, from belief in Germany, in the Führer, in the Movement and in the SS, and from loyalty."[95]

Ideology thus having been dinned into him, the SS candidate next completed his term in the Labour Service and the Wehrmacht, finally returning to the SS as a "Vollanwärter" (full candidate). If his Wehrmacht report was good, he might be finally accepted into the Order within a month.[96] When 9 November came round once more, however, there was a further ceremony at which the new SS man had to swear yet one more oath. This time he bound himself and his future family to obey the marriage law issued by the Reichsführer-SS on 31 December 1931 prescribing that SS members might marry "solely if the necessary conditions of race and healthy stock were fulfilled" and only after approval by the RuSHA or the Reichsführer-SS.[97]

Now the young member of the Order received his SS dagger and was finally admitted into this bizarre exclusive brotherhood in which the fanaticism of the religious sect, the rites and customs of a feudal age and the romantic cult of Germanism blended oddly with contemporary political and economic management and cold-blooded power politics. Himmler could now proceed to the final phase of his plan for the training of his SS-type master men—the inculcation of a corps spirit. Here he clearly followed the example of the Prussian officer corps; every order from Himmler, every little service detail was designed to instil into the SS man the conviction that he belonged to an elite and that the SS was different from all other Party organisations. Himmler intended that special prestige should attach to his Order, comparable to that of the medieval orders of chivalry.

Scharfe, the Head of the SS Legal Service, explained why the SS was an organisation apart, even within the Party: "Compared to the ordinary member of the Party, the SS man naturally occupies a special place, primarily because it is his duty to protect the Movement and its Führer, if necessary at the sacrifice of his life. This special position . . . of course means that the SS man must be dealt with in a special way."[98] From this, Scharfe drew the conclusion that no State Court, not even a Party Court, had the right to judge an SS man; this was the sole prerogative of SS Judges and SS superior Officers.[99]

So a special SS jurisdiction came into being applicable to the SD, the Verfügungstruppe, the Totenkopfverbände, the SS Cadet schools and practically every SS leader down to rank of Sturmbannführer. The SS was no longer answerable to the normal courts; centuries of European legal history were pushed aside; the SS man had his own code which he defended jealously and of which the dagger was the symbol. After the Röhm affair the SS was removed from the jurisdiction of the SA Courts of Honour and in November 1935 Himmler laid down: "Every SS man has the right and the duty to defend his honour by

force of arms."[100] So the duel, that hallmark of aristocratic arrogance, was resurrected.

Subject to the agreement of the Reichsführer, every SS
man was henceforth entitled to challenge another to a
duel. In his usual precise headmasterish manner Himmler
laid down the details in an order. The injured party, he
prescribed, must "within 3–24 hours, Sundays and holidays excepted, initiate steps to demonstrate that he intends
to obtain clarification or satisfaction." If he fails to obtain satisfaction or should satisfaction be refused him,
he should warn his opponent "that he will revert to the
incident through his representative (his second), from
whom the opponent will hear further." A second should
"where possible, be of equivalent rank to the party challenged," should "in principle appear in uniform," was to
issue his principal's challenge to a duel and agree upon
the weapons to be used. Written communication by the
second was "only permissible in exceptional cases" and
must "invariably be made by registered letter."[101]

In Himmler's view, under the special SS code of honour
suicide was also permissible. Even here the procedure
was laid down in pedantic, bureaucratic detail. An illustration is the case of Obersturmführer Johannes Buchhold, who was condemned to death for maltreating his
subordinates; on 22 June 1943 Hauptsturmführer Bleyl
recorded: "I informed Buchhold of the Reichsführer's instruction that a revolver be placed in his cell for a period
of six hours, an indication that he was thereby being
given an opportunity himself to expiate the crime he had
committed. I handed Obersturmführer Buchhold a 0.8 revolver, loaded with one round, cocked and with the safety
catch off; I then departed." The criminal was forced to
acknowledge the Reichsführer's clemency in writing: "I
confirm that the above record of hearing is correct and
append my signature, *Buchhold, SS-Obersturmführer.*"

Next a note by the Reichsführer: "The body is to be
delivered to the relatives. By his death Buchhold has
expiated his crime. The relatives are to be provided for
as if B. had fallen in action."[102]

In Himmler's eyes, however, this special jurisdiction
valid for every SS man, carried with it a threat to good
order and military discipline—it could act as a leveller
down or equaliser. In the SS the honourable estate which

the Prussian tradition had reserved to the Officer was extended to cover the most lowly ranks. To counteract this
pseudo-democratisation, Himmler was forced to re-em-
phasise the hierarchical structure of the SS.[103]

So through the body of his organisation Himmler drew
a horizontal dividing line, separating the Priests and
High Priests of the Order from the lay brothers. From
the Freemasons, of whom he had an almost superstitious
dread, Himmler learnt that imposing insignia and ranks
endowed the hierarchy of an Order with power and mystery. So in his counter-freemasonry, he introduced three
insignia.

Irrespective of rank, proven SS men were allowed to
wear a silver death's-head signet ring. Initially the ring
was intended for "old fighters" and was bestowed only
on SS men with a membership number below 10,000.
Gradually, however, the circle was widened and by 1939
practically every SS Commander who had held a senior
position for three years was a wearer of the ring.[104]

Himmler proceeded more cautiously with the dagger,
the sign of the SS Corps of Leaders; it became one of
the most important adornments of neo-German knighthood. The dagger was granted only to SS men of the
rank of Untersturmführer [Second Lieutenant] and upwards. Moreover, unlike the death's-head ring, the grant
was governed by no prescribed rule but was dependent
exclusively upon the Reichsführer's will and pleasure. Only
the young nobles of the Order, the graduates of the Cadet
schools, were given the dagger automatically on passing
their final examination.[105] The dagger was intended to
show those whom the Grand Master considered a member of the Order's hierarchy; the higher the rank, the
greater the proportion of dagger-wearers; by the end
of the war the dagger was carried by 362 out of 621
Standartenführer, 230 out of 276 Oberführer, 88 out of 96
Gruppenführer, 91 out of 92 Obergruppenführer and by
every one of the four Oberstgruppenführer.[106]

These niceties of differentiation, however, still left
Himmler's mysticism unsatisfied. From his books on ancient romantic history he had learnt that King Arthur
assembled about the Round Table his twelve bravest and
most noble knights, with whom he defended the Celtic
creed and liberties against the invading Anglo-Saxons.[107]

Here was clearly a lesson for the SS. The tale of King
Arthur must have impressed Himmler, for he never allowed more than twelve guests to sit at his table. And
as King Arthur had once chosen his bravest to sit at his
table, so now Himmler appointed his twelve best Obergruppenführer to be the senior dignitaries of his Order.[108]

For the chosen few Himmler invented yet a further
mark of distinction. In 1937 professor Karl Diebitsch,
Head of the SS office in Munich dealing with artistic matters, was ordered by the Reichsführer to design coats of
arms for the more important SS leaders.[109] The Professor
set about his task with scientific zeal but he had hardly
begun when yet another Himmler invention appeared on
the scene—the "Ancestral Heritage," a research group
primarily concerned with the excavation of old Germanic
relics. The researchers scattered far and wide digging
up raw material for Diebitsch's armorial bearings.[110]

On 17 July 1937 Gruppenführer Pohl, one of the chosen
few, was informed by "Ancestral Heritage" [Ahnenerbe]
that: "We take as our starting point the ancient coats
of arms of Germanic man; these form the basic design.
They are the symbol of the Germanic tribe and its forebears. To establish a connection with the ancient Germanic tribal signs demands the most careful research."[111]

In Wewelsburg Castle Himmler found a Valhalla where
he could set up his Round Table and place his knights'
coats of arms in a worthy setting. In Himmler's Camelot
the chosen few would assemble around the Reichsführer's
oaken table in a 100-foot by 145-foot dining hall, sitting
in high-backed pig skin chairs, each carrying the name
of its owner knight inscribed on a small silver plate.[112]
They would meet regularly for hours of conference and
meditation, reminiscent of a spiritualist session. Each of
the chosen few had his own quarters in the Castle, decorated in differing historical styles and dedicated to some
historical personality.[113]

The Lord of the Castle, described by the Armaments
Minister Albert Speer as "half schoolmaster, half
crank,"[114] had already thought out the final ceremony
for his knights. Beneath the dining hall lay a stone crypt;
its wall, five feet thick, enclosed the holy of holies of
the Order—the realm of the dead.[115]

A flight of steps in the middle of the crypt led down into a well-like cavity; in the centre of the cavity there was a stone stoop, and around the walls were twelve stone pedestals. In the event of an Obergruppenführer's death his arms were to be burnt in the stoop and an urn containing the ashes placed upon one of the pedestals. The four vents in the ceiling were so arranged that, during the burning ceremony, the smoke would ascend to the roof in a single column.[116]

Himmler intended Wewelsburg to be the setting in which he and his Obergruppenführer would work out the ideology of his Order—and the setting was a good one. Wewelsburg, named after one of its early owners, the robber knight Wewel von Büren,[117] was one of the few mountain fortresses of Westphalia and had once been a retreat of the Bishops of Paderborn, near which town it lies. In the time of the Huns it had formed a focus of Saxon resistance and in the seventeenth century had been rebuilt in massive triangular form[118]—exactly the place to capture the imagination of a man like Himmler, who lived as much in the past as in the present.

The story goes that Himmler had once heard the saying that a Westphalian castle would be the sole survivor of the next assault from the East and had therefore searched the province for this castle until he lighted upon Wewelsburg.[119]

The facts are somewhat more prosaic; the Landrat [Local Council] of Büren District, which was responsible for maintenance of the Castle, was only too glad to make it over to Himmler.[120] On 27 July 1934 the building became Himmler's property for a nominal annual rent of 1 mark. Shortly thereafter Himmler informed Schmitt, the Reich Minister of Economics: "I propose to develop Wewelsburg . . . as a Reich SS leaders' school and request the highest possible Reich grant to meet the building costs."[121] Within his personal staff he set up a Wewelsburg Office under Standartenführer Siegfried Albert Taubert, who became "Fortress Commandant" in 1937;[122] the SS Architect, Hermann Bartels,[123] was in charge of the rebuilding and the work was carried out by a detachment of the Labour Service under a staff of SS experts.

In the southern wing of the fortress, above the dining hall, were the Reichsführer's private apartments including a hall for his extensive collection of weapons, a library ultimately containing 12,000 books, a meeting hall and a courtroom for the highest SS Court. In the same wing were the guest rooms for Hitler who, however, never appeared in Wewelsburg—a fact which, perhaps, gave rise to the village rumour that one day Adolf Hitler would be buried there.[124]

By the end of the war his castle had cost Himmler 13,000,000 marks.[125]

The castle and its contrived rituals, however, were more than a mere historical charade for Himmler; he thought that ideologically history (or his version of history) might be both a bond and a driving force for the SS. Wewelsburg was not the only SS castle; in 1937 Himmler said: "It is my aim that, if possible, the area of every Standarte should include a similar cultural centre of German greatness and German history which should be restored and put into a condition worthy of a cultured people."[126]

In 1936 he founded a "Society for the Promotion and Preservation of German Cultural Monuments."[127] It was supposed to take care of historical buildings but unfortunately from Himmler's favourite periods—the early Germanic, the early medieval pagan era and the epoch of the German colonising mission in the East under the Teutonic Knights—all they could find were documents. The association deliberately gave priority, however, to the old castles of the Teutonic Knights or such places as Sachsenhain bei Verden on the Aller, the site of the memorial to 4,500 pagan Saxons massacred in 782 by Charlemagne (referred to by Himmler as "Charles the Frank").[128] This was the type of ancient monument which fitted into the SS anti-Christian and anti-Slav symbolism. Himmler commented: "These things interest us because they are of the highest importance in the ideological and political struggle."[129]

In an SS recruited from all walks of life and classes of society, Himmler looked to romanticised history, Germanic legend and paganism to provide the integrating factor; this was the background to the "Monuments Society" and many of his other creations. Pride of place among these inventions was taken by the "King Heinrich I Memorial Foundation"[130] for, as a German King of the Saxon dynasty and conqueror of the Slavs, Heinrich I (875–936) was a particular hero for Himmler, epitomising his hatred of the Poles. On 2 July 1936, the thousandth anniversary of the King's death, Himmler visited his tomb (which was empty at that time) in Quedlingburg Cathedral and swore to pursue and to complete the Saxon king's mission in the East.[131] A year later he had the bones of Heinrich I carried into the cathedral in solemn procession.[132] According to Himmler, the tomb was to be "a sacred spot to which we Germans make pilgrimage to do honour to King Heinrich."[133] On each anniversary of the King's death, at the stroke of midnight in the cold crypt of the cathedral, Himmler would commune silently with his namesake.[134]

Himmler was continually entering into contact with the great men of the past. He believed he had the power to call up spirits and hold regular meetings with them, though only, as he told Kersten, with the spirits of men who had been dead for hundreds of years.[135] When he was half-asleep, Himmler used to say, the spirit of King Heinrich would appear and give him valuable advice; he often began with the words: "In this case King Heinrich would have acted as follows." He became so obsessed by his hero that he gradually came to regard himself as a reincarnation of the King.[136]

The reason for all this occultism, however, was no mere love of history for its own sake. Contact with the past was supposed to instil into the SS Order the realisation that they were members of a select band, to lay the foundations of a historical determinism, marking out the SS man as the latest scion of a long line of Germanic nobility. Himmler's "basic features of the SS" laid down that the SS was on the march "in accordance with immutable laws as a National-Socialist Order of men of Nordic stamp and as the oath-bound community of their clans"; it continued: "We would wish to be, not only the men who fought of old, but the forebears of later generations essential to ensure the eternal existence of the Germanic people of Germany."[137]

This cult of ancestors and Germanic tribes was clearly intended by Himmler to lend the SS that ideological unity which it lacked—for even the well-reasoned mysticism of the SS Order could not conceal the fact that the SS did not possess that which distinguishes a genuine Order from the world around it—a coherent doctrine.

As far as the principles of an ideology were concerned, the SS had no more to offer than the other Nazi formations—fanatical belief in Hitler, exaggerated nationalism and racist fantasy. Himmler and Darré, the two former Artamans, had indeed introduced into the SS a few of their own special ideas, such as the peasant settlement policy; but these articles of the SS creed, which the RuSHA was intended to put into practice, remained a dead letter—at least until 1940. The demand for peasant resettlement had long since proved to be a Utopia preached by reactionary eccentrics oblivious of the realities of modern industrial society. Even in the Third Reich the requirement for men on the land was falling year by year.[138]

The fact was that the SS did not possess any distinctive ideology. The RuSHA Education Officers were always complaining of the Verfügungstruppe's lack of interest in ideology and even the Allgemeine-SS tended to yawn. Educational evenings were among the worst-attended SS gatherings. Gruppenführer Zech reported that even SS Commanders often found it more important to be present at the Wehrmacht's beer evenings than to attend the SS educational courses.[139] In January 1939 Standartenführer Dr Cäsar, Head of the SS Educational Office, complained that racial policy instruction was making little impact on SS men—"Boredom with these subjects is gradually becoming noticeable among the men and so instruction has been extended to cover the basic concepts of National-Socialist ideology." But even this did not "meet requirements."[140]

Responsibility for education was accordingly removed from the RuSHA and given to the SS Hauptamt, which instituted a new policy, playing down ideology and "placing increasing emphasis on historical themes".[141] Bowdlerised history, coloured with ideology, was the substitute used to fill the vacuum left by the absence of any original SS idea.

Further to reinforce the SS Corps spirit, Himmler instituted a curious pseudo-Germanic custom drawn from history. The SS was to differentiate itself from the outside world by a deliberate policy of neopaganism. The schoolmaster in Himmler floated uppermost, and he pried into the most intimate details of the lives of his SS men; their love life, their family life and their religion were all subject to the prior approval of the Reichsführer; in his eyes the SS was more than an association of men; it was an "Order of Germanic clans."

In an instruction issued as early as 1936 he laid down that "the SS man is expected to marry, preferably between the ages of 25 and 30, and found a family."[142] The Reichsführer-SS marriage law of 1931, to which every SS man was bound by oath, gave Himmler the power to veto unsuitable SS brides.

The SS man and his fiancée had to complete an RuSHA questionnaire, undergo a health examination by an SS doctor, provide proof of Aryan origin and submit photographs of themselves in bathing costumes. The RuSHA then decided whether both parties to the proposed marriage were worthy to be entered in the SS "clan book"; in the case of SS leaders Himmler made the decision himself.[143]

Even the marriage ceremony was governed by SS rules. Church services were taboo and, instead, after civil marriage in the Registry Office, at which only immediate relatives were present, "marriage vow ceremonies" were conducted by the local unit commander. The couple exchanged rings and received bread and salt from the SS.[144] All Himmler's rules for married life were designed to divorce his SS men from the Christian church. A man could only be promoted Commander if he turned his back on the church and declared himself "a believer in God"; no priest was allowed to be present at an SS christening or a death-bed.[145]

The local SS leader functioned as the priest; instead of baptism came carefully graduated presents from the Reichsführer, produced by the SS-owned factory at Allach near Munich—for the first child a silver breaker, a silver spoon and a blue silk shawl; for every fourth child a birthday candlestick inscribed "You are only a link in the clan's endless chain."[146]

Christmas, the Germans' favourite festival, faced Himmler with problems of theory. In 1936 he had thundered: "We will . . . lower a barrier to ensure that *Gemütlichkeit*, which has so often proved deadly to the German people,

is banished from our ranks."[147] But the SS wives continued to long for the splendour of the Christian Christmas. Himmler therefore invented a substitute—the Feast
of Midsummer. Every year the Allach Factory disgorged
on SS families a stream of "midsummer candlesticks"
and "midsummer plates." Himmler ruminated: "It is the
wives; when the church myth is taken away from them,
they want something else to take its place and gladden
the hearts of the children."[148]

The ideological hullabaloo about Christmas showed how
far the SS ideology was divorced from reality. In fact
Himmler's neo-pagan customs remained primarily a paper exercise. Even the marriage rules, which the men had
sworn to obey, remained the subject of so much controversy that many SS men disregarded them. In 1937, 307
SS men were expelled for contravention of the marriage
Order.[149] From year to year discontent in the SS increased
and Himmler was forced continuously to reduce the punishment laid down for contravention of the marriage rules.
An SS-Hauptamt order of 3 July 1935 laid down that
any man deliberately disregarding the marriage rules
would be expelled from the SS.[150] A further order on 23
June 1937, however, stated that no SS man need necessarily be expelled for this reason, provided he and his
wife subsequently satisfied the SS racial regulations.[151]
Finally, on 1 November 1940 Himmler issued an instruction that all SS men expelled for breaking the marriage
rules should be re-accepted into the Order, provided they
themselves were racially satisfactory.[152]

Equally Himmler never succeeded in implementing his
antichurch programme. Two-thirds of the Allgemeine-SS
remained in the church—54·2 per cent Evangelicals and
23·7 per cent Catholics. Himmler's "believers in God"
were in the majority only in the armed SS units—536 per
cent in the Verfügungstruppe and 69 per cent in the
Totenkopfverbände.[153] The war, however, drove the "believers" onto the defensive even in the Waffen-SS. Catholic
Chaplains appeared from time to time among the SS
troops[154] and the "Germanic volunteers" were allowed to
go to church[155]; in some units (those of Obergruppenführer
Bittrich, for instance) notices of church services were
even posted in the offices.[156]

Even more disappointing to Himmler must have been

the evident reluctance of the SS wives to raise large families. The SS birth rate hardly differed from that of the nation as a whole; instead of Himmler's much trumpeted four-child family, statistics of 31 December 1939 showed an average of 1·1 children for the 115,650 married SS men; SS officers were only marginally better with an average of 1·41.[157] Even Himmler's breeding establishment, formed in 1936 and known as "Lebensborn," with its cheap private maternity homes, failed to raise the SS birthrate. Although all the 3,500 full-time SS leaders were forced to join and contribute a defined proportion of their pay (5–8 per cent), by 1939 only 8,000 SS men were members—8,000 out of a total of 238,159 members of the Allgemeine-SS.[158] An additional—in fact the main —attraction of Lebensborn was that unmarried mothers could give birth to their children in its homes. Dr Ebner, the Head of Lebensborn, boasted: "Lebensborn is in fact the only organisation in a position to guarantee the complete secrecy of a confinement." The Reichsführer, he said, had "ordered every SS man to adopt a protective attitude to the future mother of good blood."[159] The majority of SS men, however, disregarded even this broad hint that in the interest of "good blood" all barriers of normal convention might be broken. Of 12,081 children of married SS leaders between the ages of 20 and 50, only 135 were born out of wedlock.[160]

Clearly uniformity was not to be imposed upon so bewilderingly heterogeneous an organisation as the SS merely by Himmler's neo-German rites. The anti-church propaganda, moreover, did the SS more harm than good; it deterred many from joining. The aristocracy began to turn away from the SS and seek their traditional place in the Wehrmacht.[161] Sponsoring members' contributions fell from 581,000 marks in 1934 to 400,000 marks in 1936;[162] Pohl, the SS treasurer, stated flatly: "The sponsoring member organisation . . . has passed its peak."[163] Full-time leaders began leaving the SS in increasing numbers—44 in 1938 alone.[164] On 31 December 1938 Schmitt, the Head of the Personnel Office, stated: "The fact that fulltime leaders are drifting off to industry constitutes a great danger," and noted that departures included "some of our best leaders." Particularly in Oberabschnitt Danube, he went on, many leaders had "used their position in the SS as a springboard to obtain a better job in industry."[165]

In addition the Personnel Chancellery calculated that of the medium-level leaders (Commanders of Standarten and Sturmbannen, Abschnitt Staff Officers and desk-holders in the higher-level staffs) 273 would shortly have to be relieved for inefficiency and replaced by new men. The Personnel Chancellery went on: "Of 513 full-time leaders now serving in the most important positions, it seems that in all probability only 128 (i.e. 26 per cent) are really fitted for their present employment and suitable for promotion to the higher posts."[166]

This faced Himmler with a dilemma which he was never to solve. The increasing size of his empire and the shortage of officer material meant that the recruitment of new personnel was imperative; the increased difficulty of recruiting, however, meant that he was forced to accept men bearing little relation to the SS image of the perfect nordic man.

The recruiters' difficulties would have been even greater had not the SS, in spite of its abstruse Germanic cult, offered a certain intellectual attraction to the more active brains. For the SS did possess one characteristic, and one only, differentiating it from the Party and the outer world—its own special mode of life. The hallmark of the true SS man was neither the firmness of character nor the National-Socialist fanaticism demanded by Himmler's bizarre Order; in the words of Schwerin von Krozigk, the ex-Reich Finance Minister, "unlike the Party, the aim of which is political, the SS is devoted to cultivation of a certain character."[107]

This was simply further proof that the SS had inherited the old Free Corps mentality of which Ernst Jünger, its great prophet, had once written: "The important point is not what we fight for but how we fight."[168] One of Jünger's disciples, Dr Werner Best, the one-time Gestapo official and SS-Obergruppenführer, extracted from Jünger's philosophy a notion later hallowed as one of the dominant characteristics of the SS leader—the concept of "heroic realism."[169] In 1930 Best elaborated: "The fight itself is essential and permanent; the aims of that fight are temporary and changeable. There can therefore be no question of success in our fight . . . the yardstick of the new code of morality, therefore, is not its content—not 'what' but 'how'."[170] Such an ethic, with no specific aim, opened the door to concentration upon achievement for achievement's sake and this became the focal point of the SS mentality described by Himmler with classic simplicity: "The word 'impossible' must never be heard in the SS."[171] The "worship of achievement for achievement's sake," as Hans Buchheim puts it,[172] attracted even non-Nazis, men who basically found the SS heroism claptrap repulsive. The call to energy and efficiency, the ceaseless challenge to action and trial, launched SS men into a primitive competitive struggle in which all normally accepted rules of conduct were forgotten. In 1930 Best still believed in the "good fight" and a "heroic code of morals"; his fighter was an independent personality, a true subjectivist responsible only to himself. The heroic SS fighter, however, was subject to orders from above and became a prisoner of an ethic linked to no purpose, an ethic which, ostensibly for purposes of political necessity, could suddenly order the commission of crimes and present them as goals of human technological efficiency. Buchheim says: "If a man is concerned not with what he is fighting for but only with how he fights, he is conditioned to heroic action in a criminal cause. Although such a heroic fighter imagines that he must rely on himself alone . . . he can be swept up into the service of an organisation claiming totalitarian authority—and he will perceive that this has happened either not at all or too late."[173]

Werner Best perceived it too late. The romantic ideal of heroic realism collapsed when Best found himself at Reinhard Heydrich's side building up the Third Reich's police and terror machine. Long before this, the SS had begun to turn itself into the most effective of all the tools at the disposal of the Führer dictatorship.

8

Heydrich and the Gestapo

IN the summer of 1932 Rudolf Jordan, Gauleiter of Halle-Merseburg, gave Nazi Party Headquarters a fright. The Gauleiter spied strangers; according to his information a representative of the Jewish world enemy had infiltrated into Adolf Hitler's immediate entourage.

On 6 June 1932 Jordan wrote to Gregor Strasser, the Nazi Organisation Chief: "It has come to my ears that in the Reich Leadership, there is a member named Heydrich whose father reputedly lives in Halle. There are grounds for suspecting that Bruno Heydrich of Halle, said to be the father, is a Jew. It would perhaps be wise for the Personnel Department to check this matter." To his letter Jordan attached an extract from Hugo Riemann's *Musiklexikon* in which the horrified Party functionaries read: "Heydrich Bruno, alias Süss, born 23 February 1865 in Leuben, Saxony."[1]

Strasser called for the personnel files. They showed that from 1 October 1931 a certain SS-Sturmbannführer Reinhard Heydrich had in fact been occupying a position in SS Headquarters; he was in charge of a small but top secret organisation known as the "Sicherheitsdienst Reichsführer-SS" [SS Security Service—SD].[2] Could it be, Strasser wondered, that Heinrich Himmler had entrusted to a Jew the security of Germany's most violently anti-Semitic party?

Strasser summoned Dr Achim Gercke, the Party's leading genealogist, and ordered him to trace the suspect's family tree. A fortnight later the doctor produced the results of his researches in a "Submission concerning the

182

HEYDRICH AND THE GESTAPO   183

racial origin of Lieutenant (Navy, Retired) Reinhard
Heydrich."[3] The conclusion was that: "The attached ancestry list shows that Lieutenant Heydrich is of German
origin and free from any taint of Jewish or coloured
blood . . . all the information given is based upon original sources, the reliability of which has been checked."

Gercke's memorandum was dated 22 June 1932; it
went on to explain that the rumour about Heydrich's Jewish ancestry had arisen because "Lieutenant Heydrich's
grandmother, Ernestine Wilhelmina Heydrich, nee Lind-
ner, had been married twice, her second husband being
a locksmith's assistant named Gustav Robert Süss; having
a large family by her first husband, Reinhold Heydrich,
she frequently called herself Süss-Heydrich. In this connection it should be noted that the second husband, Süss,
was equally not of Jewish origin."

Gercke continued: "This second marriage of Bruno
Heydrich's mother led to a false assumption, given currency by a note in the 1916 edition of Reimann's Musiker-
Lexikon reading 'Heydrich alias Süss'. At the request of
the Heydrich family this erroneous note was expunged
in later editions of the Lexikon."[4]

The genealogists believed that they had now cleared
up the Heydrich affair but in fact it was still in its in-
fancy. The higher Reinhard Heydrich, "the Third Reich's
evil young God of death,"[5] climbed on the National-
Socialist ladder, the more persistent became the rumour
that the number two SS man was of Jewish origin.

The tenacity with which many historians, even today,
still cling to this "Jewish ancestry" theory, is no more
than a reflection of the urge to discover some well-guarded
secret concealed behind the classically Nordic features of
Reinhard Heydrich; they feel that there must be a monster
hidden somewhere, some ineradicable stain which placed
Himmler's alter ego and head of his security police under
hypnotic pressure and turned him into the most pitiless
champion of National-Socialist doctrine, "the most fanatical of racialists" in Gerald Reitlinger's words.[6]

Somewhere, they thought, this fine figure of a man,
"one of the greatest criminals of history,"[7] must have a
chink in the armour and what more plausible than this
supposed blot on his ancestry? For a National-Socialist, after all, it was suicidal, the equivalent of a deadly sin.

So Reitlinger promptly discovered in Heydrich a "pathological Jewish self-hate" as the key to an understanding
of this supposed fanatic;[8] H. G. Adler in his *Theresienstadt
1941–1945* considered that the Third Reich offered Heydrich "unlimited power enabling him, by murdering every
Jew within reach, to exorcise the hated Jewish spot within
him."

Even Himmler secretly believed the theory, saying that
Heydrich was "an unhappy man, completely divided
against himself, as often happened with those of mixed
race."[10] Carl Burckhardt, the League of Nations Commissioner, found the same thing, saying that he could
detect a dual personality in Heydrich's face: "I said to
myself: two people are looking at me simultaneously."[11]

Burckhardt tells a story of Heydrich regaled to him
by SS men. One day, when under the influence of drink,
Heydrich staggered into his brilliantly lit bathroom and
came up against his reflection in the great wall mirror.
He snatched his revolver from the holster and fired twice
at the mirror shouting: "At last I've got you, scum!"
Burckhardt's comment is: "The man with the split personality had shot at his reflection because at last he had
met his other half—but he had met him only in the mirror
and could never get rid of him; that other half was to
accompany him to the end."[12]

But however detailed the biographers' picture of the
"blond beast" as Heydrich was sometimes called even by
the SS, the ultimate conclusion must be that it is perfectly possible to have a great deal to do with a man
and yet not know him. For Reinhard Heydrich was not
the Saint-Just of the National-Socialist revolution; he was
no racial fanatic; he was not even what Freund called:
"A professional criminal of Lucifer stature."[13]

It is, of course, attractive to compare Himmler and
Heydrich with their terrorist counterparts of the French
Revolution, Robespierre and Saint-Just. As far as crime
is concerned, the head of the SD was far ahead of his
French predecessor, but he had none of Saint-Just's doctrinaire revolutionary fanaticism or perverted idealism. In
fact Himmler and Heydrich were two archetypes of the
twentieth century raised to the *n*th degree—the ideologist
and the technologist. They frequently invoked history
and they twisted it to their own purposes but basically

Himmler and Heydrich were anti-historical figures, radical merciless rebels against tradition, morality and all humanitarian rules of conduct.

Heydrich's deity was power for its own sake; he was an incarnation of the technology of government by brute force, linked with that distrust of his lords and masters which earned him the nickname "Mr Suspicion"[14] but he did not hate. The connecting link between Saint-Just and the victims of the guillotine had been hatred, but Heydrich did not hate the Jews; in his scheme of things, they were simply the subjects for a technical planning procedure, faceless objects for a "mopping-up action" on the ghastly scale ordered by the leaders of his State. With Heydrich hatred was an expression of personal spite. Grand Admiral Raeder, for instance, who had had him cashiered from the Navy, was an object of his undying thirst for revenge; Heydrich rejected all attempts at reconciliation by his former fellow-officers.[15] Ideological hatred, on the other hand, was foreign to him, for he despised all ideologies, the National-Socialist included. Heydrich had a passion for all forms of sport; he was a fencer, a horseman, a pilot, a skier and modern pentathlon competitor; he was also SS Inspector for physical training; on occasions he would even protect Jewish sportsmen— for instance, he helped Paul Sommer, the German fencing-master, to emigrate to America and provided Kantor of the Polish Olympic team with money and papers.[16]

Heydrich obviously had none of that blind faith in Hitler which was the elixir of life to Himmler, the stimulant enabling the small-timer to grow to supernatural size. Heydrich could quite well visualise a Germany without Hitler but not a Germany without Heydrich. Those who knew him well are still convinced that, had he been alive on 20 July 1944, he might well have been found on the side of Stauffenberg—two of his fencing friends can remember him saying to them in Bad-Kreuznach in 1941 that he would be the first to do away with Hitler if "the old man makes a mess of things."[17]

Right to the end he remained a technician of power and an apostle of expediency. When, as Reich protector of Bohemia and Moravia, he was struck down by the Czech parachutists' hand grenade on 27 May 1942, the Czech conspirators were aiming not at a brutal overlord but at the sophisticated SS rationalist whose flexible stick-and-carrot policy constituted such a danger to their position that they could see no solution other than his liquidation.

Such a craftsman of pragmatism was, of course, infuriated by Himmler's interminable ideological ramblings. To his wife Lina, Heydrich would frequently unburden himself of his wrath with the Reichsführer and his racial fantasies One evening, when he had drunk too much, he yelled: "Just look at his face, his nose—typically Jewish. A real Jewish lout!"[18] Lina Heydrich egged him on, for she cordially loathed the entire Himmler family, particularly the "Madame Reichsführer." Even after the war Lina ridiculed Marga Himmler: "Size 50 knickers. That's all there was to her . . . . that narrow-minded, humourless blonde female, always worrying about protocol; she ruled her husband and could twist him round her little finger—at least until 1936."[19]

Lina Heydrich had good reason to know how strong Marga Himmler's influence was. Urged on by his wife, Himmler demanded that Heydrich should divorce Lina, whom he regarded as impossible and ungovernable. But Lina Heydrich proved stronger than the jaundiced Frau Himmler. At one of Göring's garden parites she struck back. As chance would have it, Himmler was presiding at Frau Heydrich's table. She tells the story: "They were moments of tragicomedy. I put on my most mournful expression and sat stock still. Himmler asked: 'Why are you so quiet?' To which I replied: 'Do you find that surprising?' Then we danced. Himmler danced badly. Then he said. 'Well, Frau Heydrich, everything will be all right.' You see, that was typical of Himmler; on paper he ordered us to divorce, but when face to face with me, his courage left him. The matter was never referred to again"[20]

Heydrich's vexation, however, was all the greater when he realised how dependent he was upon Himmler with his pernickety mysticism about the SS Order. Although intellectually the superior of his Chief, Heydrich never forgot to treat his Reichsführer "as a Prussian second lieutenant behaves to a senior general."[21] Kersten noted: "Heydrich behaves . . . with quite inexplicable servility. He addresses Himmler as 'Herr Reichsführer'—a thing ab-

solutely forbidden throughout the SS—instead of simply
'Reichsführer.' Heydrich's side of the conversation between them goes like this: 'Certainly, Herr Reichsführer;
if that is the Herr Reichsführer's wish, I will have the
necessary arrangements made at once and report back
to the Herr Reichsführer.' " To Lina, however, he would
rage: "Himmler is always manoeuvring and trimming his
sails; he won't take responsibility."[22]

Himmler rather dreaded his senior staff officer's appearance with some proposition. Kersten says: "Sometimes I had the impression that after one of these exposi-
tions Himmler was quite overwhelmed." Heydrich's
reports, Kersten goes on, were "masterpieces of exposi-
tion; a short sketch of the person or subject, then his
arguments perceptively built up to the decisive trump
card, which he played last of all, then his conclusion
which Himmler could hardly resist."[23]

Sometimes the intimidated Reichsführer plucked up his
courage again—once Heydrich was gone. Then he would
seize the telephone and tell Heydrich that he must first
discuss with Hitler the measures already agreed.[24] Shortly thereafter Himmler would issue a different order,
camouflaged for the benefit of Heydrich as an order from
the Führer. On one occasion Himmler had the courage
to lose his temper; he screamed at Heydrich, stuttering:
"You, you . . . and your logic. We never hear about anything but your logic. Everything I propose, you batter
down with your logic. I am fed up with you and your
cold, rational criticism." Heydrich drew back and gave
way at once. Himmler was pacified once more.[25]

Himmler always kept suspicious watch on possible rivals,
but he never regarded Heydrich as potentially dangerous.
He had detected in Heydrich characteristics which, though
admirable in a secret policeman, were hardly calculated
to further more exalted political ambitions. He was irritable, power-hungry, always ready to pounce: he was
glacial, incapable of friendship or even loyalty. Heydrich's
restlessness, his versatile, though superficial, intelligence,
his tendency to be a know-all, his urge to be top dog in
everything, whether in the SD, the fencing room or over
the bottle, could not conceal the fact that within him
there was a vacuum in which both ideologies and human
beings sank without trace.

Though he avoided making declared enemies, he equally had no friends; his only real bond with his wife was his insatiable sexual appetite. Wherever he appeared, men drew back. Even his fencing partners, though appreciating his skill, avoided him.[26]

Even today quite a number of ex-members of Himmler's staff can still be found to sing their Reichsführer's praises as a kind and thoughtful man, but there has never been a word from any friend of Heydrich, "the man with the iron heart" as Hitler called him.[27] Sepp Dietrich's coarse expression upon hearing of Heydrich's death echoed the thoughts of many SS men: "Thank God that sow's gone to the butcher."[28]

Even the Berlin prostitutes were not invariably pleased to see him. He always took an aide with him when he went night-clubbing, and there were frequent scenes when the ladies appeared to prefer the aide to the man with the sinister wolf's eyes.[29] Few realised that behind Heydrich's arrogant exterior lay a sensitivity springing from the inferiority complex of the cashiered naval officer and the actor's susceptibility to criticism, inherited from his parents. Brutality was not a basic feature of his character; when Burckhardt once visited Heydrich he said feelingly: "Abroad people take us for bloodhounds, don't they? It is almost too hard for the individual, but we must be hard as granite."[30]

So unstable a being, alternating between aggressiveness and a longing for recognition, was cut out to be Himmler's second-in-command; he would be no threat to the Reichsführer's supremacy. Both knew that neither could do without the other—for reasons of self-preservation. Without Himmler and his firm position in the Nazi hierarchy as head of the SS, the restlessly ambitious Heydrich would find his rise to power blocked; without Heydrich, his lightning intellect and his dynamism, Himmler would never hack his way through the spider's web of Nazi potentates.

Initially it seemed that the partnership between these two men would be a very one-sided affair. In June 1931, when Himmler received young Heydrich while convalescing at his home in Waldtrudering[31] and engaged him for the SD, he had clearly been a broken man who had lost the profession which he longed for—that of an officer.

Reinhard Tristan Eugen Heydrich was born on 7 March 1904 in Halle on the Saale.[32] His early career was no different from that of many middle-class young men in republican post-war Germany. He was the son of an opera singer and an actress, went to the Reform Gymnasium [High School] in Halle[33] and, at the age of 16, joined General Maerker's Free Corps—primarily to escape the poverty of his home, which had been hit by the war and inflation.[34] When he returned, he knew what he wanted to be—an officer. Like Himmler, his first choice was the Navy since in post-war disarmed Germany the best chance of satisfying his urge for self-expression and adventure was to be found at sea.

In 1922 Heydrich reported to Kiel as a naval cadet. In July 1923, as part of his training, he was posted to the training cruiser *Berlin*[35] and so met the man who later described him as "the cleverest brute of them all," Wilhelm Canaris, then First Officer of the *Berlin*. From the outset the little fastidious captain found this lanky cadet with the Mongol eyes somewhat sinister, though he admired his mathematical ability and navigational skill.[36]

Canaris' wife Erika, however, daughter of Carl Friedrich Waag, a manufacturer from Pforzheim, was artistic and she found Heydrich's violin playing delightful.[37] Aronson, Heydrich's Jewish biographer, says: "Heydrich's playing was mellow and delicate, his finger-work was first-class and he showed outstanding feeling as a violinist." When playing Heydrich could "weep for prolonged periods. This was the other side of the coin—cynicism and cruelty combined with soft sentimentality."[38]

In 1924 Canaris was posted to the Naval Staff in Berlin.[39] Heydrich meanwhile continued a normal uneventful naval career; early in 1926 he was promoted Oberfähnrich [Midshipman] and later that year Sub-Lieutenant; he attended the Naval Signal School, became signals officer of the fleet flagship *Schleswig-Holstein* and occupied various positions in the signals division of the Baltic Naval Station.[40] In 1928, by which time Heydrich had been promoted Lieutenant[41] and had also passed an examination in Russian, he was regarded as a talented naval officer; admittedly he was unpopular with his brother officers and was teased as a "nannygoat" because of his falsetto voice; among the sailors he was reckoned one of

the most unpopular officers because of his harsh, overbearing manner.[42]

Nevertheless he seemed to have an assured career in
front of him, but at this point an amorous adventure
brought it to an abrupt end. The starting point was an
evening canoeing expedition near Kiel in late summer
1930;[43] as the boat carrying Heydrich and Mohr glided
peacefully along, they saw another boat capsize. In it
were two girls; Heydrich and Mohr dived into the water
and rescued the ladies; one of them was a blonde nineteen-
year-old schoolgirl beauty, Lina Mathilde von Osten,
daughter of a schoolmaster on the Baltic Island of
Fehmarn.[44] As a result of this adventure Heydrich and
Lina struck up a friendship which culminated on 9 December 1930 in engagement—much against the will of
Lina's father.[45]

But Heydrich was a pathological womaniser and Lina
was only one more addition to his collection of young
ladies. Another soon appeared with a prior claim—a
student at the Kolonialschule in Rendsburg, daughter of a
director of IG-Farben. Heydrich rejected her coldly, but
her father had connections with Admiral Erich Raeder,
the Head of the Navy, and Heydrich's superiors were
soon pointing out to him that he would have to give up
Lina von Osten; when he refused, Raeder set the wheels of
naval justice in motion.[46]

Early in 1931 a court of honour, consisting of four
naval officers, met and examined Lieutenant Heydrich for
weeks[47]; the President and First Member of the court was
Captain Gustav Kleikamp, commander of the Baltic station and Heydrich's ex-instructor at the Naval Signal
School; he says that he "discussed the case as put forward
by Heydrich thoroughly and in detail."[48] Heydrich, however, answered his old instructor with such arrogance that
the court of honour reprimanded him for insubordination.

What primarily turned the court against Heydrich was
his blatant attempt to shift the blame on to the girl; he
accused her of lying and protested his own complete innocence. This was incompatible with the code of honour of a
great Navy. Vice Admiral Kleikamp stated subsequently:
"In view of Heydrich's inexcusable behaviour, in particular
the striking lack of candour in his presentation of his
case, the court of honour was moved to raise the question

whether the retention of such an officer in the Navy was possible; the decision on this matter, however, was left open."[49]

Raeder, a stickler for naval propriety, answered this question in the negative and threw Heydrich out of the Navy. Judgment was pronounced at the end of April 1931: "Dismissal for impropriety."[50] Rumour has it that Heydrich later told the "other girl," who was expecting a child by him, that he could not marry a girl who had given herself to him beforehand.[51]

As a result of Raeder's decision, Heydrich descended from the security of the ultra-conservative Navy into the army of the unemployed millions who were besieging Germany's labour exchanges. He revolted against the fate which he had brought upon himself. The openings seemed few; he could have become a sailing instructor, like many other ex-naval officers, and there seemed a possibility of a post with a yacht club,[52] but—as far as any form of naval uniform was concerned, even that of the merchant navy, there were no prospects. To heal his wounded pride, Heydrich had to satisfy himself with a second-rate uniform—that of the Naval SA,[53] but this did not mean that he had developed political leanings; Lina Heydrich said: "He was just a professional naval officer; he was wedded to his naval career. His only other interest was sport. He knew nothing about politics—and had never shown any great interest in them."[54]

But Lina knew her politics (Höttl describes her as "a typical example of the evil, ambitious woman in a novel");[55] she was a Hitler enthusiast and was convinced that her future husband should look to the Nazi Party for a career. Heydrich's sister Elizabeth came to the rescue. She remembered that his godmother had a son who was a senior SA leader in Munich and was about to become one of the influential personalities in the SS. "Little Karl," alias Friedrich Karl Freiherr von Eberstein, she was sure, would help "Reini"—and he did.[56]

Eberstein fortunately did not know the difference between a signals officer and an intelligence officer; Heydrich was therefore summoned to Waltrudering to meet Himmler, who was then looking for a counter-espionage man for his Security Service. Heydrich entered Himmler's house —and his life—on 14 June 1931.[57] Himmler gave him 20

minutes to draw up the outline of a future SS counter-
espionage service[58]—and this was the real genesis of the
SD. Himmler accepted Heydrich's plan and on 5 October
1931 Party Headquarters Hamburg received the following
message from Munich: "Party Member Reinhard Heydrich,
Hamburg, Membership No. 544916, will, with effect from
October of this year, be carried on the strength of Party
Headquarters as a member of the staff of the Reichsführer-SS."[59] Heydrich was given the rank of Sturmführer[60] and set to work.

Early in 1931 on Hitler's instructions, Himmler had
commenced the formation of a Security Service to protect
Nazi Leaders. His first step had been to form within SS
Headquarters an "Ic" section—in army general staff terminology Section Ic dealt with enemy intelligence. Even
after Heydrich's appointment Himmler himself remained
titular Head of Section Ic but he left the actual work to
Heydrich.[61]

Armed only with a couple of Himmler's files, Heydrich
moved into a room in the Brown House[62] and embarked
upon the career for which he was better fitted than any
other National-Socialist, that of totalitarian secret policeman. In late August 1931 he appeared at a meeting of SS
leaders in the Brown House in the capacity of future Head
of the Secret Service, and he painted a horrifying picture
of a Party riddled with innumerable spies in the pay of the
opposition parties and the police. His conclusion was that
the Nazi Party must be ruthlessly purged of all agents and
saboteurs.[63] Shortly thereafter an order was issued to all
SS units: "With immediate effect every Abschnitt will set
up an Ic desk to deal with all intelligence activities within
the Abschnitt. Subsequently an Ic desk is also envisaged
for every SS-Standarte."[64]

No sooner had Heydrich placed his men in SS units
than he moved himself out of the Brown House, whose
inmates were becoming over-curious. With three staff officers, he transferred to a two-roomed apartment at 23
Türkenstrasse, Munich,[65] where he inaugurated a curious
system obviously based upon detective and spy novels; no
more than two people were ever allowed to be present at
any discussion—Heydrich and one other.[66] Early in 1932
he had built up his staff sufficiently to seek new horizons.

Occasional contact with his spies and informers was not enough.

In April 1932 he toured Germany in order to see how his scattered staff might be concentrated into one organisation.[67] Just at this moment, however, the defenders of the Republic forced him to juggle with its title; the Reich Government banned both the SA and SS; Ic was forced to re-name itself Presse-und Informationsdienst [Press and Information Service—PID].[68]

Nevertheless Heydrich was so encouraged by his tour, that he now set up a great organisation, later to be known as "Sicherheitsdienst" (SD). He withdrew counter-espionage personnel and informers from SS units, concentrating them under his own authority;[69] he had thus formed the first specialised SS organisation. Although it had its own separate establishment, the new organisation remained a unit of the SS but, at the same time, was an SS within the SS. Heydrich set up his own territorial organisation, paralleling the SS-Oberabschnitte and Abschnitte. Its job was to track down anti-Party elements within the NSDAP and keep a watch on opposition parties.[70] Every report, every observation, every little personal detail was meticulously entered in Heydrich's card-index in the new SD Headquarters at 4 Zuccalistrasse, Munich.[71]

But Heydrich's ambition did not end there. Observation of the Party's enemies was not enough for him—other Party and SA counter-espionage services were already doing that. He was determined that the SD's work should be so outstanding that all Party rivals would be eliminated, leaving it as the sole intelligence service of the entire Nazi Party. Even this was not enough for the SS; when Adolf Hitler seized power in Berlin, Heydrich hoped that the SD would emerge from the shadows and form the new police force of the new Reich.

In astonishment verging on perplexity, Himmler, the small-timer, watched his secret-service chief drive on with merciless energy. All the self-torturing melancholy of the cashiered naval officer was gone; Heydrich drove his men with the missionary fervour of the newly converted—imperious, impatient, issuing a stream of orders in his staccato, strikingly high-pitched voice. Himmler rewarded all this industry with the requisite promotions and Heydrich climbed the ladder quickly; 10 August 1931 Sturmführer, 1 December 1931 Hauptsturmführer, 19 July 1932 formal appointment as Head of the SD, 29 July 1932 Standartenführer, 21 March 1933 Oberführer.[72] Himmler sensed instinctively that chance had given him a "born intelligence officer," "a living card index, a brain which held all the threads and wove them all together," as Kersten puts it.[73] Heydrich was ideally equipped to be head of a secret service—he was hard, he was unsentimental, his thirst for information was apparently insatiable and his contempt for his fellow-men was enough to make the flesh creep.

It was no accident that Heydrich's favourite sport was fencing. The watching and parrying, the lightning reaction to unforeseen situations, were second nature to him. Schellenberg found in him "the ever-watchful instincts of a predatory animal, always alert to danger and ready to act swiftly and ruthlessly."[74] He had an uncanny knack, almost a sixth sense, of putting his finger on the point, however intricate the situation. Himmler's files of reports from other sources often carried notes in Heydrich's angular writing: "Don't believe it" or "Simply a rumour"; when Himmler asked him whether he had investigated the report in question, he would reply: "Not yet," but that the comment was simply his feeling—and he was usually right.[75]

Himmler added: "He possessed an infallible nose for men . . . he saw the ways which friend or foe would take with a clarity which was absolutely amazing. His colleagues hardly dared to lie to him."[76] Heydrich seemed to have been born to become Head of the Secret Service in a totalitarian state. Obersturmbannführer Höttl of the SD believed that Heydrich was the first "to make Himmler aware of the potentialities of his position as Reichsführer-SS"; the idea of turning the SS into the Third Reich's Police Force originated with Heydrich.[77]

Heydrich's vision was of a close-knit system of super-vision, covering every facet of the national life and guaranteeing the total dominance of the Nazi Party; the instrument was to be none other than the Reichsführer's SD, and its Director none other than Reinhard Tristan Eugen Heydrich. He sketched out a Political Police Force which differed from its predecessors in one decisive aspect: previous police systems had been satisfied to catch enemies of the State *in flagrante delicto;* they acted when some definite danger could be detected; Heydrich's police, on the other hand, were to track down the enemy before even his thinking, let alone his actions, savoured of resistance.

The power of the police as conceived by Heydrich was limitless, embracing every aspect of the nation's life. The police force was no longer to be a defensive organisation, it was to pass to the attack—not only that; it was to be the "educator" of the people, the omnipotent purifier, cleansing the nation of all non-conformist ideas. According to Hauptsturmführer Alfred Schweder of the SD, the mission of the police was to "raise to the highest level the activity of our people's innate forces by correcting and directing their thoughts in a single direction, in the process eliminating from the national thinking all foreign, and therefore destructive, tendencies."[78] Heydrich's concept, of course, postulated disregard of all traditional legal restraint on police activity. In Werner Best's view the police should be ubiquitous "in order to suppress and avert any disturbance of governmental order in the Third Reich, even though an infringement of law and order may not, or not yet, have taken place."[79]

In other words Heydrich wished the police to be omnipotent, subject only to the "overall mission of the German Police"[80]—which was the ruthless protection of Adolf Hitler's Führer dictatorship. Obviously, however, so free a hand could not be given to a Police Force brought up under the Weimar Republic to respect the law and the constitution; still less could it be given to an administration for which, despite lip service to National Socialism, the Prussian norms of law and order still remained valid.

Heydrich knew what had to be done; in the first place the SD must occupy the key positions in the new Political Police; secondly, the specialised Police Force must then be divorced from all connection with the internal administration; finally, the entire Police Force must be merged into the SS to form a State Protection Corps. This plan contained the germ of an even more far-reaching and more revolutionary project—the formation of a purely SS administration, combining the Police, the SS and the official bureaucracy into one co-ordinated whole.

Himmler was intoxicated by Heydrich's vision. Some of

the "old fighters" such as SS-Gruppenführer August Heissmeyer, sounded the warning that if it became too closely
connected to the police, the SS Order would be hampered
in its educational mission by a heavy load of unpopular-
ity.[81] In 1946 Seyss-Inquart said: "The SS idea foundered
because Himmler misused the organisation as an executive
authority."[82] But nothing could now deter the Reichsführer
from his dream of becoming Germany's supreme policeman. In Bavaria a testing ground was already available for
Heydrich to put his ideas into practice.

Himmler and his sleuths already had a foot in the
police door as a result of the National-Socialist coup in
Bavaria on 9 March 1933; Himmler moved into Police
Headquarters as Acting Police President and Heydrich
took over the political desk in Abteilung VI.[83] A week
later the two SS men took a further major stride forward.
Himmler was nominated political adviser to the Bavarian
Ministry of the Interior and given command of the Bavarian Political Police; he hastened to summon Heydrich as
his executive deputy.[84]

The two now used Bavaria as the testing ground for
the procedure they were to follow throughout the Reich a
few years later. Himmler created in the Ministry of the
Interior an office known as "Political Police Commander,
Bavaria," while Heydrich began to build up a Bavarian
Political Police Force, manning it with personnel from his
SD.[85] Heydrich's primary object was to make the Political
Police, hitherto part of the overall police machine, independent of the Bavarian administration, and so he now
cut all administrative connections with the Bavarian Gov-
ernment. The Political Police moved out of Munich Police
Headquarters and was given the status of an independent
authority.[86]

Heydrich concentrated into one organisation the political sections of Police Headquarters [Polizeidirektionen]
and Police Offices [Polizeiämter], together with the political police desks in the Bezirke [Districts] and munici-
palities; all headed up to a single office—that of the
Political Police Commander, who was authorised to call
upon the uniformed police of Bavaria for executive duties
as occasion demanded.[87] In accordance with the theories of
Heydrich and Himmler, the authority of the Political
Police Commander was even further extended to include

certain preserves of the judiciary; Himmler was placed in charge of the concentration camps which Adolf Wagner, the rabid Nazi Minister of the Interior in Bavaria, had set up to relieve the normal prisons, overflowing with political prisoners.[88]

Meanwhile, the emergency decree "For the Protection of People and State" issued by the Reich President, empowered the police to consign citizens to "preventive custody" in a concentration camp on mere suspicion of anti-State activity;[89] as he was already in control of the concentration camps, this gave Himmler undreamed-of power and nothing could now stop his fanatical campaign for political purity. On paper he was still the subordinate of Wagner, the Gauleiter and Minister of the Interior, but his dual function as Reichsführer-SS and Political Police Commander enabled him to evade the authority of his nominal superior. Wagner, as Minister of the Interior, could give orders to Himmler in his capacity as Political Police Commander but not in his capacity as Head of the SS, for as head of a Party formation, Himmler was superior to Wagner, a mere Gauleiter; conversely, within the Party, Röhm, as Chief of Staff of the SA, which frequently obstructed the work of the political police, was superior to the Reichsführer-SS and could therefore give him orders; within Bavaria, however, Röhm could not give orders to the Political Police Commander. Himmler and Heydrich made good use of their well-nigh completely independent position. Dachau became a household word, signifying a barbaric efficiency which incensed even convinced Nazis; in Bavaria the two SS men were still filling their camps with prisoners when the first great wave of terror produced by the National-Socialist Revolution had long since died away. Himmler later recalled: "In 1933, under pressure from the Ministry, we released a large number of prisoners from preventive custody in Prussia and other German Länder. In Bavaria, however, I did not give way and did not release my prisoners."[90]

Ritter von Epp, the Reichsstatthalter of Bavaria, was disturbed by the frequent "abuse of the imposition of protective custody;" he suggested to Wagner on 20 March 1934 that such arbitrary action might "undermine confidence in the law." But Wagner would have none of it. On 14 April von Epp noted that "every sentence" of Wagner's reply was "questionable and refutable" and that it contained a series of "inaccuracies, distortions, misrepresentations and falsifications."[91]

Even Frick, the lethargic Reich Minister of the Interior, entered the lists, criticising Himmler's crude methods and his passion for placing people under arrest. On 30 January 1935 he wrote: "I have on several previous occasions drawn attention to the comparatively large number of persons in protective custody in Bavaria; I have had no satisfactory explanation from the Bavarian Political Police, nor have I seen signs of any serious effort to reduce the number of prisoners . . . I cannot allow such a situation to pass without comment; according to the latest figures, the number of persons in protective custody in Bavaria is several hundreds higher than the combined total in all other German Länder, Prussia included." But Himmler ignored these admonitions from Berlin; Frick's letter simply evoked the bleak comment: "The prisoners will remain."[92]

But Himmler and Heydrich soon found Bavaria too small for them; they cast covetous eyes on the rest of the Reich, where in the sixteen other German Länder the police were without a master or, at least, without a single guiding hand. Time was pressing, for in Prussia Göring had already set up a Political Police in the form of the Gestapo, organised similarly to Himmler's and Heydrich's machine—divorced from the administration, responsible only to one man, and independent of State and Party.

The power struggle between the National-Socialist potentates, however, brought Himmler and Heydrich a quicker victory than either had expected. Frick, a weak man but intent on reforming the Reich on centralist principles, found his way blocked by Göring's Prussian separatism and could see no other solution but to call in Himmler—he and Frick at least agreed on one point: both wanted a centralised Reich Police Force. Frick allowed Himmler to take over one Land police force after another. Prussia held out to the end. (The story of the fall of that fortress, as a by-product of preparation for action against Röhm, has been told in Chapter 5.)

So by the end of April 1934 Himmler and Heydrich had laid hands on the Prussian police. Himmler became Deputy Chief and Inspector of the Gestapo, the Prussian equivalent of the Bavarian Political Police; as deputy to the Deputy, Heydrich took over control of the Gestapa.[93] At the same time they contrived to broaden the basis of their power within the Party. The Party leadership recognised the SD as the sole Party information service, the Führer's Deputy decreeing on 9 June 1934 that thenceforth: "Apart from the Sicherheitsdienst RFSS there will be no Party intelligence or counter-espionage service, not even in the form of an internal intelligence organisation for foreign policy purposes."[94]

But the SD's victory came too soon. Heydrich had somehow lost faith in his own creature. His experience with the Bavarian Political Police had destroyed his dream of the SD as the basis of a new police force. The old-school police officials had shown themselves superior in every respect to the young upstarts of the SD. Heydrich must have sensed this early on, for only a few days before the National-Socialist seizure of power, he had cut adrift from the SD. On 27 January 1933 he resigned as Head of the SD and was appointed to the staff of the Reichsführer-SS as "Standartenführer specially employed."[95] For nine months, the SD machine ran on without Heydrich.[96]

The past and future Head of the SD was realist enough to know that, from the point of view of numbers alone, his organisation was in no position to form the cadre of a new police force. In autumn 1933 the SD totalled only 100 members; SD-Oberabschnitt South West (Stuttgart), for instance, consisted only of five men.[97] Moreover Heydrich doubted whether the SD had any future as an independent organisation. His wife told Aronson, the Jewish historian, that her husband had once said: "Now we have no further need of the Party. It has served its purpose and opened the way to power. Now the SS must penetrate the police and, with them, form a new organisation."[98]

Here then was the objective. On Himmler's instructions Heydrich, from his desk as Head of the Gestapo, now set about combining all the Länder Police Forces in Germany under the SS umbrella; his object was to turn their experienced police functionaries into loyal servants of the regime, available for any task allotted by the Führer dictatorship; of Nazism they need possess only the thinnest veneer. For Heydrich, the pragmatist, technical ability was more important than ideological purism—and he found that technical ability among a group of Munich criminal police officers who made no secret of the fact that the new-style SD was abhorrent to them.

Senior Inspector Reinhard Flesch and his colleagues, including Heinrich Müller, Franz Josef Huber and Josef Meisinger, worked in Abteilungen II and VI of the Bavarian Political Police, expecting to be displaced at any moment, by the SD upstarts. "Heini" Müller took a strong line saying: "Just let them come. We'll look after them!"[99] But, in fact, the old professionals had good reason to fear that their new masters might sack them because, with the exception of Meisinger, they had all been anti-Nazis before 1933. Meisinger was an "old fighter" who had marched to the Feldherrnhalle on 9 November 1923,[100] but every other member of the Flesch group was a supporter of some democratic party, in most cases the Bavarian Peoples' Party.

This applied even to Müller, the thickset bullnecked criminal-police inspector with the yokel's face. Born in 1900, he had been a sergeant pilot on the Western Front and a member of Munich Police Headquarters from the end of 1919. While still only an assistant in the central office, he had had to deal, as his first case, with the murders of hostages during the Red Republic period in Bavaria, and as a result had become a fanatical anticommunist.[101] During the Weimar Republic he had been in charge of the anti-communist desk in the political section of Police Headquarters; even the Headquarters of the Munich/Upper Bavaria Nazi Party Gau, where the ambitious Müller was detested, was forced to "admit categorically" that Müller was a "most violent opponent" of communism "who at times would disregard legal rules and regulations."[102]

Nevertheless the Gau Headquarters' opinion of Müller continued: "It is, however, equally clear that, had it been his job, Müller would have acted similarly against the right wing. Being incredibly ambitious. . . . he would be bent on recognition from his superiors under any system."[103] Munich Party Headquarters doubted whether a man like Müller had any professional future in the new Germany; he was a "regulation" policeman and an assiduous churchgoer, who contributed no more than 40 pfennig to the

Eintopfspende (a Nazi device to raise money); to make matters worse Dischner, the Bavarian Peoples' Party publisher, was his father-in-law.[104] He was hardly the type of police official likely to be acceptable to the Nazis.

On 4 January 1937 the Munich Gau Headquarters described Müller's character as follows: "He acts ruthlessly, uses his elbows and seizes every opportunity to display his efficiency; he is quite prepared to deck himself out in borrowed plumage."[105] The head of the local Nazi group in Munich-Pasing confirmed: "We can hardly imagine him as a member of the Party."[106] Heydrich, however, was both sufficiently imaginative and sufficiently hard-headed to take on a technician such as this—the same applied to the other members of the Flesch group. He even accepted Huber, who was loathed by the Party as the leading anti-Nazi in Police Headquarters.

Heydrich summoned Huber and produced the schedule of dismissals. Without a word, in oppressive silence he ran a finger down the list. Suddenly he looked up: "Which Huber are you?" Huber explained. A short conversation followed. When Huber left the room, Heydrich knew that he, like all the other good brave citizens of Munich Police Headquarters, would now work even more unscrupulously and dutifully for the regime whose advent they had resisted.[107]

A Munich Party Headquarters internal memorandum, dated 9 March 1937, found it incomprehensible that "so odious an opponent of the Movement" as Müller should now be one of the regime's guardians; he had always "tried to curry favour with his superiors by particularly vigilant persecution of National-Socialists"; he had once referred to the great Führer, Adolf Hitler, as an "immigrant unemployed housepainter" and "an Austrian draft-dodger."[108]

Müller and his ilk were only too ready to repay Heydrich's tolerance with "an unconditional readiness to serve." Instead of being sacked, the Munich criminal police officers found themselves unexpectedly promoted— they were accepted into the SD as a body.[109] Heydrich's cold calculation, however, threw up one unfortunate by-product, hardly noticed at the time; SS-Untersturmführer Müller, Flesch, Huber and the rest were quite prepared to sew the SD diamond on their sleeves but, right up to the

end of the Third Reich, they retained their allergy to the
SD and this was a contributory factor in its failure to gain
control of the Gestapo.

Heinrich Müller and his gang were not the only professionals recruited by Heydrich. In Berlin a similar group
was to be found, headed by Oberregierungsrat [senior
civil servant] Arthur Nebe; he was as expert a policeman
and as great an opportunist as the Bavarian Müller.

Nebe, born in 1894, was the son of a Berlin school-
teacher; he had served as a Lieutenant in the Engineers
and had been with the Berlin Criminal Police since 1920.
Later he was promoted SS-Gruppenführer but was then
involved in the 20 July 1944 plot and executed as a member of the resistance. At that time Ernst Kaltenbrunner,
Heydrich's successor, wrote a character sketch of Nebe
not unlike that given to Müller by the Munich Party
headquarters: "A two-faced character with an unhealthy
degree of ambition . . . Nebe would ruthlessly push aside
anything which stood in his path to promotion."[110] Kaltenbrunner was no doubt influenced by his hatred of the
"traitors" of 20 July but nevertheless his picture of Nebe
was basically not far wrong; on many occasions Nebe
proved himself only too willing to adopt the prevailing
attitude of cynicism.[111]

He was a suspicious inscrutable being, employed alter-
nately in the drugs and theft sections of the Berlin police,
who had been drawn to the Nazi Party in 1931[112] because,
like many police officers at the time, he found their plans
for the police tempting; National-Socialism offered what
the Weimar Republic had refused to the police—more
money and technical equipment, co-ordination of the fight
against crime, protection from attacks by the press and
increased use of preventive detention. The death-throes
of the Republic encouraged the more far-sighted to commit themselves further. Nebe became a sponsoring member of the SS, joined the SA and accepted a transfer to
the Gestapo, where he became head of the Executive
(Abteilung III) in the Gestapa.[113]

This he was soon to regret, for he became involved in
the sniping campaign between the Himmler-Heydrich team
and Rudolf Diels, Göring's protégé and first Head of the
Gestapa.[114] As already related (Chapter 5) Diels and Nebe
disliked each other; Nebe passed to Heydrich incriminating

material on Röhm, hoping thereby to work his way out of the Gestapa[115]—a hope only partially fulfilled.

In addition to these two teams of professional police officers from Munich and Berlin, Heydrich now collected a third group of educated experts, officials and lawyers from all over Germany, including the man who became Heydrich's closest collaborator and ultimately his enemy, the ex-District Judge from Hesse, Dr Werner Best.

Karl Rudolf Werner Best, born in 1903 in Darmstadt, was the son of a Post Office official. After studying law at Freiburg, Frankfurt and Giessen Universities, he entered the legal profession.[116] He was a supporter of the authoritarian State, an ardent nationalist, a disciple of Ernst Jünger and a romantic exponent of the Free Corps mentality, which (in his own words) regarded war as "a necessary and natural form of the whole scheme of existence."[117] In 1930 he published an article which read like a blueprint for a state founded on the "law of the people." He called for "passionate support of the State as the highest expression of the urge for power, transcending all individual interests"; clearly he did not accept the ideal of a liberal State founded on the rule of law, nor did he concede to the law any overall validity.[118]

In Best's eyes, therefore, the word "legality" did not imply that, all men being equal before the law, the ordinary citizen could obtain redress against the all-pervading power of the State; Best considered the law merely as a weapon to be used in the struggle for power, a "codification of the outcome of a preceding phase of struggle— accession of power on one side, loss of power on the other." He continued: "The goal of each individual authority within the State is to assure its dominance over the others; as a result all of them . . . seek to identify themselves with 'the State.' The State inevitably tends to maximise its authority; the more complete its predominance, the more perfect the State."[119]

In Best's case these were no empty words. In mid-1931, when the spectre of communist revolution was still abroad in Germany, Best attended a meeting of certain Nazis in a farmhouse named "Boxheim" near Worms and expounded both verbally and in writing his thoughts on a National-Socialist counter-revolution; they soon became notorious as the "Boxheim Documents." He proposed, for instance, that after "the disappearance of the old high-level State authorities and after the suppression of the commune," the SA and local defence formations should "seize power in the leaderless State" and ruthlessly impose "the strictest discipline upon the population"; those carrying arms should be executed "without trial and on the spot."[120] A renegade Nazi gave Best's plans away to the police, who acted forthwith; Best was forbidden to practice in Hesse but, in October 1931, the Leipzig High Court decided not to proceed further against him "on grounds of lack of evidence."[121] The National Socialist seizure of power, however, gave Best, the police state theoretician, a place in the police; his friend, Dr Heinrich Müller, was nominated Reich Commissar in Hesse and asked Best to take over the police force there. Naturally he accepted.

As Police President of Hesse, however, Best soon fell foul of Sprenger, the Gauleiter, who disliked his critical realist attitude to the Party's requirements, and in autumn 1933 Best was sacked.[122] Meanwhile, however, he had joined the SS and, on losing his job in Hesse, was placed in charge of the SD-Oberabschnitte South and Southwest;[123] his name was therefore on Heydrich's list and in late 1934, when the latter set about expanding the Gestapo, Best was summoned. Little did Heydrich think that he was engaging his most persistent "wet blanket"—as he put it.[124] For in spite of all his theoretical longings for the national authoritarian state, in his heart of hearts Best was still a lawyer; a tiny remnant of the barrister's mental approach still remained. Moreover he was too firmly cast in the official mould and his thinking was too factual to enable him to compete with the unscrupulous opportunism characteristic of the rising generation of legally-trained SD functionaries such as Walter Schellenberg.

But these shades of difference between the Nazi police officials were still in the distant future. Heydrich and his new staff were now laying the foundations for the future machine of tyranny, the instrument whose name alone made millions of Germans shudder—the Gestapo.

Heydrich deliberately played upon the horror evoked by the name. Only a reputation for omniscience and pitiless action could make the Gestapo the Führer dictatorship's great deterrent weapon and stifle all possible opposition to the regime. Heydrich once said that the Gestapo was re-

garded with a mixture of "fear and horror"[125]—betraying
the secret satisfaction of a man who had reached his
goal.

The foundations of the Gestapo were laid by Göring as
Premier of Prussia. He had hived off from the Kripo
[Kriminalpolizei—Criminal Police] its specifically politi-
cal sections together with the Political Police which dealt
with high treason, and the counter-espionage police
[Abwehrpolizei] which dealt with treason. These were all
amalgamated into a new organisation known as the Secret
State Police [Geheime Staatspolizei—Gestapo].[126] Political police tasks had originally been the responsibility of
the Prussian LKPA [Landeskriminalpolizeiamt—Land
Criminal Police Office] which maintained a so-called "Ia
Abteilung" in each police Headquarters, that in Berlin
functioning as a sort of intelligence centre for the political
police as a whole. As part of the police, the Landeskrimi-
napolizeistellen [Land Criminal Police Offices] came under the jurisdiction of the Oberpräsidenten [Provincial
Prefects] and Regierungspräsidenten [Government Presi-
dents].[127]

All this Göring altered radically. In April 1933 the
Geheime Staatspolizeiamt [Secret State Police Office],
known as the Gestapa, took the place of the LKPA and
all branches of the Political Police were brought under a
single authority; the true Political Police, the core of the
Gestapo, became Abteilung III in the Gestapa and the
counter-espionage police became Abteilung IV; to these
were added Abteilung I(Organisation and Administration)
and Abteilung II (Legal).[128]

On the middle levels similar changes were made. In the
provinces the LKPA offices [Stellen] were replaced by
Gestapo Stellen which—and here was the decisive point—
were responsible to the Regierungspräsidenten on paper
only. From the end of 1933 the Gestapo claimed to be an
autonomous authority independent of the internal administration and responsible only to the Prussian Minister-
President. A sentence in the Prussian Gestapo law of 30
November 1933 stated in so many words that the head of
a Gestapo Stelle might conform to the "wishes" of the
Regierungspräsident but only "insofar as this does not
conflict with existing directives and instructions"—from
the Gestapa.[129]

The internal administration was, in effect, deprived of any say in political police matters and from 1 April 1934 the State Police Authorities were forbidden to maintain political sections.[130] When, in addition, it is remembered that the emergency ordinance "For Protection of People and State" issued by the Reich President on 28 February 1933 had suspended all basic legal rights and empowered the police to make house searches, carry out arrests, confiscate property, tap telephones and open letters—all without a Court Order[131]—a more powerful police than Göring's Gestapo can hardly be imagined.

But this did not satisfy the secret-police perfectionist, Heydrich. He spent his time painting the dangers to the regime in the most glaring colours. In fact he followed the procedure which a dictatorship's Chief of Police invariably adopts when he wishes to initiate build-up of his terror machine—he creates an enemy of the State.

As Head of the Gestapo, Heydrich suddenly emerged from his anonymity and sounded the alarm to the world at large. In a speech early in 1935 he upbraided his Party comrades for failure to understand that, although "the enemy organisations had been smashed," the enemy had by no means been annihilated; the regime's enemies had "co-ordinated" themselves and must now be "sought out in their new positions." "The enemy motive forces," he explained, "will always be the same—world Jewry, world Freemasonry and the clergy who are to a large extent political"; more dangerous, however, than this "visible" enemy was the undercover enemy: "He works outside the law. His objective is the destruction of the leadership's unity, both in Party and State . . . the ramifications of this network are enormous."[132]

The build-up of the control machinery could now begin. The Gestapo Sections [Abteilungen] were expanded into three divisions [Hauptabteilungen] and the general staff of terror took over.

The new arrivals set out to draw Göring's police net ever tighter round the population. If, however, action against the "enemies of the State" was to be intensified, the Gestapo had to know who these enemies were. Göring had often left his officials wondering, but in general terms "enemy of the State" had seemed to be synonymous with

"Communist" or "Marxist." The new masters of the Prinz-Albrecht-Strasse, however, left no one in any doubt.

"An enemy of the State is anyone who consciously opposes the People, the Party and the State, their ideological tenets or their political actions"—said SS-Hauptsturmführer Alfred Schweder[133]; in an internal memorandum Wendzio, an ex-Criminal Police official, described the enemies of the State in terms more comprehensible to the simpler Gestapo intellects: "In detail the term covers: Communism, Marxism, Jewry, political activities by the Churches, Freemasonry, political malcontents (grousers), national opposition, reaction, the 'Black Front' (Strasser, Prague), industrial saboteurs, habitual criminals, abortionists and homosexuals (offences from the demographic point of view against the strength and defence capacity of the people, risk of espionage in the case of homosexuals), treason and high treason." According to Wendzio, this conglomeration of evil-doers had a single "goal" in common; their efforts were directed against "the spiritual and racial patrimony of the German people."[134]

A highly developed system of lists and card indexes kept track of every conceivable opponent of the regime. The Gestapa in Berlin and its out-stations in the provinces kept a so-called "A" card index, wherein "dangerous" enemies of the State (in the Gestapo sense of the word) were divided into three groups:

Group A1, distinguished by a red tab on the left of the card, consisted of opponents of the regime who were to be arrested as soon as unobtrusive preparations for general mobilisation were initiated.

Group A2 (Blue Tabs) listed persons to be arrested on a public announcement of mobilisation.

Group A3 (Green Tabs) consisted of persons who were not security risks but who, in Heydrich's words "in times of stress . . . must be regarded as so dangerous politically, that their apprehension or close supervision must be considered."[135]

Yet another system of coloured tabs enabled the Gestapo to draw even finer distinctions between their victims. Enemies of the State were further classified by a

second tab on the right of the card—dark red for a
Communist, light red for a "Marxist," brown for an
"assassin" and violet for a "grumbler." Cards were
checked twice yearly on 1 April and 1 October to ensure
that the classifications still held good.[136]

So detailed a system for keeping "enemies of the State"
under observation naturally necessitated continuous expansion of the authority and activities of the Secret
Police. The Gestapa was formed from Abteilung Ia in
Berlin Police Headquarters which had a staff of 35, but
by early 1935 it had reached a strength of 607 officials
and employees; in 1933 the Gestapo's annual budget was
around 1,000,000 marks but by 1937 it had reached
40,000,000 marks.[137]

The Gestapo "Stellen" [local offices] in each Regier-
ungsbezirk [Government Administrative District] and the
"Leitstellen" [Regional Offices], formed in 1937 at the
headquarters of each Oberpräsident or Land Government,
increased in size.[138] The counter-espionage police began to
encroach upon the preserves of the military counter-
espionage service. Gradually, the frontier control service
came under the Gestapo's wing. The Frontier Commissariats, hitherto under the LKPA, were attached to the
Gestapo and given the status of "out-station" to the local
Gestapo Stelle.[139] Later the Gestapo created its own frontier police which in fact had nothing to do with frontier
control but carried out purely secret-police functions. Its
task was to apprehend enemies of the regime on the
frontier and track down persons suspected of treason: for
this reason it came under Desk [Referat] G of Hauptabteilung III of the Gestapa, in other words the counter-
espionage police.[140]

An iron curtain descended on the frontiers of Hitler
Germany. A carefully calculated tracking system was supposed to guarantee that no fugitive could escape the
Gestapo's all-seeing eye. Various types of search warrant
were instituted—local warrants (for action by the local
police and municipal authorities) and State Police warrants. Again colours were used to differentiate between
the criminals—brick-red for escaped prisoners and white
with red stripes for deportees.[141] Eight letters were used to
signify the object of the search:

A   Arrest
B   Arrest, if no fixed address
C   Report place of residence
D   For deportation
E   Search for missing persons
F   Recover lost papers
G   Unobtrusive observation
V   Professional criminal—arrest.[142]

The greater the power of the police, the easier it became for the Gestapo to keep track of people. In later years, for instance, stateless persons due for deportation were consigned to a concentration camp by the Gestapa pending completion of the formalities. Everything, of course, had to be done in proper form; a minute from Best, dated 26 July 1937, for instance, states: "The acceptance of the stateless person into the concentration camp designated by me will take place through the Land Police Authority, under the provisions of Gestapa Form No. 240. On acceptance of the deportee, the concentration camp will forward to me the top copy of Gestapa Form No. 240, together with the index card Gestapa No. 98 carrying a photograph of the deportee." Only when some other country had signified willingness to accept the deportee was he allowed to leave the concentration camp. Best laid down: "Before passing him across the frontier, the Frontier Police Authority will obtain from the stateless person a statement in duplicate recognising that, should he return, he runs the risk of detention in a concentration camp."[143]

The authority to issue warrants for preventive arrest, and consign men to concentration camps placed a murderous weapon in the hands of the Gestapo. It undermined the rule of law in Germany and all the machinery of judge, solicitor and defence counsel was unable to prevent men suddenly disappearing behind the barbed wire of the concentration-camps.

The highest authority for the issue of preventive arrest warrants was the Gestapa; unhampered by any legal system, it had the power to consign initially every Prussian, and later every German, to a concentration camp for an unspecified period. Lower-level Gestapo offices could also place men under preventive arrest, but only for a period of seven days. If the order was not confirmed by the Gestapa, the prisoner had to be released on the eighth day.[144] As soon as Heydrich took over the Gestapo, however, the number of concentration-camp prisoners rose; in 1935–36 alone over 7,000 "Marxists" were arrested[145] on grounds explained by Dr Best as follows: "Any attempt to gain recognition for, or even to uphold, different political ideas will be ruthlessly dealt with as the symptom of a disease which threatens the healthy unity of the indivisible national organism, regardless of the subjective wishes of its supporters."[146]

However, the more menacing the growth of the Gestapo's power became, the more numerous its enemies grew. The lawyers and the bureaucrats combined to halt, or at least to retard, the Gestapo's victorious progress—and they were aiming at nothing less than the removal of the Gestapo's favourite weapon, the concentration camp. Certain courageous lawyers uncovered crimes and abuses in the concentration camps and publicised them in the hope of persuading the more moderate Nazi leaders to disband these torture factories.[147]

As early as summer 1933, when Heydrich and Himmler were setting up their trial system of terror in Bavaria, individual lawyers had begun to play a carefully concealed game. The Public Prosecutor's office of State Court II, Munich, was alerted to numerous unexplained cases of death in Dachau concentration camp; on 2 June 1933, in a memorandum to the Bavarian Ministry of Justice, it stated that "the proceedings regarding the events in Dachau Concentration Camp are to be pursued with all determination."[148] On several occasions the Public Prosecutor's office recorded its findings on murders in Dachau. In the second fortnight of May 1933 it enquired into the deaths of four Dachau prisoners (Schloss, Hausmann, Strauss and Nefzger) and found that they had been tortured to death by the camp guards. At the end of September 1933 the office insisted on a post-mortem examination of the body of Hugo Handschuch, another prisoner who had died in Dachau; conclusion—"haemorrhage originating from blows with a blunt instrument. Evidence of guilt on the part of third parties." In late October 1933 the same office attempted to clear up the supposed suicides of two further prisoners, Wilhelm Franz

and Dr Delwin Katz; judgment—"the autopsy gave
grounds for a well-founded suspicion that in the case of
both corpses force by an outside hand had been applied
... strangulation and throttling."[149]

The Public Prosecutor's office, Munich II, then requested authority from the Ministry of Justice to check
the legitimacy of the arrangements in Dachau and filed
cases for incitement to murder against SS-Oberführer
Hilmar Wäkkerle, the Camp Commandant, Dr Nuern-
bergk, the Camp Medical Officer and Mutzbauer, the
Head of the Camp Office.[150] Himmler was obliged to sack
the Camp Commandant.[151] Himmler and Heydrich, however, reacted all the more violently against any attempt
by the Public Proescutor's office to investigate other cases.
They persuaded Wagner, the Minister of the Interior, to
propose to the Cabinet that in the case of concentration-
camp crimes investigation should be refused "for reasons
of State policy."[152]

The majority of the Bavarian Cabinet, however, rejected
Wagner's proposal, so Himmler now raised another obstacle between the Public Prosecutor and the Concentration Camp. He persuaded Hans Frank, the Minister of
Justice, to issue an instruction to all Public Prosecutors
"to refrain for the time being from making an application
for the opening of preliminary investigations."[153]

The Public Prosecutor, however, persisted. On 12 July
1934 he requested the Bavarian Political Police "in consultation with the Commandant of Dachau Concentration
Camp, to clarify further the facts of the case and attempt
to discover the persons suspected as the culprits." Heydrich's Political Police commented acidly: "The latest application by the Public Prosecutor, Munich II, for production of evidence shows what far-fetched means are
employed to saddle the Dachau Concentration Camp
with alleged crimes."[154] The camp staff hastened to cover
their tracks and on 27 September 1934 Wintersberger, the
Public Prosecutor, was forced to suspend proceedings.[155]

Himmler now thought up a clever manoeuvre to tie the
hands of the Public Prosecutors. The leading light of the
anti-Dachau group was Dr Walther Steppe, the senior
State Attorney; he was a convinced National-Socialist and
Himmler persuaded him to join the SS, feeding him the
story that, as an SS-Hauptsturmführer, he would be better

placed to deal with the abuses in Dachau. So from critic of the Political Police, Steppe turned into its functionary—one year later he was its Deputy Chief.[156]

In Prussia too, brave men were found to take up the cudgels against concentration-camp crime. Diels, the first Head of the Gestapo, disbanded numerous "unofficial" concentration camps, the majority run by the SA. He planned to use the Minister's authority to suppress political crime and persuaded two National-Socialists in the Ministry of Justice, Werner von Haacke and Gunther Joel, to support him. Within the Prussian Ministry of Justice these two set up a central Public Prosecutor's Office which, though primarily occupied in dealing with the SA gangsters, from time to time contrived to attack criminals in the Gestapo and the SS.[157]

Von Haacke scored the first major success of his campaign in a battle with the Stettin Gestapo Office. SS-Sturmführer Joachim Hoffmann, the Head of the Office, maintained a concentration camp in the Vulkan Shipyard, Stettin-Bredow, where men were bestially tortured (in Gestapo slang "Vulkanised"). Haacke succeeded in arresting Hoffmann and recalls that he found standing before him, "a fanatical, sadistic intellectual with an absence of feeling such as I had never experienced before. I have only known one other man whose character, even his manner and his gestures, immediately reminded me of Hoffmann—and that man was Heydrich."[198] On 6 April 1934 No. 2 High Court Stettin condemned Hoffmann to 13 years hard labour; his assistants also received prison sentences.[159]

Encouraged by this success, other members of the legal profession began to resist the SS torturers. Dr Walther Schaeffer, the Public Prosecutor of Breslau, showed particular courage; after the 30 June blood bath, he arrested 20 SS men, including two Standartenführer, as suspected murderers and was only forced to release them after prolonged argument with Roland Freisler, the Permanent Secretary in the Ministry of Justice.[160] The departure of Diels, however, and Göring's defection to the Himmler-Heydrich camp left the lawyers without protection, half-hearted though it had frequently been. At a sitting of the Prussia, Staatsrat [State Council] in November 1934, Göring fulminated: "There are still State Attorneys who specialise in dragging senior members of the Party off to prison, but we will bring their dirty work to an end."[161]

Nevertheless some lawyers still refused to be intimidated. Early in 1935 Dr Walther, the State Attorney of Saxony, laid a charge of serious maltreatment of prisoners against an SA man, the Head of the Hohnstein concentration camp; the Gestapo was also involved and Walther prepared a separate case against Erich Vogel, the Gestapo official responsible. The concentration-camp thugs were duly condemned to several years imprisonment, but then Mutschmann, the Gauleiter of Saxony, brought pressure to bear on the Court and demanded their release. This brought a protest from Dr Franz Gürtner, the Reich Minister of Justice: "However bitter the struggle, there can be no explanation or excuse for such cruelties; they are reminiscent of oriental sadism." The Court confirmed its sentence but the Nazis soon had their revenge. The two Court assessors were expelled from the Party and the State Attorney was requested to leave the SA. Then Hitler, the supreme judge, intervened—he pardoned the accused and quashed the case against Vogel.[162]

At heart, Gürtner, the Minister of Justice, was still a liberal nationalist and such arbitrary action turned his mind towards a desperate, even foolhardy, plan; the only method, he thought, of curbing the despotism of the Führer dictatorship and the Gestapo would be to produce an abridged form of the legal code in National-Socialist style, thus preserving the essential minimum of legal norms, by which even Hitler and his minions would be bound.[163] Gürtner found an ally in the new Reich Commissar for Justice, Dr Hans Frank, the most extreme of all the National-Socialist guardians of the law. Frank's object was a fundamental de-liberalisation of the entire legal code, which he then proposed to base upon a new, somewhat hazy, notion—the protection of the so-called "popular values." Nevertheless Frank was opposed to arbitrary action by an omnipotent police force. Unfortunately not until he was under sentence at Nuremberg did he perceive "the horrifying thing about Adolf Hitler"—"that in his struggle period he had himself enjoyed the protection of the law but later, as a statesman, had shown contempt for the law and the legal profession."[164] Even on 30 June 1934 Frank had found in the Stadelheim Prison that the hands of justice were tied by the Führer dictatorship; his experience at that time sowed within him the seeds of doubt which caused him, when Governor General of Poland in 1942, to lead the most sustained public attack on Heinrich Himmler's police despotism ever made in the greater German Reich.

In late 1933, Frank and Gürtner set up an "Official Criminal Law Commission" [Amtliche Strafrechtskommission] to work out a new punishment code. Frank contributed the National-Socialist slogans, which the assiduous Roland Freisler dressed up in paragraphs; meanwhile Gürtner and his amanuensis Dohnanyi, who later became a Clerk of the High Court and was eventually executed in connection with the 20 July 1944 plot, sought means of preventing Hitler and the Gestapo from treating the law in too cavalier a fashion.[165] In the process, however, Gürtner managed to persuade Frank to support him in his major objective—the abolition of the concentration camps.

In summer 1934 Frank and Gürtner plucked up their courage "to attack Hitler direct" (Frank's words). A meeting was held in the cabinet room of the Reich Chancellery with Hitler and Himmler present and the two lawyers put forward their arguments against the concentration-camp system.[166] In his memoirs Frank says: "I proposed that the earliest possible terminal date should be set for the entire system and that an immediate halt should be called to further arrests; I further proposed that the cases of all persons still under arrest, together with all complaints of ill-treatment, should be examined under the law, in other words by the normal courts. Dr Gürtner supported me energetically but he and I were alone." Hitler rejected the proposal, saying that it was "premature" to abolish the concentration camps. Even Frank's new punishment code he later pigeon-holed.[167]

Gürtner, however, continued to search for methods of restricting the power of the Gestapo and the injustices of the preventive detention system. He amassed a wealth of evidence on unadmitted cases of death in the concentration camps and eventually demanded that persons under preventive detention be accorded the right to demand legal aid from a qualified attorney. But Himmler would have none of it, merely noting: "The concentration camps

are conscientiously run and special measures are not therefore considered necessary." He knew, of course, that he
would invariably be supported by Hitler; on 6 November
1935 he wrote to Gürtner: "On 1 November I transmitted
to the Führer and Reich Chancellor the request submitted
to us that lawyers should be permitted to intervene in
protective custody cases. The Führer has prohibited the
consultation of lawyers and has asked me to inform you
accordingly."[168]

Gürtner was weak and over-cautious and so inevitably
he failed in face of the inflexible determination of Himmler and Heydrich. Moreover many of the lawyers
brought up in the nineteenth-century school of legal positivism showed themselves incapable of thinking more
deeply; in the euphoria of the Nazi Führer cult they soon
allowed themselves to become no more than dutiful
underlings. So the opposition was doomed to failure.

The tone of the legal profession was not set by courageous champions of the law such as Schaeffer, nor by
cautious defenders of the established system such as
Gürtner; the tone was set by time-serving legal doctri-
naires such as Carl Schmitt, who hoped "to do away with
the restrictions of precedent and the compulsion to base
judgments upon findings of fact" and turn the legal profession "into creative collaborators of the Führer's will."[169]
The *juristische Wochenschrift* [Legal Weekly] of 1934[170]
cried: "Away with the pettifogging yoke of positivist law."
And Germany's judges began, with increasing lack of
scruple, to underpin the might of the Gestapo. On 2 May
1935 the Prussian Administrative High Court decided that
the actions of the Gestapa could not be contested in the
Administrative Courts; the only recourse was registration of
a disciplinary complaint with the Head of the Gestapa.[171]
On 7 October 1935 the Hamburg Administrative Court
laid down that "in the National-Socialist State, the legisla-
ture, the administration and the judiciary cannot be legally
opposed . . . the judiciary cannot, therefore, invoke
another point of view and disavow action by the State
taken as a political measure."[172]

From his desk in the Gestapa, Best observed with
pleasure the agility with which the judiciary was attempting to adapt itself; he forwarded the judgments of the
Courts to all Gestapo Stellen for information and delecta-

tion.[173] Step by step the majority of the Judges moved closer to Best's cynical definition of police action: "In so far as the police are acting in accordance with the rules laid down by their superiors—right up to the highest level—they can never be acting 'lawlessly' or 'contrary to the law.' Provided the police are carrying out the will of the Leadership, they are acting legally."[174]

As Minister of Justice Gürtner was indignant: "It is enough to drive one to despair!" He told Dr Sahm, the Burgomeister of Berlin, that he hardly dared go to a reception now, since foreign journalists were always asking him about conditions in the concentration camps. Sahm asked what Frick, the Minister of the Interior, was doing about it. Gürtner waved him away saying: "Göring and Heydrich carry a hundred times more weight than Frick."[175] Gürtner knew only too well that Frick, the timorous Nazi conservative, was trying desperately to get rid of the miracle man whom he had once called in to help him against Göring. Frick was in fact repenting bitterly that he had handed over a unified Reich Police Force to so dangerous a man as Himmler.

All Frick's efforts would have been in vain had he not been joined by two senior bureaucrats who, though supporters of the regime, refused to accept the Gestapo's claim to increasingly wide authority over the administration. Ironically the leaders of the anti-Gestapo cabal were two men ostensibly closely connected with the SS—Eggert Reeder, the Regierungspräsident of Aachen, a sponsoring member and later an SS-Gruppenführer,[176] and his counterpart in Cologne, SS-Standartenführer Rudolf Diels,[177] Göring's ex-protégé, who had contributed more than any other official to the increase of the Gestapo's authority.

Frick and the two Regierungspräsidenten played their cards well in their efforts to curb the Gestapo's influence, at least outside Berlin. The Gestapo law of 30 November 1933 had deprived the Oberpräsidenten and Regierungspräsidenten of all authority over the Gestapo Stellen;[178] the object at this stage, therefore, was to recapture some control over the Gestapa's outposts in the country as a whole. Frick opened the campaign on 16 July 1934 with a circular addressed to all Oberpräsidenten and Regierungspräsidenten;[179] it contained a singular sentence to the effect that "there was general agreement" that the in-

dependence of the Gestapo was "only a transitory phase
necessitated by the tense political situation resulting from
the Röhm revolt." Frick went on to lay down that there
must be "the closest collaboration between the Gestapo
and the Administration to ensure that Oberpräsidenten and
Regierungspräsidenten are kept continuously informed of
the activities of the Gestapo Stellen."[180] In other words,
Frick was subordinating the Gestapo to the Administration.

From Aachen Reeder wrote promptly to the Minster
of the Interior in August 1934, saying that the Regierungspräsident must "assume actual undisputed political responsibility for his District" and therefore "inevitably the
Head of the Gestapo Stelle is one of my subordinates."[181]
Diels was even more explicit; on 4 November 1934 he
wrote to Göring: "The separation of the political police
from the remainder of the Administration must, in the
long run, lead to difficulties of which you, Herr Minister-
präsident, are no doubt aware. To this 'erosion' of the internal administration are added all the difficulties associated with the predominance of the Party over the State
. . . the notion of political reliability must finally be done
away with . . . this notion is at the root of the shameful
lack of confidence which is hampering the work of the
State Administration."[182]

East Prussia's Oberpräsident, the fanatical anti-SS
Gauleiter, Erich Koch, also complained about the
Gestapo's sleuths, and called for assistance from Frick.
On 23 September 1935, referring to the situation in
Königsberg, Frick wrote to Himmler: "I consider the
present relationship between the Oberpräsident and the
head of the Gestapo Stelle to be impossible in the long term
and highly injurious to the authority of the State." Himmler replied characteristically: "The Führer has decided
that no change should be made in the position of the
Königsberg Gestapo."[183]

The bureaucrats, however, brought such pressure to
bear on the police machine that Himmler and Heydrich
eventually declared themselves ready to negotiate a new
Gestapo law with the Ministry of the Interior. After
months of haggling the law was issued on 10 February
1936. In effect it confirmed the existing situation; nevertheless in paragraph 5 it said: "Gestapo Stellen are, at

the same time, *subordinate* to the relevant Regierungspräsident, will conform to his instructions and will keep
him informed of all political police matters."[184]

To offset their concessions to the Administration, Himmler and Heydrich now demanded that the Ministry
of the Interior fulfil its promise to put through legislation
establishing a Reich Police Force. Basically the question
had long since been decided. After their capture of the
Gestapo in April 1934, Himmler and Heydrich had set
up within the Gestapa a "Central Bureau—Land Political
Police Commanders,"[185] which in practice co-ordinated
the work of the Land police authorities with that of the
Gestapo. In fact Himmler was already commanding the
political police throughout the Reich and the only
question remaining was the form in which he would exercise authority over the entire German Police Force,
including its non-political elements.

Their partial success over the Gestapo law, however,
had made the Ministry of the Interior officials bellicose
and they now prepared a further line of resistance
against the two SS men. They began toying with the idea
of placing the unified police force under the Minister of
the Interior and playing off against Himmler, whom they
regarded as too powerful already, his Berlin rival, SS-
Obergruppenführer and Police Lieutenant-General Kurt
Daluege. As early as May 1933, when commanding the
Prussian Land Police, Daluege had worked out plans
envisaging what in local jargon was called "Reichifica-
tion" of the political police.[186] The idea suited Frick and
henceforth he regarded Daluege as the future German
police chief. When the Prussian Ministry of the Interior
was absorbed into the Reich Ministry, Frick took on the
pliable Daluege as head of the new police department.
Himmler's rise to power in the summer of 1934 did not
of course help Frick's plans for Daluege; nevertheless
he asked his Ministry's legal experts to draw up a command organisation for the new Reich Police Force, as
far as possible excluding Himmler.

Frick's concept of the police command organisation
was this: the entire police force of the Reich to be
concentrated under the Reich Ministry of the Interior;
Himmler, as Inspector of the Gestapo to take over the
police department within the Ministry as the subordinate

of the Minister and with Police General Daluege as permanent deputy. According to Hans-Joachim Neufeldt, Frick's object clearly was "to relegate Himmler to a purely political and protocol role, while exercising actual command of the entire police force through Daluege."[187]

Himmler rejected Frick's proposals. On 9 June 1936, speaking in the name of his Reichsführer, Heydrich demanded overriding authority; Himmler, he said, must be given ministerial rank, be on a level with the Commanders-in-Chief of the armed forces, be entitled "Reichsführer-SS and Chief of the German Police" and be subordinate to the Minister of the Interior only "in his personal capacity"—in other words not at all. Himmler was therefore demanding undisputed control of the police machine. In a fury Frick sought an interview with Hitler but the Führer calmed the indignant Minister down; Himmler he said would not be given Ministerial rank; he would only be invited to cabinet discussions as a "State Secretary." Nevertheless, the Minister of the Interior returned a broken man—Hitler had given him to understand that Himmler's appointment as head of the police was a foregone conclusion.[188]

The Minister could now only manoeuvre in retreat. He objected that a Party office (Reichsführer-SS) should not be combined with a Governmental office (Chief of the German Police). In the draft of the law he added the words "within the Reich Ministry of the Interior" after Himmler's title in four places. He clung tenaciously to his demand that Daluege should be Himmler's permanent deputy.[189] Himmler withdrew a fraction of an inch. He abandoned his demand for Ministerial rank; he allowed himself to become the "personal and direct" subordinate of the Minister of the Interior—an almost meaningless term in the topsy-turvy Nazi phraseology; he accepted Daluege as his permanent deputy but only "in the case of his [Himmler's] absence."[190]

Hardly was the ink dry on Hitler's decree of 17 June 1936, nominating a Chief of the German Police, than Himmler showed what his interpretation of his new authority was. He not only demanded authority over the entire Police Department, but he also grabbed certain other important spheres of activity within the Ministry of the Interior—legal matters concerning the press

and the carrying of arms, arms traffic, passports, personnel questions concerning all officials of the Police Department including Police Presidents and Police Directors.[191]

Frick's candidate, Daluege, was left at the post. He
ranked only as number three, with both Himmler and
Heydrich above him, for, as in Bavaria, Himmler allotted
the key role to Heydrich. As Chief of the German Police, Himmler set up beneath him two Hauptabteilungen
entitled Hauptämter [Departments]:

Hauptamt Sicherheitspolizei [Security Police] under SS-
   Gruppenführer Reinhard Heydrich. It included the
   Gestapo and the Criminal Police.
Hauptamt Ordnungspolizei [Regular Police] under
   SS-Obergruppenführer and Police General Kurt Dal-
   uege. It included the Schutzpolizei [Urban Constabu-
   lary] the Gendarmerie [Rural Constabulary] and
   the Gemeindepolizei [Municipal Police].[192]

The entire police force of Hitler's Germany was now
in Himmler's grip. Now he and Heydrich could initiate
Phase Two of their great plan—the fusion of SS and
Police into the Third Reich's State Protection Corps.

9

The SD

ON 27 January 1937 the Prussian Landeskriminal-polizeiamt [Land Criminal Police Office—LKPA], the Headquarters of all Kripo Offices in Germany, was on stand-by alert. The LKPA teleprinters tapped out a message telling all Kripo Leitstellen and Stellen throughout the Reich what Headquarters considered to be the most urgent task in the anti-criminal campaign.

The Alexanderplatz Headquarters required "speedy transmission of a list of all criminals in your district, who in the opinion of the Criminal Police must be regarded as professional and habitual criminals or as habitual offenders against morality and who are at liberty."[1] The Kripo Stellen were ordered to draw up lists allocating a number to each known criminal. The order continued: "When the time comes, only the list number of the professional criminals concerned will be telegraphically transmitted."[2]

A month later all was ready. On 23 February the Chief of the German Police issued an instruction to the Prussian LKPA that on 9 March "some 2,000 professional and habitual criminals or dangerous offenders against morality will be taken into preventive police custody." Once more the LKPA teleprinters tapped out the orders and on 9 March the great manhunt duly began throughout Germany. The Criminal Police swarmed out and 2,000 prisoners were delivered to Sachsenhausen, Sachsenburg, Lichtenburg and Dachau concentration camps.[3]

This action directed from the LKPA ushered in the most controversial non-political measure in the history

221

of the Third Reich's police—the preventive method of
crime suppression. Heydrich's Sicherheitspolizei, which now
included the Criminal Police, labelled whole categories of
persons "anti-social malefactors" [Volksschädling] and
placed them under preventive arrest regardless of legal
considerations.

The initiative had come from the Kripo: they had
long been urging severe preventive measures to control
the habitual criminal[4] and Sicherheitspolizei Headquarters
seized on the idea. By virtue of paragraph 42 of the
Reich Criminal Code, the Courts were now authorised
to order preventive arrest in the interests of public security;[5] but in the eyes of the Sicherheitspolizei the Courts
were overscrupulous in the use of their new-found authority, their decisions too "liberalistic," too regulation."[6]

The Sicherheitspolizei therefore now claimed for themselves the right to place a so-called professional criminal
under preventive arrest—and in the Third Reich that
meant the concentration camp. As their reason they
maintained that a court could only judge how dangerous
a criminal was in the light of a single act of crime; the
police, on the other hand, possessed knowledge of all
the internal and external circumstances affecting the criminal and so could form a broader judgment.[7]

There was a difficulty here: legally the police had
no authority to place a criminal under preventive arrest;
the procedure was embodied in no law,[8] but the
Sicherheitspolizei found a way out. Best, the SD's legal
expert, later gave a lecture on the subject and his argument ran as follows: a legal basis for this police procedure did exist since, in accordance with the Völkisch
concept of law, both the authorities and individual members of the public were representatives of the people and
they "must work together for the maintenance of law
and order in accordance with rules laid down by the
leadership for the attainment of the people's aims." Even
in a case of arrest those representatives were working
together, the police being the active partner and "the
criminal who is taken into preventive custody being the
passive."[9] More cold-blooded and cynical use of seman-
tics can hardly be imagined—the criminal was assisting
the police by allowing himself to be arrested and incarcerated in a concentration camp! Use of preventive

arrest for the suppression of crime, however, meant that
the normal system of justice was deprived of its right to
conduct an unprejudiced examination of each individual
case. So a process began in which "the community was
treated like a nursery garden where the ill-grown shoot
has to be 'pricked out' and 'rooted out' at regular intervals."[10] Crime in Germany had not noticeably increased at
the time,[11] but nevertheless the Sicherheitspolizei prescribed a seasonal quota of arrests. The Chief of the
German Police, or his immediate subordinate the Chief
of the Sicherheitspolizei, simply decided when a new in-
take of criminals was due for the concentration camps.[12]

This system of preventive arrest was but a further
illustration of the power Heydrich now possessed. Since
Himmler's nomination in June 1936 as Chief of the German Police and his own appointment as Head of the
Sicherheitspolizei, Heydrich had commanded an instrument of tyranny unparalleled in German history.

In the grasping hands of Himmler and Heydrich the
words "Security Police" took on a new meaning. In legal
parlance "Security Police" had hitherto been used to
describe the police as a whole with its two main groupings, the Administrative Police (e.g. Traffic Police and
Industrial Police) and the Executive Police; the latter
was divided into four branches, the Kripo [Criminal
Police] the Schupo [Urban Constabulary], the Political
Police and the Gendarmerie.[13] Himmler, however, hived
off from the Executive Police its politically significant
branches, the Political Police and the Criminal Police,
and formed the Sicherheitspolizei [Security Police—Si-
po] under Heydrich. The remainder of the Executive Police and the Administrative Police he left to his SS rival,
Kurt Daluege; they were merged to form the new Ordnungspolizei [Regular Police—Orpo].[14]

Parallel to Daluege's Hauptamt Ordungspolizei and subordinate to the "Reichsführer-SS and Chief of the German
Police," Heydrich formed the Hauptamt Sicherheitspolizei, which ranked as a ministerial authority under the
Reich Ministry of the Interior. However, since Hauptamt
Sicherheitspolizei had no legal authority to make arrests
or order interrogations, it had to rely upon two existing
police organisations—the Gestapo and the Prussian
LKPA; as supreme Land authority the Gestapa admin-

istered the Secret State Police in Prussia and as supreme
Reich authority it administered the Political Police in all
other German Länder (Political Police terminology in the
other Länder had been brought into line with that of
Prussia on 1 October 1936); the Prussian LKPA, which
had directed the Kripo in the other Länder, was now
officially re-named Reichskriminalpolizeiamt [Reich Criminal Police Office—RKPA] and became a supreme Reich
Authority responsible for the entire German Criminal
Police Force.[15]

The Gestapo and the RKPA remained part of Hauptamt Sicherheitspolizei, as so-called "Reich Specialist
Headquarters"; Abteilung I (Administration and Legal) of
the Gestapa, however, was hived off and became a ministerial authority directly under the Ministry of the Interior.[16] Hauptamt Sicherheitspolizei therefore consisted
eventually of the Administration and Legal Department,
under Dr Werner Best, the Political Police under Heinrich Müller, the Counter-Espionage Police under Dr
Werner Best, and the criminal Police under Arthur
Nebe.[17]

Here was a vast concentration of power. The Sicherheitspolizei was continually extending its control over
different spheres of the nation's life and gradually it
created an area within which the rule of law did not
exist and into which no other official institution or legal
authority was able to penetrate. On paper Hauptamt
Sicherheitspolizei was a Ministry of the Interior authority
and Heydrich a subordinate of the Minister;[18] in practice, however, Heydrich gave Frick no insight into what
he was doing—the fact that his more important offices
were far removed from the Ministry was not accidental.

Heydrich worked tirelessly to screen his machine from
prying eyes. His quick-witted lawyers could always produce some sophism to convince the gullible citizenry
that arbitrary police action was a more exalted form of
law. The ever-inventive Best, for instance, declared that
in relation to police work legal rules were unnecessary
since Hitler's will "created law and altered existing law."[19]
Professor Reinhard Höhn of the SD went one better. He
proposed to abolish the concept both of the State and
the individual as persons in law; the State, he said, was

not an end in itself but merely a means of attaining the
people's goal as laid down by the Führer.[20]

If, however, the concept of State and individual as persons under law was abolished, the citizen had no further
redress against arbitrary action by the police. No Sicherheitspolizei measure could be contested in law, neither
before the administrative courts nor by an action for
compensation for damages, nor by a private libel suit,
and certainly not by criminal proceedings for deprivation
of liberty. Only one recourse was open to the citizen
and it was a dangerous procedure—a disciplinary complaint to the Head of the Sicherheitspolizei.[21]

The law thus being powerless, Heydrich was in effect
able to decide for himself how far his power over the
defenceless citizenry should extend. His power to order
preventive arrest and send men to concentration camps
made him absolute master of life and liberty.[22] The
Minister of the Interior's decree of 12 April 1934, laying
down the principles for preventive arrest, did indeed state
that "protective custody shall not be used as punishment
for criminal offences or offences which . . . are repre-
hensible"; these were to be "dealt with by the courts"
alone.[23] The Sipo, however, took it upon itself to amend
and increase sentences passed by the courts.

When prisoners were released from the normal gaols
on conclusion of sentence, Heydrich's men were waiting
at the gates and any who fell into the following categories
were automatically consigned to concentration camps:
persons condemned for treasonable activities; Communist officials; anyone condemned by a "Peoples Court";
and members of the banned International Bible Research
Association (whose pacifist pronouncements were regarded
by the Sipo as incitement to refusal of military service).[24]

According to the whim of Heydrich and his minions
politically suspect persons could either be handed over
to the courts or despatched to a concentration camp.
In most cases their destination was the latter, for preventive arrest, as opposed to police arrest, was subject to no
examination by the courts. On 26 February 1937 Heydrich instructed the Gestapa: "I desire that in future no
use should be made of the power to order police arrest,
so as to avoid the necessity for subsequent examination
by the courts of measures taken by the police. Imposition

of police arrest . . . is superfluous since in all these cases
the possibility of imposition of preventive arrest is open."[25]

But Heydrich did not confine himself solely to political
cases. The "enemy of the State" became an increasingly
all-embracing notion. Where political criteria did not fit
the bill, criminal police considerations came into the picture and the "enemy of the State" turned into the "anti-
social malefactor."[26] Using the preventive method of crime
suppression as a cover, the Sicherheitspolizei began to
sweep up into their net those groups on the fringe of
society who, by one method or another, had contrived to
evade the totalitarian grip of the regime. The circle of
those liable to preventive detention was drawn wider and
wider and the notion of the "anti-social malefactor" became increasingly imprecise.

Three ill-defined groups of potential concentration-camp inmates emerged: "Professional and habitual
criminals"—these were people who had been sentenced
to a minimum of six months imprisonment or hard labour
on three occasions; "anti-socials"—these were beggars,
tramps, gipsies, nomads, prostitutes, homosexuals, grum-
blers, drunkards, brawlers, traffic offenders, psychopaths,
lunatics and swindlers; "the work-shy"—these were men
who, according to Himmler, "could be proved to have
refused without adequate reason employment offered to
them on two occasions."[27] Anywhere and at any time the
Sicherheitspolizei could decide who belonged to these
categories and who, therefore, was destined for the concentration camp. Never before in Germany had men been
at the mercy of such liberty of decision on the part of the
police.

Nevertheless the apparently monolithic Sicherheitspolizei concealed certain internal weaknesses and tensions.
Heydrich's rapid rise to power had aroused the jealousy
of the more powerful SS leaders; the heads of the SS
Hauptämter were offended by his domineering manner
and even the mistrustful Himmler sometimes had to take
emergency action to slow his subordinate's headlong
progress.

In Adolf Hitler's Germany precedence belonged to the
man who could cut the broadest swathe through the jungle
of intrigue over prerogatives and spheres of authority.
The battle for authority took the place of the old parlia-

mentary squabbles; political power was measured in terms
of areas of jurisdiction, numbers of subordinates and
powers of command; mere rank and theoretical position
in the hierarchy meant little. In this jungle, however,
Heydrich's dominance was not yet complete. He could
issue warrants for preventive arrest but he did not control
the concentration camps. He accordingly suggested to
Himmler that he should take over administration of
the camps, probably calculating that if he could combine
the police and the camps under his own hand, his power
really would be total.

The concentration camp was the centrepiece of Himmler's police State; it was the silent ubiquitous threat hanging over every German. With its electrified barbed wire
and its wooden watch-towers, it lent sinister reality to
the SS-run system of police control. The very name
was intended to cast a spell over every German, to stifle
every movement of opposition. Eugen Kogon says: "Their
main purpose was the elimination of every trace
of actual or potential opposition to Nazi rule. Segregation,
debasement, humiliation, extermination—these were the
effective forms of terror."[28]

The SS masters of the concentration-camp world deliberately refused to allow the camps to become centres of
political re-education. The more gullible National-Socialists may genuinely have believed that the purpose of the
camps was to re-educate political opponents and, after
a probationary period, release them again; in practice,
however, the camps were planned from the outset as
instruments of terror for the maintenance of the regime.
Until, with the war, they became war production factories
manned by armies of slaves, the purpose of the camps
was to frighten and to deter. The torture sheds of
Dachau, Buchenwald and Sachsenhausen were intended to
demonstrate to the Germans the fate awaiting those who
opposed the Führer.

"Forget your wives, children and families. Here you
will die like dogs," was Karl Fritzsch's greeting to every
new batch of arrivals in his concentration camp.[29] Stories
which filtered through the barbed wire and were passed
on by the grapevine—of the Buchenwald "Cowstall" arranged for nape-of-the-neck shooting, of the Dachau
"Dog Kennel" where prisoners could only lie wedged to-

gether on their sides, or of the rigged accidents in the Mauthausen quarries[30]—simply increased the terror and panic which the words "concentration camp" induced in Hitler's Germany. If Heydrich was to be sole master of his machine of terror, however, he could not allow so powerful a tool of the Führer dictatorship to remain outside the Sicherheitspolizei for long. He was continually urging Himmler to place the camps under his Hauptamt, and shortly after the Gestapo law of 10 February 1936 an instruction was issued placing the concentration-camp administration under the Gestapo;[31] in his authoritative book published in 1938 Helmut Schlierbach says: "The political police in Prussia and the concentration camps were directly administered by the Gestapo through the Inspector."[32] As in the Diels period in the early 1930's the Gestapo once more appeared to have become masters of the concentration camps.[33]

But in fact Himmler had no intention of handing over the camps to Heydrich and the 1936 instruction remained a dead letter.[34] Himmler retained control of the concentration-camp system himself; they belonged to the SS as a whole. Heydrich was faced with a repetition of the events of March 1933; at that time Dachau had come under Himmler's command in his capacity as Political Police Commander Bavaria;[35] when, however, Heydrich as his deputy placed the administration of the camp under the Bavarian Political Police, Himmler barred his way with a man who refused to allow the newcomer to interfere.

This was Theodor Eicke, a failed police officer and an ex-Paymaster whom Himmler had rescued from a psychiatric clinic in Würzburg where he had been confined as a "dangerous lunatic" by his arch-enemy Gauleiter Bürckel. "Papa Eicke" was eternally grateful and consequently a pliant tool of his Reichsführer.[36]

His pleasant-sounding nickname was misleading. Eicke was an Alsatian with a grudge of explosive proportions against society, the legacy of a career which had failed at every stage: in 1919 shortage of cash had forced him to terminate his studies at the Ilmenau Technical College; in 1920 he became a police informer in Ilmenau but was dismissed without notice; he then attended the police school in Cottbus but was refused employment; he joined the Schutzpolizei in Weimar but was dismissed without

notice after a fortnight; he applied for a job at police
headquarters in Sorau but was refused.[37] For a man like
this there was only one hope left—the National-Socialist
revolution and a career in the SS. At the end of June 1933
Himmler promoted him SS-Oberführer and found him
employment for which he was totally suited—commandant of Dachau.[38]

Here Eicke found men of his own stamp, failures in
life nursing grudges which they worked off on the prisoners. Benedikt Kautsky, who was in Dachau, described
the camp staff as drawn from the stupidest and most in-
dolent section of the population who, when unemployment ended, saw no way of avoiding doing a decent job
of work other than joining the SS.[39] Under Eicke's experienced direction anyone who still retained a shred of
decency and humanity was very soon brutalised.

Later Eicke complained that on arrival in Dachau he
found "a corrupt guard detachment of barely 120 men"
and that in addition SS Oberabschnitt South had sent
him men "who for some reason or another the people in
Munich wished to get rid of." He continued: "We were
generally regarded as a necessary evil which unfortunately
cost money."[40] Eicke put his house in order with barbaric
discipline. He drew up a set of camp orders threatening
any prisoner who refused to obey with "being shot on the
spot or subsequently hanged for mutiny"; he inspired his
guard personnel with virulent hatred for the "enemies
of the State."[41]

Höss, later the commandant of Auschwitz, once heard
Eicke proclaim that pity for enemies of the State was
unworthy of an SS man; there was no room for weak-
lings in his unit and they would do well to lock themselves
up in monasteries as soon as possible; he had a use only
for hard, determined men who would carry out any order
ruthlessly; they did not wear the death's-head badge for
nothing.[42] Himmler was so delighted with Eicke's Regiment in Dachau that he decided to put the ex-Paymaster
in charge of all the concentration camps. After 30 June
1934 (when Eicke murdered Röhm) Himmler gave him
extraordinary powers; he became head of all concentration-camp guard units, the Totenkopfverbände
(Death's-head Formations—TV), and Inspector of Concentration Camps.[43]

Heydrich strove vainly to break Eicke's grip on the camps, but found himself hamstrung. Though theoretically a member of the SS-Hauptamt as "Inspector of Concentration Camps and Commander of SS Guard Formations," Eicke was Himmler's personal subordinate.[44]

Heydrich quietly collected evidence on the catastrophic conditions in the camps. Eicke had meanwhile concentrated the smaller scattered camps into four—Dachau, Sachsenhausen, Buchenwald and Lichtenburg; in 1937, when the lowest figure of concentration-camp prisoners was recorded, 4,833 TV men were keeping watch over some 10,000 prisoners.[45] Reports of ill-treatment of prisoners continued to come in; Broszat states: "The main forms of punishment were regular beatings, close arrest, hard labour, making detention conditions worse by prohibiting prisoners from writing or receiving letters, as well as tying prisoners to trees—a form of punishment originally introduced by Eicke in Dachau .... Even in this period there were instances of prisoners being maltreated and killed by SS guards."[46]

Heydrich's lawyers began to criticise the treatment meted out to prisoners in Eicke's camps—not of course for reasons of humanity but as a move in the struggle for power within the SS. In October 1935 the Gestapo issued concentration-camp regulations requiring commandants to inform the regional public prosecutors forthwith whenever unassailable medical reasons could not be given as the cause of a prisoner's death.[47] The camps, however, took little notice, for Eicke was urging them to treat prisoners with the utmost severity and ruthlessness. Any trace of pity, he said, would be taken by the "enemies of the State as a sign of weakness which they would not fail to exploit."[48]

Heydrich kept an ever-sharper watch on Eicke's camps. The Political Sections, the outposts in enemy territory, increased in size; they were staffed by Gestapo or Kripo officials who noted everything that happened within the camp, conducted the interrogation of prisoners and kept the prisoners' card index. Heydrich's emissaries were responsible to the relevant Gestapo or Kripo Stelle, and according to Kautsky, even at a later date "invariably constituted a State within a State, feared not only by the prisoners but by the camp staff."[49]

Eicke sensed danger and alerted his protector Himmler. On 10 August 1936 he wrote: "Rumours are going around in the Gestapo that in the autumn the SS Totenkopfverbände will be removed from my command and placed under the SS Oberabschnitte. These rumours originate in Dr Best's office."[50] Even worse was to come; "SS-Standartenführer Dr Best of the Gestapa has stated on various occasions that the situation in the concentration camps is disgusting and that it is high time the camps were returned to the command of the Gestapa."[51]

Eicke kept a suspicious eye on Heydrich's manoeuvres and prepared himself for battle. In February 1937 he did in fact forbid mishandling of prisoners, saying "Although as a National-Socialist I naturally sympathise with such action, I cannot and must not tolerate such behaviour; otherwise we shall run the risk of being reported by the Reich Ministry of the Interior as unfit to deal with prisoners."[52] He was continually warning his troops to be on their guard against the enemy in their own ranks, saying "Once more we are struggling for recognition and acknowledgment of our existence."[53]

Eicke need not in fact have worried, for Himmler had no intention of handing the concentration camps over to Heydrich, who was too powerful already. Eicke and his empire continued to constitute a tiresome gap in Heydrich's web.

In the police sector also Heydrich found his way blocked by one of those minefields of intrigue which did more damage to the structure of the Third Reich than all the underground work of the resistance. With Heydrich's connivance Himmler had relegated Daluege to third place in the police hierarchy but now Heydrich found Police General Daluege laying claim to command of the police.

The Chief of the Ordnungspolizei was admittedly too weak and too lethargic to declare open war on his rival Heydrich. Nevertheless he had at his disposal a police force with an *esprit de corps* comparable only to that of the old Prussian army; Prussia's green-uniformed Schutzpolizei had once been the pride of Weimar Germany and even under the Third Reich they retained this prestige— in the early stages at least. Of the original total of 150,000 men one-third went off to the new Wehrmacht, while the remainder formed the Ordnungspolizei.[54] The new regime had many attractions to offer the police— ostensible law and order, smart new uniforms and better prospects of promotion instead of hazardous political street battles and low pay. Even in face of "Gleichschaltung" the Ordnungspolizei retained a will of its own and refused to submit to complete incorporation into the SS as had the Gestapo and Kripo.[55]

Foremost among the opponents of Heydrich's plan were the civilian bureaucrats in Hauptamt Orpo. They all originated from the old bureaucracy of the Ministry of the Interior and Werner Bracht, for instance, head of the "Administration and Legal" office in Hauptamt Orpo and a senior civil servant [Ministerial Director] was even more vehement than Daluege in his opposition to Heydrich's attempts to establish his hegemony.[56]

Year by year Heydrich became more strident in his demands that "all matters of political significance are the responsibility of the Sicherheitspolizei," as he once wrote to Daluege.[57] Bracht would have none of it, saying: "In that case the policeman would eventually become simply an executive 'bobby' employed on odd jobs, without any worthwhile powers of command and used merely to carry out other people's orders."[58] Bracht and Heydrich were soon deep in a sort of trench warfare; every question of authority was bitterly disputed. Although in 1936 a clear delineation had been made between Orpo and Sipo, there were still some Orpo outposts in enemy territory. Daluege's office, for instance, dealt with all organisational questions concerning local police administration, was responsible for the Criminal Police budget and handled all accommodation problems for both Kripo and Gestapo.[59]

The sector of the front on which the most bitter battles were fought was that of control over the Kriminalpolizei. One of the numerous monstrosities of the National-Socialist regime was the fact that it created new structures while leaving the façade of the old still standing: on the higher level, for instance, the Kriminalpolizei had merged with the Gestapo to form the Sicherheitspolizei, but on the middle and lower levels the old administrative chains of command still held good. As a result the Kripo Stellen out in the country received their technical instructions from Nebe's RKPA and to that extent were organs of the Sicherheitspolizei; at the same time, however, they were part of the official police administration and therefore the Police President, the head of that administration, was automatically responsible for them; as the Police Presidents came under Hauptamt Orpo, the Kripo Stellen were also indirectly organs of the Ordnungspolizei.[60]

The battle between the two Hauptämter spilled over into provincial police headquarters. Heydrich demanded that here also authority should be divided, writing to Daluege: "The division of the head offices into two branches means that provincial police headquarters must be similarly divided."[61] Daluege would have none of it and Bracht, his strategist, gave undercover encouragement to any police president prepared to be anti-Sipo.

Heydrich accordingly launched a counter-attack. After discussion with Himmler he appointed to each Wehrkreis [Military district] an "Inspekteur der Sicherheitspolizei" [Security Police Inspector—IdS] whose job was to force through on the middle and lower levels the merger between Kripo and Gestapo.[62] The IdS developed into dangerous opponents of the Police Presidents who remained under the Orpo. Suddenly the Kripo Stellen had two masters and they obeyed the one who seemed the stronger—generally the Sipo Inspector. SS-Brigadeführer Karl Pflomm, for instance, the Police President of Dresden, complained: "Since their [the Inspectors'] arrival there has been so much interference with my activities as Police President that to some extent my authority is affected. I do not feel justified in remaining in my present position if my responsibilities as Police President are continually being whittled away."[63]

Undermining the position of Police Presidents, however, was not the only purpose of Heydrich's inspectors; they were also intended to eliminate another weakness in the Heydrich empire—lack of co-ordination between Kripo and Gestapo.

Nebe's Kriminalpolizei surrendered only too willingly to the lure of increased police authority; all the old legal scruples rooted in the Weimar system were forgotten. The Kripo had always been kept short of funds and Heydrich now offered it an undreamed-of opportunity—

a higher-powered system of crime suppression, uninhibited by considerations of publicity or legality. In Heydrich's office serious consideration was given to the abolition of public prosecutors and the transfer to the police of the initiation and conduct of legal proceedings. The abuse of the preventive arrest system had already shown how far the men of the RKPA had become infected with Sipo ideas. Nevertheless between RKPA headquarters in the Wedersche Markt and Sipo headquarters in the Prinz-Albrecht-Strasse there remained a gulf which no SS uniform could bridge.[64]

Arthur Nebe's servile attitude in face of Heydrich and his National-Socialist tirades later proved to be the deliberate sacrifice of a professional police officer determined at all costs to prevent the Kripo from becoming a dependency of the Gestapo. Nebe accepted the blame. He did at least enable non-Nazis such as his deputy Werner, and the head of the Kripo executive Hans Lobbe, together with anti-Nazis such as Gerhard Nauck, the head of the Vice Squad, to keep the RKPA largely free of Gestapo influence.[65]

The heads of the Gestapo looked with envy and suspicion on the doings of their Kripo counterparts, duly noting every fault and every failure—and well they might. Heinrich Müller and his Bavarian brigade had been recruited by Heydrich and now they were working with the blind fanaticism of the converted, but the bitter realisation was beginning to grow that they were involved in repellent business. An internal Gestapo report of 1937 bears witness to the feelings of Müller, Huber and Meisinger; the report, the author of which is unknown, compares the work of the Gestapo and Kripo saying: "The Gestapo profession is not popular with the man in the street and is frequently the target of direct attacks in the press"; the Kripo, on the other hand, was said to have "full understanding and recognition from the public."[66]

Müller seized every opportunity to taunt his "friend Arthur" with inefficiency. Both were of the same rank—Reichskriminaldirektor—and they fought a bitter battle, Nebe knowing that Müller had Heydrich's ear and was urging that the Kripo adopt Gestapo methods in the fight against crime.

Heydrich, the perfectionist in surveillance, could there-

fore feel fully confident only in the Gestapo, but that
had nothing like enough manpower to keep track of
every suspicious movement among a nation of 80 million.
Best of the Gestapo said after the war that "with the
few officials, who were always busy, anything like that
could not be carried out."[67] The gaps in Heydrich's system
of control were shown up by a vice ring story from
Bavaria where, for three years, a gang of political adventurers, alcoholics and psychopaths managed to throw
dust in the eyes of all the senior officials.

The leader of the group was Emil Traugott Danzeisen,
who played a part in the 1932 plot to murder Röhm.[68] As a
long-standing enemy of Röhm, he had clearly hoped that
when Röhm was finally murdered he would receive his
due reward. When the orders and titles failed to appear,
Danzeisen felt that he had been let down by the Party
leadership, and determined to take his revenge after his
own fashion.

He collected a circle of kindred spirits, "old fighters"
who for various reasons had a grudge against the Party;
some of them had even marched in the Munich Putsch
but had then fallen foul of the law and were therefore out
of favour with the Party. They included Albert Ampletzer,
the standard-bearer in the Hitler putsch of 1923; he had
numerous convictions against him, the latest being for
embezzlement of 16,000 marks from the Munich Boxing
Club; another was Erich Gruhl, an employee of Munich
Party Headquarters, on whom the Gestapo had reported:
"a serious psychopathic case, only kept going by narcot-
ics."[69]

Late in 1934 this distinguished company set up an
organisation designed to manoeuvre its members into lucrative posts and, at the same time, to create an intelligence organisation which would make the Party shake in
its shoes. Danzeisen had a splendid idea—it would henceforth be called "Sicherheitsdienst," in the confident ex-
pectation that, in the new Germany, no doors would remain closed to an SD man.

"SD Danzeisen" soon became a power in the land in
Munich; no one cared to disobey the orders of this
secret security service. Danzeisen soon had no fewer than
69 informers with contacts ranging from the staff of SS-
Oberabschnitt South to the political Abteilung in Munich

Police Headquarters and reaching even into the Brown House.[70] A whole group of officials and employees in these Headquarters dutifully collected information on important personalities and offices; Danzeisen even had contact men in the Bavarian Labour Office and the Labour Exchanges at Pfarrkirchen, Deggendorf, Weissenburg, Schweinfurt and Bamberg.[71]

The *éminence grise* of the Labour Office was Danzeisen's closest collaborator, ex-SA-Oberführer Hans Kallenbach. The Gestapo reported on him later: "He was generally regarded in the office as the man who had the *entrée* even to the Führer. Anyone who wished to get anywhere fell in behind Kallenbach."[72] Any of Bavaria's longstanding Nazis who obtained employment through Kallenbach were naturally willing to sign up as his contact men. Kallenbach let it be known that his job was to find positions for "old fighters." Even the Deputy President of the Labour Office thought that Kallenbach had been commissioned by the Party to find posts for the older Nazis throughout Germany.[73]

When, however, Danzeisen began to use the material provided by his contact men to blackmail senior Nazi functionaries, including the Munich Police President, the Gestapo pricked up its ears. In the spring of 1937 they uncovered the pseudo-SD's network. Even then, however, Danzeisen's friends in Police Headquarters continued to believe that they had in fact been in the service of the real SD.[74]

Heydrich was realist enough to recognise that there were gaps in his system of surveillance and control. He would not achieve his object with the Gestapo alone and so the second front must be opened. This was the moment to send into action the other organisation also responsible to Reinhard Heydrich—the SD.

The SD had long been in eclipse. The National-Socialist seizure of power had taken place without any noteworthy assistance from it; in autumn 1933 it included a mere 100 full-time personnel and 100 part-timers and was used only for low-level odd jobs.[75] It had played no distinguished part in Himmler's capture of the police machine in the Länder. In fact the SD had been disregarded for so long that many SS men hardly knew what purpose the "Sicherheitsdienst Reichsführer-SS" was supposed to serve.

SS-Scharführer Adolf Eichmann of the Dachau Guard Unit joined the SD because he thought it was Himmler's escort, saying to himself: "One gets around; one sits in the car and merely has to keep a lookout"; he was soon to be "greatly disappointed."[76] Otto Ohlendorf thought the SD was an information service; he said: "The first disappointment was to find that there was no such thing as an SD information organisation."[77]

The Party bosses did not find the SD men particularly impressive. In autumn 1933, for instance, Strenger, the Gauleiter of Hesse, dismissed Dr Best from the post of Police Chief.[78] Dietrich Klagges, the National-Socialist Minister-President of Brunswick, administered an even more humiliating snub to the SD; during the summer of 1933 the SD was intriguing against Klagges and two other SS leaders who were rivals of Himmler, the Minister of Justice, Alpers, and the Police Chief, Jeckeln; the object was to drive Klagges and his supporters from power but Klagges arraigned the SD before the Supreme Party Court. Himmler hoisted the white flag at once. The Head of the Brunswick SD was expelled from the SS and sent to a concentration camp; his most important contact man was dismissed and the director of the SD office indicted before a Party Court. Simultaneously Himmler was forced to grant senior SS Rank to the SD's enemies; Alpers, who was an SS man, was promoted to Standartenführer; Klagges, who was not an SS man, was made a Gruppenführer.[79]

The SD's prestige was temporarily so low that the Party had to give it a shot in the arm. In late 1933 Martin Bormann, presumably at Himmler's behest, issued a circular to all Gauleiter denying the rumour that the SD was to be disbanded.[80] The post-war historians, however, painted a very different picture. In their view the SD was always a sinister uncanny organisation, a ubiquitous secret society, a messenger of terror "even in the ranks of the Nazi Party itself."[81]

During the early years of the National-Socialist regime, the SD resembled a society of hyper-intelligent youth leaders rather than a serious Secret Service. Even at this stage, however, it had one important function; it was in fact the only centrally directed organisation available for use by the Party Leadership.

During the lean years of the so-called "struggle period" the Party had held together, though with some difficulty; after the seizure of power on 30 January 1933, however, it practically fell apart. The Party elite laid hands on official positions in Berlin, while the middle- and lower-level Party barons fell upon their booty out in the country and set up their little feudal empires. In the jungle of warring Party cliques the SD was the only independent organisation available to the Party leadership which was not a target for the local Party bosses' thirst for power. Frequently in collaboration with the police, the SD kept watch on the intrigues of the new lords and lordlings and began to construct a fine-spun network of surveillance and observation.[82]

The leading sleuths in this spy system could quote a directive from the Party leadership instructing them to report on and expose opposition elements within the Party. The leadership in fact kept urging the SD to be more vigilant; in June 1934 Rudolf Hess proclaimed the SD to be the sole Party counter-espionage service.[83]

The romance of a secret service and the SD's declared opposition to the "little Hitlers" attracted a group of young National-Socialist intellectuals whose object was both professional advancement and "the improvement if National-Socialism"—in the words of Gunter d'Alquen, one of the SD's most versatile brains. The SD soon became the refuge for National-Socialism's most intelligent men. They were flotsam from the wreckage left by the social disintegration which had overtaken the German middle class in the early 1930s; they were the rearguard of a bourgeoisie which had lost its faith in the pre-war standards of values. These young men, born in the 1900–1912 period, took their cue from the Völkisch wing of the German Youth Movement. They had matured in an atmosphere of disgust with the tottering democracy of Weimar and believed that in place of the "decadent" republic a better, specifically German, regime must be installed, superior to its Western counterparts.[84]

Three factors held them together: the disintegration of the bourgeoisie, the traumatic experience of Versailles, and the hallucination that only by the strictest discipline and personal self-sacrifice could the Fatherland once again be raised to its old position of power. Patriotic speeches by their professors reinforced the youngsters' blind devotion to their country. Many of them were law students and the doctrine then holding sway in the legal faculties of the German universities placed State power high in the scheme of values. As early as 1892 Bergbohm, the legal expert, had laid down that however villainous a law might be, it was binding on the legal profession if produced in proper form;[85] the young students thus grew up in a tradition of legal positivism.

These youngsters developed into legal automata, who considered that they could have no higher duty than to ensure, by a watertight system of laws and ordinances, that the demands of the State were met. For them the State was a deity to which every kind of sacrifice must be made. The law had only one function—to provide the State with the legal means to fulfil its intentions without let or hindrance.

The question was: "What sort of State did they wish to serve?" Dictatorship met youth's demand for a leader because it gave responsibility to a man of flesh and blood instead of to a faceless assembly;[86] to the Völkisch sons of the bourgeoisie nothing could be more natural than that this dictatorship should be National-Socialist. The bourgeoisie's sociological catastrophe simply increased these youngsters' readiness to accept dictatorship. Then the economic crises of the 1930s left them rootless and in revolt against the capitalist system, as their fathers had been before them.

The reaction against international banks and businesses instilled into these young intellectuals a poison which many, all too many, regarded as the antidote to all economic ills—anti-Semitism. In the minds of the National-Socialist youngsters anti-Semitism and the dogma of State omnipotence combined to produce a dynamic based on no doctrine, a technology of power serving one, and only one, supreme source of energy—the State, or more specifically the charismatic Führer. Having lost their roots in society, they gradually discarded the moral standards of the old bourgeois community. Domination, power for its own sake, became a new ethical norm, a duty to be performed by a self-elected elite which had long since outgrown the plebeian National-Socialism of the Party veterans.

In these young men's view, however, the Third Reich's Order should be "level-headed," the one-man dictatorship should answer to some rational concept, the National-Socialist revolution should not violate the basic principles of human reasoning. But what these young intellectuals frequently saw in practice was crude lust for power, ideological blather by the Party bosses or opportunists and the megalomania of the eager Party beavers. They had never imagined that the Third Reich would be like this. Then they heard that in the SD an organisation existed which had set itself the task of exposing abuses and correcting false tendencies in the State. It seemed to be fairly influential since behind the SD stood Heinrich Himmer, the coming man. The SD offered many malcontents hope and escape. One of them was a certain Otto Ohlendorf, son of a Hanoverian farmer, born in 1907, trained as a lawyer and economist and a 1925-vintage Party member.[87]

He was a member of the Institute for World Economics in Kiel where, together with his friend and teacher, Jens Peter Jessen, the Professor of Economics, he had spent months resisting what seemed to him a prostitution of National-Socialism—collectivist State socialist tendencies in the Party. He resisted so fiercely that he landed in prison under interrogation by the Gestapo.[88] In a letter to his wife he lamented: "Something inside me has been shattered. I no longer possess the old, carefree assurance with which I fought for our National-Socialism."[89] As a National-Socialist Ohlendorf was finished; the Party would have no more of his critical public speeches.

In desperation he turned to his friend Jessen, who advised him to go and see a certain Professor Reinhard Höhn who was in charge of a coordinating Abteilung in the SD Hauptamt, 102 Wilhelmstrasse, Berlin, and had a vacant post for an Economics Adviser.[90] Ohlendorf went and was astonished; Höhn told him that the SD needed critical intellects like his. Otto Ohlendorf signed up.[91]

Alongside him other National-Socialist intellectuals flooded into the SD. It already possessed a hard core of young men and experienced investigators like Dr Best, the SS Leader from Hesse, and Dr Herbert Mehlhorn, a lawyer from Saxony;[92] now there appeared an even younger cross-section of National-Socialist academics. In

October 1933, Gunter d'Alquen arrived, a racy journalist, lately on the staff of the *Völkischer Beobachter*, who had had enough of the dull uniformity imposed by the National-Socialist Press;[93] shortly thereafter Dr Hermann Behrends appeared, a lawyer from Wilhelmshaven and an old friend of Heydrich;[94] meanwhile Professor Höhn was gradually collecting around him a circle of promising National-Socialists, mostly his own acquaintances.

One contact led to another. Having levered his pupil Ohlendorf into the SD, Jessen himself fell under the spell of Höhn, the Professor of Political Science. Though Jessen did not answer the call in person,[95] Höhn was able to win over one of his colleagues, Dr Franz Six, another Professor of Political Science;[96] he in turn persuaded one of his pupils, Dr Helmut Knochen, who really wanted to become a professor of literature, to join the SD.[97] The star turn of the SD intellectual brigade was an ambitious young man from Saarbrücken named Walter Schellenberg born in 1910 and qualified in law and political science; while still a student at Bonn University he had done some spy work for the SD[98] and Heydrich, who was a good judge of men, sensed that here was a brain which he could twist to his own purposes.

The appearance of an SD elite composed of nimble intellectuals relieved Heydrich of one threat to the expansion of his police state machine. Hitherto the Gestapo had necessarily occupied a key position in his system and he was therefore in danger of becoming overdependent upon it, and on its atmosphere of officialdom. All the lip service paid to National-Socialism by the Gestapo officials could not conceal the fact that, though its methods might be new, remnants of the Prussian-German administrative tradition were still present. Even Best, the Gestapo's legal expert, had proved to be an exponent of the old official attitude and had resisted Heydrich's attempts to substitute revolutionary dynamism for the routine of the trained civil servant.[99]

The first differences between Heydrich and Best had already appeared; with his legal training Best's approach savoured too much of official impersonal objectivity to suit Heydrich. The widening gulf between the two men was first demonstrated by an innocent notice on a wall. Some of his staff had painted one of Best's own slogans

on a plaque and fixed it to the wall of his office: "In
the long run factual work gets the better of any enemy."
On seeing it when visiting Best's office one day, Heydrich
reacted acidly: "That may be good enough for the civil
servants who come here in the course of business. But
for real life that bureaucratic principle is nonsense."[100]

Gestapo appointments also produced friction. Heydrich
wished to staff the senior posts with yes-men who had
no legal training and were bound by no rules; Best, on
the other hand, maintained that only legally trained men
should be considered. Unfortunately Heydrich's opinion of
lawyers was similar to that of his Führer, who said: "I
shall not rest until every German realises that it is a
disgrace to be a lawyer."[101]

Here were the signs of a conflict and, for Heydrich,
the obvious method of solving it was to step up the
activity of the SD. Early in 1935 he initiated a manoeuvre
which has given the historians a lot of trouble; almost
overnight, the SD became a dual-purpose organisation.
As a *Party formation* it was the parent organisation for
all members of the Sicherheitspolizei, the instrument
through which the entire corps of Sipo officials was to
be incorporated into the SS. As an *intelligence organisation*[102] It was to be what Schellenberg described as "the
versatile instrument for use against all opposition circles
and in all spheres of life, the people's sense of touch
and feel."

By this master-stroke Heydrich freed himself from the
pressure of the stiff-necked Gestapo officials. Best and
the professionals such as Müller and Huber, though on
paper members of the SS in its capacity as a Party
formation, were divorced from the real SD—what other
explanation can there be for the later ludicrous situation when Best and Müller, though ostensibly SD leaders, were doing their utmost to prevent the SD from
prying into the affairs of the Gestapo? In its capacity as
an intelligence organisation, however, Heydrich now gave
the SD a completely free hand; in his scheme of things
the SD was destined to be the "Intelligence Service" of
the Great German Reich.[103]

The existing structure of the SD surveillance machine
was expanded and improved. New sections and new
senior posts sprang up in the Sicherheitshauptamt in the

Wilhelmstrasse, where SS-Standartenführer Siegfried Taubert ran the staff in Heydrich's name, Heydrich himself
remaining in the Prinz-Albrecht-Strasse nearby.[104]

The organisation alone lends substance to the statement by Shlomo Aronson, Heydrich's biographer, that the
young SD men were "fascinated by the idea of dealing
with secret intelligence and espionage affairs" and so were
caught up in a sort of James Bond world.[105] They took
their cue from the detective story and the adventure novel
rather than from books on the development of National-
Socialism, and one of the results was a ludicrous over-
estimation of the British Secret Service. Heydrich, who
was a great reader of detective stories, had somewhere
discovered that the Chief of the "Intelligence Service" was
mysteriously referred to as "C" and he now began to
imitate this habit. The mysterious "C" began to appear
in the SD files—"C" has ordered . . ." or "the decision
concerns C personally"; a rubber stamp was even made—
"Submit to C."[106] It was all intended to enhance the magic
of the almost invisible "Chief."

The mysterious signs denoting the individual offices,
branches, divisions, etc., further illustrated this naïve pleasure in playing Secret-Service games. The SD Hauptamt
was divided into three Ämter [Offices] designated by
Roman numerals—I for Organisation, II "Combatting of
Opposition," III for Foreign Countries;[107] Subdivisions
were distinguished by Arabic numerals, increasing in number with each step down the ladder—for instance I 1
indicated the Zentralabteilung [Co-ordinating Section]
"Organisation and Supervision" within Amt I, I 11 was
the Hauptabteilung [Main Section] "Organisational
Tasks," I 111 the Abteilung "Appointments" and I 1111
the Desk concerned.[108]

With few exceptions the heads of all the more important Zentralabteilungen and Hauptabteilungen were
academics holding a degree; the Zentralabteilung "Organisation" was under Wilhelm Albert, who held an engineering degree,[109] Hauptabteilung "Staff Duties" under Dr
Herbert Mehlhorn, a lawyer and economist,[110] the Zentralabteilung "Idealogical Combatting of Opposition" under
Professor Franz Six,[111] the Zentralabteilung "Reports on
Spheres of German Life" under Professor Reinhard
Höhn,[112] and the Zentralabteilung "Counter-Espionage

—Enemy Intelligence Services" under SS-Oberführer Heinz Jost.[113]

This then was the general staff of the "Intelligence Service." From it the threads ran to the staffs of the seven SD-Oberabschnitte; territorially these were geared, not to the Wehrkreise [Military Districts] like the Oberabschnitte of the Allgemeine-SS, but to the Länder.[114] Under each Oberabschnitt were two or three Unterabschnitte and these led on down to SD-Aussenstellen [Out-Stations] each responsible for a Landkreis [Rural District or major town]. These last were the most important cells in the SD Intelligence Organisation.[115]

The work of the Aussenstellen can be illustrated by the directive issued in spring 1937 by SD-Oberabschnitt "North West"; "The Head of every Aussenstelle must, under all circumstances, try to engage one or more contact men in each locality in his district; every contact man should in turn have his informer network. To take an example: suppose that Aussenstelle D is responsible for 32 Landgemeinde [parishes]. The Head of the Aussenstelle must have a contact man in each parish to represent SD interests in the area. The task of the contact man is to ensure that his area is covered by a network of informers." And a little later: "The informers should never know that they are working for the SD. It would also be a good idea to provide the contact men with message pads and get them to submit a telegraphic daily report written in indelible pencil. A contact man will soon lose interest if the Head of his Aussenstelle requires him to produce long-winded reports. Most people do not take to their pens easily."[116]

In the cities the Aussenstellen were geared to the local Nazi Party Group and distributed accordingly; in the Universities and High Schools the contact men formed so-called "SD Working Associations."[117] According to Oberabschnitt "North West" anyone could be a contact man who "had the necessary general knowledge and could think logically and practically"; "suitable people" for these posts were said to be "teachers, local group leaders, SS and SA leaders, local peasant leaders, veterinary surgeons and, if necessary, retired officials."[118]

Only a comparatively small proportion of the SD's great informer army actually belonged to the Party or the SS.

After the war one of the SD leaders, Heinz Höppner, estimated that of the full-time members of the SD only 10
per cent came from the Allgemeine SS and only 10 per
cent of the part-time assistants were SS men.[119] At times
outright opponents of the regime were used by the SD
to supply information on anti-Nazi tendencies.

The antennae of the intelligence machine penetrated
into every sphere of German society. The SD's collaborators were not solely small-time informers and spies; they
included perfectly respectable magistrates, businessmen,
artists and scientists. The Headquarters was staffed by
young academics of all disciplines; similarly in the Aussenstellen an intellectual elite worked as "reporters." In 1938,
for instance, SD-Abschnitt Koblenz had 24 part-time
workers, among them four with academic degrees; of 11
named contact men in the Abschnitt, four were local
government officials, four were police officials, one a doctor, one a teacher and one a veterinary surgeon.[120]

These secret-service intellectuals showed a curious
maidenly aversion to the word "spy." Schlierbach, the
theorist on police work who was closely connected with
the SD, wrote that it would be "unworthy of the National-
Socialist State to make use of spies and agents";[121] a
confidential Sipo Service Instruction contained the sentence: "Employment of professional agents is not permitted."[122] The staff of the SD-Hauptamt had an almost
superstitious horror of coming into physical contact with
informers. Adolf Eichmann recalled: "We knew none
of them and conversely the contact man hardly ever entered the Headquarters."[123] Only at a later stage, when
the intellectuals had long since lost their scruples, did
Walter Schellenberg put some order into the contact system; from then on every Headquarters knew its contact
men.

The Wilhelmstrasse maintained a file on every individual contact man. It was divided into two sub-files;
sub-file A, also known as the "Placement File," contained,
among other things, the man's code name, a short cur-
riculum vitae, which did not reveal the name, the outcome of the SD's internal vetting, the man's declaration
of engagement, information about his special qualifications and a record of his place in the SD network. Sub-
file B, the "Control File," contained information on the

individual missions allotted to the contact man, an estimate of the value of his reports, ranging from 1 (Excellent) to 5 (Completely useless) together with an account
of all expenses incurred. In neither sub-file was the name
of the contact man given. This was only to be found in
two places: in the contact-man card index, used to locate
the files, and in the central card index maintained by
each SD office.[124]

The density of the SD's surveillance network increased
year by year; its strands gripped the country ever tighter.
By 1937 the SD numbered 3,000 full-time members with
an invisible army of 50,000 informers.[125]

But what was the object of it all? Who was the SD
supposed to watch? What was it supposed to unearth?
Here was the great question. During the "struggle period" the SD's task had been simple; it was to eliminate
opponents within the National-Socialist ranks and discover
the intentions of Nazism's opponents. This was a plausible
story so long as the enemy controlled the police machine.
After 30 January 1933, however, the Party itself took over
the police; the enemy, whoever he might be, could therefore now be dealt with through the resources of the
police.

Initially the SD had been content to act as a sort of
auxiliary police force. On 4 July 1934 Himmler declared
it to be "the sole political counter-espionage service of
the Gestapo";[126] six months later he directed: "The SD
will discover the enemies of the National-Socialist concept and will initiate counter-measures through the official
police authorities." Executive action was therefore excluded.[127] But the SD was too proud to assume the role
of mere informer for the Gestapo and so it thought up
a new task for itself; it was to be a thought police,
the instrument of National-Socialist thought control.

Himmler spelled out the new terms of reference: "The
SD is the Party's great ideological information service,
and ultimately that of the State also. The SD is concerned only with the great ideological questions." As the
guardian of ideological purity the SD had now pre-empted
for itself a new field of activity which, according to Himmler, included: "Communism, Jewry, Freemasonry, ultra-
montanism, the activity of politically-minded religious
persuasions and reactionaries."[128] In practice this was only

another way of expressing the old "struggle period" task—"combatting of opposition," as the SD called it.

"C" put his intelligence machine into action. The SD watchers probed the community for irregularities. No opportunity was missed of reporting upon discordant tendencies among the population. The Wilhelmstrasse teleprinters ceaselessly tapped out orders and telegrams called out the Einsatzkommandos [Action Commandos].

Wherever he went the German seemed to be shadowed by the SD. On 26 January 1938 SS-Obersturmführer Grillenberger reported from the KdF [Kraft durch Freude—the Nazi holiday organisation] ship *Der Deutsche* which was on an Italian cruise: "One of the holidaymakers, Fritz Schwanebeck, born 30 March 1901, resident Mückenberg-Ferrosiedlung, makes a bad impression; when the national anthem was sung he adopted a sloppy attitude, evidencing a complete lack of interest. Sixty holidaymakers arrived late at the passport office. The general attitude was criticised at the final roll-call. Violations of currency regulations."[129]

When so-called elections were in the offing the SD was very busy. They were at work well before polling day, as an order by Aussenstelle Erfurt (dated 4 April 1938) shows; this prescribed that "all persons in your area who may confidently be expected to vote 'No' at the forthcoming election are to be reported to the SD." If the names of dissidents were available, special voting papers were prepared for the suspects; a figure was typed on the voting slip using a machine without a ribbon and the same figure entered against the name on the voting list. On 7 May 1938 Unterabschnitt Koblenz reported that by this method it had been possible "to discover the persons who had voted 'No' or spoiled their papers. Skimmed milk was used to bring out the figures."[130]

The mountain of notes and reports in the SD-Hauptamt grew as the years went by. Any movement made by a suspect was noted; Rudol Kircher, for instance, the editor of the *Frankfurter Zeitung*, was something of a nonconformist and so Abteilung II 112 began collecting his articles of the Weimar period, noting: "Very informative regarding Kircher's real political views."[131] In a report from Palestine Schwarz van Bergk, the star Nazi journalist, had the misfortune to suggest that even Jews might fight and die for their cause. Oberscharführer Hagen, Professor Six's amanuensis, found that: "In my view it is inexcusable that a journalist should openly admit, in a National-Socialist newspaper to boot, that certain happenings within the Jewish community in Palestine should be passed over in silence for propaganda reasons."[132]

Whenever opportunity offered the SD spared no effort to prove that unwanted non-Nazis were of Jewish origin. Professors Ernst and Heinrich Seraphim, for instance, both of whom came from Poland, had refuted the rumour current in the Party that they were of Jewish origin; the SD, however, spied a chance "to prove the assertion that Seraphim is of Jewish origin on the basis of the facts as set out herein." But they proceeded cautiously. An SD man named Augsburg was instructed to urge the German association in Poland to find a student willing to trace Seraphim's family tree. But again caution: "In conversation with II 112 SS-Sturmbannführer Six approved the procedure proposed by Augsburg. Care was to be taken, however, that the source of these instructions should not become known."[133]

However, the fact that his shadowy army was silently extending its grip over the whole country was not enough for Heydrich. Totalitarian thought control postulated noise, the thunder of ideological slogans, the shouting of ideological drill-sergeants and schoolmarms. So Heydrich called to his assistance the most extraordinary and most widely feared organ of the National-Socialist press—Gunter d'Alquen's weekly *Das Schwarze Korps* [The Black Corps].

D'Alquen was the son of a wool merchant in Essen. He had revolted against the solid German nationalism of his home and become one of the earliest Hitler Youth Leaders. He had very soon found out what work for the Party press entailed. He had started with the miserable *Bremer Nationalsozialistische Zeitung*—where copy arrived in longhand, the telephone was always being cut off for lack of funds and the typesetting machines were decrepit; he had then moved on to the internal policy desk of the *Völkischer Beobachter* which he found equally sterile. D'Alquen sometimes wondered whether it was possible to be a National-Socialist and a journalist at the same time.[134]

The first steps on the ladder to fame were not a success. Early in 1934 Max Amann, the Party publisher, offered him the editorship of the Berlin *Angriff* and asked him to draw up an editorial programme. D'Alquen tells the story: "And then I committed a stupidity—perhaps the greatest of my life; I told the truth. I voiced the opinion that a constructive opposition was absolutely necessary if the State was not to die of hardening of the arteries." The impudent young man was forthwith sacked by the Party.[135]

A month or so later, in the sleeping car of a train on the way to a meeting of the Silesian SS frontier district, d'Alquen met Wittje, the head of the SS Hauptamt, and told him the story of his lost job. "My dear Gunter," Wittje replied, "I will speak to Heinrich. After all the SA and every twopenny-halfpenny society has its newspaper; why not the SS?" A few days later Wittje had an interview with Himmler, who had already heard arguments on the same lines from Max Amann. Himmler already knew what the newspaper should be called— *Das Schwarze Korps*. Wittje's initiative, moreover, bore fruit; Gunter d'Alquen was given the job of "Head Leader-Writer of the special SS Newspaper."[136]

The pedantic Himmler insisted upon reading the 24-year-old Hauptsturmführer a long lecture on the business of producing a newspaper; d'Alquen's reaction was: "He simply had no idea." They could not even agree upon the paper's title; d'Alquen proposed *Die Bewegung* [The Movement] but Himmler would not change his mind. D'Alquen did not give way until two days before the appearance of the first issue, and then had to sit up day and night with the Party draughtsman, Hans Schweitzer-Mjölnir, designing the paper's heading. Meanwhile SS headquarters had concluded an agreement with the Party's publishing firm, Franz Eher, guaranteeing a 40,000-copy run.[137]

On 6 March 1935 appeared the first number of the "Newspaper of the NSDAP's SS—the organ of SS Headquarters," as the sub-title had it. D'Alquen began with a staff of only six located at 88 Zimmerstrasse, Berlin, but he soon contrived to increase the circulation of the *Schwarze Korps;* it appeared on Thursdays, initially (in 1935) in 16 pages, rising later to 20. In 1937 it sold

189,317 copies but circulation later rose to 500,000 and during the war it was running at 750,000.[138]

The success of d'Alquen's paper lay in the fact that it both shocked and fascinated the regimented Germans. Its hate campaigns against churches and Jews, its poison-pen attacks on the bourgeoisie and officialdom and its ceaseless vilification of non-conformist Germans broke all bounds of decency. Nevertheless many people could detect an undertone of a different strain; the *Schwarze Korps* was popularly known as "the only opposition news-paper," for in its pages was mirrored all the schizophrenia of the SD intellectuals as they strove to be both radical and intelligent National-Socialists. What they could not be in the hard world of official political life they tried to be on paper; they wanted to oppose—and to ex-pose—the inflated Party bosses, corruption within the Party and the brown-shirted place-seekers.

On 21 January 1937 the *Schwarze Korps* proclaimed: "After every revolution comes the danger of stagnation. History proves it. We National-Socialists have studied his-tory . . . in order to draw lessons therefrom concerning out political structure. Hence the necessity, which many will find surprising, for a new form of opposition."[139] The paper frequently did not mince its words; it observed, for instance, that "National-Socialists have had to be placed in posts for which they are neither physically nor mentally equipped";[140] it inveighed against Party "profiteers of the revolution" who "brand anyone who does not possess a membership card as a second-class citizen, as a detestable individual and probably, if he is a poor man, as a marxist."[141]

When, in summer 1935, the Munich Nazis went round breaking the windows of Jewish businesses in a sort of trial run for the 1938 "Kristallnacht," the *Schwarze Korps* castigated these "criminal machinations" saying: "The Jewish question is one of our people's most burning prob-lems; it will not be solved by terror on the streets. As for healthy popular sentiment, a competent magistrate has no need to base his judgment upon so elastic a con-cept."[142] It even had a word to say to its own police, warning them to be more careful in their use of the words "enemy of the State"—"over-savage persecution can do more harm than good . . . one day precise figures should be given for the number of cases based on denunciation and personal spite."[143]

A paper which was clearly so critical of conditions in the Third Reich gained the confidence of its readers and d'Alquen encouraged them. On 18 February 1937 he wrote: "From the outset the reader may feel confident that not only do we wish to be read but that we ourselves also take trouble to read—to read the mood, the opinions, the experiences of our people."[144]

This particular sentence gave Heydrich the idea of including the *Schwarze Korps* in his system of surveillance. It could be the mouthpiece of his thought-control system and also a channel of continuous up-to-date information on the habits and thoughts of the populace. Heydrich and d'Alquen quickly reached agreement. The SD Hauptamt fed into the *Schwarze Korps* the information produced by its intelligence machine; the newspaper's editorial office forwarded a high proportion of its reader mail to the Wilhemstrasse for evaluation. Correspondence between the Hauptamt and the editor's office became so voluminous that d'Alquen even had printed slips prepared, such as: "Attached letter from one of our readers is forwarded to you with the request that you express an opinion, take note and return. With thanks for your trouble. Heil Hitler."[145]

As an instance of how the system worked—on 7 June 1938 a Berliner named Paul Koch wrote to the *Schwarze Korps* reporting that a butcher, Gustav Schiewek, of 37 Stralsunder Strasse, invariably "handed his customers their purchases wrapped in paper carrying an advertisement for a Jewish business." Koch continued: "Could the man not be assisted by being given a reproof in the form of a thick ear?" On 21 June the *Schwarze Korps* forwarded the letter to "SD Reichsführer-SS, for the attention of Dr Six." The letter made its way to Abteilung II 112 which forwarded it a fortnight later to SD Oberabschnitt East "with a request for further recommendations." On 8 July 1938 the SD Hauptamt wrote back to the *Schwarze Korps:* "For information Paul Koch's letter has been forwarded to the relevant Gestapo Stelle. Further information on conclusion of investigations."[146]

The *Schwarze Korps* was soon being produced in the closest collaboration with the SD. The SD Hauptamt acted

as a vast information library of secrets, always on hand
to assist the leader-writers in obtaining their information.[147] The more important articles were discussed beforehand. After a conference with Rolf d'Alquen, Gunter's younger brother and Number Three in the *Schwarze
Korps* editorial office, Oberscharführer Hagen noted: "With
reference to articles on the situation of German Jewry,
it was agreed that no special initiative would be taken
and the present line would be maintained pending final
agreement with the Ministry of Economics on funds to be
made available for Jewish emigrants."[148]

The SD became all the more willing to give away its
secrets as it began to realise 'hat publicity represented a
coercive method of thought control, capable of com-
pensating for the SD's lack of executive powers. The
suggestive effect upon the ordinary citizen of the *Schwarze
Korps'* lurid polemics was often more disturbing than the
potential but invisible threat of the Gestapo; conversely
the SD information gave the newspaper an air of sinister
omniscience.

The *Schwarze Korps*, for instance, took the ultra-conservative Reich Union of German Officers aback by publishing anti-Nazi extracts from the confidential minutes
of one of their meetings.[149] The publicist Wilhelm Stapel
was put in his place by publication of one of his private
letters containing the sentence that a conservative could
only support Hitler "with a shudder."[150] A certain Werner
Grund of Zwickau wrote to Chamberlain thanking him
for his efforts for world peace; he found Chamberlain's
answer, not in his letterbox but in the columns of the
Schwarze Korps;[151] Dr Wolfgang Denk, an attorney from
Leipzig was publicly attacked for writing a confidential
memorandum defending a woman who had been sent to
a concentration camp.[152]

At times the paper would openly admit that it had denounced people or provided the necessary material. In
summer 1944 for instance, it reported: "We are pleased
to record that the Wiesbaden Court has given short shrift
to an anti-social malefactor denounced by the *Schwarze
Korps;* he was sentenced to four years hard labour and
four years loss of rights."[153]

Co-operation between the SD and the *Schwarze Korps*
would have been more profitable had Heydrich observed

the elementary rule, valid even under the National-Socialist Reich, that some limits must be set to a partnership between press and secret service. D'Alquen, who at heart was a restless demagogue, refused to allow his paper to become subject to every tactical shift on the part of SD headquarters. The *Schwarze Korps'* scurrilous attacks frequently cut across the interests of the SD—still the most controversial of the SS organisations.

In course of time the sparks began to fly between the two partners. D'Alquen refused to submit his articles for prior censorship by the SD; he refused to hand over Heinar Schilling, one of his reporters, whom the SD suspected; he protested against the mis-use of *Schwarze Korps* press cards as cover for SD secret-service operations.[154] Heydrich's people, on the other hand, warned that the *Schwarze Korps* was overdoing its attacks on actual or supposed enemies of the regime and was making less and less use of SD material. As a result the paper ran into increasing difficulties.[155]

Relations between the two later reached such an all-time low that Heydrich was forced to appoint a liaison officer, SS-Sturmbannführer von Kielpinski, to try and improve the situation.[156] D'Alquen exploded: "I am sick and tired of being treated as an outsider by SD men, who after all are supposed to be working with us."[157] In reply Ohlendorf summarised the SD's complaint against the *Schwarze Korps;* its articles, he said, "were full of false assumptions and equally false generalisations"; "in their incredibly libellous form" they were "certainly not calculated to influence those to whom they were addressed"; on the contrary "their style and tone caused decent National-Socialists to rally to the support of those whom the articles (rightly) attacked."[158]

Ohlendorf concluded that co-operation was only possible if "the *Schwarze Korps* refrains from attacking people unless the facts of the case have been established beyond doubt and the SD is available to do this"; he continued that "problems of fact should first be discussed with us in order to make use of our knowledge and material."[159] The *Schwarze Korps,* however, refused to accept the SD's claim to authority.

Heydrich had long since realised that the SD would not achieve its object through the *Schwarze Korps* publicity.

The old question raised its head once more: what was the real job of the SD? The urgency of this question increased with the ominous approach of a head-on collision between Heydrich's two engines of domination, the SD and the Gestapo.

10
The RSHA

REINHARD Heydrich scented danger. The SD and the
Gestapo, planned as two interlocking parts of his machine of tyranny, were threatening to neutralise each
other. Each was extending its sweep of power, each
was striving for control over the nation; Adolf Hitler's
Greater Germany was too small for them both. This was
the inevitable result of the failure, when reconstructing
the SD in 1935, to allot to it a logical field of activity
clearly differentiated from that of the Gestapo. Their researches covered the same area, and the SD was always
coming across the trail of its Gestapo rivals. Abteilung
IIA (Marxism) of the Gestapo, for instance, was hunting
the same Communist resistance men as Abteilung II 121
(Left-wing Movements) of the SD Hauptamt.[1]

In an attempt to curtail the battle between the two, on
1 July 1937 Heydrich issued a decree setting out their
functions. The theme was: "Let there be no rivalry; neither
is senior or junior to the other; they are mutually com-
plementary and duplication of work must be avoided."
The Gestapo was allotted Marxism, treason and émigrés;
the SD were to be responsible for science, Germanism
and folk-lore, art, education, Party and State, constitution
and administration, foreign countries, Freemasonry and
miscellaneous societies.[2]

A sufficient area of friction still remained, however,
since both were still responsible for: "churches, sects,
other religious and ideological associations, pacifism,
Jews, right-wing movements, other anti-State groups (the
Schwarze Front, the Bundische Jugend, etc.), economics

and the press." Even here some division of responsibility was attempted; the SD was to deal with "all general and basic questions," the Gestapo with "all individual cases in which secret police measures enter into consideration."[3]

The length of the SD's list of responsibilities, however, could not conceal the fact that it was under increasing threat from the Gestapo of relegation to the ideological field only, and this it refused to stomach. The SD Hauptamt central office produced well-argued theses pointing out acidely that pride of place belonged to the SD. The Gestapo, the argument ran, had come into being to meet a legal and administrative requirement of the State; the Third Reich, however, needed "a more potent guarantee of the State's security, springing from and vitalised by the will of a political movement"—and this was the SD's speciality.

The memorandum containing this sentence was entitled "The Independent Status of the SD." The unknown author laid down the principle that the Gestapo's task was to suppress "anti-State manifestations," the SD dealing with "anti-social manifestations . . . anti-State action is a legal phenomenon and is present whenever it can be proved that a person, or an action, contravenes a law protecting the State." On the other hand, "the peculiar characteristic of anti-social manifestations is that, in general, they are not amenable to criminal law; nevertheless the manifestations of anti-social action frequently constitute a far greater danger to the people, and therefore also to the State, then direct anti-State manifestations."[4]

This exercise in self-inflation, however, did not solve the SD's problem of finding new fields of activity. Eventually the Wilhelmstrasse did find two unexplored areas but they carried with them the seeds of further conflict and intrigue; they were: espionage in foreign countries and investigation of "spheres of life."

From the outset espionage had enthralled the young men of the SD. Its secret foreign intelligence service had, however, been a product of chance, a by-product of pursuit of the regime's enemies beyond the Reich frontiers. One of these enemies was Otto Strasser, the leader of the Schwarze Front, located in Prague, whence he conducted a Quixotic campaign against his former Party leader, Hitler.[5]

Strasser's "black radio" seemed particularly dangerous to the SD leaders, for it broadcast anti-Hitler speeches into the totalitarian thought-controlled Reich. The SD discovered that the transmitter was operated by an engineer named Rudolf Formis, lately senior technician of Radio Stuttgart. Heydrich was convinced that Formis must be disposed of. On 10 January 1935 he summoned his factotum, an ex-mechanic and SS-Untersturmführer named Alfred Naujocks, and ordered him to bring Formis to Berlin.[6] Naujocks drew up a plan of campaign.

The SD had established that Strasser's transmitter must be located some 15–20 miles south-east of Prague. Naujocks arranged papers for himself in the name of Hans Müller, a trader; then, together with his girl-friend, Edith Kasbach, a Berlin gym-instructress, he drove across the frontier in a Mercedes. He found what he was looking for; the "black" transmitter was located in a place called Dobris, in a room of the Zahori Hotel.[7] Naujocks and his girl-griend took room 4, close to that of Formis.[8] He made a wax impression of the key to Formis' room and telegraphed to the SD Hauptamt: "Found." Then he waited for orders. A couple of days later he prepared for action.

On 23 January at 9.30 p.m., Naujocks looked at his watch; he took a torch and swung it out of his hotel window. At the signal another SD man, Werner Goetsch, climbed the wall by a rope and jumped into the room.[9] Both were convinced that Formis was not in the hotel; they slunk along the corridor and stopped at his door. When they put the skeleton key in the lock, however, they realised that their man was inside. Naujocks took a quick decision; he knocked. A voice called: "What do you want?" Naujocks mumbled something to the effect that they had forgotten to put out Herr Formis' soap.

Formis opened the door and immediately the two SD men burst into the room and overpowered him. Formis attempted to draw a revolver. One of the intruders fired and Rudolf Formis fell dead. Naujocks and Goetsch just had time to lay a phosphorus charge on the transmitter and ignite it; then they fled as the hotel staff came running up.[10]

Back in Berlin Heydrich was furious at the clumsy

gangster-film methods which passed for secret-service work among SD men such as Naujocks. Nevertheless during the next two years the SD remained a refuge for inexperienced amateurs who drove the secret-service professionals to distraction. In spite of this, the SD penetrated further and further into the jungle of the German secret services. The SD's Aussenstellen near the frontier insisted upon collecting reports from abroad; certain SD leaders set up informer networks run by acquaintances resident in foreign countries.[11]

The SD's espionage work was under the direction of the totally inexperienced SS-Oberführer Heinz Jost and his Zentralabteilung III 2 (Enemy Intelligence Services); other sections of the Headquarters, however, also felt impelled to take a hand in the game. For instance the SD's Jewish Abteilung maintained its own intelligence network in the Middle East, collecting information on the Arab–Jew conflict in Palestine.[12] The main collecting centre here was the office of Dr Reichert, the German News Agency's correspondent in Tel Aviv; he had informers in both camps: on the Arab side the Nationalist leader Ibrahim Chanti, editor of the newspaper *Al Difah*, and on the Jewish the Zionist leader Feivel Polkes, one of the commanders of the Jewish Secret Army, "Haganah."[13]

A note in one of the SD Hauptamt files says: "Provided adequate support is forthcoming, Dr Reichert has undertaken to work only with the SD on the more difficult cases; he will transmit all material of intelligence importance either via Herr von Ritgen of the German News Agency under code sign H or to the addressees indicated by Oberscharführer Hagen." Reichert's information service registered one or two successes. (In 1937 he laid hands on a letter from the ex-Prime Minister Stanley Baldwin alluding to a secret Anglo-Turkish treaty; the Italian Secret Service offered £150,000 for it.[14])

But the further the SD penetrated into the secret-service under growth, the more it came into collision with Military Intelligence under Admiral Wilhelm Canaris. He was a diplomatic officer and so far had contrived to maintain cautiously good relations with his ex-midshipman, Heydrich; they were wrecked, however, by the SD's expansion.

During the early years (1932–4) when the Abwehr

[Military Intelligence] was run by Captain Patzig, it had frequently clashed with the Gestapo; then the Wehrmacht leaders had thought that in Canaris they had found the ideal officer to rub along with Heydrich.[15] Canaris, born in 1887, was, after all, a Naval Captain and ex-U-boat commander; he had been an outspoken opponent of the Weimar Republic and had the reputation of being on good personal terms with Heydrich. Canaris and Heydrich could reminisce about their time on board the training cruiser *Berlin;* Canaris' wife, Erika, had long missed Heydrich's violin-playing at her musical evenings. Even after his appointment as head of the Abwehr in January 1934, Canaris had kept in close contact with Heydrich.[16-18]

On official matters Canaris and Heydrich initially reached a working arrangement. On 21 December 1936 Canaris and Best, the head of the Abwehrpolizei, signed an agreement (known as "the Ten Commandments") laying down the spheres of the Abwehr and Gestapo respectively. The Abwehr was to deal with espionage abroad and counter-espionage at home; the Gestapo was to be responsible for "investigation of culpable actions under para. 163 of the State Police Ordinance (Treason) and the necessary followup action." Canaris had therefore conceded a certain technical preponderance to the Gestapo. In peacetime, moreover, the Abwehr had no military police and so the Gestapo had to be called in as executive agents even in cases dealt with by the military. At the same time, however, the Canaris-Best agreement gave a certain precedence to the requirements of Military Intelligence, for it included the following: "in dealing with individual cases the interests of the Secret Intelligence Service and of counter-espionage take precedence over executive action by the Abwehrpolizei." The Gestapo was bound "at the request of the relevant Wehrmacht Abwehr office to refrain from proceeding with their measures until, in the judgment of the Wehrmacht Abwehr office, neither Military Intelligence nor counter-espionage has any further interest in the case."[19]

The Abwehr's privileged position was now imperilled by the expansion of the SD, who began to meddle in the network of foreign secret services and upset the Abwehr's plans. Even on such subjects as other countries' economic potential and armaments industries the collisions between

Abwehr and SD became increasingly violent.[20] A breach between Canaris and Heydrich was obviously coming; it was accelerated by an affair which, for the first time, showed Canaris how totally lacking in scruple the SD dilettantes were.

Late in 1936 Heydrich received information via SD channels that an opposition group was forming in the Soviet Union, whose object was to bring Stalin down by force; the leader of the group was said to be Marshal Tukachevsky, Deputy Commissar for War of the Soviet Union. Heydrich had a fantastic idea: suppose it were possible to feed this information to Stalin, giving it verisimilitude by means of one or two forged documents. It might then be possible at one stroke to annihilate the entire Soviet Army leadership—and to do so with the assistance of Stalin and the Soviet Secret Police.[21]

Heydrich already had an outline plan. In the immediate post-war period relationships between the Reichswehr and the Red Army had been close; there ought, therefore, to be documents, notes and letters bearing the signatures of the Soviet generals now suspected of conspiring against Stalin. If these old papers were given a new look by the addition of a few sentences, they could be made to give the impression that Soviet generals were in league with German officers against the Kremlin. Heydrich summoned Naujocks, who was in charge of a false papers and passports factory in the Delbruckstrasse, Berlin, and let him into the secret. SS-Standartenführer Hermann Behrends, the SD Commander East, was also informed confidentially and the forgers got to work.[22]

SS-Hauptsturmführer Erich Jahnke, one of the few professional Secret Service men in the SD, sounded a warning. He did not believe that the Tukachevsky story was genuine; it could all well be a trick by the Soviet Secret Service. The reason for his suspicion was that the story originated from a certain Russian exile living in Paris who was working both for the SD *and* for the Soviet Secret Service.[23] But Heydrich thought he knew better: he placed the tiresome Jahnke under house arrest. The false papers took only four days to prepare and Heydrich then obtained Hitler's agreement to pass them across to the Soviets.[24]

Behrends took the documents to Prague and, through

various contacts, persuaded Benes, the Czechoslovak
President, to advise Moscow of their existence. The
Soviets reacted and immediately sent a special delegate to
Berlin to negotiate with Heydrich. According to Schellenberg, Moscow paid a sum of 3,000,000 roubles for them
—but in notes which unfortunately proved to be as good
forgeries as the documents themselves.[25]

On 11 June 1937 the Soviet news agency *Tass* reported that Marshal Tukachevsky and seven Red Army
Generals had been condemned to death by a special tribunal because "the accused had maintained treasonable
relationships with leading military circles of a foreign
power which was pursuing a policy hostile to the Soviet
Union. The accused were working for this Power's espionage service."[26] The execution of Tukachevsky and his
companions heralded the bloodiest political purge in the
history of Stalin's Russia. In a single year almost half the
entire officer corps—35,000 officers—was eliminated; 90
per cent of the Soviet generals and 80 per cent of the
colonels were liquidated or cashiered—3 out of 5 marshals, 13 out of 15 army commanders, 57 out of 85
corps commanders, 110 of 195 divisional commanders
and 220 out of 406 brigade commanders.[27]

A few months later the Ausland-SD submitted to Heydrich a secret report entitled "Political Situation in the
Red Army." It contained this: "The new arrivals will
inevitably take time to overcome the effects of so far-
reaching a purge in the higher ranks of the Soviet Army.
The new Commanders are inadequately trained and
prematurely promoted; it is difficult to underestimate their
efficiency."[28] Heydrich was jubilant. He went round telling a story repeated by all the SS memoir writers from
Walter Schellenberg to Wilhelm Höttl, publicised in the
film *Canaris* and believed even by Winston Churchill and
Nikita Khrushchev[29]—that the SD had lopped the head
off the dreaded Soviet Army.

At about this time a certain War Ministry staff officer
stopped Lieutenant-Colonel Karl Spalcke in the corridor
and asked whether he had heard that Heydrich was boasting of having brought down Tukachevsky. Spalcke, who
had the Russian desk in the Abteilung "Foreign Armies"
(T 3), simply laughed saying: "Pure bragging by Heydrich."[30] He was at the time the only man who suspected

the truth for, in fact, Tukachevsky was not brought down by Heydrich and the SD. In 1937 Spalcke could not substantiate his suspicions but today the proof is there that Heydrich was no more than a small, unimportant pawn in a Soviet Secret Service game.

The fact was that in Stalin's opinion Tukachevsky had become overpowerful and a threat to his personal dictatorship; Stalin had decided to put an end to the Marshal long before Heydrich started his document gambit; he had been preparing his blow against the military ever since late 1936. In December 1936 Yezhov, the Head of the Russian Secret Police, set up an "Administration for Special Tasks" known as the "Special Bureau" and this undertook the initial investigations against Tukachevsky.[31] Shortly thereafter Yezhov had General Vitaliy Putna, one of Tukachevsky's closest collaborators, arrested.[32] On 27 January 1937 the first reference to the Marshal as a friend of the "traitor" Putna was made at the fake trial of Karl Radek, the right-wing deviationist.[33] On 3 March, in a speech to the Central Committee of the Communist Party, Stalin referred to the enormous damage "which a handful of spies in the ranks of the Red Army could do to the country."[34] On 11 May Tukachevsky was dismissed as Deputy Commissar for War and put in cold storage as Commander of the remote Volga Military District.[35] Three weeks later he was arrested.[36]

Comparison of this sequence of events with the accounts of the SS memoir-writers shows how small was the SD contribution to the Tukachevsky affair. Höttl of the SD says that "the systematic work of forgery" began on Heydrich's instructions in April 1937[37]—by which time, Putna, Tukachevsky's friend, had already been publicly denounced and Stalin had spoken of the "handful of spies" in the Red Army. Schellenberg states that the forged documents were handed over to the Soviets in mid-May 1937[38]—Tukachevsky had already been dismissed on 11 May.

Any attempt to ascribe to the SD some major hand in the liquidation of Tukachevsky presupposes that the Societ Secret Service was working through several channels simultaneously. In any case it may reasonably be assumed that Yezhov's Special Bureau would have looked for incriminating material in Germany, a country with which Tukachevsky had Service relations. In the post-war period he had frequently visited Germany; he had been a guest of the Reichswehr at their manoeuvres and he had shaken Hindenburg's hand.[39] What more natural source of incriminating material for Yezhov than the National-Socialist Regime, which had never approved of military collaboration with the Bolshevist "world enemy"? The Soviets, however, obviously had to conceal their interest in this incriminating evidence and, for this purpose, Skoblin, a double agent with the panache of an ex-civil war general, was exactly the right man to lure Heydrich into a game which the omniscient "C" never perceived.

One regularly repeated feature of the Tukachevsky story is, however, totally untrue—that Heydrich asked his opposite number Canaris for the Reichswehr's correspondence with the Soviet Army and, when the Admiral refused, obtained it by breaking into a Wehrmacht office.[40] Spalcke, the Russian expert, confirms that Canaris knew nothing of Heydrich's plans up to the time of Tukachevsky's death. When Spalcke reported to the Admiral on the Tukachevksy affair, the latter was completely unsuspecting.[41]

Canaris used to go riding with Heydrich in the mornings and was, no doubt, informed of the SD's stroke of genius on one of these occasions. The news must have shaken him for it revealed to him the existence of a world of crooks, capable of dragging the whole Reich down to ruin. Abshagen, Canaris' biographer, considers that the Tukachevsky affair was the turning point in the Admiral's attitude both to Heydrich and to the regime.[42] Barely a year later Canaris had become determined that the entire leadership both of the Sicherheitspolizei and the SD must go.

Here then were the first signs of conflict between the Wehrmacht and the SD/SS. The SD's second new field of activity, however, aroused the suspicion of an authority far more dangerous to it than the Wehrmacht—the Party. The Ausland-SD had already broken the letter of the law contained in the Canaris-Best agreement; now the work of the Inland-SD violated the spirit of an unwritten agreement subordinating the SD to the Party—Rudolf Hess had declared the SD to be the sole intelligence and counter-espionage organisation of the National-Socialist Party.[43]

This unique position had been granted to the SD only

on the understanding that it would not interfere in internal Party affairs. The SD, so the formula ran, was an enemy intelligence organisation—in other words its job was to uncover opposition within the Party but not to concern itself with internal Party questions.[44]

Himmler and Heydrich had issued strict instructions forbidding any SD man to take part in internal Party discussions in any way. Reporting of Party matters was forbidden; any unauthorised reports were to be forwarded at once, and unprocessed, to the Party Chancellery.[45] The Party, and especially the Gauleiter, kept jealous watch to ensure that the SD did not develop into an organisation of Party snoopers.

Since the reconstruction of the SD, however, there were two men working in the Wilhelmstrasse in whose eyes this—maintenance of a watch on the Party—was exactly what the SD was for. In the view of Professor Reinhard Höhn, Head of Zentralabteilung II 2 in the SD Hauptamt, and of Otto Ohlendorf, his staff director, the SD was the National-Socialist dictatorship's corrective, the voice of criticism.[46]

At their very first meeting in May 1936, Höhn had told Ohlendorf that, since public criticism was no longer allowed, it was the task of the SD "to inform the leading organisations of the Party and State about National-Socialist developments and especially wrong developments, wrong tendencies, etc."[47] The professor found a willing pupil in Ohlendorf; he was an "old fighter" and had long been searching for an opportunity of countering what seemed to him a catastrophic trend in National-Socialism. Ohlendorf was a fastidious creature, regarded by many Party members as typical of the neurotic sharp-tongued intellectual know-all;[48] he maintained that two mortal dangers threatened the health of National-Socialism from within—collectivist tendencies in economic and social policy and absolutist tendencies in constitutional policy. The former he loosely described as "Bolshevism"; he regarded Robert Ley, the Head of the Labour Front, and SS-Obergruppenführer Walther Darré, the peasant ideologist, as its protagonists. The opposite tendency he labelled "Fascism," categorising as its supporters all who preached a National-Socialist form of imperial authority untrammelled by rules and institutions—Carl Schmitt, the Professor of Law, for instance.[49]

Ohlendorf and Höhn seriously believed that through the SD they could influence the development of National-Socialism. Höhn had already made the first organisational preparations. Even before Ohlendorf joined, Zentralabteilung II 2 had transferred its attention from anti-opposition action to a new concept—that of so-called "spheres of life" observation.[50] Höhn declared that it was the SD's job to investigate opinion in all spheres of the national life and to discover the reaction of the population to measures taken by the Government and Party organisations, only thus could the leadership of the State know whether the people were in tune with its policy—it was a sort of National-Socialist version of the Gallup poll.[51]

Höhn opened his "spheres of life" reporting campaign in an area familiar to the political economist—the High Schools and Universities. But the results he achieved were moderate. When Ohlendorf joined the SD, he found that Höhn's office consisted of "about twenty young people without any office help, any registration, without any means at all."[52] Ohlendorf took over the Hauptabteilung "Economics" and rapidly built up a staff of expert economists from all parts of the country; they collected reports on the economic situation and subjected the over-all results to critical analysis.[53] The main purpose of their work was summarised by Ohlendorf in a memorandum entitled "The Economy in the National-Socialist State."

The rearmament of the Reich, Ohlendorf said, was leading to "unparallelled strains" in the economy, for instance "expansion of big businesses and contraction of others, elimination of private initiative in numerous fields and its replacement by major purchasing and distribution organisations with all their disadvantages, such as interference with the prices and wages structure." It was therefore now the "task of the political and economic leaders to recognise the limits which these stresses and strains must not exceed if the purpose of the economy as a whole is not to be prejudiced . . . through its system of reporting on the situation, the climate of opinion and abuses, the SD has here a task of quite extraordinary importance."[54]

Höhn was so pleased with the sober factual reports

from Ohlendorf's section that, in April 1937, he appointed him director of the entire staff of Zentralabteilung II 2.[55]

Ohlendorf expanded his reporting system, hitherto confined to the economy, to cover all facets of the national life. Soon hardly a sphere of activity remained uncovered by Ohlendorf's and Höhn's office. Three large-scale staffs sprang up in the Wilhelmstrasse charged with investigating the true state of the nation: Hauptabteilung II 2 1—Culture, Science, Education, the Community; Hauptabteilung II 2 2—Law and Administration, Party and State, High Schools and students; Hauptabteilung II 2 3—All Aspects of the Economy.[56]

The deeper Ohlendorf's investigators delved, however, the more critical their reports became. The SD reporters did not mince their words, referring for instance to increase of the power of big business, unchecked deficit spending by the State, collectivist tendencies in the Labour Front, denigration of the middle class, arrogance and megalomania in the Party. Earlier than they had foreseen, the investigators were at loggerheads with the Party hierarchy. The party functionaries soon realised that they were being subjected to examination by the SD. A process began later referred to by Ohlendorf as "a continuous struggle, defeats, victories and again defeats for the SD and for me."[57]

In summer 1936, however, Höhn put a foot seriously wrong and the SD's enemies seized on the opportunity to out-manoeuvre him. He had been intriguing against Professor Walther Frank, the leading National-Socialist historian, in an attempt to infiltrate SS experts into key positions in the writing of German history.[58] With the assistance of Julius Streicher, who loathed the SD, Frank struck back. He discovered certain earlier anti-Nazi remarks by Höhn as for instance: "It was primarily Hitler with his National-Socialist Movement who created an anti-intellectual current of opinion"; such remarks rang so ominously in National-Socialist ears that, according to Lammers, the Head of the Reich Chancellery, even Hitler expressed "the most serious doubts regarding Professor Höhn."[59] Himmler and Heydrich were forced to relieve Höhn of his office; he was dismissed from the SD and

disappeared to Sweden for a few months to escape the
threat of expulsion from the Party.[60]

Hardly had Höhn disappeared, however, than Ohlendorf
came under fire. Initially Himmler had been pleased with
Ohlendorf's detailed reports.[61] As the Party's suspicions increased, however, the ever-cautious and opportunist
Reichsführer kept his distance; moreover he began to
dislike the doctrinaire manner of "Nazism's Knight of the
Holy Grail," as he called Ohlendorf.

Rudolf Brandt, Himmler's secretary, lamented: "He
[Ohlendorf] doesn't know how to cope with the Reichsführer. Really to get into contact with him he ought to
bring him a rune stone from time to time and chat with
the Reichsführer about his Germanic ideals. Instead of
that he's very cold and superior in his manner as he goes
into some matter of which the Reichsführer has little
knowledge; he makes the gloomiest prophecies with a
deadly serious face."[62]

Himmler even did something which he was normally at
pains to avoid—he bypassed Heydrich, summoned Ohlendorf and reprimanded him.[63] Ohlendorf was given to
understand that the SD's "spheres of life" investigations
were illegal and would never be countenanced by the
Party; the SD was only authorised to deal with enemy
intelligence and everything else was contrary to SS interests. Heydrich followed suit. Ohlendorf was relieved as
staff director of Abteilung II 2 and relegated to his
original sphere, economics.[64] On 4 September 1937 Heydrich issued a decree: "Situation reports on spheres of life
can have only one purpose—to report the progress made
by National-Socialist ideology in the individual spheres of
life and to indicate the resistance encountered and, if
necessary, from whom; cultural, material or other matters
affecting the life of the community will only be reported
from this viewpoint."[65]

Under these circumstances Ohlendorf had no further
wish to remain in the SD and he asked Heydrich to be
allowed to resign. Heydrich refused;[66] he did not wish to
deprive himself of Ohlendorf's expertise, nor of a possible
tool for the expansion of his power. Himmler also, in spite
of his fear of Party criticism, clung to Ohlendorf.

Not until spring 1938 was Ohlendorf able to work his
passage out of the SD Hauptamt. Hitherto he had only

been a part-time Standartenführer in the SD; now he was permitted to join the "Reich Group Commerce," one of the Nazi economic pressure organisations, where he became managing director.[67] He did not completely sever his connections with the SD, however; he continued to work part-time (some two hours a day) in his old Hauptabteilung in the Wilhelmstrasse.[68]

Ohlendorf's was not an isolated case. Messages from all parts of the SD network poured into the Wilhelmstrasse, all expressing anxiety for the future. The Ohlendorf crisis had once more emphasised the fact that the SD's future was as opaque as ever. Schellenberg noted: "An increasing volume of 'reports from the front' [a term peculiar to the SD referring to the lower levels of the intelligence organisation supposed to be in direct contact with the enemy] refer to growing uncertainty regarding the SD's future; psychologically the effect of this is catastrophic. Simultaneously a wave of resignations by full-timers has started."[69]

Himmler and Heydrich found themselves faced with the necessity ultimately to produce some fundamental clarification in the status of the SD. Even before Ohlendorf's resignation a mammoth scandal had shown how insecure their machine of tyranny was. This scandal could be laid at the Gestapo's door and it bade fair to break both Heydrich's power and the partnership between him and Himmler.

The background to this affair went back as far as May 1936—in the office of the examining magistrate, Berlin Police Court, Police Headquarters. Ernst, an assistant judge, was examining an old habitué of the Berlin courts and prisons, a labourer named Otto Schmidt with a record of many previous convictions.[70] Schmidt's card showed: Otto Schmidt, aged 29; 1921–22 three convictions for theft, sentenced to two weeks, three weeks and 30 days imprisonment respectively; 1924, four months imprisonment for theft; 1927, one month for embezzlement; 1928, four months for blackmail and in the same year six months for blackmail and extortion; 1929, two weeks for fraud.[71] In 1935 Schmidt had been arrested by the Criminal Police on suspicion of further blackmail. At his first interrogation by Justus, a clerk of the court, he had admitted a couple of minor acts of blackmail but denied anything larger.[72] So Schmidt finally landed in the office of the interrogating magistrate. Ernst succeeded in loosening his tongue. He suddenly became voluble, chattering about having blackmailed a lot of people—"hundreds"—with well-known personalities among them. The majority had been homosexuals whom he had caught *in flagrante delicto*. He gave names. They included Rüdiger Graf von der Goltz, the lawyer son of the Baltic Free Corps commander, SS-Standartenführer Graf von Wedel, the Police President of Potsdam, Funk, the Reich Minister of Economics and also a "General" Fritsch.[73] Ernst pricked up his ears: which Fritsch? But Schmidt was saying no more.

A very ordinary case of blackmail had suddenly turned into a homosexual case with every sort of political implication; such affairs were the responsibility of the "Reich Co-ordinating Office for the Suppression of Homosexuality" located in the Gestapa and directed by Kriminalrat [Criminal Counsellor] Josef Meisinger. So the Schmidt files were sent across to the Prinz-Albrecht-Strasse. Meisinger read the files and he too caught his breath at the name Fritsch. Could this, he wondered, be the Commander-in-Chief of the Wehrmacht, Colonel-General Werner Freiherr von Fritsch, the secret hope of the conservative opposition in Germany and the declared enemy of all attempts by the SS to use the Verfügungstruppe to break the Wehrmacht's monopoly as an armed force? Meisinger summoned Schmidt from prison and had him interrogated by Hausser, a captain in the Schutzpolizei.[74]

On 8 or 9 July 1936 Hausser confronted Schmidt with a collection of photographs assembled by Meisinger, from which Schmidt, who was all for making a name for himself, picked out the man with the most honourable title.[75] Meisinger, who was hardly an exponent of the niceties of police work, had entered beneath each photograph the name and official title of the person concerned. When Schmidt read: "Colonel-General Freiherr von Fritsch, Commander-in-Chief of the Army," he gestured saying: "That's him."[76] Then he recorded a statement: "One evening in November 1933 he had observed in the vestibule of the Wannsee Station Berlin a man dressed in dark overcoat with brown fur collar, dark hat, white scarf, and wearing a monocle. The man had left the station with a youth of no fixed address named Martin

Weingärtner and had gone into the unlit private railway road. There he, Schmidt, had observed a homosexual act between the two."[77] After a time, Schmidt went on, the man had returned and gone to the Ring Station on the Potsdamerplatz nearby; there he, Schmidt, had confronted the man, presenting himself as "Kriminalkommissar Kröger."[78] The man had said that he was General von Fritsch and had shown him an identity card. The name "von Fritsch" was easily legible on the top right-hand corner of the card. Negotiations on the blackmail money then began; the man had said that he did not wish to be unfair—a couple of thousand marks meant nothing to him; unfortunately he had only 100 marks on him. Together they had gone to Lichterfelde where the man had disappeared into No. 21, Ferdinandstrasse. Ten minutes later he returned and pressed 500 marks into Schmidt's hand, promising a further thousand for the following day. Schmidt had collected this money and been promised yet a further thousand marks. These he had received in mid-January 1934 in the second-class waiting room of the Lichterfelde-Ost Underground station; on this occasion he had been accompanied by a friend named Heiter, whom he had presented as his chief. He, Schmidt, had given Heiter 500 marks."[79]

So much for Otto Schmidt's statement in early July 1936. Meisinger was triumphant; chance had placed in his hands a deadly weapon against von Fritsch, the Commander-in-Chief of the Army, and with it he, Josef Meisinger, would rid the SS of one of their most dangerous enemies. Meisinger pursued the case. In August Schmidt was interrogated once more, this time by Löffner, another criminal police official, and he embroidered his story; on 20 August Heiter, his accomplice, corroborated the tale.[80] Meisinger now had no doubts; Schmidt's von Fritsch was the abominable Colonel-General von Fritsch.

Meisinger forthwith reported his happy discovery to his superiors and Himmler went off at once to tell his Führer. In the Reich Chancellery, however, he met with a disappointment. Hitler cast a cursory glance over the eight-page record of the interrogation and ordered him to burn "this muck."[81] Von Fritsch, the military technician, whom Hitler had once said that he "loved,"[82] was far too useful to Hitler the rearmament fanatic to be sacrificed over such a trifle.

Unfortunately for Himmler he had shown the dictator the Fritsch file just at the moment when, in the words of the Chancellor's military aide, Colonel Friedrich Hossbach, Hitler was treating the Commander-in-Chief of the Army "with respectful discretion," allowing him in general a free hand and refraining from direct critisism of the army leadership.[83] Himmler received one of those snubs which Hitler was then reserving for anyone who dared to criticise the Wehrmacht and even more its generals. He had, after all, once said to Admiral Boehm "Then someone from the Party may come to me and say 'Alright, my Führer, but General So-and-So both speaks and works against you.' Then I shall say 'I don't believe it.' And if the man then says 'But I can show you proof my Führer,' then I shall tear the bumf up, for my faith in the Wehrmacht is unshakable."[84]

So Himmler and Heydrich had to tear up their "bumf." Heydrich had the Fritsch file destroyed—but not before he had carefully taken extracts.[85] Presumably he expected to be able to use them one day when playing for high stakes. That day came quicker than he had hoped, for in the meantime a scene had been enacted in the Reich Chancellery which must be reckoned as one of the decisive turning points in the history of the National-Socialist regime. On the afternoon of 5 November 1937 it had been borne in on Hitler that von Fritsch and Field Marshal Werner von Blomberg, the Defence Minister, were hesitant to follow him in his increasingly reckless adventurist policy and were likely to prove a restraining influence.[86]

Hitler had assembled six of his closest collaborators—Göring, Raeder, the Commander-in-Chief of the Navy, and Freiherr von Neurath, the Foreign Minister, in addition to von Fritsch, von Blomberg, and Hossbach; he had revealed to them future plans which he regarded as so important that, as Hossbach recorded in the minutes, they were to be regarded "as a political testament." They amounted to this: by 1943 at the latest Germany must have expanded her "Lebensraum" by force, Austria and Czechoslovakia must be under German control.[87] Blomberg and Fritsch raised objections, though of course only on technical military grounds; the Czechoslovak frontier defences, they said, presented a most difficult problem; even if Italy and France were at war, the presence of a strong French army on the German western frontier must be assumed. War could not be waged unless British and French neutrality could be guaranteed.[88] Hossbach noted "At times the discussion became extremely heated, primarily during an argument between Blomberg and Fritsch on the one side and Göring on the other, Hitler mostly adopting the role of attentive listener."[89]

Hitler had heard enough to form an opinion. If this was the attitude of his military men the warlike phase of National-Socialist foreign policy would get off to a bad start. Hitler's relations with his leading military advisers cooled abruptly—suddenly Meisinger's Fritsch file was a matter of interest once more. Possibly the decision to reopen the case came from Hitler himself but this seems unlikely; there was someone else with far more interest in letting the Gestapo thugs loose on the Commander-in-Chief of the Army—Göring; during the scene in the Reich Chancellery von Fritsch had accused him of dilettantism; although he had the rank of Colonel-General, he invariably felt himself ridiculed in professional military circles—and on paper he was still head of the Prussian Gestapo. In autumn 1941 Meisinger told Fritz Wiedemann, Hitler's former political aide, that the order to reconstitute the Fritsch file had come to him from Göring.[90] The only obscure factor is the timing.

The Gestapo's interest in the Fritsch case must have been reawakened immediately after the Fritsch-Göring argument in the Reich Chancellery, for when Fritsch left for a trip to Egypt on 10 November 1937 he was already being shadowed by two Gestapo agents whose brief was to confirm whether the General visited homosexual dives.[91] In mid-January 1938 Meisinger set his policemen going again, subjecting Schmidt's evidence to yet another crosscheck.[92] Inspector Fehling of Meisinger's staff in fact came near the truth; on 15 January he discovered that a certain Captain (retired) von Fritsch lived next door to 21 Ferdinand Strasse where Schmidt's victim was supposed to have disappeared—this trail was so hot that he promptly lost it again![93]

Göring's definitive order to reconstruct the Fritsch file,

however, only came later—when von Helldorf, the Berlin
Police President, came to him with a revelation highly
embarrassing to the military and so offered him the possibility of satisfying his life's ambition—to become Reich
Minister of War.

Field-Marshal von Blomberg had been a widower since
1932—with two sons and three daughters. On 12 January
1938 he had married Erna Gruhn, a shorthand typist in
the Reich Egg Marketing Board.[94] The wedding had been
a small one with Hitler and Göring as witnesses and the
happy couple had forthwith set off on their honeymoon.[95] Shortly afterwards Curt Hellmuth Müller, head
of the Reich Identification Office in the RKPA received a
batch of lewd photographs sent over by his colleague
Gerhard Nauck of the "Morality Crimes" desk. Müller's
secretary, Burkert, drew his special attention to certain of
the photographs and Müller examined them more
closely.[96]

Müller recalls: "I noticed that someone had inked in
names on the photographs of the two naked bodies and so
I called Nauck and asked him whether he was interested in
knowing who they were. He thought that at the moment
this was not necessary. I was sure, however, that I had
read the name of the woman somewhere but could not
think who it might be." So he searched in his fingerprint
index "and lo and behold the woman concerned appeared
two or three times in our register."[97] He went to Mesch,
the head of the domicile registration office, to find out
who the woman might be. From a steel tray Mesch drew
a registration card—it was that of Blomberg's wife.[98]

Müller hurried off to his chief, Arthur Nebe, who exclaimed: "Good God, Müller, and this woman has kissed
the Führer's hand!"[99] Nebe proceeded cautiously and took
Helldorf, the Police President, into his confidence. On the
morning of 23 January Helldorf appeared in the office of
General Wilhelm Keitel, the head of the Wehrmacht office
in the Reich Ministry of War and Blomberg's closest
confidant.[100] He asked the General to confirm whether
the lady referred to on the index card was the new Frau
von Blomberg. Keitel, however, said that he was in no
position to do so, since he had never seen the lady. He
called the Minister's office but Blomberg was not at home.
Then Keitel had a fatal idea; he advised Helldorf to go

and see Göring; he, after all, had been a witness at the wedding and must therefore know Blomberg's new wife.[101]

So from that moment on the evening of 23 January 1938 when Helldorf let him into the secret of the Blomberg case, Göring held a decisive trump card in his hand. He realised at once that the scandal would lead to Blomberg's dismissal. Who would then move into the Bendlerstrasse? None other than Göring's rival, Colonel-General von Fritsch. And that Göring was determined to prevent under all circumstances.

Göring had to wait 24 hours before he could strike, for Hitler was not expected back from the Berghof in Bavaria before the evening of 24 January.[102] Hitler had hardly reached the Reich Chancellery, however, when Göring arrived, lamenting to Hossbach that he always had to be the bearer of bad news. He gave Hossbach an indication of what the bad news was; it had something to do with Blomberg, the Minister of War. He said not a word about the Commander-in-Chief of the Army.[103] Göring seems to have mentioned the Fritsch case only at his meeting with Hitler and then merely in passing. When Göring had left, Hossbach found his Führer "in a great state of agitation but neither anxious nor depressed."[104]

Göring must therefore have ordered Meisinger to reconstitute the Fritsch file during the night 24/25 January. When he visited the Reich Chancellery on the evening of the 24th he had not got it with him but by the next morning it was on Hitler's desk.[105] It therefore seems a reasonable assumption that it took shape during that night. (Gestapo officials invariably state that the work of reconstituting the file took place "at high pressure and at night."[106]) A telephone call from Schaub, Hitler's aide, to Hossbach at 2.15 a.m. on 25 January ordering him to come to the Chancellery forthwith, also fits into the picture.[107] Presumably Meisinger's Fritsch file had just arrived.

The Hitler whom Hossbach met a few hours later was almost unrecognisable. There was no doubt that the double Blomberg-Fritsch affair had hit the dictator hard; it had perhaps shaken a lifetime of naïve trust in the Prussian/German military man. Wiedemann, Hitler's aide, says: "Throughout the whole four years during which I served him, I have never seen him so downcast. He paced slowly up and down in his room, bent and with his hands behind his back, mumbling that if a German Field-Marshal could do something like this, then anything in the world was possible."[108] General von Rundstedt found Hitler "in a fearful state of excitement such as I had never seen before. Something had cracked in him; he had lost all confidence in men."[109]

Was it all play-acting? Initially, certainly not. Soon, however, Hitler's predatory instinct asserted itself; here was an opportunity with one blow to deprive the Wehrmacht top level of its authority and to place himself at the head of the army. Henceforth no soldier would be able to stop his career of foreign policy adventure.

So Hitler now changed front and played off Göring against the military. When the courageous Hossbach continued to protest Fritsch's innocence Hitler commissioned his henchman to check the truth of Schmidt's statement. Twice Göring drove over to the Prinz-Albrecht-Strasse and obtained confirmation of what he and Hitler wished to hear—that Schmidt stuck to his evidence.[110] Hossbach then took the initiative. Contrary to Hitler's express order, during the night of 25/26 January he went to Fritsch and told him what was brewing. Von Fritsch seemed paralysed, shouting "It's a stinking lie!"[111]—nothing more.

This was the moment which proved that, when its great crisis came, the men in charge of the Wehrmacht were obsessed by a sense of discipline and blinded by the Führer cult; their motto might well have been the adage of the French Marshal MacMahon: "Of all people in the world the Generals are those who have the least courage to act."[112] This applied with special force to Fritsch; his contemporaries have wrongly labelled him as a secret opponent of Hitler but in fact, perhaps more than any other general, he had fallen under the spell of the Führer. Right to the end he could not understand what his Führer had done to him, could not see the abyss into which he would have fallen had his fellow generals not dragged him back. He now simply resigned himself to his destiny. His destiny?—it was that of Germany. Later he wrote of Hitler: "This man is Germany's destiny for good or ill and this destiny will go to the end of the road; if it

leads us into the abyss he will take us all with him—
there is nothing to be done about it."[113]

Nevertheless military men were still to be found who
were not prepared to abandon themselves to their fate
with such supine resignation. Once more Hossbach stood
up for his Commander-in-Chief. He argued with Hitler at
such length that the latter eventually agreed to receive von
Fritsch.[114] On the evening of 26 January the Colonel-
General was summoned to the Reich Chancellery. Fritsch
hastened to his Führer, hoping eventually to see "the pig,"
and was at once confronted with Schmidt who had also
been summoned. Schmidt said at once: "That's him." Von
Fritsch gave his word of honour "I do not know this
gentleman."[115] Meanwhile Hossbach was waiting in the
little dining-room of the Reich Chancellery; he says:
"After waiting alone for a long time I suddenly heard
footsteps pounding from the library to the little dining
room; the door swung open; Göring rushed in, both hands
up to his face, howling at the top of his voice; he threw
himself on the sofa shrieking over and over again 'He did
it, he did it!' "[116]

Hitler declared that even the Colonel-General's word of
honour did not satisfy him.[117] Now Göring saw his moment. He took Wiedemann, Hitler's aide, aside and said:
"Listen—you might talk to the Führer. Tell him to give
me the army as well. I am ready to give up the
Four-Year Plan."[118] But one intermediary was not enough
for Göring. On hearing that Keitel had been summoned
to Hitler at 1 p.m. on 27 January he called and asked
him to look round. He asked who Blomberg's successor
would be. Keitel replied: "There can be no question of
anyone other than you, for you, as C-in-C of the Luftwaffe, would not serve under another army General."
Göring could of course only applaud such delicacy of
feeling,[119] but he apparently recruited yet a third member
of the team—Blomberg; he too regarded Göring as his
natural successor.[120]

But Hitler had no intention of allowing Göring to
ruin his own plans; in his inimitable way he produced
three different reasons for refusing Göring's candidature.
To his aide Wiedemann he said: "No question of it. That
fellow Göring does not understand how to carry out
even a Luftwaffe inspection. I know more about it

myself."[121] He told Keitel: "There could be no question of it; he had given him [Göring] the Four-Year Plan; he must retain the Luftwaffe because no better man could be found and as his [Hitler's] successor he must play his proper part in State business."[122] Blomberg later recalled that Hitler made "one or two unpleasant remarks about Göring: he was too easy-going—the word 'idle' may even have been used—and in any case there was no question of him."[123]

At this point—4 p.m. on 27 January 1938—the disgraced Minister for War was seized with hatred for the military caste which had always shown its aversion to Hitler's protégé and now, in accordance with its stiffnecked code of honour, refused any gesture of sympathy to a fallen Field-Marshal. Blomberg was bent on revenge; he would ensure that the military bitterly regretted their insulting behaviour. And take his revenge he did; at his farewell visit to Hitler he suggested that the Führer and Reich Chancellor should himself take over the post of Reich Minister of War.[124] Hitler concealed his feeling of triumph. At about the same time General Alfred Jodl, Head of the "National Defence" Section in the Reich Ministry of War, was writing in his diary: "One has the impression that this is a fateful moment for the German people. How great is the unconscious influence a woman can exert on the fate of a people and hence of the world!"[125]

Hitler had taken his decision. The next day Keitel was told that Hitler himself would take over the War Ministry, transformed into an "Oberkommando der Wehrmacht" [High Command of the Armed Forces—OKW]; "I was to remain his Chief of Staff; I must not and could not leave him in the lurch in this situation."[126] On 4 February 1938 the nation heard the news that all the sceptics regarding Hitler's policy had been removed: von Blomberg and von Fritsch had retired, Freiherr von Neurath, the Foreign Minister, had been replaced by the outsider Joachim von Ribbentrop, sixteen generals had been retired, 44 others posted, the War Ministry had been disbanded and renamed OKW.[127] The Propaganda Ministry's slogan for this German version of the Tukachevsky affair was: "Concentration of powers."[128] The road to catastrophe was now open. Adolf Hitler was untrammelled Dictator of Germany.

The case of Fritsch, however, remained to be solved. A few days before his compulsory retirement Hitler had worked out a most convenient plan: Fritsch was to hand in his resignation, nothing was to be said on either side and there were to be no legal proceedings.[129] The Commander-in-Chief of the Army, however, refused to accept, so Hitler had a new idea: the case should be decided by a special court,[130] but now the military and legal professions took a hand and weighed in on the side of the General. On 27 January Dr Heinrich Rosenberg, head of the Wehrmacht Legal Section in the War Ministry, said that a special court for Fritsch was out of the question; an officer was entitled to a military court and in fact paragraph 11 of the Military Legal Code laid down that for officers of the rank of Lieutenant-General and above the President and members of the court should be appointed by the Führer. Keitel was horrified; he did not relish the idea of putting such proposals to Hitler. Hesitantly he replied: "You must bear in mind that these men are children of the revolution and their standards are different from ours."[131]

Nevertheless Rosenberg gained his point, for he was supported by the Reich Minister of Justice.[132] At last Gürtner saw a chance of calling a halt to the growing power of the Himmler-Heydrich machine. He hoped that Fritsch's case could be used to prove that if the police alone could condemn a man, the Reich was heading for a situation in which arbitrary action could replace the rule of law.[133] Hitler himself had summoned Gürtner and asked for his opinion. The Minister of Justice pored over twenty-two files of court proceedings, seven Gestapo files and two additional records of interrogations.[134] Then he reached his decision, though he expressed it in the cautious terms characteristic of National-Socialist bureaucracy; he wrote to Hitler: "I must not and cannot pronounce judgment on guilt or innocence; irrespective of the status of the person concerned, his rank or his position, this must remain a matter for the judgment of the court."[135]

The Dictator now had no alternative but to agree to the convening of a Court Martial. He nominated a Supreme Commander's Court consisting of the Commanders-in-

Chief of the Army, Navy and Luftwaffe together with the Presidents of the two Divisions of the Supreme Military Court; he charged two Judge Advocates, Biron and Dr Carl Sack, with the preliminary investigations.[136] At the same time Hitler introduced one or two safety devices into the legal machine: Göring was nominated President of the Court and the Gestapo was authorised to conduct a parallel investigation.[137] The struggle between SS and Army had begun.

At first the Gestapo seemed to be in the lead. Before Sack, the official investigator, had even started work von Fritsch suddenly and on his own initiative appeared in the Prinz-Albrecht-Strasse and submitted himself to a Gestapo interrogation.[138] Fritsch's friends were thunderstruck. For years the Army had dinned into every recruit, however junior, that the Gestapo had no right to arrest a soldier nor even summon him for interrogation; for years the Wehrmacht had insisted upon the principle that its territory was forbidden ground to any Gestapo official, however high his rank—and now here was the Commander-in-Chief of the Army losing his nerve, disregarding the restrictions which he himself had laid down and allowing himself to be interrogated by the Gestapo.

Fritsch went to the Gestapo not once but twice. On 27 January SS-Oberführer Werner Best interrogated him in the presence of Kriminalrat Franz Josef Huber; on 28 January Best confronted him with Schmidt, the witness for the prosecution.[139] The Fritsch interrogations were among the longest in the history of the Gestapo. But Best was a lawyer by profession and he was assailed by a curious feeling of unease. Admittedly Fritsch gave an irresolute impression; he was obviously nervous and became hopelessly entangled in an attempt to explain away the origin of the homosexual story by various nonsensical tales about two so-called NSV [National-Socialistische Verein—a Nazi association] youths whom he had once put up in his apartment.[140] Best was also disgusted by Fritsch's prolonged arguments with Schmidt.

Nevertheless Best could not bring himself to believe Schmidt's story. After all many of his other so-called revelations had proved to be figments of the imagination. Finally Best's doubts got the better of him, and he poured them out to Himmler who, however, waved him away,

saying: "There is such a thing as honour among thieves."
In other words—even a crook would not lie in so delicate
a situation.[141] So Schmidt's statements were checked yet
once more but this time the Gestapo must have realised
that they had been hoaxed.

Hans-Bernd Gisevius, Nebe's confidant, maintains that
Nebe told him on the evening of 30 January "that the
'case' of Fritsch was a matter of mistaken identities.
Heydrich and Himmler knew this but had taken every
imaginable measure to cover up the fact."[142] Schellenberg
also confirms that "when Heydrich began to have doubts,
the files were already on Hitler's desk."[143]

An iron curtain of silence descended on the Prinz-
Albrecht-Strasse. Not a word was spoken or indication
given which might lead the other side to suspect the truth
of the Fritsch case. The Gestapo initiated a bold diver-
sionary manoeuvre, as if they were still convinced of
Fritsch's guilt. Heydrich's minions swarmed into the
barracks and interrogated any soldier who had ever acted
as batman to von Fritsch.[144] The General's ex-aides were
also interrogated. Even the mothers of the two youngsters whom Fritsch had once fed and housed were
plagued by the Gestapo.[145]

Nevertheless the Police Chiefs were now nervous—so
nervous that it was noticeable to the outside world. Himmler's confidence in his talented head of the Sipo and SD
was shaken; Heydrich lamented that he would probably
be put to the sword.[146] General Jodl noted in his diary:
"Himmler must be depressed that senior Wehrmacht
officers are casting unheard-of aspersions on him."[147]
Every day messages arrived in the Prinz-Albrecht-Strasse
giving Himmler and Heydrich to think that the army
officers were closing their ranks and toying with the idea
of breaking the Sicherheitspolizei's grip. For Heydrich,
credence was lent to these messages by the fact that
Admiral Canaris had now become one of his bitterest
opponents.[148]

One day Schellenberg received a cry of alarm from his
master. Heydrich ordered him to provide himself at once
with a revolver and ammunition and report to his office.
Schellenberg found "C" very uneasy: together they went
to the Gestapo mess. Hours passed, Heydrich becoming
increasingly nervous. Suddenly he looked at the clock and

said: "If they don't start marching from Potsdam during
the next hour and a half, the danger will have passed."
It was Schellenberg's first intimation that Heydrich had
seriously thought that the Potsdam Wehrmacht garrison
might take action against the Gestapo headquarters in the
Prinz-Albrecht-Strasse.[149]

Certain officers had actually been considering plans of
this nature but the generals recoiled and contented themselves with pathetic gestures. Beck, the Chief of the
General Staff, was slow to grasp the deeper implications
of the Fritsch affair;[150] the new Commander-in-Chief,
Colonel-General Walter von Brauchitsch, protested
against Gestapo intrusions into the barracks;[151] Fritsch
challenged Himmler to a duel, but General von Rundstedt,
his second, never delivered the challenge and kept it at
home as a souvenir.[152] The battle against the SS was re-
lentlessly pursued only by Colonel Hossbach and Canaris,
the Head of the Abwehr; their staunchest allies were
Rüdiger Graf von der Goltz, Fritsch's defence counsel,
and Sack, the official attorney. Gradually their investigators
succeeded in penetrating the Gestapo's secret.

Sack and von der Goltz set out to disprove Schmidt's
statements. They were able to show that von Fritsch had
never possessed the identity card referred to by Schmidt
and had never lived in the neighbourhood of the Ferdi-
nand-Strasse; moreover, the General had never been a
smoker (as was Schmidt's Fritsch) and did not possess
an overcoat with a fur collar.[153] Gradually, however, it
began to dawn on Fritsch's defenders that the incident
described by Schmidt must actually have happened.
Schmidt's description of the locality was clearly correct.

Then von der Goltz had an idea: he searched through
the telephone book for the name Fritsch or something
similar. And there he found it: "von Frisch, Captain retired"—and he lived at number 20 Ferdinandstrasse! Sack
and his assistant hurried to that address and the riddle
was solved.[154] Everything fitted: Captain von Frisch admitted the incident at the Wannsee Station; he had an
overcoat with a fur collar; he was a heavy smoker—and
finally he produced the receipt for the blackmail money
drawn on his account.[155] Von der Goltz drove at once to
his principal and without even greeting him blurted out:

"General, you can rest assured; the real Fritsch has been found; the case has been cleared up without question." But the ex-C-in-C was doubtful: "Even that won't satisfy the Führer. He will not wish to believe anything like that."[156] Fritsch's fatalistic assumption was almost borne out in practice. The Gestapo laid hands on the Captain and seemed to have every intention of causing him to disappear, for Frisch was the repository of a secret which, for the Gestapo, could be mortal: he knew (and had told Sack so) that Inspector Fehling of the Gestapo had visited him as early as 15 January 1938 and had checked his bank statements.[157] Von Fritsch's friends, however, were alive to the possibilities. Sack intervened and insisted that the Captain be released by the Gestapo.[158]

On 10 March the Supreme Commander's Court, sitting in the Berlin Preussenhaus, opened the main proceedings against Werner Freiherr von Fritsch.[159] Though the real accused was the Gestapo, the start of the case was, from Fritsch's point of view, unpromising. After only a few hours the proceedings were suspended, Hitler having summoned the Commanders-in-Chief of the Services to the Reich Chancellery. Confidentially von Fritsch was given the reason; Adolf Hitler had ordered the move into Austria.[160] A week later the trial was resumed.[161] Schmidt, the Gestapo's witness made every effort to stick to his story, but then Göring, the President, intervened; although, more than anyone other than the Gestapo, he had made great play with the Fritsch case, with a couple of powerful outbursts of rhetoric he now drove Schmidt into such a corner that the blackmailer confessed everything.[162] On 18 March 1938 judgment was given: "In the case against Colonel-General (retired) Werner Freiherr von Fritsch, the Supreme Commander's Court has pronounced as follows on the basis of the main hearing: the main hearing has proved that Colonel-General (retired) Freiherr von Fritsch is innocent on all counts."[163]

Himmler and Heydrich went to ground. Surely, they thought, the Wehrmacht must strike now; surely the soldiers would play their trump card. But the Wehrmacht kept its mouth shut. Only Hossbach and Canaris produced a "draft of demands" which the Army should put to Hitler. Canaris dictated it:

(a) Public reinstatement of Colonel-General Freiherr
von Fritsch in the most impressive manner possible; the
true reason for the General's retirement to be given
wide publicity.

(b) Considerable changes in senior Gestapo appointments. In the first instance the following to be considered:

> Himmler, Heydrich, Jost (of the SD), Best,
> Meisinger, Fehling and others.[164]

Once more the Generals drew back. Beck studied the
Canaris-Hossbach paper and pigeon-holed it.[165] Politically the Blomberg-Fritsch crisis had broken the Wehrmacht's back. Moreover Hitler made a gesture to the
military. He summoned an assemblage of Generals and
rehabilitated von Fritsch, though without re-appointing
him to his office, merely nominating him Commander of
the 12th Artillery Regiment;[166] with this regiment Fritsch,
the fatalist, the "target" as he called himself, fell in action
near Warsaw on 22 September 1939.[167] Himmler, on the
other hand, had Schmidt, the blackmailer, shot.[168] He
arraigned Inspector Fehling before a disciplinary Court
and transferred him to an inconspicuous post.[169] Kriminal-
kommissar Eberhard Schiele, one of the experts working
on the Fritsch case, was dismissed from the Gestapo[170]
and even Meisinger was deprived of his "office for the
suppression of homosexuality"; in 1939 Himmler sent him
off to German-occupied Poland.[171]

Himmler took some time to forget the Fritsch setback.
He remained extremely susceptible to Wehrmacht accusations that he was campaigning against the Generals. When
SS-Gruppenführer Streckenbach was enquiring into the
case of a certain SS Commander accused by the Wehrmacht, Himmler said: "Examine everything; omit nothing
so that people cannot go on accusing me of disrespectful
behaviour towards the Wehrmacht."[172] Even to the SS-
Verfügungstruppe Himmler thought it advisable to deny
any complicity in the Fritsch case. In a speech to VT
Commanders he said that he had been the victim of in-
competent officials. Hausser, the VT Inspector, commented:
"We gave him that much."[173]

The Reichsführer was clearly in some trepidation and
kept anxious watch to ensure that neither the police nor

the SS voiced criticisms of the Wehrmacht. Anti-military comments were forbidden even at secret SS Commanders' conference. In January 1939, when SS-Brigadeführer Leo Petri submitted notes for an address to be made at a Gruppenführer conference in Berlin containing sly allusions to the Blomberg-Fritsch crisis, Himmler's green pencil was used with every indication of ill-humour; he noted on the draft: "must not be put in this way," and made numerous mollifying corrections.[174]

Heydrich also felt that his position had been affected; Lina Heydrich says that her husband lived under severe nervous strain at this period.[175] Heydrich realised a fact which has escaped the majority of historians: the police machine had not gained in strength as a result of the Blomberg-Fritsch affair. The case had of course set the seal upon the final transition to the total dictatorship of Adolf Hitler. In the relative positions of police and Wehrmacht, however, nothing had changed: the new Army leaders showed the same reserve and hostility towards the SS as their predecessors.

If anything, the conflict had sharpened. Although military intelligence was officially forbidden to report on political matters, Heydrich's enemy, Canaris, and even more Lt-Col Hans Oster, Head of the co-ordinating Abteilung in the OKW Ausland Abwehr [Foreign Intelligence], allowed their organisation to extend their activities into this field; moreover they were continually assisting enemies of the regime to escape the clutches of the Gestapo and SD.[176] Even Hitler's yesman, General Keitel, the head of OKW, considered one of his primary tasks to be the prevention of SS and Police interference in military matters. One day Halder, successor as Chief of the General Staff to Beck, who had been dismissed shortly after the Fritsch crisis, reproached Keitel for invariably giving way to Hitler; tears came into Keitel's eyes and he retorted: "Halder, I do it only for your sake after all. Do try and understand me."[177]

Heydrich knew only too well that his authority was unlikely to be accepted unquestioningly. He must therefore subject his machine to even stricter centralised control and eliminate all sources of friction within his empire. The Gestapo's loss of prestige in spring 1938 and the SD's crisis of confidence led him to develop a plan for merging the two halves of his surveillance system into one co-ordinated whole—in short he proposed combination of the SD and Gestapo into a Reich Security Service.[178]

The impulse was given by Himmler. In summer 1938 he stepped up the tempo of his great project—the merger of SS and police into "a consolidated State Protection Corps of the National-Socialist Reich," in the words of a Himmler decree of 23 June 1938.[179] Himmler visualised a two-stage merger: members of the Ordnungspolizei were to join the Allgemeine SS, even forming combined SS/Police units in the major cities; members of the Sicherheitspolizei, on the other hand, were to join the Party Organisation, the SD.[180] Himmler had already worked out (at least on paper) a detailed system for this personnel merger, the object being to bind the SS and Police indissolubly together. In autumn 1936 Commanders of SD-Oberabschnitte were nominated "Inspectors of the Sicherheitspolizei and SD" [IdS], in order to promote the gradual fusion of Gestapo, Kripo and SD.[181] In late 1937 Commanders of SS-Oberabschnitte were nominated "Höhere SS- und Polizeiführer" [Senior SS and Police Commanders—HSSPF]; in the event of mobilisation they were to assume direction of all SS, Ordnungspolizei and Sicherheitspolizei units in their Wehrkreis [military district].[182]

Himmler's plan for a State Protection Corps, however, threatened to undermine the independent status of the SD. The proposal that Sipo personnel should join the SD as the party organisation implied a new influx of men into the SD and they necessarily originated primarily from the Gestapo; as far as their official activities were concerned they were the SD's competitors in intelligence. In addition police officials now came flooding into the SD and, although they did not hold even junior SS ranks, they were now given rank corresponding to their status in the Police Force; for instance, a "Kriminalobersekretär" became an SS-Untersturmführer, a "Kriminalrat" an SS-Hauptsturmführer and a "Regierungsdirektor" an SS-Standartenführer.[183] The old SD men therefore saw the day approaching when they would be swamped by newly nominated "rank-parity" officials from the Gestapo. The potential numbers of ex-Gestapo candidates were enormous; in mid-1936 only 244 out of 607 Gestapo officials belonged to the SS and by the outbreak of war only 3,000 out of 20,000.[184]

The majority of the older SD men, moreover, were in no position to compete, for the members of the Sipo and SD were drawn from different backgrounds. The Sicherheitspolizei consisted primarily of the traditional police officials and administrative law experts; the SD intelligence organisation, on the other hand, was a bustling, heterogeneous collection of men, thrown up by the arbitrary SS career regulations—a further reflection of the fact that the SD was a Party organisation and the Sicherheitspolizei a State institution.

Heydrich now decided to put an end to this disparity. He proposed to amalgamate the SD's intelligence organisation with the Sicherheitspolizei and, at the same time, to give the SD official status; this would eliminate two major disadvantages from the SD point of view: its dependence on the Party and the lack of an official career structure with assured pension facilities.[185] The arguments over the SD's "spheres of life" activity had already shown that politically the SD was entirely dependent upon Party goodwill.

The SD's permanent shortage of funds was a further and even more aggravating proof of its dependence on the Party; every year it had to send a begging letter to the Party Treasurer. In 1936, for instance, Oswald Pohl wrote to Franz Xaver Schwarz, the Party Treasurer:[186] "Please do not be taken aback by this request; SS Headquarters funds are completely exhausted. Savings and reserves have been completely expended. The safes are empty. In recent months the financial situation has frequently been worse than catastrophic. During the last four months liquid funds available to the SS have averaged 3,000 marks!!!"[187] From time to time Schwarz went on strike, reproaching the SD with asking for more money than all the Party Members' contributions put together (in 1934 it was demanding 700,960 marks per month). Continuous SS promotion did not move Schwarz to loosen the purse strings. The Führer's Deputy and Party Headquarters frequently had to intervene to tide the SD over its difficulties.[188]

Heydrich was determined to rescue the SD from the

position of suppliant. Late in 1938 he commissioned Schellenberg to examine the problem of merging SD and Sipo,[189] salient points of the proposed reform being: "The SD to become a State Organisation independent of the Party—its budget to be borne by the Reich." Time was pressing, for the rumour was rife throughout the country that the SD's days were numbered. On 4 April 1939 Schellenberg wrote: "These rumours have built up until there is now general talk of the SD's disbandment or its absorption by the Sicherheitspolizei; the inevitable conclusion drawn is that all SD members who are without a career recognised by the internal administration, in particular those without full legal training, will lose their means of livelihood."[190]

These rumours were no figment of the imagination. At one moment Himmler had, in fact, toyed with the idea of disbanding the entire SD Intelligence Organisation.[191] He was only prevented from doing so by considerations of power policy; his position within the Party rested upon the fact that the SD was the sole Party intelligence organisation. If he abolished the SD, some other Party power group might set up a new intelligence organisation—and it would be independent of the Reichsführer-SS.

The way was therefore open for Schellenberg to proceed to design a new super-organisation. To Himmler's concept of a State Protection Corps—the SS plus the Police, he now added the notion of a Reich Security Service—the SD plus the Sicherheitspolizei. He therefore proposed amalgamation of the SD Hauptamt (a Party Organisation) with the Hauptamt Sicherheitspolizei (a State institution) to form a Reichssicherheitshauptamt. In each Wehrkreis it would maintain Security Service Inspectors in charge of Security Service Abschnitte, thus bringing all Sicherheitspolizei and SD units under one authority. Nevertheless—and here was the decisive point—the SD was not to be absorbed into the Sicherheitspolizei but was to retain its "specialised" character.[192]

Schellenberg's proposal, in fact, amounted to this: the SD would have all the advantages of becoming a State organisation, independent of the Party; members of the SD and of the Sicherheitspolizei would have equal status, but at the same time the SD would remain closed to the ex-Gestapo civil servants. Schellenberg's nightmare was the prospect of SD freedom of action being hampered by administrative lawyers. Like his master Heydrich, he was fanatically opposed to the lawyer's normative habits of thought. Though a lawyer himself, he had an almost pathological mistrust of administrative lawyers; in his view they lacked that unthinking tractability which must be characteristic of the new master-men; the type of functionary envisaged by the SD must be uninhibited by laws laid down by society or the State; they must be prepared to carry out unquestioningly every whim of the Dictator, including even the most criminal order from Adolf Hitler. In Schellenberg's view the new machine must "put aside all inhibiting or traditional notions—it must at last possess that flexibility which the government of a state must have if it is to administer a country smoothly in accordance with the directives which the Führer sees fit to issue."[193] An old-style lawyer like Werner Best, however, was incapable of such flexibility; in his view the administrative lawyer must continue to occupy a key position and so he revolted against the "deofficialisation" of the police envisaged by Heydrich and Schellenberg. He therefore proposed new career regulations, under which the SD man would be a servant of the State and full legal training a condition of employment.[194]

Between Schellenberg and Best a sniping war developed and it was not confined to the four walls of the Prinz-Albrecht-Strasse. In April 1939 Best published an article in the periodical *Deutsches Recht* clearly aimed at Heydrich's anti-legal advisers.[195] In the Third Reich, Best said, the lawyer's calling must be envisaged as "that of a monitor within the structure of society, a man who has mastered the technique of giving and executing orders in civil life and who possesses such knowledge of the tasks both of the leadership and of the community that he is in a position to carry out his monitoring function in every sphere. Within the present-day structure of society the legal profession is therefore the 'most political' profession in existence."[196]

Heydrich was so furious over Best's article that he immediately commissioned Schellenberg to draft a retort[197] and the latter set to work with his usual acumen. He criticised Best's article as "a question of personal taste." On 25 April 1939 he commented: "This implies

nothing less than a perpetuation of the arrogance shown
towards the leadership by the expert on forms of words
and it is this which leads to the present criticisms. It must
also lead to perpetuation of the disadvantages associated
with a period which we thought was past . . . highly
doubtful whether this is the moment to defend the 'lawyers' . . . failure to prove innocence . . . presumption."[198]

Best continued to demand, however, that if he became
a member of the Sicherheitspolizei, the SD man must be
subject to the normal rules of State Administration. He
continued to insist that senior officials must have had
some legal training, drawing from Heydrich the remark:
"Oh, you and your assessors' kindergarten!"[199] All this
arguing, however, proved unnecessary, for Schellenberg's
ambitious project foundered on the rock of Himmler's
timidity. He was not confident of his ability to defend the
proposal for a Reich Security Service against the Party's
objections. A tentative enquiry from Rudolf Hess had convinced him that the Party leadership would never permit
combination of a Party organisation with a State institution
to form a new official super-authority.[200] The Party was
still keeping jealous watch to ensure that no State
authority, although manned by the most ardent of
National-Socialists, should have any insight into Party
matters.

In its final form the Reichssicherheitshauptamt (RSHA)
was no more than a feeble compromise. An organisation
with this title did, indeed, come into existence on 27
September 1939 but it was never allowed to use the
name in public; the instructions laid down that the letter-
heading "Reichssicherheitshauptamt" was not to be used
in correspondence with other authorities.[201]

The RSHA, in fact, led a shadowy existence; officially
no one was supposed to know of it. It remained an
organisation valid for internal purposes only; the only title
appearing on the surface was that of "Chief of the Sicherheitspolizei and SD" (CSSD).[202]

Even the dream of combining the SD with the Sicherheitspolizei came to nothing. Party and State refused to
mix.

The RSHA "Ämter" were formed from the Abteilungen
of the SD Hauptamt and Hauptamt Sicherheitspolizei, but
even these "Ämter" led a comparatively independent

existence, some being Party institutions and others State
authorities. Amt I (Administration and Legal) was formed
from the Legal and Organisation sections of both
Hauptämter; its Head was Dr. Werner Best; it was a
State Authority.[203] Amt II (Ideologicial Investigation) was
formed from Zentralabteilungen I 3 and II 1 of the SD
Hauptamt; its Head was Professor Franz Six; it was a
Party Organisation.[204] Amt III (Spheres of German Life or
Inland-SD) was formed from Zentralabteilung II 2 of the
SD Hauptamt; its Head was Otto Ohlendorf; it was a
Party Organisation.[205] Amt IV (Suppression of Opposition)
was formed from Abteilungen II and III of the Gestapa
and Zentralabteilung III 2 of the SD Hauptamt; its Head
was Heinrich Müller; it was a State Authority.[206] Amt V
(Suppression of Crime) was identical with the RKPA and
the Kripo office in Hauptamt Sicherheitspolizei; its Head
was Arthur Nebe; it was a State Authority.[207] Amt VI
(Foreign Intelligence Service or Ausland-SD) was formed
from SD Amt III of the SD Hauptamt; its Head was
Heinz Jost; it was a Party Office.[208] (After Best's departure
in 1940 the RSHA Ämter were re-organised once more;
Best's Amt I was split into two new Ämter—I (Personnel)
and II (Organisation, Administration and Legal), the
original Amt II becoming a new Amt VII.)

The SD was in fact still dependent upon Party goodwill.
Apart from certain SD offices incorporated into RSHA
Ämter I and IV (and therefore financed by the State), the
idea of making the SD budget official misfired;[209] even the
Inland SD continued to work in the semi-official capacity
to which it had been relegated ever since embarking upon
its "spheres of life" investigations. The Inland-SD in fact
became a mere façade, maintained in being solely to
ensure that no one else in the Party should have the bright
idea of setting up an intelligence organisation. Even the
SD-Hauptamt officially remained in being as a Party Organisation[210] although it had, in fact, long since been disbanded. Ohlendorf gave the reason: "As the Reichsführer-SS did not intend to develop the 'spheres of life'
intelligence service, since he had had so much difficulty
with it . . . the solution of an external façade was
sufficient."[211]

The SD would have sunk into complete insignificance
had not Ohlendorf and his people gone on striving to

expand their sphere of activity, frequently in opposition to Himmler's declared policies. This naturally led to fresh conflicts with the Party and eventually, in 1944, Himmler threw the SD to the Party wolves. Henceforth it had only two real functions—to carry on espionage abroad, and to form the parent organisation for the leaders of the Einsatzgruppen [Action Groups] and Sonderkommandos [Special Detachments] which carried political terror and genocide into Adolf Hitler's new Europe during the Second World War.

The man who had laid the foundations of this fearful machine of tyranny, however, was not involved in the issue of orders for organised terror. Werner Best had realised that, peculiar though his concept of the legal profession was, there was no place for it in the SS world. He seized the first opportunity to resign from the Sicherheitspolizei. In May 1940 he asked Heydrich to release him to go to the front—in the Wehrmacht.[212] Heydrich was only too relieved to be rid of his millstone. He told Best: "Whenever I had a good idea, I risked finding you standing in my way and proving to me, with your legalistic arguments, that it could not be done or should be done some other way."[213]

The two parted amicably but, as time went on, Heydrich's aversion to the RSHA renegade grew. Aversion turned into hatred. Wherever Best appeared, Heydrich put obstacles in his path. In a letter to Heydrich, Best lamented: "I once promised your wife, who has always been very sensitive to atmosphere, that I would be a true friend to you. But you do not want a friend. You want a subordinate."[214] Heydrich never answered the letter.[215] He rejected all approaches by his former legal adviser, writing to Daluege, the Head of the Orpo: "In my office, the lawyer . . . is not allowed so-called power of decision on all matters . . . but is merely an adviser and an assistant . . . this, as you know, was in essence the reason for my disagreement with Dr Best."[216]

Best, the lawyer, had resigned from the Sicherheitspolizei. It was almost symbolic. Even under Best's control, the rights of the people had been curtailed, the liberal notion of individual liberty had disappeared, but some vestiges of normality and certain salient points of what is

normally meant by the word "law" had remained. Even these were now no longer valid; Heydrich's juggernaut had no braking system any more. The period of war and mass murder was at hand.

11

The SS and Foreign Policy

ON Tuesday 22 August 1939 the military elite of the Reich, the Commanders-in-Chief, Chiefs of Staff and Commanding Generals of the Wehrmacht, were summoned to the Berghof to hear from Hitler's own lips a momentous decision—the decision to go to war.

Hitler's opening words were: "I have called you together in order to give you a picture of the political situation so that you may have some insight into the individual factors upon which my irrevocable decision to act is based."[1] His monologue continued for hours; from it the military gathered that never had the situation been so favourable to Germany—England was "most seriously threatened," the position of France had "equally worsened," Soviet Russia was prepared to sign a non-aggression pact with Germany. Hitler concluded: "No one knows how long I shall live. Therefore better to have the showdown now."[2]

From minute to minute, Hitler's bellicose frenzy increased; his eyes bulged and he screamed: "Close your hearts to pity! Act brutally! Eighty million people must obtain what is their right."[3] Suddenly he recovered himself, and announced calmly that next day he would lay down the date for the attack on Poland.[4] War was to come by hook or by crook—"I shall give a propagandist reason for starting the war—never mind whether it is plausible or not. The victor will not be asked afterwards whether he told the truth. In starting and waging a war, it is not right that matters but victory."[5]

As the military dispersed, none of them knew that the

293

men who were to create Hitler's "propagandist reason
for starting the war" were already standing by. Hitler
had selected Heinrich Himmler for this task: the operation links him for all time with the blood and tears of the
Second World War.

The only man in the Berghof with any inkling of
Hitler's plans was Halder, the Chief of Staff of the Army.
On 17 August 1939 he had noted somewhat cryptically
in his diary: "Canaris . . . Abteilung I. Himmler–Heydrich,
Obersalzberg. 150 Polish uniforms with accoutrements . . .
Upper Silesia."[6] This recorded that via Admiral Canaris,
the Head of the Abwehr, Halder had heard of a conference
held by Hitler in the Obersalzberg; the Dictator had discussed with Himmler and Heydrich an incident planned
to take place in Upper Silesia, the props for which were
150 Polish uniforms. Such was the overture to a drama
which eventually cost the lives of 55,000,000 men.[7]

The idea came from Heydrich. During the Sudeten
crisis of 1938 he had proposed that the Reich should
create a prctext for the move into Czechoslovakia by
faked frontier incidents.[8] Only the Western Powers'
capitulation in face of Hitler's threats and the subsequent
Munich Conference had prevented the plan from being
carried out. The forthcoming showdown with Poland now
tempted Heydrich to produce his plan afresh. By early
August he had worked out how the world could be made
to believe that Germany had been provoked into war by
Poland.

Heydrich's plan was that during the night preceding the
German attack, SD detachments dressed as Polish
soldiers and guerillas should engineer incidents along the
German-Polish frontier. The pseudo-Poles were to occupy
the German radio station at Gleiwitz for a few moments
and shout, in Polish, one or two anti-German slogans
into the microphone;[9] they were also to attack the
Forestry Station at Pitschen, north of Kreuzburg[10] and
destroy the German Customs building at Hochlinden between Gleiwitz and Ratibor.[11]

The most horrifying feature of Heydrich's plan was the
fact that, to lend realism to the SD's war game, actual
blood was to be shed. The journalists of the world's press
had to be convinced, and so bodies must be found on the
battlefield. Heydrich commented: "Actual proof of Polish

attack is essential both for the foreign press and for
German propaganda."[12] But where to get the bodies?
Heydrich, the cynic, knew the answer to that too. The
"fallen" were to come from the concentration camps; for
the greater glory of the Third Reich, certain concentration-camp prisoners were to be given lethal injections on
D-Day and then made ready to play their part on the
Upper Silesian stage. In the repulsive Gestapo jargon,
they were referred to as "canned goods."[13]

Early in August Himmler and Heydrich submitted their
plan to the Führer and he leapt at it. The SD Hauptamt
teleprinters were soon tapping out orders to SS Standarten
23 and 45 stationed in the Gleiwitz-Beuthen-Oppeln area,
instructing them to despatch to 102 Wilhelmstrasse, Berlin,
men with knowledge of the Polish language for employment on a secret mission.[14] At about the same time SS-
Oberführer Dr Herbert Mehlhorn was ordered to report
to the Chief of the Sicherheitspolizei and SD. Heydrich
initiated him into the secret and commissioned him to
prepare the incident in the Hochlinden area.[15] The next
visitor to come heel-clicking into Heydrich's office was
SS-Sturmbannführer Alfred Naujocks, Heydrich's old crony
from the early SD days; he was placed in charge of the
attack on the Gleiwitz transmitter.

Heydrich explained that "merely for the sake of ap-
pearances, we must place the blame for forthcoming
events on other shoulders"; Naujocks took the point at
once. Heydrich ordered him to take six men, go to the
Gleiwitz area, reconnoitre the ground, and wait for the
code word "Grandmama dead."[16] He warned: "First: you
are not to get in touch with any German authority in
Gleiwitz about this business. Second: none of your men
will carry any form of identity papers which might indicate membership of the SS, the SD or the Police, or the
possession of German nationality."[17]

This took place on 10 August. Naujocks selected five
men from his office, obtained a Polish-speaker for the
proposed anti-German announcements, and set off for
Gleiwitz with his men.[18] They took rooms in two hotels,[19]
and Naujocks set about reconnoitring the position of the
transmitter. It was situated outside the town on the
minor road to Tarnowitz and proved to be surrounded by
six-foot-high wire netting; the general area of the station

and the two attached blocks of living quarters were practically unguarded.[20]

Meanwhile Heydrich had collected the other key figures in the business and discussed final details with them. The various roles were distributed: Polish uniforms to be obtained by SS-Brigadeführer Heinz Jost, Head of the Ausland-SD; the attack on the Pitschen Forestry Station to be led by SS-Oberführer Dr Otto Rasch; SS-Oberführer Dr Mehlhorn to clear the Wehrmacht from the Hochlinden area and co-ordinate the attack/defence game; the attackers consisted of a detachment dressed in Polish uniform which was to move against Hochlinden from the south (i.e. from the direction of Poland) under SS-Obersturmbannführer Ottfried Hellwig; SS-Standartenführer Dr Hans Trummler commanded the Frontier Police and the Hochlinden "defenders"; finally SS-Oberführer Heinrich Müller, the Head of the Gestapo, was to convey the "canned goods" from the concentration camps to the various battlefields.[21]

By mid-August preparations were so far advanced that Himmler and Heydrich could report to Hitler once more. An order from the Führer gave the SD the run of the Wehrmacht's secret clothing stores. On 17 August 1939 the diary of Amtsgruppe Abwehr in OKW noted: "The Führer has given Admiral Canaris, the Head of the Amtsgruppe, the following instructions: Hold ready 250 Polish uniforms for an operation under the Reichsführer-SS Himmler." Captain Dingler, Counter-Espionage Officer of VIII Corps Headquarters in Breslau, was instructed to hand the uniforms over to representatives of the SD; Canaris' office provided Polish weapons and paybooks.[22] Jost, who was in charge of this side of the business, assembled all the material in the SD School at Bernau, where the men detailed by the Upper Silesian Standarten began practising night attacks and Polish words of command.[23]

The majority of the men training at Bernau were given Polish uniforms with a rifle and thirty rounds per man; the SS men detailed for the attacks on the Forestry Station and Customs House, however, were dressed as guerillas. Hauptscharführer Josef Grzimek, one of the Bernau men, later said "for these men clothing consisted of green shirts, long trousers and civilian jackets of varying colours. On their heads they wore civilian caps and hats."[24]

By 20 August all was ready. Mehlhorn collected all his men in the lecture hall of the SD School and issued detailed orders for the top secret "Frontier Mission."[25] Then they moved off in closed trucks to their assembly areas. Grzimek reported: "Before moving off, we were strictly forbidden to look out of the vehicles, to speak to anyone, or to engage in any form of conversation."[26] Two days later, reports reaching Heydrich showed that action might be required at any moment. On 23 August Hitler decided that the Polish campaign would start at 4.30 a.m. on 26 August.[27]

Heydrich would have been somewhat less sure of himself had he known that exactly at this moment the regime's opponents in the Abwehr were engaged in compiling a record of Hitler's 22 August speech to the generals; in addition to certain verbatim quotations it contained the apocryphal, though basically correct, statement that the Dictator intended to use one or two companies of troops to make simulated attacks on the German frontier in Upper Silesia. These so-called minutes reached Hermann Maas, the opposition Youth Leader, and he, via Louis Lochner, head of the Associated Press office in Berlin, passed them to the British Embassy. As early as the afternoon of 25 August 1939, therefore, the British Government was aware that Hitler was preparing to start war against Poland by means of simulated frontier incidents.[28]

Danger threatened Heydrich's operation from another quarter, however, and of this Hitler was totally oblivious when, at about 3.0 p.m. on 25 August, he issued the final order to start war against Poland next morning.[29] Heydrich seized the telephone and gave his final instructions; Naujocks was told not to leave his hotel and to be ready for the executive order at any moment; Mehlhorn was instructed to dispatch Hellwig's detachment to the frontier; Müller set in motion his lorries carrying the dead prisoners.[30]

Then something happened on which Heydrich had not reckoned at all—Hitler called off the war. In late afternoon two messages reached the Reich Chancellery which gave the Dictator pause; the Italian Ambassador transmitted the news that the Duce felt unable to participate in this war-like adventure; London reported that England had just concluded a mutual assistance agreement with Poland. Hitler summoned Colonel-General Keitel and ordered him: "Stop everything at once; get Brauchitsch [C-in-C Army] immediately; I need time for negotiations."[31]

Keitel rushed off to the telephone—it was now 6.30 p.m.—and informed the Commander-in-Chief of the Army: "Operation White, which has already started, will be halted at 8.30 p.m. owing to changed political circumstances." The war machine had already begun to roll and was only brought to a standstill with the greatest difficulty.[32] Heydrich followed suit. Orders sped to Upper Silesia ordering the frontier action to be halted forthwith but Mehlhorn could no longer contact Hellwig's men for they had long since crossed into Poland. Hellwig's detachment duly attacked the Hochlinden Customs post and opened fire, which was promptly answered from the German side; fighting was only brought to an end by Müller's intervention.[33]

Mehlhorn and Hellwig could never subsequently agree who was responsible for this bloody incident. Hellwig had clearly taken Mehlhorn's warning as the definitive order to act; the ever-suspicious Heydrich, however, regarded the incident as more than a mere misunderstanding. In fact it was surprising that Heydrich had allotted Mehlhorn such a key role in the operation. Mehlhorn was an attorney from Chemnitz, one of the oldest and cleverest members of the SD staff, but regarded in the SD-Hauptamt as a "scruples merchant"—one of the old-style intellectuals opposed to the complete lack of principle or scruple shown by Heydrich and his people. He had been head of the "Staff Duties" division in the SD-Hauptamt but, as an opponent of Heydrich, had been relieved in 1937 and sent off to the Reich Ministry of the Interior, whence he had been despatched on a study trip to America and Japan. Nevertheless in Heydrich's schizophrenic mind Mehlhorn was worth including in the SD's war game as a guarantee that the action would be carried out cautiously and circumspectly. When, however, Heydrich heard that Mehlhorn had referred to the entire operation as an "historical crime" and when the 25 August misfire threatened to affect his prestige, he jettisoned Mehlhorn. He was relieved by Müller, dismissed from the SD and never allowed to enter the SD Hauptamt again; in fact Heydrich feared him more than any other of his subordinates, and he was never further promoted. Hellwig too was dismissed, and Standartenführer Trummler, hitherto in charge of the "defence," took over his part in the scenario.[34]

Everything went better second time round. On 31 August Hitler issued his new and final date for the attack: 1 September at 4.45 a.m.[35] Heydrich immediately alerted his secret army on the German-Polish frontier once again; about 4 p.m. the telephone rang in Naujocks' hotel room in Gleiwitz and a high-pitched metallic voice said: "Call back." That was all. Naujocks called Heydrich's office in the Prinz-Albrecht-Strasse Berlin and the same high-pitched voice told him: "Grandmama dead."[36] Naujocks collected his men and arranged that they should leave for the Radio Station at 7.45 p.m.[37] At a villa in Oppeln Müller started up his trucks. He had to hurry to get the corpses to the scene of action in time. He had one "piece of canned goods" ready for Naujocks and it must be lying at the gate of the Gleiwitz transmitter by 8.20.[38]

Meanwhile Naujocks and his team were roaring down the Tarnowitz road towards the transmitting station. Shortly before 8 p.m. one of the engineers, named Foitzik, saw five men enter the station engine room and go up the stairs to the broadcasting room. Foitzik was about to ask what they wanted when he found himself staring into the muzzle of a revolver. Naujocks greeted the remainder of the station personnel with "Hands up!"[39] He then gave a signal and his men began to make a noise. Telling the story later, Naujocks said: "We fired our pistols in the broadcasting room. We loosed off a couple of warning shots into the ceiling in order to make a bit of a shindy and frighten people."[40]

The station staff were handcuffed and carted off to the cellar. Naujocks continued: "We then had a feverish search before we could get our broadcast through." For a moment the intruders were at a loss, for they did not know how to interrupt the broadcast already in progress in order to put their political diatribe on the air. Finally they discovered the so-called storm microphone, normally

used by the announcers to inform listeners of interference
with the programme in the event of a storm. Naujocks
pulled out his Polish manuscripts and a few minutes later
thousands of German listeners heard a confused babble
of voices, obviously speaking Polish, interspersed with
one or two shots. The broadcast lasted four minutes and
then Naujocks withdrew with his men.[41] When he reached
the road he found the body of one of the concentration-
camp prisoners laid out in front of the gate. Two of the
Naujocks team had collected the corpse from Müller.
Naujocks gave him a passing glance and then signalled
for home.[42]

Similar scenes were enacted at the other places. As
Josef Grzimek came stumbling out of the Hochlinden
Customs House, which his detachment had meanwhile
devastated, he fell over something in the dark. He records:
"I bent down and saw several men lying motionless on
the ground; they were wearing Polish uniforms and . . .
their heads were shaved. I knelt down because I thought
they might be some of our people. When I tried to pick
one of them up, I found that he was completely rigid."[43]
But Himmler did not worry his head over one or two
dead concentration-camp prisoners. He had provided his
Führer with what the latter required to initiate the Second
World War—Polish provocation. Though Adolf Hitler's
soldiers and tanks had long since moved into Poland, the
press of the Third Reich hastened to register well-orches-
trated indignation, to report to the world the monstrous
happenings on the frontiers of greater Germany. "Polish
insurgents cross the German frontier" was the *Völkischer
Beobachter* headline on 1 September 1939; the paper
continued that the Gleiwitz crime was "clearly the signal
for a general attack on German territory by Polish guer-
rillas."[44] Another paper had apparently discovered that
"detachments of the Sicherheitspolizei on frontier duty
had opposed the intruders. Fierce fighting is continuing."[45]

The leaders of the Third Reich took up the story with
enthusiasm. In his 1 September speech to the Reichstag
announcing the outbreak of the Second World War, Hitler
declared that there had been fourteen frontier incidents
the previous night—three of them serious;[46] von Ribbentrop told the French Ambassador that the Polish Army
had entered Reich territory at three points.[47] Even Göring,

who had had his doubts about Hitler's war policy, "after some hesitation" told Birger Dahlerus, the Swedish mediator, that: "War had broken out because the Poles had attacked the Gleiwitz Radio Station."[48]

To support the lamentations of the press and the potentates, Gestapo Müller had to return to the scene of action, though in a different role. He and his Kripo colleague, Arthur Nebe, appeared with a murder squad to establish the facts of the Polish onslaught in proper criminal-police form.[49] To impress neutral visitors, Nebe even had an elaborate scale model of the frontier incident constructed; it could be seen by all visitors to the RKPA; on pressing a button, concealed bulbs lit up and camouflaged model machine guns chattered. When such shows were given, Heydrich would stand by murmuring: "Yes, yes. That's how the war started."[50]

The SD's war game on the German-Polish frontier showed that the SS was well on the way to establishing for itself a key position in the Third Reich's expansionist policy. The fact that the road to foreign-policy adventure should be opened by shots from SS men was little less than a portent. Those shots were the signal for Hitler's Germany to set forth towards the new horizons opened up by a policy of limitless conquest. But Gleiwitz was only a stage in Himmler's great plan; he was determined that, one day, he would dictate the course of German foreign policy. A man like Himmler, obsessed with the world mission of the Germanic master race, could have no object other than to open the door to world-wide expansion for his master men—and this implied that, one day, the SS must be the deciding factor in German power-policy and German foreign policy.

Nevertheless Himmler had to proceed with caution. He was not yet strong enough to impose his will on the other rival power groups struggling in the jungle of the Third Reich's hierarchy. His power was, of course, enormous. Next to the Wehrmacht he controlled the most powerful machine in the State—the Police; he commanded 258,456 SS men,[51] including four regiments of armed Verfügungstruppe;[52] he was in charge of the only political secret service in the Reich. On that level, however, on which the Dictator allowed his senior henchmen a free hand, this power was not enough to enable Himmler to dictate the political line. The power of the SS was overriding only when it was acting on express instructions from the Führer; when acting in its own interests it paled into impotence.

The struggle for control of foreign policy showed how small was the prospect of the SS carrying the day in the jungle warfare of National-Socialist authorities and cliques. Even in the early days of the regime, the ambitious SS foreign-policy experts had become bogged in the morass of intrigue peculiar to National-Socialism; worse still in 1933–4 they had plunged the regime into its worst foreign-policy crisis so far, hinging on the murder of Dollfuss.

At the time the Austrian Anschluss had been first on the list of new German foreign policy demands. There were no fewer than five contestants for control of German policy in Austria; the Foreign Ministry under the professional diplomat, Freiherr von Neurath; the External Policy Office of the NSDAP under Alfred Rosenberg; the so called "Ribbentrop bureau," a Party-run organisation under Hitler's adviser, Joachim von Ribbentrop, whom the Foreign Ministry regarded as an outsider; the Foreign Organisation of the NSDAP under Gauleiter Wilhelm Bohle; and finally the headquarters of the Austrian Nazi Party, in exile in Munich under Theo Habicht whom Hitler had nominated Inspector for Austria. In the autumn of 1933, however, the SS accidentally became involved in the Austrian problem and so plunged, as the sixth contestant, into this tangle of warring groups.

In summer 1933 Dollfuss, the authoritarian right-wing Catholic Chancellor of Austria, had banned the Austrian Nazi Party.[53] Dollfuss' police were tough and so thousands of Austrian Nazis fled to Bavaria—straight into the arms of Himmler, who was looking for new recruits for his army. The SS formed the fugitives into an "Austrian Legion" under SS-Brigadeführer Alfred Rodenbücher; it trained at the military camp of Kloster Lechfeld and was armed by SS Headquarters.[54] More important from the SS point of view, however, was the fact that the more active Nazis remaining in Austria turned to the SS. In the Austrian Party, the political and SA leaders had been at loggerheads and so an increasing number of Austrian Nazis opted for the Reichsführer-SS. One of them was Fridolin Glass, an ex-Sergeant-Major in the Austrian

Army, who had formed a Nazi group of soldiers and been dismissed from the Army when the Party was banned in the summer of 1933.[55]

The men of Glass's Nazi cell were dismissed at the same time and so he formed them into a "Military Standarte" of six companies. Initially he placed the unit under SA-Obergruppe XI, but he soon found that neither the rules nor the mentality of the SA were to his liking, so he went to Berlin and offered his unit to the SS.[56] By spring 1934 he had won over Gruppenführer Wittje of the SS-Hauptamt to his plan to incorporate his "Military Standarte" into the SS. Himmler agreed and Glass's unit became Standarte 89 of the Allgemeine SS.[57] Glass's action was to have devastating consequences for the Austrian Nazis. An SS investigation commission later stated that "Glass's behaviour was regarded as treachery by SA Headquarters, Austria."[58]

Glass, who had meanwhile been promoted SS-Sturmbannführer, had a plan to rid the Austrian Nazis of the Dollfuss regime by force, though whether he divulged this at the time to SS Headquarters in Berlin is not clear. He proposed to bring the Vienna Government down by a putsch. The plan was nothing new. In summer 1933 a group of National-Socialist police officials in Vienna had plotted to eliminate the Austrian Government by force but the plan had come to nothing owing to Hitler's opposition; in October 1933 Austrian Nazi Headquarters in Munich had informed the conspirators that the foreign policy situation was not yet ripe for a putsch.[59]

Glass, however, had no intention of accepting a permanent veto from Hitler, and he worked out a new putsch plan. With 150 men of his Standarte he proposed to arrest the Vienna Government during a ministerial council in the Federal Chancellery, occupy the Radio Station and proclaim a new Government, whereupon the SA throughout the country would rise.[60] Habicht, the senior Austrian Nazi and Hitler's main contact for all Austrian questions, heard of Glass's project and summoned him to Munich early in June 1934. Glass was confident that part of the Vienna police force and also some Army units would support a National-Socialist putsch. Habicht gave the conspirators the green light.[61]

This brought Glass into contact with Habicht's closest

collaborators—ex-Captain Dr Rudolf Weydenhammer, Director of the Austrian Nazi Office, and the Vienna SS-Sturmbannführer, Dr Otto Gustav Wächter, Habicht's Deputy in Austria. Habicht's entourage took up the putsch idea with enthusiasm;[62] they allotted responsibilities: Wächter was to be the political leader of the putsch and Glass the military; Weydenhammer was to maintain contact with the outside world.[63] On 25 June 1934 they all met Habicht in Zürich and fixed the preliminary details. Glass was charged with preparing the action "under all circumstances" and, even more important, with ensuring that the Vienna police and military would collaborate. Weydenhammer was to obtain the weapons and groom Dr Anton Rintelen, Dollfuss' Christian Socialist opponent and Austrian Ambassador to Rome, for the role of opposition Chancellor.[64]

Preparations gathered momentum, and developments seemed promising. Rintelen declared himself ready[65] and Lieutenant-Colonel Sinzinger, the Vienna Garrison Commander, joined the plot. He undertook to make uniforms available for Glass's men who were to enter the Federal Chancellery and arrest the Ministers.[66] When the conspirators met for a further council of war on the evening of 16 July in Habicht's apartment at 60 Kunigundenstrasse, Munich, they fixed the date of the putsch.[67] The last Ministers' meeting before the summer holidays was scheduled for the afternoon of 24 July in the Federal Chancellery and this was the moment when the conspirators would strike.

Although failure would obviously have a disastrous effect on German foreign policy, they clearly cared little about what Chancellor Hitler might say of their venture. Wächter later put it on record that never for one moment had the idea entered his head that he might not be acting in accordance with Adolf Hitler's ideas. In fact Habicht had divulged the plan to his Führer and obtained Hitler's agreement[68]—but in such vague terms that Hitler was able subsequently to deny all responsibility and in 1938 even to arraign Wächter before the Supreme Party Court for having "deliberately acted against the declared will of the Führer."[69]

The Dictator was once more playing that double game which allowed his right hand to be ignorant of what his left hand was doing. While conniving at Habicht's intrigues against Dollfuss, he was urging von Neurath's Foreign Ministry to warn the Austrian Nazis to refrain from any ill-considered action against the Dollfuss regime. While the conspirators were meeting in the Kunigundenstrasse, Dr Reith, the German Minister in Vienna, was drafting a telegram to the Foreign Minister, informing him that Austrian National-Socialists were planning a putsch against Dollfuss.[70]

An Austrian Nazi named Hans Kohler, a post-office official in Heinfeld, had handed a memorandum to the legation with the request that it be forwarded to Hitler; it amounted to a demand for the arrest of the entire Austrian Government. The legation telegraphed: "Herr Kohler was told by the Legation that the ideas contained in the memorandum were prejudicial to the policy of the Reich and he was requested, moreover, to prevail on his collaborators to desist from the plan. The memorandum was retained to prevent it from falling into the wrong hands. Since it cannot be ascertained here whether Herr Kohler is pursuing his plan further, in spite of the fact that he was warned against it, I suggest that appropriate steps be taken to stop this action."[71]

The Foreign Ministry bureaucrats were just as disturbed as the Minister in Vienna. The Foreign Ministry wrote forthwith to Habicht, requesting him to "prevent any such plans that might possibly exist."[72] It is not known whether, for the delectation of his fellow conspirators, Habicht read them the Foreign Ministry's letter. Nevertheless at the conspirators' table sat a man who was determined to cause the *coup d'état* against Dollfuss to fail; Wächter later called the result "the most shattering experience of my life."[73]

SA-Obergruppenführer Hermann Reschny, head of Austria's proscribed SA, could not reconcile himself to the fact that in their plans for a coup Glass and Wächter, both SS Commanders, had allotted the SA no more than a subordinate role; the SA was only to emerge when the decision had already been reached in Vienna. Reschny sensed in this a deliberate insult to the SA. It seemed to him no accident that SS men should once more relegate SA interests to second place. Back in Germany the SS had destroyed the SA's unique position; they had murdered the SA old guard. Now the SS seemed to be demanding the predominant position in Austria too. They had already filched from the Austrian SA its most powerful unit, Glass' Standarte.

Moreover Reschny could not forget that on that bloody Saturday of 30 June 1934, a mere month before the Austrian putsch, when Röhm and his retinue had been liquidated, only chance had saved the head of the Austrian SA from the SS thugs. Could it be that he was now destined to avenge his murdered SA comrades—now that the SS was apparently girding its loins for a further expansion of its power?

By his tactics Habicht unconsciously made things easier for Reschny. He had laid down that on the day of the revolt, though they would strike in unison, the SA and SS would march separately. Wächter stated: "Comrade Habicht told me that I was not to get in touch with the SA. The SA was separately commanded and, on receipt of the code word, would be used as a body under Obergruppenführer Reschny."[74]

Reschny concluded from this that, should the SS putsch fail in Vienna, there would be no repercussions on the SA, since the two groups were to act completely separately. Without appearing in the open himself, he cautiously fed information about the putsch plans to the Austrian security services.[75]

Reschny used two "trusties" who had already, on several occasions, contacted the Dollfuss Government on his behalf—SA-Sturmbannführer Friedrich Hamburger, Liaison Officer to the SA-Obergruppe in Vienna, and his friend, Captain Schaller. When Schaller was tried in 1935, Wächter, basing his comments on the material brought in evidence, stated: "In 1933 and 1934 the Austrian governmental offices were kept fully informed of everything which the Party wished to keep secret from them."[76] After Habicht's conspiratorial council of war, Reschny summoned his two "trusties" to Munich for an SA-Obergruppe Commanders' Conference and discussed the putsch once more in complete detail.[77]

Schaller took the point; he noted down all the details and passed them to the Federal Chancellery via a Vienna security official named Cyhlar.[78] But Reschny, apparently, wished to make doubly sure. Schaller later stated on oath that Hamburger had given him further detailed instructions to pass to the Austrian police—names and personal details of the putsch leaders, Glass, Wächter and Weydenhammer.[79] So the Austrian Secret Police knew all about the putsch. In 1935 Cyhlar stated: "As regards Wächter, during the final months Schaller kept me continuously informed about the July putsch."[80]

The Government was nevertheless taken by surprise: the historian Hellmuth Auerbach ascribes this to be extraordinary contortions of the Viennese spy world. "The agent business" in Austria at the time, he says, was "so highly developed that it cancelled itself out."[81] Wächter was placed under observation by the Austrian State Police; wherever he went he was shadowed by two secret policemen. One thing, however, Weiser, the Vienna Police Chief, did not know—Wächter's shadows were National-Socialists and every evening he and they would get together to draft the observation report for the police.[82]

So Wächter and Glass still seemed to have a chance of bringing off their putsch. 24 July, the day of the final ministerial council in the Ballhausplatz, approached. Rintelen was holding himself in readiness in the Imperial Hotel, Vienna; the 150 SS men of 89 Standarte prepared for action; the senior conspirators hurried off to the agreed assembly points.[83] Then, on the afternoon of 24 July, Weydenhammer heard from Rintelen that the Ministers' meeting had been postponed and fixed for 11 a.m. the next day.[84] Rintelen wished to quit but the Nazi leaders insisted that now, at last, they must strike.[85] A fresh order was issued to the SS men detailed for the attack on the Chancellery: "89—12.45 p.m., Gymnasium, 11 Siebensterngasse—do not approach the Siebensterngasse via the Breitegasse."[86]

Punctually on the next day, 25 July 1934, 30 SS men arrived at the German Gymnastic Association's great gymnasium to fit themselves out as soldiers. A lorry rumbled up bringing uniforms of the Deutschmeister Regiment obtained by the conspirators from Army stocks. Glass hurried his men along, for the changing process seemed to be taking too long[87]—the lorry full of pseudo-soldiers was due to leave for the Federal Chancellery at 12.30. Eventually it left, fifteen minutes late. Every man knew the cover story which was to gain them the entrée to

Dollfuss—President Miklas had ordered them to the Chancellery for a special mission.[88]

While Glass and his men were on the way to the Ballhausplatz, Wächter, the political leader, took up position in the Tischler restaurant in the Schauflergasse near the Chancellery, ready to intervene if necessary.[89] He was only to appear later: his job was to conduct negotiations with the arrested Ministers and instal the new Government. Neither Glass nor Wächter, however, knew that the putsch was, in fact, a failure before it had ever begun. It had been betrayed—and not by the SA. One of the Wächter-Glass conspirators, Johann Dobler, a District Police Inspector and ex-Economic Director in the Brown House, had lost his nerve and given away the whole thing.[90]

Before the Ministers' meeting ever began, Emil Fey, the Heimwehr [the Austrian right-wing defence formation] Minister was informed that a group of Nazi extremists was planning an attack on the Federal Chancellery.[91] Unfortunately he was an ambitious man and so, instead of alerting Dollfuss and the Army, he called his own private army, the Heimwehr, out on to the streets and sent them off on a cops-and-robbers-style hunt to track down the conspiracy.[92] When at last he bethought him of his duty, valuable minutes had been lost. He hurried into the Ministers' meeting only shortly before midday, took the Chancellor into a corner and whispered the news into his ear. Dollfuss was incredulous but determined.[93] He said to the Ministers: "Fey has just told me something but I don't yet know whether there is anything behind it. But it's perhaps better that we should interrupt the session and that every Minister goes back to his own office. I will let you all know when we can continue."[94] The Ministers left, thoroughly baffled. The only people to remain in the Chancellery were Dollfuss, Fey and Karwinsky, the Permanent Secretary in charge of security.[95]

Karwinsky ordered police reinforcements to the Ballhausplatz. Unsuspectingly he looked down into the courtyard as a lorry turned in at the gate. That will be the police, he thought: in fact it was the conspirators.[96] A few minutes later a captain rushed in and told Dollfuss that armed men had broken into the Federal Chancellery. Dollfuss hurried out of his study into the hall next door to look out of the window into the courtyard. A Criminal Police officer reported that the intruders were soldiers, to which Dollfuss replied: "Oh? Soldiers?"[97] Hedvicek, the doorkeeper, then came pounding into the room and seized the Chancellor's arm, shouting: "Chancellor, quick!" He knew a secret spiral staircase leading out of the building; it could be reached from a corner room near the Chancellor's study.[98]

Hedvicek and his charge had hardly reached the corner room, however, when eleven SS men led by Otto Planetta burst in from the stairway and came across to the Chancellor.[99] The intruders stood still for a moment and then all shouted hysterically: "Hands up!" The Chancellor looked them straight in the eye saying: "What do you want from me?" He made a gesture of impatience. Planetta drew back and pulled the trigger of his automatic. Dollfuss collapsed and fell back, blood streaming from his chest.[100]

The conspirators laid the wounded man on a sofa. After a moment Dollfuss opened his eyes and asked in puzzlement: "Little ones, what on earth's happening? A major, a captain and several soldiers suddenly come in and shoot me."[101] Gradually Dollfuss realised that he had not long to live; he collected the men around him and there began what Gordon Shepherd called "a curiously placid political discussion" between Dollfuss and the rebels.[102]

Dollfuss opened with: "I always tried to do the best I could and I always wanted peace." An SS man retorted that the Chancellor had it in his power to bring about peace with Germany. The dying man answered: "Children, you simply don't understand."[103] Glumly the SS men looked down at their victim; no one said a word. At 3.45 p.m. Austria's Chancellor breathed his last; his final words were: "Little ones, people have been so good to me. Why aren't the others like that? All I have wanted is peace. We have never attacked but we had to defend ourselves. The good God will forgive you."[104]

Nevertheless the putschists did not give up. The coup against the ministerial council had failed and the arrest of all the Ministers, the essential feature of the whole action, had misfired. Only the occupation of the radio station had been successful.[105] Wächter raced off through

Vienna to get help. This, he thought, was the moment when the SA must strike; now Obergruppenführer Reschny must call his cohorts out onto the streets and send them into action against the Government. Finally Wächter reached the Saint James Hotel where the leaders of the Austrian SA were assembled, and presented himself to SA Brigadeführer Turk.[106] Wächter describes the sequel: "After I had given a short account of the situation and asked the SA to move, Turk issued in my presence an order alerting the SA Groups in Vienna and Lower Austria. In answer to my question, he declared that the SA would be on the march to the centre of the city within an hour."[107]

But Turk was of the same mind as his master, Reschny. When Wächter rushed off to another appointment, Turk cancelled the orders and instructed the Vienna SA, which had already been alerted, to return to its billets. Not an SA man moved to assist the hard-pressed SS putschists. Shortly thereafter Turk let it be known that: "The putsch of 25 July is an operation peculiar to SS-Standarte 89, for which the SA disowns all responsibility."[108] The SA looked on unmoved while Austria's police and army put an end to the Vienna putschists. Planetta and six of his fellow conspirators were executed; the remainder were sentenced to long periods of imprisonment.[109]

Hitler, however, now found himself unexpectedly faced with a wave of international protest. For the first time since the formation of the Third Reich, Adolf Hitler was now regarded by the world at large as an out-and-out murderer, against whom it was the duty of any responsible statesman to mobilise all the forces of the civilised world. "We are faced with a second Sarajevo" Hitler screamed, when urging his ex-Vice Chancellor von Papen to go as Ambassador to Vienna and use his reputation as the principal Catholic member of the regime to patch matters up.[110] Hitler made a clean sweep; Habicht was relieved of his post; the "Austrian Legion" was disbanded and an official Party enquiry into the conspiracy was held.[111] The hardest hit by the débâcle, however, was the Reichsführer-SS, who had to swallow a severe loss of prestige.

It was useless for Wächter to rage that the SA "used traitorous methods to further their policy, which was aimed at SA predominance in Austria" and that "anything was possible with leaders who, for their own selfish motives, could hand over their comrades to the enemy."[112] The damage to the reputation of the SS was not to be made good so easily. Hitler's confidence was shaken and the SS had to work its passage back.

The SS had learnt one lesson—in the struggle between the National-Socialist potentates power groups were to be found prepared to achieve thier ends by the use of naked force and without regard to the supposedly unifying influence of common belief in National-Socialism. The battle of cliques and power groups within the Party and, since 1933, within the State-Party machine, had become so habitual a pastime with its brown-shirted masters that even an appeal to their common interest in averting the regime's threatened self-frustration would not stop it. People were prepared to give way to a political opponent rather than renounce any shred of authority or power in favour of some rival within the Party. In 1932, for instance, Röhm had allied himself with the Social-Democratic Reichsbanner rather than compromise with his internal Party enemies; in Austria Reschny preferred to see a National-Socialist putsch fail rather than concede victory to the SS; back in Germany Lutze, the Chief of Staff of the SA, rather than bury the hatchet after the Röhm upheaval, dreamed of combined SA-Wehrmacht action against his *bête noire*, the SS.

In this tussle of unyielding interests, locked in a sort of trench warfare, the SS was only one force among many and could make no worthwhile breakthrough on its own. In the field of German power policy and foreign policy it could inch its way forwards only when under the protection of the sole source of power recognised on all sides—the authority of Adolf Hitler and the Party leadership installed by him. The latter was now embodied in Rudolf Hess, the "Führer's Deputy," and it was he who eventually allowed the SS to take a hand in a secondary theatre of German foreign policy, where full rein could be given to Himmler's racial and biological hallucinations—the field of German "Volkstum" [racial or demographic] policy.

From the earliest days the Party leaders had realised that the islands of German nationals on and beyond the frontiers could form bastions of a future German great-power policy; their manpower resources were considerable and they had increased in number as a result of the frontier rectifications decreed at Versailles. There were many links, some visible and some invisible, between the NSDAP and the "racial Germans," primarily those in eastern and southeastern Europe.

In 1931 Party Headquarters had set up a "Foreign Section" to deal with all persons of German nationality resident abroad. The Section [Abteilung] later became known as the "Auslands Organisation" [Foreign Organisation—AO] under Gauleiter Wilhelm Bohle; in 1937 it had over 51,000 members.[113] The Organisation soon became such a factor in foreign policy that von Neurath took the precaution of appointing Bohle State Secretary in the Foreign Ministry, hoping thereby to keep a tighter rein on him.[114] Bohle's organisation, however, was only one among many power groups intruding into the sphere of traditional German diplomacy. Rosenberg's "External Policy Office" dealt with German students from abroad[115] and the Verein für das Deutschtum im Ausland" [Association for Germanism Abroad—VDA], officially a private organisation but long since Nazified, maintained contact with "racial Germans" throughout the world.[116]

The intrigues between these various organisations eventually became so intolerable that in 1936 Hitler charged Hess with control of all matters concerning Germans abroad. Hess, in turn, nominated Otto von Kursell, an "old fighter," to head a "Volksdeutsche Mittelstelle" [Reference Office for Racial Germans—VOMI]; it was responsible to the Party leadership and was intended to act as a sort of undercover headquarters co-ordinating the work of all governmental and Party offices concerned with questions affecting Germans resident abroad.[117] Kursell, however, lacked the authority to bring to heel all the various organisations which were locked in the battle for spheres of influence. Hess suddenly had an idea for saving the situation. The only Party formation which could help was the one whose leaders were supposed to possess discipline and organising ability—the SS. Hess asked the Reichsführer-SS to select a man capable of bringing some order into the confusion and Himmler at last spied a chance to lay hands on some aspect of German foreign policy. He detailed SS-Obergruppenführer Werner Lorenz to take charge of the "Germans Abroad" front.

Lorenz was one of the most personable and adroit SS leaders. Born in 1891, he had been a Cadet Officer and Air Corps pilot in the Imperial Army; he owned an estate in Danzig and had finally ended as Commander of SS-Oberabschnitt "North West" in Hamburg; his daughter had married the Hamburg publisher, Axel Springer. He was regarded as the SS *bon viveur,* with the manners of the old Prussian officers' mess and the air of a master of backstairs intrigue.[118] Subsequently Himmler probably regretted his choice, for Lorenz was a power-seeker and soon succumbed to the temptation to profit from the triangular battle between Party, Foreign Ministry and SS to create his own private army—and it was by no means always used to further the ambitions of the Reichsführer. In any case, from the SS point of view, a great gulf was fixed between the two men; Lorenz was a traditional nationalist and invariably treated his master's racial fantasies with condescending pity.[119] Himmler was well aware of this, but not until the outbreak of war was he able to force Lorenz out of his dominant position in German racial policy and incorporate VOMI, which had become far too independent, into his empire as a new SS Hauptamt.

Nevertheless VOMI enabled the SS to take a major step forward in the field of German racial policy and consequently also in that of foreign policy. Originally intended as a Party co-ordinating office, it developed into an SS centre of power, absorbing an increasing number of fields of activity and organisations concerned with racial policy.

Lorenz began in January 1937 with a small organisation of only 30 men[120] but he contrived to gain control of one institution after another. In July 1938 Dr Steinacher, who headed the VDA and had become over-powerful, was dismissed and VDA business was taken over by one of Lorenz's close associates;[121] shortly thereafter VOMI took under its wing the influential "Bund Deutscher Osten" [League of Germans in the East—BDO];[122] as the BDO was responsible for the frontier areas, VOMI was assured of a preponderant position in the leadership and financing of the German minorities in Eastern Europe.[123] The SD made good use of VOMI's manifold connections with the German racial groups beyond the Reich frontiers and set up a network of listening and observation posts, using

VOMI representatives as cover. VOMI and the SD worked closely together. The appointment of Dr Hermann Behrends, a senior SD official and close associate of Heydrich's, to be Lorenz's Deputy in VOMI was no accident.[124]

The network of SS and SD contacts began to impinge more and more perceptibly upon the official work of the Foreign Ministry. SS men began to appear in the higher ranks of the numerous cultural organisations and societies dealing with the countries of south-eastern Europe. For instance, SS-Oberführer Ewald von Massow became President of the "German Bulgarian Society" and Lorenz took over the Chairmanship of "Inter-State Contacts."[125]

Himmler and Lorenz kept in specially close touch with the man to whom VOMI was theoretically subordinate. This was SS-Gruppenführer Joachim von Ribbentrop, the "Deputy for External Political Questions on the Staff of the Führer's Deputy," to give him his official title;[126] the SS had high hopes that through Ribbentrop they might make a major breakthrough into the control of foreign policy. Relationships between Ribbentrop and the SS were so close that many people regarded the future Foreign Minister as the "SS spokesman" on foreign policy.[127] Correspondence between Himmler and Ribbentrop was full of glowing phrases: "You know my attitude to your SS and how I admire the way you have built it up entirely by your own efforts. I shall always regard it as a special honour to be a member of this proud corps of leaders which is of such decisive importance for the future of our great German Reich" (Ribbentrop to Himmler in July 1940).[128]

The two men had known each other since the end of 1932; and that time von Ribbentrop, demobilised as a Lieutenant in 1919, an ex-champagne merchant and married to the heiress to the Henkel champagne fortune, had made available his villa in Berlin-Dahlem for secret negotiations between Hitler and von Papen.[129] Himmler's job at the time had been to assist Hitler to evade the reporters by climbing over the back garden wall of Ribbentrop's property and then to demonstrate by his polished behaviour at table that even Nazis were fit to be included in the Government.[130]

Himmler's demonstration at least convinced his host von

Ribbentrop, for shortly thereafter the latter joined the Nazi Party and asked Himmler for the favour of permission to belong to the SS. On 30 May 1933 he was given the rank of Standartenführer and Himmler was henceforth a welcome guest in the Ribbentrop villa.[131] Ribbentrop sat at Hitler's feet and successfully worked himself into favour with the dictator, becoming his special adviser on foreign affairs; the further he advanced, the more closely did Himmler cling to the coat-tails of this dilettante upon whom fortune was clearly smiling. On Hitler's instructions Ribbentrop later set up a bureau in the Wilhelmstrasse opposite the Foreign Ministry; it created its own reporting system to cross-check the work of the Foreign Ministry, which Hitler found suspect. Himmler provided both money and personnel to assist his friend.

In 1937 SS-Oberführer Rolf von Humann-Hainhofen joined the "Ribbentrop Office" as Director;[132] he was the forerunner of that type of SS diplomat who was to be found in increasing numbers in Ribbentrop's entourage. SS-Oberführer Rudolf Likus, Ribbentrop's old school-friend,[133] and SS-Standartenführer Werner Picot, who dabbled in secret-service affairs,[134] were among the most trusted Ribbentrop men. Ribbentrop and the SS worked so closely together that when the former was nominated Foreign Minister in February 1938, Himmler was justified in considering the appointment a major prestige victory for the SS.

As Foreign Minister Ribbentrop continued to cling to the SS; all his "adjutants" were SS commanders[135] and he sent his son, Rudolf, into the Leibstandarte Adolf Hitler.[136] One day he had a splendid idea, which horrified the Foreign Ministry diplomats; he informed all the senior bureaucrats that he had agreed with Himmler on their acceptance as a body into the SS.[137] Everyone now had to put on SS uniform. Freiherr von Weizsäcker, the Permanent Secretary, turned into an SS-Oberführer,[138] Ernst Woermann, the Under Secretary, into an SS-Standartenführer,[139] von Dörnberg, the Chief of Protocol, into an SS-Obersturmführer.[140] According to Erich Kordt, an opponent of Hitler masquerading as an SS-Obersturmbannführer, nothing gave Ribbentrop greater pleasure than "to appear in the office in the uniform of an SS-Gruppenführer with his great jackboots. He presumably thought

that this gave him the greatest resemblance to his predecessor, Bismarck, whom he always pictured as a man
who usually went about in a cuirassier's tall, uncomfortable jackboots."[141]

The Führer's Bismarck could not have enough SS-uni-
formed men around him; at times he even reproached
his "Dear Himmler" for failing to make sufficient numbers
of SS men available for the Foreign Ministry, writing:
"since taking over the Foreign Ministry, I have not received a single first-class staff officer from the SS; in view
of the good relations between my office and the SS,
together with our close personal friendship, it would be
more than regrettable if the SS were conspicuous by its
absence."[142]

Ironically, however, the struggle for power within the
bureaucracy brought the two partners into collision and
turned them into bitter enemies. The man who had introduced the SS uniform into the Foreign Ministry would
later fly into a paroxysm of rage if he ever saw any of his
diplomats wearing it.[143] The fact that he wore an SS-
Gruppenführer's uniform did not prevent von Ribbentrop,
as Foreign Minister, from becoming involved in those
intrigues which were the daily bread of the Nazi potentates.
For he had become head of an authority which could not
but resist SS penetration into its preserves, if it did not
wish to lose to the SS the technical control of German
foreign policy.

The occasion of the quarrel was a decision by Hitler
pregnant with consequences for the history of the world.
After the occupation of Austria the Dictator decided to
expand the German sphere of influence and, regardless of
the risk of war, to play up the problems of the German
minority groups in Czechoslovakia and Poland, both
fraught with potentialities of crisis. This, however, brought
the racial problem into the forefront of German foreign
policy and, in that field, the SS had already achieved a
position through VOMI. The Foreign Ministry diplomats
found themselves being pushed to one side by the SS
racial experts.

In the Sudeten crisis engineered by Hitler in the summer
of 1938 the Foreign Ministry in fact played only a
secondary role. Ernst Eisenlohr, the German Minister in
Prague, being opposed to Hitler's annexation policy, was

deliberately left in ignorance,[144] while Lorenz, the head of VOMI, on Hitler's instructions discussed the detailed moves against the Czechoslovak Government with the Sudeten German leader, Konrad Henlein.[145] However, independently of, and sometimes in opposition to, VOMI, another SS authority now took a hand in the game— Heydrich's Ausland-SD; it was destined to become a nightmare to the Foreign Ministry for it was pursuing an entirely different aim—to bring down Henlein. The SD had managed to convince itself that Henlein was a compromiser and a weakling who did not promote the Führer's interests with sufficient energy. Certain of the Sudeten Party leaders, such as Walter Brand, Wilhelm Sebekowski and Heinrich Rutha, were regarded with suspicion by the SD as being supporters of the Catholic Authoritarian State theory; they had no wish to join Hitler's Germany; they simply hoped that the great powers would assist them to obtain improved minority status *within* Czechoslovakia.[146] In 1934 even Henlein himself had said: "We do not hesitate to state that a fundamental difference exists between us and National-Socialism. We will never renounce the freedom of the individual."[147] Incorporation of the Sudentenland into the Reich was supported only by a small group of National-Socialist extremists—and on them Heydrich set his sights.[148]

In late 1937 Heydrich decided to bring Henlein down by means of a Party revolt. Henlein was too quick for him, however; Heydrich's main allies consisted of a circle of politicians centred around the newspaper *Der Aufbruch* and these Henlein expelled from the Party.[149] Early in the summer of 1938 Heydrich spied another chance. He had meanwhile established contact with Carl Hermann Frank, Henlein's principal Party opponent and leader of the Sudeten Nazi Party, which had been banned and absorbed into Henlein's Organisation. Frank was not averse to capturing leadership of the Party, even with the assistance of the SD.[150]

Henlein must have sensed the danger, for he escaped from the SD's clutches by precipitating matters. He had, in any case, come to the conclusion that the intransigence of the Prague Government, together with the disappearance of Austria, left him no other choice than to collaborate with Germany; accordingly at the end of July 1938, he went to the German Gymnastic Festival in Breslau and there reached agreement with Hitler, who was also present.[151] The Dictator forbade the SD to intrigue further against Henlein. Henlein was therefore saved, though the price demanded was high. The SS, on the other hand, was left to draw the necessary conclusions from the changed situation—Henlein, the ex-critic of the Nazis, was given the rank of SS-Gruppenführer.[152]

The Foreign Ministry diplomats, however, had now been shown how far the SS had already penetrated into their foreign-policy preserve. Von Ribbentrop did manage to prevent Lorenz of VOMI being nominated Secretary for German minority questions,[153] but this only increased the SD's greed for diplomatic privileges. The next foreign policy crisis saw the Foreign Ministry completely out-pointed by the SD. The Dictator left it to his own trusted Secret Service men to lay on the scenario—the destruction of the "remainder of Czechoslovakia" in March 1939.

Hitler had worked out a sophisticated plan. The leaders of the ultra-conservative and clericalist Slovak Peoples' Party were to be urged to declare their country's secession from the centralised Czechoslovak State; simultaneously the Czechs were to be encouraged to suppress the Slovak revolt. In the resulting upheaval Hitler would emerge as arbiter and take both countries under his control. The "remainder of Czechoslovakia" was to form the Reich Protectorate of Bohemia and Moravia, Slovakia remaining as a theoretically independent State under the "protection" of the Greater German Reich.

Early in 1939 SS-Gruppenführer Wilhelm Keppler, together with SS-Standartenführer Edmund Veesenmayer and a troop of SD agents, travelled to Bratislava and established contact with the Slovak politicians.[154] These secret emissaries had strict instructions from Hitler that under no circumstances were they to allow the Foreign Ministry to know the purpose of their journey.[155] Keppler and his gang arrived just in time; the Prague government, weary of continuous friction with the semi-autonomous provincial Government of Slovakia, had just invited the Slovaks to a conference of reconciliation in the capital. The men from Berlin, however, persuaded Josef Tiso, the Slovak Minister-President, to reject the invitation from

Prague and make immediate preparations for Slovak independence.[156]

At this point, one of the most prominent of the Slovak politicians threw a spanner in the works. Dr Karel Sidor, the Slovak Minister of State in the Prague Government and Commander-in-Chief of the Hlinka Guard (a sort of Slovak SA) rejected the Germans' separatist plan. This gave the remaining Slovak politicians pause. The Germans negotiated with Sidor but he refused to budge.[157] The SD therefore turned to its normal solution in such situations —criminal methods.

Alfred Naujocks, the SD troubleshooter, was ordered to Slovakia with a sabotage squad. He was to engineer incidents apparently the work of the Slovak Nationalists.[158] All was going well—the first bombs had gone off in a Bratislava chocolate factory, Prague had swallowed the German bait, deposed the Tiso Government and declared a state of emergency in Slovakia—when suddenly an amateur diplomat took a hand unscheduled in the programme.[159]

Josef Bürckel, the Gauleiter of Vienna and another SS Gruppenführer, called on Sidor, whom Prague had meanwhile nominated Minister-President of Slovakia in place of the separatist Tiso, and tried to get him to change his mind. But "these remarkable efforts on the part of the Gauleiter" (Keppler's caustic description) failed.[160]

Back in Berlin Hitler was becoming nervous. Time was pressing. Suspecting that the Germans were playing a double game, Hacha, the Czechoslovak President, had announced his arrival for a visit to Hitler on 14 March[161] and this meant that the dictator was forced to obtain the Slovak declaration of independence not later than the evening of the 13th; without it Hitler would not obtain the capitulation which he intended to force on the Czechs. On 11 March Keppler went to Tiso once more, imploring him to agree to a split with Prague. During the night of 12–13 March Tiso gave way.[162] Hardly had he given his agreement than an invitation to Berlin reached him from Hitler. A few hours later he was in Hitler's presence, just in time to lay Slovakia at the feet of the overlord of Central Europe before Hacha arrived.[163]

For the first time the SD had shown its mettle as the executor of Hitler's will in a matter of foreign policy.

From Vienna Bürckel protested that the SD had shown themselves downright bunglers in Slovakia; if only he, Bürckel, had been given more time to negotiate with Sidor, everything would have passed off far more smoothly; but the Führer ignored him. Even this, however, led to an internal SS quarrel; after the victory in Slovakia harsh words passed between SS Commanders unable to agree upon whose the victory was. SS-Gruppenführer Bürckel deluged Hitler, Göring and Ribbentrop with memoranda about the inefficiency of SS-Gruppenführer Keppler. SS-Gruppenführer Keppler retorted that SS-Gruppenführer Bürckel had nearly caused irreparable damage to the Reich. In a letter to Himmler Keppler complained: "I trust that you will not misunderstand me if, in pursuing this matter further, I take as little account of Bürckel's SS membership as he has done of mine; it seems to me likely that I shall have to defend myself against gross slanders."[164]

Hitler now placed unlimited confidence in his SD. It was not therefore surprising that he allotted it the "honour" of lighting the spark which set off the Second World War. The actions on the German-Polish frontier described earlier in this chapter were only part of the SD's war provocation; simultaneously no fewer than twelve SD commandos moved into Poland with orders to initiate 200 individual actions by the end of August, all to be ascribed to Polish extremists.[165]

The SD became increasingly prominent in affairs of foreign policy. In Hitler's field headquarters SD reports were frequently used in place of the regular Foreign Ministry diplomatic despatches. Ribbentrop later lamented that "Hitler, without informing me, would take immediate decisions based on false information" (from the SD).[166] There was hardly an area of foreign policy where Ribbentrop was in sole charge. In January 1939, without any consultation with the Foreign Ministry, Himmler had assisted General Oshima, the Japanese Ambassador in Berlin, to dispatch to the Soviet Union ten Russian emigrés armed with bombs to murder Stalin.[167] Similarly, during the war, the SD pursued a policy all their own; on their own initiative, for instance, and in face of the Foreign Ministry's opposition, SD representatives tried to lure Castillo, the President of Argentina, into an alliance with the Third Reich directed against the USA;[168] in Spain they attempted to bring down Franco and replace him by a Falangist leader more sympathetic to National-Socialism;[169] in Rumania, they attempted to manoeuvre the fascist organisation, the Iron Guard, into power.[170]

An even more serious threat to any further independent existence for German diplomacy was the fact that in the first hectic days of the war, Ribbentrop gave his agreement to a new proposal from the RSHA, something which the Foreign Ministry was to rue for many a long day— the inclusion of so-called Police Attachés in diplomatic missions. On 26 October 1939 Ribbentrop agreed that the SD might make use of German Embassies and Legations as cover for their work in foreign countries; in any particular country the head of the SD intelligence network was to be given diplomatic status and entitled Police Attaché. As a *quid pro quo* the SD promised not to interfere in matters of foreign policy.[171] The Police Attachés, however, soon began to criticise their Ambassador's or Minister's policy and spy upon the Mission's personnel. The Foreign Ministry could do nothing, for Ribbentrop was still set upon the closest possible collaboration with the SS and had given Himmler and Heydrich the right to instal SD agents "direct"—in other words without prior reference to the Foreign Ministry; their reports, moreover, went direct to the RSHA. These SD reports frequently contained violent criticism of German diplomats. In his memoirs Ribbentrop said: "On one occasion, for instance, secret SD reports direct to the Führer led to the sudden order that I should recall three Heads of Mission—those in Spain, Portugal and Sweden."[172]

Nevertheless Joachim von Ribbontrop was not a man to lie down under such an invasion of his preserves. He barricaded himself behind his prerogatives and initiated a dogged war of outposts against his erstwhile comrade Himmler. The Foreign Minister soon became a doughty exponent of internecine National-Socialist strategy.

As the opening shot in his counter-offensive Ribbentrop astutely made use of an order from the Führer. On 3 September 1939 Hitler had laid down that "For the duration of the War all representatives of civil authorities or Party offices located abroad . . . will be subordinated to the German Head of Mission in the country concerned. These representatives or delegates will report to the Foreign Ministry through the Head of Mission."[173] Ribbentrop proposed to use this Hitler ukase to bring the SD agents abroad under the control of the Foreign Ministry. Nevertheless he had to proceed with caution; so long as the SD was working on Hitler's instructions and adhering strictly to Hitler's orders, the Foreign Ministry had no hope of regaining even a minimum of authority over its work abroad. Ribbentrop had to wait until the SD made a gaffe which shook its prestige even in the Führer's headquarters. He waited.

Shortly after the Police Attaché agreement of 25 October 1939 an incident had occurred which showed how unwise it still was to voice criticism of the SD's behaviour in Hitler's presence. Ribbentrop had heard that the SD was planning one of the greatest kidnappings in secret-service history to take place on the German/Dutch frontier—and he was worried.

In mid-October 1939 Walter Schellenberg of the SD received instructions from Heydrich to initiate a Secret Service operation against the much-admired British Intelligence Service in Holland, at the time still a neutral country. Heydrich hoped for great things from this particular gambit—insight into the methods of the British Intelligence Service, into the degree of co-operation between the British and Dutch Secret Services, and into the German internal opposition's contacts abroad.[174] A certain German emigré in Holland named Dr Franz worked for the SD under the code number F479 and he had good contacts with the British Secret Service, in particular with Captain S. Payne Best, the "Intelligence Service" representative in Holland; Best was particularly interested in signs of opposition to Hitler among the German generals. F479 promised to obtain information.[175]

Via Franz, the Ausland SD (alias Amt VI of the RSHA) provided Best with carefully prepared false information. Meanwhile the RSHA began to think that it might perhaps be worthwhile to hear a few more details from the Intelligence Service representative. For this task Heydrich selected his best man, his confidant Schellenberg. The latter quickly turned himself into Captain Schemmel of the

OKW Transport Section, wearer of an eyeglass and bearer of important secrets regarding internal German opposition.[176] F479 arranged a meeting and on 21 October Schemmel, monocle in eye, was sitting opposite Best (who also affected a monocle) somewhere in the Netherlands.[177]

Best took Schellenberg/Schemmel in his Buick to Arnhem, where two more Intelligence Service men were waiting, the British Major Stevens and a Dutch staff officer who called himself Copper though his real name was Klop.[178] The three foreigners found the revelations of their new German friend extremely interesting. Schellenberg presented himself as the confidant of a general who, together with other military men, was planning a *coup d'état* against Hitler.[179]

They agreed to meet again on 30 October when Schellenberg once more travelled to Holland.[180] Copper/Klop had arranged to have Schellenberg temporarily arrested in error, in order surreptitiously to examine the German's papers; the British, however, were fully confident in the SS man[181]—they even gave him a radio set for urgent communications, with the call sign ON4.[182]

Meanwhile the two British officers had given the impression of being the repositories of such valuable secrets that Heydrich had the idea of kidnapping Best and Stevens and carrying them across the Dutch frontier into Germany.[183] This was the moment chosen by Ribbentrop to tell his Führer of his anxieties over SD methods. The moment was badly chosen in any case; Adolf Hitler was in no mood to listen to criticism of his SD. He reacted with such ill humour that Ribbentrop executed one of his well-known somersaults, stammering: "Yes, my Führer, that has always been my opinion, but these bureaucrats and lawyers in the Foreign Ministry are so tedious."[184]

In fact Ribbentrop withdrew just in time, for irrationality now took control of Schellenberg's secret-service game. As a result of an assassination attempt by a lone-wolf cabinet-maker, Stevens and Best became labelled for ever more in Hitler's mind as the central figures of a traumatic experience.

On the evening of 8 November 1939, Martin, the Police President of Nuremberg, stopped the "Führer Special" as it was moving out of Munich station with Hitler

and Himmler on board. Martin clambered onto the train
and reported that a few minutes after the Führer's traditional Bürgerbräu speech in Munich a bomb had exploded in the "Old Fighters'" Assembly Hall; the ceiling
of the hall had fallen in, ten or twelve Party members were
feared dead, and the criminal was still unknown.[185] Immediately it flashed through Hitler's mind that this was
the doing of the British Secret Service and that Stevens
and Best were behind it. Himmler got the point. He hurried
to the telephone and alerted the RSHA. Then he dialled
a number in Düsseldorf. The telephone rang in Schellenberg's room and an excited Himmler was on the other
end of the line: "This evening, just after the Führer's
speech in the beer cellar, an attempt was made to assassinate him . . . the Führer had left the cellar a few minutes
before . . . there's no doubt that the British Secret Service
is behind it all."[186] Himmler then passed on Hitler's order
to arrest Stevens and Best forthwith and bring them to
Germany. Schellenberg did as he was told. He had been
ready for the operation for days: Naujocks from the SD
was standing by with an armed squad and Schellenberg
had agreed to meet the two British officers on the afternoon of the next day in the Dutch frontier town of
Venlo.[187]

At 3.00 p.m. the next day, 9 November, Schellenberg
installed himself in a Venlo café close to the frontier. The
minutes dragged by interminably. Schellenberg looked out
of the window and kept a watch on the street—the coup
must take place before the two British officers entered
the café. Then Schellenberg saw Best's Buick drive up.
With a great show of geniality he went out to welcome
his visitors. Best and Stevens approached.[188]

At this moment an SS convertible roared up, crashed
through the frontier barrier and stopped in front of the
two British officers. Submachine-guns fired and the two
Englishmen drew their revolvers. Naujocks and his men
jumped out of the car and overpowered them; Klop,
though severely wounded, was carted along too. Schellenberg meanwhile hurried off to his own car, parked behind the café, and in a few moments all was over. The
coup had succeeded.[189]

The next day the German propaganda machine went

into top gear. The Germans were told that the Reich Security Services had succeeded in arresting the manipulators behind the abominable attempt upon the Führer's life. SS-Oberführer Walter Schellenberg received from the Führer's own hand the Iron Cross First Class for his bravery in violating international law; the Dictator even invited him to dinner in the Reich Chancellery with the heads of SS.[190] The precocious Schellenberg, however, had a disappointment in store for his master during the meal. He voiced his opinion that the attempt upon the Führer's life had not been the work of the British Secret Service and certainly not of his two prisoners, Stevens and Best; in his view only one man had the crime upon his conscience —the man under arrest, Georg Elser.[191]

Himmler intervened immediately to say that this was only Schellenberg's personal opinion.[192] In fact it was the unanimous view of the RSHA. Schellenberg had taken the precaution of studying the RKPA files and they led only to one conclusion—Elser was a lone-wolf operator.[193] During the night of 9 November Nebe, the head of the Kripo, together with the members of the Special "Assassination Commission" (Heydrich, Gestapo Müller, Lobbes, Nebe's deputy, and explosives experts) had flown from Döberitz airfield to double-check the clues in the Bürgerbräu, Munich.[194] But Nebe discovered little which the Kripo Leitstelle Munich had not already noted.

All the indications and scraps of evidence showed that the coup had been prepared over a long period. The criminal had used a timebomb with an explosive charge of no more than 20 pounds, which had been concealed in one of the wood-panelled ferro-concrete pillars of the Bürgerbräu. Soon the man responsible was cowering in front of the Gestapo's interrogation arc-lights; he had been arrested on the evening of 8 November while attempting to cross the Swiss frontier illegally. He was Georg Elser, an apprentice cabinet-maker and watchmaker from Königsbronn, aged 36, a worker both by inclination and principle, who wanted no more than peace and a quiet life and so did not like Hitler's war.[195]

He described his actions in detail: "Using a padsaw, I cut the wooden panelling of the pillar, fixed a couple of hinges and then replaced the piece of wood in the

form of a little door. Later I lined this door with 2 mm
thick iron plate. The plate served two purposes. In the
first place in the event of anyone tapping the pillars it
would conceal the existence of a cavity behind; secondly,
in the event of redecoration of the hall it would prevent
some accidental nail damaging the clockwork." Then he
brought along his dynamite charge connected to a timing
device: "on the evening of 5 November between 9 and
10 p.m. I went to the Bürgerbräu with the timing mechanism in a box. I went up into the gallery . . . and hid
myself behind a pillar. There I waited until the lights were
put out and the hall was shut. As a precaution I waited
a further half hour. Then I went to the pillar with the
timing mechanism, opened the little door, and checked
that the clockwork parts would fit into the front part of
the chamber. Finally I set the two watches."[196] It was as
simple as that. But the simple truth did not satisfy the
Führer of the Great German Reich; he was convinced
that this was a gigantic conspiracy by the British Secret
Service, a widespread net of intrigue in which all his deadly
enemies had had a hand—the Jews, the British, the Freemasons and, last but not least, Otto Strasser. Himmler
was in a state of panic. Where were the masterminds?
When Nebe could not find them, he was dismissed and
recalled to Berlin.[197] Almost in tears, Himmler lamented:
"Schellenberg, what we have to do is to find the people
behind this thing. The Führer simply will not believe that
Elser did it alone."[198] On the record of the first Elser
interrogation which produced the lone-wolf theory, he
wrote indignantly: "What idiot conducted this interrogation?"[199]

With the rage of desperation characteristic of the panic-
stricken subordinate, Himmler descended upon the unfortunate prisoner Elser who by this time was almost beside himself. Dr Bohme, the head of the Kripo Leitstelle
Munich, witnessed the scene in the Wittelsbach Palace,
the Gestapo Headquarters: "With wild curses Himmler
drove his boots hard into the body of the handcuffed
Elser. He then had him removed by a Gestapo official
whom I do not know and taken to the lavatory leading
off the head of the Gestapo Leitstelle's office where he
was beaten up with a whip or some similar instrument

until he howled with pain. He was then brought back at the double to Himmler, who once more kicked him and cursed him."[200]

But Georg Elser stuck to his story. Himmler ordered another top investigator to Munich, Franz Josef Huber, head of the Vienna Gestapo. He too failed to find the master-minds. Huber called Müller in Berlin and told him of the conclusions he had reached, but the head of the Gestapo was indignant: "Good God, how can anyone think that!"[201] One after the other, however, they came to recognise that Elser was in fact a lone wolf. Even Heydrich was forced to accept the truth.[202] Himmler alone continued to chase the phantom master-minds; on 4 December SS-Gruppenführer Karl Wolff, head of Himmler's personal staff, wrote to SS-Oberführer Zimmann: "We are not satisfied with the single man."[203] But a single man it remained.

Finally, Himmler had to accept from Hitler's own lips the reproach which he most feared—that of having failed. Hitler never forgave the Reichsführer-SS for withholding from him the real criminal of 8 November 1939: these were sufficient grounds for Himmler to preserve Elser as the most valuable witness to police efficiency—he was the only man who might be able to confirm that Himmler's minions had not in fact failed.

For Himmler's rival, Ribbentrop, however, the Elser affair provided a most encouraging pointer: the power of Himmler's machine was unassailable only so long as it was carrying out Hitler's orders and wishes to the letter; if it diverged, even by only a hair's-breadth, from the Dictator's line, the SS was fair game for any criticism. The Foreign Minister waited patiently for the moment when he could prove to his Führer that the SS was not a totally reliable instrument of the Führer's will. That moment came a year later. The SD proved itself so undisciplined that Hitler flew into a rage, screaming that he would "smoke out the black plague" if it did not toe the line.[204]

The reason for the Dictator's wrath was an attempted rising by the SD-backed Iron Guard in Rumania, the object of which was to bring down Hitler's ally, the ultra-conservative Minister-President, General Antonescu. German policy in Rumania was a particularly ludicrous illustration of the tug-of-war between Foreign Ministry and SD. For years the SD had been supporting the Iron Guard, a nationalist revolutionary party with Fascist leanings, which Himmler's and Heydrich's emissaries regarded as first cousin to the Nazi Party.[205] In September 1940, however, General Antonescu, a Balkan leader equally averse to fascism and democracy, stepped into power just ahead of the Iron Guard.

Antonescu had good reason to be grateful to the Germans; in July 1940 he had been arrested by King Carol and had only been released as a result of representations by German diplomats.[206] Since the Iron Guard, moreover, possessed no personalities of note, the Berlin Foreign Office put its money on Antonescu as the future Dictator of Rumania.[207] This called for no great decision from Hitler, since initially Antonescu made common cause with the Iron Guard and ruled Rumania with its assistance. But the alliance between the reactionary and the revolutionaries was short-lived and two months later Horia Sima, the head of the Iron Guard, was girding his loins for revolt against Antonescu, confident of the assistance from Germany promised him by his SD advisers.

On 21 January 1941 the Iron Guard struck in Bucharest. Almost all the capital's important open spaces and buildings fell into their hands, Antonescu retaining control only of the Minister-President's office.[208] His situation was desperate; this was the moment when only Hitler could help. On 22 January, via the German Legation, Antonescu enquired whether he still enjoyed Hitler's confidence. The reply flashed back from Ribbentrop: Yes; Antonescu should act as he thought fit; the Führer advised him to treat the legionaries as he, Adolf Hitler, had once dealt with the conspirators in the Röhm putsch.[209]

Antonescu struck back and put down the revolt, pursuing his enemies ruthlessly. But suddenly the SD intervened, rescuing the leaders of the Iron Guard, including its Chief, Horia Sima and fourteen Commandants; Sima was hidden in the house of the German minority leader, Andreas Schmidt.[210] When the Rumanian police abandoned their hunt for the fugitives, the SD smuggled them out of the country disguised in German uniforms and travelling in ambulances.[211]

As soon as Ribbentrop heard of the SD's Rumanian extravaganza he worked Hitler into a rage. He painted a picture of a gigantic SS conspiracy against the official foreign policy of the Reich; the head of the SD in Rumania had encouraged Horia Sima to revolt; SS-Obergruppenführer Lorenz, the Head of VOMI, had installed Schmidt as minority leader and Schmidt had provided Sima with a hiding-place. According to Ribbentrop, the entire SS Headquarters was involved in the plot, for Schmidt's connections reached back to Himmler's immediate entourage; Gruppenführer Gottlob Berger, Head of the SS Hauptamt, was Schmidt's father-in-law.[212]

Ribbentrop despatched a new German representative to Bucharest with full plenary powers; he immediately dismissed the SD Commander attached to the Embassy and ordered him back to Germany. An arrest warrant awaited him and he spent months in the Gestapo prison.[213] Such inroads had been made into the SD's prestige that Ribbentrop finally plucked up his courage to bring the sinister Police Attachés to heel. In April and June 1941 he wrote three letters to Heydrich, amounting to a demand for a new working arrangement between the Foreign Ministry and the RSHA in view of continued SD interference in the field of foreign policy.[214]

Ribbentrop now revoked the 26 October 1939 agreement, basing his case on Hitler's instruction that all German representatives abroad must act under the authority of the head of mission concerned, and demanded that, like everybody else, the Police Attaché conduct his official correspondence only through the head of mission.[215] Himmler gave way. On 9 August 1941 he concluded a new agreement with Ribbentrop, providing that all correspondence between Police Attachés and the RSHA should be seen by the head of mission; in addition, the SD was not to interfere in the internal affairs of the country concerned.[216]

Whether or not the SD took such agreements seriously, this development in the power struggle clearly constituted an invitation to Ribbentrop to be more insistent in his demands upon the SS. He missed no opportunity to remind the Reichsführer-SS of the Foreign Minister's prerogatives. On one occasion Himmler was invited to Italy by the Italian Foreign Minister; Ribbentrop pointed out to him that "applications for authorisation for foreign travel by leading personalities of the State and the Party should be transmitted in writing and in good time to the Foreign Ministry." Only if Himmler would inform him of the exact purpose of his journey to Italy, could he, as Head of the Foreign Ministry, decide whether he could recommend this journey to the Führer. He continued: "If you are basing yourself upon the assumption that your functions within Germany give rise to some form of special authority to take action abroad, I would point out that on my side I could under no circumstances recognise any claim to authority in relation to foreign countries such as might affect the external policy of the Reich."[217]

In south-eastern Europe, where SS contacts were particularly numerous, Ribbentrop now put a stop to any further SS foreign-policy adventures by allying himself to a force which had already, on several occasions, stood in the way of Himmler's foreign-policy ambitions—the SA. In summer 1941 he filled all Embassy and Legation posts in the Balkans with SA leaders, deliberately selecting survivors of the Röhm putsch. SA-Obergruppenführer Seigfried Kasche from Lower Saxony became Minister in Zagreb, SA-Obergruppenführer von Jagow from Berlin Minister in Budapest, SA-Obergruppenführer Manfred Freiherr von Killinger from Central Germany Minister in Bucharest, SA-Gruppenführer Hans Ludin from Swabia Minister in Bratislava and SA-Obergruppenführer Adolf-Heinz Berkerle from Hesse Minister in Sofia.[218] None of these men had forgotten that they were once near to death at the hands of the SS.

Ribbentrop, in fact, drew a line which Himmler was never allowed to pass. When SS-Gruppenführer Werner Best joined the Foreign Service, Ribbentrop told him that from now on he must be his, Ribbentrop's, man, not Himmler's.[219]

But his erstwhile friend's pinpricks could now no longer hurt the Reichsführer-SS. He had long since realised that the longer the war went on, the less foreign policy mattered. The field of independent foreign policy was growing ever smaller; the world of neutral and independent states was shrinking. Occupation policy was taking the place of foreign policy. In the West, and even more important in the vast open spaces of the East, a new field of activity was opening. There Himmler, with his prophet's eye, saw a promised land—the world of the German master-race.

12

Racial Policy in the East

HEINRICH Himmler took every known precaution to safeguard the secrecy of his precious document. No unauthorised person was to read it; only a select few of the Third Reich's most senior officials were allowed to know of its contents. The reason was not far to seek; on its six pages were set down Himmler's most private day-dreamings—fevered ravings, but they were to dictate the fate of millions of men.

On 28 May 1940 Himmler noted: "The Führer directed that only a limited number of copies should be made, that it was not to be reproduced and that it was to be treated as top secret." Only a few Nazi potentates were initiated into the mystery—one or two Gauleiters, two Ministers of the Reich, the Governor-General of Poland, the HSSPF [Höhere SS- und Polizeiführer—Senior SS and Police Commanders] and the Heads of the SS Hauptämter. To the latter the file was brought by hand of officer, who waited while it was read and demanded a written acknowledgment from the reader.[1]

The document was written by Himmler and submitted to Hitler in May 1940; it was entitled: "Some thoughts on the treatment of foreign populations in the East."[2] This was the secret which the Reichsführer-SS was so anxious to conceal even from the most orthodox National-Socialist eyes, for it amounted, to a proposal, in Himmler's dry bureaucratic language, for the destruction of the Eastern peoples in order to make room for the German master race.

As the ultimate goal of German policy in the East, the

author proposed that what had once been Poland with its numerous races (Poles, Ukrainians, White Russians, Jews, Gorals, Lemkes and Kashubs) should be "broken up into the largest possible number of parts and fragments." The "racially valuable elements should be extracted from this hotch-potch" and the residue left to wither slowly away. Himmler continued: "If these measures are consistently carried out, over the course of the next ten years the population of the Government General will necessarily be reduced to a remnant of substandard beings. It will consist of a leaderless labour force, capable of furnishing Germany with casual labourers annually, together with the manpower required for special projects."[3] The peoples of the East were gradually to be reduced in number and driven further eastwards; the Jews were to be "completely eliminated by means of a major deportation operation to Africa or some colony"; "in our area" it should be possible "to cause the Ukrainians, the Gorals and the Lemkes to disappear as racial entities. Making allowance for the larger area involved, the same should apply . . . in the case of the Poles."[4]

But how to destroy a racial entity? Himmler's answer was: elimination of its upper classes and "screening" of its youth; children were to be classified in two categories: "racially valuable" to be carried off to the Reich and Germanised, "the remainder" were to be deliberately left to vegetate. Himmler prescribed: "No higher education than that provided by a four-class primary school will be allowed for the non-German population of the East. The aim of this primary school should be to teach the pupil solely: how to count up to a maximum of 500, how to write his name, that it is God's command that he should be obedient to Germans, honourable, industrious and brave. I regard reading as unnecessary."[5]

No flatter statement of National-Socialist determination to dominate can be imagined; the old German "Drang nach Osten" was being resumed in a far more virulent form. But Himmler's memorandum carried a further implication. It was proof of the SS claim to control of German policy in the East; it was a reflection of that imperious SS demand succinctly expressed by SS-Gruppenführer Otto Hofmann of the RuSHA: "The East belongs to the SS."[6]

As it so happened Hitler's initial victories had in fact placed the SS in a key position in the Eastern territories; the real master in that area appeared to be Himmler. For the first time he could visualise the possibility that his long-standing dream might really come true, that his SS, his neo-German order of knighthood, might carve out a new kingdom of teutonic knights and found a strong teutonic state; his SS would form the breakwater damming the rising Slav tide and standing guard over fertile settlement areas filled by a German peasant population.

Ever since he became capable of coherent thought, Heinrich Himmler had been preparing himself for exactly this mission. No one, he thought, could be more ideally suited to fulfil this sacred mission, to lead the Germans eastwards and turn them back into a nation of peasants. One day he returned overjoyed from a conference in the Führer's Headquarters, saying to his masseur, Felix Kersten: "You won't understand how happy I am . . . the Führer not only listened to me . . . he went so far as to approve my proposals . . . this is the happiest day of my life." The proposal which Himmler had laid before his Führer was his project for the construction in the East of a network of SS settlements manned by armed peasants. He continued: "The Germans were once a farming people and must essentially become one again. The East will help to strengthen this agricultural bent inherent in the German nation—it will become the everlasting fountain of youth replenishing the lifeblood of Germany whence it will, in its turn, be continuously renewed."[7]

Himmler had always seen himself in this role of great Germanic peasant leader. In his bizarre dream-world the romantic historical picture of medieval eastern settlements combined with his biological horror of dark-haired bullet-heads to produce the crazy notion that Germany's salvation lay in a sort of feudal peasant aristocracy settled in the East. He never tired of propagating his theory of German settlement in the East. At heart he was still the Artaman who, with his friend Walther Darré, had once tried to stem the influx of low-paid Polish workers on to the East German estates; now he was continually drumming into his SS men the necessity for Germans to recapture their roots in the soil and win new settlement areas for themselves.

Himmler and Darré, the Head of the RuSHA, had been quick to lay hands on responsibility for German settlement policy. In 1934 SS-Gruppenführer Darré had been promoted Reich Minister of Agriculture;[8] SS-Standartenführer Dr Horst Rechenbach had become Head of the Reich "Office for Settler Selection";[9] all the leading officials of the Reich Food Organisation had been made honorary SS Commanders.[10] Nevertheless the hard facts of modern industrial society torpedoed the sociological Utopia envisaged by these two reactionary enthusiasts and in the process terminated the friendship between Darré and Himmler. Darré clung to his theory of a "blood-and-soil" aristocracy and in February 1938 Himmler dismissed him as "too theoretical."[11] Himmler, the opportunist, waited until his Führer's policy presented him with new settlement areas in which to instal the great German Reich's new peasantry.

In March 1939 when the first foreign people, the Czechs of the "remainder of Czechoslovakia," were incorporated into the Greater German Reich, Himmler saw a chance to revive his old plans. In June he dispatched SS-Oberführer Curt von Gottberg to Prague to set up a Real Estate Office.[12] The idea was that in the rich agricultural areas of the "Reich Protectorate of Bohemia and Moravia," von Gottberg should dispossess Czech landowners and settle Germans on the farms thus made vacant; even Hitler was already talking of deporting six million Czechs.[13] But von Gottberg's mission was a failure. The German armament industry was relying largely on Czech industrial and labour potential and it refused to hear of any major deportation measures in the Reich's back garden. The Prague Real Estate Office had to content itself with preparations for the settlement of one or two SS families in Bohemia and Moravia.[14]

Not until the outbreak of World War II could Himmler, the anti-Slav peasant mystic, see the promised land before him. Disappointingly, entry could, initially, only be gained by the back door. Although the Dictator had summoned his most faithful disciple before the start of the Polish campaign, what he wanted from him was not the missionary zeal of the settler, but the ruthless action of the policeman.

Adolf Hitler had decided upon a solution of the "Polish

question." In his eyes the Polish war was far more than
the violent settlement of the Danzig and Polish corridor
problems; now was the moment to fulfil the prophecy
made years before in *Mein Kampf* "We begin where we
left off 600 years ago. We put an end to the perpetual
Germanic march towards the South and west of Europe
and turn our eyes towards the lands of the East. We
finally put a stop to the colonial and trade policy of pre-
war times and pass over to the territorial policy of the
future."[15] In the path of this "territorial policy," however, stood a foreign people already cultivating the soil.
But on this subject too Hitler knew his own mind as early
as 1928; the Reich, he wrote, must "either sterilise these
racially foreign elements to ensure that its own people's
blood is not continually adulterated or . . . remove them
altogether and make over to its own people the land thereby released."[16]

Translated into 1939 terms this meant that the Poles
were to be reduced to the level of a nation of helots,
deprived of their upper class, of their existence as a nation
or a State, and of their culture. The proud Polish people
were to become a nation of slave labour, condemned to
serve one purpose only—to work for their German masters. From the 22 August conference in the Obersalzberg
Germany's senior soldiers knew that Hitler was set upon
the destruction of Poland. Field-Marshal von Bock recalls
that Hitler said that "things would be done of which the
German generals would not approve. He did not therefore
wish to burden the army with the necessary liquidations
but . . . would have them carried out by the SS."[17]

This was the reason for Hitler's summons to Himmler
and this is why, for all time, the SS must remain indissolubly linked with the Polish tragedy. Hitler gave
Himmler the task of forming "Einsatzgruppen" [Task
forces] to follow the German troops as they advanced
into Poland and liquidate Poland's upper class wherever
it was to be found.

Einsatzgruppen of the Sicherheitspolizei had so far been
a regular feature of every stage of National-Socialist expansionist policy. During the move into Austria Heydrich's
"Sonderkommandos" [Special detachments] had gone in
with the troops;[18] Einsatzgruppen had moved into
Czechoslovakia when that country was broken up.[19] The

Einsatzgruppen were mobile advanced detachments of the Sicherheitspolizei and SD, and their purpose was rapid intervention in intelligence and security police matters. Once their immediate task was ended, they turned themselves into static outposts of the two organisations on the lines of those known in the Reich as Gestapo Leitstellen and SD Abschnitte;[20] they also provided the personnel for further Einsatzgruppen.

Heydrich formed his five Einsatzgruppen for the Polish campaign at high speed; their members wore the service uniform of the SS-Verfügungstruppe with the SD diamond on the left sleeve;[21] they were allotted one to each army and each was sub-divided into four "Einsatzkommandos" [Action Commandos] of 100–150 men; these, in turn, were sub-allotted to army corps.[22] All the senior posts were occupied by SD Commanders—Bruno Streckenbach,[23] Dr Emanuel Schaefer,[24] Dr Herbert Fischer, [25] Lothar Beuthel,[26] and Ernst Damzog.[27]

However, if Heydrich and Himmler were to carry out Hitler's order for mass liquidation of the Polish elite and to do so undisturbed by the Wehrmacht, this RSHA on wheels had to be extremely careful not to divulge its hand to the military. The Wehrmacht had numerous opportunities of controlling the Einsatzgruppen; throughout the operations zone Heydrich's units were under army command, although they did of course receive their technical instructions from the RSHA in Berlin; moreover they were subject to Wehrmacht jurisdiction.[28] In addition the Army Commander-in-Chief had persuaded Hitler to agree that, on conclusion of operations the military should retain plenary powers in occupied Poland.[29] Provided Germany's generals showed sufficient political acumen, these powers could considerably restrict Himmler and Heydrich in their terror campaign.

The two SS men had to trim their sails carefully. They gave the military only the bare minimum of information; in an order of 9 September 1939, for instance, 8th Army described the task of the Einsatzgruppen as: "suppression of all anti-Reich and anti-German elements in rear of the fighting troops, in particular counter-espionage, arrest of politically unreliable persons, confiscation of weapons, safeguarding of important counter-espionage material, etc."[30] The necessity to camouflage the real purpose of the

Einsatzgruppen made Himmler and Heydrich uneasy; they were murdering Polish aristocrats, priests and intellectuals and, in the long run, this could hardly be kept secret from the soldiery. They found themselves caught on the horns of a dilemma; either they must betray Hitler's secret or resign themselves to being labelled by the military as an undisciplined gang of murderers.

Months later Himmler and Heydrich were still bemoaning the invidious position in which Hitler had placed them. Himmler adroitly attempted to place the blame on the Führer, protesting pathetically to the Generals: "I am doing nothing which the Führer does not know about."[31] In an office minute Heydrich later admitted that there had been serious differences of opinion with the Army in occupied Poland, because the "directives governing police activity were exceptionally far-reaching—for instance, the liquidation of numerous Polish leading circles running into thousands of persons was ordered; such an order could not be divulged to the general run of military headquarters, still less to members of the staffs; to the uninitiated, therefore, the action of the police and SS appeared arbitrary, brutal and unauthorised."[32]

The military soon realised what had really brought the Einsatzgruppen to Poland. On 8 September Admiral Canaris of the Abwehr reported to General von Stülpnagel, Deputy Chief of Staff I in Army Headquaters, that SS Commanders were boasting of shooting 200 Poles a day. Executions were in most cases carried out without trial and the victims were primarily Jews, aristocrats and priests.[33] Three days later Canaris was in the Führer Special near Illnau and reported to Keitel, the Chief of DKW. He warned: "The world will one day hold the Wehrmacht responsible for these methods since these things are taking place under its nose." Keitel was unimpressed. He took refuge behind Hitler's primitive logic: if the Wehrmacht did not want to do "these things" it must not complain when the Sicherheitspolizei and SS undertook the work of liquidation.[34]

The Wehrmacht resigned itself to the unworthy role of spectator. Canaris and his staff continued to amass evidence of the horrors perpetrated by the Einsatzgruppen but they need not have troubled; before the eyes of the military, Poland was subjected to a wave of terror reminiscent of the fearful days following the Nazi seizure of power in Germany. Hitler had said: "Whatever we can find in the shape of an upper class in Poland is to be liquidated; should anything take its place, it will be placed under guard and done away with at an appropriate time";[35] the men of the Einsatzkommandos went off on their manhunt to make his words come true.

Armed with previously prepared lists, Heydrich's thugs rounded up Polish teachers, doctors, officials, priests, landowners and businessmen. On arrest they were herded into reception camps which frequently proved to be places of execution. The Torun grease factory, Muhltal near Bydgoszcz, Soldau Camp, Stutthof and Fort VII in Poznan[36] —all became synonymous with terror and death for thousands of Poles. SS-Sturmbannführer Dr Roeder, Commander of the Bydgoszcz Einsatzkommando, declared: "It is planned to liquidate the radical elements"[37]—the word "radical" covered any Polish nationalist; mere membership of the Westmarkenverein (an association of Polish chauvinists which demanded annexation of additional German territory and had, in fact, been of great assistance to Hitler's Polish policy) was enough for the liquidators to pronounce sentence of death.[38]

Gradually the Polish elite was decimated. In the diocese of Chelm-Pelplin two-thirds of the 690 priests were arrested and 214 executed, including almost the entire cathedral chapter of Chelm-Pelplin.[39] Roeder reported to Berlin: "A high proportion of the Catholic clergy has been eliminated in view of their well-known radical Polish attitude."[40] Martin Broszat, the expert on German policy in Poland, gives "some tens of thousands" as the figure of victims for the first month of German rule.[41] On 27 September 1939 Heydrich stated: "Of the Polish upper classes in the occupied territories only a maximum of 3 per cent is still present."[42]

The Einsatzgruppe liquidation squads worked on a cold, rational plan, but alongside them now appeared another SS organisation governed not by a secret order from the Führer, but solely by hatred and thirst for revenge. Fanatical members of the German minority streamed out in their thousands, primarily in Danzig and West Prussia, unable to forget that they had recently been fair game for the Polish chauvinists.

Incensed by Hitler's "back-to-the-Reich" propaganda and prey to a panic-striken spy mania, when war broke out the Polish authorities and organisations had fallen upon the German minority. The Germans of Poland were martyred; an avalanche of arrest warrants descended on their heads—red for imprisonment in the local gaol, pink for incarceration in an internment camp and yellow for deportation to central and eastern Poland. Every nationalist organisation had its black list and took independent action against the "Germans," the "Hitlerites" or the "Swabians."[43]

50,000 members of the German minority were driven from their homes in western Poland and deported to the east; thousands disappeared behind prison bars;[44] roaming bands of Poles sacked German houses and farms, murdering the inmates; thousands of Germans were killed and others died as they ran the gauntlet of screaming, spitting mobs in the villages. The German authorities subsequently stated that by 1 February 1940 they had discovered the bodies of 13,000 murdered Germans.[45] The figure is probably exaggerated; nevertheless, a memorandum drafted in 1954 by the Polish "West Institute" in Poznan, mentions a figure of "several thousands."[46] Broszat is probably nearest to the truth; he gives a figure of 4,000–5,000 Germans murdered, together with a further 2,000 deaths directly attributable to the war.[47]

The Polish murders, however, differed from the German crimes in one important aspect; they were not the product of a co-ordinated plan nor were they carried out at the behest of the State; many Poles, including a number of officers, protected Germans from the wrath of the mob. The German minority, however, prepared to take revenge upon their persecutors. No sooner had the war rolled by than the German-speaking minority in each locality formed itself into a self-defence organisation. Initially defence alone was the object, for the Germans in Poland genuinely feared that they might once more be attacked by the Polish majority and this volunteer militia was intended for their protection.[48]

Soon, however, nationalistic spite became the governing factor; Albert Forster, the Gauleiter of Danzig, moved into West Prussia with his own Home Guard and a newly formed organisation known as "SS-Sturmbann Eimann," raising the tempo of the anti-Polish racial battle.[49] West Prussia soon became the scene of a pitiless anti-Polish campaign in which deliberately inflamed passions were combined with cold calculation. The Danzig racial fanatics, brought up in the revolutionary tradition of the SA, worked off years of suppressed anti-Polish feeling; they were adroitly directed by the ambitious Forster, whose aim was to present himself to his Führer as the first Eastern Gauleiter with an area "clear of Poles."[50]

Himmler had long regarded Forster as one of the more serious competitors for Hitler's favours and so this evidence of the Gauleiter's ambitions put him on the alert. Under no circumstances could Forster be allowed to become master of the self-defence organisations and he therefore despatched SS-Brigadeführer Gottlob Berger, the Head of his Recruiting Office, to organise the self-defence units into a "racial German" SS.[51]

Berger took with him a number of racial German SS leaders and they assumed command of the German self-defence organisation in occupied Poland. The militia was divided into four self-defence regions, sub-divided again into so-called inspectorates responsible to the relevant HSSPF.[52] In general the self-defence organisation was used as an auxiliary police force; the only areas where murderous man-hunts still continued were West Prussia and later Lublin.

The head of the self-defence organisation in West Prussia was SS-Oberführer Ludolf von Alvensleben; he was a fanatical National-Socialist and in his area he instituted a regime of tyranny reminiscent of that to which the democrats and republicans had been subjected by the SA thugs of the Karl Ernst school with their "wildcat" concentration camps.[53] Von Alvensleben was master of life and death in his region. Mere denunciation by a German or a tiny tick on a list were enough for his men to appear and cart some Pole off to a cellar, a garage or a copse and murder him.

Even many Nazis gradually found the persecution of the Poles too savage for their liking. In a letter of protest to Göring, Lily Jungblut, a Party member and wife of a German landowner in the Hohensalza district, complained that "thousands upon thousands of innocent men were being shot."[54] Even Heydrich grumbled about "certain intolerable and uncontrolled acts of revenge" on the part of the self-defence organisation—though he was worried about discipline rather than humanity.[55]

All that mattered to Himmler, however, was the "success" of his operation, the figures of Poles liquidated or, in the current jargon, "subjected to special treatment." In mid-September he despatched a new murder squad, the "Special Duty" Einsatzgruppe under SS-Obergruppenführer Udo von Woyrsch, to liquidate Poles and Jews in the Katowice area.[56] He had been Himmler's partner in the Röhm manhunt and was intended to initiate a new phase of SS policy in eastern Upper Silesia—deportation of the 50,000 Jews of Danzig, West Prussia, Poznan and Upper Silesia into the interior of Poland.[57]

Von Woyrsch's Einsatzgruppe was clearly designed as a form of shock unit to strike terror and panic into the Jews of Upper Silesia and force them to move in the general direction of Cracow. No sooner had the campaign opened than Heydrich paid a visit to Army Headquarters to initiate Eduard Wagner, the Deputy Chief of Staff, into the secret of the new plan. In the eastern territories now once more under German rule, he said, it was proposed to concentrate *all* Jews in ghettos in Poland for shipment abroad in due course.[58] Wagner raised no objections. Twenty-four hours later, on 21 September, Heydrich instructed the Einsatzgruppen to start deportation of Jews into the heart of Poland.[59]

Heydrich's prior warning to the Army, however, proved to be an error, for the soldiers suddenly began to kick over the traces. A military occupation regime had meanwhile been set up in conquered Poland with Commander-in-Chief East, Colonel-General Gerd von Rundstedt at its head. Poland was divided into four military districts, each under a General to whom some trusted National-Socialist functionary was attached as head of the civil administration;[60] the military were responsible for public security and order and they were determined to fulfil the Army's solemn proclamation to the Poles: "The Wehrmacht does not regard the civil population as enemies. All provisions of international law will be respected."[61] But the savage terror imposed by the SS units, primarily the brutal actions of von Woyrsch's Einsatzgruppe, were now making a mockery of the Army's assurances. For-

tunately officers were still to be found ready to raise
their voices against the SS murderers.

On 20 September 14th Army Operations Section reported that the troops were becoming restive "because of
the largely illegal measures taken in the Army area by
Einsatzgruppe Woyrsch (mass shooting, particularly of
Jews). The troops are especially incensed that, instead of
fighting at the front, young men should be demonstrating
their courage against defenceless civilians."[62] Von Rundstedt thereupon declared that Woyrsch's Einsatzgruppe
would no longer be tolerated in the Operations Zone.
Himmler gave way and von Woyrsch had to bow to
the wishes of the military. In addition, the army demanded
that anti-Jewish measures already under way should cease.
Once more Himmler complied.[63] On 1 October Army
Headquarters informed Corps HQs in Poland: "Order No.
II (reference No. 288/39G dated 21 September '39)
issued to Einsatzgruppen by the Chief of the Sicherheitspolizei should initially give rise to preparatory measures
only. A fresh instruction on these lines is being issued to
Einsatzgruppen by the Reichsführer-SS."[64]

Had the Wehrmacht been determined to maintain pressure upon Himmler, it might possibly have stopped arbitrary action in the East—but Hitler knew his Generals.
He quickly brought military Government in the East to
an end, confident that his senior soldiers would heave a
sigh of relief.

On 5 October Gauleiter Forster presented himself to
Hitler and complained of the continuous vexation caused
him by the military in West Prussia. That very day Hitler
issued an order removing West Prussia from military jurisdiction and placing it under Forster.[65] This snap decision
started an avalanche which ultimately swept away all
military government in the East. In mid-October, with a
stroke of the pen, Hitler set up a complete new system
of rule in German-occupied Poland, a new maze of
competing authorities and a fruitful field for intrigue
among those Nazi potentates who had a finger in the
Eastern pie. Danzig and West Prussia were amalgamated
and incorporated into the Reich as a new Gau under
Gauleiter Forster. A new Reich Gau named Wartheland
(Poznan) was formed under Arthur Greiser, Forster's
rival in Danzig where he was Deputy Gauleiter and Presi-

dent of the Senate; certain small Polish areas bordering
on East Prussia were placed under another of Forster's
rivals, Erich Koch, the Gauleiter of Königsberg; Upper
Silesia was incorporated into Silesia under Gauleiter Josef
Wagner (in 1941, it became an independent district under Gauleiter Fritz Bracht); the remainder of Poland,
now isolated both from the Germans in the West and
from the Russians in the East, was placed in a straitjacket,
known as the "Government-General" under Dr Hans
Frank, the Nazi legal adviser who was given unusually
extensive plenary powers.[66]

The military might have been expected to rise in wrath
against the rape of their powers in the East, to protest
against Hitler's abandonment of his promise that overriding authority was the prerogative of the Wehrmacht. But
not at all. The Generals were only too glad for the
Dictator to relieve them of responsibility for murder; in
any case Hitler had adroitly taken the precaution of painting them a horrifying picture of Poland's future. On 17
October, with Keitel present, he had outlined his policy
towards Poland. The horrified military scribbled down:
"increased severity of the racial struggle permits of no
legal restriction; methods used will be incompatible with
our principles . . . ensure that the Polish intelligentsia
cannot throw up a new leader class . . . Jews, Poles
and similar trash to be cleared from the old and new
Reich territories."[67]

The military turned their backs with a shudder. How
right Hitler's calculation had been was shown by the attitude of von Rundstedt: when he learned that Frank,
the ultra-Nazi, was to be Governor-General, he handed
in his resignation.[68] The Generals were in such a hurry
to bring their Military Government to an end that the
build-up of the new administration could hardly keep pace
with the military withdrawal. In Broszat's words a "legal-
ised vacuum of anarchy" appeared: Himmler filled it with
his SS and police units.[69]

Even before the new governmental dignitaries were at
their desks, an SS shadow Government had already spread
its net over Poland. The Einsatzgruppen transformed
themselves into static Gestapo Leitstellen and SD Abschnitte, responsible in each district of the Government-
General to a "Kommandeur der Sicherheitspolizei und des

SD" [Local Security Police and SD Commander—KdS];
the KdS in the five districts of Poland were under a
"Befehlshaber der Sicherheitspolizei und des SD" [Secur-
ity Police and SD Commander—BdS] who, in turn, was
the direct subordinate of the RSHA.[70] Parallel to this organisation another police chain of command ran through
occupied Poland, that of the Ordnungspolizei. On the outbreak of war the Orpo had been mobilised and a number
of Police Battalions had taken part both in the Polish
campaign and in many Einsatzgruppe operations. The
Orpo hierarchy paralleled that of the Sicherheitspolizei;
in each district of the Government-General was a Kommandeur of the Ordnungspolizei, an Orpo Befehlshaber
was responsible for the Government General as whole
and he, in turn, was responsible to Hauptamt Orpo.[71]

Real power, however, lay in the hands of the HSSPF,
since they covered both chains of command. In Germany
the HSSPF had existed since 1937; they were generally
the commanders of SS-Oberabschnitte whom Himmler
had nominated to represent him in the Wehrkreise. In
theory they were to co-ordinate the operations of all SS
and Police units in the event of mobilisation; in practice
they were intended by Himmler to guarantee the SS/
Police integration for which he was striving. In Germany
itself, however, Himmler's representatives led a wretched
existence; the civil administration refused to countenance
the intrusion of SS functionaries who had no official
place in the police hierarchy and the Reichsführer was
compelled to confine his HSSPF to purely formal representative duties.[72]

However, in Greater Germany's colony, Poland, leaderless and deprived of any traditional bureaucracy, Himmler was able to give his HSSPF more power. There they
were to supervise all Police and SS formations, form a
counterweight to the over-powerful position of Heydrich
within the SS and set up a special political police administration destined in Himmler's eyes to be the real agent
of the Führer's will.[73]

For Himmler success or failure in the East might well
depend upon his HSSPF; he therefore chose three hard-
working, ambitious SS Commanders, dynamic personalities, yet not strong enough to be dangerous to him. As
HSSPF Vistula/Danzig he nominated Gruppenführer Rich-

ard Hildebrandt, an "old fighter" regarded as an opponent of the "Little Hitlers" (Himmler had once had to relieve him of all his SS offices for quarrelling with Gauleiter Streicher).[74] HSSPF Warthe (Poznan) was Gruppenführer Wilhelm Koppe, an energetic operator.[75] As HSSPF East (Cracow) Himmler chose one of the most unpopular SS leaders, Obergruppenführer Friedrich-Wilhelm Krüger, loathed by the SA for his treachery in the Röhm affair; he was a scandalmonger and a pedant, whose tales of supposedly deviationist comrades even Himmler found hard to stomach.[76] HSSPF in Poland were allotted a new category of subordinates not found elsewhere—the "SS- und Polizeiführer" [SS and Police Commanders—SSPF],[77] one to each district of the Government-General. They were to guarantee SS/Police integration on the provincial level.

Himmler used the rapid expansion of the SS and Police system in the East to lay claim to the leading role in German occupation policy. Without consulting the Wehrmacht, he began to take action against remnants of the Polish armed forces and newly formed partisan groups; under cover of the anti-partisan war, the extermination campaign against the Polish upper class proceeded. Arrests of Poles continued and, from time to time, whole groups of them would be liquidated; the operation culminated in the "special pacification action" of spring 1940, when 3,500 Poles were shot.[78]

Himmler's units now began to play the role of occupation force with such frequency that even the Wehrmacht generals reacted angrily. Although the yes-men, such as Keitel of OKW, or the fatalists, such as Rundstedt, were quite ready to renounce any political role in the East, the Army as a whole was not prepared to be elbowed out of its dominant position as occupation force. Too late the SS leaders realised that the new Commander-in-Chief East, Colonel-General Johannes Blaskowitz, "felt himself complete master of the situation and the man who was really in command," as Brigadeführer Berger put it.[79]

The Wehrmacht's position in the Government-General was a strong one. Under a Hitler decree it was in sole command in the event of internal unrest; it was responsible for all measures connected with external defence; it was in control of the traffic and communications networks; it supervised all factories and businesses important to the war effort.[80] The Wehrmacht was therefore not prepared to allow itself to be elbowed out by some Himmler. Only a spark was needed to bring the officers' wrath to the boil and this was provided by the accelerated extermination campaign conducted by the Sicherheitspolizei and SS units. Blaskowitz launched the first, and perhaps only, Wehrmacht campaign against the SS murderers and did so, in the words of the Munich historian Helmut Krausnick, "in a language unparalleled in German military history."[81]

Blaskowitz collected reports on SS crimes in Poland and collated them in a memorandum dispatched to the C-in-C of the Army in mid-November 1939. By 18 November the Blaskowitz memorandum was on Hitler's desk.[82] Captain Engel, Hitler's Wehrmacht aide, summarised the contents in his diary: "Great concern over illegal shootings, arrests and confiscations; risk to the discipline of the troops who see these things happening; local discussions with SD and Gestapo fruitless—reference to instructions from SS Headquarters; request for re-establishment of the rule of law—in particular executions only to be carried out on sentence by a court."[83] Hitler rejected such "childish ideas" on the part of the Army. He had never had confidence in General Blaskowitz, he raged, and now it was high time to relieve the man of his appointment.[84]

But Blaskowitz was undeterred by his Führer's explosions of rage and continued to collect evidence against the SS. Unit reports poured in from all sides. To cite a few examples—report by General Petzel, Wehrkreis Commander Warthegau, 23 November 1939: "In almost all major localities, the organisations referred to (SS and Police) carry out public shootings. Selection is entirely arbitrary and the conduct of the executions in many cases disgusting. Arrests are almost invariably accompanied by looting."[85] Report of incidents in Turck town on 30 October 1939: "A number of Jews were herded into the synagogue and there were made to crawl along the pews singing, while being continuously beaten with whips by SS men. They were then forced to take down their trousers so that they could be beaten on the bare buttocks. One Jew who had fouled his trousers in fear was

compelled to smear his excrement over the faces of other
Jews."[86] Letter from General Ulex, C-in-C Frontier Sector
South, 2 February 1940: "The recent increase in the use
of violence by the police shows an almost incredible lack
of human and moral qualities; the word 'brutish' is almost justified. The only solution I can see to this revolting situation which sullies the honour of the entire German
people, is that all police formations together with all their
senior Commanders . . . should be dismissed in a body
and the units disbanded."[87]

Blaskowitz drew up a new list of SS crimes; it cited
33 incidents proved in every detail, maltreatment of Jews
and Poles, rape, looting, murder.[88] On 6 February Blaskowitz summarised: "The attitude of the troops to the
SS and Police alternates between abhorrence and hatred.
Every soldier feels disgusted and repelled by these crimes
committed in Poland by nationals of the Reich and representatives of our State."[89] Blaskowitz' new attack drove
the SS and Police on to the defensive. Even Hitler's
military disciples such as von Reichenau, joined the
anti-SS ranks; in the Führer's headquarters, no Wehrmacht
officer would shake the hand of an SS leader. To save
his face, even Himmler had to make some gesture and
therefore he ordered the Chief of the Ordnungspolizei and
the Hauptamt SS-Gericht to investigate Blaskowitz' "complaints."[90] Frank, the Governor General, now came to the
assistance of the hard-pressed Reichsführer—an action
which he was later bitterly to regret. On 13 February he
presented himself to Hitler and asked for something upon
which the Führer had long since decided—the dismissal
of that tiresome critic, Blaskowitz.[91] Three months later
Himmler was rid of his military enemy. Blaskowitz was
transferred to the West and with him went the main
body of the German Army located in the Government-
General. They were destined for the Franco-German
frontier, for 10 May 1940, the opening of the Western
campaign, was only a few weeks away.[92]

May 1940 was the month in which Himmler dictated his
memorandum on "treatment of foreign populations in the
East." The way was open; from the moonscape of the
devasted Polish State Himmler could now begin to carve
out his SS Order's promised land, the Utopia of the future
race of German peasant-warriors.

The May memorandum marked a new phase in Himmler's eastward drive. The mass liquidator of the Polish upper class became the nurseryman of the Germanic ideal, the Chief of the German Police turned into the "Reich Commissar for the Strengthening of Germanism" [Reichskommissar für die Festigung deutschen Volkstums —RKF]. A new SS invading army was poised for action, though with highly unwilling auxiliaries. SS re-settlement staffs set themselves up, refugee camps appeared, racial commissions drew up questionnaires—the greatest migration in German history was in course of preparation, directed by the SS in accordance with a master plan.

Soon the men whom the SS intended to use to validate their claim to be overlords of the East were on the move, the unsuspecting victims of unscrupulous power policy, summoned—lured—by the "home-to-the-Reich" propaganda; 120,000 Germans came from the Baltic States, 136,000 from Soviet-occupied Eastern Poland, 200,000 from Rumania and thousands from Yugoslavia and Slovakia.[93] They were to be settled in the German Eastern territories. The propagandists told them that they were answering the call of their blood; in practice, however, the lords of the regime had decided upon their repatriation for a much more prosaic reason: Greater Germany's labour force was inadequate; the country of the "people without space" had insufficient manpower to keep its industry and agriculture running at full blast.

As early as 1937 Göring, the plenipotentiary for the Four-Year Plan, had calcuated that the Reich was short of 150,000 workers.[94] As Chief of Police Himmler had thereupon been ordered by Göring to do what he could to ensure that the labour requirement was met. So within his personal staff Himmler set up a "Four-Year Plan office" and at its head he placed an SS Commander regarded as one of the leading brains among the SS technocrats.[95] This was Ulrich Greifelt, son of a Berlin chemist; he had been a member of a Free Corps, a business manager, once an anti-Nazi and was now an SS-Oberführer; he was more at home in the world of statistics, production figures and sales records than in that of ideology; only when alone would he allow himself the relaxation of a little sentimentality.[96]

By January 1939 the labour shortage had risen to more

than 500,000 men[97] and at this point Greifelt explained how the labour shortage problem could be solved. His answer was repatriation of the thirty million Germans and "racial Germans" resident abroad; they were the natural reservoir of labour which must be tapped to meet the shortage.[98] Six months later Greifelt had occasion to put his suggestion into practice. Hitler and Mussolini had agreed to eliminate a tiresome piece of grit affecting the smooth running of the Axis machine—the German-speaking population of South Tyrol; in July 1939 the two Governments agreed upon the repatriation of this minority to the Reich. It was Greifelt's job to arrange their transportation.[99]

Greifelt set up a staff of 20, known as the "Controlling Office for Immigrants and Repatriates" located at 142 Kurfürstendamm, Berlin.[100] The first repatriates were just arriving in the Reich when Himmler found a far more important task for his planner—Greifelt was to resettle German-occupied Poland with "racial Germans" from Eastern Europe.[101]

The loss of hundreds of thousands of German workers to the army and the growing requirements of the armaments industry had led Hitler and Göring to adopt Greifelt's solution to the labour problem. At the end of September the Reich concluded an agreement with the Soviet Union and the Baltic States providing for transfer to the Reich of the Germans resident in that area.[102] Hitler summoned his direct subordinate, SS-Obergruppenführer Lorenz, the Head of VOMI, and charged him with control of the re-settlement operation.[103] The choice was a natural one, since all political and financial dealings with racial Germans abroad had been channelled through VOMI since 1938.

No sooner had Himmler heard of the good fortune of his friend Lorenz, however, than he hurried along to his Führer. He pointed out that so important a field as racial policy could hardly be left in the hands of a single Obergruppenführer; it was the task of the SS as a whole.[104] Hitler gave way and allowed Himmler to assume overall control of the business. By 29 September Himmler already had on his desk the draft of a secret decree from the Führer, charging him with the "strengthening of Germanism." It laid down three tasks for the Reichsführer-

SS; "Repatriation of persons of German race and nationality resident abroad and considered suitable for permanent return to the Reich; elimination of the injurious influence of those sections of the population of foreign origin constituting a danger to the Reich and the German community; formation of new German settlement areas by transfer of population, in particular by giving land entitlement to persons of German race or nationality returning from abroad."[105] The decree also gave Himmler such wide plenary powers that he was, in effect, in a position to lay down the law in the East; he was authorised "to make use of the existing authorities and institutions of the Reich, the Länder and the Gemeinde [Municipalities] as also of other public bodies and existing re-settlement associations."[106] Providing he made full use of the overriding authority now given him, he could very soon be overlord of the conquered territories in the East.

He knew only too well, of course, that he was headed straight for a minefield of National-Socialist intrigue; a whole collection of brown-shirted would-be imperialists had turned the corpse of Poland into an arena for the exercise of neo-feudal ambitions. Himmler could not challenge the lordlings of the East all at the same time. He had to gather the reins of power as unobtrusively as he could. He could not afford to create a sensation until his new invading army was in position.

He gave himself the portentous title of Reich Commissar for the Strengthening of Germanism (RKF).[107] At the same time, however, he was careful not to set up a mammoth organisation. As the general staff of the racial offensive he selected Greifelt's "controlling office," re-christened "RKF Office" (in 1941, it was raised to the status of "Stabshauptamt" [Staff Department]).[108] He then distributed the work among several SS organisations; the RKF Office was to be responsible for planning the re-settlement of German repatriates and providing re-settlement areas by confiscation of Polish or Jewish property.[109] VOMI would transport the repatriates, accommodate them in reception camps and supervise the political leadership of individual immigrant groups;[110] the RuSHA would keep an eye on racial purity;[111] the RSHA was to deal with the requisitioning of property of "anti-state" persons, deportation of the Poles and their so-called "re-settlement" in the Government-General.[112]

All was now ready. Lorenz and his staff had meanwhile been concluding their preparations for the repatriation of the German Balts and on 20 October the first settler ships arrived from Estonia;[113] the Balts were due to be accommodated in the Danzig area. However, if Himmler thought that his new access of power had passed unnoticed by his rivals, he was soon disillusioned. One of the Reichsführer's bitterest enemies who, to make matters worse, was entitled to wear the uniform of an SS-Gruppenführer, refused to allow the RKF to interfere in his kingdom in any way—this was Gauleiter Forster.

To ensure that all the various authorities co-operated in the repatriation exercise, it had been Himmler's intention to nominate the most senior personality in each area as his representative. Forster, however, who was in charge of the Danzig–West Prussia Gau, refused to take orders from Himmler and the latter had to nominate the HSSPF as his representative.[114] No persuasion could bring Forster to co-operate with the RKF. When VOMI personnel, assisted by the Sicherheitspolizei, began to earmark whole areas of West Prussian towns for the reception of immigrants, Forster summoned the VOMI representative and threatened him with arrest if he did not immediately order his people to stop.[115] Forster proved so inhospitable that the repatriate ships heading for Danzig were re-routed to Stettin.[116] He only changed his attitude after a couple of telephone calls from Himmler, and even then he would only allow the returning Balts the most transient accommodation in his area.[117]

Himmler was compelled to postpone settlement of the German Balts to the following year. Owing to Forster's obstruction and the inefficiency of the VOMI organisation, the repatriates' situation was so miserable that another critic of Himmler's racial policy appeared, the National-Socialist ideologist Alfred Rosenberg, who was a German Balt himself. In a letter to Himmler he complained that "the manner in which the Balts are treated is reminiscent of the Bolshevik period." VOMI, he went on, had turned the German Balts into "a disorganised mob of disappointed, embittered and hopeless men."[118] But Forster and Rosenberg were not Himmler's only rivals and opponents.

Others were on the scene to dispute his authority over the settlement area upon which the whole success of his operation depended.

Gauleiter Koch of East Prussia, for instance, was also in charge of certain ex-Polish territories now incorporated in his Gau and known as "New East Prussia"; he refused to allow his area to be used for the re-settlement of the RKF's German repatriates. When Professor Konrad Meyer-Heterling, Greifelt's senior area planner, initiated a survey, Koch threatened to have him thrown out of East Prussia.[119] Others found more subtle methods of opposition. For instance Himmler set up a Central Real Estate Office to direct the requisitioning of Polish land; hardly had he done so than Göring's Four-Year Plan office organised a "Haupttreuhandstelle Ost" [Main Trust Office for the East—HTO]. Here was the Reich's Number Two staking his claim to control of all Polish-Jewish property—precisely the land which Himmler's Central Real Estate Office wished to reserve for its settlers.[120]

Göring immediately rubbed into Himmler the fact that he was not regarded as an equal. Alerted by the formation of the HTO, Himmler promptly made representations to Göring in his capacity as head of the Four-Year Plan; Göring, however, referred him to the Head of the HTO, Max Winkler—a mere burgomaster. Only after endless discussions did Himmler reach agreement with Göring's representative: the HTO to retain control of all Polish industrial and urban property, Himmler being allowed only confiscated agricultural property in German-occupied Poland.[121]

Yet even now Himmler was not in full control of his new settlement area. He had had to concede some voice in the business to Darré, his disillusioned friend of the old Artaman days, now Minister of Agriculture.[122] Moreover, Darré now reinsured via Göring's newly constituted organisation in the East. He set up his own office for the management of requisitioned Polish estates and placed it under Göring—clearly in the hope of strengthening his hand vis-a-vis the RKF.[123]

In face of such resistance Himmler had to manoeuvre with caution if he was to achieve his object. The National-Socialist rule of self-frustration would soon have brought the RKF to an end, had Himmler not been able to rely

upon his police machine in the East—and this had work
to do: as early as 8 November 1939 HSSPF East had
held a meeting in Cracow with the Commander of the
Government-General's Sicherheitspolizei at which they had
discussed what, in SS terminology, was euphemistically
called the "negative" aspect of racial policy—in other
words, the deportation of Poles and Jews from the ex-
Polish territories now "re-incorporated" in the Reich.[124]
(See Appendix 4.)

In Lodz the Sicherheitspolizei set up a so-called "Deportee Centre" [Umwanderungszentralstelle—UWZ]   responsible for planning the deportation to the Government-
General[125] of unwanted Poles and Jews from the new
"Germanised" areas. With their usual ruthlessness the
Sicherheitspolizei proceeded to eject all Poles on their list
and by February 1940 300,000 Poles had been "re-
settled" in the Government General. The Sipo's deportation figures climbed faster and higher—120,000 Polish
landowners deported from Warthegau, 35,000 from Dan-
zig-West Prussia and 15,000 from Eastern Upper Silesia.[126]
By the outbreak of the war against Russia a million Poles
had been driven from their homes.[127] The SS re-settlement staffs were quick to introduce their "racial German"
immigrants and distribute them to the deserted Polish
properties—though only after complicated checking by the
RuSHA.

By mid-1941, 200,000 German repatriates had been
provided with new homes.[128] Greifelt's office distributed
Polish property; of Poland's 928,000 farms, comprising
245,000,000 acres, German settlers inherited in all 47,000
farms, comprising 23,000,000 acres. By the end of 1942
German settlers had been allotted some 20 per cent of the
60,000 Polish business concerns and Reich Germans 8
per cent; 51 per cent already belonged to indigenous Germans and 21 per cent were controlled by German trusts.
Of the small craftsman businesses some 2,000 were transferred to German immigrants, the bulk (80 per cent) remaining with their Polish owners.[129]

The recall to the Reich of the true racial Germans
and their resettlement in the East, however, was not
enough for Himmler, the racial fanatic. True to his memorandum of May 1940 he now began to extract from
the Polish population every drop of German blood; racial

commissions travelled round seeking out concealed members of the German race; Himmler had a "German racial list" prepared on which was entered every inhabitant of German origin in the East. They were divided into four categories: Category 1—Proven "racial fighters"; Category 2—passive "racial Germans" who had at least a 50 per cent knowledge of the German language; Category 3—persons of doubtful German orgin; Category 4—anti-Nazis of German origin who had taken part in measures directed against the German minority.[130]

Racial investigation, however, was not confined to persons of German origin; many Polish nationals had to pass under the microscope and if any nordic traits were detected the "re-Germanisation" mechanism was set in motion. In accordance with the crazy doctrine of racial purity and in the words of an SS memorandum entitled "The Use of Human Material," the object was to "recover for the German community German blood available in the East," even though it might run in Polish veins.[131] In Himmler's view no foreign race existed which did not include "nordic representatives" capable of germanisation. He stated that "in course of time" even Gorals, Lemkes and Huzuls should be "germanised," since "their Germanic origin or, at least, their German descent" could be established.[132]

Himmler was especially persistent in his pursuit of Polish children, regarding them as ideal candidates for germanisation. A rumour current in Poznan was that, in the early days of the war, the Poles had kidnapped German children and hidden them in orphanages. The RKF promptly issued an order for the disbandment of all Polish orphanages and the transfer of their inmates after racial examination to German children's homes. Later, children were even torn from their families and carried off to Germany.[133] On 13 June 1941 Himmler wrote to Greiser, the Gauleiter of Warthegau: "Racially pure children of Poles should be brought up by us in special kindergartens or children's homes. The parents can be told that this is being done for the children's health."[134]

Six months later Himmler brought "Lebensborn," the SS maternity organisation, into the game; its homes were to be used for the reception of Polish children, later to be distributed to childless SS families. A large-scale kidnapping operation was instituted (code name Haymaking) as a result of which thousands of Polish children disappeared into Germany.[135] Those who refused to allow their children to be germanised were subjected to severe reprisals by the Sicherheitspolizei. Brunhilde Muszynski, for instance, the German wife of a Polish officer, refused to allow her children to be brought up in Germany. The Zamosc Immigration Centre [Einwandererzentralstelle— EWZ], an RuSHA office, decreed: "her children will be sterilised and accommodated somewhere as foster children."[136]

Such cases, however, were rare; in general both Poles and racial Germans complied with Himmler's germanisation procedure, 100,000 pure Poles allowed themselves to be germanised, a million men registered in categories 1 and 2 of the "racial list," and a further two million in categories 3 and 4.[137]

The greater the success of Himmler's re-settlement and Germanisation policy, however, the larger the number of his enemies grew. Josef Wagner, the Catholic Gauleiter of Silesia, expressed fears lest Himmler force the entire Polish skilled labour force to leave Upper Silesian heavy industry; his counter-measures were largely successful in reducing the severity of the deportation measures ordered by Greifelt's office.[138] Even the Economic Office of OKW appealed to Himmler to reduce the tempo of re-settlement.[139] In Danzig Forster openly ridiculed "certain theorists" who had no conception of racial policy; the local Sipo Inspector reported that he had expressed himself "very cynically." It was abundantly clear that he was referring primarily to the SS.[140] In letters to the Reich Chancellery, the Government-General complained heatedly that "the re-settlement policy was gradually becoming impossible and was no longer tolerable in view of its catastrophic consequences." A letter of 25 June 1940 stated that the continued influx of Polish deportees into the Government-General had led to a "hopeless food situation."[141]

Himmler found himself confronted by so many jealous rivals and critics that he could only hope for some miracle to give him new freedom of manoeuvre. That miracle was provided by Adolf Hitler; on 22 June 1941 all German radio networks announced that the Army of the Reich had set forth on its crusade against the Bolshevik world enemy.

The Russian campaign opened up for Himmler vast new territories in which to deploy his energies. That which Forster, Wagner, Koch and Göring had so far prevented, he could now do in the limitless expanses of Russia; vast new settlement areas were there for the taking. Himmler and his SS leaders were intoxicated by the prospect of the endless steppes and vast woodlands. Bemused by the continental expanse of Russia, the SS planners seized their drawing boards and drew up fantastic visions of the future—grotesque, unreal, pathological daydreams.

As early as January 1941, at a meeting in Wewelsburg, Himmler had confided to SS-Gruppenführer Erich von dem Bach-Zelewski that the German master plan for the East necessitated the elimination of thirty million Slavs.[142] The racial experts now foregathered in Group IIIB of the RuSHA to plan the German Eastern empire of the future.[143]

Their dreamings were committed to paper in the shape of the "master plan East." The entire area as far as the line Leningrad–Lake Ladoga–Valdai Hills–Briansk–bend of the Dnieper was to be settled by Germans; fourteen million people of other races were to be deported; fourteen million were to be allowed to remain in the settlement area but must be germanised within a period of 30 years. The Government-General and the Baltic States were to be completely "re-populated"; 85 per cent of the twenty million Poles and 65 per cent of the West Ukrainians were to be deported to Western Siberia to make room for German immigrants. These were to arrive in several waves—840,000 "for immediate settlement," followed by a second wave of 1·1 million; the RuSHA plans provided for an influx of 200,000 annually over the next ten years and a total of 2·4 million Germans moved during the following two decades.[144]

But how were such comparatively small numbers to maintain themselves in the face of the numerical superiority of the other races? How were they to establish the dominant position which Himmler's Order postulated? The answer, on paper at any rate, was provided by SS-Oberführer Professor Konrad Meyer-Hetling, Senior Settlement and Area Planner and Director of the Institute

for Agriculture and Agrarian Policy in the University of
Berlin. On 28 May 1942 the Professor submitted to the
Reichsführer-SS a memorandum outlining the German
master race's wonderland.[145] The great area of the East
was to be carved up into settlement provinces ("Marks")
under the supreme authority of the Reichsführer-SS; he
was to be the liege lord of the East, directing the settlers to
the areas provided for them and granting them fiefs of
varying types—"life fiefs," "hereditary fiefs" and "special
status properties."[146] Provincial "headmen" appointed by
the Reichsführer-SS were to supervise the "Marks"; after
a 25-year pioneering period their population should be 50
per cent German. The Baltic States and Poland were to be
fully germanised; besides these, Meyer-Hetling envisaged
three "Marks"—the area west of Leningrad (to be known
as "Ingermanland"), the Crimea–Kherson area (to be
known as "Gotengau") and the Memel-Narev area.[147] The
German colonial empire in the East was to be protected by
a system of 26 strong-points. In these areas the population
was to be only 30 per cent germanised; in Himmler's
words the strongpoints were to guard "the intersections
of German arteries of communication; they were to consist of small towns of about 20,000 inhabitants surrounded
by a ring of German villages at a distance of 2–5
miles."[148]

The Reichsführer was overjoyed. Here, at last, the
world of his dreams was taking shape—the world of
armed peasant settlers under the sole authority of Heinrich Himmler. "Just imagine," he said to Kersten, "what
a sublime idea! It's the greatest piece of colonisation the
world will ever have seen linked with a most noble and
essential task, the protection of the Western world against
an irruption from Asia."[149] He was continually producing
maps and plans showing the warrior-peasant settlements
and explaining the layout to Kersten—here were the 30
to 40 farmhouses constituting a village—there the leader's
mansion around which the village was grouped—there the
SS peasant-warrior "Sturm" to which all male inhabitants would belong. Kersten remembers Himmler saying:
"We will instil a fighting spirit such as has never been
seen before; it will guarantee the indestructibility of the
resulting community."[150]

Himmler had already selected the SS leader to turn this

dream world into reality—the SSPF Lublin, Brigadeführer Odilo Globocnik. Globocnik was the son of a Trieste cavalry captain, a builder by trade and a long-standing Nazi; he was one of Himmler's least educated and most hot-headed disciples; his display of unflagging enthusiasm was designed to curry favour with his Reichsführer—and for good reason; he had only been accepted into the SS as a result of Himmler's influence, after being described by Schwarz, the Party Treasurer and certainly no prude, as one of the most dubious characters ever to wear a Party badge. In 1933, when a deputy Gauleiter, he had fled to Germany after murdering a jeweller in Vienna; in 1939, by which time he had become a Gauleiter, he was dismissed for trafficking in currency.[151] He made good his lack of respectability by dog-like devotion. The SS Personnel Department noted: "His impetuosity frequently leads him to break the rules and forget the restrictions imposed upon him by the Order."[152]

Like Himmler, Globocnik, the future mass murderer of Jews, was captivated by the prospect of vast racial biological experiments. In the south-eastern part of Lublin District he had come across traces of early German settlements and the discovery inspired him with the notion of re-creating a German settlement area; the Polish population was to be deported and German settlements created in each district using SS and Police units; Globocnik proposed to begin with the towns of Zamosc, Tomaszow and Hrubieszow.[153]

Globocnik, of course, knew that Frank, the Governor-General, was unlikely to agree to deportations on so large a scale since they would inevitably aggravate Poland's already catastrophic economic and communications situation. Staking his luck, however, upon the rivalry between Frank and Himmler, he submitted his plan to the Reichsführer and Himmler seized upon it. A glance at the map must have shown him that Globocnik's proposed experimental area lay at the base of the elongated quadrilateral on which Himmler proposed to centre his SS re-settlement policy.

This quadrilateral was bounded by Lublin, Zhitomir, Vinnitsa and Lwow, each a special centre of SS activity; Lublin was the headquarters of Globocnik, in Zhitomir Himmler had set up his command post during the first

phase of the eastern campaign and had opened a settlement centre for German Ukrainians; Vinnitsa was on the
edge of Transnistria where a further German settlement
area was planned; Lwow, capital of Eastern Galicia, now
incorporated in the Government General, was the Headquarters of SS-Brigadeführer Wächter, who had been involved in the Dollfuss putsch.[154] The American historian
Robert L. Koehl, one of the outstanding experts on SS
racial policy, says: "In this quadrilateral, straddling two
different German administrative areas and the Polish-
Ukrainian ethnic frontier, an SS State might have arisen
some day if the Germans had been victorious in Russia."[155]

In autumn 1941, Himmler gave Globocnik the green
light,[156] obviously calculating that Frank was unlikely to
resist the Lublin deportation plan. In fact, however, he
touched off a violent power struggle which proved, yet
again, how little influence the SS, acting alone, could exert
on the Third Reich's policy.

Without informing the Government-General, Himmler
paid a visit to Lublin and announced that Zamosc district
would be the first major German settlement area.[157] He
promptly found himself in opposition to a man who had
hitherto concealed from the outer world that he had no
intention of allowing the RKF to interfere in his sphere
of authority—Dr Hans Frank, the Governor-General of
Poland, Reich Minister without Portfolio, Reich Legal Adviser and a Party Reichsleiter (the highest-ranking Nazi
functionary).

Nothing had so far given anyone reason to suspect
that Frank was nursing a hatred against the SS which
was now at boiling point. He was regarded as one of the
most radical Nazi leaders; he had proposed to divest the
legal code of all its liberal provisions; he followed Adolf
Hitler with a blind, fanatical devotion, with that subservience, indeed, which frequently binds misfits and homosexuals to some virile authoritarian father-figure. Gilbert,
the American psychiatrist, described Frank as "one of the
most intelligent of the 'old fighters' as well as one of the
most unstable emotionally."[158] He had come to Poland determined to carry out his Führer's programme ruthlessly;
his diaries contain excerpts from his speeches redolent of a
diseased mania for power—"we will hold on to the Gov-

ernment-General and will never give it up again[159] . . . I admit, quite openly, that this will cost the lives of several thousand Poles, primarily from the intellectual upper class[160] . . . We liquidate things in this country. We will do so in the manner which proves simplest[161] . . . Our primary object here in this area is to fulfil National-Socialism's great mission in the East. It cannot, therefore, be our object to set up here a State based on the rule of law[162] . . . Anyone suspected by us should be liquidated forthwith."[163]

Nevertheless, Frank was too intelligent not to realise that it was impossible to rule by brutality alone. In his view if the Poles were to be mobilised in the service of the Reich, the Government-General must become a model of economic development, a German ruling class must be introduced into the country and the peoples of other races, such as the Ukrainians and the Kashubs, must be used as a counter-weight to the Poles.

Himmler's racial policy, however, wrecked Frank's plan. The Sicherheitspolizei drove into the Government-General a million Poles from the areas incorporated in the Reich, thus playing havoc with the food position in Frank's kingdom; Himmler then lured into the Warthegau 30,000 of the 90,000 racial Germans resident in the Government-General,[164] thereby ruining Frank's dream of a German ruling class; finally the RKF began to germanise the Gorals, the Lemkes, the Kashubs and the Huzuls, the minorities whom Frank wished to use as a counter-weight to the Poles. But worse was to come; SS formations and the Sicherheitspolizei initiated a pitiless campaign against actual or suspected Polish resistance fighters, driving thousands of innocent peasants into the woods or into the ranks of the partisans. SS and Police Courts passed blanket sentences of death without regard to the Government or any normal form of legal procedure.[165]

Gradually Frank began to suspect that Himmler's real purpose in despatching his HSSPF, Friedrich-Wilhelm Krüger, to Cracow was "to put an end to Frank"—as Gottlob Berger now openly admits.[166] Signs multiplied that an SS and Police administration, distinct from that of the Government-General, was forming and setting itself up as the real ruler in Frank's kingdom.

In impotent rage the hard-pressed Governor-General

cursed and swore at the SS invaders. He despatched a
stream of protest letters to the Reich Chancellery;[167] at
almost every "cabinet meeting" in Cracow, he took occasion to demonstrate to Krüger, verbally at any rate,
that he was master in the Government-General. "I have
never left anyone in any doubt that it is only possible to
rule here if he who carries the responsibility carries it in
full," Frank stormed at Krüger. "It is therefore clear that
the HSSPF is my subordinate, that the police form an
integral part of the Government and that the SSPF in
districts are subordinate to the Governors."[168] And on
another occasion: "No organ of the Reich is empowered
to take action, directly or indirectly, in this area. Orders
are issued solely by the Governor-General as the Führer's
direct representative and by no one else."[169]

But Himmler's minions were entirely unruffled by
Frank's homilies. They awaited their moment and, in late
autumn 1941, they thought it had come; the Sicherheitspolizei was on the trail of a corruption scandal in which
Frank himself was involved.[170]

SS-Untersturmführer Lorenz Löv, Head of the Governor-General's Central Administrative Office in Warsaw,
had fallen under suspicion of running a highly profitable
black market in furs and other articles stored in a warehouse under his control. He was brought before SS/Police
Court VI in Cracow and sentenced to life imprisonment
for embezzlement by the SS judge, Dr Günther Reinecke.[171] In the process the investigators stumbled upon
the fact that the Governor-General and his family were
busily engaged in feathering their nest and had clearly
been using official funds to purchase articles, said to be
"for representational purposes." Frank's family was evidently particularly interested in furs.

Immediately after Löv's arrest, Frank closed down the
fur warehouse and the contents were sold at bargain
prices. On 1 December 1941 Reinecke reported to Himmler: "The Governor-General's wife procured from the
warehouse a number of fur coats (at least ten) far in
excess of her personal requirements. But even this by no
means satisfied her need for furs! From Apfelbaum in
Warsaw she ordered a moleskin jacket, a beaver coat, a
musquash coat, an ermine coat, two broadtail coats, an
ermine jacket, a silver fox cape, a blue fox cape and

other furs. According to SS-Sturmbannführer Fassbender, the persons making these purchases on behalf of the Governor-General's wife were members of the Governor-General's office and they simply fixed the price at approximately 50 per cent of cost price."[172]

The Governor-General had also used his position to divert certain other articles into his own possession; according to Reinecke, the Frank family had picked up from the Jews of Warsaw rings, gold bracelets, gold fountain pens, tinned food, picnic hampers, coffee machines and groceries "at staggeringly low prices."[173] From his official estate at Kressendorf in Poland, Frank shipped both property and produce to Schobernhof, his private estate in Southern Germany; it included 200,000 eggs, a whole year's produce of dried fruit, sheets, blankets and furniture.[174] In November 1940, two whole convoys of foodstuffs left for Schobernhof. The first contained 150 lb of beef, 50 lb of pork, 20 geese, 50 chickens, 25 lb. of salami, 30 lb of ham sausage, 25 lb of ham; the second: 175 lb of butter, 110 lb of cooking oil, 30 lb of cheese, 1,440 eggs, 50 lb of coffee beans and 120 lb of sugar.[175] Simultaneously Frank took sculptures, figures of the Madonna, angels and icons from Polish churches and dispatched them to the Schobernhof private chapel.[176] Reinecke summarised: "This affair constitutes a case of corruption of the basest sort, all the more deplorable in that it shows that Germans are misusing their positions as senior political leaders of the Reich to enrich themselves personally by exploiting the circumstances arising from the war."[177]

Himmler seized upon this affair to strike at Frank. One of Frank's closest collaborators, Dr Karl Lasch, the Governor of Radom, had meanwhile been brought down by the Sicherheitspolizei because of a corruption scandal,[178] so Himmler now thought that he could force his enemy to his knees. On 5 March 1942 Frank was summoned to appear before Lammers, the Head of the Reich Chancellery; in Lammers' special train he was subjected to an inquisition; the other members of the tribunal were Bormann, the Head of the Party Chancellery, and Himmler. The Reichsführer made the speech for the prosecution. In his meticulous, pedantic manner, he detailed every one of Frank's peccadilloes, starting with his brother-in-law,

Heinrich Herbst, who had suddenly assumed Swedish nationality, and ending with Frau Frank's fur coats.[179]

Frank had to do obeisance before they would let him
go. The price: acceptance of Krüger as Secretary of
State in his Government, agreement that Krüger should
receive instructions direct from the Reichsführer-SS, and
an undertaking to dismiss Zörner, the anti-SS Governor of
Lublin.[180]

But Himmler's inquisition did not achieve its object.
No sooner had he returned to Cracow than Frank showed
that he intended to continue the battle. On 10 March he
sent an almost impertinent letter to Lammers, in effect
withdrawing everything to which he had agreed in the
special train. "To-day I can state," he said, "that among
the Germans in the Government-General, there exists an
impeccable official economic and social order which only
the basest slander can dispute. Primarily I would wish to
refute most vehemently any suggestion that an accusation
of major corruption can be substantiated."[181]

Frank then proceeded to act as if nothing had happened. He was, indeed, compelled to nominate Krüger as
Secretary of State, but Zörner remained at his post.[182]
Both in speeches and ordinances he resumed his attack on
the SS and the Police. He had it recorded in the cabinet
minutes, for instance, that the SD reports were "the worst
type of spy product, bearing no relation to objective truth
and being little more than a manifestation of hatred for
the work of the officials of the Government-General."[183]
When Globocnik in Lublin finally began to deport the
Poles and settle Germans in their stead, all without the
agreement of the Cracow Government, Frank's wrath exploded. Regardless of the consequences, he launched a
campaign against Himmler unparalleled in the history of
the Third Reich.

The truth had dawned on Frank—shortly before his
death he said: "Comprehension finally came to me in
1942."[184] On 30 June 1934 in Stadelheim prison a still,
small voice had spoken; during his struggle against the
continued existence of the concentration camps it had
become louder; now he knew. The Führer's legal adviser
began warning the Germans against the poison spread by
the totalitarian state. He accepted invitations to lecture in
German Universities; he peregrinated from rostrum to

rostrum. Berlin, Vienna, Munich, Heidelberg—in all of them his shocked audience heard a message never before voiced in public: Away with arbitrary action by the Police and SS.

Berlin University, 9 June 1942: "Without law—or contrary to law—no German Reich is conceivable. A people cannot be ruled by force, a community without law is unthinkable . . . it is intolerable that the State should be able to deprive a member of the community of honour, liberty, life and property, declare him an outlaw and condemn him, without first giving him an opportunity to reply to the accusations made against him."[185] Vienna University, 1 July 1942: "I shall continue to assert, with all the force at my command, that it would be bad if the Police State were to be presented as the ideal of National-Socialism. Nowadays many people say that humanity is an out-of-date notion, something incompatible with the severity of this period. That is not my opinion. The principle which every State, including our own, must follow, is that its methods must be designed to meet the historical tasks which any State must fulfil but that, in no circumstances, can a State be endangered by being humane."[186] Munich University, 20 July 1942: 'Even in wartime, a mode of life based on the rule of law is important for the development of our community. We must not give the impression that in our Reich the law is powerless. The law is the personal safeguard of our people . . . force alone cannot make the State strong. Brutality is never synonymous with strength . . . I say: only the man who does not fear the law is strong."[187] Heidelberg University, 21 July 1942: "The Police State must never exist—never! I reject it. As a National Socialist and leader of the German legal profession I therefore feel it my duty to protest against these continual disparagements of the law and its servants. I protest against a profession being attacked and slandered simply from spite or a permanent nagging desire to criticise."[188]

The initiated held their breath. By his self-destructive criticism of the SS, they thought, Frank was inviting the final blow; nobody and nothing could now save a man who thus challenged Himmler. The blow fell. From the rostrum Frank proclaimed: "Führer, protect the legal profession also!"[189] Hitler gave him his answer: he stripped

Frank of all his Party offices and dismissed him as Minister of the Reich.[190] On 24 August 1942 Frank handed in his resignation as Governor-General of Poland.[191]

But then came a curious phenomenon. Perhaps out of respect for the courage of his old comrade-in-arms, or perhaps to prevent the police machine from becoming over-powerful, Hitler allowed Frank to remain at his post in Cracow. He was there from 1942 to 1944—in fact he remained until called to the gallows in Nuremberg. By contrast Frank's SS enemies fell by the wayside. In autumn 1943 Himmler withdrew Globocnik from the anti-Frank battle for dealings which even he found too shady;[192] Globocnik was followed by Krüger, the HSSPF, who had regarded himself as successor to the tottering Frank.[193]

Himmler had to swallow this loss of prestige, but his Führer gave him little time to ruminate upon it. Hitler had already selected him for a new task compared to which the martyrdom of Poland was no more than a feeble overture. To the Reichsführer-SS was reserved the most grisly executioner's task in recorded history—the annihilation of European Jewry.

13

The Jewish Question

ON 11 November 1941 Kersten, Himmler's masseur, noted in his diary: "To-day Himmler is very depressed. He has just come from the Führer's Chancellery. I gave him treatment. After much pressure and questions as to what was the matter with him he told me that the destruction of the Jews is being planned."[1] This was the first Kersten had heard of the "Final Solution of the Jewish Question." "I was horrified," he says,[2] and he spoke up vehemently against this fearful plan. But Himmler, normally so talkative, was curiously reserved.

Shortly afterwards Kersten returned to the charge. On 16 November he noted: "In these last few days with Himmler I have been constantly trying to return to the fate of the Jews. Contrary to all his habits he only listens to me in silence."[3] A year later, however, on 10 November 1942, Himmler's tongue was looser: "Ach, Kersten, I never wanted to destroy the Jews. I had quite different ideas. But Goebbels has it all on his conscience."[4] And he went on: "Some years ago the Führer gave me orders to get rid of the Jews. They were to be allowed to take their fortunes and properties with them. I made a start and even punished excesses which had been committed by my people, which were reported to me. But I was inexorable on one point: the Jews had to leave Germany . . . up to the spring of 1940, Jews could still leave Germany without any trouble. Then Goebbels got the upper hand."

"Why Goebbels?" Kersten asked.

Himmler replied: "Goebbels' attitude was that the Jewish question could only be solved by the total extermination of the Jews. While a Jew remained alive, he would always be an enemy to National-Socialist Germany. Therefore any kindness shown them was out of place."[5]

This conversation with Himmler, recorded by that assiduous diary-writer Kersten, does not square with the picture which many of Himmler's contemporaries and the majority of the post-war world have formed for themselves of the origins of the so-called "Final Solution" of the Jewish problem. The annihilation of European Jewry is so closely bound up with the history of the SS that in centuries to come it will probably be the only single event which the letters SS will call to men's minds; consequently the natural (but erroneous) assumption has been made that the agents of the greatest mass crime in history were also its instigators.

After the war Rudolf Diels held that the "Final Solution" had "taken shape in the brains of Himmler and Heydrich" in 1942;[6] Paul Schmidt, the Foreign Ministry's ex-interpreter-in-chief, was equally convinced that "the 'Final Solution' originated from the Heydrich-Himmler-Streicher group."[7] Even serious historians have accepted this view. Leon Poliakov, for instance, considers that Heydrich was the first highly-placed National-Socialist to plan the annihilation of the Jews and that he did so before the outbreak of war.[8] The American Henry A. Zeiger maintains that Hitler and Göring only decided upon the "Final Solution" in 1941 as the result of a proposal from Heydrich to kill every Jew in Europe.[9]

There is no concrete proof of this theory. It springs, in fact, from the self-evident conclusion that the men who slaughtered millions of Jews in any orgy of blood and sadism can hardly have been transformed overnight from peaceful citizens into mass murderers—in other words the annihilation of the Jews was present in the hearts and minds of the SS long before the actual order was issued. Other indications, however, lead to the conclusion that the decision to murder the Jews originated elsewhere than in SS headquarters.

Hitler's decision must have been taken in early summer 1941 and no earlier document from any SS organisation has been found foreshadowing the physical annihilation of European Jewry. In his famous memorandum of May 1940 on "Treatment of foreign populations in the East,"

Himmler had characterised "the Bolshevist method of physical extermination of a people as un-Germanic and impossible" and had therefore rejected it "from inner conviction."[10]

One undisputed fact alone is enough to demolish the theory that Himmler was the originator of the "Final Solution." Hitler's decision wrecked an entirely different policy which the SS had been pursuing for years—the expulsion of the Jews from Germany, euphemistically called the "Emigration Policy." Pitiless this SS Jewish policy may have been, but, at least up to the outbreak of war, there was one notion it did not contain—that of physical liquidation of the Jews. The occupants of the Jewish desks in SS Headquarters were infuriated by the crude incitements to murder issuing from the Jew-baiting Gauleiter Julius Streicher and his weekly newspaper *Der Stürmer*. Ever since the SS had become the Führer dictatorship's primary instrument its leaders had supported a Jewish policy differing in many respects from the Party's crude anti-Semitism, though they naturally subscribed to the inhuman thesis that the Jews were a sort of racial blot and a manifestation of evil; they would have agreed with the comment by Buch, the Senior Party Judge: "The Jew is not a human being. He is a symptom of putrefaction."[11]

Following the economic crises of the early 1930s, anti-Semitism became even more firmly established as an SS article of faith; their livelihood gone, the sons of the farming and lower-middle classes streamed into the SS; having been taught to regard the Jew as the root of all evil, they saw in him the real cause of their economic misfortunes. These SS youngsters had inherited from their fathers an anti-Semitism tinged with socialism but in their minds it was overshadowed by a more sophisticated form of anti-Semitism—social Darwinism. The protagonists of this doctrine were believers in the laws propounded by the British biologist, Charles Darwin (1809–1882)—natural selection and the struggle for existence; these they transposed into the sphere of State policy.

More than any other Nazi organisation, the SS subscribed to the theory culled from Darwin and adapted to their own purposes, that a people's valuable characteristics could be increased and improved by a process of selection. The SS racial mystics recognised only one criterion of

value—the Nordic Germanic race.[12] The political twist
given to Darwin's biological theory presented his concept
of the struggle for existence in a new light. What Darwin
had regarded as a law of nature, the social Darwinists
wished to impose from without through measures of
coercion decreed by the authoritarian State; this culminated in the belief that the superior and stronger race
had the right to eliminate racially inferior beings.

The aim of any normal civilised State's social policy
was inverted. The normally accepted task of any State is
to protect the weak, the handicapped and the minorities;
here, however, the rule was to reinforce the "good blood"
and root out those elements of the race considered incapable of maintaining themselves. The SS looked upon
nations not as formed entities but, in Bucheim's words, as
"a plantation overgrown with weeds, which must be
cleared by isolating the incorrigible, cutting out the 'fer-
ment of decomposition,' cultivating the worthwhile elements and allowing the sub-standard to wither."[13]

Even the early social Darwinists had kept the notion of
race in the forefront of their minds. As early as 1903
Wilhelm Schallmayer, the biologist, had proposed "fer-
tility selection"; in his view good racial characteristics
could be cultivated by methods of racial selectivism, such
as control of banning of marriages and sterilisation of
inferior members of society.[14] This was clearly the forerunner of Himmler's racial fantasies with his "clan oaths,"
marriage permits and racial hygiene examinations. In his
social-Darwinistic phraseology Himmler once said: "Unless
the blood of leadership in German veins, by which alone
we stand or fall, can be increased by the admixture of
good blood from elsewhere, we shall never achieve world
mastery."[15]

It was at this point that anti-Semitism springing from
economic difficulties merged with social Darwinism based
on racialism to produce the hatred of the Jews characteristic of the SS philosophy. The Jew became symbolic of
the foreign body or inferior being against whom men of
good race must hold their own. Himmler proclaimed that
the anti-Jewish crusade was "a struggle between humans
and sub-humans"; it was "a law of nature, just as men
fight some disease or a healthy body fights the plague
virus."[16] The SS man was subjected to a torrent of anti-

Semitic indoctrination lectures; the fact that the Jew was
a foreign body was dinned into him at every turn. A
standard lecture for SS units issued in 1936 contained the
following: "The Jew is a parasite. Wherever he flourishes,
the people die. From the earliest times to our own day
the Jew has quite literally killed and exterminated the
peoples upon whom he has battened, insofar as he has
been able to do so. Elimination of the Jew from our
community is to be regarded as an emergency defence
measure."[17]

But how to "eliminate" the Jews? For the Nazi anti-
Semites this was the national problem upon which opinions differed. The young intellectuals, primarily those in
senior SD posts, displayed unmistakable horror at the
crude official Party solution—"down with the Jews." For
some time, however, they knew only what they did *not*
want. They did not want the methods advocated by the
Stürmer and Julius Streicher; they would have none of his
wild campaign of hatred and jealousy motivated by sex
and economics; in the final analysis this could only let
loose the basest instincts and deprive the Jews of all right
to existence.

The SD intellectuals wanted to be thought radical National-Socialists, but they also wanted to be regarded as
"decent," and this type of anti-Jewish action seemed to
them "harmful anti-Semitism," in the words of a *Schwarze
Korps* headline.[18] Inciting street mobs against the Jews
seemed to the SD leaders to be unintelligent folly; breaking Jewish shop windows, they argued, damaged the new
Germany's reputation in the world without advancing
the solution of the Jewish question one inch. On 5 June
1935 the *Schwarze Korps* proclaimed: "The National-
Socialist Movement and its State opposes these criminal
machinations with all its energy. The Party will not tolerate prostitution of its sacred struggle for the good of the
nation by street riots and destruction of property."[19]

The men of the SD were too intelligent to accept the
Party's crude anti-Semitic propaganda, and if they had
had their way most of it would have been suppressed.
Their sole object was to solve the so-called Jewish problem
in a cold, rational manner. They censored much of the
literature produced by the anti-Jewish Nazi fanatics. In
autumn 1935, for instance, the Berlin publisher Paul

Schmidt produced a leaflet, folded in the form of a caricature Jewish head, blaming the Jews for the Abyssinian
war; Abteilung II 2 B of the Gestapa commented: "The
contents of the leaflet are arrant nonsense. Reinke of the
Berlin Gestapo has been instructed by telephone to arrange its confiscation forthwith."[20]

Even the *Protocols of Zion,* the stock-in-trade of every
anti-Jewish propagandist, awoke no echoes in the SD
though they were regarded as suitable mental fodder for
the SS rank and file and references to them were retained
in the Allgemeine-SS education courses; SS-Untersturmführer Edler von Mildenstein, who occupied the Jewish
desk in the SD, regarded them as mere "poppycock."[21]
On 21 July 1938 SS-Oberscharführer Herbert Hagen, the
SD's Jewish expert, referring to books produced by the
Hochmut firm, wrote them off as insignificant produc-
tions, "quite apart from the fact that reference is made to
the *Protocols of Zion.*"[22] Commenting upon a brochure entitled *Der Judenspiegel (The Jewish Mirror)* produced by
the Party's Central Press and written by Rudolfs, Hagen
noted: "This over-zealous author is determined to see the
hand of Jewry in every development; he does so even
where something perfectly natural has occurred which
would have led to some sort of result, whether or not
Jewry had had a hand in it."[23]

In criticising the cruder anti-Semitic outbursts, the SD
memo-writers took no account of the author's Party se-
niority. The most notorious production from the Streicher
camp, for instance, was a book for the young entitled
The Poison Pill written by Ernst Hiemer, the editor of the
Stürmer; it was the subject of much laudatory comment;
Amann, the Party publisher, wrote: "should be read by
every German boy and girl"; Lutze, Chief of Staff of the
SA: "This is a unique book, well calculated to clarify the
Jewish question"; Gauleiter Wächter: "A guarantee that
Germans will adopt a correct attitude to Jewry in future."[24] The SD-Hauptamt, on the other hand, commented
drily: "Cannot agree with the view of most commentators;
quite apart from its contents, the style of the book is by
no means impeccable; in my view it is therefore unsuitable for children's education."[25]

Unmistakable though their disquiet was, however, the
SD elite gave little open expression to it until the summer

of 1935 when Edler von Mildenstein, later an SS-Untersturmführer, began to formulate a Jewish policy peculiar
to the SS. Born in Prague, von Mildenstein, though a
qualified engineer, was at heart a globe-trotter to whom
Heydrich's attention had been drawn by an article he had
written for the Berlin newspaper *Der Angriff* describing a
trip to Palestine and giving a reasoned view of the prospects of a Jewish state there.[26]

Von Mildenstein was no more anti-Jewish than his ham-
fisted amanuensis Adolf Eichmann or Reinhard Höhn,
Head of the SD Zentralabteilung; the latter, in fact, had
published a book in 1929 in which he referred to anti-
Semitism as a "poisonous agitation."[27] Von Mildenstein
was friendly with a number of Zionist leaders and a regular attendant at Zionist Congresses; at one of these he had
become convinced that emigration to Palestine was the
only solution to the Jewish problem and he therefore
established contact with the Zionists. He laboured under
the delusion that their anti-Semitism could and would lead
the Nazis to support emigration. Knowing that SS Headquarters was largely opposed to the arbitrary and incon-
sistent Jewish policy pursued by the Party, he turned to
the SS for help.

The Party had never been able to make up its mind
how to put its anti-Semitism into practice. In *Mein Kampf*
Hitler had not adumbrated any actual anti-Semitic legislation; in 1933 Achim Gercke, the Nazi racial expert,
thought it "premature from all points of view to work
out plans.[28] Alfred Rosenberg took refuge in the formula
that the "Jews must be recognised as a nation resident in
Germany" but "excluded from all positions of authority in
politics, culture and industry."[29]

SS-Standartenführer Dr Conti (later to become Reich
Health Leader) even declared that the new Germany was
averse to any form of racial hatred and that the Jews
were "not an inferior but a different race."[30]

Many recent historians have formed the theory that the
inconsistency of these Nazi statements was no more than
cover for a centrally planned, phased and increasingly
savage extermination campaign. Any attempt to read so
much logic into the actions of the Third Reich, however,
misses the point that the system of National-Socialist rule
was inherently structureless and contradictory. These dif-

fering statements were in fact reflections of the views of
the various anti-Semitic factions within the Party. There
were at least three: first a "Völkisch" group which desired
to restrict Jewish influence in politics and culture but allow them almost unlimited freedom in the business world;
among the leaders of this group were Dr Walther Gross,
Head of the Party Racial Policy Office and Dr Bernhard
Lösener, who occupied the Racial Desk in the Reich Ministry of the Interior. The second group consisted of the
anti-Semitic mystics and racial theorists led by Alfred
Rosenberg; the third, of the pornographic neurotic Jew-
baiters such as Julius Streicher, later joined by Josef
Goebbels. The history of German Jewry's sufferings from
1933 onwards shows clearly which of the various groups
was in the ascendant at the time.

During the first months after the Nazi seizure of power
the regime's anti-Jewish measures were governed by the
anti-Semitism of the Streicher group. The bloody attacks
on the Jews of March 1933, the boycott of Jewish businesses on 1 April, the dismissals of Jewish officials, doctors
and lawyers, the aryanisation of Jewish businesses and
the exclusion of Jews from swimming pools, concert halls
and art exhibitions—all these bore the unmistakable mark
of Streicher.[31]

In 1934 the anti-Jewish terror eased. The running was
taken up by somewhat more moderate anti-Semites such
as Hans Frank, the Nazi head of the legal profession; he
stated that the regime wished "to introduce a certain
limit on the further pursuit of its quarrel with the Jews."[32]
The Jews began to raise their heads once more; on 9 May
1935 the *Völkischer Beobachter* reported that of the Jews
who had fled from Germany, nearly 10,000 had returned.[33]

Inexorably, however, in 1935 the anti-Jewish pendulum
swung back. Josef Goebbels was now setting the pace.
Speaking on 29 June 1935 he screamed: "We want no
more Jews!" He then proceeded to fulminate against the
"stupid, absurd statements of middle-class intellectuals to
the effect that the Jew is a human being."[34] Gradually
German Jewry's possibilities of existence shrank. Jewish
citizens were assaulted on Berlin's Kurfürstendamm, Jews
were forced to leave the Wehrmacht and the Labour Service, placards reading "Jews not wanted" began to appear.

All this culminated in the most shameful series of laws in German history, the Nuremberg Laws, classifying German Jews as a group of outcasts and declaring all intercourse between Jews and non-Jews a crime against the State.[35]

A year later, however (1936), the grip of the anti-Semites loosened once more; the grumbling anti-Jewish campaign of denigration continued but the dominant voice was now that of Göring, Head of the Four-Year Plan, and he was clearly hesitant to exclude the Jews from industry altogether (he was thought at one time to have been a member of the "Völkisch" anti-Semitic group).

Von Mildenstein's object was to put an end to this interplay between the Party's anti-Semitic factions and solve the Jewish problem in the only way capable in his view of furnishing a reasonable and lasting settlement—Jewish emigration. There was nothing new about the idea but practical steps had invariably been blocked by the unwillingness of other countries to accept large numbers of Jews. SD Headquarters' proposal, therefore, was that Germany's 503,000 Jews should be shipped off to the country which both the SS and the Zionists regarded as Jewry's home—Palestine. (See Appendix 5.)

But von Mildenstein's Palestine plan encountered a serious difficulty—only a minority of Germany's Jews showed any desire to go there; in 1933 only 19 per cent of Jewish emigrants from the Third Reich went to Palestine; a year later the figure had risen to the exceptional level of 38 per cent but then it fell rapidly once more—36 per cent in 1935, 34 per cent in 1936, 16 per cent in 1937.[36] In spite of harassment, slander and terror the mass of German Jewry clung on in desperation; the *CV Zeitung*, the mouthpiece of the Central Union of German Citizens of the Jewish Persuasion, voiced the view: "With dignity and courage we shall manage to endure in our own home country the pitiless measures taken by Germans against German Jews."[37]

Alongside this majority, however, a small group of Zionist spokesmen was at work, and their object was to turn the minds of German Jewry away from their traditional German patriotism and direct them towards Palestine. Initially therefore they regarded the advent of National-Socialism as by no means a catastrophe; in their eyes it presented Zionism with a unique opportunity to fulfil its object, the return to a Jewish State and Jewish national consciousness. The rise of anti-Semitism in Germany exerted a curious fascination over the Zionists, for in it they saw the defeat of westernised Jewry which, they considered, was striving to identify itself with the non-Jewish industrialised peoples. After the Nazi seizure of power the Zionist newspaper *Jüdische Rundschau* proclaimed on a note of triumph: "An ideology has collapsed; we will not lament it but will think of the future."[38]

Many were tempted to regard 30 January 1933 as a favourable turning-point in Jewish history—"Jewry for the Jews" could become the watchword once more. This remark was to be found in an article entitled "We Jews" written by a young Rabbi, Dr Joachim Prinz. (Hans Lamm, the historian of German Jewry under the Third Reich, described it as "a curious, almost apologetic, interpretation of the anti-Semitic phenomenon.") Prinz considered that "there can be no further evasion of this Jewish problem; emancipation has forced the Jew to accept anonymity and deny his Jewish nationality." But this, he continued, had not profited the Jews at all. "Among those who nevertheless realised that a man was a Jew, this anonymity gave rise to the tensions generated by mistrust and the sense of contact with a foreigner." What solution could there be to the Jewish tragedy other than to take the road to Palestine? Prinz continued: "No subterfuge can save us now. In place of assimilation we desire to establish a new concept—recognition of the Jewish nation and Jewish race."[39]

For the Jewish nationalists the prospect was tempting; under the pressure of German racialism and with its assistance the Zionist ideal might win that victory denied it in the humanitarian and democratic atmosphere of the Weimar republic. If both the Zionists and National-Socialists regarded race and nationhood as universally valid criteria, some common ground must be discoverable between the two. As early as 13 June 1933, the *Jüdische Rundschau* had come out into the open: "Zionism recognises the existence of a Jewish problem and desires a far-reaching and constructive solution. For this purpose Zionism wishes to obtain the assistance of all peoples, whether pro- or anti-Jewish, because in its view, we are dealing here with a concrete rather than a sentimental problem, in the solution of which all peoples are interested."[40]

At this point von Mildenstein stepped in. The task of the SD, he argued, was to turn the German-assimilated Jews back into "conscious" Jews, to promote "dissimilation" in order to awaken in the breasts of the largest possible number of Jews the urge to go to Palestine, the only country open at the time to large-scale Jewish immigration. Himmler seized on Mildenstein's plan and set him to work. Within the SD Hauptamt Mildenstein set up a Jewish desk (entitled II 112); a period of SS Jewish policy began in which, according to Hans Lamm, "the adoption or affectation of a pro-Zionist attitude" was in order.[41]

The new SS policy made its first appearance in the columns of the *Schwarze Korps;* in place of the paper's anti-Jewish tirades references began to appear to the "sensible, totally unsentimental Jew" of the Zionist movement. The paper forecast: "The time cannot be far distant when Palestine will again be able to accept its sons who have been lost to it for over a thousand years. Our good wishes together with out official goodwill go with them."[42]

Although Jewish emigration to Palestine was officially the responsibility of the Gestapo and the Reich Ministry of the Interior, the SD now began to force the pace. Between 1933 and 1937 24,000 Jews had left for Palestine; the SD now increased its pressure upon those still willing to emigrate.[43] Von Mildenstein gave all possible support to the Zionist organisation's re-training camps, where young Jews were trained for the farm work which they would have to do in Palestine's kibbutzim.[44] He kept close watch on the work of the Zionists, and maintained large-scale maps in his office showing the progress of Zionism among German Jewry.

The staff of Section II 112 in the SD Hauptamt regarded every Zionist success or failure as its own. With some pride they recorded that one of the results of the Nazi seizure of power had been "to turn a section of German Jewry back to Jewish nationalism."[45] They noted with regret "that a high proportion of ostensibly enthusiastic Zionists were only "pseudo-Zionists, on whom the Zionist ideal has made no real impact."[46] The SD's Zionist observers regarded the activities of the anti-Zionist Jews with suspicion; for instance the athletic association of the patriotic Reich League of Jewish Front-line Soldiers was said to "dominate Jewish sport both numerically and by the results it achieves—a most unwelcome situation and further proof that the Zionist idea has not taken root among the majority of Jewish youth."[47]

Among the observers of the Zionists was a young SS man named Adolf Eichmann. He had been born in 1906 in Solingen; his family had then moved to Upper Austria, where he had worked at the coal face, as a salesman of electrical goods, and as a commercial traveller in oil products; accidentally finding himself on the German side of the frontier, he served for a short while in the SS-Verfügungstruppe and then joined the SD. His SS superiors discovered him in a window bay of the Johannis Hall in the Wilhelmstrasse Palace (SD Headquarters) occupied in sticking on the wall old seals from masonic lodges. He caught the eye by the ludicrously subservient manner with which he greeted any senior officer; his rule was to regard any SS Commander as a superior being, and whenever an officer passed through the hall (and a good many did) he sprang to attention and clicked his heels.[48] Von Mildenstein could make good use of so zealous an assistant and Eichmann was asked whether he would like to work for Section II 112. He nodded stiffly; he could think of no reason why he should not work on the Jewish question though later he said: "I would have said yes to anything to get away from sticking those seals on."[49] Eichmann was detailed to the Jewish office.

Anti-Semitism had played no noticeable part in Eichmann's previous existence. He had had difficulty in making up his mind whether to join the SS or a masonic lodge; he did not really know what to think of the Jews. He had no more anti-Jewish prejudice than the next man—rather less, in fact; he had many Jewish acquaintances and a Jewish girlfriend; he owed his modest career in business to the good offices of Jews.[50] Nevertheless under Mildenstein's guidance he rapidly developed into an anti-Semitic expert and soon became an indispensable member of the Jewish section's staff. Von Mildenstein, however, whose unorthodox methods were disapproved of by Himmler's staff, resigned after 10 months in the SD Hauptamt and later joined the Foreign Ministry.[51]

In Section II 112 Eichmann was given the "Zionist Or-

ganisation" desk;[52] he trotted out Hebrew words and
Zionist clichés so convincingly that rumour in the SD
Hauptamt had it that Eichmann was an ex-Palestinian
German with detailed knowledge of the country and its
people.[53] In fact he had crammed himself with a few
exiguous ideas by laborious nocturnal study of Theodor
Herzl's *Der Judenstaat* and a Hebrew grammar.[54] Nevertheless this knowledge sufficed to give him the entrée to
the Zionist organisations and parties and he soon produced
a memorandum entitled *The Zionist World Organisation*,
issued in October 1936 as an SS pamphlet.[55] While drafting this *magnum opus* Eichmann and SS-Oberscharführer
Herbert Hagen (a journalist who had succeeded von
Mildenstein) realised for the first time the difficulty for
which SS emigration policy was headed.

In fact the SS was faced with an ideological dilemma
which it was never to resolve; on the one hand it wished
to ship all Jews to Palestine; on the other, its hair stood
on end at the prospect of a strong Jewish state. Eichmann's 1936 brochure contained this: "The work of the
'Zionist World Organisation' carries with it a growing
danger—a strong Jewish Palestine. For all time world
Jewry will remain an enemy of Germany; a strong Jewish
Palestine could be an important factor in its struggle."[56]
But the danger did not end there; Zionism threatened to
challenge German anti-Semitism on its own ground and
this it would do as soon as a Jewish state had been formed
in Palestine and could take the German Jews under its
protection. As Hagen saw it: "It is axiomatic that Germany cannot approve the formation of such a monstrosity
of a state; otherwise the day might come when all the
stateless Jews in Germany would be given Palestinian
citizenship, call themselves a minority and demand repre-
sentation in the German Government."[57]

Hagen and Eichmann were not prepared, as Ohlendorf
was later, to concede minority status to the Jews;[58] they
were left only with the vague hope that Britain, the mandatory power in Palestine, would never permit the formation of a Jewish state; but no one could be sure. The SD
decided to place the Zionist organisations under much
stricter surveillance.

Orders were issued that a sharp watch be kept upon
the doings of the Zionist Union for Germany [Zionistische

Vereinigung für Deutschland—ZVfD] and the Zionist Movement "Hechaluz." An SD internal order stated: "The work of ZVfD Headquarters, No. 10 Meinekestrasse, Berlin W, telephone number J 1 90 31, requires particularly strict vigilance." In the case of Hechaluz, Section II 112 ordered: "The work of the Hechaluz re-training camps and their subsidiary organisations is to be watched as closely as possible; nominal rolls of those attending the courses should be prepared. On conclusion of the courses it should be ascertained whether those attending, in so far as they are resident in the area of the Oberabschnitt, do in fact emigrate."[59]

Mere control of the Zionists in Germany, however, did not satisfy Hagen and Eichmann. If they were really to estimate the chances of formation of a Jewish state, they had to force their way into the nerve centre of the Zionist movement.

The opportunity to do so came via an old friend of von Mildenstein. This was Otto von Bolschwingh, a Party member, an SD informer and an experienced salesman in the motor trade; he was in contact with a group of Palestinian Germans who lined their pockets by certain extramural intelligence activities. Among them was Dr Reichert, the German News Agency's Jerusalem correspondent.[60] Reichert, in turn, possessed contacts with one of the leaders of a secret Zionist organisation, the Hagana, which (with the exception of the "British Intelligence Service") fascinated the SD more than any other institution. Eichmann's comment on the Hagana in his 1936 brochure had been: "All parties and formations included in the Zionist World Organisation are kept under observation by a central counter-espionage and supervisory office which plays an extraordinarily important role in Jewish political life. This office is known as 'Hagana' (translated—self-defence)." The Hagana was not only the Jewish settlers' military defence organisation but, in addition, maintained a widespread espionage system.[61] On the headquarters staff of this secret army there was a chartered accountant named Feivel Polkes, born in Poland on 11 September 1900, who drew considerable sums from Dr Reichert for occasional scraps of information.[62] He carried the rank of Commander in the Hagana and according to Hagen was responsible for "running the entire self-defence organisation of the Palestinian Jews."[63]

Section II 112 evinced interest in the Hagana Commander and in February 1937 he journeyed to Berlin. On 26 February he and Eichmann met; on the first occasion Eichmann entertained him at the Traube restaurant near the zoo;[64] during the return match Polkes invited Eichmann to Palestine.[65] Polkes was, of course, no ordinary agent. His object, he explained to Eichmann, was to accelerate Jewish immigration into Palestine so that the Jews in their homeland might outnumber the Arabs; for this purpose he was already working with the British and French Secret Services and was only too willing to co-operate with Hitler Germany.[66]

On 17 June 1937 Eichmann's office noted: "He [Polkes] was prepared among other things to give powerful support to German foreign policy interests in the Middle East . . . on condition that German currency regulations were relaxed for Jews emigrating to Palestine."[67] Gradually the SD realised that Polkes had not made the journey to Berlin on his own initiative—he was patently representing the immigration policy of the Hagana. Eichmann minuted: "As a *quid pro quo* the following assurances could be given to Polkes: pressure would be exerted upon the German Jewish leaders to place an obligation upon all Jews emigrating from Germany to go to Palestine and not to any other country. Such a measure is completely in line with German interests and preparatory steps have already been taken by the Gestapa."[68]

At 8.50 a.m. on 26 September 1937 Eichmann and Hagen boarded a train and set off to crown these first cautious steps towards an SS–Hagana alliance.[69] Heydrich had given Eichmann permission to accept Polkes' invitation to Palestine.[70] Their cover was amateurish; Eichmann travelled as a correspondent of the *Berliner Tageblatt* and Hagen as a student.[71]

On 2 October the *Romania* with the two SD men on board docked in Haifa, but here the Jews' Arab enemies put a spoke in the wheel of the Jews' German enemies. In late September the Arab nationalists had risen once more, forcing the Mandatory Power to declare a state of siege and close the frontiers of Palestine.[72] The meeting with Polkes had to take place in Cairo. Polkes declared himself satisfied with a monthly salary of £15 sterling and delivered his first batch of information.[73] Hagen recorded Polkes as expressing the opinion that "in Jewish nationalist circles people were pleased with the radical German Jewish policy, since the strength of the Jewish population in Palestine would be so far increased thereby that in the foreseeable future the Jews could reckon upon numerical superiority over the Arabs in Palestine."[74]

Eichmann rated the results of his Palestine journey as "meagre";[75] Himmler and Heydrich, on the other hand, regarded their Zionist expert's work as so promising that six months later, after the move into Austria, they placed him in charge of the whole Jewish emigration problem. For the first time the SD was formally involved in the regime's Jewish policy. Eichmann, who had been promoted Untersturmführer in January 1938, was dispatched to Vienna as Jewish Adviser to the Inspector of the Sicherheitspolizei and SD;[76] his primary task was to promote Jewish emigration by all available methods.

Hitherto emigration had been more or less voluntary. Now, however, Eichmann brought Sicherheitspolizei pressure to bear and so harried the Jews that emigration became almost synonymous with deportation. Organisation was his passion and he suddenly discovered that he was now entitled to plan and give orders. He had an idea. He wished to put an end to the crossing of wires between police, State and Party authorities, all of whom had some responsibility for Jewish emigration, and to concentrate all those concerned—both German authorities and Jewish representatives—into one organisation. One office only should be responsible for the compulsory Jewish emigrants; in Eichmann's words "it should be a conveyor belt—you put the first document followed by the other papers in at one end and out comes the passport at the other."[77]

The conveyor belt took the form of the Central Office for Jewish Emigration, headed by Eichmann and located in an old Rothschild palace at 20–22 Prinz-Eugen-Strasse, Vienna. With him arrived a staff later to provide the ambassadors and couriers of genocide—the brothers Hans and Rolf Günther, Franz Novak, Alois and Anton Brunner, Erich Rajakovich, Stuschka, Hrosineck—all cold-blooded and indefatigable strategic planners for the expulsion of the Jews.[78]

Eichmann's new office used blackmail to give impetus to the Jewish exodus. The majority of Austria's 300,000 Jews were destitute and could not produce the minimum capital demanded by the receiving countries; the Nazi regime, on the other hand, was short of foreign currency and could provide no funds. The richer Jews were accordingly compelled to subsidise the exodus from their own resources.[79] Heydrich later explained the procedure: "We worked it this way: through the Jewish community we extracted a certain amount of money from the rich Jews who wanted to emigrate . . . The problem was not to make the rich Jews leave but to get rid of the Jewish mob.[80] Simultaneously Eichmann allowed the leaders of Austrian Jewry to travel abroad to obtain money for the emigration from Jewish aid organisations; in spring 1938, for instance, the American Joint Distribution Committee provided $100,000.[81]

Such methods enabled Eichmann to report record figures to Berlin. By late autumn 1938 his office had organised the emigration of 45,000 Austrian Jews; in a bare 18 months he had driven 150,000 Jews from their homes.[82] His merciless policy of compulsory emigration, however, could only succeed provided both the frontiers of the receiving countries and the coffers of the Jewish Aid Organisations remained open, and neither would do so unless the SS technocrats could keep the deportations running smoothly. The Party extremists now set out to sabotage this machinery; annoyed by the SD's intrusion into Jewish policy, they initiated a fresh anti-Jewish atrocity campaign in the summer of 1938.

The opening shots were fired by Julius Streicher's *Der Stürmer*. In increasingly strident tones the newspaper called for the exclusion of the Jews from the few positions still remaining to them in business and industry; it called on the countries of Europe to unite in the battle against the Jews and close their frontiers to "World Enemy No. 1."—the same frontiers which Eichmann was trying to keep open for his emigrants.

In vain Eichmann strove to change *Der Stürmer's* line. At the end of May 1938 Hiemer, the editor, visited Vienna and Eichmann took him to task, explaining the SS emigration policy and giving him what he called "a two-hour briefing."[83] He arranged to visit Streicher in

Nuremberg in order (as he noted in the file) "to use the opportunity to bring about a different line on the part of *Der Stürmer*."[84] His efforts were fruitless. A two-page article by Hiemer on Viennese Jewry showed Eichmann and Hagen "how wrong we were in our opinion that we could bring about a change of heart by such methods."[85]

On 28 June 1938 Hagen wrote to Eichmann: "Of all the crazy things—he [Hiemer] refers to the highly satisfactory fact that many Viennese Jews are returning to the Jewish faith and then adds the following in brackets 'to a religion which recognises the teachings of the Talmud as the supreme law! the Talmud which permits any crime against non-Jews!' When I see something like that, I tear my hair. What are they after! Perhaps *Der Stürmer* supports the radical solution—off with their heads to ensure that they cannot get the praiseworthy idea of admitting once again that they are Jews."[86] Relations between Streicher and the SD became so bad that Heydrich ordered Eichmann to excuse himself from any further visit. Obersturmbannführer Six noted: "C desires that for the moment Untersturmführer Eichmann should refuse any further invitation, saying that he has just gone on leave."[87]

A few weeks later the opponents of the SS Jewish policy received a far more formidable reinforcement in the person of Goebbels, the Reich Propaganda Minister. He had long been waiting for an opportunity to lay hands on the regime's Jewish policy; his propaganda machine was already standing by to launch a new wave of anti-Semitic measures.

Goebbels' opportunity came when Polish and German anti-Jewish leaders began sniping at each other. On 6 October 1938 the Polish government issued a decree invalidating all Polish passports unless by the end of the month holders had had them franked with a special stamp obtainable only in Poland.[88] The Berlin Foreign Ministry at once suspected that the Warsaw government's purpose was to rid themselves in one operation of the numerous Polish Jews resident in Germany. The reaction of the Nazi regime was typical. On 28 October Heydrich had 17,000 Polish Jews arrested, crammed into railway wagons and shipped to the Polish frontier. During the night of 28–29 October these victims of the Third Reich's first mass deportation of Jews were driven across the frontier

—against the muzzles of the Polish frontier troops' machine guns.[89]

Among those wandering between the German and Polish frontiers was a tailor from Hanover named Grunspan whose 17-year-old son heard of his father's plight while in Paris. On 7 November he bought himself a revolver and with five shots laid low Ernst vom Rath, Third Secretary in the German Embassy.[90] The murder of a German diplomat by a Jew was just what Goebbels had been waiting and hoping for. His propaganda machine began to operate. On 8 November the *Völkischer Beobachter* thundered: "It is clear that the German people will draw its own conclusions from this new deed."[91] In the Gaue of Kurhesse and Magdeburg-Anhalt Nazi-directed mobs were already gathering and looting Jewish shops.[92]

For Goebbels this was the moment. On 9 November each year Hitler's oldest comrades-in-arms forgathered in Munich's Old Town Hall to celebrate the Hitler Beer Cellar Putsch of 1923. Everyone of note in the Party would be there—and, Goebbels thought, one incendiary speech from him would suffice to launch the Party into the final battle against the Jews. Berlin's wits christened the sequel the "Reichskristallnacht" [plate glass night], a reference to the thousands of Jewish shop windows smashed that evening. It has gone down to history as a night of shame—men were officially ordered by their regime to carry out a pogrom.

In the context of the internal history of the Hitler regime, however, "Kristallnacht" has another significance. It is a typical example of the Nazi system of rule. Like the Röhm affair and the Blomberg-Fritsch scandal, it illustrates how nonsensical, chaotic and structureless was the jungle which served as a system of government in the Führer state. An ironic and sinister sidelight on this episode is that the later mass murderers of Jews were opposed to Goebbels' coup. A factor in the action of 9 November 1938 was internal Party indignation against the dominant role played by the SS in Jewish policy.[93] It was no accident that Himmler and Heydrich only heard of the action when it was well under way—under the control of the Reich Minister of Propaganda.

Goebbels had gone to Munich on 9 November with the definite purpose of inciting the "old fighters" to initiate an anti-Jewish program. Chance came to his assistance. The old Nazis had hardly sat down to dinner in the Town Hall when the news arrived that Ernst vom Rath had died of his wounds at 4.30 p.m.[94] SS-Obergruppenführer Freiherr von Eberstein, the Police President of Munich, said in evidence: "Hitler was very strongly affected by this and refused to speak as he had always done before." Hitler and Goebbels put their heads together; they seemed to Eberstein to have a "very serious discussion."[95]

Undoubtedly this was the moment when the decision was taken. As Head of State Hitler could not be involved in the pogrom but Goebbels was only too willing to take control. The Dictator left the hall, whereupon Goebbels made a speech saying everything and nothing; the text has not survived but it must be reckoned as one of the master-pieces of National-Socialist demagogy. Baldur von Schirach, the Reich Youth Leader, later recalled that "the speech was definitely of an inflammatory nature and one was free to assume from this speech that Goebbels intended to start some action."[96] The speech was all things to all men; some took it as an instruction not to stand in the way of action against the Jews, others as an order actively to engineer a pogrom, still others as an invitation to set fire to synagogues and finally some as a command to hunt the Jews out of the city.[97]

But what had Goebbels actually said? Simply this: he, Goebbels, had informed the Führer that in certain areas anti-Jewish demonstrations had already taken place. The Führer had thereupon decided that such demonstrations were neither to be prepared nor organised by the Party; should they occur spontaneously, however, no action was to be taken to stop them.[98] This was all that Goebbels said. The "old fighters," however, were used to reading between the lines of their leaders' speeches. The subsequent judge-ment of the Supreme Party Court read: "All the Party leaders present took the verbal instructions of the Reich Propaganda Minister to mean that the Party must not out-wardly appear to be the instigator of the demonstrations, though in reality it should organise and execute them."[99]

The "old fighters," the majority of whom were leaders of Party formations, rushed to their telephones and alert orders sped to their units all over the country. At last they could feel themselves masters of the Jewish problem; at last the Party could once more assert its right to be heard; at last the SA saw the moment approach when it could emerge from its shadowy existence and avenge itself for the Röhm affair. And the man in full control was Dr Josef Goebbels. Tirelessly he dictated messages to the Party propaganda offices, telephones rang uninterruptedly and aides bustled in and out taking the Propaganda Minister's orders.

The official directors of National-Socialist Jewish policy, however, knew nothing of what was brewing. Göring, officially in charge of the Jewish problem, was on an overnight train to Berlin;[100] Himmler and his SS commanders were on the way to the SS recruits' oath-taking ceremony in front of the Feldherrnhalle;[101] Heydrich and his cronies were sitting in a room in the Four Seasons Hotel, Munich.[102] Werner Best, who had accompanied his master Heydrich to the traditional meeting of Nazi dignitaries, later stated that Heydrich was "completely surprised" by Goebbels' action; "I was with him when, only a few metres from the hotel where we were staying, a synagogue went up in flames."[103]

Heydrich and his companions were still puzzling over the background to the assault on the synagogue when the riddle was solved by a telephone call from the Gestapo Leitstelle, Munich. At 11.15 p.m. the Duty Commander reported that he had just been informed by the Munich/Upper Bavaria Party Propaganda Office that Jewish pogroms had been ordered; the Gestapo was not to intervene to prevent them.[104] The Commander asked for orders but Heydrich did not know what to say. He immediately dispatched Gruppenführer Karl Wolff, the Head of the Reichsführer's Personal Staff, to find Himmler and tell him the news. It was 11.30 p.m. when Wolff found his master in Hitler's private apartments in the Outer Prinzregentenstrasse.[105]

No one could have appeared more astonished than Adolf Hitler. The unsuspecting Himmler later noted: "When I questioned the Führer I had the impression that he knew nothing of these events."[106] Nevertheless Hitler quickly recovered from his well-simulated surprise. He ordered the SS not to become involved in the action; the Gestapo was merely to secure Jewish property. Wolff passed on the order to Heydrich.[107] There is nothing to show what happened during the next few minutes—Himmler was meanwhile on the way to the Feldherrnhalle with Hitler. It may be assumed, however, that Heydrich instructed Gestapo Müller, who was still in Berlin, to alert all Gestapo offices. Heydrich himself, whose information on the background to these events was extremely hazy, avoided giving detailed orders pending Himmler's return. He clearly wished to hear from his master what attitude the SS should adopt to Goebbels' coup. At 1 a.m. on 10 November Himmler finally arrived in the Four Seasons and issued his orders to Heydrich and the assembled Oberabschnitt Commanders of the Allgemeine SS.[108]

In an urgent teleprinter message to all Gestapo and SD offices Heydrich ordered: "Jewish business and houses are not to be damaged or looted. The Police have been instructed to ensure that this order is carried out and to arrest looters." In business quarters special care was to be taken "that non-Jewish businesses are protected from damage under all circumstances" and "foreign nationals, even if Jews, are not to be inconvenienced."[109] No sooner had Himmler issued his orders, however, than fury with his enemy Goebbels became the uppermost thought in his mind. From the outset he had realised the implications of the 9 November pogrom: it was a shot across the bows of the rational SS Jewish policy; it was an attack upon the dominant position of the SS in all Jewish emigration questions; it was sabotage of the only solution of the Jewish question which the SS thought feasible. Himmler summoned Untersturmführer Luitpold Schallermeier, Wolff's personal assistant, and at 3 a.m. dictated to him a note for the file which he placed in a sealed envelope. Himmler pronounced: "I presume that Goebbels in his lust for power and foolhardiness, which has struck me for some time, has sponsored this action at a time when the situation as regards foreign policy was at its worst."[110]

Himmler was not the only SS leader to be infuriated by Goebbels' action. According to a non-political student friend, Otto Ohlendorf, later head of the Inland SD, was "highly indignant" over the pogrom.[111] Gruppenführer Wolff admitted to the Indian politician Hafiz Khan that Germany had lost "a moral battle";[112] von Eberstein, the Police President of Munich, forbade his SS units to have anything to do with the business and regarded the whole

action as "downright indecent."[113] But—was this all that
the SS did to register their protest? The answer is that it
was—or very nearly. It never crossed the mind of any SS
Commander to go on strike and refuse to co-operate in an
undertaking regarded as crazy by the SS Jewish experts.
The SS paraded and did as it was told.

Rumour has it that Himmler did actually make a more
effective gesture of protest. Popitz, the Prussian Minister
of Finance, heard that Himmler had told Hitler that he
was unable to obey the Führer's orders;[114] Günther Schmitt
of the SS told the ex-Ambassador Ulrich von Hassell that
the Reichsführer had "disapproved of the pogrom and
confined the Verfügungstruppe to barracks for two
days."[115] The only particle of truth in all this is that
Himmler patiently collected evidence of the damage and
looting perpetrated by Goebbels' mobs and then pointed
out to the Dictator the stupidity of the entire affair, demanding the dismissal of his enemy from all his offices of
state.

Once the bill of devastation had been compiled, Himmler prepared to do battle against Goebbels. On 11 November Heydrich produced preliminary totals: 815 business premises damaged, 29 warehouses demolished, 171
houses destroyed, 76 synagogues devastated and a further
191 set on fire; 36 Jews murdered, 36 severely wounded,
171 looters arrested.[116] The prudent Reichsführer-SS
looked around for an ally against the mighty Propaganda
Chief. He found such an ally in Göring, who also saw his
own position in Jewish policy threatened by Goebbels.

As soon as the first reports of the pogrom arrived,
Göring hurried to the Reich Chancellery and implored
Hitler to stop the action forthwith.[117] His arguments were
similar to those of Himmler—not of course of a humanitarian nature—the Head of the Four-Year Plan was interested only in material damage. "I am sick of these
demonstrations," he said.[118] Hitler defended his Propaganda Minister but Göring pursued his campaign. When they
next met he used "very sharp words" to Goebbels[119] and
Himmler meanwhile produced yet another complaint in
the hope of bringing Goebbels down. Goebbels' irrespon-
sible pogrom, he said, had done the Reich irreparable
harm abroad.[120]

The anti-Goebbels battle reached its height on 14 November. On that day Carl Burckhardt, the League of Nations Commissioner in Danzig, had requested an interview with the Minister of Propaganda; but on reaching the Ministry was told that Goebbels could only receive him later. Burckhardt soon found out why.[121] Lipski, the Polish Ambassador, told him that "a spontaneous anti-Goebbels movement had taken place" in the Reich Cabinet; from an "eye-witness source" Burckhardt learnt that "the immediate dismissal of the Propaganda Minister had been demanded."[122] On 13 November the battle was still undecided, but by the morning of the next day Hitler had opted for Goebbels. About 11 a.m. he drove down to Goebbels' private apartment and assured him of his continued confidence; that evening Berlin and the world learnt that Hitler had accompanied Goebbels to a play in the Schiller theatre.[123]

Burckhardt returned to Danzig puzzled. On arrival, however, he found a message to say that Himmler had called, asking him to go urgently to Berlin.[124] Himmler was still pursuing his anti-Goebbels battle and thought that capital was still to be made of the argument that damage had been done to German foreign policy. However, von Ribbentrop, the Foreign Minister, had lined up with Goebbels, assuring him that there was no question of any damage to the Reich's foreign-policy interests.[125] In this situation Burckhardt was the only man who might help, for he was known to be an energetic supporter of any Nazi leader whom he regarded as a potential restraining influence on Hitler's adventurist policy.

But when Burckhardt appeared in the Prinz-Albrecht-Strasse, Himmler had already given up the struggle. Instead of the Reichsführer-SS Burckhardt was received by Gruppenführer Karl Wolff. His master was unfortunately sick, Wolff said; the events of the last few weeks had been a severe strain on Himmler's nerves. Nevertheless—the Reichsführer condemned the ruinous methods employed against the Jews. "The internal situation in this country has become intolerable," Wolff shouted; "something must happen. Goebbels is responsible for it all; his influence upon the Führer is catastrophic. We had hoped to bring him down on the pretext of his propaganda during the

Czech crisis and this time we definitely thought we were sure of success. But once more the Führer has saved him. This cannot continue; we shall have to act."[126] As he returned to Danzig, Burckhardt was completely at sea, comforting himself with the thought that Himmler must after all be "more astute than his appearance or his acts would lead one to think."[127] He did not, of course, know that his invitation to Berlin was Himmler's last move in a battle already lost to Goebbels. Nevertheless Goebbels had to pay a high price for his survival. He remained in office but was forbidden to meddle further in the Jewish question. Hitler had decreed that Göring alone should carry responsibility in this field—should now "concentrate the decisive steps under one central authority" as Göring put it in typical Nazi jargon.[128]

What this meant was increased pressure on German Jewry, complete exclusion of the Jews from industry and commerce, and above all increased emphasis on the SD's emigration policy. On 24 January 1939 Göring issued an order to Heydrich that Jewish emigration should be promoted by all possible means. Expropriation of Jewish property and expulsion of Jews continued.[129]

Heydrich now set up in Germany a larger-scale replica of Eichmann's Austrian organisation. A Reich Central Office for Jewish Emigration was created in Berlin; like its Vienna predecessor it included representatives both of the Reich Authorities and (compulsorily) of German Jewry (from the Reich Association of Jews in Germany); all were supposed to collaborate in the exodus of non-Aryans.[130] The office came under Heydrich in his capacity as Chief of the Sicherheitspolizei; he in turn nominated as Director SS-Standartenführer Heinrich Müller, Head of Abteilung II in the Gestapa.[131] New forms of pressure were brought to bear on the Jewish leaders to compel their people to emigrate.

The Reich Central Office demanded that the Jews of Berlin submit a daily list of 70 families prepared to emigrate and the Jewish representatives applied the spur; in summer 1938 they had already stated in public that 200,000 German Jews would have to go.[132] Heydrich's and Müller's offices were soon able to show record figures. In 1939 78,000 Jews left Germany compared with 40,000 in

1938.[133] Meanwhile Eichmann, who had by this time set up a further Office for Jewish Emigration in Prague, could record only 30,000 forced to emigrate from the Protectorate of Bohemia and Moravia.[134]

Heydrich's emigration experts missed no opportunity to ship Jews out of the country. They even established contact with a secret Zionist organisation whose aim, like that of Eichmann and Hagen in their 1937 conversations with Feivel Polkes, was mass emigration of German Jews to Palestine. But the plan was thwarted by the British Mandatory Government. After the bloody incidents between Arabs, Jews and the Mandatory Power in autumn 1937, the British Government had adopted a policy of strict limitation of Jewish immigration into Palestine.[135]

The first regulations were issued in December 1937; in 1938 the British Government took new restrictive measures summarised in a British White Paper of 17 May 1939, providing for the acceptance of 75,000 Jews into Palestine over the next five years. London, however, reserved the right to issue definite immigration quotas every six months covering the succeeding six months.[136] To fight England's new immigration policy, a Zionist Resistance Group was formed supported by the Hagana (of which Polkes, it will be remembered, was a member); the group was named Mossad le Aliyah Bet (Immigration Bureau); it had been formed in 1937 by Eliahu Golomb, the powerful Hagana leader.[137]

Throughout Europe Mossad set up a network of contact men to smuggle Jewish immigrants into Palestine in small ships. Its representatives combed every country of Europe for young Jews ready to accept the hard life of Palestine. Inevitably their eyes turned to the Third Reich as a priority target and Golomb's men were sufficiently hard-boiled to use even the SS as an instrument to obtain Jews for Palestine; in the words of the British journalists Jon and David Kimche, they were prepared to risk a "pact with the devil."

At about the time of "Kristallnacht" two representatives of Mossad, Pino Ginzburg and Moshe Auerbach, journeyed to Adolf Hitler's Reich to offer the SS their assistance in the matter of Jewish emigration.[138] They were prepared to accelerate the Zionist re-education pro-

THE JEWISH QUESTION 393

gramme for Jews willing to emigrate, and to ship the Jews to Palestine. Emigration figures had already begun to fall and so the SD leapt at the idea and guaranteed Mossad their co-operation. Untersturmführer Hagen noted that "receiving countries were raising increasing barriers against immigration"; on 15 June 1939 he further recorded: "Objects of German Jewish policy: promote emigration by all means available. Jewish immigration becoming more difficult. Promote all plans for emigration no matter whither."[139]

The SD was prepared to show its gratitude to anyone ready to ship German Jews abroad but the SS could hardly be seen in open collusion with the Zionists. Ribbentrop's Foreign Ministry was opposed to any immigration into Palestine and the Party Foreign Organisation was also intriguing against the incomprehensible SS policy which was apparently helping to build up a Jewish state. A Foreign Ministry circular issued on 25 January 1939 to all German diplomatic missions and consulates summarised the views of the anti-Israel camp, saying that instead of promoting an "internationally recognised increase of power" for world Jewry, the object of German policy must be continued "fragmentation of Jewry."[140]

The SD accordingly imposed a secret condition—under no circumstances must Palestine be given as the destination of Mossad's emigrant ships. The line-up was a curious one: the SD was now in league with the Zionists, first against the Foreign Ministry and Party radicals, and secondly against England—England had now reinforced her naval patrols off the Palestine coast and was stopping any illegal immigrant ship.

Nevertheless Pino Ginzburg moved into Zionist Headquarters in the Meinekestrasse, Berlin and began to assemble his convoys.[141] Heydrich's Emigration Office demanded that he organise 400 Jews per week for emigration and ship them to Palestine;[142] later the Office even engaged a German-Greek shipowner, but unfortunately his ships soon proved to be no better than miserable hulks.[143] Golomb, who was planning the operation from Palestine, therefore looked round for better means of transport; initially he had had to content himself with small boats carrying only 50 passengers; now he began to charter ships carrying 800 in spite of the fact that the Mossad office in Germany lacked the funds to pay for them.[144]

Despite these difficulties, in March 1939 Ginzburg managed to organise his first convoy. It consisted of 280 emigrants destined, according to the SD, for Mexico. They were joined by a further group from Vienna organised by Auerbach, and together they boarded the *Colorado* in the Yugoslav port of Susak. Off Corfu they were transshipped to the *Otrato*, another Mossad ship, and taken to Palestine.[145] Mossad's convoys now began to flow more smoothly and the number of immigrants began to rise. In summer 1939 the *Colorado* put to sea with a further 400 immigrants, followed shortly afterwards by the *Dora* from Holland with another 500.[146]

The British reacted strongly against this illegal immigration. The Admiralty stationed a destroyer flotilla off the coast of Palestine and ordered more intensive air reconnaissance; British Secret Service agents appeared in European ports to report the departure of immigrant ships.[147] On the diplomatic network Britain urged the Greek and Turkish Governments to refuse to accept refugee ships in their ports. The British Mandatory Government then proceeded to impose a "penalty"; all quotas for Jewish immigration during the next six months were cancelled.[148] To a chorus of protest from the Opposition Malcolm MacDonald, Secretary of State for the Colonies, reported many a victory over the helpless immigrants. On 21 July 1939 he told the Commons that British forces had arrested 3,507 illegal immigrants in two months. In June the *Astir* carrying 724 Jews was arrested. In August the Royal Navy stopped five ships carrying 297 German Jews, and shortly thereafter a further ship with 800 illegal immigrants on board.[149]

The more the British authorities reacted, however, the more forthcoming did Heydrich's Central Office become. In mid-summer he allowed Ginzburg to route his ships to Emden and Hamburg to enable emigrants to leave the country without trans-shipment; Ginzburg had already chartered four ships for October and under his new programme 10,000 Jews were to leave the country.[150]

At this point, however, Adolf Hitler's World War II terminated the uneasy partnership between SS and

Zionism. The last real chance to save the Jews of Europe
vanished amid the thunder of the guns and the scream of
the Stukas.

The outbreak of war put an end to the SD's independent
Jewish policy. The Jewish question now became the sole
responsibility of the Gestapo, where officials were more
prone to apply ruthless police-state standards to all
political problems and to regard human beings as mere
objects to be disposed of at any time by the all-embracing
power of the State. The SD intellectuals of the Herbert
Hagen type had at least attempted to see the Jewish question other than in black and white, to move towards a
solution which, while conforming to National-Socialist
dogma, bore some relation to reality. The men of the
Gestapo, however, were barrack-square officials, brainwashed by Reinhard Heydrich, nurselings of the Führer
cult and frequently bent on concealing their lack of
National-Socialist fervour by an excess of zeal in their
official duties; for them the Jewish question was simply an
aspect of State security; the political leadership would
decide how far they should or should not go.

The shining example of this drill-sergeant attitude of
mind was Hauptsturmführer Adolf Eichmann, who was
shortly to head the Gestapo version of Jewish policy. In
October 1939, Gestapo Müller had relinquished his post
as Director of the Reich Central Office for Jewish Emigration, proposing Eichmann as his successor.[151] Eichmann
came unwillingly. "I resisted," he told his Israeli interrogator: "I much preferred life in the provinces."[152] But
Eichmann would not have been Eichmann had he not
dutifully clicked his heels and accepted his new assignment
with alacrity. Obedience and acceptance of orders were
the limits of his capabilities.

In some astonishment that the great SS-Oberführer
Müller should think him worthy of notice, Eichmann
rapidly climbed the Gestapo ladder. He was assigned to
Amt IV (Gestapo) of the RSHA where he was given
Desk IVD4 (Emigration and Evacuation). Later he was
transferred to IVB4 (Jewish Affairs—Evacuation
Affairs).[153] He summoned his former staffs from Vienna
and Prague; he took a suite of rooms in a four-storey
house at 116 Kurfürstenstrasse, Berlin; it had marble stair-

ways and great halls—"quite unsuitable for an office," as Eichmann said.[154] Little did he know that he had entered the headquarters of the future annihilation campaign.

The last and most grisly phase of the "Final Solution" was of course still some way off; initially Eichmann imagined that he would be continuing his emigration policy. Gradually, however, even he perceived that extremely few Jewish applicants were reporting to the Kurfürstenstrasse—"the general trend is listless, I must say."[155] Nevertheless he clung to the emigration idea, for he knew of no other way to solve the Jewish problem. Then the Polish campaign seemed to him to offer an opportunity. He and SS-Brigadeführer Walter Stahlecker had already drafted a programme summarised by Eichmann in the words; "Give the Jews land and then the whole problem is solved for them all."[156]

The idea was to set up a Jewish reserve in the extreme eastern area of German-occupied Poland, where all Jews would be concentrated. Eichmann and Stahlecker went to Poland to look for an area of adequate size and they found it south-west of Lublin near the little town of Nisko on the San. Like a prophet viewing the promised land, Eichmann exclaimed: "We saw a vast area; we saw the San, villages, markets and little towns—and we said to ourselves 'This is it.' Then we said to ourselves—'Why should we not re-settle the Poles and give the Jews a vast territory here?' "[157]

Without realising it, Eichmann and Stahlecker had given SS Jewish policy a further inhuman twist. Gradually the concept became more pitiless and its methods less humane. Initially the Jews had been permitted to emigrate "voluntarily," then emigration had become compulsory, now came intensive expulsion and deportation. Heydrich explained the new plan of campaign to his staff on 21 September 1939; his orders were noted down in telegraphese: "Jews into the towns as soon as possible; Jews out of the Reich to Poland; systematic evacuation of Jews from German areas by goods train."[158]

In full this meant: the Jews in the ex-Polish areas annexed by Germany, together with those in German-occupied Poland, were to be concentrated in towns east of Cracow; "councils of elders" or "Jewish councils" were to be formed in the ghettos to be reponsible later for administration of the proposed Jewish reserve.[159] In an express letter to the heads of the Einsatzgruppen responsible for concentrating the Jews in the east, Heydrich outlined the area of the proposed Jewish reserve: "This decree does not apply to the area of Einsatzgruppe I, i.e. the zone east of Cracow bounded by Polanico, Jaroslav, the new demarcation line and the former Slovak-Polish frontier. In this area, only summary registration arrangements need be made."[160] In the centre of this area lay Nisko; this was Eichmann's future Jewish state.

Early in October the first train, carrying building materials, engineers and 4,000 settlers rounded up by the Sicherheitspolizei from the Jews of Czechoslovakia and Vienna, began to roll to Eichmann's Utopia in Nisko.[161] Then the Sicherheitspolizei set off on their great manhunt in the eastern territories. Ruthlessly the Jews were driven from their homes and hunted into the Government-General—6,000 from Vienna and Moravska Ostrava, 87,000 from the so-called reincorporated territories.[162] Train after train carried the Jews into Ecihmann's far-eastern land of dreams, there to meet an unknown fate.

Eichmann already saw himself as the future Governor of a Jewish State, lord of a Jewish settler people in the east. At this point unfortunately he was made aware of a basic principle of National-Socialist Jewish policy, which he described sadly as follows: "Every office meddled in it; it became fashionable to have a hand in Jewish affairs."[163] The first to "meddle" was Hans Frank, the Governor-General. He disliked being the sole receptacle for Jewish refugees; in addition the ambitious SS Jewish policy upset the already precarious food situation in the Government-General; in fact Heydrich's and Eichmann's increasingly bold re-settlement plans threatened to destroy the economy of the country completely. So Frank rebelled against the evacuation policy. On 12 February 1940 he went to Berlin and complained to Göring of the chaotic manner in which Jews were being shipped to the Government-General. His protest was successful. Göring ordered the transport of Jews to stop;[164] from the end of March Jews might only be despatched to Poland with Frank's permission. And that permission was seldom given. Eichmann's dream collapsed and, on 13 April 1940, the Jewish hutted town of Nisko was broken up.[165]

To take the place of this Jewish Paradise Lost in the East, the anti-Semitic Utopians thought up an even more fantastic plan. During the French campaign Nazi diplomats had toyed with the idea of settling all Europe's Jews on the East African island of Madagascar. The main protagonist of the plan was Franz Rademacher, a foreign service officer, Head of the Jewish Desk in the German Abteilung of the Foreign Ministry. France, he proposed, should cede Madagascar to Germany; under the peace treaty, all Frenchmen resident there should be re-settled and a "giant ghetto for four million Jews created and placed under the Sicherheitspolizei."[166] Eichmann seized on the idea and prepared learned theses which met with the approval of Himmler and Heydrich. He worked feverishly; with his friend Rajakovich, he travelled to the Tropical Institute in Hamburg to discover the climatic conditions on this far-off island,[167] he dispatched Theodor Dannecke, one of his staff, to the French Ministry for the Colonies to obtain information about Madagascar.[168] He burrowed in history books and discovered that many politicians from Napoleon to Bonnet, the French Foreign Minister, had had the idea of shipping Jews to Madagascar.[169]

Talking to Dr Bernhard Lösener, a counsellor in the Reich Ministry of the Interior, he said that after the war some six million Jews would be sent to Madagascar under a five-year plan—in "non-German shipping" of course. Lösener noted: "The Jews were to be productively employed down there. Production and trade would be managed by German-run organisations. There would be purely German and purely Jewish businesses. The merchant bank plus the issue and transfer bank would be German. The trading bank and production organisation would be Jewish."[170]

Once more Eichmann could see himself as Governor-General of a Jewish State; his macabre dream caught the imagination even of the most senior dignitaries in the State and the SS. At a meeting with Mussolini on 18 June 1940 Hitler declared: "One could found a State of Israel in Madagascar."[171] But once more Eichmann's promised land evaporated. He was soon at "the critical point where I said to myself: no more beating about the bush; away with dreams; no good."[172] In fact the Madagascar plan was the death spasm of the SS emigration policy, the end of an idea.

The sequel was genocide.

14

The "Final Solution"

HITLER is recorded as saying to the Czechoslovak Foreign Minister, Chvalkovsky on 21 January 1939: "Our Jews will be destroyed";[1] nine days later he forecast that, if war came, "the result would be, not the bolshevisation of the world and therewith the victory of Jewry, but the annihilation of the Jewish race in Europe."[2] Hitler was determined to make these statements come true; he was prepared to exterminate an entire people. We do not know exactly when he gave the order for the "Final Solution of the Jewish question"; no document reveals the date of this frightful decision.

There does exist, however, an order from Göring, dated 31 July 1941, requesting Heydrich to "send me, as soon as possible, a draft setting out details of the preliminary measures taken in the organisational, technical and material fields for the achievement of the 'final solution' which we seek."[3] Hitler's basic order had thus been issued earlier than this. Krausnick, the historian, has summarised all that can be said with certainty concerning the genesis of the "Final Solution" plan: "What is certain is that the nearer Hitler's plan to overthrow Russia as the last possible enemy on the continent of Europe approached maturity, the more he became obsessed with the idea—with which he had been toying as a 'final solution' for a long time—of wiping out the Jews in the territories under his control. It cannot have been later than March 1941, when he openly declared his intention of having the political commissars of the Red Army shot, that he issued his secret decree for the elimination of the Jews."[4]

Documentary evidence exists for a sort of warning order: on 3 March 1941 Hitler dictated to General Alfred Jodl a general directive for the forthcoming war against the Soviet Union and this contained the first intimation that the Reichsführer-SS, Heinrich Himmler, would assume responsibility for the extermination of the Jewish/Bolshevist ruling class in the East. Jodl noted: "The Bolshevist/Jewish intelligentsia must be eliminated as having been the 'oppressor' of the people up to now." The primary task was to liquidate "all Bolshevist leaders or commissars," if possible while still in the operations zone; "the necessity for employment of organisations responsible to the Reichsführer-SS, in addition to the Field Security Police, to be examined with the Reichsführer."[5]

The mass crime thereby announced was not, of course, openly stated. Initially Hitler referred "only" to the annihilation of the Jewish Soviet ruling class; his directive contained not a syllable to show that in practice every Jew would be handed over to the extermination machine—following the Nazi Jew-baiters' obscure reasoning that Bolshevism was a typical manifestation of Jewry. Hitler tightened the SS murder screw only by degrees. At first only Jewish "Bolshevist leaders" were to be exterminated but gradually the circle of victims widened; political functionaries were followed by the intelligentsia, the intelligentisa by all officials, officials by persons suspected of partisan activities—and finally the circle spread to every individual Jew.

The military knew nothing of this grisly process of inflation. As Hitler had indicated that the Reichsführer-SS would have a key role to play in the East, they were quite content to negotiate with Himmler and leave the dirty work to the SS, provided they did not infringe the Wehrmacht's prerogatives. On 13 March Major-General Eduard Wagner met Heydrich to find out how the RSHA proposed to co-operate in the East. Heydrich was only too willing to tell him: as in the Polish campaign, the Reichsführer-SS would use Einsatzgruppen of the Sicherheitspolizei and SD.[6]

The only point left undecided was the measure of control over the Einsatzgruppen to be exerted by the fighting formations. Heydrich deputed Gestapo Müller to negotiate with the Army High Command [Oberkommando des

Heeres—OKH] but the uncouth Gestapo man behaved with such arrogance that discussions soon reached an impasse.[7] The military were forced, however, to reach some agreement with the police, for on 30 March Hitler assembled 200 senior Wehrmacht officers in the Reich Chancellery and explained to them that the Eastern campaign would be the most barbaric of all time. "Bolshevism is a sociological crime," he screamed. "We must abandon any thought of soldierly comradeship. Commissars and OGPU men are criminals and must be treated as such."[8] Hitler's diatribe heralded the most criminal order in German military history, the notorious "commissar order" which made it the duty of army formation commanders to treat political and secret service officers captured from the Red Army, not as soldiers, but as political criminals to be liquidated or handed over to the Sicherheitspolizei for execution. Since hardly a single general was prepared to offer active resistance to Hitler's ukase, the temptation was all the greater to leave the "special treatment" to Himmler's police.[9]

The OKW international lawyers had just started drafting the commissar order when, on 4 April, Wagner sent Heydrich the draft of an agreement on the role of the Einsatzgruppen in the Eastern campaign.[10] This showed that the army was prepared to concede them well-nigh unrestricted activity. The draft proposed that in the Rear Army Area the Einsatzgruppen should be under orders of Armies "for movement, rations and accommodation"; for disciplinary matters and technical instructions they would be under the RSHA. The Commander-in-Chief of an Army, however, might forbid action by the Einsatzgruppen in areas where this might have adverse effects upon operations. But from Heydrich's point of view the overriding sentence of the Wagner draft was "The Sonderkommandos (or Einsatzgruppen) are authorised, within the framework of their task and on their own responsibility, to take executive measures affecting the civilian population." Heydrich accepted Wagner's draft.[11] He could see the way clear for his murder squads.

Had the army thereby given its agreement to wholesale murder of Jews by the Einsatzgruppen? The answer is that it had not. Everything goes to show that the military knew nothing of the "Final Solution of the Jewish Question" as

ordered by Hitler. Wagner set out the tasks of the Einsatzgruppen as follows: "In the Rear Army Area: prior to
the opening of operations, listing of certain concrete objects (material, archives, card indices of anti-German or
anti-Government organisations, associations, groups, etc.)
and certain important individuals (leading émigrés, saboteurs, terrorists, etc.)"; and "in the communications
zone: discovery and eradication of anti-German and anti-
Government movements in so far as these do not form
part of the enemy's armed forces, provision of general
information to the commander of the communications
zone regarding the political situation."[12]

Here, in black and white, was an example of that curious
military schizophrenia which so greatly facilitated the work
of the Einsatzgruppen. The generals regarded Heydrich's
shock troops as normal counter-espionage organisations
designed to deal with the enemy in rear of the front; at the
same time, however, they did at least know that the Einsatzgruppen in the East had "special tasks" of a political
nature—but the military were only too glad to leave those
"special tasks" to Heydrich's people.[13]

Initially, the men of the Einsatzgruppen were similarly
deceived; Heydrich thought it best to reveal the murder
order to his thugs in small doses. When he summoned the
RSHA Heads of Division in April 1941, he spoke only of
a "heavy task," explaining that the problem was to "secure
and pacify" the Russian area using Sicherheitspolizei and
SD methods. He concluded: "I need real men and hope
that my Heads of Division will place themselves unreservedly at my disposal."[14]

Arthur Nebe, the Head of the Kripo, stepped forward,
clicked his heels and announced: "Gruppenführer, you can
count on me." Heydrich nodded—the first Commander of
an Einsatzgruppe had reported for duty before it had even
been formed.[15] Nebe was later in touch with the resistance
and so his present-day friends have been at pains to explain why he thus volunteered. In his book *Wo ist Nebe?*
(Where is Nebe?), for instance, Hans Bernd Gisevius attempts to show that Nebe only assumed command of an
Einsatzgruppe after much cogitation and on the advice of
the Beck-Goerdeler resistance group.[16] Gisevius even attempts to clear his friend Nebe by saying that the "outsize
deeds of horror only occurred after he had returned"

(from Russia).[17] The fact remains that Nebe's Einsatzgruppe reported the liquidation of 45,000 Jews.[18] Gisevius'
arguments in fact are reminiscent of those of defence
counsel during the Nuremberg War Crimes Trial which
the US prosecutor, Robert Kempner, countered with the
question: "Tell me now, Mr Resistance Leader, how many
Jews did you really have to liquidate in order to offend
against humanity?"[19] In Nebe's case the truth was somewhat simpler—he thought that by promptly volunteering
for duty in the East, he would earn himself the clasp to the
Iron Cross First Class and curry favour with the unpredictable Heydrich. Initially, however, Nebe certainly did
not know that "employment in the East" was synonymous
with the greatest mass murder in history.

Of the leaders of the Einsatzgruppen, Nebe was the only
volunteer. Hardly one of them came of his own volition;
each had cogent personal reasons for obeying Heydrich's
order. Otto Ohlendorf, for instance, the Head of the Inland
SD, did so because he was National-Socialism's cantankerous, argumentative "knight of the holy grail" and had
consequently fallen into disfavour with Himmler; he had
twice refused to go to the East and now complied only
to avoid the reproach of cowardice.[20] SS Brigadeführer
Walther Stahlecker was an opponent of Heydrich's who
had transferred to the Foreign Ministry and hoped to win
his way back into the RSHA by commanding an Einsatzgruppe.[21] SS-Brigadeführer Dr Otto Rasch was kicking his
heels in the SD East Prussian Abschnitt, and thought that
a display of zeal in the East would give him a chance of a
senior appointment in the Berlin Head Office.[22]

Ironically enough, the only commanders actually to
carry out murders of Jews in the East were the two uncon-
ventional Heads of Division in the RSHA, Nebe and
Ohlendorf. Their colleagues were more expert at finding
loopholes; Franz Six (Advance Commando Moscow) and
Heinz Jost (Einsatzgruppe A) left their units after only a
few weeks in the East;[23] the remaining Heads of Division—
Heinrich Müller, Bruno Streckenbach, Walter Schellenberg
and Dr Nockemann—contrived to avoid any call to SS
heroism.

The middle-level Commanders, the Sturmbannführer
and Obersturmbannführer, were little more enthusiastic.
Heydrich had selected them from all branches of the police

organisation and, in the majority of cases, they came from
intellectual professions. The Jew-liquidators in fact were
a curious collection—highly qualified academics, ministerial officials, lawyers and even a Protestant priest and an
opera singer. Several availed themselves of some opportunity to leave the murder machine. Just as Six and Jost left
their posts with or without the agreement of Heydrich, so
some Einsatzkommando leaders such as Erwin Schulz or
Karl Jäger avoided the worst consequences of the racial
frenzy.[24] Even the lower levels sometimes managed to
evade the murder order. SS-Oberscharführer Mathias Graf
refused to take command of a sub-commando in Russia;
he was arrested and returned to the Reich.[25] Professor Six
testified: "One could at any rate *try* to get posted away
from an Einsatzgruppe. At least no one was shot for
doing so."[26]

Even among the rank and file, enthusiasm for Heydrich's duty in the East was so small that he had to comb all
the Gestapo, Kripo and SD offices to obtain the necessary
personnel. He was even compelled to scratch men out
from the Ordnungspolizei and Waffen-SS; a Berlin Police
Battalion was disbanded and distributed by platoons to the
individual Einsatzgruppen.[27]

Nevertheless, by May 1941 Heydrich had assembled
some 3000 men whom he formed into four Einsatzgruppen.[28] Stahlecker assumed command of Einsatzgruppe
A which was to follow Army Group North through the
Baltic States towards Leningrad; Nebe was in charge of
Einsatzgruppe B attached to Army Group Centre, operating between the Baltic States and the Ukraine. Rasch
commanded Einsatzgruppe C, operating in the west, north
and east of Army Group South's area. Ohlendorf's Einsatzgruppe D was responsible for the southern part of
Army Group South's zone between Bessarabia and the
Crimea.[29] (See Appendix 6.)

An Einsatzgruppe was of approximately battalion
strength; Einsatzgruppe A for example, consisted of 9
per cent Gestapo men, 3·5 per cent SD men, 4·1 per cent
from the Kripo, 13·4 per cent from the Ordnungspolizei,
8·8 per cent foreign auxilliary police personnel and 34
per cent from the Waffen-SS; the remainder consisted of
technical personnel and clerks.[30] The strength of an Einsatzgruppe varied between 990 men in Einsatzgruppe A

and 500 men in Einsatzgruppe D.[31] Each Einsatzgruppe was divided into two sections—a number of Einsatzkommandos or Sonderkommandos of about 70–120 men each attached to an Army, and sub-commandos of about 20–30 men.[32]

In late May Heydrich assembled the 120 Einsatzgruppe and Einsatzkommando leaders in the Frontier Police School at Pretsch on the Elbe near Wittenberg, to train for their annihilation campaign against the racial enemy.[33]

Slowly Heydrich increased the pressure of ideological indoctrination; RSHA instructors schooled the men in genocide, their language increasing in savagery. In mid-June Heydrich paraded the 3000 men of the Einsatzgruppen near the little town of Duben on the Mulde. The Head of the Sicherheitspolizei and SD faced his murder brigade drawn up on three sides of a square. He made a vigorous speech, though he kept it vague, speaking only of a task which demanded "unparalleled hardness."[34]

Later, addressing the Einsatzgruppe Commanders in the old baroque castle of Pretsch, he was more explicit. Even after the war Standartenführer Dr Walter Blume could still remember him saying that "Judaism in the East is the source of Bolshevism and must therefore be wiped out in accordance with the Führer's aims."[35] Years later Ohlendorf remembered that Heydrich had passed on to them a Führer order including the sentence that "Communist functionaries and activists, Jews, gipsies, saboteurs and agents must basically be regarded as persons who, by their very existence, endanger the security of the troops and are therefore to be executed without further ado."[36]

Did any of them revolt against this monstrous order? Did anyone refuse to obey the Dictator? Ohlendorf says that while in Pretsch, "in the presence of all the assembled Einsatzgruppe and Sonderkommando commanders, he protested loud and clear against the order for mass execution"; nevertheelss it was his duty "to obey the orders of my Government, no matter whether I regarded them as moral or immoral."[37]

Similarly Martin Sandberger, Commander of Sonderkommando 1A and a doctor of law, stated that, although he rejected the Führer's order, he considered it "legal" since Hitler "represented the supreme authority in the State."[38] Blume argued similarly; he had wished to resist the Führer's order but "for me an order from the Führer was the means of making war."[39]

No one rebelled, everyone obeyed. The men of the Einsatzgruppen moved happily off to their assembly areas. On 23 June 1941, one day after Adolf Hitler had let loose his war on Russia, Heydrich's messengers of death set off on their most grisly adventure—3,000 men hunting Russia's 5,000,000 Jews.[40]

The murderous impact of the Einsatzgruppen caught Russian Jewry totally unprepared. Only a few Jews in Russia, where anti-Semitism had been dormant under Stalin, realised the mortal danger represented by the German form of the disease; National-Socialist anti-Semitic atrocities had hardly been reported in the Russian press. In some towns (in the Ukraine, for instance) the Jewish community compared Adolf Hitler's soldiers to those of the Kaiser in 1918 and welcomed the Germans as liberators. "The Jews are remarkably ill-informed about our attitude towards them," Sonderführer [Detachment Commander] Schröter reported from White Russia on 12 July 1941.[41] The impact of Heydrich's murderers was all the more cruel as a result.

To gain the advantage of surprise, the Einsatzgruppen followed close behind the advancing troops, their main objectives being the Russian cities where over 90 per cent of Russian Jews were concentrated.[42] In many cases advanced detachments of the Einsatzgruppe had started their murderous task while fighting was still going on around the town. The RSHA murder commandos frequently entered alongside the German troops. Kovno, Yelgava, Riga and Reval fell to the Einsatzgruppen and the Army simultaneously; as they moved on Zhitomir the leading tanks were followed by three vehicles of Einsatzgruppe C; Einsatzkommando 4A occupied Kiev on the day the city fell (19 September 1941).[43]

No sooner had an Einsatzgruppe unit reached a town than a deadly stranglehold gripped the Jewish inhabitants claiming thousands upon thousands of victims day by day and hour by hour. For Heydrich's men no brutality was too base, no trick too mean, no barbarity too disgusting, if it allowed them to raise their grim tally. Report after report testified to the murderers' fanatical zeal—reports couched in cold, official language as if recording production figures for refrigerators or numbers of vermin destroyed.

Einsatzgruppe D report No. 153: "Area of the sub-commandos, primarily in smaller localities, reported cleared of Jews. During period covered by this report 3,176 Jews, 85 Partisans, 12 looters, 122 Communist functionaries shot. Total 79,276."[44] Einsatzgruppe C report No. 17: "In accordance with RSHA instructions, liquidation of all state and party functionaries undertaken in the above-named White Russian town. As regards Jews, orders similarly carried out."[45] Report from Einsatzgruppe C: "To deal with this situation [risk of epidemic] 1,107 adult Jews shot by Commando 4A and 661 Jewish adolescents by the Ukrainian militia. Up to 6 September 1941, therefore, Sonderkommando 4A has dealt with 11,328 Jews in all."[46]

Kill, kill, kill. Einsatzkommando 6: "Of the remaining 30,000 approximately 10,000 were shot."[47] Einsatzgruppe D: "In the period covered by this report 2,010 persons were shot."[48] Einsatzkommando 8: ". . . liquidated 113 Jews."[49] Advanced detachment of Einsatzkommando 4A: ". . . in all 537 Jews (men, women and children) apprehended and liquidated."[50] The news of the Einsatzgruppe horror spread like a forest fire. The further German troops penetrated into the interior of Soviet Russia, the more panic-stricken became the flight of Jews from towns in the path of the German advance. At last the Jews had been warned and the "final solution" became more difficult to put into operation. One Einsatzkommando reported in vexation: "Rumours from other areas regarding the shootings have made action considerably more difficult. Information regarding our action against the Jews is gradually filtering through via fugitive Jews, Russians and talkative German soldiers."[51]

The manhunters developed numerous ingenious methods of catching their victims *en masse;* for instance: "The Jews of the town were invited to present themselves at a certain spot for registration and subsequent accommodation in a camp. Some 34,000 reported, including women and children. After being stripped of their valuables and clothing all were killed, a task which demanded several days."[52] In Kiev, Einsatzgruppe C reported: "The Jewish population was invited by poster to present themselves for re-settlement. Although initially we had only counted on 5,000–6,000 Jews reporting, more than 30,000 Jews appeared; by a remarkably efficient piece of organisation they were led to believe in the re-settlement story until shortly before their execution."[53]

The cold, bureaucratic language of the reports naturally gave no indication of the atrocities attendant upon the annihilation of Russian Jewry. Even the accounts of independent eye-witnesses, however great their revulsion, cannot give a true picture of the horror—the calvaries of thousands and hundreds of thousands, the mass graves, the columns of naked women with babies in arms, the murderous scene at the edge of the grave.

In late July 1941 Major Rösler, commanding 528 Infantry Regiment, was alerted in his billet in Zhitomir by a wild fusillade of rifle fire. He went out to look and climbing an embankment, came upon "a picture of such barbaric horror that the effect upon anyone coming upon it unawares was both shattering and repellent." Rösler was looking down into a pit in which were heaped innumerable bodies of Jews of all ages and both sexes; soldiers and civilians stood around staring curiously into it. He continued: "In this grave lay, among others, an old man with a white beard clutching a cane in his left hand. Since this man, judging by his sporadic breathing, showed signs of life, I ordered one of the policemen to kill him. He smilingly replied: 'I have already shot him seven times in the stomach. He can die on his own now.' "[54]

Hearing of the approach of a murder commando, the Jews of one Russian village had gone into hiding; when the commando reached the village, the only person whom the SS men saw in the street was a woman with a baby in her arms. She refused to tell them where the Jews were hidden. One of the men snatched the baby from her, gripped it by the legs and smashed its head against a door. An SS man recalls: "It went off with a bang like a bursting motor tyre. I shall never forget that sound as long as I live." Beside herself, the woman gave away the hiding place.[55]

In Riga an SS man saw two Jews carrying a log of wood; calmly he pulled out his revolver and shot one of them, saying: "One's enough for that job!"[56] Similarly while clearing a Latvian ghetto, an SS Commander, seeing

sick Jews being carried out on litters, went from one
to another with his service revolver and shot each in
turn.[57]

Pitilessly the Einsatzgruppen decimated Russian Jewry.
By winter 1941/42 they had reported the following figures
for Jews liquidated: Einsatzgruppe A—249,420, Einsatzgruppe B—45,467, Einsatzgruppe C—95,000 Einsatzgruppe D—92,000, a total of almost half a million.[58]

The first wave of Einsatzgruppen was soon followed
by a second batch of SS murderers. Behind the front a
German civil administration had meanwhile been established under Alfred Rosenberg who was entitled "Reich
Minister for the Occupied Eastern Territories"; he was
responsible for two Reich Commissariats known as "Ostland" and "Ukraine"; these were again sub-divided into
"Commissariats-General." Within this civil administration
the Reichsführer-SS occupied a key position, for a Führer
decree of 17 July 1941 had charged Himmler with "police
security in the newly occupied territories" and empowered
him "in discharging his responsibility to give instructions
to the Reich Commissars."[59] Himmler had already nominated HSSPF [Senior SS and Police Commanders] as his
principal representatives in Russia: Gruppenführer Hans
Prützmann as HSSPF North in Riga, Gruppenführer Erich
Kiev; in mid-1942 they were reinforced by Brigadeführer
Gerret Korsemann as HSSPF Caucasus.[60]

Each of Himmler's senior representatives controlled a
regiment of Ordnungspolizei and certain Waffen-SS units
reinforced by half-trained "auxiliary volunteers" from the
Baltic States and the Ukraine. They were given liquidation tasks similar to those of the Einsatzgruppen—anything which the initial murder brigades had missed was
to be steam-rollered by the formations of the HSSPF.
The latter soon started a sinister race with the Einsatzgruppen for numbers of Jews liquidated. The eventual
winner turned out to be Jeckeln who, for the month of
August 1941 alone, reported a total of 44,125 executions, primarily of Jews.[61]

Actual numbers of Jews killed by units under the HSSPF
during the early months of the Eastern Campaign cannot
be accurately established. It is known, however, that when
the Einsatzgruppen and HSSPF formations suspended
operations at the end of 1941 to gather strength for the

following spring, 500,000 Jews had been murdered, 300,-
000 by the Einsatzgruppen.[62]

In spite of these "successes" the SS murderers were
now showing clear signs of exhaustion. In September
Schulz, a Commando leader, had requested a posting;[63]
Rasch, commanding an Einsatzgruppe, had gone on leave,
never to return;[64] in November Nebe had told his deputy,
Werner, that he was for home (Werner's comment was
"Arthur, if you can't go on, I'll release you"); Gisevius
says that Nebe was "a mere shadow of his former self,
nerves on edge and depressed";[65] Nebe's driver, Köhn from
the Kripo, had shot himself in horror at the anti-Jewish
atrocities.[66]

A few months later even Himmler's most aggressive
Eastern minion became a victim of the nightmare—von
dem Bach-Zelewski was taken to the SS hospital in
Hohenlychen, suffering from a nervous breakdown and
congestion of the liver. Haunted by his guilt, he would
pass his nights screaming, a prey to hallucinations. Dr
Grawitz, the Head SS doctor, reported to Himmler: "He
is suffering particularly from hallucinations connected with
the shootings of Jews which he himself carried out and
with other grievous experiences in the East."[67] When the
doctor asked him why he was in such a state of fear,
Bach-Zelewski growled: "Thank God, I'm through with
it. Don't you know what's happening in Russia? The entire
Jewish people . . . is being exterminated there."[68] Yet
when Bach-Zelewski asked the Reichsführer whether the
Jewish business in the East could not now be brought to an
end, Himmler replied angrily: "That is a Führer order.
The Jews are the disseminators of Bolshevism . . . if you
don't keep your nose out of the Jewish business, you'll see
what'll happen to you!"[69]

Even so fanatical a devotee of the Führer's orders as
Himmler must have known that, apart from a small
minority of natural sadists and killers, the men of the
Einsatzgruppen felt like Bach-Zelewski or Brigadeführer
Eberhard Herf, Head of the SS Personnel Hauptamt, who
wrote that he "wished to get out of the East, since
frankly I've had more than enough of it."[70]

Nevertheless in the Einsatzgruppen a determined army
of death had arisen, unparalleled even in the SS. Wholly
dedicated to achievement, "hardness" and camaraderie,

they reached a degree of insensibility surpassed only by those soulless automata, the concentration-camp guards. Here was to be found the elite of that barbaric type of mankind, intoxicated by its own achievements, which Himmler exalted as the SS ideal; it was indeed an Order of the Death's Head, divorced from the world of ordinary mortals and from their moral standards, ready to undertake any mission ordered by its masters, and prisoner of a community claiming the sole right to decide the SS man's social and ethical standards. For years their leaders had drummed into the men now forming the Einsatzgruppen that they should yield themselves to the intoxication of power, that they should savour the elite's feeling of superiority and consider themselves a class above the mass of Party members, too superior to conform to their moral standards—they even claimed for themselves the right to turn men into subjects for biological laboratory experiments.

Both by background and training, therefore, no one could have been more eminently suited to be Jew murderers than the men of the SS Order. Moreover the deeds demanded of them took place in the vast expanses of Russia, so far distant from their normal environment that the whole murder business seemed like a dream; those who had such a thing as a conscience could pretend, by a process of self-deception, that what occurred had never really taken place. Nevertheless—when faced individually with the thousand-fold murders they themselves had committed, all their façade of neo-German heroism collapsed. The Germanic knights shrank back into what they had always been—inflated mediocrities, carrying on their bestial handiwork with typical German self-pity, all the while thinking, with sentimental tears in their eyes, of their wives and children at home.

While mowing down their Jewish victims, the Einsatzgruppen believed that they were entitled to the sympathy of all good Aryans. "The job is not a pretty one," Gruppenführer Turner lamented, while proceeding with his murders in Serbia.[71] After the war Paul Blobel, leader of Einsatzkommando 4A, maintained that the real unfortunates were the liquidators themselves: "The nervous strain was far heavier in the case of our men who carried out the executions than in that of their victims. From the psychological point of view they had a terrible time."[72] Fritz Jacob, a Gendarmerie Commander, bewailed the fact that he had to do his Jew liquidations so far from home; his superior, Gruppenführer Querner, had to remind him of his duty to the fatherland; Jacob promised to do better: "I thank you for your warning. We men of the new Germany must be hard with ourselves even at the price of prolonged separation from our families."[73]

Himmler was only too well aware of the sufferings of his little men. He seized every opportunity to encourage the men of his Einsatzgruppen—in sonorous pseudo-patriotic phraseology, calculated to make even the most cynical of his audience believe that he was participating in a mighty world plan, almost incomprehensible to human intelligence, designed to save the German people and the Nordic race.

For instance—"Most of you will know what it means to see a hundred corpses—five hundred—a thousand—lying there. But seeing this thing through and nevertheless—apart from certain exceptions due to human infirmity—remaining decent, that is what has made us hard. This is a never-recorded and never-to-be-recorded page of glory in our history."[74] His imagination worked overtime in the effort to prove that mass murder was no crime. Nevertheless his speeches to the SS liquidators contained an element of self-exculpation and self-justification; at a meeting of Reichsleiter and Gauleiter, Himmler declared that the "Final Solution" had become "the most painful question of my life."[75]

Even to his closest collaborators, he attempted to minimise the true enormity of the Jewish massacres, using every known argument to cover up the horror of the reality. In his heart of hearts he felt himself an outcast like his minions, saw himself an object of world detestation—the daily flood of requests for mercy for individual Jews was there to prove it. "Remember," Himmler said to the Gauleiter, "how many people, Party members included, send their precious plea for clemency to me or some other authority; they invariably say that all Jews are, of course, swine but that Mr So-and-so is the exception, a decent Jew who should not be touched. I have no hesitation in saying that the number of these requests and the number of differing opinions in Germany, leads one to conclude that there are more decent Jews than all the rest put together."[76]

There was only one possible escape from this sense of isolation; he had to convince himself and his executioners in the East that they were the instruments of a great historical mission, the creators of a work surpassing all human comprehension. Himmler told Kersten: "You oughtn't to look at things from such a limited and egotistical point of view; you have to consider the Germanic world as a whole . . . a man has to sacrifice himself."[77] He was continually encouraging his Einsatzgruppen to fulfill their "heavy task," continually speaking words of comfort to his unhappy executioners in the East: "I can tell you that it is hideous and frightful for a German to have to see such things. It is so, and if we had not felt it to be hideous and frightful, we should not have been Germans. However hideous it may be, it has been necessary for us to do it and it will be necessary in many other cases."[78]

Himmler toured the Einsatzgruppen to raise the sinking morale of his executioners. In Minsk he attended the execution of 200 Jews, but was so shocked by the disgusting scene that Wolff, the Head of his Personal Staff, barely managed to prevent him from collapsing. "Good for him to see what he expects people to do," Wolff commented.[79] Gradually Himmler recovered and began his pathetic "must-see-it-through" speech. The men would no doubt have observed, he said, that he "hated this bloody business," but everyone must do his duty, however hard it might be. He then told Nebe, the Head of the Einsatzgruppe, that a new method of killing must be found.[80] This incident heralded the birth of the gas vans.

The actual heads of the Einsatzgruppen, however, were not prepared to rely on Himmler's mealy-mouthed exhortations. The nightmare that haunted Ohlendorf, Rasch, Nebe and Stahlecker was a breakdown of discipline and a chain reaction starting from individual acts of sadism by uncontrolled Jew murderers. Precise regulations were laid down to ensure that executions passed off rapidly and effectively before the executioners had time to realise what they were doing.[81]

In Einsatzgruppe D Ohlendorf carried out his executions in military form. It was a macabre perversion of the military tradition, but the reasoning behind the policy was sound: the individual man of the Einsatzgruppe should have no contact with his victim; he should feel himself part of a unit acting as such and acting only on the orders of his superiors, thus eliminating any individual sense of guilt. No individual was allowed to do the shooting; moreover Ohlendorf took care to ensure that the victims remained calm up to the last minute, for any uproar carried with it the danger that the liquidators might start firing wildly into the crowd and running amok —and that prospect Ohlendorf feared more than a mass escape by the Jews. Anxiety on this score rather than any considerations of humanity caused Ohlendorf to recoil before the employment of gas vans. The gas vans, he thought, would produce "an intolerable psychic burden" for his men, for after the execution they would have to unload the distorted bodies—frequently covered in excrement—and so the executioners would be brought face to face with what they had done—the moment of truth from which Ohlendorf wished to save them.[82]

Dr Otto Rasch, Head of Einsatzgruppe C, adopted other tactics. In his view every man of the Einsatzgruppe must partake of its collective guilt; scenes of horror witnessed in common were to form the bond of comradeship holding the unit together; collective blood guilt was to be its cement.[83] Rasch insisted that every man of his Einsatzgruppe take part in executions; the individual had to "overcome himself."[84] There was hardly a man in this Einsatzgruppe who did not suffer from "the most horrible dreams," an eyewitness reported.[85] Nevertheless, the aim was achieved—the camaraderie of guilt.

Every trick of psychology was employed to ease the work of the executioners. Even terminology played its part. In the murderer's vocabulary the word murder did not appear; instead he used a picturesque selection of ostensibly innocent code words—"special actions," "special treatment," "elimination," "execution activity," "cleansing," "re-settlement." An unending stream of propaganda, even more intense in Russia than elsewhere, aimed to eradicate any feeling among the executioners that the Jew was a human being; he was presented as a pest or vermin.

Nevertheless for the leaders of the Einsatzgruppen even

this ghastly propaganda was inadequate. The American historian Hilberg, who has made a meticulous study of the actions of the Einsatzgruppen, considers that "psychological justifications were an essential part of the killing operations. If a proposed action could not be justified, it did not take place."[86] The two most commonly used excuses were fear of epidemics and prevention of collaboration between the Jews and the enemy. In Balti, for instance, the Jews were liquidated for "attacks" on German troops.[87] In Novoukrainka for "encroachments,"[88] in Kiev for "arson" and in another town for "a spirit of opposition."[89]

In 1942 Himmler admitted to Mussolini: "In Russia we had to shoot a considerable number of Jews, both men and women, since there even the women and older children were working as couriers for the partisans." The Jews, he said, were "everywhere primarily responsible for sabotage, espionage and resistance, as also for the formation of partisan bands."[90]

The theory that all Jews were partisans ushered in a new annihilation programme, beginning in 1942. It was a clever idea, for murder of Jews could now take place under cover of the anti-partisan war and some of the responsibility for the greatest crime of the century therefore inevitably attached to the Wehrmacht.

On occasions the army had used the Einsatzgruppen for military purposes such as dealing with scattered enemy units; from the outset, therefore, the commanders of the fighting formations were on good terms with Heydrich's people. Einsatzkommando 4B, for instance, reported: "Armed forces, surprisingly, welcome hostility against Jews";[91] Einsatzgruppe A considered that relations with 4 Panzer Army were "very close—yes, almost cordial."[92] As a result of the Jewish panic and the partisans' early activities, the military uged the Einsatzgruppen to take more severe measures against the Jews. In September 1941 17th Army requested Einsatzkommando 4B to exterminate the Jews of Kremenchug; the reason was that Army cables in Kremenchug had been cut on three occasions by persons unknown.[93] In August XXX Corps Field Security Police requested a detachment of Einsatzkommando 10A to take action against the Jews in the Ukrainian town of Kodyma, because Captain Kramer of the Field Security Police had been told that the Jews were planning an attack on German army units.[94]

Many (though not all) military men regarded the liquidation of Jews as nothing unusual. In an order of the day to the soldiers of 6th Army, for instance, Field-Marshal Walter von Reichenau told them that they were "the standard-bearers of an inexorable popular concept" and so must have "full comprehension for the necessity of this severe but justified atonement required from the Jewish sub-humans."[95] The army did indeed comprehend: 17th Army issued an order that when those responsible for acts of sabotage could not be traced, Jews, and particularly Jewish Komsomol members, were to be shot; [96] Einsatzgruppe A reported that by December 1941 Army Group Centre had liquidated 19,000 partisans and criminals, the majority of them Jews.[97] The army in Russia even organised concentration camps. As a defence against partisan attacks, the Commanding General of XXX Corps decreed that hostages should be taken and held in a concentration camp. Infantry Regiment 124 maintained a concentration camp in Kutschuk Muskomja, Infantry Regiment 226 another in Warmutka and No. 72 Anti-Tank Battalion yet another in Foros.[98]

The military reacted nervously to any signs of unrest among the Jews in their area. The local Commander of Dzhankoy, for instance, fearing an epidemic among the Jews in the concentration camp for which he was responsible, asked Einsatzgruppe D to liquidate all Jews in the camp; but the Einsatzgruppe was short of personnel and required much persuasion before it was prepared to help the Field Security Police to do his bidding.[99] So persistent were some of the military in their demands for additional liquidations that Sturmbannführer Lindow exclaimed indignantly that the Gestapo was not, after all, "the Wehrmacht's hangman."[100]

As the Russian-organised partisan war increased in intensity, the military became yet more eager to call in the Einsatzgruppen. When Halder, Chief of Staff of the Army, assembled Army Commanders at Orscha in December 1941, they were unanimous in their praise of the Einsatzgruppen: "These people are worth their weight in gold to us. They guarantee the security of our rear communications and so save us calling upon troops for this purpose."[101]

The first to be used in the partisan war was Einsatz-gruppe A. In late September 1941 Soviet partisans were sighted in the Leningrad area and by the end of the year most of Stahlecker's Einsatzgruppe was concentrated on the northern front for anti-partisan operations. Stahlecker himself was killed in the process early in March 1942.[102] Himmler was quick to seize the opportunity of using the partisan war as cover to step up his anti-Jewish campaign —in July 1941, after all, Hitler had said: "This partisan war has some advantagess for us; it enables us to wipe out everyone who opposes us."[103]

Himmler camouflaged his army of executioners as a semi-military anti-partisan force, officially known as "anti-Partisan Formations." The Einsatzgruppen turned themselves into static Sicherheitspolizei command posts, the Heads of Einsatzgruppen A and C becoming Befehlshaber (BdS) and the commanders of Einsatzkommandos Kommandeure (KdS).[104] This heterogeneous army of anti-partisan units was later placed under a "Chief of Anti-Partisan Formations" in the person of Bach-Zelewski; to them were added five regiments of Ordnungspolizei and the indigenous militia of the German-occupied Eastern territories.[105] The overall strength by the end of 1942 was 14,953 Germans and 238,105 auxiliaries.[106]

Thus carefully camouflaged, the murderers returned to the attack, supported as occasion required by the Army and the Waffen-SS. Jeckeln, who had been transferred to the Northern Front as HSSPF, was the first to get going. In February and March 1942 he initiated an anti-Jew and anti-partisan operation known as "Action Marsh Fever." At the end of it he was able to report: 389 partisans killed, 1,274 persons shot on suspicion and 8,350 Jews liquidated.[107]

This combined operation was the forerunner of a series of murderous sweeps whereby, under cover of military necessity, Himmler continued his extermination of Jewry. No fewer than five major operations were initiated: the purpose of all of them was the annihilation of the Jewish people.[108] Simultaneously, the net was drawn tighter round those Jews who had not taken refuge with the partisans. The liquidators had driven the mass of the Jews into ghettos and concentration camps; in "Ostland," for instance, 100,000 Jews were still alive, of whom 68,000 were in the towns.[109] A further deadly blow against them was in course of preparation.

The new extermination campaign was concentrated upon the White Russian Commissariat-General, re-christened "White Ruthenia" by its new masters. Town after town was combed by the Police Battalions and Auxiliary Brigades; ghetto after ghetto fell to the liquidators' sub-machineguns. The SS hierarchy, from HSSPF through BdS to KdS, could soon calculate when the last Jew in White Ruthenia would have disappeared. At exactly this moment, however, the civil administrators of the Reich Commissariat "Ostland" developed a proprietary and protective instinct which turned even long-standing Nazis into opponents of the Thousand Year Reich's racial policy. Leading the revolt was one of the most corrupt of Party functionaries—Gauleiter Wilhelm Kube, Commissar-General of White Ruthenia.

Like other Nazi colonial governors in the East, Kube based his case upon the fact that over-hasty anti-Jewish action by the SS and Police formations had ruined the country's economy. Even Stahlecker, after all, had once warned: "The immediate removal of all Jews employed in industry is not possible, particularly not in the larger cities."[110] The "Final Solution" expert in White Ruthenia, however, SS-Obersturmbannführer Dr Eduard Strauch, the KdS, continued his fanatical campaign of liquidation and the infuriated Kube found himself facing an economic breakdown in his area, for the White Russian Jews were the only craftsmen and skilled workers in the country. Even more vexing to Kube, however, was the fact that the SS Commanders were descending upon the Jews without informing him beforehand. His anger had been at boiling point even before the latest offensive by the murder brigades.

On 27 October 1941 the adjutant of No. II Police Battalion reported to Carl, the Area Commissar in Slutsk, and told him that within the next few hours the Battalion would start liquidation of all Jews in the town.[111] Carl was horrified. He begged the Commander of the Police Battalion to leave the Jewish craftsmen alone, but the Police ignored his request. The Jews of Slutsk were exterminated. On 30 October Carl reported to Kube; "The whole picture was worse than disgusting. With indescribable brutality, both German Police officials and, even more, the Lithuanian partisans (Auxiliary Police) herded the Jews out of their houses. Shots were to be heard all over the town and in some streets the bodies were piled high." Carl and his staff had attempted to "save what might be saved. On several occasions I had to drive German policemen and Lithuanian partisans out of business premises, literally revolver in hand."[112]

Kube filed a case for undisciplined behaviour against the entire officer corps of No. II Police Battalion.[113] Burying alive Jews who had been shot—as had happened in Slutsk—was a "bottomless infamy," he wrote; "law and order in White Ruthenia will not be established by such methods."[114] Kube was a long-standing anti-Semite; in 1934 he had said: "This plague virus must be exterminated."[115] He would therefore not have objected to an "orderly" annihilation of Russian Jewry and would have been quite prepared to participate, as he had done before, in the murder of Jews. Now, however, he suddenly saw thousands of Jews from Germany being deported to Minsk for killing;[116] when he saw German Jews arrive, his entire ideology collapsed—Kube the anti-Semite became Kube the protector of the Jews.

Kube discovered that among the German Jews were men who had served in the First World War and had been decorated. He compiled a list of their names and appealed to the RSHA as if the "Final Solution of the Jewish question" was something new to him. Heydrich retorted angrily that everything was in order; moreover "in wartime there were far more important things to do than run around after a bunch of Jews, prepare time-wasting reports and thereby prevent my staff getting on with other and more important jobs." He concluded: "I find it regrettable that six and a half years after the issue of the Nuremberg laws, I have to justify these measures."[117]

But Kube refused to accept the situation. He placed the German Jews under his personal protection and as soon as he heard that the Sicherheitspolizei under Obersturmbannführer Strauch, was preparing to take the final step, Kube hurried to see him. "A remarkable attitude towards the Jewish question," Strauch scoffed;[118] he had

not yet realised that one of the Third Reich's first Gauleiter had turned into a protector of the Jews. The bottom
was falling out of Strauch's world; he noted: "I emphasised that it was incomprehensible to me why Germans
should fall out over a few Jews. I was continually hearing
myself and my men accused of barbarity and sadism
whereas all I was doing was my duty."[119] According to
Strauch, Kube countered with: "This sort of action was
unworthy of a German or of the Germany of Kant and
Goethe. The fact that Germany's reputation was falling
all the world over was our [the SS] fault. Moreover,
he said, it was quite true that my men actually took pleasure in these executions."[120]

Kube did not confine himself, however, to public denunciation of the executioners as barbarians. He replaced the
SS guards on his office building by ST men.[121] He was
always on the spot if some SS man committed a crime
against a Jew.[122] Wherever he could, he sabotaged the
liquidation programme. 1 March 1943, for instance, had
been earmarked by Strauch for a killing operation in the
Minsk ghetto; 5,000 Jews were ordered by the Sicherheitspolizei to assemble at a certain spot for "re-settlement." The plan was betrayed by Kube. He arranged for
the Jews to be warned of Strauch's real intentions, and
all Jews employed in the General-Commissariat Offices
were told indirectly not to go into the ghetto. A furious
Strauch found only a few Jews to arrest.[123] As a result
riots took place and the Commissar-General protested
once more. Strauch reported: "He cursed several of my
men savagely, using expressions such as 'filthy brute' and
'you'll hear more of this.' "[124]

Kube became such a thorn in Strauch's flesh that
the latter alerted his superiors. Himmler complained to
Rosenberg, the Minister for the East and Kube's ultimate
superior, who promised to give Kube a warning.[125] But
Kube refused to give way; he was reinforced in his attitude by the knowledge that Heinrich Lohse, the Reich
Commissar for Ostland and therefore his immediate superior, loathed the SS as much as he did. When a further
mass liquidation of Jews, camouflaged as anti-partisan
operations (code word "Major Undertaking Kottbus"),
took place, Kube seized the opportunity for general criticism of the tactical methods used by SS formations. In

a letter to Rosenberg he warned that the political repercussions of such operations would be "devastating," since
many of the Russians liquidated by the Police were not
partisans at all but simply harmless peasants. "If only 492
rifles are found on 4,500 enemy dead, that is, to my
mind, proof that among those dead were numerous ordinary peasants," Kube reported.[126] On 18 June 1943 Lohse
noted on Kube's report: "What is Katyn* compared to
this? Think of what would happen if the enemy found out
about these things and made use of them! I suppose such
propaganda would be ineffective because listeners and
readers would simply refuse to believe such things."[127]

The masters of the terror machine were at their wits'
end to know how to get rid of their enemy in Minsk
but finally Soviet partisans came to their aid: during the
night of 22 September 1943 Wilhelm Kube was blown
up by a bomb which his maid-servant, who was a partisan
agent, had placed under his bed.[128] Himmler was radiant;
Kube's death, he stated, was a blessing for the fatherland.[129]

He could afford to take it calmly, for the "Final Solution" in Russia was drawing to a close. Much had been
accomplished; of the 2·5 million Russian Jews unable to
escape from the Germans, 900,000 had been liquidated.[130]
It remained to erase the evidence before the Soviet armies
began to drive back the German invaders; this was the
task of Standartenführer Paul Blobel, commanding a special detachment known as "Commando 1005." He opened
the mass graves and burnt the bodies on oil-soaked grids;
any remaining bones were ground up in special machines.[231] The burning bodies illuminated an eerie scene,
the final act of a perverted militarism unparalleled in the
history of war.

Yet even before the extermination of Russian Jewry
had ended, Himmler had issued the order for a new
phase of mass murder. The mobile killing units were to
turn into static death factories; bullets gave way to gas—
the grisly era of the gas chambers had begun. The initiative had come from SS-Gruppenführer Arthur Greiser,

---

* On entering the Soviet Union, German troops found the
mass graves of some 10,000 Polish Officers at Katyn, near
Smolensk; they had been murdered by the Russians in 1940.

Reichsstatthalter of Warthegau. In autumn 1941 he asked Himmler and Heydrich for an assignment of trained executioners to enable Wartheland to be "cleared of Jews" as soon as possible. 100,000 Jews still remained in his area, he said, almost all in the Lodz ghetto, and they should be liquidated quickly.[132]

Himmler and Heydrich agreed at once and despatched Hauptsturmführer Lange. Heydrich allotted him the most ghastly invention at his disposal—the gas vans already used in Russia. By the end of the year Lange had set up near Lodz the first murder factory in human history. In the woods of Kulmhof (Chelmno), 40 miles northwest of Lodz, he found an old, isolated mansion, ideally suited for his bestial task. In December 1941 Commander Lange set to work with three gas vans.[133]

In a steady stream the Jews were brought from Lodz to Kulmhof Station and carted off to the mansion; there they were made to strip and climb into a closed van, supposedly to go to the showers. But their journey was to death, not to a bath hut. As soon as the doors of the van were closed behind them, the exhaust gases were diverted into the van by a concealed pipe, killing the inmates. Meanwhile a special detachment of selected Jews stood ready to heave the dead into the waiting mass grave and to remove their last valuables. Such service earned many Jews the privilege of existing for a few weeks longer in the cellars of the mansion, waiting for the next convoy of unfortunates.[134] The system was a primitive one, however, and the liquidators often had trouble with it; the gassing did not always work. The RSHA service instructions said that all should be over in 15 minutes, but often it lasted for hours. Sometimes a few of the victims were still alive when the doors of the death van were re-opened.[135]

Reports of the mass horrors in Kulmhof must have reached Müller in Gestapo Headquarters, for one day he summoned SS-Sturmbannführer Adolf Eichmann, his Jewish expert, and said to him: "Go down there. I'd like to know what goes on." Eichmann arrived at Lange's mansion and saw the Jews being driven into the death vans and carted off to the mass grave. Later he told his story: "I followed the van and then came the most horrifying sight I've ever seen in my life. The van drew up alongside a long pit, the doors were opened and the bodies thrown out; the limbs were still supple, as if they were still alive. They were thrown into the pit. I saw a civilian pulling out teeth with a pair of pliers and then I took off. I rushed to my car and departed and said no more. I was through. I had had it. A white-coated doctor said I ought to look through the peephole and see what went on inside the vans. I refused. I couldn't. I couldn't speak. I had to get away. Frightful, I tell you. An inferno. Can't do it. I can't do it. That's what I told him [Müller]."[136]

The horrors of Kulmhof heralded a macabre competition between the technicians of murder and the gas specialists. The success of Lange's installation was the signal for the opening of a new chapter in the Final Solution, a new chapter of racial frenzy—the mass annihilation of Polish Jewry, the largest group of Jewish people whom the second World War had brought under the shadow of the swastika.

A 1931 Polish census had shown a total of 3,000,000 Jews, of whom 2,300,000 were in the German-occupied areas.[137] During the first months of the Nazi occupation, almost all had been forced into ghettos designated by Heydrich and initially intended as collecting points for the planned Jewish emigration; since the initiation of the Final Solution, however, they had turned into the anterooms of death. "We must annihilate the Jews wherever we find them," Hans Frank, Poland's Governor-General, shouted at his staff. "We cannot shoot these Jews, we cannot poison them, but we can undertake operations which will somehow lead to successful annihilation in connection with . . . major measures."[138]

The "major measures" had already been thought out by Heinrich Himmler. He intended to solve the problem after his own fashion and the Kulmhof experiments had shown him the way: on the territory of what had once been Poland, both in the Government-General and in the so-called incorporated territories, a chain of death factories was to be set up, designed to eliminate every Jew in Poland and, indeed, in Europe. Chance had made available to him the necessary highly specialised executioners; even before Greiser had asked for assistance in the liquidation of "his" Jews, another murder operation had

just ended; it was known as "Euthanasia" and had succeeded in killing 100,000 men who were either mentally
handicapped or, in the Nazi phrase, "unfit to live."[139]

The Reichsführer-SS and Chief of the German Police
had loaned to operation "Euthanasia" a number of SS
commanders and Criminal Police Officials, and they had
proved to be experts in killing their victims with gas.
Their leader was a self-opinionated ogre, Kriminal-
oberkommissar [Criminal Police Inspector] Christian
Wirth; in the Führer's Chancellery, the headquarters of the
euthanasia plan, he was regarded as head executioner.[140]
In the death factories of the Euthanasia project Wirth
had been working with carbon monoxide gas which
killed quickly and silently. When, early in 1942, Himmler
asked Dr Ernst Grawitz, the SS Medical Officer-in-Chief,
how one could most quickly liquidate one million Polish
Jews, the Doctor referred him to Wirth, who was then
out of a job.[141] Himmler summoned the gas expert and
ordered him to continue his work in Poland. Shortly
thereafter Wirth reported to Odilo Globocnik, the SSPF
Lublin, whom Himmler had commissioned to liquidate
the Jews ("Operation Reinhard").[142] Wirth set to work.

. Wirth, the specialist, regarded Lange as a mere bungling
amateur. Instead of the Kulmhof-type mobile gas chambers he constructed static chambers into which he piped
exhaust gases from diesel engines. The death chambers
masqueraded as "inhalation and bath rooms." An observer noted that the system of death chambers looked
somewhat like "a sort of bath house" with "geraniums,
then a little stairway and then, on each side, three rooms
16 ft $\times$ 16 ft $\times$ 6 ft with wooden doors like a garage.
The rear wall was formed by large wooden folding doors.
As a 'thoughtful little witticism' a Star of David was
painted on the roof."[143] Around these murder installations Wirth constructed the normal trappings of National-
Socialist concentration camps—huts, parade grounds,
barbed wire and more barbed wire. A chain of these
extermination camps soon extended along the river Bug,
all, with the exception of the Lublin camp, under SS-
Brigadeführer Globocnik. One after another the death factories sprang up. The first of Wirth's installations opened
on 17 March 1942—Belzec Camp on the Lublin-Lwow
railway; it was equipped with six gas chambers and could

deal with 15,000 men a day.[144] It was followed in April
by Sobibor Camp, near the frontier of the Ukraine Reich
Commissariat; its maximum output was 20,000 persons
a day.[145] Three months later Treblinka appeared, 75 miles
north-east of Warsaw; this was Wirth's largest camp,
equipped with 30 gas chambers and capable of dealing
with 25,000 men a day.[146] Finally in autumn 1942 a set
of gas chambers was added to the existing Lublin Concentration Camp, known after the war as Maidanek.[147]
Wirth was now in technical control of all SS extermination installations on Polish territory.[148] He was continually
raising the death figures, testimony to a ghastly efficiency
which earned him the title of uncrowned king of Poland's
Jew liquidators.

Meanwhile in the eerie extermination-camp world competitors appeared with their eyes on Wirth's position. Competition came primarily from Auschwitz in Upper Silesia,
the largest concentration camp in the German-occupied
East and also designated as an extermination factory;
there the staff was determined to discover new methods
to topple the gas expert, Wirth, from his lonely pedestal.
The Commander of the Auschwitz protective custody
camp put his Treblinka rival in the shade by discover-
ing a new killing agent, entirely compatible with the
theory that murdering Jews was equivalent to pest control; this was the prussic acid gas, Zyklon B, sold on the
market as an anti-vermin substance by Degesch [Deutsche
Gesellschaft für Schädlingsbekämpfung GmbH —German
Pest Control Company Limited].[149] Zyklon B was better
than Wirth's gas in that the operator, provided he was
protected by a gas mask, had only to open the tin and
scatter the contents—and in a few minutes the victims
were dead. Wirth's process took much longer.[160]

A number of SS leaders got together to topple Wirth
from his throne. In August 1942 SS-Obersturmführer Kurt
Gerstein, who was in the prussic acid trade, together
with Rolf Günther, Eichmann's No. 2, appeared in Belzec Camp to put Wirth's methods to the test. Gerstein
later wrote up his experiences:[151]

"The train arrives; 200 Ukrainians fling open the doors
and hunt the people out of the trucks with ox-hide whips.
Instructions come through the loudspeaker: strip com-

pletely, including artificial limbs, spectacles, etc. Then the
women and girls go off to the barber, who, with two or
three strokes of his shears, cuts off all their hair and
stuffs it into a potato sack. Then the procession starts,
an extremely pretty girl in the lead. So they move down
the alleyway, all naked, men, women and children, artificial limbs gone . . . They mount the steps, hesitate,
and enter the death chambers. The majority say not a
word. One Jewess, aged about 40, eyes blazing, calls down
upon the murderers the blood which is being shed here.
She gets five or six strokes of the whip across the face
and disappears into the chamber like the rest. The chambers fill up, packed tight—that's Wirth's order. People are
treading on each other's toes . . . at last I understand
why the whole set-up is known as the Heckenholt system.
Heckenholt is a little technician who drives the diesel
motor and also constructed the installations. The victims
are to be killed by the diesel's exhaust gases."

The start of the motor, however, was Wirth's most
humiliating moment; the engine refused to fire. Gerstein
took out a stop watch and measured the extent of Wirth's
defeat in seconds, in minutes, in hours. "Wirth arrives.
He is clearly extremely embarrassed that this should happen just on the day when I'm here. Yes, indeed! I can
see the whole thing! And I wait. My stop-watch ticks
faithfully on—50 minutes 70 seconds and still the diesel
won't start! The men in the gas chambers are waiting.
In vain! One can hear them sobbing and weeping . . .
Wirth strikes Heckenholt's Ukrainian assistant 12 or 13
times across the face with his riding crop. After 2 hours
and 49 minutes—measured exactly on the stop watch—
the diesel starts . . . a further 25 minutes pass. Correct
—many are dead. One can look through the peephole
when the electric light in the gas chambers is on for a
moment. A few are still alive after 28 minutes. Finally
after 32 minutes they're all dead. Men of the labour
detachment open the wooden doors from the other side.
Jammed in the chambers, the dead are still standing there
like marble pillars. There's no room for them to fall or
even bend over."[152]
The Zyklon B enthusiasts such as Günther had seen
enough and Wirth had lost his leading position as a tech-

nician of murder. From this moment a state of war existed between Auschwitz and Wirth's camps. The pest control method was eventually introduced into Auschwitz and no one was happier than Rudolf Höss, the Commandant. In his autobiography he says: "I must admit that the gassing process had a calming effect upon me. I always had a horror of the shootings, thinking of the number of people, the women and children. I was relieved that we were all to be spared these blood-baths."[153]

High-pressure extermination of Polish Jewry could now begin. Himmler gave the green light. The Ordnungspolizei, foreign auxiliaries and the German-organised Jewish Law and Order Service drove the Jews from the ghettos to the six extermination camps. On 19 July 1942 Himmler wrote to Obergruppenführer Krüger, HSSPF East in Cracow: "I command that the re-settlement of the entire Jewish population of the Government-General shall have been carried out and completed by 31 December 1942."[154] The miserable processions of victims were already on the way to the murder factories and one ghetto after another was already being emptied when, once again, an outside authority threatened to bring the mills of death to a halt. For the second time in the short history of German occupation of Poland, the Wehrmacht rose in wrath against the lunacy of the Final Solution.

Unlike their comrades in Russia, many of whom had been unnerved by the partisan war, the German army in Poland set out to protect the Jews, come what might. They deployed an argument calculated to impress even the racial fanatics—the closing phase of the Final Solution would deprive the Wehrmacht of the Jewish labour essential to keep the armaments industry in the East functioning. The objection had already been foreseen by Heydrich. On 4 October 1941 he had stated that there was a risk "that primarily on economic grounds many a claim will be made, that the Jews are an indispensable labour force and that no one will make any effort to obtain alternative labour to take the place of the Jews."[155] General Curt Freiherr von Gienanth, C-in-C of the Polish Wehrkreis, and Colonel Freter, the Head of the Warsaw Armaments Commission, were determined to do exactly what Heydrich had anticipated.

They were under no illusion that the so-called "re-settlement" of the Jews was, the fact, cover for a murder campaign; Globocnik, after all, had said: "This entire matter is one of the most secret things with which we have to deal at the present time."[156] In July Captain Friedrich Wilhelm Hassler asked Colonel Freter whether it was true that the Jews were to be liquidated. Freter said nothing, but Hassler persisted: "What is happening here is legally a crime and from a Christian point of view, a sin. One day there will be a reckoning." Freter pointed out to him that he had three alternatives: he could express his opinion openly but must then reckon that his life would be forfeit; he could report sick; or he could stay with him, Freter, and help the Armaments Commission to do what it could for the Jews. Captain Hassler stayed.[157]

Krüger, the HSSPF, realising what the military were up to, got a jump ahead of them. He agreed with the OKW Armaments Inspectorate that they might temporarily retain their Jewish labour force but that the Jews employed in factories or camps must be quartered in barracks under SS command.[158] This, Krüger hoped, would gradually deprive the military of any authority over the Jews. Even these modest concessions, however, were too much for Himmler, who was continually urging Krüger not to give an inch to the Wehrmacht. He also brought pressure to bear against the military in another quarter, urging OKW to order the soldiers in the Government-General to pipe down.[159]

As so often happened in the case of political disagreements, Field Marshal Keitel of OKW let his officers down. While the Armaments Commission in the Government-General was struggling tenaciously for every Jew, on 5 September 1942 Keitel issued an order that all Jewish labour was forthwith to be replaced by Poles.[160] Von Gienanth angrily turned against the yes-man in the Führer's Headquarters. On 18 September he dispatched a memorandum to the OKW Operations Staff setting out his view, supported by statistics, that "immediate removal of the Jews would lead to a considerable reduction of Germany's war effort; supplies to the front and to the troops in the Government-General would be held up—at least for the time being."[161]

Gienanth continued: "It is requested that Jews working in industry be exempted from evacuation till then [completion of certain important production tasks]."[162]

For better or for worse Keitel was forced to show Gienanth's memorandum to Himmler. His reaction was one of fury against the military saboteurs of his new annihilation programme. On 2 October he thundered: "I have ordered that ruthless steps be taken against all those who think that they can use the interests of war industry to cloak their real intention to protect the Jews and their own business affairs."[163] The intimidated Keitel hardly waited for Himmler's reaction but, via his staff, cracked down on the rebels in Poland. General von Gienanth was relieved at once.[164] On 10 October a teleprinter message from the OKW operations staff reiterated the decision: "OKW is in entire agreement with the principle laid down by the Reichsführer-SS that all Jews employed by the armed forces in auxiliary military services and in the war industries are to be replaced immediately by Aryan workers."[165]

So the Wehrmacht had capitulated. Between 13 and 15 October 1942 the Communications Zone commander in the Government-General was ordered to dismiss his Jewish labour. As a result, in the words of the historian Hanns von Krannhals, "All Jews in the Government-General were delivered into the hands of the SS."[166] The murderers could now go on their way unhindered. Hour by hour, day by day, week by week, the SS and their local auxiliaries drove Jews into the gas chambers, beating, tormenting, insulting and torturing.

The death factories in the East ground remorselessly on, every hour and every victim adding to the list of German crime. Even today the figures from the murder factories stagger the imagination; in Kulmhof 152,000 Jews died, in Belzec 600,000, in Sobibor 250,000, in Treblinka 700,000, in Maidanek 200,000 and in Auschwitz over 1,000,000.[167] Hundreds of thousands of Jews were overwhelmed by a murderous wave of unbridled sadism. Gomerski, the Sobibor executioner, used an iron water pot to batter in the skulls of Jews who had fallen sick during the journey;[168] children's heads were smashed against barrack walls; these savages in SS uniform were capable of every form of infamy in their "extramural activities."[169]

A prisoner named Max Kasner was a disposer of bodies in Auschwitz. One day he was ordered to the courtyard of one of the blocks: "On the left were lying some 70 dead women, real goodlookers too—even in death. All their breasts were cut off and from all the fleshy parts, such as the thigh all the meat was removed with great, deep incisions. The courtyard sloped steeply and the drain became blocked with blood; we were wading in blood way above our ankles."[170] Every day came reports of guards firing on children. Professor Ludwik Hirszfeld of Warsaw saw "a little girl trying to slip past the guard. The sentry called, slowly he took his rifle from his shoulder. The child was clasping his boots and begging for mercy. The sentry laughed and said: 'You needn't die but you won't do any more smuggling'. Then he shot the child through the feet. Both had to be amputated later."[171]

In the evenings Oberscharführer Oswald Kaduk, the Auschwitz Rapportführer [NCO in charge], would hunt a number of prisoners into the bath house and there make them jump, stark naked, over a walking stick which he held about 2 ft 6 in high. Anyone who stumbled was directed to the left and then taken off to be gassed. If too many prisoners managed to do the jump, Kaduk would beat them till they fell.[172] Lederer, one of the prisoners, described "another of Kaduk's specialities": at the so-called louse inspections, any prisoner on whom a louse was found was made to lie on the floor and a pole, used for carrying the food containers, was placed across his throat; Kaduk would then place a foot on either end and rock from side to side until the prisoner was dead."[173]

Kurt Franz, Commandant of Treblinka, regularly set Bari, his savage Saint Bernard, on to prisoners. Jews were hung head downwards from a gallows and mangled by the dog. Franz maintained an execution spot camouflaged as a hospital; attached to it was a grave 25 ft $\times$ 10 ft in which a fire was kept burning continuously. Every day Franz would hold three roll calls and on each occasion select ten Jews to be liquidated by him personally. Jakubowicz, one of the prisoners, reported that he "drove them into the hospital with a whip and shot them there. It was an automatic procedure—shoot and into the grave—shoot and into the grave."[174]

Oberscharführer Wilhelm Boger of the Auschwitz Political Section invented the most notorious torture known to Europe's largest extermination camp; after the war Oberscharführer Perry Broad described it as follows: "Two tables were placed side by side about a yard apart. The victim was made to sit on the floor, draw up his knees and place his hands in front of them. His wrists were then tied together. A large pole was then slipped between his elbows and knees and its ends placed upon the tables. He was now hanging helpless between the tables, head downwards. He was then beaten upon the buttocks and the soles of his bare feet. The blows were so violent that the victims almost described a full circle. Whenever the buttocks were in the right position another blow would descend with all Boger's force. If the screams became too ear-splitting, the sadist would put a gas-mask on him . . . after about 15 minutes, the victim's convulsions would cease. He could not speak. His trousers were dark red and blood was dripping on the floor. Finally his head hung down motionless; he had fainted. But this did not shake Boger at all. With a knowing grin he would take a flask of smelling salts from his pocket and hold it to the prisoner's nose. After a few minutes, the man would regain consciousness."[175]

As a result of such bestialities, the post-war world has been misled into the belief that sadism was at the root of the mass-extermination phenomenon. The executioners are depicted as dehumanised beings, a horde of monsters whose only pleasure was destruction and murder. This is too simple a picture. Dr Ella Lingens-Reiner, who was a prisoner in Auschwitz, testified: "I know hardly a single SS man who could not say that he had saved someone's life. There were few sadists. No more than five or ten per cent were criminals by nature. The others were perfectly normal men, fully alive to good and evil. They all knew what was going on."[176]

The shattering revelations, during the West German War Crimes trials, of the torments imposed upon their victims by the mass exterminators threatened to obscure a truth propounded as early as 1944 by Hannah Arendt, the German-American sociologist; she submitted that the mass extermination organisation was manned "neither by fanatics nor by natural murderers nor by sadists. It was manned solely and exclusively by normal human beings of the type of Heinrich Himmler."[177] The fact that brutes and sadists made use of the extermination machine does not mean that they were typical of it. The most diverse characters have always been attracted by crimes of this nature—witness the guillotine during the French Revolution and the fanatical purges of the Soviet OGPU.

The sensational fact, the really horrifying feature, of the annihilation of the Jews was that thousands of respectable fathers of families made murder their official business and yet, when off duty, still regarded themselves as ordinary law-abiding citizens who were incapable even of thinking of straying from the strict path of virtue. Sadism was only one facet of mass extermination and one disapproved of by SS Headquarters. Himmler's maxim was that mass extermination must be carried out coolly and cleanly; even while obeying the official order to commit murder, the SS man must remain "decent."

Briefing Sturmbannführer Franke-Gricksch, Himmler said: "The SS Commander must be hard but he must not become hardened. If, during your work, you come across cases in which some Commander exceeds his duty or shows signs that his sense of restraint is becoming blurred, intervene at once. Anyone who finds it necessary to dull his senses, or forgets himself in face of the enemy who is handed over to him, shows that he is no true SS Commander."[178] Himmler even issued definite instructions forbidding his minions to torment their victims; an order of August 1935 laid down: "Any independent, individual action against the Jews by any member of the SS is most strictly forbidden";[179] the concentration-camp guards had to sign a declaration every three months, acknowledging their duty to refrain from maltreating prisoners.[180]

In autumn 1942 the Hauptamt SS-Gericht [SS Legal Department] posed the hypothetical question of how unauthorised shootings of Jews should be dealt with. Himmler's answer was: "If the motive is purely political there should be no punishment unless such is necessary for the maintenance of discipline. If the motive is selfish, sadistic or sexual, judicial punishment should be imposed for murder or manslaughter as the case may be."[181]

On occasions he actually had SS sadists punished. In June 1943 an SS Untersturmführer was condemned to death for bestial ill-treatment of innumerable Jews. On 9

June 1943 the Supreme SS and Police Court pronounced judgment: "He succumbed to the temptation to commit atrocities unworthy of a German or an SS Commander. These excesses cannot be justified by saying, as does the accused, that they are a just recompense for the damage done by the Jews to the German people. Necessary though the annihilation of our people's worst enemy may be, it is not in the German manner to use Bolshevist methods to do so. And the methods adopted by the accused border upon those of Bolshevism.[182]

When sadism was combined with corruption, then Himmler let the hounds of justice loose, for he regarded both as crimes against the SS—sadism undermined its discipline and corruption destroyed its ideology. The temporary clean-up which Konrad Morgen, the SS Judge, was allowed to conduct among the SS liquidators was a good illustration of Himmler's Jekyll-and-Hyde character; the Reichsführer's dual personality was suddenly exposed—the lower-middle-class citizen with his strict moral upbringing clashed with the automaton, the fanatical agent of the Führer's commands. It was an absurd spectacle; one or two "unauthorised" murders of Jews were investigated—by a whole squad of SS legal experts—inside the extermination camps where thousands were being murdered daily!

Dr Konrad Morgen was the son of a railwayman, born in 1910 in Frankfurt-am-Main. His professional legal career had ended when he refused to accept a judgment by his provincial magistrate, but he had then been appointed to the SS/Police court in Cracow as Assistant Judge to deal primarily with cases of corruption. After quarrelling with Krüger, the HSSPF, he had been posted to the SS "Viking" Division as a punishment. In 1943 he was transferred to the RKPA but forbidden to deal with political cases.[183] There he stumbled across a case of widespread corruption in the concentration camps.

One day the RKPA group "Financial Crimes Office," to which Morgen belonged, received a call for assistance from Kassel, where SS Police Court XXII was located. The Court, which was responsible for Buchenwald concentration camp, wished to clear up an old corruption case with ramifications extending into the camp itself.[184] Emil Holtschmidt, a young Criminal Police Officer, had been keeping a watch on Bornschein, the local Nazi Group leader in Weimar; he was a provisions merchant who had run various profitable rackets in partnership with Karl Koch, the Commandant of Buchenwald. When Holt-schmidt became over-inquisitive, Bornschein joined the Waffen-SS and got himself posted to the headquarters staff of Buchenwald.[185] The SS/Police Court took up the case but could do nothing, since such Courts had juris-diction over the Waffen-SS (to which the concentration-camp guard units theoretically belonged) only in the ca-pacity of a sort of court martial; within the camp itself, however, so-called legal officers were in charge and they were responsible not to the Hauptamt SS-Gericht but to the highest legal authority concerned with the concentration camps, Obergruppenführer Oswald Pohl, Head of the SS Wirtschaftsverwaltungshauptamt [Economic and Admin-istrative Department—WVHA].[186]

The SS/Police Court Kassel now brought the RKPA into the game. It asked for Criminal Police assistance against the Koch gang, specifying as a condition, however, that the selected RKPA official must carry officer rank in the Waffen-SS—no one else would have the smallest pros-pect of penetrating into Buchenwald concentration camp.[187] Morgen, being an Obersturmführer in the Waffen-SS, was allotted the job and went to Weimar where he installed himself in the Elephant Hotel and initiated un-obtrusive investigations. He soon succeeded in convicting Bornschein.[188] Then, however, he found himself uncovering the murkiest secrets of Buchenwald Camp. Though not officially authorised to do so, he checked Koch's ac-counts in Weimar banks and intercepted letters between Koch (who had meanwhile been appointed Commandant of the Lublin extermination camp) and his wife Ilse, who had remained in Buchenwald.[189] The deeper he delved, the more clearly he perceived that a network of corruption existed with ramifications extending into the other con-centration camps.

From corruption the case developed into one of multi-ple murder, for Morgen discovered that Koch had not only been blackmailing rich Jews who had landed in his concentration camp after the 1938 Kristallnacht, but had also been causing awkward witnesses among the pris-oners to disappear. Morgen determined to bring to justice

the entire blackmail and murder gang centred around
Koch. When, however, he submitted the results of his researches to Nebe, his Kripo master was appalled by the
over-enthusiasm of his sleuth. Nebe foresaw frightful consequences from Morgen's campaign and was unwilling to
take responsibility. Morgen, however, hot on the trail of
his prey, chased from one SS leader to another. He explained the case in detail to Gestapo Müller, who sent him
to the Head of the RSHA. The latter passed him on to
the Head of the Haumptamt SS-Gericht who could think
of only one solution—Himmler.[190]

Morgen proceeded to the Reichsführer's Field Headquarters but could not get in touch with Himmler. With
one of Himmler's personal staff, to whom he told the
whole story, he drafted an innocently worded telegram;
provided it was delivered, Himmler's agreement seemed
certain. The telegram was delivered.[191] No one can say
what caused Himmler to give the go-ahead for action
against the Koch gang. Perhaps it was his permanent
mistrust of Obergruppenführer Pohl and his corrupt hang-
ers-on, or he may have underestimated the chain reaction
which the Koch case was bound to produce. The fact remains that, for a short instant, Himmler (in his lower-
middle-class role) could congratulate himself on putting
his house in order.

Morgen seized his chance. He ordered Koch to Buchenwald and subjected him to so severe an interrogation that
the ex-king of the camp finally broke down and confessed
everything. The case for the prosecution became longer
and longer; it included murder of two prisoners, Krämer
and Peix, embezzlement and actions detrimental to the
war effort.[192] Morgen also got his hooks on Koch's accomplices—Sommer a sadist in charge of one of the barrack blocks, Dr Waldemar Hoven, the camp doctor,
Hauptscharführer Blanck and last, but not least, the
"Queen of the Camp," Ilse Koch. The indictment included murder, manslaughter, and assault with intent to
murder.[193]

But Morgen and his assistants were not prepared to be
satisfied merely with the elimination of the Koch gang.
On his initiative the Kassel SS/Police Court had been
turned into a "special" court with the right to investigate
all crimes in concentration camps.[194] Morgen had discov-

ered new clues and they led eastwards, straight into the top-secret extermination camps. He unearthed what he was not supposed to unearth, the million-fold murders of Jews in the death factories of the East. In Lublin and in Auschwitz he suddenly stumbled across the gas chambers and realised that he had been hunting one or two cases of murder in places where millions were being slaughtered.[195] But how did he react to his discovery? The answer he gives to-day shows that he also suffered from his Reichsführer's schizophrenia. There were at the time, he would have us believe, three types of murder: the officially decreed murders of Jews "against which nothing could be done because the orders issued from the Führer's Chancellery within the framework of the 'Final Solution' and were given by Hitler himself"; the Euthanasia killings, which were equally official; finally "arbitrary killings" of prisoners.[196] Only against the third category of murders did he set the SS judicial machine in motion.

In practically every concentration camp Morgen and the RKPA installed Commissions of Inquiry to investigate cases of corruption and "arbitrary killings."[197] Pohl's minions, however, put up fierce resistance to the entry of the investigators; looking for sadists in a concentration camp was a dangerous business, for the camp staff reacted savagely, sometimes even with murder. One of the Oranienburg prisoners named Rothe, who was an RKPA informer, was only saved in the nick of time[198] from a public execution arranged by the camp staff as a warning to other prisoners not to collaborate with Morgen.[199] In another camp a hut containing RKPA files was burnt down and in Auschwitz Hauptscharführer Gerhard Palitsch, whom Morgen had dispatched to investigate the doings of Höss, the Camp Commandant, vanished into a punishment cell.[200]

Nevertheless Morgen registered numerous successes. 800 cases of corruption and murder were dealt with and 200 resulted in sentences.[201] Well-known names from the sinister concentration-camp aristocracy figured on Morgen's list: Karl Koch, Commandant of Buchenwald and Lublin—two death sentences for murder—executed;[202] Hermann Florstedt, Commandant of Lublin—condemned to death for murder and executed;[203] Hermann Hackmann, in charge of protective custody in Lublin—condemned to death for murder but eventually posted to a penal unit;[204] Hans Loritz, Commandant of Oranienburg —proceedings initiated on suspicion of arbitrary killings;[205] Adam Grünewald, Commandant of Hertogenbosch —sentenced for maltreatment of prisoners and posted to a penal unit;[206] Karl Künstler, Commandment of Flossenburg —dismissed for drunkenness and debauchery;[207] Alex Piorkowski, Commandant of Dachau—accused of murder but not sentenced;[208] Maximilian Grabner, Head of the Political Section in Auschwitz—accused of murder but not sentenced.[209]

The deeper the men of the RKPA delved into the secrets of the concentration-camp world, however, the more uneasy did Himmler become. As early as mid-April 1944 he ordered Morgen to confine himself to the Koch case; all other investigations were to be stopped.[210] The order illustrated the conflict of principle between Himmler the mass liquidator and Himmler the apostle of rectitude. He ordered that Pohl should personally supervise Koch's execution; the other miscreants, however, must report their crimes voluntarily; anyone who came forward of his own free will could be sure of clemency.[211] Himmler withdrew into his world of illusion. At a meeting of SS-Gruppenführer as early as 1943 he had said: "All in all we can say that we have completed this painful task (the annihilation of the Jews) out of love for our people. In our own selves, in our souls and in our character we have suffered no damage therefrom."[212]

It was no accident that Himmler closed down Morgen's campaign just at the moment when investigations were starting against Höss, the Commandant of Auschwitz. Rudolf Höss was an outstanding exponent of the hygienic mass-murder system, the clinically clean automatic process; he was the ideal SS man, for whose "purity" Himmler had been so concerned when he authorised this short period of housecleaning. The system and the rhythm of mass extermination were dictated not by the sadists such as Boger or Kaduk but by men like Rudolf Höss—worthy family men brought up in the belief that anti-Semitism was a form of pest control, harnessed into an impersonal mechanical system working with the precision of militarised industry and relieving the individual of any sense of personal responsibility.

Martin Broszat, the historian, describes mass extermination as "the work of ambitious, straight-laced philistines, men obsessed with a sense of duty, faithful servants of the powers that be; they had been brought up in a spirit of soulless conformity; they were incapable of criticism and devoid of imagination; so in all good faith and with a clear conscience, they persuaded themselves, and allowed themselves to be persuaded, that the 'liquidation' of men in hundreds of thousands was a service to their people and their country.[213] The machine of extermination was served by modern production-line employees whom Hannah Arendt, for want of a more precise sociological expression, calls "John Citizen."[214] They were sinister illustrations of the gulf which existed between public and private morality; refusal to admit of any connection between their official duties and their private existence, together with an ineradicable self-righteousness, prevented them regarding themselves as murderers.

On the contrary—from their grotesquely exaggerated sense of righteousness in the fulfilment of their civic duty sprang the notion that basically in the midst of all this murder they were men of compassion who had every sympathy with those who must die, with the "existing and the perishing"—Höss's hypocritical description of mass murder.[215] "Nothing is more difficult," Höss said, "than to have to make one's way through this business cold, unsympathetic and without pity."[216]

Like the men of the Einsatzgruppen, the death-camp technicians entrenched themselves behind a spurious self-pity which enabled them seriously to believe that in fact they were tragic figures. Höss, for instance, says: "There was no escape for me. I had to carry on the process of extermination, of mass murder, to live with it, to be an unemotional spectator of something at which my whole soul revolted."[217] In emotional terms he continued that, if some particular incident had moved him, "I could not go home to my family. I would get on a horse and let the fresh air blow away the picture of frightfulness; alternatively at night time I often went through the stable and found peace among my beloved animals."[218]

No sooner, however, had a dent been made in their armour of philistine self-righteousness, than these men relapsed into whimpering sentimentality and, as a rule, took refuge in alcohol. In his cups even so barbaric a Jew exterminator as Globocnik admitted to a friend: "My heart's no longer in it but I am so deeply involved in these things that I have no alternative but to ride to victory with Hitler or go under.[219] At the graveside of his children, who had died of diphtheria, Hermann Höfle, Globocnik's minion who had been responsible for the deportation of more than 200,000 Jews, sobbed: "This is Heaven's punishment for all my misdeeds."[220]

Through all these burgeoning doubts, however, one sheet-anchor remained to them—they had received an order. Höss says: "I had no second thoughts at the time; I had received an order and had to carry it out. When the Führer himself had ordered the 'final solution' of the Jewish question, a long-standing National-Socialist could have no second thoughts, still less an SS officer. 'Führer, befiehl, wir folgen' [Führer, command—we follow thee] was for us no empty phrase, no mere slogan. We took it with deadly seriousness."[221] The official order was their idol, their justification and their final refuge. When Gilbert, the American psychologist, later asked Höss if he had ever considered whether the Jews whom he murdered had deserved their fate "he tried patiently to explain that there was something unrealistic about such a question because he had been living in an entirely different world. 'Don't you see, we SS men were not supposed to think about these things; it never even occurred to us'."[222]

When, however, the order was no longer unequivocal, when it contradicted, indeed condemned, what had hitherto been an article of faith, what was to happen then? The mass murderers were then abandoned, lost in a maze from which there was no exit. Exactly this occurred during the final stage of the extermination programme; before Polish Jewry had been completely annihilated an SS authority appeared bent on reducing the tempo of extermination and preserving the Jews as slave labour for Greater Germany's war effort.

This was the headquarters of the SS economic enterprises, the WVHA, under Oswald Pohl, a newcomer to the world of concentration and extermination camps. Originally the camps had been under the authority of Theodor Eicke, the Inspector of Concentration Camps, who on paper came under the SS-Hauptamt; when Eicke

transferred to the Waffen-SS, his successor Richard Glücks
was placed under the SS-Führungshauptamt [Waffen-SS
Headquarters].[223] In 1942 Himmler re-organised the concentration-camp command system yet again; Glücks and
his staff were transferred to Pohl's WVHA, where the Inspector of Concentration Camps became Head of Amtsgruppe [Division] D.[224]

This transfer into the realm of the managerial and production enthusiasts gave the concentration-camp system a
new twist. Hitherto the camps had aimed solely at the
punishment and extermination of so-called enemies of thc
State and the race; the theorists of the WVHA, however,
could see no purpose in them other than to provide
armies of slaves for the SS business empire. On 30 April
1942 Pohl wrote to Himmler that the increased armaments requirements necessitated "mobilisation of all prisoner labour" and required "measures involving gradual
transformation of the concentration camps from their
previous purely political form into an organisation capable
of meeting our economic requirements."[225]

Hitherto prisoners had been treated with unrelenting
brutality, the object being to get rid of them; now preservation and maintenance became the order of the day.
Glücks ordered prisoners to be sent out to work and "in
this connection it is axiomatic that it is forbidden to
strike, kick or even touch a prisoner."[226] Himmler added
that the prisoners' work output must be raised "by reasonable (if necessary, improved) food and clothing; prisoners must be encouraged to take interest in thc cconomic
enterprise concerned; co-operative prisoners should be
held up as an example to the listless majority."[227] The
German Excavation and Quarrying Co. Ltd, a WVHA
concern producing building materials, instituted courses
to train skilled prisoner labour. To attract prisoners who
showed interest, promises of lucrative employment were
made, including prospects of special accommodation or
even release from the camp and continued employment
as civilian workers.[228] Some of the SS concerns seriously
planned to house considerable numbers of released prisoners in housing estates near their firms.[229]

Simultaneously, however, the WVHA increased the severity of the prisoners' working conditions; Pohl's slaves
had to work an average of 11 hours a day, undernourished

and frequently wretchedly clothed. The WVHA's army of involuntary workers appeared in all sectors of SS and private industry. Of the 600,000 prisoners in WVHA camps in December 1944, 250,000 were working in privately owned armament firms, 170,000 in firms directly under the Ministry of Armaments and Munitions, 15,000 in building firms, 12,000 for firms constructing a new Führer Headquarters in Thuringia, 50,000 for firms under Amtsgruppe C of the WVHA and 130,000 in agriculture and the distributive trades.[230]

Earlier than he had foreseen, Himmler found himself faced with the ideological and practical consequences of this change of policy, and they threatened his Final Solution programme. The WVHA pragmatists cast greedy eyes on the mass of Jewish death candidates. German Armaments Works Ltd, the controlling organisation for all wood- and metal-working concerns within the concentration camps, was already putting out its feelers for Polish Jewry's surviving labour force.[231]

By the end of 1942 three-quarters of Polish Jewry had been murdered, leaving 700,000 alive.[232] These men were languishing in the innumerable labour camps maintained by the SSPF in the Government-General and at regular intervals they furnished their quota to the death factories. The WVHA business tycoons, however, soon brought the Polish camps under their control. In March 1943 Pohl's experts formed Eastern Industries Ltd to exploit Jewish labour and take over such businesses as still survived within the ghettos. A number of ex-Jewish concerns came under its control—the peat-cutting industry in Dorohueza, the brush factory in Lublin, the armaments works in Radom-Blizyn and the tannery in Trawniki.[233]

The Final Solution fanatics, however, found this desire for Jewish labour highly disturbing, for it threatened to jeopardise their work of extermination. SSPF Warsaw summarised their feelings: on seeing a WVHA man arrive he explained: "Eastern Industries! I only have to hear the word 'industry' to be nauseated."[234] The technicians of murder in fact bore their WVHA colleagues so much ill-will that they dealt Eastern Industries a mortal blow. Hardly had the concern got going than they deprived it of all its Jewish labour. On 3 November 1943 "Eastern Industries" Jews were summoned to the gas chambers.[235]

Obersturmführer Dr Max Horn, Deputy Director of Eastern Industries, lamented: "As a result of the withdrawal
of Jewish labour all our work of organisation and expansion has become totally valueless."[236]

The Eastern Industries case was the start of a quarrel
between the WVHA and the RSHA which was to last
until the end of the Third Reich, the RSHA trying to
liquidate as many Jews as possible and the WVHA to
retain all those fit for work. Höss commented: "In the
view of the RSHA every new labour camp and every
additional thousand workers increased the risk that one
day they might be set free or somehow contrive to remain alive." Nevertheless Pohl was in the stronger position,
for Himmler supported him with increasingly urgent demands for prisoners for the armament industry.[237] The
more violent this quarrel, the more perplexed the men in
control of the gas chambers became. Hardest hit by the
battle was Adolf Eichmann, the RSHA's senior liquidator; to add to his troubles, resistance from the European
States was growing stronger and an increasing number of
SS leaders were suffering twinges of conscience.

Initially it looked as if a series of surprise actions would
enable Eichmann and his minions to sweep up the Jews
of Europe and pack them into the death trains for Auschwitz. In January 1942 Heydrich had held a conference,
known from its location as the Wannsee Conference, at
which he had ordered the inclusion of all European Jews
in the murder programme.[238] From that moment Adolf
Eichmann had only one aim in life—to be death's most
reliable and indefatigable collector and transport agent.

The centre of the web was Gestapo Desk IV B 4 with
Obersturmbannführer Eichmann at its head, located in the
cavernous, gloomy, rooms of No. 116 Kurfürstenstrasse,
Berlin, formerly a masonic lodge. From this building ran
the strands which enmeshed the entire continent to draw
European Jewry to its doom. At Eichmann's side was a
staff of cold-blooded executioners, ready at any moment
to carry his orders abroad. His organisation had its repercussions on other German and foreign institutions; as he
opened his drag-net campaign Eichmann was assured of
the support of German diplomacy, which brought pressure
to bear on foreign governments to hand over their Jewish
nationals; the Reichsbahn provided the deportation trains;

Eichmann had representatives attached to the Sicher-heitspolizei Commanders in the occupied territories and to German diplomatic missions abroad. All were standing ready to act at any moment on orders from the Kurfür-stenstrasse. (See Appendix 7.)

The death-march of the Jews from central and western Europe had begun even before the Wannsee conference. The first trainloads of German Jews had been dispatched by Eichmann's Headquarters in October 1941; by November Jews from Germany proper and from Austria were reaching the Minsk, Riga and Lodz ghettos, all of which were scheduled for destruction.[239] One or two deportee trains were enough to decimate German Jewry. The Final Solution juggernaut then turned westwards, the first victims being the Jews of Holland. There Reichskommissar Arthur Seyss-Inquart was in charge of the German civil administration and he did not wear the uniform of an SS-Obergruppenführer for nothing. The way was clear for the liquidators. From May 1942 the Jews of Holland were forced to wear the Star of David; a month later Eichmann's deportation trains began to arrive and by July they were on their way eastwards. Dutch Jewry was exterminated with unparalleled precision—of 110,000 Jews deported, only 6,000 survived.[240]

Eichmann's men then turned their attention southwards —to Belgium and France. Here, however, hunting became more difficult, for in both countries Wehrmacht Generals were in charge and one could never be sure whether they would not, even at this stage, oppose the liquidation programme. As in Poland and Russia the fate of the Jews depended to large extent on the attitude of the Wehrmacht and once again, as in the East, the response from the military was uneven. Fortunately for the Jews of France and Belgium it was less definite than that in the Balkans; there the partisan war turned the German military commanders into virtual accomplices of the "Final Solution"; the battle against the Serbian partisans was so savage that the liquidators felt safe in leaving the military to shoot the 20,000 Serbian Jews held as hostages.[241] Martin Luther, an Under-Secretary in the Foreign Office and its senior anti-Semite, commented sneeringly: "In other territories other Military Commanders have taken care of considerably larger numbers of Jews without even mentioning it."[242] The soldiers simply did as they were told. On 2 October 1941, for instance, a motorised column of 342 Infantry Division was ambushed by partisans near Topola;[243] thereupon General Franz Böhme of the Mountain Troops, Commanding General in Serbia, had 2,100 Jews shot in reprisal.[244] By the end of the month, the figure had risen to 5,000—all liquidated by the Wehrmacht.[245] But the military were unwilling to execute the remaining 15,000 Jewish women and children because— as Gruppenführer Dr Harald Turner, Head of the civil administration, obligingly explained—"It was contrary to the viewpoint of the German soldier . . . to take women as hostages."[246] The RSHA gas vans did the rest—hardly a Serbian Jew survived.[247]

The German Generals in Greece were in equally close touch with the RSHA minions. Lieutenant-General von Krenzki, C-in-C Salonika-Aegean area, was the first to strike against the Jews in the German occupation zone; there were 55,000 of them (in the remainder of Greece, occupied by the Italians, there were 13,000 Jews and in the north-east corner, occupied by the Bulgarians, 5,000). Von Krenzki rounded up 7,000 Jews for work on fortifications;[248] then early in 1943 Eichmann sent to Greece two emissaries, Dieter Wisliceny and Anton Brunner, to organise transports to Auschwitz and again the military helped;[249] the army was used to clear the Salonika ghetto,[250] Jews were moved north-eastwards in Wehrmacht trains;[251] the German "Admiral Aegean" made shipping available to carry the last remaining Jews from the Greek islands to the gas chambers.[252]

The German Generals in Western Europe, on the other hand, differed from their Balkan counterparts. C-in-C Belgium and Northern France was General Alexander von Falkenhausen who "till his own arrest in July 1944, more than held his own against Security Police interference."[253]

Belgium was the first country where the tempo of extermination began to slacken. Eichmann's executioners could report only partial successes to Berlin; of the 52,000 Jews living in Belgium, 24,000 were murdered, but hardly a single Jew possessing Belgian nationality was handed over to the death factories in the east.[254]

General Carl-Heinrich von Stülpnagel, the Military

Governor, France, was equally unwilling to assist the annihilation programme, repeatedly refusing to make troops available to SS-Standartenführer Dr Helmut Knochen, the Sicherheitspolizei Commander in France.[255] Nevertheless Stülpnagel could hardly have saved the French Jews from the fate of their countrymen in Serbia and Greece had not the French themselves been determined to protect the Jews from Knochen's thugs. Even the puppet Government in Vichy refused to assist in the Final Solution; although Pierre Laval, the wily Head of the Government, did not yet know that murder was the purpose of Jewish "resettlement" in the East, he barred the way to the hunters. Nevertheless he had to pay a considerable price—as a last resort he was ready to sacrifice the stateless Jews, but under no circumstances would he hand over French citizens of Jewish descent.[256]

On 6 July 1942 Hauptsturmführer Theodor Dannecker, Eichmann's representative in Paris, triumphantly reported to Berlin that the French Government was prepared to relinquish the stateless Jews.[257] But the rejoicing was short-lived. 12,000 Jews from Paris were, indeed, shipped eastwards[258] but in the provinces Eichmann's death wagons remained empty. The Sicherheitspolizei was compelled to rely upon the co-operation of the French Gendarmerie and so the French could sabotage Eichmann's programme. In Bordeaux, for instance, a major operation against the stateless Jews was arranged for mid-July but the Gendarmes only produced 150 victims.[259] Dannecker's section received a furious call from Eichmann; Obersturmführer Heinz Röthke took it and on 15 July noted down Eichmann as saying: "Such a thing had never happened to him before. The matter was very 'blameworthy.' He must consider whether to abandon France altogether as a forwarding area."[260]

Six months later, however, Eichmann saw an opportunity to get his claws on his prey. In November 1942 the Allies landed in French North Africa and German troops thereupon moved into unoccupied France—the last remnant of French autonomy had disappeared. Eichmann's manhunters promptly moved into Southern France. There, however, the much-despised Italian Army taught them a lesson, proving that even in the era of mass murder, humanity and the honour of an officer still had some meaning; the Italians were now occupying Southern France east of the Rhone and their officers cried halt to the annihilation of the Jews.

The Italian Army's refusal to take action against the Jews in the areas which it occupied (Greece and Croatia for instance), had already been made plain. The Chief of the Italian General Staff had told a Todt Organisation leader; "Anti-Jewish excesses are not compatible with the honour of the Italian Army"[261]—a sentiment one would have wished to hear from the mouth of a German General. In innumerable cases the Italian soldiers had assisted the Jews: in Greece General Geloso, commanding the Italian Second Army, refused to sanction the wearing of the Star of David in his occupation area; in Athens he posted a guard on the Synagogue and the Jewish Community Centre to deter a Greek anti-Semitic organisation from instigating anti-Jewish riots.[262] In Salonika, which was German-occupied, the Italian Consulate saved hundreds of Jews by granting them Italian nationality.[263] In summer 1941, on the pretext of pursuing partisans, an Italian unit penetrated into Inner Croatia to save a group of Jews from murder by the Croat fascists; following a protest by the Croat Government, the unit's officers were court-martialled but sentenced only to a few days' arrest.[264]

In their new occupation zone in France the Italian Army authorities stopped any anti-Jewish action. Assisted by the French Administration, the Germans had begun to arrest Jews but the Italians reacted immediately. In February 1943, for instance, the Police Chief of Lyons placed 300 Jews in an internment camp for subsequent transport to Auschwitz; an Italian General promptly compelled him to release them.[265] Early in March the French gendarmerie arrested a number of Jews in the Italian zone, but the Italians prevented them being carted off to Germany;[266] Italian troops surrounded the gendarmerie barracks in Annecy until the arrested Jews were released.[267]

Knochen, the local Sicherheitspolizei Commander, lamented: "Throughout France the 'Final Solution of the Jewish question' decreed for the whole of Europe is being seriously hampered by the Italian position," and he appealed to the German C-in-C West to bring the Italians to reason.[268] Suddenly, however, the German Generals seemed to be of the same mind as their Italian colleagues. Lieutenant-General Blumentritt, Chief of Staff to C-in-C West, informed Knochen: "If the Italian Government appears to have other views, C-in-C West can take no decision in this matter."[269]

Eichmann thereupon appealed to the Foreign Ministry for help. Ribbentrop dutifully got busy, complaining to Rome about sabotage by the Italian Generals and asking Mussolini for his assistance.[270] Instead of clearing the matter up, however, the Duce proved a vexation to his allies; he dispatched to Southern France Guido Lospinoso, the Inspector General of the Italian Police, but the latter's primary object seemed to be to avoid all contact with the Germans.[271] Eichmann and his people soon realised why. Lospinoso had brought with him an assistant named Donati, President of a Franco-Italian bank and a confidant of the Vatican. Assisted by the Holy See, Lospinoso and Donati intended to pass across into Switzerland the 30,000 Jews who had meanwhile taken refuge in the Italian zone.[272] The Jew-murderers reacted violently, for Obersturmführer Röthke had the horrifying suspicion that "Donati is possibly even a full Jew."[273] Röthke produced a plan to kidnap Donati from the Italian Headquarters in Nice and carry him off to Marseilles. Before it could be carried out, however, Donati had taken an aeroplane to Rome.[274]

The capitulation of Italy in the summer of 1943 of course deprived the French Jews of their Italian protectors. Nevertheless the humanity of the Italian Generals had assisted 80 per cent of the 300,000 Jews of France to escape the extermination camps.[275] Moreover, Italian resistance to the Final Solution marked a turning point; it coincided with two events which reduced both the tempo and the scope of the murder programme—these were Adolf Hitler's sinking fortunes of war and the revelations, issuing primarily from the Vatican, of the true nature of Eichmann's "re-settlement" in the East.

When Nazi Germany's opportunist allies realised that they were passengers in a sinking ship, the SS murderers' spell was broken. In quick succession Germany's satellites withdrew from the Jewish pogrom: in autumn 1942 the Slovak Government stopped all deportations of Jew's to the East; the official reason given was that, via the Vatican, information had filtered through concerning the real fate of the Slovak Jews deported to Poland supposedly for "re-settlement"; moreover Eichmann had refused to allow a Slovak Commission of Inquiry to visit supposed Jewish settlements in the East.[276] In December 1942 the Government of Rumania, whose anti-Semites had been even more murderous than the German, refused any further surrender of Jews to Germany.[277] In April 1943 Czar Boris III of Bulgaria ordered all deportation of Jews to stop—not a single Bulgarian Jew was delivered to the mass exterminators.[278]

The remainder of the annihilation programme proceeded only in fits and starts. As a reprisal for Italian sabotage Eichmann planned to arrest all the Jews of Rome during the night of 16–17 October 1943, but even this did not succeed—of the 8,000 Roman Jews only 1,259 could be found.[279] Obersturmbannführer Herbert Kappler, the Police Attaché in charge of the operation, wired on 17 October: "Attitude of Italian population definitely one of passive resistance; numerous cases of active assistance to Jews. No sign during operation of anti-Semitic section of population; normal man-in-street only; even some instances of attempts to drag police officers away from Jews."[280]

Europe's resistance to the Final Solution was undoubtedly growing. Even some of Himmler's immediate entourage were affected and—carefully camouflaged of course—joined the ranks of the "decent." The first was Himmler's masseur, Felix Kersten. When, on 15 July 1942, he heard that Hitler was now demanding surrender of Finland's Jews and that Himmler was to visit Helsinki to put this requirement to the Government, Kersten at once warned the Finnish Legation in Berlin.[281]

On 29 July Himmler, accompanied by Kersten, flew to Finland but before Himmler could open his conversations with the Finnish Government, Kersten went to Witting, the Foreign Minister, and suggested a method of parrying Himmler's attack: he should say that the Jewish problem was so important a question that it could only be decided by Parliament—which, however, did not meet again until November. The Finns adopted Kersten's tactics and Himmler was persuaded to wait until November. On 14

December the Reichsführer once more reverted to the
Finns and asked Kersten what was happening to the
Finnish Final Solution. Kersten had a new argument
ready: the Finnish war situation was so bad that the
Government dared not recall Parliament and submit to it
so thorny a problem. On 18 September 1943 Himmler
returned to the charge yet again. He growled angrily to
Kersten: "What does this twopenny-halfpenny state think
it's doing, refusing to comply with the Führer's desires!"
The Finnish Jews were saved—the first move by Kersten,
to whom thousands and thousands of European Jews were
later to owe their lives.[282]

SS-Brigadeführer Eggert Reeder, Head of Military Administration at the Headquarters of C-in-C Belgium and
Northern France, also had second thoughts about the
programme. As early as March 1942 he had rejected
Knochen's proposal to introduce the Star of David in
Belgium;[283] in September 1943 he took it upon himself to
order the release of Belgian Jews assembled in the Dos-
sin barracks at Malines for transport to Auschwitz.[284]

Even hardened supporters of Hitler like SS-Gruppenführer Wilhelm Stuckart, State Secretary in the Reich
Ministry of the Interior, attempted to salve their con-
sciences. Under gentle pressure from Dr Bernhard Lösener, his Counsellor, he attempted to save two fringe categories of German Jewry whose fate had not yet been
finally decided—the 107,000 "Mischlinge" ["half-castes"]
and the 28,000 Jews "in mixed marriages."[285] The Ministry
of the Interior held several laborious conferences with
Eichmann and the exterminators of the RSHA in an attempt to stop them liquidating the "Mischlinge."[286] When
the RSHA refused to give way, Stuckart took refuge in a
last desperate proposal—sterilisation instead of killing. In
September 1942 Lösener drafted a personal memorandum
from Stuckart to Himmler;[287] it is a typical illustration of
the extreme methods and deceptive phraseology which
anyone wishing to help Jews in Germany had to use.

Lösener made adroit use of Himmler's devotion to the
cult of his Germanic ancestors. In Stuckart's name he submitted that in the case of the "Mischlinge" it must be remembered that "deporting the half-Jews would mean not
only abandoning that half of the blood which is German
but actually making a present of it to the enemies of

Germany"; in addition the "Mischlinge" had "in most cases made every effort to work for German interests." Moreover the "psychological and political repercussions" must be considered since, if the "Mischlinge" were treated as Jews, "an increased psychological burden for their parents and relatives would result." Lösener concluded: "I cannot therefore regard the evacuation plan as being in the true interests of Germany and would prefer to see the half-Jews sterilised and so die out naturally". The sting came in the tail: "neither evacuation nor sterilisation could of course be undertaken until after the war."[288]

The Stuckart-Lösener letter caught the Reichsführer in a weak moment. Himmler forbade liquidation and the majority of the "Mischlinge" were saved. Even the Nuremberg War Crimes Tribunal accepted Stuckart's letter, particularly as he was able to prove something which he had carefully concealed when writing it—he had previously been assured by SS-Gruppenführer Dr Conti, State Secretary for the Health Service, that sterilisation of the "Mischlinge" was in fact impracticable.[289]

The most striking example of the scepticism from which many SS leaders were now suffering, however, was that of SS Gruppenführer Dr Werner Best, the Gestapo's ex-Legal Adviser and now Reich Plenipotentiary in Copenhagen, who played an active part in sabotaging the extermination of Danish Jewry. Early in September 1943 Best learned that Hitler had ordered the evacuation of the 6,500 Danish Jews.[290] He immediately dispatched a telegram to the Foreign Ministry arguing against the operation: "The King and Parliament would cease to take part in the Government of the country. In addition we cannot discount the possibility of a general strike."[291]

Nevertheless Hitler and Himmler insisted upon striking their blow against the Danish Jews. On 18 September Best gave a further warning: "From the political point of view the evacuation of Jews will undoubtedly lead to a serious increase in the state of tension in Denmark. There may be riots and possibly a general strike."[292] Ribbentrop was so impressed by Best's gloomy prognostications that he submitted them to Hitler. The answer came back via Ambassador Hewel, the Foreign Ministry's representative in the Führer's Headquarters: "The Führer doubts whether the operation will have the results anticipated."[293] The operation proceeded. Two Ordnungspolizei battalions were dispatched to Denmark and the *Wartheland* docked in Copenhagen to take the Jewish prisoners on board.[294]

Best then decided to resist. The Reich Plenipotentiary rebelled against his Führer—naturally after his own manner, cautiously feeling his way and with not a little cynical double-dealing. As soon as he heard the date of the operation, he let his shipping expert, Georg Ferdinand Duckwitz, into the picture and told him to warn the Jews. Although he was an old Party member formerly on the staff of Alfred Rosenberg and wearing the Golden Party Badge, Duckwitz lost no time in doing so. On 27 September he met the Danish Resistance leaders in Copenhagen and asked them to alert the leaders of the Danish-Jewish community.[295] By the grape-vine the word went round through synagogues and Jewish homes. The Jews went to ground and then, in one of the most remarkable rescue operations which a nation has ever undertaken for a minority, were shipped across the Kattegat to safety in Sweden.[296]

Best did something else to protect the Jews. He instructed the Sicherheitspolizei Commander that his men were not to enter Jewish houses but merely to ring the door-bell. He justified his action later by arguing that "since the vast majority of Jews are no longer living in their own houses, breaking into empty dwellings would have made an unpleasant impression and might have given rise to thefts which would then have been laid at our door."[297] The anti-Jewish action of 1 and 2 October 1943 was therefore inevitably a failure. The Sicherheitspolizei captured only a few of the older Jews whom Best's warning had not reached. Only 477 Jews were evacuated—out of 6,500. Best contrived to arrange that these Jews were sent to the so-called Old Peoples' Concentration Camp, Theresienstadt, where most of them survived to the end of the war.[298]

As an ex-Gestapo pen-pusher however, Best could not forego his little camouflage joke. As if the Sicherheitspolizei had just carried out a large and successful operation against world Jewry he dutifully reported to Berlin: "1. Anti-Jewish action in Denmark carried out without incident during the night 1/2 October, 1943. 2. As of today Denmark can be regarded as free of Jews."[299] When the Berlin exterminators screamed to high heaven that only very few Jews had been arrested, Best, with his tongue in his cheek, replied on 5 October 1943: "The Sicherheitspolizei Commander and I had foreseen that only very few Jews would be caught. Since the real object of action in Denmark was to free the country of Jews rather than have a good man-hunt, it must be recorded that the operation achieved its object."[300]

Adolf Eichmann could no longer understand what was going on. First there had been Wilhelm Stuckart and now here was another SS leader wrecking what was supposed to be the Final Solution. He told his Israeli interrogator: "I remember this very well because I was astounded at the time and said: 'Now, that same Dr Best was once Head of Amt I in the RSHA and at that time he gave us a great talk about the tasks and aims of the police'; and then I said to myself: 'But, look you, now he's in Denmark and now he's against his master's orders.' "[301]

Eichmann's very ordinary, petty but evil little brain was incapable of understanding such curious goings-on. One even more bitter disappointment, however, awaited him before he ended his career as a hangman; when he came to deal with Hungarian Jewry, he found that they had another protector—and his name was Heinrich Himmler.

15
The Impotence of Power

THE destruction of European Jewry demonstrated even to the sceptics the frightful power over defenceless human beings possessed by the SS in Adolf Hitler's Germany. With its numerous organisations the SS wrapped its tentacles round the Reich like an octopus. With the SD and the Gestapo, the Waffen-SS and the "Reich Commissar for the strengthening of Germanism," Ahnenerbe [Ancestral Heritage] and "Lebensborn," concentration camps and industrial enterprises, hardly an aspect of the nation's life was closed to Himmler's bureaucrats and minions. The structure of the SS organisations became increasingly labyrinthine, the whole SS machine increasingly complex and convoluted.

The extent of SS influence was largely concealed by the continuous switching of responsibility from one part of the vast organisation to another. The Party's or Allgemeine [General] SS had long since sunk into insignificance; the Army had swept up 60 per cent of its members[1] and the remainder either paraded for evening instruction or lined the streets—in either case without much enthusiasm; they were practically indistinguishable from the Nazi veterans of the SA or NSKK [National-Sozialistische Kraftfahr Korps—the Party Motor Transport Organisation]. But specialised SS organizations appeared in place of the Allgemeine SS, less obtrusive but far more influential.

The success story of the RSHA is perhaps the clearest indication of the extent to which the SS ruled the life of Germany. Under the pressure of the RSHA security machine, the legal rights of the German citizen shrank with each year of war. On the outbreak of war the RSHA claimed the right to order summary executions to "correct" sentences by the normal courts, blocking protests from the Ministry of Justice by the statement that under a Führer order the Reichsführer-SS was entitled to use all methods to guarantee the security of the State, including summary executions for offences against defence regulations.[2] So long as Dr Franz Gürtner, a German Nationalist whom Hitler treated with some respect, was still Minister of Justice, the power of the RSHA was kept within bounds. On Gürtner's death in January 1941, however, his place was taken by Franz Schlegelberger, the Permanent Secretary, a weak man with only acting rank, and the RSHA seized the opportunity to deal the judiciary a blow from which it never recovered.

In autumn 1942 Heydrich, in addition to all his other offices, was appointed acting Reich Protector of Bohemia and Moravia. The Czechs were restive and Hitler had told him to act ruthlessly, so Heydrich proposed to usher in his regime with a spectacular trial designed to show the Czech serfs that their new overlord meant business. As candidate for the dock, Heydrich selected General Alois Elias, head of the Protectorate's puppet government in Prague. The SD had long suspected that he was secretly working both with Czech resistance and with the émigré Czechoslovak Government in London.[3]

Ever since mid-1940 the RSHA had been urging the dismissal of Elias and his trial before a summary court, but Freiherr von Neurath, the Reich Protector, who was a moderate, had resisted and refused to take proceedings against him. Even Ernst Lautz, a Nazi lawyer and senior State Attorney of the Peoples' Court, regarded the RSHA's evidence against Elias as inadequate to justify a trial.[4]

But Heydrich had his own plan. He knew that Dr Otto Thierack, an "old fighter," the first National-Socialist Minister of Justice in Saxony and now President of the Peoples' Court, was an ambitious man and that his aim was to become Reich Minister of Justice; Heydrich calculated that Thierack would be quite prepared to join in a little intrigue if he thought that it would bring him the coveted appointment. On 27 September 1941 Heydrich and Thierack agreed on the arrest of Elias and his arraignment before the Peoples' Court; Lautz, the sceptical attorney, was to be kept out of the proceedings and the case for the prosecution would be conducted by the Sicherheitspolizei.[5] At one stroke the RSHA had thus almost fulfilled one of their long-standing dreams: the man who was about to become Reich Minister of Justice had in effect agreed that State Attorneys, the men whose thinking was conditioned by the normal legal system, should be completely excluded from the case; he was therefore a supporter of complete freedom of action for the police and they would now be able to appear in court in the role of State Attorney. Thierack in fact was prepared to sell the Law down the river. When it was all over he told Rothenberger, the Ministry's State Secretary, that he had agreed with Heydrich that "should he become Reich Minister of Justice, he would make over to the Reichsführer the duties of the State Attorneys."[6]

The drama in Prague was staged exactly as agreed in Berlin. Thierack waited until his unsuspecting State Attorney went off for the weekend; meanwhile in Prague Heydrich arrested Elias, and SS-Obersturmbannführer Dr Hans Geschke, Head of the Gestapo Leitstelle in Prague, took over the case for the prosecution.[7] Before the legal experts in Berlin had realised what was happening in Prague, Heydrich had hustled through his grim travesty of justice. Elias was arrested on 28 September; the next day Geschke indicted him; on 30 September Division I of the Peoples' Court moved to Prague; on 1 October at 10 a.m. sharp proceedings against Elias opened; four hours later sentence was pronounced. The verdict was death for attempted high treason together with action in aid of the enemy.[8]

Otto Thierack had given good service and so could claim his reward; on 20 August 1942 the grateful dictator appointed him Reich Minister of Justice.[9] The new Minister of course kept in close touch with the SS. Although the rank-and-file lawyers prevented him handing over all the duties of State Attorneys, he contrived to make over a whole series of the judiciary's preserves to the Reichsführer-SS. In an agreement with Himmler dated 18 September 1942, Thierack conceded to the RSHA the privilege of "correcting" sentences of the courts by means of Gestapo "special treatment"; he also agreed that persons sentenced by the normal courts to more than eight years imprisonment should be handed over to the police;[10] at the beginning of November 1942 Thierack handed over to the Sicherheitspolizei complete judicial responsibility for Poles and Jews in the re-incorporated Eastern Territories;[11] in summer 1943 he agreed that all Jews under German sovereignty should come under the jurisdiction of the RSHA.[12]

Though theoretically under the Reich Ministry of the Interior, the power of the RSHA grew unchecked. Certain of the traditionally-minded bureaucrats in the Ministry had made some attempt to bring it under control but from August 1943 even this internal opposition was silenced, for Himmler was then appointed Minister of the Interior in succession to Wilhelm Frick, who was anti-SS and had fallen out of favour.[13] Many of the Ministry's most important responsibilities were thereupon transferred to the RSHA. Abteilung I of the Ministry, for instance, lost to its Prinz-Albrecht-Strasse rivals all real authority in the constitutional, legislative and administrative fields.[14]

One of the chief sufferers from Himmler's new access of power was Hauptamt Orpo. Hitherto its traditionalist officials, lawyers and officers had kept their distance from the RSHA and the Sicherheitspolizei; as a result of an internal streamlining operation, however, euphemistically termed "clarification of responsibilities," Hauptamt Orpo had to relinquish to the RSHA all control over the criminal police.[15] Worse still, the police reporting and registry system, general questions of police law and police organisation, all of which had been Orpo responsibilities, were swallowed up by the RSHA. Politically Hauptamt Orpo was now completely in the shade.[16]

No sooner had he become Minister of the Interior than Himmler disbanded the Administration and Legal Section in Hauptamt Orpo; its self-willed head, Werner Bracht, had obstructed him often enough. The tiresome nest of lawyers was turned into an "economic and administrative office," at the head of which Himmler placed an "old fighter," SS-Gruppenführer August Frank.[17] At about the same time Kurt Daluege, the head of the Orpo and one of Himmler's rivals, fell seriously ill and so the Reichs-führer was able to abolish the last remnants of Orpo inde-pendence.[18] In summer 1944 Orpo welfare questions were transferred to the SS and even administrative police law was removed from it and given to the RSHA.[19]

The expansion of the RSHA, however, was only one indication among many of the growing power of the SS. Himmler's organising ability had produced another colossus which showed how deeply embedded the SS had become in the whole Nazi system of tyranny—this was the WVHA [Wirtschaftsverwaltungshauptamt—Economic and Administrative Department].

The WVHA originated from the SS administrative office—part of the SS-Hauptamt which had dealt with all administrative questions concerning the Allgemeine-SS ever since 1934.[20] To head it Himmler had appointed Oswald Pohl, an ex-Naval Paymaster and a slick but dogmatic tyrant; he looked like Mussolini, whose unscrupulous ambition he shared. Brigadeführer Pohl proved to be an inventive organiser and his empire was soon expanding. At an early stage he assumed administrative responsibility for the Totenkopfverbände and the Verfügungstruppe; he finally became financial administrator of the entire SS, taking over the "Hauptamt Haushalt und Bauten [Budget and Buildings Department] of the Reichsführer-SS and Chief of the German Police within the Reich Ministry of the Interior"—a state institution which gave him the rank of Director in the Ministry.[21]

By 1939 Pohl, who had meanwhile been promoted SS-Gruppenführer, had become so powerful a figure that Himmler freed him from the strait-jacket of the SS-Hauptamt, giving him his own Hauptamt, known as "Verwaltung und Wirtschaft" [Administration and Economics].[22] Three years later, by which time administration of the concentration camps had also been placed under Pohl, Hauptamt Verwaltung und Wirtschaft was amalgamated with Hauptamt Haushalt und Bauten to form the WVHA.[23] So in a remarkably short time, Pohl had worked himself up until, Heydrich excepted, he was the most powerful man among the Heads of the SS Hauptämter.

Four potent departments placed Pohl's hand firmly on the levers of power in the SS empire: he was in charge of the entire administration and supply of the Waffen-SS; he controlled the 20 concentration camps and 165 labour camps;[24] he directed all SS and Police building projects; he was in charge of all SS economic enterprises. In fact

Pohl could see his Hauptamt developing into one of the most powerful economic forces in Germany—primarily because the SS business concerns could call upon the pool of labour provided by the concentration-camp prisoners.

SS-owned firms had been launched early on by qualified businessmen such as the brothers Georg and Hans Lörner, and SS-Hauptsturmführer Franz Eirenschmalz, a building tycoon.[25] By the outbreak of war there were four great SS concerns: the Deutsche Erd-und Steinwerke GmbH [German Excavation and Quarrying Company Ltd] producing building materials; it owned 14 stone, brick and clinker works with a total turnover in 1943 of 14,822,800 marks;[26] second, the Deutsche Ausrüstungwerke GmbH [German Equipment Co. Ltd]; this owned all plants located in the concentration camps and dealt with a variety of trades from bread-making to cutlery, woodworking and iron foundries;[27] third, the Deutsche Versuchsanstalt für Ernährung und Verpflegung GmbH [German Experimental Establishment for Foodstuffs and Nutrition Ltd]; for Himmler, with his belief in the medicinal qualities of herbs and his insistence upon surrounding the concentration camps with gardens of herbs, this was a favourite concern; later, however, it also dealt with Estates, Forestry and Fisheries where experiments were carried on with new but more innocuous foodstuffs;[28] fourth, the Gesellschaft für Textil- und Lederverwertung GmbH [Society for Exploitation of Textile and Leather Work Ltd]; this concern was centred on Ravensbrück women's concentration camp and its primary activity was the production of uniforms for the Waffen-SS; its turnover in 1943 was over nine million marks.[29]

Pohl grouped all these four concerns together into one holding company, Deutsche Wirtschaftsbetriebe [German Industrial Undertakings—DWB].[30] The formation of the DWB was typical of the technique of capitalist infiltration used by the WVHA to establish a hold over many fringe areas of the German economy. Outwardly the SS did not appear either as owner or manager of these firms; in the case of the DWB, for instance, the members of the board were shown as a certain ministerial director named Oswald Pohl and a businessman named Georg Lörner.[31] Only by thumbing through the SS lists was it possible to elucidate that SS-Obergruppenführer Pohl was head of the

WVHA and SS-Gruppenführer Lörner his deputy.[32] Enno
Georg, who has written a valuable and exhaustive account
of these SS economic undertakings, points out that by
various commercial-law subterfuges, the SS were highly
successful in concealing their interest in the firms, at the
same time reaping all the advantages of a major business
undertaking by presenting them as privately organised
cartels under public law.[33]

Pohl was realistic enough to know that he could not
force his way into all areas of the economy. He therefore
drew up a priority programme, setting out those branches
of production in which he intended to establish an SS
monopoly. First on the list was the mineral-water business,
which was centred in the Sudetenland and was mostly in
Jewish or British ownership; under cover of the Aryanisation decrees, Pohl's representatives took possession of a
number of such firms—Grün and Heinrich Mattoni, for
instance.[34] He then turned his attention to German firms,
laying hands on Niederselters and Apollinaris.[35] By 1944
Pohl was in control of 75 per cent of the German mineral-
water market.[36]

The Sudetenland was also the scene of the second and
equally successful venture by the WVHA capitalists. Emil
Gerstel, the largest furniture manufacturers in Czechoslovakia, also fell into their hands as being an ex-Jewish undertaking; it formed the foundation for an SS-owned
furniture industry. In this case, however, the WVHA had
to cover their tracks carefully. The Reich Ministry of
Economics had laid down that Gerstel should be taken
over not by the SS but by a company to be formed by
established German furniture manufacturers: Dr Kurt
May, a furniture manufacturer from Stuttgart, together
with two others in the same line of business, accordingly
set up a German firm to take over Gerstel. What the
Ministry of Economics did not know, however, was that
in his spare time May was an SS-Untersturmführer and
head of Amt WIV in the WVHA. He and his two henchmen forthwith made over their interests in the new company to the SS (through the DWB).[37] By taking over a
number of other firms including the major Jewish concern of Drucker, the SS built itself up to a predominant
position in the furniture market,[38] eventually forming
Deutsche Heimgestaltung e.V. [German Home Furnish-

ing Ltd]; this put cheap home furnishings on the market and drew up a production programme to which many non-SS furniture firms adhered.[39]

The third area to be invaded by the SS captains of industry was that of building materials. Here they could make use of the concerns in the German-occupied Eastern territories and the workshops in the Jewish ghettos of Poland. A Company known as Ostdeutsche Baustoffwerke GmbH [East German Building Materials Ltd] was set up in Poznan, running no fewer than 313 ex-Polish or ex-Jewish brickworks in the re-incorporated territories; in 1943 its turnover was 11,000,000 marks.[40] In Eastern Upper Silesia and the Government-General, Klinker-Zement GmbH [Roughcast Cement Ltd] formed by Pohl took over brickworks, lime kilns, cement works and china factories.[41] Until the last frightful phase of the "Final Solution" Ostindustrie GmbH [Eastern Industries Ltd], formed in 1943, did its best to make use of Jewish labour and businesses in the ghettos.[42] The Deutsche Ausrüstungswerke GmbH, one of DWB's subsidiaries, took over woodworking firms and iron foundries in Poland and even made inroads into textiles, printing and shoemaking.[43] In fact there was hardly a field of business activity in which Pohl's minions did not try their luck. Shale oil, bookbinding, estate management in Russia, jam factories—Pohl's Hauptamt had a finger in them all.

All this was under the control of Amtsgruppe W (Industrial Directorate) in the WVHA. Amstgruppe C was no less successful; it laid the foundation of an SS armaments industry. Amtsgruppe C was in charge of the SS/Police building programme and at its head was one of the most unscrupulous careerists ever to wear SS uniform.

His name was Hans Kammler, he was a qualified engineer and his ambition was abnormal even by SS standards; he would build gas chambers in Auschwitz or launching ramps for flying bombs with equal attention to detail. He eventually became a Gruppenführer but in spite of his exalted position bore no loyalty to the SS; for him the Order was nothing but a ladder for his own advancement.

This did not worry Pohl; he was quite prepared to recruit into the WVHA men who cared nothing for the SS and he kept them as long as they seemed useful, Amtsgruppe W, for instance, was run by a totally apolitical chartered accountant, Dr Hans Hohberg, who never belonged to any Nazi formation and never wore SS uniform;[44] Kammler also came from outside the SS. He was a civil servant who had long held the post of Director of Works in the Reich Ministry of Civil Aviation; in 1941 Himmler persuaded him to transfer to the SS, together with a staff of construction experts from the Luftwaffe.[45] He was given the rank of SS-Standartenführer and took over Amtsgruppe C in the WVHA where he produced an ambitious building programme which, by 1942, was already employing 175,000 men from the concentration and prisoner-of-war camps.[46]

Construction of supply depots, concentration-camp gas chambers, ammunition storage and barracks for the Waffen-SS was not enough to satisfy Kammler. He flew higher. Speer, the Armaments Minister, recalled: "When Kammler took on his first job, I did not realise that it was he who had been earmarked as my successor."[47]

Himmler's and Kammler's ambitions coincided: one of the former's dreams was to build up his own armaments industry and so make the SS units independent of equipment allocations from the ever-mistrustful Wehrmacht; Kammler saw himself at the head of a super-Ministry of Armaments. Both these ambitions were to be at least partially satisfied.

From 1943 Kammler was under orders to accelerate construction of arms factories, including underground workshops in the more important cases.[48] With his expert building gangs, his army of concentration-camp slaves and the extensive SS training areas available to him in the east, he soon became an indispensable figure in SS armament planning. He set up the Kammler Special Staff, gradually divorced Amtsgruppe C from the rest of the WVHA and refused to take orders from anyone other than the Reichsführer himself.[49] By 1944 Gruppenführer Kammler was calling himself "Representative of the Reichsführer-SS." On many occasions his construction experts paved the way for Himmler into the innermost recesses of armaments policy. Kammler's tasks were legion: construction of an underground Führer headquarters in Thuringia, construction of underground hangars for assembly of aircraft and flying bombs, participation in the manufacture of the Me 262 jet fighter and, finally control of the top secret miracle weapon to which Greater Germany was to look for salvation—the V1 and V2 rockets.[50]

When Himmler became Commander-in-Chief of the Replacement Army after 20 July 1944, he handed over to Kammler technical direction of the V2 weapons which had been developed by the Army; in September 1944 Himmler took over tactical command of the two Army Missile Units, Group North and Group South.[51] By 31 December 1944 1,561 V2 rockets had been fired on London and Antwerp.[52] Early in 1945 the Luftwaffe relinquished to Kammler command of 5 AA Division and with it control of the V1 programme; he was now entitled to call himself "General Commanding a Specialised Army Corps" and to register the greatest prestige victory possible for an SS man—he became responsible to Hitler personally.[53]

Kammler's meteoric career was an illustration of the central position to which the SS and its leaders had risen among the power groups of the Third Reich. Almost every SS organisation could tell a success story similar to that of the RSHA or WVHA—and inevitably therefore the idea was mooted that the day might not be far distant when the SS would take over the entire State. Its accumulation of prestige, exalted positions and highly placed dignitaries has led certain historians to ascribe to the SS such omnipotence that the entire Third Reich has been made to appear as a tributary of the SS Order.[54] Any such notion, however, betrays a misunderstanding of the practice of leadership in the totalitarian state.

The majority of historians have read into the Third Reich's system of government a degree of planning, organisation and system, in other words a degree of orderliness, which was in fact totally foreign to the rulers of Hitler Germany. The Führer dictatorship was essentially based, not upon authority and organisation, but on a complete lack of any hierarchy or structure. Nothing was more abhorrent to Hitler than the appearance of new organisational structures, for they would inevitably exert a constricting influence upon what was known as "the dynamic will of the leadership." Deliberately and instinctively, Hitler refused to permit any intervening hierarchical level between himself and the masses—any such intervention could only have detracted from the unique and supreme position of the Führer.

The hallmark of the Nazi regime was "absence of system" (Masaryk's description of the Stalin regime)[55]; the weight of power was continually shifting among the paladins; communication and co-ordination between lower-level leaders was barred: the rivalries among the Nazi potentates were artificially kept alive. Hannah Arendt says: "the will of the Führer can be embodied everywhere and at all times and he himself is not tied to any hierarchy, not even the one he might have established himself."[56] Refusal to permit devolution of authority to the lower levels was a method of guaranteeing the personal dominance of the Führer—for dynamism was then his prerogative alone. Though outwardly resembling a pyramid of power, the hierarchy of Party functionaries in fact possessed no inherent authority; in the words of Hannah Arendt, the expert on totalitarianism, an action was legitimised "not because it was done in execution of orders issuing from this or that authority but because it was done in 'fulfilment of the will of the leadership'."[57]

In this unsystematic system the SS and its numerous organisations might occupy powerful positions but the absence of established authority continually allowed counterweights to emerge to prevent the SS from attaining any overriding position of predominance. Whether it was the Party, the SA or the Wehrmacht, there were always rivals to apply restraints and prevent the power-hungry SS from flying too high. Even the Wehrmacht, which had been politically emasculated as a result of the Blomberg-Fritsch crisis of 1938, invariably found ways and means to offset any SS claim to predominance. Right to the end of the war the Wehrmacht retained its privileged position. Nevertheless there was clearly a latent conflict between SS and Wehrmacht and this was first reflected in the field of occupation policy for German-occupied Europe; as soon as the German armies moved into Poland, this conflict arose.

From the outset the Wehrmacht had demanded full powers in occupied Polish territory; it had also insisted that the Sicherheitspolizei's Einsatzgruppen working in Poland should (at least during operations) be subordinate to the Wehrmacht. A military administration was in fact set up but disagreements between the Wehrmacht and

Himmler's murder commandos became so acute that the senior soldiers were only too glad when responsibility for government in Poland was removed from them by Hitler.[58] Nevertheless on the next occasion the Army's demands, as put forward by its Commander-in-Chief, Colonel-General von Brauchitsch, were even stiffer. Before the Norwegian Campaign he submitted to Hitler a demand that plenary powers should once more be accorded to the Wehrmacht; Einsatzgruppen were not to be allowed in Norway.[59]

Ostensibly Hitler accepted the military demands and Heydrich's bloodhounds were not permitted to take part in the Norwegian campaign. Only ten days after the conclusion of operations, however, the Dictator broke his word, appointing a Reich Commissar, the fire-eating Gauleiter Josef Terboven. Terboven was admittedly one of the anti-SS Party members, but simultaneously an HSSPF was appointed to Oslo, and he immediately summoned a number of Einsatzkommandos.[60] The process was repeated after the attack on Holland; Einsatzkommandos were only admitted after nomination of a Reich Commissar by Hitler. This time, however, the appointment was a clear victory for the SS: the Reich Commissar in question was Dr Arthur Seyss-Inquart and he wore the uniform of an SS-Gruppenführer.[61]

In Belgium and France, on the other hand, the military contrived to maintain their position of authority. No Einsatzkommandos were allowed while operations were in progress; OKH [Army High Command] eventually agreed to accept a Sicherheitspolizei detachment of ten men but only after representations from Göring and on condition that the men wore Wehrmacht uniform.[62] The detachment commander was SS-Obersturmbannführer Dr Helmut Knochen; he set up headquarters in the Hotel du Louvre, Paris, but General Otto von Stülpnagel, the Military Governor, France, with 2,500 men of the Field Security Police under his command, set out to ensure that Knochen's activities were severely restricted.[63]

Heydrich's nightmare was that "led by the retired and reserve officers in the counter-espionage offices who were not always politically reliable," the Army might set up its own police organisation independent of the RSHA.[64] He therefore produced the standard RSHA demand for all occupied territories—appointment of an HSSPF to command the local police units and be responsible to Himmler alone.[65] The Army refused; it was, however, willing to accept a "representative of the Sicherheitspolizei and SD." SS-Brigadeführer Dr Max Thomas was appointed,[66] but he soon became too active for the liking of the military, and they booted him out again.

The SS leaders had good reason to adopt cautious tactics towards the Wehrmacht since additional occupation areas were now under the latter's control. After the Balkan campaign, for instance, Military Governments were installed in Greece and Jugoslavia and they were not prepared to concede the SS much voice in affairs.[67] With growing suspicion SS Headquarters watched the Wehrmacht's attempts to insulate itself from SS influence. Himmler did in fact think that he had a reliable Fifth Column inside the military organisation in the shape of the Senior SS Commanders who acted as Military Administration Advisers in certain of the military districts in western and southeastern Europe. But the SS luck was out. Hardly one of them proved effective. The worst thorn in Himmler's flesh was SS-Brigadeführer Eggert Reeder, Head of Military Administration on the staff of C-in-C Belgium and Northern France.

Reeder was an ex-Regierungspräsident and an uncompromising supporter of the well-tried Prussian-German bureaucratic tradition. Himmler and his numerous emissaries were continually finding it necessary to remind Reeder that he was an Honorary SS Commander and that his policy should therefore be palatable to the SS.[68] The Prinz-Albrecht-Strasse was particularly incensed by Reeder's comparatively mild occupation policy and in this he was supported by the anti-Nazi von Falkenhausen, the military commander. Himmler was continually having "to remonstrate about matters to which I do not normally have to refer in the case of SS officers," as he wrote to Reeder on 16 February 1943;[69] SS-Gruppenführer Gottlob Berger, Head of the SS Hauptamt and Himmler's most reliable mouthpiece, said that Reeder appeared "not to realise that his policy was a Belgian one; he should change his policy and make it a 'Reich policy.' "[70]

Reeder simply shrugged off Himmler's admonitions. He relied largely upon his adviser, an Administrative Officer

[Oberkriegsverwaltungsrat] named Franz Thedieck, a right-wing Catholic and anti-Nazi, who scandalised the SS leaders by demonstratively going to church in Wehrmacht uniform (he later became State Secretary in the Federal Ministry in Bonn). Himmler complained again. "You had promised SS-Gruppenführer Berger that by 31 December 1942 you would dismiss your staff officer,[71] whom we regard as undesirable if not downright mischievous in the capacity of adviser on political matters in Belgium. This promise has not been kept." Reeder never kept it.[72]

Himmler was equally disappointed by SS-Brigadeführer Dr Werner Best, head of the Military Section on the staff of the Military Governor, France; though he had been a co-founder of the RSHA, Best was all too frequently found on the side of the more cautious occupation policy adopted by the military. Nevertheless in July 1942 the soldiers got rid of him by an organisational subterfuge. On the arrival of Oberg as HSSPF France, the military decided to clear their decks of SS men. The administrative staff, Paris, was reduced in size and Best, who was an ex-Under Secretary [Ministerialrat], found himself doing a tuppeny-halfpenny job as a desk officer. He departed of his own accord.[73]

In Serbia the military adopted similar tactics against SS-Gruppenführer Dr Harald Turner, a fanatical National-Socialist and anti-Semite, head of the Military Administration on the staff of the Plenipotentiary Commanding General, Belgrade. On 31 March 1942 SS-Obsturmbann-führer Dr Georg Kiesel, Turner's staff officer, reported to Berlin: "There is no doubt that attempts are now being made by the Wehrmacht to force Gruppenführer Turner out of the military administration; the fact is that he does not suit them because, being an SS Commander, he is regarded as too dangerous."[74] From an informer in the office of C-in-C South-East, Kiesel had heard that, as in Paris, the administrative staff was to be downgraded to an administrative section in order to force Turner out of Serbia. The reason adduced was the same as in Paris: appointment of an HSSPF.[75]

The military now opened a "personal insult" campaign against Turner, described by Kiesel as a "war of nerves."[76] C-in-C South-East proposed to throw Turner out of his official residence, forbade him to sign administrative

documents and refused to forward one of his reports because "it contained certain criticisms of the Military
Command which are regarded as subversive."[77] Then
Colonel Hermann Foertsch, Chief of Staff to C-in-C South-
East, delivered the *coup de grâce,* writing to Turner: "I can
foresee that in the long run the development of the situation in Serbia will neither satisfy nor provide adequate
employment for a man of your experience and capabilities."[78]

Turner complained to the Reichsführer and Himmler
succeeded in preventing the army from carrying out its
proposed staff reorganisation.[79] The soldiers had more or
less given the game up for lost when they found an unexpected ally in the HSSPF Serbia, Gruppenführer August
Meyszner; he apparently preferred to side with the military
rather than his fellow SS man. The two SS Commanders
became involved in so bitter a struggle about prerogatives
and prestige that in Turner's words "interested parties in
Belgrade could hardly conceal their satisfaction."[80]
Whether the subject was control of the local Serbian
Police, disposal of the property of murdered Jews, or
priorities in the anti-partisan war, the HSSPF was continually making representations to the military to call
"their" Chief Administrative Officer to order.[81]

Meyszner was clearly one of those SS Commanders—
mostly ex-police or ex-army officers—who had never
overcome a secret longing to rejoin their old military
comrades-in-arms. Neither the splendour of the SS uniform
nor the SS elite mystique could quite stifle their private
conviction that basically the Wehrmacht was the only
force in the country which could legitimately bear arms.
Even Karl Wolff, the most senior HSSPF once said that
"as an ex-regular Guards officer he had always been torn
between his duty to the SS and his attachment to the
Wehrmacht."[82] Arthur Nebe, who was an ex-Lieutenant in
the Engineers, was similarly inclined; when commanding
Einsatzgruppe B he tended to pay far more attention to
the view of anti-Nazi officers on the staff of Army Group
Centre than to his orders from the RSHA.[83] Even
Gruppenführer Oberg, the HSSPF France, could never
conceal the esteem in which he held his wartime fellow-
officer, the anti-Nazi General Carl-Heinrich von Stülpnagel. After the collapse of the 20 July plot in 1944 he

saved many of the conspirators from the Gestapo and Stülpnagel himself said: "If Oberg could have done as he liked, I believe he would have been on our side."[84]

For many SS leaders the Wehrmacht was still the oracle on military matters and they would frequently accept a General's opinion without question, regarding him as the expert. This attitude of mind became almost an insidious disease sapping the arrogant self-confidence characteristic of so many SS leaders. The most striking example was perhaps Gruppenführer Gerret Korsemann, HSSPF Central Russia, whose behaviour caused Himmler some embarrassment. In summer 1943 the word went round that Korsemann had made an over-hasty getaway during the retreat from the Caucasus and had behaved "like a frightened rabbit or just a plain coward."[85] He evidently considered that there was nothing out of order in asking the Wehrmacht to give him a clean bill of health. On 30 June 1943 he wrote a lengthy letter to Field-Marshal von Kleist under whose command he was: "Honoured Field-Marshal," the letter began; the Field-Marshal's "obedient servant" then "permitted himself to submit" that the Field-Marshal might "write a short letter showing that I remained at my post not only as long as was necessary but in fact considerably longer and that I only withdrew with the Field-Marshal's agreement and when in practice I had no further task to perform."[86] Berger of the SS-Hauptamt exploded: "The stupidity and ingratiating tone of this letter are an insult to the SS in general and the Reichsführer in particular";[87] Himmler was so incensed that Korsemann was relieved and despatched to the Waffen-SS as a punishment.[88]

Himmler punished any "ingratiating attitude" towards the Wehrmacht with all the more severity since he suspected that the generals were exploiting their established position to expand their sphere of influence and block the growth of the SS. Moreover, alongside the Wehrmacht the Reichsführer saw another enemy of the SS emerging, a force which for years had been searching for an ally in its anti-SS campaign—the SA.

The unhappy survivors of the Röhm putsch had been relegated to the status of an old comrades association but the SA's hatred for the SS murderers was still boiling. Even Viktor Lutze, the Chief of Staff of the SA, would never forget Hitler's bloody excursion. He was determined to revenge himself on the SS murderers who had assassinated SA men in rows in the cellars of the SS torture houses. But the SA was too weak to challenge the SS unaided. Lutze could think of only one sure ally—the Wehrmacht.

Lutze had wanted the SA and Wehrmacht to strike against the SS immediately after the fall of von Blomberg and von Fritsch. In May 1938 at the foundation-stone laying ceremony of the Volkswagen factory in Wolfsburg, he had drawn aside General Ulex, a well-known anti-Nazi, and told him that the Fritsch case must be used to bring down Himmler who, he said, was already building up a private army in order to seize the succession from Hitler.[89] When the General asked what the attitude of the SA would be in the event of Wehrmacht action against the SS, Lutze exclaimed spontaneously: "Unconditionally on the side of the Wehrmacht!" What if Hitler supported Himmler, Ulex asked. Lutze replied: "The Führer must of course be spared as far as possible." Ulex took Lutze's answer to mean: "If he will not go along, he must go down too." Ulex declared himself ready to transmit Lutze's plan to von Fritsch and his successor, von Brauchitsch, but stipulated that Lutze first provide proof that the Gestapo had used force to extract evidence against von Fritsch from Schmidt, the blackmailer.[90]

"A week or two later," Ulex records, "the Commander of SA Standarte Feldherrnhalle came to see me. On Lutze's instructions he informed me that his Chief was now in a position to bring proof that Schmidt's statements had been made under pressure from Himmler." Ulex thereupon went to von Fritsch and von Brauchitsch but neither was willing to take part in Lutze's plans for a putsch, Brauchitsch saying: "If these gentlemen want to do it, they must do it alone." The Commander-in-Chief of the Army, torn between his aversion to the regime and his sense of military duty, was once more placing his confidence in Hitler. But his credulity did not last long. He was later to have many occasions to recall his remark to Ulex: "I assure you that I will not rest until I have cleaned out the Himmler pig-sty."[91]

Lutze made continuous efforts to win over the vacillating C-in-C Army to his plan. His wife was related to the

General[92] and so he was continually hanging around him pouring anti-SS poison into his ear. The more menacing the war situation became and the more dangerously the power of the SS grew, the greater the urgency with which Lutze pressed his case. Senior members of the Party were well aware that Lutze was hand-in-glove with the military. Goebbels noted in his diary: "Unfortunately Lutze allowed his wife and the family's friendship with Brauchitsch to manoeuvre him into excessive opposition to the SS. Everywhere he criticises and grumbles. Everywhere he feels that his SA has been put in the shade. He has got into the wrong hands."[93]

As early as 12 March 1940 Berger noted: "The attitude of Lutze, the Chief of Staff, is gradually becoming a danger to the SS, if not to the Party. His 'communal evenings' particularly those attended by the Wehrmacht, are invariably used for anti-SS propaganda—and in a form unworthy of any decent person."[94] Berger continued that, when meeting Wehrmacht officers in public, Lutze "adopted an intolerable attitude towards the Reichsführer" and he ended: "In my view it is necessary to place Lutze under observation."[95]

Himmler's minions watched their enemy's every move. Not a detail escaped them. Lutze, for instance, had referred approvingly to a remark by Kerrl, the Reich Minister for Church Affairs, to the effect that Hitler had broken his promise of religious tolerance;[96] Lutze kept too many horses in his stables;[97] Lutze had ridiculed the SS as dagger-carrying numbskulls saying "We want ideas-merchants, not dagger-merchants"[98]—everything was noted down and reported to the Party Chancellery. SS Headquarters did not fail to observe that Lutze had meanwhile found a new ally—Hans Frank, the overlord of Poland and another enemy of the SS; Frank was only too willing to play off the SA against the tiresome SS/Police formations in the Government-General.

Initially Frank had set up a so-called "special branch," a sort of private police force responsible to him alone and available for use by any Head of a District. After a two-year battle, however, Krüger, HSSPF Cracow and Frank's bitterest rival, had succeeded in removing control of the "special branch" from the Governor-General.[99] At this moment—the end of 1942—the SA offered itself to

Frank as a new security service. Oberführer Pelz, the SA officer responsible for the Eastern territories, even attempted to take over Krüger's police duties, proposing that the SA be allowed into the Government-General in formed units to act as an auxiliary police force, clearly in the hope that the SA might counter-balance the SS and police formations.[100] On Himmler's instructions Krüger returned a flat negative.[101] But the SA had another card up its sleeve. Pelz offered his unit to the Headquarters of Air Region VIII, located in Cracow. This manoeuvre would have put the necessary weapons (machine guns and anti-aircraft guns) into the hands of the SA but at the last moment Krüger heard of the plan and managed to persuade the Air Region to withdraw its agreement.[102] Yet again the SA returned to the charge; it applied to the Reich Ministry for the East for approval to set up a construction service in all occupied Eastern territories. Berger, the watchdog, described the application as "illegal" and once more Himmler was able to scotch his adversary's intrigue.[103]

When, however, in February 1943, Himmler heard that Lutze had gone off to Frank's "kingdom" and had taken up residence in the Governor-General's villa in Bad Kryniza, he was seized with something approaching panic.[104] On 26 February 1943 he wrote a letter of complaint to Bormann: "I regard Lutze's visit to a spa in the Government-General as unfortunate; I consider it would be better if he took his cure in some German spa."[105]

A few months later Lutze was killed in a road accident.[106] The SS had lost a dangerous enemy; nevertheless the SA remained as a centre of anti-SS opposition to whom anyone involved in a struggle with the SS turned for assistance. Alfred Rosenberg, the Minister for the East, together with SA leaders and prominent Party members, was the next to take up the cudgels against excessive SS influence in the German-occupied East. Berger spied another dangerous anti-SS conspiracy forming. "I note to my astonishment," he reported to Himmler, "that a whole collection of Gauleiter are ranging themselves around Rosenberg and that he is regarded by the SA as the ultimate 'defender of the rights of man.' There are many senior Party leaders who consider the Reichsführer's position to be too powerful and who regard the development of the SS with a jaundiced eye."[107]

The Russian neo-colonialists closed their ranks firmly against the SS. Of the ten Commissars-General in the Eastern administration, two were Gauleiter, two SA-Obergruppenführer, one an NSKK Obergruppenführer, one a senior Party official, two officials of the Labour Service, and two civil servants—there was not a single SS man.[108] Enemies of the SS were everywhere, and opponents were to be found even in the most senior posts. In the Ukraine there was Reich Commissar Erich Koch, whom the SS had tried to sack in the mid-1930s;[109] in the Reich Commissariat "Ostland" there was Gauleiter Hinrich Lohse, whom Berger described as "a man without the smallest intelligence" and inspired by "limitless hatred for the SS";[110] the Reich Commissar-designate Moscow was SA-Obergruppenführer Siegfried Kasche, a Röhm putsch survivor who would seize any opportunity to sabotage the SS.[111]

Motives for the antipathy of all these men to the SS were as varied as their personalities. Koch, for instance, was a crude neo-imperialist and a savage oppressor of the Slav "sub-humans"; he disliked the SS because he suspected that it did not appreciate his master-race airs. Lohse resisted the SS because its methods bore an unpleasant similarity to those of the OGPU.

When HSSPF Ostland began exporting children from the Baltic States for "germanisation," Lohse reprimanded him for exceeding his authority and for political ineptitude; on 13 April 1942 he protested that he found "this kidnapping of children by the police both provocative and questionable; the Bolshevists also use their police to deport children for Bolshevist education."[112] In the Ukraine Koch felt that his HSSPF, Obergruppenführer Prützmann, was spying on him and missed no opportunity of snubbing the man; he was continually trying to reduce Prützmann's authority and even forbade him to accept orders from Himmler. There were frequent shouting matches which would bring Koch's staff running up. Prützmann reported one argument on 27 December 1942 as follows: "Koch replied that I was his subordinate and should accept orders only from him. Moreover he would have to get rid of me since he wanted an HSSPF who would do what he said. In addition to criticising my official actions, Koch

made a number of insulting personal accusations; this he
clearly did deliberately in order to increase the acrimony
of the discussion. Finally I bowed myself out, since Koch
declared at the top of his voice that he did not believe a
word I said."[113]

This sniping war between Koch and the SS did however
illustrate one thing: the Nazi internal quarrels in the East
did not spring solely from sheer lust for power on the part
of the SS; SS criticism of the corruption and arrogance of
the brown-shirted bosses also played its part and this inevitably brought the SS into increasingly open opposition
to the Party.

As a result of the change in the fortunes of war in the
East some of the more moderate SS leaders were having
second thoughts about the whole master-race concept and
felt that the Eastern peoples should be treated with more
circumspection. In the summer of 1943 even Berger
himself emerged as the champion of a more moderate
Eastern policy; he joined the Ministry for the East as Head
of an "operational staff in charge of political affairs" and
became one of Rosenberg's strongest allies against the
autocratic Koch.[114] The more the SS Eastern policy-
makers veered towards tolerance, the more violent became
their conflict with Koch and his supporter Bormann, the
Head of the Party Chancellery. The SD began to keep
records of Koch's atrocities.

The SD reports became so critical and Koch's protests
to Himmler so shrill that SS Gruppenführer Thomas, late
of France and now Sicherheitspolizei and SD Commander
Ukraine, forbade the SD representative on his staff to
report further on the Reich Commissar.[115] When the SD
reports on Koch continued, Himmler intervened: "These
SD reports must now finally cease; if they do not, the
SD will be disbanded and the officer responsible imprisoned."[116] The reports on Koch ceased.

The fact was that Himmler had suddenly glimpsed a
bottomless pit yawning in front of him and he recoiled.
The one thing which could really worry him was a head-
on collision with the Party.

Ever since the fortunes of war had ceased to smile
upon Adolf Hitler the centres of power within the regime
had crystallised with increasing clarity. As the months
went by SS and Party, starting from opposite poles, had

been gnawing their way through the timbers of the Reich towards the central focus of political power—and the moment could not be far distant when they would meet each other face to face. In the words of Professor Trevor-Roper "Throughout the war the Party machine like the SS had grown; like the SS it had encroached on the functions of the armed forces, especially in matters of administration and supply, fortification and evacuation; like the SS it had become more formidable and more indispensable with every defeat of German arms."[117] Moreover, since Hess had vanished to England the Party had found in Martin Bormann a leader determined to keep the SS at a distance from the Third Reich's ultimate levers of power. His methods were as unobtrusive as they were dangerous; he sat in the innermost sanctum of the Führer's headquarters, he was the channel of correspondence between Hitler and the Party, he ruled over the serried ranks of Gauleiter and Party functionaries—inconspicuous, ubiquitous and efficient.

For Himmler, the timorous small-timer, there could be no more torturing thought than the possibility that one day he might find himself involved in a duel with the Party. He knew only too well that the Party had no love for him. As long as he could do so without detriment to the prestige of the SS he must avoid open warfare. He had never managed to establish good relations with the Party bureaucracy. The majority of the Party activists were greedy schemers, avid for high-sounding titles and gold-braided uniforms and they despised this moralising schoolmaster, this desiccated inhuman figure with his clap-trap about an SS Order and Germanism. However many uniformed minions he collected around him, to the Party he remained an outsider. Powerful though he might appear, therefore, the Reichsführer reacted with extreme sensitivity to any criticism from the Party. Though privately he might growl that order would only return to Germany when the last Gauleiter had been hung from a lamp-post,[118] the Party hierarchy had only to clear its throat for Himmler to take fright.

Any number of examples of Himmler's susceptibility on this point can be quoted. He was repeatedly sending to the SD written orders to refrain from investigating Party functionaries or meddling in Party questions.[119] When Bormann's Chancellery complained about anti-Party sallies in the *Schwarze Korps*, he passed the complaints on—to the editors and in writing—with every evidence of vexation. When Gertrud Scholtz-Klink, the Reich women's leader, complained about the *Schwarze Korps* because Michel Mumm, the editorial office wag, had headed a perfectly ordinary announcement of the birth of a child to a local Nazi Group leader with the humorous comment "Our numbers rise,"[120] an office minute from Himmler gave it to be understood that: "The Reichsführer-SS desires that no more of Michel Mumm's efforts be published in the *Schwarze Korps* since they all too often lead to complaints."[121]

Whenever anyone complained, the editors of the *Schwarze Korps* could be sure that a reprimand from Himmler would arrive on their desks. Reichsleiter Karl Fiehler, for instance, objected that "as used to happen in Jewish rags" the paper was "seizing avidly upon any opportunity, possible or impossible, to label whole groups of officials as old-fashioned bureaucrats"[122] and Bormann demanded that attacks on individual Party members should cease.[123] On 2 May 1941 Himmler accordingly wrote: "The reason is that this once highly respectable newspaper has sunk to a kitchen gossip level. Once and for all stop these stupid little digs at people; they interest no one except, one supposes, the gentlemen who write them and who apparently derive some inner satisfaction therefrom."[124]

Himmler had a compelling private reason for remaining on good terms with Bormann. By 1940 he had lost all affection for his nervy shrewish wife Marga, and his ex-secretary Hedwig Potthast, an attractive girl from Cologne whom he had known since 1937, had become his mistress.[125] She was twenty-eight, the daughter of a businessman, and after graduating at the Industrial College in Mannheim, had joined the Reichsführer's personal staff as a secret.. y in the mid-1930s;[126] she soon came to exert a humanising and relaxing influence on the stiff prim Himmler.[127] Initially Himmler wished to get a divorce but could not quite bring himself to do so. The liaison had the usual results and early in 1942 Hedwig Potthast was expecting the birth of her first child, Helge (another daughter, Nanette Dorothea, was born in 1944).[128]

This produced a tricky problem for Himmler. Hedwig was lodging with a family, but she obviously could not continue there now that she was pregnant; he had to find her somewhere to live.[129] The problem was all the more urgent since Hedwig's parents, not realising how far the affair had gone, were continually urging her to give Himmler up.[130] Being a married man, they said, Himmler could never provide a respectable home for Haschen. Hedwig's sister-in-law Hilde, whose husband had been killed on the eastern front, became the intermediary between the girl and her parents. "For your parents' sake I would wish to see you married as soon as possible," she said[131]—and in another letter: "I fear, Hedwig, that there can never be a reconciliation [with the parents]. They would forgive everything at any time if you would give him up or if he would make himself a free man for your sake. What they cannot swallow is that you should go on living with him."[132] Hilde rubbed the point home: "He is after all married and your parents regard your relationship as dishonest towards his wife and disrespectful towards you. Your mother asked me whether his wife knew about it and unfortunately I had to tell her that as far as I knew this was not yet the case. She regarded this as proof of cold feet. Your parents are quite terribly distressed about it all."[133]

If Himmler was not to lose his Hedwig he had to find her somewhere to live. But how? He was lord of the SS empire, he was master of the SS economic enterprises and he was ruler of the greatest police machine in German history—but he had no private capital. He could think of nothing other than to do what other Party members did— apply for a loan to the Party Chancellery. Bormann was generous and allowed Himmler 80,000 marks[134] and with this sum he built a house for Hedwig Potthast in Berchtesgaden-Schönau near the Königssee.[135] It was named "Haus Schneewinkellehen" and was the basis of a temporary alliance between Himmler and Bormann, for Himmler's lonely mistress became friendly with Bormann's wife Gerda, who lived nearby.[136]

Like their womenfolk, Bormann and Himmler kept in close touch. One of Gerda Bormann's letters to her husband says "Oh Daddy, it doesn't bear imagining what would happen if you and Heinrich didn't see to everything.

The Führer would never be able to do it alone. So you two must keep well and take care of yourselves."[137] Martin Bormann took care. He took care that "Uncle Heinrich" did not become over-powerful, he encouraged him when he was having an attack of depression, he upbraided him if he ever allowed himself to criticise The Chief (Hitler). On one occasion Himmler lamented that Hitler was being unfair to him; he was apparently thought good for nothing but to raise new divisions for the Führer. Bormann calmed him down but at the same time warned him not to carry criticism of Adolf Hitler too far; to Gerda he wrote: "His chilly way of criticising is unpleasant. When all is said and done the Führer is the Führer. Where should we be without him?"[138]

So long as no vital SS interest was at stake, the Reichsführer had no intention of allowing the rapacity of his underlings to bring him into collision with this mentor who also controlled the only door to his wayward demigod, Hitler. Himmler forbade any criticism of the Party.

But Himmler had not reckoned upon the overweening ambition of those of his subordinates who had no private reasons to treat the Party gently—and of these the outstanding example was Otto Ohlendorf whose ideas on the Party were quite different. He was the archetype of the schizophrenic SS intellectual; in the same breath he could direct a vast army of spies and dream of the disbandment of the Party to make way for a cultural Order of National-Socialist noblemen. He was one of the most controversial characters in the entire SS world; Himmler regarded him as an intelligent machine but for the historian he is a puzzle—he directed the murder of 70,000 Jews[139] and at the same time was appalled by the crude methods of the brown-shirted bosses. To Himmler's misfortune this was the man at the head of the Inland-SD.

Ohlendorf's friends later tried to present him as a sort of resistance fighter inside the SS, as the mouthpiece of a "positive opposition."[140] They carefully omitted to mention that this opposition was involuntary; Ohlendorf was the victim rather than the master of a chain of events which he himself had initiated. As already related, Ohlendorf had had the idea of instituting a sort of secret Gallup poll to produce unvarnished accounts of all movements of opinion within Germany and these were made known to senior leaders in the "Reports from the Reich" issued two or three times per week. Here inevitably lay the germ of serious conflict; the SD was forbidden to investigate the Party; if, however, the SD "Reports from the Reich" were to cover all so-called "spheres of life," how could they omit the most important political sphere of life—the Party?

With satisfaction mixed with consternation, Ohlendorf realised that hardly a detail of the Party's squabbles escaped his observers. The SD faithfully recorded the megalomania and arrogance of the bosses, the ineffectiveness of Party propaganda and mismanagement by Gau or District Headquarters. Vainly he sought to put a brake on the mechanism which he himself had set in motion, assuring senior SD leaders that "by far his greatest worry" was the fear lest the SD reports give the impression that the Party was "something negative or hostile" and that "the Führer, the Reichsführer and the SS were opposed to the Party bureaucracy."[141]

In every order he protested that the whole purpose of the SD was to reinforce the rule of National-Socialism. "The legal position," he said in an SD directive of 1941, must "invariably be consonant with the political and ideological principles of National-Socialism." He proclaimed that the law "had not yet succeeded in bringing the administration of justice entirely into line with the political requirements for the security of our order of society."[142]

On the basic question of human liberties his thinking hardly differed from that of the barbaric manipulators of the law like Roland Freisler. In a draft for a lecture to be given in October 1942 he described Hans Frank, the opponent of the police state, as an accomplice of British plutocrats and with his own perverse brilliance proved that the illegal was merely a superior form of legality. The object of the law, he argued, was to protect the community, not the individual; the protection of the law was synonymous with the protection of the Reich; wherever the latter was endangered by ideologically unreliable judges, the police must undertake the "correction of inadequate sentences" and "counteract the prevailing leniency in the administration of justice." He referred to the protection of the law as "that well-worn phrase."[143]

In the light of such fanatical National-Socialist orthodoxy Ohlendorf, the puritan, spied all sorts of inadequacies, stupidities and depravities disfiguring his idealised picture of National-Socialism. He could not share the calculated optimism of those around him; every fresh report from his informers reinforced his conviction that the Party was suffering from a cancer which would infect the still healthy parts of the regime. Himmler ruminated: "He has trouble with his liver and gall-bladder. His reports are always gloomy; he has the pessimistic outlook which goes with physical suffering. Liver and gall-bladder troubles always have that effect on the mind."[144] It never occurred to Himmler that the cause of Ohlendorf's suffering was the gloomy reading made by the SD daily reports. Every page proved that public opinion was turning against the Party and the regime.

A report from SD Aussenstelle Bunde, 13 May 1941 read: "Hardly anything has produced so paralysing a shock as the news that the Führer's Deputy [Hess] has flown to England. The craziest rumours are going round and people simply do not believe that some mental aberration can in fact have been the reason. Other people talk of a moral defeat, of another major breach of faith by one of the 'old fighters.' "[145]

Report from SD Aussenstelle Minden, 24 July 1941: "The initial effect upon the majority of the population of Sunday's event—war with Russia—has been one of paralysis. Moreover the fact that the Führer called for God's blessing upon this struggle has contributed to the state of public opinion, which can hardly be described as rosy."[146]

The more the fortunes of war turned against Germany the more pessimistic the SD reports became and the more often was their criticism directed primarily against the propaganda put out by Goebbels and the Party. Report of 12 January 1942: "According to the attached reports from SD Aussenstelle Erfurt the population's reaction to the propaganda appearing in the press over the last few weeks has been particularly unfavourable. Especially in the *Thüringer Gauzeitung* both the headlines and the comments on individual reports have been so unrealistic and the conclusions drawn so fanciful that the newspaper can hardly continue to be taken seriously."[147]

"The article by Dr Goebbels in *Reich* of 11 January 1942 has evoked no applause from the population. His statement that Churchill's place is on the variety stage and not at the head of an empire is liable to lead to underestimation of our enemy. As German propaganda's supreme director Dr Goebbels should really now cease to indulge in such fatuities."[148] Goebbels in fact became the standard Aunt Sally of the SD reports; on another of his articles SD Erfurt commented: "Such remarks might perhaps have been acceptable from a street warden during an air-raid practice; coming from the Reich Minister of Propaganda they can only be described as sub-standard."[149]

Ohlendorf's "Reports from the Reich" soon became known in the Party and the Party organisation men took fright. A wave of Party indignation, touched off by certain prominent Gauleiter, descended on the SD's investigation system. Leading Nazi functionaries were continually complaining to Martin Bormann and accusing the Reichsführer-SS of allowing the SD to exceed its authority. As the months passed the tone of the complaints became sharper until they might have been referring to agents of a foreign power. Hans Frank, the Governor-General of Poland, for instance, voiced "most serious misgiving concerning the so-called confidential information reports about the Government-General which the so-called SD continuously brandishes about the Reich." They were "simply low-level spy stories."[150] On 30 November 1942 Gauleiter Albert Florian fulminated: "My suspicion, hitherto unfortunately lacking evidence, that the SD was in fact rummaging around in Party matters is now fully substantiated. I am therefore compelled to take my own measures. I propose to forbid any political director or member of my staff to undertake any duty on behalf of the SD; alternatively I shall make such action dependent upon approval by the District Governor concerned or by myself."[151]

On 22 January 1943 Gauleiter Carl Weinrich stated: "I refuse once and for all to allow the SD to poke its nose into my affairs. After all we are not in Russia and do not need to be shadowed by an OGPU."[152]

The SD now found itself the target for a general attack by the Party functionaries, employing every form of subtlety and designed to uncover and paralyse its informer network. At a meeting of his local Group leaders Kampe,

the Kreisleiter [District Leader] of Danzig, called out
"Who among you is a so-called contact man for the SD?"
When Pohle, the local Group leader from Praust, admitted
as much, Kampe loosed a flood of invective on his head;
Richard Hildebrandt, the HSSPF, reported that "Kampe's
description of the contact man compared him to a stateless, characterless intelligence agent." Kampe's anti-SD
outburst was greeted with thunderous applause by the
other local Group leaders, one shouting "Spy!" and
another "Cheka methods!" One Group leader confided to
Hildebrandt: "I must say that I was really astounded at the
hatred of the SS among the political leaders."153

Any SD informer discovered by the indignant Party
sleuths was faced with an ultimatum—to make up his mind
whether he belonged to the Party or the SS—and some
Nazi officials imposed a complete boycott on the SD.

As the Party complaints increased in vehemence Himmler gave way. On 18 March 1943 he sent a letter to
Bormann assuring him that "as before" the SD had "the
strictest orders not to concern itself with internal Party
matters."154 Bormann declared himself satisfied with
Himmler's assurance—he knew that Himmler disliked the
intellectual Ohlendorf more than any other SS leader.

"To be quite frank," Himmler confided to Kersten, "I
don't care for the man. He has no sense of humour. He is
one of those unbearable people who always know better.
Having his Gold Party Badge and being one of the first
recruits to the SS, he regards himself as the Galahad of
National-Socialism."155 Rudolf Brandt, Himmler's personal
assistant, said that Himmler "feels that Ohlendorf is continually watching over him like a second Reichsführer; he
is a man who always knows better and has the ability to
Ohlendorf was undoubtedly the last man for whom
Himmler would risk a quarrel with the Party. He cut the
SD down to size; SD planning was continuously being
upset by some pronouncement from Himmler.

The "Reports from the Reich" frequently came back to
Ohlendorf mangled by Himmler; the Reichsführer repeatedly threatened to have Ohlendorf arrested and the
Inland-SD disbanded if it continued to deal with Party
matters.157 Although they were probably the most realistic
reflections of the true position, he refused to show the
reports to Hitler, saying to Kersten: "They are usually so

pessimistic that this is quite out of the question; they would only impair the Führer's capacity for action."

"Supposing they are true?" Kersten asked.

"That doesn't matter," Himmler replied. "Details which are unhelpful must be kept from the Führer, however important they may appear."[158]

But Ohlendorf showed no inclination to obey his Reichsführer's orders and the SD continued to keep watch on the Party functionaries. The much-abused Goebbels, together with Martin Bormann, thereupon decided that a steam-hammer must be used to crack this nut. Goebbels demanded that the "Reports from the Reich" either be banned or at least co-ordinated with the reports of the Reich propaganda offices—which of course were under his orders. The readers of the SD reports, Goebbels said, who included officials in Government offices, were being given information about Party matters and this was the responsibility of the Party Chancellery alone.[159]

Goebbels fired the first shot in the anti-SD campaign—he banned distribution of the reports within his Ministry; Hans Fritzsche, the Director of Broadcasting, remembers him saying that they were "calculated to give to leading Party and State circles a defeatist impression of the people's morale and the prospects of the war."[160] Himmler withdrew an inch or two. On 12 May 1943 Goebbels noted in his diary: "Himmler is now ready to have the SD report stopped . . . as its effect is too defeatist."[161] Here, however, Goebbels was being premature—Himmler waited to see what Bormann would do.

For some time Bormann had made no move but then something happened which radically altered his relationship with Himmler—in August 1943 Himmler was appointed Reich Minister of the Interior. Party and SS were now face to face; the confrontation between the two power groups began.

It was soon borne in on Himmler that something had changed. Bormann now joined the anti-SD ranks and demanded strict adherence to Party orders—and these prescribed that both the formulation of opinions on internal Party matters and evaluation of the political reliability of Government officials were the business of the Party alone. Gradually the SD's enemies closed in; in summer 1943 the distribution list of the "Reports from the Reich" was severely restricted and a year later the reports were banned altogether.[162] Simultaneously Bormann forbade both full-time and part-time Party functionaries to work with the SD and shortly thereafter the Labour Front followed suit—the SA, as we have seen, had already done so.[163]

One would have expected Himmler to protest against the emasculation of his SD and at last mobilise the power which he undoubtedly possessed. But he did nothing of the sort: he made no move at all. Ohlendorf raged; "He had power but in practice he made no use of it in Germany; he and his power were a pricked balloon."[164] Himmler, the tactician, could think of only one method of saving the SD: negotiations with the Party Chancellery for a new SD field of activity had already begun, and he allowed them to drag on, hoping for some miracle to appear. At the end of the war he was still negotiating.[165] Evidently he had no faith in their success, for he had long since lopped certain responsibilities in the field of Police Law off the Reich Ministry of the Interior and given them to the SD in order to ensure that it had something to do and therefore some justification for existence.[166]

This withdrawal by Himmler was a good example of a flaw in the SS system which was usually concealed by the façade of totalitarian solidarity. The SS never dared to wage open warfare against the Party because its leaders did not really agree where their true interests lay. The monolithic unity of the SS was in fact no more than a myth carefully cultivated by the SS propagandists.

Himmler was under no illusions that his dream of unshakable SS unity was anything but a figment of the imagination. As early as 1940 he had confided to the officers of the Leibstandarte the "anxieties which sometimes beset me . . . This Waffen-SS will live only if the SS as a whole lives—if the entire Corps becomes a real Order living according to these laws and realising that one part without the other is unthinkable."[167] Speaking to SS-Gruppenführer in Poznan in October 1943 he was even more explicit: "Doom!—if a split develops between the SS and the police. Doom!—if some well-meaning but misguided notion of their responsibilities leads the Hauptämter to try to make themselves independent each with their own channel of command to their subordinates. I sincerely believe that if that were so and if one day I were to be shot down, it would be the end of the SS," and he continued with his gloomy picture of the decline of the SS: "Doom! —if the separate Hauptämter or the individual heads of department have a false picture of their mission . . . Doom!—if we ever allow these ties [between the various SS organisations] to loosen; then you may be sure that in a generation or less all would sink back into its old mediocrity."[168]

Such desperate appeals for unity showed that Himmler resembled the entrepreneur obsessed with the expansion of his business who sets up ever more numerous and ever larger installations and then finds that he is in danger of losing control of them all. Similarly Himmler, a timorous and mistrustful being anyway, must sometimes have wondered whether he was still master in his own house. The more dynamic and rapacious the SS empire became, the more obvious it was that its component parts were gathering a momentum of their own and visibly divorcing themselves from Himmler; the more self-assertive subordinates acted as if they were independent authorities. Moreover the continuous growth of the SS organisation forced Himmler to accept into his Order men who by no means measured up to the standards of pure-blooded National-Socialism.

Even the senior ranks gradually became filled with so heterogeneous a collection of men that the SS turned into a curiously pluralistic organisation for a totalitarian dictatorship under the Führer. It resembled a gigantic sponge, sucking up men of the most contradictory characters—so contradictory that it frequently had difficulty in presenting a solid front to the outside world. Andreas Schmidt, leader of the German minority in Rumania and son-in-law to Gottlob Berger, complained indignantly: "It is unfortunately a fact that in difficult times even members of the SS do not present a common front; when times are difficult they intrigue all the more, thus considerably increasing already existing difficulties."[169]

The multifarious interests of the SS subsidiary organisations, and the conviction dinned into them over the years that they belonged to a superior and select group of men, had built up a superiority complex which at times worked against the overall interests of the Order. Thirsting for

power and prestige, SS leaders often fought each other
to the detriment of the SS as a whole and there were
even instances of naked cabalistic intrigue causing senior
SS commanders to oppose the interests and orders of
Himmler. The appointment of the HSSPF [Höhere SS-
und Polizeiführer—Senior SS and Police Commanders] is
a good illustration of Himmler's difficulty in asserting his
authority in the jungle of the warring SS cliques. The
HSSPF were his most important representatives and yet
it was all he could do to ensure that they were treated with
proper respect; in many instances insults and contempt
were the order of the day.

Himmler had created the post of HSSPF in 1937 with
two objects; on the "Land" level (paralleling Himmler at
the centre) to amalgamate the SS and police into one
State Protection Corps; secondly, as Himmler's representatives, to supervise all SS units.[170] By creating the HSSPF
Himmler had hoped to keep ahead of developments. As
the SS continued to expand and spawn fresh organisations,
Himmler was haunted by the nightmare that the individual
components of the SS empire might claim their independence and the senior bureaucrats of the subsidiary organisations, the heads of the SS Hauptämter, might undermine
his position as the supreme autocrat. Himmler therefore
regarded the HSSPF not only as the cement binding
together the pluralist SS society but also as the counter-
weight to the growing power of the Hauptämter.

The Berlin Hauptämter accordingly left no stone unturned to reduce these viceroys of the SS Sultan to the
status of delegates with sonorous titles but without power.
Moreover the traditionalist official administration refused
to allow the upstart HSSPF any disciplinary authority
under administrative law, and to conceal his purpose from
the recalcitrant administration Himmler was forced to
restrict the HSSPF to purely representative functions.[171]
Accordingly their SS rivals initially had an easy run.

In occupied Europe, however, where the obstacle of an
established administration did not exist, Himmler could
give his HSSPF more authority; yet even here pretending
that the HSSPF did not exist became a recognised sport
for local SS units. The SS and Police Hauptämter took
precautions to ensure that the HSSPF did not become
over-powerful. Hauptamt Orpo, for instance, repeatedly re-

fused to grant them authority to punish or promote
personnel of the Ordnungspolizei;[172] the Chief of the Ordnungspolizei insisted that in Russia the HSSPF were
subordinate to him.[173] SS Commanders repeatedly showed
that they did not take Himmler's representatives very
seriously. The local concentration-camp Commandant in
Hamburg, for instance, refused to tell his HSSPF how
many prisoners he had, saying that he was pledged to
secrecy; SS-Oberführer Leo von Jena, Commanding 8 SS
Totenkopf Standarte, disputed the right of Krüger, the
HSSPF, to demand from him reports on the strength,
dispositions and morale of his troops.[174]

The fiercest resistance against the attempts by the
HSSPF to exercise command authority came from the
Waffen-SS. When Krüger ordered von Jena to take up
new positions for a proposed operation against Polish
partisans, Jena refused and referred Krüger to the Inspector General of Reinforced Totenkopf Standarte, who
alone was authorised to order changes of this nature.[175]
Himmler was so vexed by the unruliness of his subordinates that he issued additional orders concerning the
authority of the HSSPF; in the case of the Waffen-SS, he
said, it appeared that existing orders "in practice" permitted the HSSPF "to assist the Waffen-SS" but that
"otherwise they were looked upon as tiresome outsiders."[176] On 16 March 1942 Himmler warned the
refractory heads of the Hauptämter: "I would like all my
heads of department to think whether they would themselves wish to be an HSSPF under such degrading
conditions of impotence. I would also ask them to consider
what the SS and police would look like in ten years time if
I allowed such a state of affairs to continue."[177] Himmler
then armed his satraps with increased plenary powers. In
their areas the HSSPF were given authority over all
Allgemeine-SS offices, commanders of the Ordnungspolizei, the Sicherheitspolizei and SD, and overall representatives of VOMI and the RKF Staff Department.[178]
A draft order of January 1943 prepared by Himmler's
Personal Staff, laid down that the HSSPF were "responsible
for seeing that all offices of the Allgemeine-SS, the Waffen-
SS, the Ordnungspolizei and the SD act in a manner
worthy of the SS and present a good appearance."[179] So
the HSSPF were now entitled to claim that they alone

were responsible for all that went on within the SS in their respective areas.[180]

Nevertheless the Hauptämter contrived to chip away at the authority of the HSSPF; "provisional service regulations" for HSSPF dated 8 January 1943, for instance, stated that all members of the SS were under the HSSPF "for matters of general behaviour in accordance with SS standards"; "orders and instructions on technical matters," however, could be issued "to those SS members for whom they were technically responsible" only by the Hauptämter.[181] When the HSSPF complained that they were still being sabotaged by the Hauptämter, Himmler extended their authority yet again. Local SS leaders were ordered to report to their HSSPF before any duty trip to their Hauptamt, and applications for leave also had to be countersigned by the HSSPF.[182] Nevertheless Himmler was only too well aware that the authority of his HSSPF was often as fictitious as the unity of the SS. In 1943 he declaimed: "This SS Order with all its ramifications, all its basic organisations . . . must continue even under the tenth Reichsführer-SS . . . all must remain as one block, one body, one Order."[183] The files of the innumerable disciplinary and arbitration Courts, however, show that in practice the Order was little better than an arena in which the most diverse and antagonistic elements struggled for mastery—hardly a single senior SS leader was not accusing one of his colleagues of disloyalty to the policy or ideology of the SS.

In such a maze of individual and factional interests true solidarity was hardly possible. Even Himmler could not impose unity on such perplexing multiplicity. The SS leaders' rugged individualism was proof even against the person of the Reichsführer himself. In fact "Reichsheini" with his inelegant semi-comic figure, found it difficult to assert his authority when face to face with his subordinates. For this reason Himmler disliked receiving several people at a time; he felt more secure behind his mountains of files and the incessant barrage of orders which he loosed upon his realm.

However, Himmler had his own methods of curbing the impetuosity of his subordinates. Reprimands in severe schoolmasterish style, a spy system covering even the most senior SS leaders and the distribution of orders to the widest possible circle of his subordinates, combined to form a control system calculated to nip in the bud the growth of any new centres of power within the SS. His continuous warnings and scoldings were intended constantly to remind the SS leaders that the Reichsführer was the sole source of their power.

Himmler to SS-Brigadeführer Hintze: "I have given you this chance to be an HSSPF; if your lack of self-control, drunkenness and megalomania prevent you making use of it, it is your own fault if you get no further."[184] Shortly thereafter a further reprimand: "Report to SS-Obergruppenführer Jeckeln as instructed. Don't make so many speeches and get on with your job."[185] To SS-Oberführer Professor Arnold Waldschmidt, "as an old Party member and SS man, I expect you in future to represent the views of the Führer faithfully and without question. Although you have done great damage to the reputation of Germanism and of the SS, I do not propose to proceed further on this occasion. Until further notice, however, you will not receive authorisation for journeys abroad."[186]

Even the most reliable Obergruppenführer received their reprimands. To HSSPF South West: "In this serious moment I request you at last to display that energy and drive necessary to avert panic situations."[187] To Oberstgruppenführer Kurt Daluege, his old crony and rival: "I implore you to strike with an iron hand and abolish totally that spirit of officialdom still to be found here and there; have it out by the roots."[188] He even intervened in the private lives of his officers; on 16 May 1944 he wrote to HSSPF Denmark: "Dear Pancke, I request you to discipline your wife and to stop her voicing her opinions loud and clear in the most improbable places concerning this or that political occurrence in the Gau or concerning the Gauleiter himself. In general I have the impression that in your marriage you do not exert sufficient control and that you have not educated your young wife in the manner which I have a right to expect from an SS leader."[189]

Senior SS officers were kept under observation and any irregularity in their private lives was noted. Many of them were persecuted by anonymous letters which Himmler took with extreme seriousness.

One SS leader kept watch upon another. Obergruppenführer Wolff faced Gruppenführer Kaltenbrunner with a report to the effect that he was misusing Government petrol for journeys to his home;[190] Brigadeführer Ohlendorf presented Obergruppenführer Wolff with a report showing that official vehicles were delivering an extraordinary number of geese and ducks to Wolff's house.[191] Himmler distrusted even the older SS commanders, employing outsiders to keep an eye on them. In 1940 he discovered a super-watchdog who was not even a member of the SS and who rapidly became its most hated and most exploited figure.[192]

The whipping-boy was named Dr Richard Korherr, a devout Catholic and one of the most brilliant statisticians in the Reich. Nazi District Headquarters Würzburg described him as "a timorous personality somewhat shy, irritable and sensitive"[193]—hardly the man to clamp down on the forceful self-seekers of the Hauptämter. Exactly this, however, was what Himmler proposed to the unsuspecting Korherr; as "Inspector for Statistics attached to the Reichsführer-SS and Chief of the German Police and Reich Commissar for the strengthening of Germanism," he was to check information and reports coming from the Hauptämter. In a solid phalanx the heads of the Hauptämter prepared to run this intruder out of business. Even the dutiful Berger, normally so concerned for his Reichsführer's prestige, attempted to muzzle Himmler's watchdog, saying "you, Korherr, join me. I will make you a Standartenführer." But Korherr refused.[194]

Korherr soon uncovered the falsehoods, both great and small, with which the heads of the Hauptämter embellished their success stories to Himmler. He told Himmler "Without the smallest detriment to the work of the offices I could now extract from the SS Hauptämter three battle-strength divisions";[195] he pointed out that a report from Lebensborn on infant mortality was a "stinking lie from beginning to end."[196] Dr Gregor Ebner, the head of Lebensborn, had reported that the infant mortality rate in his maternity home was 4 per cent, 2 per cent lower than the average in Germany at the time. Korherr discovered that the actual mortality rate in the Lebensborn homes was 8 per cent. Furiously Ebner demanded that the tiresome Korherr be placed under arrest.[197]

Finally one of the Hauptamt Chiefs resorted to physical

violence. On 12 August 1943 Obergruppenführer Richard Hildebrandt, the new Head of the RuSHA, summoned Korherr and accused him of claiming the right to pass judgement upon the Hauptämter. The subsequent scene was reported to Himmler by Korherr as follows: "I made as if to go, when Obergruppenführer Hildebrandt said 'I will have no more of your insolence.' I threw back: 'The insolence is on your side,' saluted and made for the door. Obergruppenführer Hildebrandt followed and gave me two resounding smacks, one on each cheek. As far as I remember he then said 'And now get out,' though I could not swear to it. I departed without a word or any attempt to retaliate."[198]

Seething with anger, Korherr awaited satisfaction, but the weeks went by and the Reichsführer made no move to support his statistician. All Himmler could extract from Hildebrandt was a half-hearted apology addressed, not to Korherr, but to Himmler: "Honoured Reichsführer, I respectfully request you to express my regret to Oberregierungsrat Doctor Korherr for the physical assault which I made upon him. Heil Hitler! Yours: Hildebrandt."[199]

Richard Korherr had learned his lesson. Himmler was clearly in no position to protect his own inspector. Korherr took himself off to the neighbourhood of Regensburg where, on Himmler's orders, he set up a scientific statistical institute—out of reach of the Heads of the Hauptämter.[200] The Korherr episode showed how independent the Hauptämter had become within the SS. In fact they only closed their ranks if some common danger threatened; in normal circumstances they operated separately and each went its own way. After the war SS-Oberführer Reinecke said: "Instead of working more closely together, as Himmler had intended, these organisations, due to their varied tasks, steadily drifted away from each other."[201]

Frequently they pursued totally contradictory policies, for instance: the RSHA pressed for the total annihilation of all Jews but the WVHA advocated the preservation of all Jews capable of work;[202] in occupation policy in Russia the RSHA clung to the "Russian subhuman" theory whereas the SS Hauptamt pressed for the formation of a Russian shadow army under German leadership;[203] on questions of State security (such as monitoring enemy broadcasts) the Gestapo adopted a much tougher line than the SD;[204] the WVHA strove to exempt its various concerns from all control by the State, whereas a group of SS officers led by Ohlendorf visualised stricter supervision of SS economic undertakings by the Reich authorities.[205] In Rumania there were no fewer than four lines of SS policy: the SS Hauptamt wished to recruit the maximum number of "racial Germans"; VOMI thought similarly but was even more radical; the VDA [Verein Deutscher in Ausland—Union of Germans Abroad] was opposed to VOMI; and finally the Consul General (an SS-Oberführer) pursued a policy of his own.[206] The clearest example, however, of the tendency towards independence shown by the various parts of the SS is the story of the Führungshauptamt [Operational Headquarters], the headquarters of the armed force which carried the SS terror onto the battlefields of Europe, and yet increasingly divorced itself from the ideology of the SS Order: this was the Waffen-SS.

16

The Waffen-SS

IN March 1942 the RSHA forwarded to Himmler a secret SD report showing what the Germans thought of Adolf Hitler's most merciless and most feared force of armed men. "Basically," the report said, "it may be stated that by its achievements the Waffen-SS has won its place in the popular esteem. Particular reference is made to the good comradeship and excellent relations between officers, NCOs and men."

On the other hand, the SD indicated "voices are to be heard saying that the Waffen-SS possesses no trained officers and that SS men are therefore 'recklessly sacrificed.' The Waffen-SS is said to 'rush on regardless' because it thinks that it must 'get ahead' of the Wehrmacht." Worse still: "Critical voices are to be heard saying that the Waffen-SS is a sort of 'military watchdog.' SS men are trained to be brutal and ruthless, apparently so that they can be used against other German formations if necessary." General impression: "The Waffen-SS is the most ruthless force; it takes no prisoners but totally annihilates its enemy."[1]

The popular picture of the Waffen-SS as presented by the SD was accurate; this force, which more than any other SS formation reflected the heterogeneous character, the horror and the idealism of Himmler's Order, was regarded by many Germans with a mixture of admiration and fear. The Waffen-SS was the Imperial Guard of the National-Socialist regime; in the Second World War its soldiers scored one military success after another, but its commanders were too rugged and too independent to accept their Reichsführer's ideological fantasies without demur.

The Waffen-SS had been conceived as the Party's Brigade of Guards; it had been trained for the merciless fanatical war of ideology; but as the years went by its divorce from the remainder of the Order became increasingly obvious. The daily grind of World War II turned the Reichsführer's legionaries into practically normal soldiers, almost indistinguishable from those of the Wehrmacht. The collective judgment of the Nuremberg Court, however, branded the Waffen-SS as an "Army of Outlaws" (Felix Steiner's title) and a collection of political fanatics. The Waffen-SS soldiers found themselves stripped of their military character and equated with the RSHA's murder commandos and the concentration-camp torturers.

The ex-Wehrmacht officers could have corrected this distorted picture of the Waffen-SS but the majority preferred to hold their tongues. Many were apparently unable to remember that they had once been glad to have the elite Waffen-SS Divisions fighting alongside them. Some even contributed to this blanket condemnation of the SS troops. Field-Marshal Kesselring described the formation of the Waffen-SS as "the game of a spoilt child";[2] General Westphal complained that the Waffen-SS had "diverted the best-quality reinforcements and newly trained men from the Army";[3] Field-Marshal von Manstein grumbled that it "paid a toll of blood incommensurate with its actual gains."[4] Some of the senior soldiers apparently suffered from lapses of memory. During the defensive battles west of Kharkov in August 1943 von Manstein acknowledged that by throwing back the Soviet forces which had broken through in the Bielgorod-Valki area, the SS Division "Das Reich" had made a German counter-offensive possible. In his memoirs, however, he is silent on the subject.[5]

Such deliberate discretion provoked a counter-offensive from the ex-Waffen-SS commanders; as memoir-writers the SS Generals proved worthy competitors of the Wehrmacht—at least insofar as calculated loss of memory was concerned. The leading Waffen-SS apologists were Oberstgruppenführer and Colonel-General (retired) Paul Hausser, his late fellow-General Felix Steiner and the spokesmen of the "Mutual Aid Society for ex-soldiers of the Waffen-

SS," all of whom attempted to prove the unprovable—that the Waffen-SS, had never been anything but a purely military force. The worst offenders were the "Mutual Aid Society"; by quoting fictitious extracts from Hitler's speeches and falsifying dates, they have attempted to prove that the background to the Waffen-SS and its predecessor the SS-Verfügungstruppe (VT) was entirely non-political. The VT, they say, was formed only after the proclamation of universal military service in 1935 and was a "fourth arm of the Service," a "modern experimental force."[6]

In fact the history of the Waffen-SS goes back much further—to the first months following the National-Socialist seizure of power, when the SS started to form armed units. Even at this early stage battle groups armed with personal weapons appeared in the Abschnitte and Oberabschnitte of the Allgemeine-SS; they were designed to ensure that the SA army treated the SS with proper respect and to terrorise the democratic opposition which, though defeated, was still active.

As a general rule in each SS Abschnitt some 100 armed SS men formed themselves into a so-called "Headquarters Guard," a title which in itself shows that initially the primary purpose of these units was to satisfy some local SS leader's desire for martial pomp and circumstance; in many cases Himmler was not even consulted. Once a headquarters Guard was fully trained it called itself a Sonderkommando [special detachment] and acted as an auxiliary police force, the object here being to get its pay carried on the local police budget.[7] If a Sonderkommando rose to more than company strength, it was entitled to call itself a Politische Bereitschaft [Political Alarm Squad]; it was then organised on full military lines with sections, platoons, Stürme [companies] and Sturmbanne [battalions].[8]

The entire country was eventually covered by a network of Politische Bereitschaften training armed SS men for the practice of political terror on the home front. In Wolterdingen, Arolsen, Ellwangen, Leisnig, Württemberg and Saxony, for example, Politische Bereitschaften practised for the German civil war,[9] which for a few hours on 30 June 1934 threatened to become a gruesome reality.

Among these political warriors from the Allgemeine-SS, the best-known unit was one created by Adolf Hitler himself. He had formed a "Headquarters Guard" for his personal protection and placed at its head a shrewd and effective Upper Bavarian SS-Gruppenführer, Josef ("Sepp") Dietrich. Dietrich, born in 1892, had had a varied career—farm labourer, waiter, NCO in a tank unit, policeman, foreman in a tobacco factory, customs officer and petrol-pump attendant;[10] he was one of those quick-witted Bavarian toughs who rode in Hitler's Mercedes during his oratorical tours of Germany, and whom the Party wags dubbed the "chauffeureska."[11] Hitler found a variety of jobs for his versatile bodyguard to do; when he joined the Party in 1928, Dietrich worked as a despatcher in the Nazi-owned publishing firm, Franz Eher of Munich; he then organised the SS in Southern Bavaria and in 1931 became head of SS Oberabschnitt North in Hamburg; on the Nazi seizure of power he was summoned to the Chancellery as Hitler's chief bodyguard.[12]

On 17 March 1933, on Hitler's instructions, Dietrich formed the "SS Headquarters Guard Berlin" consisting of 120 selected men from Hitler's former bodyguard in Munich; initially it was housed in the Alexander Barracks near the Friedrichstrasse underground station.[13] From this unit sprang the most memorable force in National-Socialist military history—the "Leibstandarte Adolf Hitler." Initially its development hardly differed from that of the other Politische Bereitschaften; it grew to a strength of two companies and was then organised as an SS Sonderkommando; in spring 1933 it was re-named "Guard Battalion Berlin" and moved to the barracks of the former Cadet College, Berlin-Lichterfelde; shortly thereafter it was reinforced by three additional companies trained in the military manoeuvre area at Jüterbog.[14]

No. 9 Infantry Regiment Potsdam took care of the Leibstandarte's military training,[15] for the requirements of modern war were well beyond the capacity of ex-Sergeant-Major Dietrich. The sceptics subsequently required much convincing that the first Colonel-General of the Waffen-SS possessed any great military qualities. Dietrich's friends were reduced to arguing that he had once served in a tank regiment, undoubtedly possessed exceptional moral courage, and his rugged independence and nonchalant disregard of orders from Himmler made him highly popular with his men; he was therefore a sort of natural soldier, they said. In fact he was barely fit to command a regiment. Wilhelm Bittrich, the ex-Obergruppenführer, recalls: "I once spent an hour and a half trying to explain a situation to Sepp Dietrich with the aid of a map. It was quite useless. He understood nothing at all."[16]

Such failings on the part of his guard commander left Hitler unmoved. The new unit was intended to be, not a military fighting formation but the Third Reich's Household Troops, and ceremonial unit. Very soon it assumed responsibility for the protection of Hitler's person in a manner obvious for all the world to see. Later it provided the personnel on duty inside the new Reich Chancellery. The double sentries in their black uniform with white belts, white gloves and white shirts posted at the entrance to Hitler's study[17] symbolised the opening of a new era—the formation of a second armed force parallel to the Wehrmacht.

At the Nuremberg Party Rally in September 1933 Hitler named the guard battalion after himself; henceforth it was permitted to call itself the Leibstandarte Adolf Hitler.[18] Two months later, on the tenth anniversary of the Munich beer-cellar putsch, the Leibstandarte swore eternal allegiance to its patron.[19] Hardly a soul perceived, however, that both in military and in constitutional terms a miniature revolution had taken place; the men of the Leibstandarte had sworn their oath to the Chancellor, Adolf Hitler, whereas constitutionally the President of the Reich was sole Commander-in-Chief of all armed forces; nowhere was it laid down that the Reich Chancellor might maintain a private army.[20] Though the Leibstandarte was only a few hundred strong at the time, Hitler's action illustrated the duality which was to be the hallmark of the later Waffen-SS; he had created a unit under his exclusive personal command—one day he could use it as a military force, the next as an instrument of political terror, if necessary even against the nation's constitutional armed forces, the Reichswehr.

Anyone who doubted whether this was in fact the case was given his lesson on that bloody Saturday, 30 June 1934. Two companies of the Leibstandarte moved to Bavaria with orders to seize and arrest the SA leaders

assembled in Bad Wiessee.[21] Then in the courtyard of
Stadelheim Prison, Munich, a special detachment under
Dietrich mowed down six prominent SA commanders,[22]
while in Berlin roving commandos of the Leibstandarte
hunted anti-Nazis and executed them in the courtyard of
the Lichterfelde Barracks. The Politische Bereitschaften
also took part in the bloody chase. Politische Bereitschaft
SS 3 (Saxony) murdered nine unpopular Party members;
other Bereitschaften in West and South Germany arrested
suspect SA leaders.[23]

The intervention of the Politische Bereitschaften
whetted Himmler's ambition to form a large-scale armed
force. Hitler agreed and promised the Reichsführer sufficient equipment from confiscated SA stocks to form a
sizable body—and this in spite of the fact that the Reichswehr Generals were already grumbling that the SS was
starting to compete with them as a military unit. Hitler
proceeded with sufficient caution, however, to avoid open
criticism from Reichswehr Headquarters; he allowed
Himmler only three armed SS regiments and, with his
eye on the Wehrmacht, vetoed a proposal to form them
into a division with artillery and pioneer units.[24]

Subsequent instructions both from Hitler and Army
Headquarters prescribed that the primary task of the
future SS-Verfügungstruppe was the *internal* security of
the regime; the Verfügungstruppe remained part of the SS
and therefore of the Party; only in the event of war was it
to be used for military purposes, for which the Reichswehr
was responsible for training it; its actual role was to be
decided only on mobilisation "in the light of the existing
internal political situation and the level of efficiency
reached by the SS regiments"—in the words of an instruction of 24 September 1934 from the Reich Defence
Minister (as the Minister of War was entitled at the time).
Nevertheless this same instruction recognised the right of
the SS to form "a standing armed force for such special
internal political tasks as may be allotted to the SS by the
Führer."[25]

Here was the formal admission that the Verfügungstruppe was intended to be the regime's armed State
Police. Himmler now only needed to amalgamate the
Leibstandarte and the Politische Bereitschaften into a
single force and the foundation would be laid for the

future SS army. It was soon borne in upon the Reichsführer, however, that he was not going to be able to form
his force from the men of the Allgemeine-SS alone. He
needed the craftsmen of war, the military experts; under
Sergeant-Major types like Sepp Dietrich his troops would
never be an elite.

Here he was faced with a dilemma. He required experienced professional soldiers, but they were unlikely to
join a force hardly distinguishable from the police. He was
therefore forced to camouflage the real purpose of the
Verfügungstruppe and turn it to purposes of a more
traditional nature than Hitler's and the Reichswehr's instructions visualised—there can be no other explanation
for the fact that even today the senior Waffen-SS commanders seriously believe that from the outset they were
serving in a normal military force.

This deceptive picture of a new Imperial Guard
attracted certain ex-officers into the ranks of the Verfügungstruppe. Paul Scharfe, the SS Judge, even recruited a
real Reichswehr General; during SA manoeuvres in Oden-
wald he met his old war-time comrade Paul Hausser
masquerading in the uniform of an SA-Standartenführer;
Scharfe enquired whether he would like to join the SS.
Hausser would.[26]

A greater contrast to the bull-necked Dietrich could
hardly be imagined. Hausser was a tall lean Brandenburger,
born in 1880, son of an officer, reared in the Prussian
cadet corps and a qualified General Staff Officer; out-
wardly he was the typical Prussian officer—elegant,
educated and with a gift for sarcasm which had made him
many enemies in the Reichswehr.[27] His military career had
been one of normal promotion and prescribed routine—
infantry training, staff college, staff officer with troops on
the Western and Eastern fronts in the First World War,
Chief of Staff Wehrkreis II, Commanding Officer 10 Infantry Regiment, Infantry Commander Magdeburg and
finally, in January 1932, retirement in the rank of Lieutenant-General.[28] As an ultra-conservative retired officer
he could think of nothing better to do than join the German nationalist ex-soldiers association, "Stahlhelm," where
he was immediately appointed local Commander Berlin-
Brandenburg—a post which in his own words was "a
'natural' for a retired Reichswehr General."[29] When the

Stahlhelm was forcibly amalgamated with the SA he happily accepted from Röhm the rank of reserve SA-Standartenführer; equally happily he accepted from Himmler the uniform of an SS-Standartenführer.[30]

Himmler sensed that this ex-Reichswehr General possessed the craftsman's technical ability which he must have for the early stages of his programme. On 14 December 1934 he had issued a directive reorganising the Politische Bereitschaften into battalions and amalgamating them with the Leibstandarte to form the SS-Verfügungstruppe.[31] Standartenführer Hausser was a key figure in this reorganisation; he was to instil into the SS soldiers that which they lacked—discipline, obedience, drill, battleworthiness—in other words military know-how.

Early in 1935 in one of the Duke of Brunswick's old castles Hausser opened an SS Cadet School to train the young entry who one day would assume command of the regiments and battalions of the SS army. It was not the first of its kind; on 1 October 1934 Paul Lettow, another ex-Reichswehr officer, had already initiated the first course at the Bad Tölz SS Cadet School.[32] Hausser quickly realised that only by adopting the training methods and outlook of the Reichswehr could he create an effective force: "I considered that the SS force must be formed on the well-tried training regulations of the Reichswehr."[33]

Hausser's solid groundwork in Brunswick attracted a sufficient number of ex-police officers, time-expired Reichswehr sergeant-majors and young military enthusiasts to form the officer and NCO cadre of the future SS Army. The cadres were distributed to the scattered battalions and these were gradually formed into regiments. In Munich three Sturmbanne went to form No. 1 SS Regiment, the "Deutschland," organised and equipped as a horse-drawn infantry regiment; in Hamburg another three Sturmbanne formed No. 2 SS Regiment, the "Germania"; in Berlin the Leibstandarte expanded into a motorised infantry regiment and in 1938 the fourth Infantry Regiment formed in Vienna—3 SS Regiment, "Der Führer."[34] By mid-summer 1936 the Verfügungstruppe had so far taken shape that Himmler felt himself entitled to appoint an official head of his miniature SS army: on 1 October 1936 SS-Brigadeführer Hausser was appointed Inspector of the Verfügungstruppe.[35]

In spite of this sonorous title, Hausser was by no means master in his own house. He created a sort of divisional staff to supervise the equipment and training of his troops, but on paper he was under the SS-Hauptamt and the SS military princelings were not initially prepared to recognise his authority too easily. The Oberabschnitt commanders of the Allgemeine-SS were reluctant to relinquish control of their armed units—they had, after all, formed them as Politische Bereitschaften.[36] A Himmler order of 17 September 1936 laid down that the powers of the Inspectorate covered training only and would not affect the "territorial prerogatives of the SS-Oberabschnitt over the VT units located in their areas."[37] Even though backed by Himmler, Hausser had to exercise caution in asserting his authority over the SS Oberabschnitte.

Hardly had he settled his outside quarrels, however, than an obstreperous opponent appeared within his own ranks: Dietrich, the Commander of the Leibstandarte, evinced no inclination to be ordered about by the Prussian, Hausser. Even Himmler was hesitant to call Dietrich to order. In his Directive on the Verfügungstruppe he had prudently laid down that inspection of the Leibstandarte was his own prerogative and that the Inspector was merely "authorised to attend Leibstandarte parades"[38]—proof enough that Himmler was resigned to the fact that Dietrich's guardsmen were not going to obey his orders. "Reichsheini's" authority frequently ended at the barrack gate of Lichterfelde.

Himmler once wrote in agitation: "My dear Sepp, this is of course another impossibility. Your officers are good enough to recognise me personally; otherwise, however, the Leibstandarte is a complete law unto itself; it does and allows anything it likes without taking the slightest notice of orders from above."[39] Vexations caused by the Leibstandarte were endless—frequent brawls with Wehrmacht soldiers,[40] insulting remarks to other members of the Verfügungstruppe,[41] recruitment of national servicemen without the Wehrmacht's approval.[42] The Head of the SS-Hauptamt tore his hair: "If, contrary to all orders, instructions and assurances, the Leibstandarte chooses to act in this arbitrary manner, I foresee great difficulties."[43] Once more Himmler warned Dietrich: "For the last time I ask you to stop these things. I can no more admit to the

Wehrmacht that I am unable to get the Leibstandarte to conform to the orders and instructions valid for the entire Verfügungstruppe than I can tolerate continuance of these extravagances on the part of the Leibstandarte."[44]

Although the "Asphalt Soldiers," as the Verfügungstruppe nicknamed the Leibstandarte, lacked any basic military training, Dietrich's refusal to co-operate forced even Hausser to withdraw for a time. Nevertheless, as they were continuously employed on parades and sentry duty, it soon became abundantly clear that the Leibstandarte was devoid of even the rudiments of battle training.[45] Finally even Dietrich realised that no soldier was taking the Leibstandarte seriously and he was eventually persuaded to allow Hausser more freedom of action. In 1938 he agreed to an exchange of battalion and company commanders between the Verfügungstruppe and the Leibstandarte. Gradually Hausser's training staff managed to put some military order into the unit.[46]

Ex-General Hausser, however, was not to be allowed to set the military tone for the Verfügungstruppe all by himself. Ex-soldiers and National-Socialist hotheads were soon pouring into the Verfügungstruppe and, unlike Hausser, they thought it by no means desirable to ape the Reichswehr. The newcomers believed that the Verfügungstruppe's mission in life was to form the core of the new Reich's revolutionary army, destined to take over from the supposedly hide-bound Wehrmacht. They brought to the Verfügungstruppe a certain dynamism and the arrogance of the elite Imperial Guard; the blind fervour of the growing Hitler Youth generation combined with the reforming zeal of ex-officer heretics to produce a sense of mission and superiority.

The leading brain among the military reformers was SS-Sturmbannführer Felix Steiner; he was an ex-Reichswehr officer whose experiences on the Western Front in the First World War had turned him into a rebel against the conservative doctrines of the Army. During the breakthrough battles of 1918 he had witnessed the failure of the static mass armies and the advent of a new military formation—the assault detachment or mobile battle group.[47]

To escape from the deadly immobility of trench warfare with one mass army facing another in a mutual

battle of attrition, the German front-line officers had hit
upon the idea of withdrawing their best men from the
trenches and forming them into battle groups. These so-
called "storm battalions" were to stiffen the spine of the
mass army, to be the keep of the defence and the spear-
head of the attack. The battle groups were trained for
fighting at close quarters; they were equipped with flame-
throwers, machine guns, pistols, hand grenades and spades,
and they quickly learnt what was later to be known as
"military teamwork"—co-operation on the sub-unit
level.[48] At the time twenty-year-old Second Lieutenant
Steiner from East Prussia, son of an émigré family from
Salzburg and now Company Commander of a machinegun
marksman detachment,[49] was lying behind his machine
gun; he thought he could see the dawn of a new era in
military history; he believed that the future belonged
neither to the amorphous mass nor to the traditional
single-combat champions but to an elite fighting in groups.

But Steiner was wrong. The post-war Reichswehr generals thought as did the later SS-Brigadeführer Hausser: in
their view the storm battalions had been an emergency
measure and could never be more than temporary and
exceptional expedients within the framework of a normal
army.[50] Steiner, promoted Captain in 1927 and serving as
a company commander in No. 1 Infantry Regiment in
Königsberg from 1932, found himself increasingly in opposition to the Reichswehr doctrine.[51] The Generals wished
to wage the next war as they had the last one—with a
citizen army based on universal military service. Steiner,
however, was still a believer in the idea of a military elite.
Total war, Steiner thought, required mass armies only for
defensive operations; the decisive role belonged to mobile
operational formations of high-class elite troops, to a
select ultra-modern force which "by blows of lightning
rapidity would split the enemy into fragments and then
destroy the dislocated remnants."[52]

For Steiner, with his elite theory, Hausser's Verfügungstruppe was the logical destination; it was the specialised
force of the future of which he had always dreamed. He
was given command of the proposed VT regiment
"Deutschland" and in a matter of months had become
the intellectual counterbalance to Hausser, the Reichswehr
traditionalist.[53] Initially Steiner tried out his reforms with

one battalion only. He demoted mechanical barrack-square drill from its place of primary importance and centred his training on sport and athletics, aiming to turn his soldiers into cross-country experts of the "hunter-poacher-athlete type" described by Liddell Hart as the ideal modern infantryman.[54]

He was also insistent upon reducing the distinctions between officers and the rank and file, thereby promoting a spirit of comradeship in face of the hardships and discomforts of battle training or of war itself. Officers, NCOs and men competed in teams against each other—a further method of eliminating differences in rank.[55] The officer selection system also promoted a unit spirit. The SS cadet schools had abandoned the Wehrmacht system whereby officer candidates were accepted at an early age provided they could show the requisite educational qualifications. The future SS officers had to serve for two years in the ranks before going to the Military Academy; no preference was given to education or background—before 1938 40 per cent of SS cadets had not matriculated.[56] Steiner and his fellow SS commanders made it abundantly clear that they were abandoning the Wehrmacht's ways: in SS barracks, doors of rooms and cupboards were left open as a matter of principle,[57] administrative officers had to undergo a period of military training before being released to their technical schools[58] and in the words of the American historian George H. Stein, they "fostered among officers, NCOs and enlisted men a sense of fellowship and mutual respect generally unknown in the Army."[59]

In his training for war Steiner introduced numerous innovations. Unlike the Wehrmacht the basic military unit in his view was not the section but the battle group; Steiner wished to organise his entire regiment in battle groups, sufficiently mobile to come rapidly to grips with the enemy but nevertheless capable of retaining their regimental organisation.[60] Instead of the Wehrmacht's regulation rifle he introduced handier and more mobile weapons, primarily sub-machine guns, hand grenades and explosives. A new battledress, the camouflage blouse and camouflage suit, replaced the field service dress of the Army.[61] Gradually Steiner created a force of military athletes, a "supple adaptable type of soldier, athletic of bearing, capable of more than average endurance on the march and in combat," as Steiner later described his men.[62] Even the Wehrmacht's eyebrows rose. Troops who could cover three kilometres (1•88 miles) in twenty minutes—such a thing was unheard of.[63]

The success of Steiner's modernisation was so obvious that the Verfügungstruppe began to look upon him as their real commander. Himmler too, always easily influenced by anything new, made Steiner "definitely his favourite baby," as Hausser put it.[64] To begin with, at any rate, Himmler was prepared to overlook the fact that Steiner treated his Reichsführer with scant respect, refused to marry and also refused to leave the Church—a "must" for any senior SS officer:[65] Himmler was almost invariably ready to tolerate the ideas of his cantankerous soldier.

For years Steiner held his place as the star turn of the Verfügungstruppe because he was one of the very few professional soldiers in the SS. Even the euphoria of the Verfügungstruppe expansion could not conceal the fact that the new force lacked experienced officers with the aptitude for command and the social standing born of generations of military service. In the Reichswehr 49 per cent of the officer corps came of military families but in the Verfügungstruppe the proportion was only 5 per cent; barely 2 per cent of the Wehrmacht officers came of peasant stock, but 90 per cent of the Verfügungstruppe commanders had been brought up on the land.[66] The Verfügungstruppe never made its mark on the bourgeoisie and the town-dwellers; it remained an army of peasants and artisans. In Schleswig-Holstein, Lower Saxony, Franconia and the Saar, one out of every three farmer's sons joined the Verfügungstruppe or, later, the Waffen-SS.[67]

The Verfügungstruppe's recruits and its new commanders sought to compensate for their lack of military tradition by enthusiasm and devotion to the Hitler cult; many of them therefore came to believe that in contrast to the "reactionary" Wehrmacht, the Verfügungstruppe was the only reliable armed force in the National-Socialist State. Steiner's tactical reforms had implanted in his men the idea that they were a military elite far superior to the Wehrmacht; similarly the new commanders, brought up in the Hitler Youth and indoctrinated in the SS cadet colleges, instilled into their troops a National-Socialist ideological fervour which brought them into barely con-

cealed opposition to "the old fogeys," as Röhm had once
called the Reichswehr Generals. Enmity towards the army
became almost an elixir of life to the Verfügungstruppe,
for in the early stages the Wehrmacht succeeded in tying
the hands of this unwelcome competitor.

The Army Generals had never recognised the
Verfügungstruppe as a fourth arm of the service; on the
contrary, they feared that a second force under the control
of Himmler, already in charge of the entire police machine, might rapidly develop into a deadly threat to the
existence of the Wehrmacht.[68] There were many little signs
—brawls between members of the Verfügungstruppe and
Wehrmacht, slanderous gossip in SS messes against General Freiherr von Fritsch, the anti-Nazi C-in-C of the
Army, incidents between the Army and the SS when
sharing manoeuvre areas; for Army Headquarters all these
indicated a threat that one day the Army might lose to
the SS its monopoly as the sole bearer of arms within the
nation.[69] On 1 February 1938 General von Fritsch noted:
"all sources agree that the attitude of the SS Verfügungstruppe towards the Army is frigid if not hostile. One cannot avoid the impression that this hostile attitude is deliberately cultivated."[70]

Fritsch and the Army Generals had pressed Hitler so
hard that the Dictator temporarily forbade any further expansion of the SS troops and even denied them full recognition as military formations. So the Verfügungstruppe
found its way blocked by the Wehrmacht; it was not
allowed to form a Division;[71] it was refused artillery;[72]
it was forbidden to publish recruiting notices in the
Press;[73] the Army had the right to inspect SS units.[74]
To cap it all, these provisions were valid only until the
outbreak of war; then Hitler would decide whether to
place the Verfügungstruppe under the Army as a formed
body or disband it and distribute its members individually
to Wehrmacht units.[75] No more bitter fate could threaten
a military formation, particularly one which prided itself
on being both an elite and the core of the future German
defence force.

An unexpected crisis within the Wehrmacht now came
to the assistance of the Verfügungstruppe. In February
1938 its enemy von Fritsch and the Reich Minister of
War, von Blomberg, both fell and Hitler seized command

of the Wehrmacht. Six months later the Verfügungstruppe's anxiety over its future was at an end: on 17 August 1938 Hitler signed a decree which in effect announced the birth of the future Waffen-SS, for it recognised the Verfügungstruppe as a permanent force both in peace and in war. The VT was to be available for "certain special internal political tasks which are the responsibility of the Reichsführer-SS and Chief of the German Police, and these I reserve the right to allot to him myself as occasion demands; in addition certain formations should be available for mobile employment under the Army in the event of war."[76] The Verfügungstruppe had arrived. Brigadeführer Leo Petri of the SS Hauptamt noted in triumph: "the Wehrmacht has been forced to recognise that the pertinacity of the Reichsführer-SS in the pursuit of his aims is stronger than its own resistance to the innovations of the Third Reich."[77]

Even at the time, professional soldiers such as Hausser and Steiner probably subscribed to the Hitler decree only with considerable reservations; after all, for them it closed the door to their only object in life—to be soldiers following a purely military profession. Hausser, Steiner and the other ex-professional soldiers may have differed on technical military questions but they had one thing in common—they wanted to devote themselves to an exclusively military job; they wanted to be soldiers "like the rest"; nothing could have been more foreign to them than Petri's triumphal cry about the victory of the "party troops," nothing could have seemed to them more degrading than their Reichsführer's concept of the Verfügungstruppe as merely one among many links in the chain of his precious State Protection Corps.

Nevertheless the Verfügungstruppe became and remained a force for the protection of the regime; all ideological instruction drummed into Himmler's soldiers the notion that they must be ready, if necessary, to protect Adolf Hitler's State even against their own fellow-countrymen. In the words of an official SS document, they were told that the Verfügungstruppe was "the visible armed force of the National-Socialist Party"; recruiting pamphlets urged every "healthy young man of German blood" to join the Verfügungstruppe, but with the proviso that unconditional acceptance of National-Socialist ideology was essential.[78] Educational instruction was designed to ensure that the Verfügungstruppe soldier was a fanatical Nazi, unquestioningly obedient and ready to carry out any order from the Dictator-Chancellor. A flood of anti-Christian propaganda was loosed on the heads of the men to compel them to renounce all the rules of bourgeois Christian morality and to sever all ties with the Church.

The Verfügungstruppe became a stronghold of that atheism peculiar to the SS which, in their perverse terminology, the Nazi propagandists christened "Gottgläubigkeit" (belief in God). By the end of 1938 53·6 per cent of Verfügungstruppe men had left the Church, a figure surpassed only by the even more rabid Totenkopfverbände with 69 per cent.[79] Many men were literally compelled to leave the Church. A typical case was that of one Franz Waldmann from Spessart, a Catholic, whose troubles later even came to the ears of OKW. He had volunteered for the Verfügungstruppe because, as his Catholic priest later wrote, his father thought it was "like joining the Guards."

The priest's report to his Diocese continued: no sooner had Waldmann joined than "pressure was brought to bear upon him to leave the Church. He told his mother that some 30 of them refused. They were then subjected to a martyrdom which young men could hardly be expected to endure. On every parade and during every instructional period the cry was 'One pace forward anyone who has not yet left the Church!' Every opportunity was taken to humiliate and ridicule them. Franz countered by saying that religion was not the point; what mattered was how he did his duty. One by one his fellows gave way under the pressure until Franz was alone. About this time one of his friends wrote to his father saying that Franz could not stand it any longer. Even he was now weary of the struggle." Shortly thereafter the priest heard that Franz Waldmann had left the Church. In October 1942 he was killed in Finland. During his last leave he had told his mother: "Day by day I was compelled to renounce my faith. I would never go back to my unit, even though I like the life. After the war I want to be free again, to be like I was before."[80]

The SS unit of Radolfzell (about one thousand strong) provided a good illustration of the progress of anti-Church propaganda in the Verfügungstruppe and the later Waffen-

SS; of 300 Catholics the church-leavers totalled 4 in 1937, 3 in 1938, 67 in 1940 and 129 in 1942.[81] In a letter of protest to OKW, Kosch, the Vicar-General in the Archbishop of Freiburg's Chancellery, complained: "In these barracks mass exits from the Church are the regular sequel to an ideological course of instruction. This can hardly be due to individual crises of conscience."[82] The young Verfügungstruppe officers were continually called upon to prove their uncompromising opposition to the Christian message of reconciliation and tolerance, which the SS regarded as un-German. From the outset they were ordered to abjure the Christian faith as a destructive, effeminate and "Jewish" doctrine. On leaving the Cadet School the young officers had to write essays on such subjects as "Responsibility of Christianity for the decline of the Ostrogoths and Vandals" or "Effect of Christianity on Ancestor Worship among our people." Himmler called such exercises "advanced education";[83] they were supposed to ensure that mentally as well as physically the Verfügungstruppe officers belonged to an "ideological force."

The men of the Verfügungstruppe were told that they must be ready at any moment to act ruthlessly within their own country in order to prevent another November 1918. Educational material still being distributed to the SS Panzergrenadier Division "Hohenstaufen" in October 1943 stated that the lessons of history "showed the necessity for an unflinching force at the disposal of the leadership of the Reich in any situation, even when this implies maintenance of order at home by the use of all methods."[84] This was no empty statement. On 9 November 1938, when barbarism engulfed the Jews of Germany, one of Heydrich's urgent teleprinter messages ordered the Verfügungstruppe into the most shameful operation yet undertaken by Germans in uniform.[85] On 14 November 1939 SD-Oberabschnitt Danube in Vienna reported to the SD-Hauptamt Berlin: "Mobile detachments of the Verfügungstruppe drove up to the synagogues and placed stocks of hand grenades in position preparatory to setting fire to the buildings." In the "Kristallnacht" story, participation by the Verfügungstruppe was the exception; nevertheless this incident showed the type of function SS Headquarters thought suitable for the VT.[86]

Himmler had never regarded the Verfügungstruppe as anything other than an instrument of internal political power. It was to protect the regime and form a counterweight to the Wehrmacht, which he never regarded as totally reliable; in the event of a military putsch the Verfügungstruppe, together with the police and Allgemeine SS units, would suppress a *coup d' état*. But the idea of the Verfügungstruppe as a political force was destroyed by Hitler's World War. The Dictator's adventurist policy drove it onto the battlefield—as a military fighting formation.

On 19 August 1939 OKW transmitted to the Verfügungstruppe Inspectorate an order from Hitler: "With immediate effect, units of the SS-Verfügungstruppe are placed under the Commander-in-Chief of the Army. The Commander-in-Chief of the Army will lay down their employment in accordance with the directives given by me."[87] For one campaign at least the men of the Verfügungstruppe were permitted to nurse their illusion that they were no different from normal soldiers. Hausser, the Inspector, arranged to be posted as liaison officer to Major General Werner Kempf's division (a normal Army formation) and never returned to the world of the SS-Hauptämter in Berlin.[88] His frustrating days as Inspector were over; now Paul Hausser could once more be what he had always wanted to be—a General commanding troops.

Steiner's Infantry Regiment, "Deutschland," an artillery regiment and other units of the Verfügungstruppe were also included in Kempf's semi-armoured division.[89] The Leibstandarte Motorised Infantry Regiment and the "Germania" Regiment were incorporated in army formations for the attack on Poland.[90] Steiner's unit distinguished itself during 3rd Army's advance on Mlava and Modlin;[91] the Leibstandarte took part in the battle of Bzura in central Poland;[92] "Germania" moved forward on Lwow with 14th Army.[93]

The army critics, however, found the SS troops' performance unsatisfactory. The Verfügungstruppe suffered considerably heavier losses than comparable army formations, and it soon became evident that the SS troops were not trained to fight as part of a Division, nor were the Verfügungstruppe officers capable of commanding their men in complicated operations.[94] The Verfügungstruppe could justifiably retort that in the Polish campaign the army had starved them of heavy weapons and kept them short of supplies; nevertheless, even the SS military were dissatisfied with the performance of their troops.[95] There was only one solution: the Verfügungstruppe must form a Division with its own heavy weapons and supply services—but this solution was blocked by the OKW Generals, still determined to keep Himmler's force as small as possible.

OKW could in effect dictate the numerical strength of the Verfügungstruppe. Each year it laid down the numbers from each annual class to be allotted to individual arms of the service by the local Wehrbezirkskommando [Defence District Headquarters—WBK], the mustering authority for national servicemen; the last word lay with the WBK; no man could be called up to a unit until the WBK concerned had released him.[96] This rule also applied to the Verfügungstruppe. OKW could not deny the SS the necessary replacements for their field units but the Wehrmacht could lay down a ceiling sufficiently low to prevent the Verfügungstruppe from expanding—and the OKW Generals made full use of this privilege.[97]

At this point the Verfügungstruppe commanders received a powerful reinforcement in the shape of an energetic Swabian who was both sufficiently astute and unscrupulous to free the Verfügungstruppe from its Wehrmacht shackles —SS-Brigadeführer Gottlob Berger appeared on the scene, and he was the real founder of the Waffen-SS. Since the end of the Thousand-Year Reich, however, he has been treated by the ex-SS Generals as a kind of leper: "Berger? He had nothing whatsoever to do with the Waffen-SS," Felix Steiner exclaimed shortly before his death;[98] ex-Obergruppenführer Bittrich shuddered at the mere name: "A mountebank, a swindler."[99]

Such vitriolic reactions give one to suspect that Berger did not fit into the "we-were-all-simple-soldiers" theme of the Waffen-SS apologists. The "Duke of Swabia," as the SS called Berger,[100] was one of the earliest recruits to National-Socialism and the SA[101] and he regarded the SS units primarily as the military arm of the Party and of National-Socialism. Born in 1896, son of a saw-mill owner, Berger had volunteered in the First World War and had been severely wounded as a Second Lieutenant commanding a battle group; he was an expert athletics instructor and well-versed in military affairs[102]—yet the professional officers of the Verfügungstruppe always kept him at arm's length. They disliked him for his typically Swabian loquacity and for his position as Himmler's *éminence grise*. For years he had been regarded as the most faithful of a faithful band, a man who thought it his duty to warn his Reichsführer of any disloyalty among his closest collaborators, and in particular among the Verfügungstruppe military men. He once wrote in a minute to Himmler, for instance, that in many regiments "and in particular on the staff of the Verfügungstruppe" people had "attempted to bypass the Reichsführer-SS— I have witnessed this myself and as a result clashed with Hausser at the time."[103] With a mixture of machiavellianism, shrewdness and frankness Berger became Himmler's principal adviser; he weaned his master away from many a crazy idea (particularly on Eastern policy) but he clung to him, for "my Reichsführer confides in me and tells me things personally which he would never do unless he was completely at ease"—as he wrote to Himmler on 9 March 1943.[104]

He clung faithfully to Himmler because his career depended upon that of his master. He had already failed in the SA; in spring 1933 he had been involved in a quarrel with the younger SA element, had been brought before an arbitration court and had subsequently resigned; after the Röhm upheaval he had spied an opportunity to recapture some leading position in the SA.[105]

Berger had given SA Headquarters the written assurance that "I shall always regard the SA as Number One and shall never be on the side of those who wish to destroy the SA."[106] Only a week or two later, however, he had become someone else's disciple; he accepted a post under SA-Obergruppenführer Krüger (who later transferred to the SS) who was regarded as a traitor by the SA because of his equivocal role in the Röhm putsch; one year later Berger had finally joined the SS.[107] On 7 December 1934 SA-Gruppenführer Hanns Ludin, once a friend of Berger, explained to the special Court convened by Supreme SA Headquarters that Berger suffered from "a not inconsiderable self-conceit," was "loud-mouthed" and gave evidence of a "deplorable lack of self-criticism and soldierly modesty."[108] Between the SA leaders and the renegade Berger there developed an implacable hatred which was to have dire consequences for the Waffen-SS. At a later stage three SA-Gruppenführer (Ludin, von Jagow and Beckerle), all members of the SA Arbitration Court which had sat on Berger's case,[109] were in charge of German legations in the Balkans; they sabotaged Berger's Waffen-SS recruiting programme—and without the assistance of the Foreign Ministry Berger was powerless to obtain any "racial Germans" for his units.

Recruitment for the SS troops was one of Berger's most important tasks. In 1938 he had become head of the recruiting office in the SS Hauptamt[110] and he shared Himmler's ambition to build up the Verfügungstruppe into a full-scale army; he had accordingly given much thought to the expansion of the armed SS units. When, therefore, the Wehrmacht's opposition threatened to torpedo the Verfügungstruppe's expansion programme, Berger knew what to do. In the formations responsible to the "Reichsführer-SS and Chief of the German police" three categories of men were exempt from service in the Wehrmacht; first, the concentration-camp guards, the "Totenkopfverbände," secondly their war-time reinforcements (the so-called "police reinforcements" or "Reinforced Totenkopf Standarten"), and thirdly a section of the Ordnungspolizei.[111] Two Hitler orders now gave Berger the opportunity to build up the Waffen-SS from sources over which the Wehrmacht had no control; a decree of 17 August 1938 provided that parts of the Totenkopfverbände would reinforce the Verfügungstruppe in the event of war; a further decree of 18 May 1939 permitted Himmler to call up 50,000 men of the Allgemeine SS as "Reinforced Totenkopf Standarten."[112]

The plan which Berger proposed to Himmler provided for immediate duplication of the armed SS and formation of two full battle-strength divisions; in addition, if Hitler would sanction transfer of the Totenkopfverbände and Ordnungspolizei units into the Verfügungstruppe, Himmler would then have three to four divisions available in a very short time.[113] Hitler approved Berger's plan, since theoretically the proposal did not infringe the recruiting rules laid down by the touchy Wehrmacht. Berger and the Verfügungstruppe Inspectorate were therefore free to start formation of an entirely new army; it was also given a new name—Waffen-SS.[114]

Berger's subterfuge, however, linked the Verfügungstruppe with the most disreputable organisation in the entire SS, a process which many Verfügungstruppe commanders regarded as an insult to any soldier. Under SS-Gruppenführer Theodor Eicke the Totenkopfverbände had been deliberately schooled in the antithesis of militarism. They and the Verfügungstruppe originated from the same source, the Politsche Bereitschaften,[115] but since then no love had been lost between the two members of the family. The Verfügungstruppe was trying to be a military force, whereas the Totenkopfverbände affected an anti-military outlook; the result had been many a tavern brawl.[116]

Eicke was an irascible Alsatian, the murderer of Röhm and the inventor of bureaucratised concentration-camp terror. One of his objects in life was to turn his Totenkopfverbände into a sort of counterforce to the Verfügungstruppe. As an ex-paymaster in the Imperial Army he was imbued with an undying hatred of the professional officers whom he now saw in command of the Verfügungstruppe as well as the army.[117] He had been dismissed from the army, had been a failure in the police and was written off by the Party as a querulous individual—so he instilled into his men all the pent-up resentments for which he himself could find no outlet. They were willing pupils; the uneducated yokels and embitted unemployed, who provided the majority of his army of thugs, accepted without demur "Papa" Eicke's hate tirades against Jews, Marxists and professional soldiers.

The brown uniform which Eicke's men wore, in place of the regulation SS black, showed that they possessed some sort of special status. Himmler had given his head concentration-camp guard almost complete autonomy; as "Inspector of Concentration Camps and Commander of SS Guard Formations" Eicke was responsible to the Reichsführer-SS alone.[118] He formed a guard unit in each concentration camp, outside the control of the Allgemeine-SS and initially entitled a Sturmbann. On 29 March 1936, by which time they totalled 3,500 men, they were officially designated "Totenkopfverbände."[119] In April 1937 Eicke formed his five Sturmbanne into three Totenkopf-Standarten—"Oberbayern" located in Dachau, "Brandenburg," located in Oranienburg, and "Thuringia," located in Weimar for Buchenwald; in 1938 a fourth Standarte was added—"Ostmark" located in Linz.[120]

Eicke kept jealous watch to ensure that no professional officer infiltrated into his organisation to dispute his command of the Totenkopfverbände; he was continually warning his men against the "ludicrous attempt to ape a military organisation."[121] In 1937 one of his orders stated: "We belong neither to the army nor to the police nor to the Verfügungstruppe . . . men of the Totenkopfverbände consider themselves members of the Allgemeine-SS and cannot therefore be commanded either by officers or NCOs . . . henceforth commanders who act like officers, junior officers who act like NCOs, and men who act like private soldiers will be posted to the Allgemeine-SS."[122]

Such was the mentality in which Eicke had schooled the corps of thugs which was now to be combined with the Verfügungstruppe. But with their eyes set on their own expansion the SS military brushed the problem aside, just as Himmler ignored the lack of ideological reliability among the men streaming into the Waffen-SS from the Ordnungspolizei. "They are no National-Socialists," he said, "they are neither SS men nor selected personnel . . . they were simply called up like men of some construction battalion."[123]

Though the Waffen-SS was fast becoming a remarkably heterogeneous force, Berger and his organisers formed division after division. The SS army gradually took shape; in late September 1939 SS-Brigadeführer and Police Major-General Karl Pfeffer-Wildenbruch formed an SS/Police Division from members of the Ordnungspolizei together with certain specialised army units.[124] On 10 October SS-Gruppenführer Hausser commenced formation of a motorised Verfügungstruppe division (later named "Das Reich") from the three SS regiments "Deutschland," "Germania" and "Der Führer."[125] On 1 November SS-Gruppenführer Eicke formed the "Totenkopf" division from certain of his Totenkopfstandarten and parts of the "police reinforcements."[126] The Leibstandarte initially remained as a motorised infantry regiment, only becoming a division in 1942.[127]

So at one stroke Berger had succeeded in creating a

sizable SS armed force. When it left for the Polish campaign the Verfügungstruppe had been 18,000 strong; now Himmler had no fewer than 100,000 armed men.[128] Simultaneously Berger created the "Waffen-SS reinforcement office," for the vital question now was whether he would be able to obtain adequate replacements for the SS field formations and the Totenkopfstandarten. Berger set up recruiting offices in the seventeen SS Oberabschnitte and opened negotiations with the Wehrmacht;[129] his object was to persuade OKW to agree to the formation of larger SS reserve units in the hope that one day he might be able to expand the Waffen-SS yet again.

But the Wehrmacht at first refused to recognise the Totenkopfstandarten as military units—they had after all originally been intended for police work. OKW was prepared to release only a limited number of conscripts as replacements for the Totenkopfstandarten or the police units; it allowed Berger to recruit 20-year-olds for the Waffen-SS field units,[130] but reserved the right to decide whether a man so recruited should in fact be released for service in the SS. The Wehrmacht had thus placed a further spoke in Berger's wheel; however many applicants might report for service in the Waffen-SS, the Wehrbezirkskommando released on average only one-third of them.[131]

The more persistently Berger pressed the Wehrmacht, the more firmly did OKW reject his plans for expansion. On 8 March 1940 OKW laid down the units which it would henceforth recognise as part of the Waffen-SS— the Leibstandarte, the three SS divisions, the Totenkopfstandarten, the replacement units and the cadet schools.[132] Even Hitler supported his generals in this case. In his eyes the Waffen-SS was still a militarised police force of elite National-Socialists and it must be ready at any time to defend the regime.

Hitler was counting upon a short war and a rapid victory; in addition he had no wish to scare his professional soldiers with the bogey of a second Wehrmacht. Accordingly (at least until June 1942) he opposed all the major expansion plans of the Waffen-SS. He forbade formation of an SS army corps, he laid down that the strength of the Waffen-SS was not to exceed 5–10 per cent of the peacetime strength of the army.[133] He was continually emphasising what the Waffen-SS was *not* to be—a purely military force. In a secret decree issued on 6 August 1940 he gave his own view on the "necessity for the Waffen-SS"; the expansion of the Greater German Reich, he said, necessitated "the creation of an armed state police capable, whatever the situation, of representing and enforcing the authority of the Reich in the interior of the country."[134]

The rebuff administered by the Führer's headquarters was clear enough but Berger was not to be deterred. His own position had meanwhile grown in importance; on 1 June 1940 he had been promoted Head of the SS-Hauptamt and had thus become the man mainly responsible for the Waffen-SS.[135] After the western campaign command of the Waffen-SS had been divided between two Hauptämter. On 15 August 1940 the Verfügungstruppe Inspectorate had turned into the Führungshauptamt, the "headquarters for the military command of the Waffen-SS," in the words of the basic order;[136] the SS-Hauptamt, however, remained responsible for ideological education, recruiting and, most important of all, replacements for the Waffen-SS.[137]

Berger therefore looked around for new methods of expanding his army. Since the Wehrmacht refused him any further replacement units, he must now draw his recruits from some source outside the control of the OKW generals. He found just such a source. Beyond the borders of the Reich, primarily in the Balkans, lived hundreds of thousands of "racial Germans," who were citizens of other states but nevertheless intoxicated by Hitler's campaigns of conquest and captivated by the propaganda on "greater Germany." These were the men to be drawn into the Waffen-SS; no Wehrmacht general could forbid their recruitment as a gigantic reserve for Himmler's legions.

Berger started with his own family—his son-in-law was Andreas Schmidt, leader of the German minority in Rumania. He was an ultra-Nazi, typical of the immature young fanatics intoxicated by the Hitler cult and he immediately promised his father-in-law that he would recruit the Germans of Rumania into the Waffen-SS. In the spring of 1940 Schmidt, assisted by Berger's minions, contrived to smuggle 1,000 Germans out of Rumania under the noses of the Rumanian authorities, who were keeping sharp watch to ensure that no Rumanian liable for military service deserted to some foreign army.[138] Berger was so elated by his successes in Rumania that in August 1940 he proposed to Himmler that all the Germans in southeastern Europe fit for military service (there were 1,500,000 of them) be directed into the Waffen-SS—with or without the agreement of their Governments.[139]

Berger's methods of press-ganging the "racial Germans" into the Waffen-SS were highly imaginative. The SS "volunteers" were camouflaged as casual labourers, they were hidden in German hospital trains, they were swept up by the supply columns of the SS divisions as they carved their way across south-eastern Europe.[140] Berger's Hauptampt later concluded agreements with various foreign Governments permitting Germans to volunteer for the Waffen-SS and officially leave their country of origin on certain agreed conditions. The Balkan states did not always observe the agreements and in such cases Berger's minions would re-start their recruit-smuggling operations.[141]

In Berger's empire, however, volunteering was an elastic notion. Where the siren song of propaganda failed, strong-arm squads came to the assistance of the Nazi minority leaders. Berger commented "If a minority is even passably well led, all will volunteer; those who do not volunteer will have their houses broken up."[142] In the later years of the war sheer press-gang methods were used. Germany forced upon the Balkan states agreements providing that all men of German blood should legally complete their military service in the German army—for preference in the Waffen-SS.[143] By the end of 1943 25 per cent of Waffen-SS manpower was "racial German" and by the end of the war 310,000 of them, drawn from all parts of Europe, were serving in SS units.[144]

Meanwhile Berger had had the idea of tapping a new and even more remarkable reservoir of recruits—the countries known to the SS as "Germanic." The early German blitz victories had electrified many of the young men of northern and western Europe; in a matter of weeks a whole world, the world of bourgeois democracy, had collapsed before their eyes. To many of the simpler minds the conquerors who marched through the streets of Oslo,

Brussels or The Hague, were the youthful standard-bearers of a new era.

In many a young Belgian, Dutchman or Norwegian there awoke the urge to conform, the desire not to miss the opportunity of climbing on the band-wagon of the new era. They were not of course invariably the blue-eyed idealists of Waffen-SS legend. As well as the urge for adventure a powerful motive was the prospect of a career and of becoming "warrior peasants" ruling millions of "Slav sub-humans." Political ideas were decisive only for a minority; of the 125,000 West Europeans who fought in the Waffen-SS barely a third belonged to the pro-Nazi nationalist parties where subservience to the new German masters was to be seen in its crudest form.[145]

Whatever their motives, men streamed into the recruiting offices which, from mid-1940, Berger set up in all the occupied countries of Western and Northern Europe—little did he think what political and ideological results the introduction of so diverse a collection of races would have on the SS and on its relationship to Adolf Hitler. He was concerned solely with numbers, and on this score he was more than satisfied. By the end of 1940 the SS-Hauptamt had set up a training camp at Sennheim in Alsace where SS volunteers from all the countries of Europe were drilled—both in arms and in ideology.[146] By spring 1941 the first major non-German formation had been constituted, the SS Division "Viking" composed of Flemish, Dutch, Danish and Norweigan volunteers with German commanders and cadres.[147]

The "Germanic" Waffen-SS soon turned into a sort of European Army; new nationalities were continually being brought in—and diluting the purity of its National-Socialism in the process. Berger even recruited in the East; fezzes and Cossack caps lent a curious appearance to Himmler's army of ideological puritans. The Reichsführer's anti-Slav prejudices had to be circumvented—initially the sight of "Eastern sub-humans" in the uniform of the Waffen-SS seemed to Himmler a shameful breach of faith with Germanism. The persuasive Berger, however, eventually argued Himmler into acceptance of all Eastern Europeans as German plunder; first came the Baltic peoples, then the Ukrainians and finally even Russians and other races, culminating in the Balkan Moslems. Eventually no fewer

than 200,000 members of these races were serving in the
Waffen-SS.[148]

Year by year Berger's recruiting list lengthened; year
by year the Waffen-SS army swelled to more explosive
proportions—mid-1940—100,000 men, 1941—220,000,
1942—330,000, 1943—540,000, 1944—910,000.[149] Berger's influx of recruits eventually enabled the officers of the
Führungshauptamt to bury the detested label of armed
State Police; the Waffen-SS entered upon a victorious
career of which there are few parallels in the history of
the war. Even in the 1940 campaign in the West the SS
proved that it could hold its own with the crack divisions
of the army. The SS military athletes stormed through
Holland, Belgium and France—fanatical, irresistible, dis-
dainful of losses and impelled by a blind fury in the
assault which distinguished Himmler's army from all other
formations of the German Wehrmacht. The first Iron
Cross of the campaign was won by SS-Obersturmführer
Kraas of the Leibstandarte;[150] it was the shadow of things
to come—again and again SS units spearheaded the attack
and swept the German invasion forward. Sepp Dietrich's
Leibstandarte in particular displayed a nonchalance, towards both the enemy and its own superior officers, that
was totally foreign to the Wehrmacht.

During the pursuit of the British forces towards Dunkirk
the Leibstandarte was ordered to cross the heavily defended Aa Canal and seize the town of Watten. On the
afternoon of 24 May 1940, however, the Führer's Headquarters countermanded the crossing. Dietrich simply disregarded Hitler's order and a few hours later his troops
were over the canal.[151] At a later stage of the campaign
the Leibstandarte headed the pursuit of the beaten enemy;
as advance guard to Colonel-General von Kleist's Panzer
Group it stormed southwards to prevent the French from
forming a line of resistance along the Loire. In a wide
southward sweep the regiment reached St Etienne, leaving the main body of the German army far behind.[152]

The other SS formations were equally successful; the
"Der Führer" Regiment forced the Grebbe line in Holland;
the Verfügungstruppe Division chased the enemy right up
to the Spanish frontier; the Totenkopf Division seized a
crossing over the Seine and bridgeheads over the Loire.[153]

The army generals observed the SS thirst for battle with

mingled admiration and dismay; to the traditionally minded
these new soldiers seemed to herald a new form of warfare which made a mockery of all reasonable and cal-
culable tactics. Many regarded the SS troops as did Werner
Picht, the sociologist, who commented that they were
"not a new form of front-line soldier but an oath-bound
community, available to the Führer for any mission."[154]
General Erich Hoepner, an armoured-formation commander, gave perhaps the crispest expression to the regular officers' criticism of the SS; when Eicke, commanding
the Totenkopf Division which was under Hoepner at the
time, reported that a certain order to attack had been carried out and that in doing so human life had counted for
nothing, the ex-cavalryman retorted: "That's a butcher's
outlook."[155]

Army officers were appalled by the fact that the Waffen-
SS commanders had clearly never learnt to exercise any
form of caution in the use of the men entrusted to them.
Many, though of course not all, SS commanders simply
put into practice in the field the lesson they had learned
in the cadet schools—that the soldier's supreme duty was
to deal out and to accept death.[156] The SS formations
accordingly suffered losses on a scale unknown to the
army. Just before the Battle of France began officer
casualties in the SS Divisions were found to have been so
heavy that replacement officers had to be drafted in
straight from the cadet schools.[157]

Despite these obvious failings on the part of the SS
the Wehrmacht leaders sensed danger. A rival to the Wehrmacht had appeared on the battlefield and its *élan* inevitably impressed the Dictator in his Field Headquarters. On
19 July 1940 in a speech to the Reichstag Hitler publicly acknowledged that "the brave Divisions and Standarten of the Waffen-SS" had been used.[158] Praise from
the Dictator, their own successes and, even more, the
aloofness of their military rivals reinforced the corps spirit of the SS—and it was an arrogant spirit, looking down
upon the military world around it with the guardsman's
traditional contempt for the common soldiery. With each
battle the Waffen-SS visibly reinforced its claim to the
mantle of the nation's military elite. Though the SS soldiers had been schooled to be especially faithful and uncompromising fighters for National-Socialism, in their own

eyes they were no different from the American "Leather-necks" or the later French "Paras"—surrounded by an aura of toughness and masculinity, inspired by a sense of belonging to an aristocratic minority, a closed community with its own rules and loyalties.

SS-Gruppenführer Hans Jüttner, the Chief-of-Staff and later Head of the Führungshauptamt, was insistent that the Waffen-SS formations must meet the standards and requirements of the Wehrmacht and that all traces of their former police character must be eliminated. The main stumbling-block here was Eicke, whose pseudo-revolutionary anti-militarism no longer squared with the imperial-guard concept. With increasing severity the Führungshauptamt demanded that the Totenkopf Division Commander adhere strictly to the orders of Waffen-SS Headquarters (formed in summer 1940).[159] Eicke complained to Obergruppenführer Wolff that there was a "hate against him" in Berlin—"ever since I left Germany certain circles have been doing their best to undermine the Reichsführer's confidence in me, which I have enjoyed for years."[160]

Jüttner in fact considered that, for the sake of the reputation of the Waffen-SS, the dilettante ex-paymaster should be relieved of command of his Division. Too much explosive evidence was piling up: the Totenkopf Division had been guilty of the first major war crime in the West—on 26 May 1940 a company commander of No. 2 Regiment had shot one hundred British prisoners-of-war during the fighting in north-west France;[161] in many units of the Division the barbaric methods characteristic of the concentration-camp guards persisted; Eicke secretly obtained additional weapons for his Division from the Dachau and Oranienburg concentration camps;[162] he made unauthorised purchases of trucks in unoccupied France because the Wehrmacht refused to motorise his Division, which was still horsedrawn.[163] Finally in August 1940, when certain men of his division were to be released, Eicke demanded a declaration from them binding them never to voice complaints regarding conditions within the Division. This was too much for Jüttner, and Eicke was called to order. Waffen-SS Headquarters ordered him to withdraw the declarations immediately.[164] On Jüttner's orders SS legal officers interrogated the men who had

carried out Eicke's secret weapons forays and all the
Division's unauthorised vehicles were confiscated. Simultaneously Jüttner threatened that, in the event of further
insubordination, Eicke's weapons traffickers would be summoned before the competent SS-Police court.[165]

In a fury, Eicke retorted that hitherto he had in principle been responsible to the Reichsführer alone and that
Jüttner should therefore regard any agreement to conform as a concession. He continued: "The tone adopted
towards a senior SS officer and Divisional Commander
in the letters from your office is not that to which even
hardened soldiers are accustomed."[166] But Jüttner persisted.
The Führungshauptamt interrogated ex-members of the
Division and compiled a comprehensive critique of Eicke's
methods of command. Once more Eicke protested, writing to Jüttner of attacks "by expert pen-pushers on your
staff and silly gossip by their spiteful friends." He concluded: "When enquiries are made regarding conditions
in an SS operational division which has left 23 officers
and 370 NCOs and men dead on the battlefield, and
when the purpose of the enquiry is simply to obtain
incriminating evidence against decent SS officers and
men, this is pure Marxism and the result is to undermine
confidence."[167]

At times even Himmler took part in the anti-Eicke
campaign. One of Eicke's Divisional Orders showed that
"for general edification" even regimental commanders
were being punished for trivial offences, and the names
of senior officers who contracted venereal disease were
being announced in public. Himmler blew up: "Dear
Eicke, when I read something like this, I doubt your
reason. These are moments when I question your capacity to command a division."[168] Nevertheless Himmler
would not allow Jüttner to relieve Eicke of his command. Eicke swallowed the reproof and retained his division.

Meanwhile the Führungshauptamt pushed on with the
expansion of the SS army and by spring 1941 it consisted
of four divisions and one brigade. At this point World
War II turned eastwards; the SS formations were summoned to the Balkans and once more SS troops spearheaded the German invading armies. The Leibstandarte
broke through from southern Serbia into Albania, stormed

through Thessaly and forced the passage into the Peloponnese. In central Serbia "Das Reich" took Belgrade by *coup de main* and overran the Bacska.[169]

The SS formations had hardly come to rest, however, before the Führer's Headquarters teleprinters were tapping out new orders. Adolf Hitler had decided to attack the Soviet Union.

Himmler's army now numbered 160,000 men;[170] it moved into its assembly areas on the eastern frontier of the German zone ready for the Third Reich's final catastrophic adventure. The Leibstandarte and the "Viking" Division were allotted to Army Group South, "Das Reich" to Army Group Centre, and the Totenkopf and Police Divisions to Army Group North.[171] On 22 June 1941 at 3.15 a.m. the Waffen-SS set foot upon the battleground of its greatest achievements; the real saga of the SS army was about to open. Before it did so, however, a shadow had fallen upon the Waffen-SS of which it was never to rid itself: Himmler had issued an instruction indirectly linking all forces of the Waffen-SS with the murkiest corner of the entire SS empire—the concentration camps.

On 22 April 1941 Himmler laid down the units which he intended to regard as part of the Waffen-SS. Hitherto he had accepted OKW's decision that the Waffen-SS consisted solely of the fighting formations, their replacement units, the Totenkopf Standarten and the three cadet schools in Brunswick, Bad Tölz and Klagenfurt. But now, on the eve of the Eastern campaign and in control of four divisions, Himmler felt himself strong enough arbitrarily to extend the meaning of the term "Waffen-SS." In a Führungshauptamt directive he set out 179 units and agencies all now to be considered an integral part of the Waffen-SS—and they included the concentration camps, their administrative staffs and the Totenkopf guard units,[172] in other words all those organisations which had been formed in 1939 when Eicke's Totenkopfverbände were relieved from concentration-camp duty; their personnel consisted of men unfit for service from the Allgemeine-SS, the Kyffhäuserbund and the SA.[173]

From now on the concentration-camp guards ranked as members of the Waffen-SS. They carried the same pay-books, they wore the same uniform as the true Waffen-

SS[174] which, with its fighting formations at the front, had never been implicated in the terror regime of the concentration camps. Moreover the hangmen and the soldiers had something else in common—the Führungshauptamt was responsible for the equipment and military training of the guard units, and all transfers between concentration camps now had to pass via Waffen-SS Headquarters. Worse still—pending transfer to the WVHA —the Concentration Camp Inspectorate, the headquarters of all concentration camps, was temporarily included in the Führungshauptamt (from autumn 1940 to spring 1942).[175]

But did the Waffen-SS soldiers protest against this insult? Did they rise in wrath when their military organisation was equated with the executioners of the torture factories and extermination camps? They accepted Himmler's order without a word: they fell into line, held their tongues, and remained dumb—as they had done at the end of 1939 when the Verfügungstruppe was amalgamated with Eicke's 6,500 thugs from the concentration camps and the Waffen-SS thus received an injection of the poison of an inhuman and barbaric attitude to prisoners learnt and practised over the years.[176] They remained dumb— as they did later when the 50,000 men of the "Reinforced Totenkopf Standarten," also trained in the concentration camps and the standard-bearers of political terror throughout German-occupied Europe, joined the Waffen-SS as cadres for new divisions.[177] They remained dumb as they did later in the war when many a sinister figure from the eerie empire of terror and mass extermination was transferred to the Waffen-SS—Hauptsturmführer Bothmann with his liquidation commando which had murdered 300,000 Jews in the Kulmhof gas vans[178]—the 2,500 men from the extermination staff of Auschwitz[179] —the 1,500 guards from Sachsenhausen.[180]

The Waffen-SS commanders probably comforted themselves with the thought that the discipline and sense of honour of their troops would enable them to keep their distance from the SS political underworld. But they could not keep the slate quite clean: the Waffen-SS had to provide units (some 1,500 men) to assist in forming the Einsatzgruppen murder squads;[181] certain of their reserve units took part in the more grisly SS operations such as the suppression of the Warsaw ghetto revolt;[182] they had to accept official Waffen-SS status for a penal brigade composed of poachers, professional criminals and men under sentence of court martial, commanded by a friend of Berger's Doctor Oskar Dirlewanger.[183]

Nevertheless the SS military still thought that they could keep their escutcheon clean and in this they were supported even by Himmler; early in April 1941 he made a gesture showing that he still wished to keep the Waffen-SS fighting formations separate from the machine of terror.[184] He created a sort of Waffen-SS within the Waffen-SS, a private army which he intended to use for his own political strategy.[185] Immediately they entered the operations zone, the Waffen-SS fighting formations came under command of the army; this special force, however, was subject to Himmler alone; he could, of course, make it available to the army but equally he could remove it at any time he thought fit.[186] The main body of Himmler's army consisted of the Totenkopf Standarten, which OKW had initially refused to recognise as Waffen-SS units. Himmler organised the majority of the Standarten into infantry and cavalry brigades under the direct orders of the Reichsführer-SS.[187] He chose SS-Brigadeführer Knoblauch as Chief of Staff and in May 1941 formed the "Headquarters Staff Reichsführer-SS" [Kommandostab];[188] the troops were for use in rear of the front against partisans and Jews.

But the martial dreams of Himmler's middle age melted away as quickly as had those of his youth. The eastern campaign demanded more and more formations. Regiment by regiment Himmler's private army was swallowed up and by mid-1942 all its units had been incorporated in the field army.[189] As a result of the formation of the "Headquarters Staff," however, the gap between Himmler and the professional commanders of the Waffen-SS widened. Moreover the further the SS divisions penetrated into the endless expanses of Russia, the more visibly did Himmler's military men become divorced from the orders and fantasies of their Reichsführer.

The SS soldiers were living in another world, a cruel remorseless world, aeons removed from the ideological verbiage of the SS. Driven by belief in their Führer and in the ultimate victory of Germany, the SS formations stormed through the steppes, marshes and forests of Russia, both heroes and victims of a ghastly chapter of human error and hallucination. They won for themselves a select place in the annals of war. Whether in the south, the centre or the north, wherever the enemy recovered sufficiently from his surprise to stand and fight, wherever he launched a counter-attack and tore gaps in the German attacking front, orders went out for the SS formations.

Once more the SS divisions spearheaded the German armies. The Leibstandarte seized a bridgehead over the Dnieper; it broke through the Soviet defences of the Crimea at Perekop and stormed Taganrog and Rostov.[190] The "Viking" division pursued the enemy to the shores of the Sea of Azov; "Das Reich" broke through the Moscow defences south of Borodino and came within a few miles of the Soviet capital.[191] Then, when the Soviets launched their first major counter-attacks late in 1941, the Waffen-SS provided an unparalleled example of tenacity. Hammered by "Stalin organs," tanks and massed infantry, the SS more than justified their reputation as the eastern army's fire brigade.

In January 1942 after the Soviet breakthrough west of Moscow, strong Soviet forces moved forward in rear of Army Group Centre. General Model, C-in-C 9th Army, thereupon moved the SS regiment "Der Führer" under Obersturmbannführer Otto Kumm into the bend of the Volga near Rzhev. The regiment was to form a thin screen linking the front with the army formations further west and it was to hold until Model had concentrated sufficient troops in the south to deal the enemy an annihilating blow. In a temperature of minus 52 Centigrade the SS men held on, driving the enemy back day after day, hour after hour. By 18 February Model had won his victory. When his regiment was relieved, Kumm met his Army Commander. Model said: "I know what your regiment must have been through, Kumm. But I still can't do without it. How strong is it now?" Kumm pointed to the window: "My regiment is on parade outside!" There stood 35 men, all that remained of 2,000.[192]

Even Theodor Eicke now proved that he could turn soldier. Since being promoted SS-Obergruppenführer the ex-concentration-camp guard had become a changed man.

He shut himself up in his billet for days at a time, cut the tactical signs out of the situation maps and played a war game with them on the floor of his room—all in deadly secret lest his senior general staff officer notice his suddenly acquired taste for military matters.[193] When Soviet forces cut off the Totenkopf division and five other army divisions at Demyansk south of Lake Ilmen on 8 February 1942, they found that in Eicke they were facing a tough, clever opponent.[194] Field-Marshal Busch described the fact that the Germans encircled at Demyansk held out for months primarily to "the energetic leadership of Obergruppenführer Eicke."[195] Then the SS soldiers showed their offensive spirit once more; together with army formations they broke through into the pocket and relieved the defenders of Demyansk.

Demyansk, Rzhev, the Mius River, Lake Ladoga, Volkov —all these names were linked with the military exploits of a force which had gained an almost legendary reputation on both sides, evoking superstitious fear on the one hand and jealous admiration on the other. Both friend and foe were agreed that the Waffen-SS possessed military qualities equalled by few other forces and surpassed by none.

When taken prisoner in autumn 1941 the Russian Major-General Artemenko, commander of XXVII Army Corps, said that the SS division "Viking" had shown greater fortitude than any other formation on either side; the Russians had breathed a sigh of relief, he said, when the division was relieved by army units.[196] General Wohler, C-in-C of the German 8th Army, thought similarly, becoming almost lyrical in his praise of the SS formations under his command; they had "stood like a rock in the army," he said and had withstood the enemy "with unshakable fortitude."[197] In a letter to Himmler, General von Mackensen, commanding III Panzer Corps, extolled the Leibstandarte for its "discipline, refreshing, cheerful energy and unshakable steadfastness in crisis." "A real elite unit," he concluded.[198]

Not all army officers, however, were prepared to agree with such panegyrics. Rivalry and jealousy were the feelings uppermost in the breasts of many professional soldiers as they saw the Waffen-SS pushing itself into the forefront and clearly obtaining favoured treatment from the leaders of the State. The army's aversion to the Waffen-SS was an open secret. Waffen-SS commanders already suspected the army of deliberately allotting the most dangerous hot-spots to the Waffen-SS in order to "burn up" their tiresome rival.

Eicke fulminated that the SS would "emerge from these battles so weak that it would never get on its feet again";[199] even Himmler later detected an intention "on the part of many people of ill-will" to "butcher this unwelcome force and get rid of it for some future development."[200] SS-Oberführer Simon, a regimental commander in the Totenkopf division, had positive proof that the staff of II Corps had deliberately withheld orders from the Führer's Headquarters for the relief of the Danish volunteers and the cadres of No. 2 Totenkopf infantry regiment in order to avoid having to relieve these units with army troops.[201] Eicke grumbled that it was high time that "our men were released from the grip of a malicious, jealous gang."[202]

In the case of many officers, however, jealousy was not the only reason for their frosty reserve. The military detected in this new force a fanaticism foreign to the military tradition and directed not only against the enemy in the field but also against helpless prisoners and the civilian population. In many cases Waffen-SS units broke the rules of military ethics which those soldiers with any feeling for tradition were trying to preserve despite all the bestialities of this war. Stories of barbaric treatment of prisoners-of-war and civilians by SS units were as numerous as the tales of SS bravery. Apologists for the Waffen-SS later protested that the troops were merely reacting to the inhuman Soviet methods of warfare. German troops had in fact found in captured files orders by Soviet Army and Corps headquarters proving that German prisoners had been murdered by the Russians. For instance—report from Headquarters Russian 26 Division, 13 July 1941: "The enemy left about 400 dead behind on the battlefield; about 80 men surrendered and were shot."[203] Report from 33 Army, 8 December 1941: "100 prisoners of war captured by the GM Infantry Division were shot by orders of the Commissar of the Division in view of the complicated situation."[204] Liquidation of German prisoners of war became so widespread that order No. 0068

of 2 December 1941 from the Chief of Staff Soviet
Coastal Army Sebastopol contained this: "As a rule the
troop formations exterminate prisoners without interrogation and without transferring them to the divisional staff.
Prisoners may only be exterminated in the case of resistance or escape. Besides, the shooting of prisoners at the
place of capture or at the front line, which is being practised most extensively, acts as a deterrent to soldiers of
the enemy wanting to desert to us."[205] On 29 March 1942
the Leibstandarte War Graves Officer reported that in
the courtyard of the former GPU headquarters in Taganrog six members of No. 3 Company of the Leibstandarte
had been found murdered; all had been thrown down a
well shaft; the medical report stated: "Four fingers of
the right hand missing (presumably hacked off), skull
smashed (presumably when thrown down the well) . . .
Spine broken . . . chest smashed in."[206]

The SS apologists ignore the fact that both sides were
guilty of crimes against prisoners of war; moreover the ag-
gressor, who in this instance had decided upon the liquidation of whole categories of prisoners *before* operations
commenced (the Commissar Order), could send his prisoners to the rear more easily than the disorganised defender. In any case the brutal reprisals for Soviet crimes
taken by Waffen-SS soldiers were out of all proportion,
and repugnant to many of their fellow-countrymen. In
fairness, however, it must be said that senior Waffen-
SS commanders, including even Sepp Dietrich, tried to
prevent reprisals against prisoners—"We owe it to the
title on our sleeve," Dietrich said.[207] But the order did
not penetrate to each individual soldier.

As a result of the introduction of unsoldierly types
drawn from the cesspool of political fanaticism—the
former members of the Totenkopfverbände or the exchange
personnel from the concentration camps for instance—
combined with the fury of battle and a certain relaxation of discipline, the Waffen-SS became apt to use all
types of inhuman methods of warfare. Its military record
was continually being tarnished by crime; a fortnight after the opening of the Russian campaign the "Viking"
division shot 600 Jews in Galicia as a reprisal for Soviet
crimes;[208] in summer 1943 the "Prinz Eugen" division
liquidated the inhabitants of Kosutica because Einsatzkom-

mando 2 reported that the troops had "apparently" been
fired on from the church;[209] in spring 1944 the SS/
Police division destroyed Klissura in northern Greece after one of their units had been ambushed;[210] in June
1944 a company of "Das Reich," searching for an SS
commander who had been captured by the *maquis*, destroyed the village of Oradour-sur-Glane in south-west
France, killing the entire population;[211] two months later
during the battles in Normandy the SS Panzer division
"Hitlerjugend" shot 64 Canadian and British prisoners of
war.[212]

Explicable though such brutalities may be, the fact
remains that similar crimes were seldom committed by
the Wehrmacht. Reports on Wehrmacht and Waffen-SS
misdemeanours collated by the Allgemeine Wehrmachtamt
[General Armed Forces office—AW] of OKW underline the difference. On 2 August 1943 AW stated: "In
the period covered by this report 151 cases of this nature
came to notice. In 19 cases the culprits belonged to the
army, in 53 cases to the Waffen-SS, while in 79 cases
the culprits' unit could not be established. The number
of cases of rape is high. After interrogation of the victims
and of witnesses, the Field Security Police and in certain
instances the SS Patrol Service [Streifendienst], reported
18 proven cases of rape. In 12 cases the culprits were
members of the Waffen-SS; in the other 6 the culprits'
arm of the service could not be clearly established."[213]

In parts of the Ukraine the Waffen-SS behaved with
such savagery that the people deserted their villages and
took refuge with the Soviet army. The AW noted: "The
inhabitants of this town and the surrounding district are
in a state of permanent indignation over thefts of live-
stock, assaults on inhabitants and rape of women and
girls."[214] On 30 May 1943 two Russian officials begged
the Town Major of Rogosyanka to order the Waffen-SS
"not to beat up the population, to refrain from requisitioning and to cease plaguing the villagers." They concluded:
"Prior to the arrival of the SS the population was most
favourably disposed towards the troops and towards Adolf
Hitler."[215]

From other areas also reports of brutality and high-
handed actions by the Waffen-SS began to arrive. In November 1942 the Rumanian General Staff protested that

532 THE ORDER OF THE DEATH'S HEAD

"racial German" members of the Waffen-SS were beating
up Rumanian officials, violating Rumanian laws and intriguing against the authority of the Rumanian State. A
telegram from Böhme, the Police Attaché, Bucharest,
stated: "Based on these proven instances, the Rumanian
Great General Staff asserts that these misdemeanours and
incidents are the work primarily of members of the Waffen-SS . . . the Great General Staff considers it necessary
that both sides should respect the good order and discipline
prevalent in this country."[216] In the Balkans even the
RSHA Einsatzkommando protested against the inhuman
methods of warfare of the SS divisions. On 15 July 1943
SS-Sturmbannführer Reinholz of Einsatzkommando 2 reported that the Waffen-SS methods had "begun to have
an injurious effect upon German interests in this area."[217]
In conversation with a Croat Minister SS-Brigadeführer
Ritter von Oberkamp, commander of the "Prinz Eugen"
division, attempted to pass off some outrage committed
by his unit as an "error"; SS-Oberführer Fromm, who was
also present, threw back at him: "Since you arrived there
has unfortunately been one 'error' after another."[218] Many
of these "errors" were due to the fact that as the Waffen-
SS swelled and division after division was formed, discipline inevitably relaxed—and the SS swelled because its
successes, together with his own sinking fortunes, caused
Adolf Hitler to lift all restrictions on it. As the years
went by the Waffen-SS became the tyrant's last hope;
Hitler clung in desperation to the belief that only the
invincible SS troops could save him from catastrophe.

As early as the spring of 1942 Hitler had agreed to the
formation of a new SS division, the "Prinz Eugen";[219]
shortly thereafter the "Florian Geyer" division was
formed from the SS cavalry brigade[220] and by that autumn
Hitler was allowing the Waffen-SS to do as it liked. The
result was the "Hohenstaufen" Panzergrenadier division,
initially consisting of 70 per cent conscripts;[221] then the
"Frundsberg,"[222] a new "Germanic" division named "Nord-
land,"[223] the "Hitlerjugend"[224] and a Bosnian division[225]
—the Waffen-SS grew and grew. Moreover the SS now
managed to break the OKW stranglehold on equipment.
The army had so far been careful to ensure that the
Wehrmacht had priority over the Waffen-SS in the distribution of modern weapons, but Hitler now reversed the

position, allocating to the Waffen-SS all the latest equipment from assault guns to armoured troop carriers.[226]

Finally the Waffen-SS succeeded in eliminating the deficiency to which it ascribed its heavy losses in men and material—lack of armour. Even in late 1941 Arthur Phleps, the ex-Rumanian General and at the time a regimental commander in the "Viking" division, had implored Felix Steiner to "get us tanks; without them this magnificent force will be ruined."[227] Slowly, and in the face of continual resistance from the Wehrmacht, the three original Waffen-SS divisions (the Leibstandarte, "Das Reich" and "Totenkopf") were re-equipped as Panzer divisions;[228] and the first SS Panzer Corps allowed to the Waffen-SS was constituted under the command of Paul Hausser.[229] Additional Panzer Corps followed.[230] In March 1943 Obergruppenführer Hausser at the head of his armoured formations charged through the Ukraine and fulfilled Hitler's wildest hopes. The Corps repulsed a major Soviet attack in the Kharkov area and in summer 1943 spearheaded the southern front in the last major German offensive in Russia.[231]

A year later the Waffen-SS divisions had become the crack formations on the eastern front. In the view of Stein, the American historian, they "had on two separate occasions prevented another Stalingrad"[232] by breaking up menacing Soviet envelopment moves: at Cherkassy in January 1944 Soviet forces had surrounded two German Corps; they were relieved by army formations together with the SS division "Viking"; at Kamenetz-Podolsk an entire German Panzer Army was surrounded and eventually relieved by Hausser's Corps, which had in the meantime been moved to France and recalled.[233] Stein says: "Wherever they were committed they attacked; sometimes with great success and sometimes with little or none. But whatever the outcome of the individual action, the end result was to delay the enemy advance."[234] The military triumphs of the Waffen-SS, however, could not conceal the fact that the force had long since been "burnt to a cinder," in the words of Steiner, the commander of the "Viking" division.[235] The armour had come too late. By 1943 one-third of the original Waffen-SS divisions had fallen in Russia.[236] They had suffered losses which would have broken the back of any other force. Between 22 June and 19 November 1941 they lost 1,239 officers and 35,377 men, of whom 13,037 were killed.[237] During the break-out from the Cherkassy pocket "Viking" lost all its tanks, all its equipment and half its men.[238] In February 1943 Eicke, commanding the Totenkopf division, fell near Kharkov and similar casualties in other divisions began to affect efficiency. On 15 November 1941 "Totenkopf" reported: "The losses so far suffered in battle have deprived this formation of nearly 60 per cent of the vital officer and NCO cadre. Losses in NCOs are catastrophic . . . a company which has lost its old experienced NCOs and section commanders cannot attack. It is unreliable in defence because its backbone is not there. There are already companies in this division incapable of reconnoitring in front of their sectors."[239]

As their manpower losses mounted, the SS divisions' cries for assistance became more strident; moreover the quality of the replacements provided by the SS-Hauptamt recruiting centres was so low that both the fighting efficiency and quality of the force were affected. The early Waffen-SS soldiers had gone to war with enthusiasm, inspired by the Hitler cult and in the conviction that they were serving a new, more egalitarian Germany. They were young idealists under the spell of a sort of ecstasy, and nothing seemed more natural to them than to devote themselves and sacrifice themselves to what they called "Führer and Reich." The seal was set on their tragic error—the error of an entire generation—by the graves and wooden crosses in the lonely expanses of Russia. Behind these early crusaders followed a new wave of actual or ostensible volunteers, but they lacked the naive credulity of their predecessors, now dead. Many of them had been press-ganged or lured into service and they soldiered with reluctance. They had joined the Waffen-SS without enthusiasm, they were badly trained and they had turned into sceptics; they brought to the Waffen-SS a mentality far removed from that of the Verfügungstruppe pioneers.

With righteous National-Socialist indignation the Führungshauptamt recorded in spring 1943: "Morale is bad. Unmistakable signs of home and church influences. General attitude: if I am conscripted I can do nothing about it but volunteer I will not. Fear of active service."[240] Berger could no longer provide the replacements required by the military for his sources had long since been exhausted. The reservoir of volunteers had dried up as quickly in the case of the Waffen-SS as in that of the Wehrmacht and from 1942 onwards the Waffen-SS had to rely on conscripts.[241] Every report from the recruiting centres confirmed that, horrified by the reports of its savage methods of warfare and its towering casualty figures, the Germans were now anti-Waffen-SS.

In February 1943 Waffen-SS headquarters collated thirteen reports from the recruiting centres and they told a story of total failure.[242] Recruiting Centre South-east (Breslau): "Readiness to enlist not good. No enthusiasm for military service. Young men do not wish to volunteer. Instances of a definite anti-Waffen-SS attitude."[243] Recruiting Centre South (Munich): "Readiness to enlist leaves much to be desired, sometimes giving impression of passive resistance. Men do not wish to volunteer but to wait until they are conscripted."[244] Recruiting Centre Main (Nuremberg): "Readiness to enlist small, at times catastrophic. The young men are not only anti-Waffen-SS but basically opposed to any form of military service."[245] The anti-Christian propaganda so long drummed into the Waffen-SS now began to boomerang. Parents and churches paralysed recruiting; even fear of the Gestapo did not prevent men from opting out of Himmler's army.

SS Recruiting Centre North-east: "Influence of parents and church negative."[246] Baltic II: "Home influence unfavourable."[247] South: "Many youngsters forbidden by their parents to join the Waffen-SS."[248] Hamburg: "Parents generally anti-Waffen-SS."[249] Vienna: "Church influence very strong. One man said: 'The priest told us that the SS was atheist and if we joined it we should go to hell.' "[250] Berger reported to Himmler that at a Leibstandarte passing-out parade almost all officer cadets had refused to become Waffen-SS officers. One, a youngster from Hanover, had said: "We didn't want war. We had enough to eat and still have. Let those who haven't enough to eat carry on with this war." Berger added: "Reichsführer, these are not isolated instances."[251]

Gloomily Himmler accepted Berger's jeremiads. On 14 May 1943 he lamented: "In my view the overall conclusion is that the youth of our people has clearly and deliberately been poisoned by Christian education and we have obviously not countered it by sufficiently positive ideological education, particularly now in wartime."[252] Nevertheless Berger refused to accept that all recruiting was at an end and he found two allies prepared to hound their members into volunteering: the pre-military training camps of the Hitler Youth and the Labour Service Camps; here he was free to recruit at his will.[253]

To be sure that he was ahead of the Wehrmacht's mustering commissions in the hunt for new recruits, Berger ordered all members of certain annual intakes to present themselves for preliminary mustering for the Waffen-SS. SS recruiting officers appeared, determined to force every young man in the Labour Service into the Waffen-SS. On 24 February 1943 a number of young men failed to appear for a Waffen-SS lecture in a Labour Service agricultural school at Halle. An SS officer commented: "If these people joined the SS they would forthwith be shot; this is nothing else but sabotage and desertion."[254] Others at the school were confronted with printed forms pledging them to join the Waffen-SS. When one man objected that he must first talk to his father, the SS officer replied: "We don't have anything more to do with those old fogeys. You've all got to sign or I shall let no one leave." To another man he said: "You pigs seem to think that others are being shot to bits out there for the pleasure of allowing you to skrimshank here." Practically everybody signed.[255]

Writing to his father a Labour Service man complained: "Dear Papa, today I have witnessed the dirtiest trick I have ever seen." Three SS men and a policeman had appeared in the camp demanding that all the inmates register on the Waffen-SS recruiting list. The letter continued: "About 60 men were forced to sign, failing which they were given a reprimand or three days under arrest. All sorts of threats were used. Everybody was frightfully indignant. One or two just departed, some even through the window. The policeman stood at the door and would let no one out. The whole camp is furious. I've had enough; I've changed completely." The father sent the letter on to Himmler.[256]

The headquarters of the Moselle Gau reported to the Party Chancellery: "We understand that all Labour Service men over 5ft 5in were paraded and a certain number selected; whether they wished to or not, they were then forced to 'volunteer' for the Waffen-SS on the pretext that the SS delegation had come direct from the Führer's headquarters."[257] On 30 March 1943 the acting commander of V Army Corps reported "numerous complaints that the Waffen-SS is using unauthorised recruiting methods."[258] Report from Sassbach-Achern: "When no one came forward even after the demand had been repeated five times, it was stated that no one might leave the hall who had not volunteered for one of the Waffen-SS formations."[259] Canvassing among apprentices in a Mulhouse factory, SS officers threatened that "in the case of refusal their parents would be expelled from Alsace."[260]

The units, however, were horrified when they saw the replacements with which they were expected to face the increasingly severe fighting in prospect. In August 1941 and again in March 1942 Jüttner protested to Berger against the "totally unacceptable replacements" provided by the SS-Hauptamt.[261] In September 1942 he was even more outspoken, referring to crude recruiting methods which produced men either obtained on false pretences or simply press-ganged. Units were continually being plagued by complaints from families demanding the return of relatives press-ganged into the Waffen-SS.[262]

In addition commanders complained about the miserable training standard of their recruits. "A considerable proportion of the men reach the front knowing nothing," Eicke reported: "their listless uninterested faces are eloquent. One can see that they have had no strenuous training to fit them for battle."[263] The fighting commanders may have been dissatisfied with the replacements mustered from Germany but Berger's protégés, the "racial German" volunteers, were worse. Headquarters of the "Florian Geyer" SS cavalry division observed in 1943 that the racial Germans showed "a striking indifference and mulishness" which was affecting the morale of the troops.[264]

Initially the racial German volunteers from Rumania and Croatia had been glad to join the Waffen-SS (unlike their counterparts from Hungary) but they were soon disillusioned.[265] The headquarters of the "Florian Geyer" division thought it "perfectly possible that many of the racial German volunteers do not regard this war as their own nor consider service in the Waffen-SS as their duty to the German people."[266] Eicke's opinion of them was even lower: "A large number of the racial Germans can only

538 THE ORDER OF THE DEATH'S HEAD

be described as intellectually substandard. Many can neither write nor read German. They do not understand the words of command and are inclined to insubordination and malingering. Orders issued are generally not carried out, the excuse being that they did not understand what their officer wanted. This is an invitation to cowardice."[267] Fighting efficiency was eventually so badly affected by the attitude of the racial Germans that a low percentage of racial Germans was considered the mark of a good SS division.[268]

In the eyes of the SS commanders this vexatious recruiting situation was partially offset by the enthusiasm for the Waffen-SS shown by the European volunteers. The 200,000 non-Germans in the Waffen-SS gave it a multiracial aura and reintroduced some of that idealism which the commanders found so sadly lacking. But the daily wartime grind quickly damped enthusiasm. Even the cry of "anti-Bolshevist crusade," to which all could subscribe, could not conceal the fact that the Waffen-SS was not, as it liked to think, the political and military expression of a spontaneous European movement.

Drawn from a variety of countries and with a variety of ideologies, the SS volunteers suddenly found themselves under training by a force of strict Prussian drill-sergeants reared in the blinkers of totalitarianism. In the Waffen-SS these foreigners were thrown together with men who had no understanding of the habits and views of other races. Complaints soon began to pile up that officers and NCOs of the Waffen-SS were treating their foreign volunteers in the most overbearing master-race manner. Resistance to the over-Germanic training methods of the Waffen-SS came primarily from the Flemish, the Norwegians and the Dutch.[269] Even Himmler castigated the "iniquitous and psychologically mistaken treatment" of his non-German Germans and threatened that "officers and NCOs who offend against the future of Germanism must be ruthlessly demoted and expelled."[270] In Norway ex-Waffen-SS men banded together to keep out Berger's recruiting officers;[271] from early 1943 applications by Dutchmen, Danes and Belgians for release from the Waffen-SS increased sharply.[272]

"It is simply incomprehensible how little influence Waffen-SS methods have had upon the men's ideological attitude," Amt VI of the SS-Hauptamt lamented in October 1942.[273] In many cases outright enemies of the SS were wearing Waffen-SS uniform. The field postal censorship office, for instance, intercepted a letter from a Dutch SS cadet named 't Veer telling a friend in Amsterdam that he was "twice as optimistic since our friends [the Allies] have established a foothold on Italian soil." Himmler ordered: "This man must immediately be brought before an SS court."[274] Leon Degrelle, the Rexist leader and Belgian Waffen-SS hero, an SS-Sturmbannführer decorated with the Oak Leaves, had in fact only joined the Waffen-SS in order to thwart Himmler's plan to separate Flemish-speaking Belgium from the rest of the country and incorporate it in the Reich.[275] Voorhoeve, the director of National-Socialist propaganda in Holland, was anti-German and opposed to SS Germanic policy; he told a friend that only by joining this "squad of damned idiots" could SS plans be countered.[276] Rauter, the HSSPF, warned: "Acceptance of this man into the Waffen-SS is highly dangerous. Should he return to Holland as a 'hero' it would be very difficult for us to oppose so distinguished a front-line soldier."[277]

Even the more simple-minded among the European volunteers began to realise that they had been lured by promises which were not being kept. Many of them had joined the Waffen-SS because they believed in the promises made by Berger's recruiting squads that by serving the Germans in war they would assure their country's independence in Adolf Hitler's new Europe. The Waffen-SS commanders supported these aspirations, but the door was soon closed by Hitler. As the months went by, therefore, the officers' position vis-à-vis the European volunteers became more and more untenable. Commanders took refuge in a variety of expedients: the Bad Tölz cadet school was turned into a European military academy[278] where non-Germans were even permitted to criticise the National-Socialist Party programme; in Holland it was proposed to erect a "memorial to the Germanic warrior";[279] plans for a pan-European future appeared—and all the time these officers knew that they were drawing for their men a picture of a future which would never materialise.

The world in which the Waffen-SS commanders had once believed collapsed. The ideological lifeline linking the

army of Steiner, Hausser, Bittrich and Dietrich to the SS
parted—not suddenly but gradually, becoming more tenuous and tattered month by month. With their faith in
Hitler wavering, despairing of final victory, handicapped
by second-rate reinforcements and wrestling with a crisis
of conscience over the European volunteers, the SS army
fell a prey to ideological doubts, unsure whether it still
belonged to the SS. The SS formations were now following
only their own banners and they were led by commanders
whose loyalty to the leadership of the state was faltering.

They still trotted out the stereotyped phrases about
Führer and Reich, loyalty and final victory, but in their
heart of hearts they withdrew into themselves and became
a force owing allegiance to none—no longer SS and not
yet Wehrmacht. In this they shared the traditional fate of
an imperial guard which, in the words of Rolf Bigler,
the Swiss sociologist, is invariably characterised by "a
special relationship to official authority and consequently
to the government."[280] So among the hardships and disappointments of war, for the men of the Waffen-SS the unit
became their real home; the divisional symbol, the bitter
battles, the memory of fallen comrades formed a mystical
bond holding the unit together, a closed circle into which
no stranger might penetrate. It was the same with the
commanders. Seldom have German formations been led
by more self-assured or haughtier generals. The SS generals gave many examples of robust self-reliance.

In February 1943, for instance, Paul Hausser and his
II SS Panzer Corps were ordered to stop the enemy then
massing against Kharkov and to hold the city at all costs.
By 12 February, however, the Russians had succeeded in
working round behind the German formations and Hausser's corps was faced with encirclement at any moment.
Hausser thereupon asked permission from Lanz, his Army
Commander, to evacuate Kharkov and withdraw. Lanz's
headquarters refused, pointing out that Hitler had forbidden any retrograde movement. On 15 February OKH sent
a radio message to Kharkov referring once more to the
Führer's order and forbidding Hausser to evacuate Kharkov. Then Hausser took his own decision. About 12.50
p.m. on 15 February he gave the order to withdraw—
contrary to his Führer's explicit instructions. As a result
his Panzer corps was saved from annihilation and Field

Marshal von Manstein was able to use it later for a counter-offensive. Hitler grumbled about the insubordinate SS general but left him undisturbed.[281]

SS generals frequently disregarded the orders of the army. During the German advance in southern Russia OKW accused Dietrich, the commander of the Leibstandarte, of "charging into Rostov" contrary to orders "purely to gain a prestige victory"—as Berger noted in the file;[282] the insubordination of another SS commander drew an order from Field Marshal von Kleist in classic terms. "The commander of the 'Viking' division," he radioed, "is 1: to be informed that the army will not have positions occupied contrary to orders; 2: to report how it comes about that, without reporting the fact, he has occupied a position other than that expressly ordered by Corps Headquarters."[283]

Few had more reason to complain of the SS Generals' independent ways than Himmler himself. Suspiciously he watched the Waffen-SS withdrawing into its own world. On 23 November 1942 Maximillian von Herff, Head of the SS Personnel Office, commented on the senior officers of the Führungshauptamt: "There is a circle centred around Jüttner which must be watched, since it could become dangerous one day. This is the Petri-von Jena-Hansen group. Neither their thoughts nor their desires are those of the SS. They simply wish to be an imperial guard; anything else is a side issue in their eyes."[284]

The Reichsführer-SS had never had any very close relationship with his troops but he was sufficiently sensitive to perceive the increasing estrangement between his fighting force and the rest of his Order. It can hardly have surprised him. As early as 5 March 1942 he had prophesied: "I see here a major danger—that the Waffen-SS will start to lead its own existence, pleading 'exigency of war' just as the Wehrmacht used earlier to plead 'national defence requirement.' "[285] On many previous occasions the Reichsführer-SS had been worried by the fact that the Waffen-SS led its own existence. There were many small signs—the manifest aversion of Waffen-SS officers to social contact with men of the Allgemeine-SS, the tendency to use Wehrmacht instead of SS ranks, contrary to Himmler's order, and the alacrity with which Waffen-

SS units placed themselves under Wehrmacht orders, again contrary to the Reichsführer's explicit instructions.

When 600 Waffen-SS men placed themselves under the Wehrmacht Commandant Berlin during an air-raid, Himmler was furious: "If a single other Waffen-SS man places himself under the command of the Wehrmacht and the Waffen-SS thereby stabs me, the Reichsführer-SS, in the back, I shall have the SS Garrison Commander Berlin not only relieved at once but arrested."[286] But the Waffen-SS officers were not to be persuaded to renounce what Himmler called the "Wehrmacht outlook." Sturmbannführer Loh, Waffen-SS Garrison Commander Nuremberg, refused on principle all contact with offices of the Allgemeine-SS and SD. On 10 October 1941 the SD Abschnitt Nuremberg reported: "As SS Oberabschnitt Commander, SS-Brigadeführer Dr Martin has done all in his power to weld the SS as a whole into one block . . . his attempts to include the Waffen-SS have failed in face of the obdurate and incomprehensible attitude of the above-named SS-Sturmbannführer Loh."[287] In vain Himmler drew the attention of his soldiers to the fact that the SS Order was the real home of the Waffen-SS. In August 1941 he commanded that only SS badges of rank be used in the SS Divisions.[288] Steiner was reprimanded for invariably signing his Corps Orders "General Steiner."[289] On this point, nevertheless, Himmler had eventually to give way somewhat to his military men. He agreed that senior Waffen-SS officers from Brigadeführer upwards might use Wehrmacht ranks in addition to their SS titles.[290] But he was more outspoken in criticising ideological backsliding on the part of his Generals. Sharply worded orders descended on Waffen-SS Headquarters urging every SS officer to train his soldiers "to be more fanatical and convinced standard-bearers of the National-Socialist ideology and of the concept of our Führer Adolf Hitler"; and then a threat: "I shall judge capacity to command a unit not only by ability to train it well militarily but also by ability to educate every individual officer, NCO and man to be a convinced, steadfast ideological fighter in every situation."[291]

Hardly a single SS General took any notice. Berger found it astonishing "that there are people in the SS who simply take no notice of an explicit order from the Reichsführer."[292] In many divisions the ideological instruction ordered by Himmler simply did not take place and the more assiduous SS Commanders who tried to carry it out became a laughing stock. In 1944 the ideological instructor of 13 SS Division complained that his "honour as an SS leader and officer had been impugned" because his political work "was largely disregarded by the divisional staff."[293] On 2 October 1943, a secret SS-Hauptamt informer put it more crudely: "It's enough to make you vomit. I'm always hearing: 'SS spirit! Shit! It's non-existent'."[294]

As the frequency of such reports increased, so did Himmler's suspicion that he was surrounded by ungrateful generals who already had a foot in the other camp—that of the Wehrmacht. One after another he saw his generals as apostates from the SS Order.

Berger noted that Obergruppenführer Phleps, commanding the SS Mountain Corps, had become "most peculiar"; he excluded from his staff conferences non-military National-Socialists such as Andreas Schmidt, the minority group leader.[295] Obergruppenführer Höfle's servile attitude to the Wehrmacht so infuriated Himmler that, although he was an old comrade from the days of the November 1923 putsch, Himmler ceased to address him with the familiar "du" and threatened him with the direst punishments. "Herr Höfle. This letter is the final warning before I dismiss you. As a subordinate you are as indisciplined as you are weak in carrying out your orders. I have the impression that you are complete wax in the hands of your staff. You will notify concisely and convincingly in writing—without any excuses or explanations—whether you are now prepared to obey your instructions and to pay more attention to the orders you receive from me than to the whisperings of your staff or the directives of the local army authorities."[296]

His Reichsführer's outbursts of rage left Höfle unmoved. Similarly Obergruppenführer Bittrich, now commander of II SS Panzer Corps, when dismissed by Himmler for critical utterances after the Normandy battle, refused to leave his post and was supported by the Commander-in-Chief West, Field-Marshal Model.[297] Particularly exasperating to Himmler was the fact that his one-time favourite, SS-Obergruppenführer and Waffen-SS General Felix

Steiner, now joined the ranks of the Reichsführer's critics.

"You are my most insubordinate general," Himmler once exclaimed, after hearing that Steiner had referred to him as a "sleazy romantic."[298] Henceforth Himmler watched the crusty East Prussian with mistrust. He had already observed that Steiner had surrounded himself with SS officers who did more than merely ridicule the spindly-legged figure of "Reichsheini" in uniform. As early as 1940 Himmler had been taken aback when Steiner, then commanding the "Deutschland" Verfügungstruppe regiment, had voiced loud criticism in the officers' mess of Hitler's strategy in the Western Campaign—so loud that Himmler had despatched Höfle to tell him to hold his tongue.[299] Himmler was also incensed by the critical comments of SS-Sturmbannführer Reichel, Steiner's senior staff officer, who, according to the Reichsführer, exercised "an extraordinarily unfortunate influence on morale among the officers of the [Viking] division."[300] He gave Steiner his reasons in August 1942: "In particular I regard it as impossible in the long run that Reichel should shoot his mouth off, criticising the actions not only of the authorities in general but even of the Führer and also of myself."[301] Standartenführer Gille, Steiner's Artillery Commander, was also in the Reichsführer's bad books. Gille was an entirely non-political officer who would have nothing to do with ideology. To Obersturmbannführer Fick, the divisional ideological observer, he growled: "Wearing of the brown shirt is not permitted in this aristocratic artillery regiment. I'll put a clean-out squad into your room."[302]

Himmler did his best to bring his one-time favourite general to heel. He threatened. He coaxed. He implored. He appealed to Steiner's sense of gratitude. He despatched emissaries to talk the General round. "I think it is generally recognised," he confided to Berger, "that I have always shown the greatest possible leniency towards the vainglory now characteristic of the soldiers and in particular of the average General."[303] Appealing to Steiner's gratitude Himmler pointed out that "he must realise that he had become an Obergruppenführer and Waffen-SS General at the age of 47, whereas in the army I doubt whether you would have become a General at all." Would he therefore be so good as to "cease call-

ing himself General, taking his SS rank of Obergruppenführer for granted, and use 'Gruppenführer' or 'Obergruppenführer,' the ranks to which he has been promoted as
a revolutionary commander."[304] And more threateningly:
"The Reichsführer desires that he [Steiner] put a stop once
and for all to the scandalous expressions used about me,
the Reichsführer, by many in the 'Viking' Division when
talking in the mess, etc. I will no longer tolerate these
things."[305]

But Himmler's admonitions fell on deaf ears. Berger
gave up the struggle, recognising "that SS-Gruppenführer
Steiner is simply not to be controlled. He does what he
wants and will not be talked to."[306] The last straw was
the news that Steiner was now greeting his men simply
with "Heil" instead of the obligatory "Heil Hitler" and was
even criticising the SS "Russian sub-humans" policy: Berger was instructed "to establish whether Steiner is lacking in loyalty towards the Reichsführer."[307] Berger was
able to reassure Himmler.[308]

But loyalty was an elastic term in the Waffen-SS. Himmler and Berger were unaware that a few days earlier
(June 1943) in a Berlin café Felix Steiner had met an
old friend, the one-time Nazi and now anti-Nazi Fritz Diet-
lof Graf von der Schulenburg, lately Vice President of the
Berlin Police. Steiner and Schulenburg had been friends
ever since they had served together in No. 1 Infantry
Regiment in Königsberg. Schulenburg divulged dangerous
thoughts to his friend: "We shall have to kill Hitler before he ruins Germany totally."[309] SS-Obergruppenführer
Steiner departed deep in thought. The Waffen-SS was
headed for the great parting of the ways. The moment
of truth—20 July 1944—was only a year away.

17

The SS and German Resistance

IN autumn 1942 information reaching the RSHA caused SS-Gruppenführer Müller, the Head of the Gestapo, to prick up his ears. The Gestapo Leitstelle Munich reported a currency case which, though it seemed at first sight an ordinary misdemeanour, was to have considerable effects upon the whole structure of power in the Third Reich.

On orders from the Customs Investigation Office in Prague, a man named David had been arrested on the old Czechoslovak frontier for carrying 400 dollars without authorisation. David stated that he was acting on behalf of an Officer of Military Intelligence [Abwehr] under Admiral Wilhelm Canaris and that he had been commissioned to wind up certain financial dealings with Jews in the Protectorate.[1] From David the trail led to two sources of money, both in the pay of the Abwehr Office Munich—Captain Ickrat and his friend Wilhelm Schmidhuber, a German exporter. Both were placed on the suspect list for breaking currency regulations.[2]

Under pressure Schmidhuber dictated to the Gestapo interrogating officials a statement which showed that this apparent currency offence had political implications. He referred to similar transactions undertaken by Dr Hans von Dohnanyi, a State Attorney working in the Abwehr Central Office under Major-General Hans Oster.[3] Thinking that they had stumbled upon a further Abwehr affair, the Gestapo investigated further. They discovered that von Dohnanyi had provided Jews with papers and money

546

from the Abwehr and allowed them to travel to Switzerland as agents.[4]

Meanwhile Schmidhuber had been arrested by the Gestapo and "persuaded" to talk further. He indicated that there was some connection between his activities and the efforts made by Lieutenant Josef Müller of the Munich Abwehr to persuade the Vatican to mediate between Germany and the Allies.[5] Gestapo Müller immediately realised the implications of the Munich report; for the first time the Gestapo had succeeded in penetrating the mighty Abwehr which had so far prevented Müller's organisation from becoming Germany's sole secret service and protected the Wehrmacht from the prying eyes of the Gestapo. Moreover in the Gestapo's mind, Major-General Oster, Lieutenant Müller and Dr von Dohnanyi were suspect; they had long been convinced that the OKW Ausland/Abwehr office contained a group of determined enemies of the regime who under Wehrmacht cover—and therefore out of the Gestapo's reach—were planning the downfall of the National-Socialist regime.

Ever since the RSHA had clamped its controls on Germany, it had been at daggers drawn with the Abwehr. Although officially the two organisations collaborated, Abwehr officers were always criticising the unscrupulous Gestapo methods of suppressing so-called enemies and they thwarted all attempts by SS Headquarters to amalgamate the political and military secret services (SD and Abwehr) under the RSHA. The RSHA had already compiled what Heydrich called the "ammunition pack" which the Gestapo brains trust would open when the time seemed ripe to give the enemy the *coup de grâce*.[6] The "pack" contained secret dossiers recording numerous indications of anti-regime activity by Oster, Dohnanyi and Müller. Oster was a monarchist and a sort of Chief of Staff of the Abwehr; he had organised an internal political information service which provided the leaders of German resistance with reports of anti-regime sentiment; it was so effective that von Hentig, a foreign service officer, had referred in somewhat highly-coloured terms to "supervision of the entire Party by the Wehrmacht's Abwehr."[7] Dr von Dohnanyi, a lawyer, had been on the RSHA's black list ever since 1938, when he had helped to uncover the Gestapo intrigue against Colonel-General von Fritsch;

he was also known to be in close contact with the anti-Hitler circle led by Ludwig Beck, the late Army Chief of Staff, and Carl Goerdeler, the ex-Burgomaster.[8] Lieutenant Josef Müller was a Catholic, later a co-founder of the Christian Socialist Union; he had long been under Gestapo and SD observation on suspicion of having divulged to the Belgian Legation in the Vatican the date of the German offensive in the West (10 May 1940).[9]

All this led Gestapo Müller to think that the Munich currency case offered an opportunity to disgrace the Abwehr. But nothing must reveal his true political motives; the Gestapo must give the impression that it was simply enquiring into a breach of currency regulations. Since the Gestapo could not pursue its investigations inside the Abwehr, Müller handed the case over to the Wehrmacht but at the same time ensured that the Gestapo had a hand in the game by appointing an observer, Kriminal-kommissar Sonderegger.[10] The Reich Military Court, oblivious of the Gestapo's manoeuvre, nominated as investigating officer the senior Judge Advocate, Dr Manfred Roeder, who had already shown his ability as an investigator of anti-Nazi resistance in the case of the Soviet "Rote Kapelle" espionage ring.[11]

On 5 April 1943 Roeder and Sonderegger presented themselves to Canaris. Roeder produced an arrest warrant for Dohnanyi and explained to the Admiral that he was authorised by the Reich Military Court to search Dohnanyi's office.[12] A few minutes later the three men were in Dohnanyi's room. Roeder's unexpected visit exposed a fatal weakness to which the anti-Hitler conspirators were prone. Only a few days earlier Arthur Nebe, the Head of the Kripo, who had been in contact with the internal German resistance for years, had warned the Abwehr that Gestapo Müller was planning a coup, but Dohnanyi was still taken by surprise. Roeder went to Dohnanyi's desk and extracted a disorderly pile of documents. Among them was a file on Dohnanyi's Jewish agents in Switzerland and notes on peace talks in Rome and Stockholm undertaken by Abwehr officers together with Pastor Dietrich Bonhoeffer, who was already under Gestapo observation.[13] Sonderegger noticed that Oster was staring at Dohnanyi's desk as if transfixed. A file lay upon it. Dohnanyi hissed to Oster "Those papers;

those papers." Slowly Oster drew nearer to the desk and reached out to snatch the papers.[14] "Stop," Sonderegger shouted, pointing to Oster. Roeder turned round and grasped the position at once. He requested Admiral Canaris to order Oster to relinquish the papers and after some initial hesitation Oster complied.[15]

Roeder read the paper. On it Dohnanyi and Oster had worked out a code by which a meeting between Bonhoeffer and certain pro-Allied politicians, planned to take place in a foreign country, could be presented as perfectly harmless. This scene in Dohnanyi's room heralded the end of the Abwehr's independence. Oster, the opposition's most important informant next to Nebe, was dismissed and cashiered; Dohnanyi, Josef Müller and Bonhoeffer were arrested.[16]

In January 1944 the Gestapo brought off another coup against the imprudent Abwehr conspirators. Gestapo Müller broke up a resistance ring centred around Hanna Solf, the widow of the former Ambassador to Japan, and in the process arrested certain members of the Abwehr office; they included Kiep, the ex-minister, Graf von Moltke, a military administrative officer and Captain Gehre.[17] Hardly had the Abwehr recovered from this new blow than it fell victim to its own weakness once more. The Abwehr representatives in Switzerland, Sweden and Turkey deserted to the Allies.[18]

When the desertions were reported to Hitler, he heaped curses on the head of the Abwehr. He was heard to say that Admiral Canaris' organisation had failed all along the line. SS-Gruppenführer Fegelein, Himmler's representative in the Führer's Headquarters and Hitler's future brother-in-law, partly as a joke remarked that "the whole business" ought to be handed over to the Reichsführer-SS. Hitler seized on the idea and summoned Himmler.[19] In a matter of minutes the fate of the Abwehr was decided: at the end of February 1944 Himmler was commissioned by his Führer to amalgamate the Abwehr and the SD. The Wehrmacht had lost a decisive battle to the SS.[20] The mighty German Wehrmacht had lost its intelligence organisation and become the only army in the world without its own secret service. Military counter-espionage was henceforth a prerogative of the SS—which of course was jubilant.

Curiously enough, however, the victor did not take his anticipated revenge. Gestapo Müller, who was eager to clean out the "gang of traitors" in Canaris' office, was not placed in charge of the Abwehr; instead the job went to Müller's bitterest rival, SS-Brigadeführer Walter Schellenberg, Head of Amt VI (Ausland-SD) in the RSHA. The relationship between Schellenberg and Admiral Canaris had long been curiously ambivalent; the Admiral appreciated the young man's exceptional intelligence; his feelings were almost paternal. In return Schellenberg respected Canaris as a man—an unusual attitude for the cold SD intellectual.[21]

Even during his most violent quarrels with Heydrich, Schellenberg's master, the Admiral would listen to the young man's advice. "Was I too outspoken again?" he would often ask when he met Schellenberg on his morning ride in the Berlin Tiergarten.[22] Canaris knew that, as far as he was concerned, there were certain rules of loyalty which Schellenberg would never break. The Foreign Ministry Head of Intelligence, an ultra-Nazi of the Ribbentrop school, once asked Schellenberg whether Canaris was really a crafty old fox or a geniune supporter of the Nazi regime. Schellenberg cut him short, saying that there was no doubt of the Admiral's loyalty.[23] (Schellenberg never wavered in this conviction—not even on 23 July 1944 when Müller deliberately selected him to arrest the Admiral as an accomplice of the 20 July conspirators.[24] Schellenberg knew better. Perhaps he even knew of the telephone conversation between Canaris and Graf Stauffenberg who made the attack on Hitler; when, on the afternoon of 20 July, Stauffenberg informed the Admiral of the supposedly successful attack on Hitler, Canaris exclaimed: "Dead? Good God! Who did it? The Russians?")[25]

Nevertheless Schellenberg regarded the end of the Abwehr as a personal triumph, a victory for his Ausland-SD. At last his dream looked like coming true—a unified super secret service; he could visualise himself as the master mind of an espionage empire which would put the much-envied British "Intelligence Service" in the shade.[26] Here was further proof of the fact that Walter Schellenberg was one of the most ambitious and unpredictable figures in SS Headquarters; even the other RSHA

heads of division regarded him as a dangerous outsider
who was best avoided. Through the SD's spy system this
Saarbrücken lawyer had worked his way first into the SS
and then into favour with Heydrich, to whom he was bound
by a sort of love-hate relationship.[27]

The RSHA had initially regarded Schellenberg as Heydrich's office factotum; later, however, they realised that
behind the almost feminine sensitivity of this well-groomed
and well-read barrister lay a strength of will capable
of asserting itself even in face of the fearsome Heydrich.
Moreover he had contrived to reinsure with Himmler; the
Reichsführer liked this wily "Benjamin," as he used to call
Schellenberg.[28] During a flight to Vienna Schellenberg had
once seized his Reichsführer by the tunic when Himmler
thoughtlessly leant back against the door handle.[29] Himmler had felt confident in Schellenberg's sense and circumspection ever since.

In spite of these close ties with the most powerful
personalities in the SS, Schellenberg was shrewd enough
not to "lay at the feet of the totalitarian state the tribute
of his loyalty unto death."[30] He had no intention of
shedding his last drop of blood for the National-Socialist
State. The versatility and adaptability which had won
this penniless son of a middle-class family a place among
the SD elite enabled him to turn his back on the Hitler
regime as soon as he saw the writing on the wall herald-
ing the Nazi "Götterdämmerung." He had been aware of
the Reich's real situation ever since he had forced his way
into the higher echelons of the SS Intelligence Service.
In 1940 he had taken over the Abwehr Polizei [Counter-
Espionage Police] when Werner Best was dismissed, but
had then fallen out so badly with his master, the sour,
brutal, Gestapo Müller,[31] that he must have been only too
glad to take over the Ausland-SD in 1942 as successor
to Heinz Jost.[32]

As Head of the Foreign Intelligence Service, Schellenberg displayed such talent that when Himmler was given
the task of amalgamating the SD and the Abwehr, his
mind turned to his "Benjamin" and so in spring 1944 Schellenberg set to work to form a unified Secret Service
under the RSHA.[33] But he did not parade his sense of
triumph before the vanquished Abwehr. He dismantled the
Abwehr machine with the utmost caution; almost to a

man Canaris' old staff was carefully given its niche in the RSHA.[34] On the surface nothing had changed except, apparently, the senior posts.[35]

Even Canaris was initially left in peace by the Gestapo. He was the first confined in Burg Lauenstein under a sort of parole, but after a discussion with Schellenberg he was allowed to return to Berlin as head of the OKW Special Staff for Economic Warfare.[36] The SS even brought themselves to sing the praises of their fallen enemy. Early in May 1944 in a castle near Salzburg Himmler and Keitel, the Chief of OKW, celebrated the birth of the new era for the Secret-Service in the presence of a crowd of SS leaders; on this occasion the Reichsführer referred to "the valuable work of the Military Abwehr."[37] The majority of the Abwehr officers had no inkling why Schellenberg was treating the Canaris men with such leniency. Only gradually did the fantastic truth emerge—Schellenberg, the Head of the SD, was pursuing a policy surprisingly similar to that of the Abwehr conspirators.

On this eve of 20 July 1944 hardly a soul knew that the Abwehr and the Ausland-SD were working on parallel lines. Both had ceased to believe in an ultimate German victory; both wanted a separate peace with the Allies; both were ready to do away with Adolf Hitler in the interests of German survival.

The Abwehr's critical analyses of the war situation checked with the SD's enemy intelligence and morale reports. Moreover both organisations were equally frustrated. Canaris had continually complained that his situation reports were no longer read in the Führer's Headquarters; from mid-1944 the SD was not even allowed to submit its "Reports from the Reich" which were intended for the top-level leaders.[38] In their search for an escape from Hitler's war, SD and Abwehr often found themselves using the same deep dark paths, the same intermediaries, the same Allied agents.

At least in some degree the two were heading in the same direction; on the one hand the conscience of the German officer corps was in revolt, on the other the cold-blooded rationalists of the SD were taking avoiding action. So close was their alliance that the SS apologists later maintained that the two wanted the same thing; after the war, Werner Best considered that the same tragic fate had overtaken both the Abwehr and the SD. "It was a tragedy for both of us," he said, "that for the sake of our people we created a regime which made a good start and registered considerable initial successes but then, for unforseen reasons—Hitler's obsession with his gift of prophecy—led us to catastrophe."[39]

This reading of the situation, of course, ignores the vast moral difference between the conspirators of 20 July, who acted primarily on ethical grounds, and the SS technologists of power; nevertheless Best's words reflect the bitterness and disillusionment into which the drab reality of the Third Reich had plunged the lieutenants of the Führer dictatorship. Best's remark about "Hitler's obsession with his gift of prophecy" provides a clue to the attitude of the SS, or at least certain of its leaders, up to 20 July 1944. In their heart of hearts many SS leaders had lost faith in the man to whom they had sworn blind, fanatical loyalty—Adolf Hitler.

Devotion to this "greatest brain of all time," as Himmler called his idol,[40] was the only thing which lent the SS Order any sense or purpose in the eyes of its leaders. To guard the life of Adolf Hitler, to carry out his orders ruthlessly, to be the executors of his last will and testament—for them this was the sacred mission of the SS. Many of its leaders had been disgusted by the kaleidoscope of the Weimar democracy with its apparent disorder, so they dreamed of an orderly "Völkisch" state directed by the genius of a Führer towering over his century and administered by a technologist class of unsentimental "realists" (their favourite expression) translating into action the directives of the leadership. For them the totalitarian state was the only salvation; they hoped that it would bring about the much-trumpeted orderliness and national discipline. But close proximity to the regime's manipulators of power brought many SS leaders down to earth. They soon perceived that the democratic party struggles had been replaced, not by single co-ordinated direction from the Führer dictatorship, but by wranglings about precedence among a plethora of Nazi potentates whom Hitler rode on a long rein in order to maintain his own position as the supreme autocrat.

For the SD intellectuals the most disillusioning aspect was that the Dictator proved by no means the supremely realistic statesman they had envisaged in their clinically efficient world. Instead of rationalism, instead of the SD's golden rule of realism, they found their Head of State possessed by a brutal urge to conquer, an uncontrollable lust for power, drawing his inspiration from the crudest nineteenth-century biological nationalism and ruled by a racialist colonising mania which broke all bounds of nationalistic doctrine, even as interpreted by the SS leaders.

The first tiny crack, noticeable only to the initiated, in the relationship between Hitler and the SS leaders, occurred when the Dictator, intoxicated by his success, incorporated into his empire the first non-German people— the Czechs of the "remainder of Czechoslovakia." The rape of Prague staggered not only the outside world but certain SS leaders as well. SS-Standartenführer Reinhard Höhn, for instance, met Oberführer Best on a morning ride in the Berlin Tiergarten in March 1939: "Höhn, my friend," Best confided to him, "this is the end. So far people have believed us when we said that National-Socialism was the incarnation of the racial concept and that this racial concept had certain limits. With the move into Prague, however, National-Socialism has turned to imperialism."[41]

Of course neither the thoughts nor the deeds of the SS leaders showed any trace of these fleeting doubts in public; the SS followed Hitler into his world of fantasy; it followed him in his campaigns of conquest and genocide. Nevertheless, it was symptomatic that even Himmler, insulated though he was by his ecstatic Hitler worship, at times showed signs of an unmistakable unease— and that as early as summer 1939. In his heart of hearts Himmler was a timorous being and Hitler's suicidal career into the abyss of war gave him food for thought. During the 1938 Sudeten crisis he had been a front-ranking jingoist, egging the Dictator on in his policy of aggression; but when Hitler engineered the Danzig quarrel Himmler was assailed by a feeling that his master was gambling too high.

On the Danzig question Himmler allied himself with Göring, who was opposed to Hitler's policy of naked force; consequently he came into collision with Ribbentrop, whom he regarded as the most sinister of all Hitler's advisers. Early in April he journeyed to Danzig to counsel moderation to Albert Forster, the bellicose Gauleiter and overlord of the Free Port.[42] Baron Guy de la Tournelle, the French Consul General, reported to Paris that Himmler was determined to oust Forster[43] but in spite of the support of Greiser, the President of the Danzig Senate and Forster's rival, he did not succeed. At this time even the Polish Ambassador to Berlin ranked Himmler as one of the opponents of war.[44] On 26 July 1939 Burckhardt, the Swiss League of Nations Commissioner in Danzig, wrote to the Secretary-General that there was talk abroad "that Hitler was now isolated by Himmler and Goebbels. This was inaccurate but it was true that since the autumn and particularly since the November Jewish pogrom, Himmler had changed front; he now stood much closer to Göring and was opposed to Goebbels and his propaganda methods."[45]

Later Himmler dutifully fell in behind Hitler's war policy but he retained his aversion to Ribbentrop, on whose shoulders he placed responsibility for Germany's fateful course towards war—to absolve his idol Hitler from any blame. Certain of Hitler's entourage were labouring under the delusion that peace with the Allies could be quickly achieved if only Ribbentrop could be got rid of. Göring once said: "This is not our war; it's Ribbentrop's!"[46] And many in SS Headquarters thought this way. In October 1939 Ulrich von Hassell, the ex-Ambassador and one of the leaders of German resistance, heard of it. When he met Graf Welczek, the ex-German Ambassador to Paris, he told him that they were trying to end the war as soon as possible. Hassell noted: "His [Welczek's] sphere of activity includes members of the SS High Command—Stuckart and Höhn. He maintained that these two men thought fundamentally as we [the opposition] do and were already considering whether Ribbentrop should not be thrown to the wolves. The formation of a new Cabinet was under consideration there."[47]

Such little indications, sporadic though they were, showed that the men of SS Headquarters by no means shared that blind confidence in victory of the thousands upon thousands of young SS men whom they despatched to face the horrors and massacres of the Second World War. Even at the height of the German victories Hassell noted: "Since the SS view the outcome of the war very realistically, that is sceptically," SS Headquarters was unable to subscribe to the regulation Nazi jingoism.[48]

Not that they had any doubts about the essential validity of Hitler's power policy. As always, the SS stood ready to carry out even the most barbaric order from its Führer. Whether the task was to annihilate the Jewish people, to launch a fresh offensive on the battlefield, to liberate Mussolini from captivity or prevent the defection of a German satellite, the SS never hesitated.

Many an SS leader found that common sense prevented him from placing himself unreservedly at the disposal of the Führer dictatorship. The SD elite was simply too intelligent to swallow the poisonous doctrine of naked force preached from the Führer's Headquarters by the apostle of "Lebensraum." In occupation policy, certain significant shades of difference appeared between the SS concept of rule and Hitler's simple master-and-slave concept. The coldly calculating technicians of power, whose task was to rule conquered Europe with their police machine and at the same time to pacify it, found their task complicated by Hitler's uncompromising "Lebensraum" imperialism; inevitably its naked policy of conquest would one day rouse the subject people to resist their German masters.

Hitler's instructions for the treatment of occupied Russia were in general valid for the rest of Europe; the basic point he said, was "to carve up the gigantic cake so that we may first dominate it, secondly administer it and thirdly exploit it."[49] His world contained, apart from Germany, no autonomous peoples or states but simply a collection of satrapies under a centralised super-dictatorship. Speaking to the Reichsleiter and Gauleiter in 1944 Hitler had said that the "rubbish of small states" must be liquidated as soon as possible; "the Germans alone" could really organize Europe. He was not prepared to allow the occupied states even a minimum of national autonomy,[50] saying: "The road to self-government leads to independence; one cannot keep by democratic institutions what one has acquired by force."[51]

The SS version of this programme was a more intelligent, though morally no less questionable, policy, best described by the current phrase "stick and carrot." The SS occupation policy experts hoped to produce a grudging

consensus between rulers and ruled by continuous alternation between severity and leniency. Werner Best's ideas,
for instance, were very different from those of his master
with his scorn for the "rubbish of small states"; in 1942
Best wrote in the periodical *Reich, Volksordnung, Lebensraum:* "as regards the relationship of a great power to
other peoples in an area, it must be remembered that in
the long term no people has been able to exercise leadership without or against the consent of the led . . . men
can be neither coerced nor duped . . . The highest degree
of self-expression to which a people can aspire is to be
the strongest among a group of peoples living in the
same area, to work towards the same destiny in close cooperation with its allies, to have as its object the creation
of a single great demographic area in which it will still
be the leader in accordance with the natural laws of
existence; by this means lasting natural development can
be assured instead of decline, the inevitable consequence
of a short-term master-race hallucination."[52]

Heydrich was the first to put this specifically SS occupation policy to the test. In September 1941, although
already Head of the SD and Director of the RSHA, he
was nominated acting (and in practice actual) Reich
Protector of Bohemia and Moravia.

Heydrich introduced himself to the Czechs with a wave
of terror which earned him the name of the "Butcher
of Prague." He engineered the first fake trial in Nazi
history, having the Czech Premier, Alois Elias, condemned
to death within a few hours. Meanwhile Gestapo commandos broke up the Czech resistance groups and arrested opposition elements;[53] shortly before his arrival
the pro-Western and Communist resistance groups had
combined, but in a bare two weeks Heydrich had practically destroyed the Czech resistance movement.[54] Daily
he reported the "victories" of his terror campaign to the
Führer's Headquarters.

No sooner had he achieved his immediate purpose, however, than Heydrich brought the summary courts of justice to an end. The Reich Protector presented a new face
to his terrorised subjects. Heydrich the butcher was replaced by Heydrich the benefactor. He declared political
persecution at an end and began to woo the Czech workers and peasants, playing them off against the bourgeois

intelligentisia whom he regarded as the main focus of potential resistance.[55] Having been commissioned to raise Czech industrial and agricultural production, he abolished many of the regulations stamping the Czechs as second-class citizens.

Heydrich raised the fat ration for 2,000,000 Czech industrial workers, released 200,000 pairs of shoes for workers in the armaments industry, and requisitioned luxury hotels in Bohemia's world-famous spas as holiday homes for Czech workers.[56] Simultaneously he reorganised the Czech social-security system, which was far inferior to the German. Charles Wighton, Heydrich's British biographer, says that "for the first time even in democratic Czechoslovakia he made them [the workers and peasants] socially acceptable."[57] With his wife Lina, the Protector received a stream of Czech delegations, giving many the erroneous impression that the Czechs had accepted German domination.[58]

In London the Czech Government-in-exile under Eduard Benes was taken aback by the reports of Heydrich's achievements. Peace in the Protectorate threatened to paralyse the Czech émigré democrats, for the more the population of Bohemia and Moravia seemed prepared passively to accept their German masters, the more untenable did the position of the Government-in-exile become in negotiations with the Allies.[59] Only if there was an active resistance movement in the Protectorate could the Government-in-exile assert any claim to Allied consideration of Czech interests in a post-war settlement. However, so long as the Germans under Heydrich continued their flexible occupation policy, there would be no resistance. The Czech exiles drew the sober conclusion—Heydrich must be liquidated; only the murder of the mighty Reich Protector was likely to call forth that German brutality without which Czech resistance had neither purpose nor incentive.

In December 1941 the émigré cabinet in London decided that Heydrich must die. Two Czech NCOs, Jan Kubis and Josef Gabcik, were selected for the task of murdering the Protector and shortly after Christmas they were dropped into the Protectorate from a British aircraft.[60] Kubis and Gabcik had been well prepared for their mission. They had been sent to a school for spies near

Manchester, had been trained in sabotage at Cambusdar-roch in Northern Scotland and been given final training at the Villa Pellasis near Dorking; they planned to murder Heydrich somewhere along his short daily drive to Prague from Panenske-Breschen, his summer residence.[61]

As the assassination spot Kubis and Gabcik chose the Prague suburb of Holešovice, where the Dresden-Prague road traces a hairpin bend down to the Troja bridge. While negotiating the bend Heydrich's car, which was always unescorted, would naturally have to reduce speed. This was the moment which Kubis and Gabcik, now reinforced by two more saboteurs, intended to use.[62] The four men distributed themselves around the curve, each armed with a Sten gun and a supply of hand grenades concealed under their mackintoshes. Valcik, another of the gang, was posted three hundred yards before the turn to give warning of Heydrich's arrival by whistle signal.[63]

On the morning of 27 May 1942 all was ready; 9.30 a.m., Heydrich's usual time of arrival, passed and the Protector's green Mercedes convertible did not appear. An hour went by and they were becoming nervous. Then Gabcik and Kubis heard the signal. Gabcik unbuttoned his coat, grasped his Sten gun and sprang into the roadway. As the Mercedes turned the corner, he raised his gun and aimed. He could see everything quite clearly through the windscreen—Heydrich's pale face and the head of Klein, the driver. He pressed the trigger—nothing happened, he cocked the gun again—again nothing. A desperate shout came from Kubis standing behind him. Kubis pulled out a hand grenade and lobbed it at the car as it slithered to a halt. The bomb hit the back of the car and wrecked it.[64] Apparently unharmed, Heydrich leapt out of the convertible roaring something to his driver. At the first sight of Gabcik he had stood up in the car and dragged his service revolver out of the holster. Now he jumped out into the road and set off, shouting and shooting, after his attackers who were now on the run; he was "the central figure in a scene which might have been taken from any Western."[65] Heydrich was gaining on Kubis when the Czech saw his chance; two trams were approaching from opposite directions and Kubis managed to slip behind one of them before Heydrich reached him. He jumped on a bicycle which had been

left in readiness and escaped. Heydrich then turned on
the second attacker. Gabcik had been slow to recover
from his dismay at the failure of his sub-machine gun;
now he suddenly realised his danger. Drawing his revolver from his pocket he jumped back, firing as he went;
turning and shooting, diving from cover to cover,
he fled.[66] Then he saw Heydrich throw his revolver to
the ground; his ammunition was exhausted. Suddenly he
clapped his right hand to his hip and staggered. Gabcik
made good his escape. Now at last it became clear that
the attackers had not missed Heydrich; Kubis' grenade
had driven leatherwork and steel springs from the car's
upholstery into Heydrich's ribs and stomach; particles of
horsehair had even penetrated the spleen. The doctors
were unable to save Reinhard Heydrich: on 4 June 1942
he died of his wounds.[67] All that remained of the lord
of the greatest system of terror in German history was
his death mask, a picture of a machiavellianism peculiar
to the SS. One of the first to see the mask was Dr
Bernhard Wehner, a criminal police official ordered to
Prague to investigate the affair; he noted later: "Deceptive features of uncanny spirituality and entirely perverted
beauty, like a renaissance Cardinal."[68]

The government-in-exile in London, however, got what
it wanted. A wave of terror descended on Bohemia and
Moravia, one of the most agonising in the history of the
Third Reich. 10,000 Czechs were arrested; at least 1,300
were shot, including all male inhabitants of the village
of Lidice near Prague which was supposed to have harboured Heydrich's attackers. The village was razed to the
ground. Heydrich's assailants were in fact among the
victims of these wild, fanatical reprisals, but this was
purely a matter of chance.[69] After the war the British
Labour MP, R. T. Paget, pronounced "Partisans often
deliberately provoke reprisals in order that hatred of the
occupier may be intensified and more people may be
induced to resist. This was our general idea when we
flew in a party to murder Heydrich in Czechoslovakia.
The main Czech resistance movement was the direct
result of the consequent SS reprisals."[70]

Among those who fell heir to Heydrich's occupation
policy, one at least was determined to avoid such barbaric
reprisals in future. Ironically, among the men destined

both to continue and refine the policy initiated by Hey-drich was one whom he had hated more than any other SS leader—Dr Werner Best, Heydrich's co-founder of the Gestapo machine, now an SS-Gruppenführer and, since August 1942, a Director in the Foreign Ministry.[71]

As the result of a German-Danish crisis in late 1942 Best had been dispatched to Copenhagen. Though oc-cupied, the Danes had retained their constitutional ma-chinery and Hitler felt that he had been publicly insulted by the Royal House and the Danish Government; he proposed to take the opportunity to insist upon ac-ceptance into the Government of the small group of Danish Nazis. In the autumn the Dictator broke off rela-tions with the Danish Royal House and recalled his two most important representatives, the Reich Plenipotentiary and the German Military Commander. He proposed to appoint a more rabid National-Socialist as Reich Pleni-potentiary who was to demand the resignation of the Danish Government and acceptance of the National-So-cialists into a new Cabinet.[72]

For this task von Ribbentrop selected SS-Gruppen-führer Best; he had, after all, a reputation as an energetic operator. Best, however, soon realised that Hitler's demands were bound to wreck German occupa-tion policy in Denmark. The Danish Parliament would never agree to the nomination of Nazi Ministers. Best accordingly did what no other Foreign Ministry diplomat had dared to do—he ignored the Führer's order and came to an agreement with the Danish politicians; they formed a new Cabinet, dropping one or two ministers who were suspect to the Germans and Best, as a *quid pro quo*, did not insist on the inclusion of the Danish Nazis;[73] in fact he made clear to them that they were hindering rather than helping German occupation policy. When Parliamentary elections were held in March 1943 and the Nazis won only three seats, Best persuaded their lead-er, Frits Clausen, to leave Copenhagen and more or less to retire into private life.[74]

Best quietly and unobtrusively pursued the policy which seemed to him most effective. He was determined to ensure good order and stability in his area and to do so was prepared to act against all disturbers of the peace, the Allies, the Danish resistance—and Hitler.

His flexible policy, based on cold logic though it was, soon encountered resistance from Hitler. The Führer's Headquarters had accepted the sacrifice of the Danish Nazis, but the supposedly weak-kneed treatment of the Danish resistance infuriated the Dictator. In fact a course of events similar to that in Prague now repeated itself in Denmark. Danish resistance fighters trained in England started guerilla warfare against the German occupation authority in Best's model protectorate. Again the primary object was to provoke German reprisals against the still hesitant population. Best the diplomat, however, avoided all unnecessary severity. He allowed the military and the Sicherheitspolizei to carry out only transient, limited reprisals. In his reports to the Foreign Ministry he even tended to minimise the real extent of the resistance to avoid some wild reaction on the part of Hitler. That he feared more than he did the partisans.[75]

Meanwhile, however, the situation reports from the military commander Denmark to the OKW operations staff painted so black a picture of Danish resistance that Hitler began to suspect his plenipotentiary of deceiving him. Furiously he demanded the most severe reprisals against the Danish partisans, for Denmark was important to him as a bridge to Norway.[76] Best was ordered to present the Danish government with an ultimatum demanding the institution of summary courts to deal with the resistance and the introduction of the death penalty for attacks on the German occupation forces. Best declared at once that the Danish government would never accept this ultimatum[77] and a few days later he was proved right; the Danish Cabinet rejected it and on 29 August 1943 resigned in a body. The German military commander thereupon proclaimed a state of emergency.[78]

Looking at the situation soberly and realistically Best, the technician of power, was convinced that Hitler's policy of force could be of help only to the partisans. When, therefore, the Dictator proceeded to introduce into Denmark the standard savage anti-partisan methods, it was clear that a collision was unavoidable. On 30 December 1943 Best was summoned to the Führer's headquarters. Hitler explained that the terror in Denmark could only be broken by intensified counter-terror; he therefore ordered that sabotage by the Danish resistance should be answered by German reprisals; for every German attacked, five partisans, or persons who had assisted them with money or otherwise, were to be liquidated. Best objected that counter-terror was not the way to deal with the Danes. With so law-abiding a people, he said, the best method of making the saboteurs unpopular was to take action only against terrorists who had been arrested and condemned under the laws of war. Hitler, who anyway regarded lawyers as the most despicable people on earth, was infuriated by Best's legal arguments. The order for counter-terror was confirmed.[79]

A wave of severe German reprisals descended upon Denmark and, however great his scepticism regarding the policy, Best could not avoid becoming involved with other leading German functionaries in some responsibility for the crimes committed. He was in fact forced to take part in a programme of reprisals which he found abhorrent. Nevertheless he continued to try to reduce the tempo of the terror campaign. In collusion with the Commander of the Sicherheitspolizei he reduced Hitler's reprisal ratio from 5:1 to 1:1 and gradually introduced German Courts Martial.[80]

His Plenipotentiary's evasive manoeuvres did not escape Hitler's notice. On 3 July 1944 Ribbentrop cabled to Best: "In view of the reports on the situation in Denmark, the Führer has voiced very sharp criticism of the policy you have so far adopted towards the Danes. The Führer considers that the institution of legal courts is responsible for present developments in Denmark." Threateningly Ribbentrop demanded an immediate detailed report, in particular on the question why "contrary to the Führer's instructions you have continued to deal with sabotage activity by legal proceedings instead of simply by counter-terror."[81] Once more Best was summoned to his Führer and on 5 July found himself facing Hitler: "These gentlemen always think they are cleverer than me," the Dictator growled. Hitler renewed his order for counter-terror and insisted that the Reich Plenipotentiary had no business to follow a policy of his own. When Best started to object, Hitler screamed: "I will not listen." SS-Gruppenführer Best saluted and left the room.[82] A few hours later he had glaring proof of the illogicality of the Nazi totalitarian state. When he explained

the position to Ribbentrop, the latter suddenly turned
pensive and then gave him the grostesque advice: "Do
what you think is right and sensible. But the Führer's
orders must be carried out."[83]

The Best episode was the first clear demonstration
that, where occupation policy was concerned, Hitler's
ideas and those of the SS were not invariably identical.
The next area in which differences began to appear was
the treatment of the so-called "Germanic" peoples; though
both Hitler and the SS used the phraseology of Nazi
dogma, the two were in fact working on different principles. In spite of all the Germanic claptrap, Hitler was
still the German nationalist of the Imperial era, who regarded any supra-national institution as a betrayal of
Germany; the SS leaders, on the other hand, were genuinely striving for a Great German Reich which, in a
vague sort of way, they hoped and believed would produce a new epoch of international brotherhood transcending national boundaries—though under German leadership, of course.

In one of his moments of enthusiasm, Himmler said
that he could quite well imagine that the next Reichsführer-SS might not be a German; Hitler, on the other
hand, would ridicule Himmler's passion for Germanic experimentation;[84] in his view, unless he had been ideologically brainwashed, every non-German SS volunteer must
"feel himself a traitor to his people."[85] These two remarks alone give one to think that in contrast to Hitler's
nationalistic programme, the SS leant "toward a policy
conceived in quite different terms: one of greater autonomy" (Paul Kluke's phrase). Kluke also found Himmler
"far more prepared to remove the Nordic elements from
the non-German races, in other words to carry out those
biological fishing expeditions among other peoples which
Hitler himself found so dubious."[86]

As Himmler became more deeply involved in his Germanic programme and came to occupy a key position
in occupation policy in relation to those countries which
the SS called "Nordic-Germanic," the divergence between
the SS and Hitler inevitably became more pronounced.
The requirement for "Germanic" volunteers for the Waffen-SS and the tangle of warring Nazi cliques in the
German-occupied territories had caused Hitler to appoint

Himmler as a sort of overlord for the Germanic countries. A Führer decree stated: "The Reichsführer-SS carries sole responsibility for negotiation on common Germanic Völkisch requirements with the Germanic Völkisch groups in the occupied territories."[87] A "Germanische Leitstelle" [Germanic Office—GL] was set up in the SS-Hauptamt under Dr Franz Riedweg, a Swiss military medical officer and son-in-law to the Field-Marshal von Blomberg who had been dismissed in 1938.[88] The GL maintained out-stations in Oslo, Copenhagen, The Hague and Brussels, and set up a network of pan-German SS cells.

The GL out-stations canvassed for Waffen-SS recruits, they checked "Germanic" applicants for the Allgemeine-SS, they set up educational establishments, they bought up publishing firms, they published newspapers, they kept touch with local Nazi leaders who were opposed to their official Party Headquarters.[89] Already the SS Germanic fanatics could see the great Germanic empire forming. Gottlob Berger, Head of the SS-Hauptamt, said: "The Germanic volunteers in the Waffen-SS, together with the members of the Germanic SS, will one day form the foundation upon which the Germanic empire will be built."[90] The minutes of a Commanders' Conference in the SS-Hauptamt, on 8 October 1942, laid down the SS programme: "Responsibility for the entire Germanic area will be conferred on the Reichsführer. It must therefore be our task to prepare the way for our leader in order that later he may be able to unite the Germanic countries in the Germanic empire. These countries should enter our Germanic empire without renouncing their nationality or their culture."[91]

The Dictator's innate nationalistic instincts, however, ran counter to the imperialistic illusions of the SS Germanists; Hitler showed no inclination to grant the Germanic countries even that measure of autonomy which the SS leaders were prepared to concede. The majority of the German-occupied countries were still legally in a state of war with the Reich and with Hitler unwilling to make any definite pronouncement about the measure of national sovereignty to be allowed these countries in the proposed "Germanic Empire of the German Nation," the

SS "Greater Germany" propaganda naturally proved totally ineffective.

The problem was not one of ideology alone; Hitler's refusal to make any pronouncement affected the actual practical work of the SS—and that on a subject which was difficult anyway. Since the dictator refused to speak the saving word, the Waffen-SS recruiters found themselves paralysed by Adolf Hitler. The GL reports continued to emphasise that unless Hitler soon gave the Germanic countries some assurance regarding their national independence, SS recruiting would come to a complete standstill. In 1943 Berger reported on the situation in Norway: "The supply of volunteers has dried up completely. In spite of all our efforts, we are no longer in a position to obtain volunteers because the basis for recruitment is lacking." As the months went by, he continued, Norwegian SS men were asking with increasing urgency "the old question: what will become of us after the war?"[92]

Desperately Berger urged his Reichsführer to ask Hitler to conclude a peace treaty with occupied Norway. Writing to Himmler on 25 September 1943 he said: "Since it is essential that we tap the manpower resources of the Germanic countries, I believe that in view of the forthcoming recruiting campaign, I am justified in re-opening this question, in spite of the fact that the Führer has previously given a negative reply."[93] Once more Hitler refused. Only later was he persuaded to allow Terboven, the Reich Commissar in Norway, to issue a declaration holding out to the Norwegian people some prospects of internal sovereignty—but its terms were vague and the future to which it referred even more nebulous. The SS leaders were not taken in by Hitler's meaningless verbiage. A combined report from Amt III of the RSHA and the GL Norway set out what the Norwegians thought of Hitler's declaration: "It is so elastic that whoever is in power can make it mean what he likes. In practice, therefore, it has changed nothing."[94]

Hitler's policy of silence tempted SS leaders to take the law into their own hands and make political promises to their Germanic subjects. As early as summer 1942 Obergruppenführer Jeckeln, the HSSPF Ostland, was telling Latvian officers that "in a great Germanic empire

the Latvian people too would have their place in the sun."
He was even more explicit: "Latvia has already been
granted self-government; no restrictions are placed upon
its cultural life; even its economy is already beginning to
revive. After the war Latvia will continue to enjoy similar
independence and in close association with the Reich will
once more blossom in every way."[95] The Ministry for
the East indignantly refused to accept such political extravagances on the part of SS leaders. On 14 August 1942
Meyer, the acting Minister, protested: "It cannot be the
business of an HSSPF to give public expression to views
about the possibility of development in the status of Latvia
under constitutional law."[96]

Jeckeln was not the only SS leader to realise that if
the ground was not to be cut from under his feet, he
must use his own initiative to offset Hitler's blanket orders.
Other local SS governors walked the tightrope between
officially authorised policy and the wrath of the Dictator.
SS-Gruppenführer Wächter, Governor of Galicia, for instance, considered that the Poles should be treated with
moderation, whereas the orders from on high called for
deportations to make room for German settlers;[97] his
colleague, Curt von Gottberg, Commissar-General in
White Ruthenia, demanded a measure of self-government
for the Russians, whereas Hitler's theme was that any
internal autonomy would undermine German rule.[98]

The last great drama which, more than any other single
event, finally loosened the ties between Hitler and the
SS and produced an unconscious change in the mentality
of many SS leaders, was the war against Russia. It
carried the SS to the Baltic States, Galicia and White
Ruthenia and the story of events in these areas leads
direct to the 20 July plot.

Initially Hitler and SS Headquarters had been completely at one in their ideas on Russia. Both wished to
carve up the "gigantic Russian cake" to decimate the
peoples of the East and settle Germans in the areas thus
released. The SS ideological instructors preached that the
Slav millions were uncultured sub-humans with the habits
of vermin. A brochure entitled *The Sub-Human,* issued
by Berger's ideological craftsmen, explained to SS men
why the Slavs were not in fact human beings. "To the
outward eye the sub-human is biologically an entirely

similar creation of nature; he has hands, feet and a sort
of brain with eyes and a mouth. In fact, however, he is
a totally different and a frightful creature, a caricature
of a man with features similar to those of a human
being but intellectually and morally lower than any animal. This creature is actuated by a ghastly chaos of
savage, unrestrained passions—limitless destructiveness,
primitive lust and shameless vulgarity."[99]

The murders by the Einsatzgruppen, the mass shootings of Soviet prisoners-of-war by the Gestapo, atrocities
by individual soldiers and units of the Waffen-SS against
the Russian civilian population—all this proved that the
theory down in black and white was meant in deadly
earnest. The SS became the scourge of German-occupied
Russia. Thousands of SS eyes watched to ensure that no
German soldier fraternised with the Slav sub-human. The
RSHA's spies and detachments were busy frustrating every
effort by the German soldiers and administrators to persuade the inhabitants of the East to work for the Reich
by guarantees of some measure of self-government. In
Himmler's eyes such efforts were a betrayal of the German mission in the East. He saw anyone prepared to
accept Russians as auxiliaries or, still worse, allies in the
anti-soviet crusade, as a saboteur of his programme for
German rule in the East. Systematically he opposed any
tendency to grant the Eastern peoples a measure of self-
government. SS-Einsatzkommandos broke up the Ukrainian National Government which had been formed by
agreement with the Wehrmacht, and arrested its leaders;[100] in White Ruthenia the Sicherheitspolizei liquidated
a nationalist group which Gauleiter Kube, Gottberg's
predecessor, hoped to use to build up an indigenous
administration;[101] SS Headquarters rejected all offers by
captured Soviet Generals to fight with the Germans against
Stalin.[102]

Even the strictest ideological vigilance, however, could
not prevent the Germans from being confronted with the
realities of the situation. Two sobering years of bloody
war in Russia provided cruel proof of the falsity of the
tale about "sub-humans." As early as August 1942 in its
"Reports from the Reich" the SD noted that the feeling
was growing among the German people "that we have
been victims of delusion. The main and startling impres-

sion is of the vast mass of Soviet weapons, their technical quality and the gigantic Soviet effort of industrialisation— all in sharp contrast to the previous picture of the Soviet Union. People are asking themselves how Bolshevism has managed to produce all this."[103]

The Waffen-SS commanders were among the first to protest against the false doctrine that the Russians were "sub-humans"; every day spent in the slime and mud of the Russian front proved to their men what fighting against Russians really meant. Anger at the claptrap of the ideologists gave rise to bitter memoranda to the Reichsführer. Felix Steiner, for instance, commanding the "Viking" Division, told Himmler that the war could only be won if people such as the Ukrainians were granted autonomy and allowed to fight at the side of the German army against the Soviet enemy. Himmler rejected the idea: "Do not forget that in 1918 these splendid Ukrainians murdered Field Marshal von Eichhorn."[104] When Gunter d'Alquen's SS war reporters began to criticise the stale "sub-human" theme and advocate "Europe" as the new slogan, Himmler exploded, referring to "stupid twaddle about a European community in which even the Ukrainians and Russians would be included . . . I refuse once and for all to allow the SS to subscribe in any way to this policy . . . which has been specifically rejected by the Führer."[105] Himmler's attitude, however, was not dictated by ideology alone; he feared the Dictator's wrath. Hitler refused to meet the national desires of the eastern peoples in any way and he had already clashed with Himmler over a statement concerning autonomy for the Baltic States.

The origin of the disagreement was a plan to raise recruits for the Waffen-SS in Estonia, Latvia and Lithuania. Himmler's international lawyers persuaded him that general mobilisation was incompatible with the status of an occupied country and so he set to work to obtain a measure of autonomy for the Baltic States.[106] The three Baltic countries were to be given their own sovereignty under the "protection" of the Greater German Reich, which would continue to control military and foreign affairs. But in the Führer's Headqarters Himmler failed to gain his point. On 8 February 1943 Hitler turned down the proposal, to the relief of Bormann, the Head of the Party Chancellery, who feared that such an expansion of the SS might affect the position of the Party.[107]

As time went on, however, a sort of conspiracy of commonsense involved the SS ever more closely in the problem of German occupation policy in the East; in face of the realities of the Eastern campaign the SS anti-Russian dogma began to look more and more part-worn. The next stage of the struggle for autonomy for the Baltic States provided a good illustration; under the leadership of Rudolf Bangerskis, ex-Minister of War in Latvia, so many Baltic volunteers were streaming into the Waffen-SS that Himmler felt that he owed it to his Baltic brigades to take up the struggle for autonomy once more.[108] In November 1943 he faced his Führer again but again Hitler refused. Rosenberg, the Minister for the East, noted: "In the course of the discussion the Führer repeatedly interjected that it was self-evident that he could not evacuate these coutnries, that there could of course be no talk about this. He was also inherently opposed to making such far-reaching concessions in difficult times."[109]

So Himmler had lost once more. Nevertheless, "this breach in the 'anti-Eastern' stand of the SS was to provide an important precedent."[110] Himmler's appetite for new SS recruits drawn from the populations of the East had been whetted and now there was no holding him; step by step he retreated from the "sub-human" ideology and Germans drawn from a series of races were press-ganged into the SS.

After the Balts came the turn of the Ukrainians. In spring 1943 SS-Brigadeführer Dr Otto Wächter, the Governor of Galicia, had begun to recruit Ukrainians into an SS volunteer division entitled "Galicia."[111] Himmler agreed, for in his eyes Galicia had no connection with Ukrainian nationalism since it consisted of the West Ukrainian areas which had formerly been part of the Austro-Hungarian Monarchy and reputedly had always been pro-German.

When no fewer than 100,000 Ukrainians volunteered, Wächter petitioned Himmler to change the name "Galicia" to "Ukraine."[112] Himmler was horrified—this sounded like encouragement of Ukrainian nationalism; it sounded like betrayal of the German colonising mission in the East. And what would the Führer say? On 14 July 1943 he decreed: "To all Heads of Hauptamt. In referring to the Galician Division, I forbid use of the term 'Ukrainian Division' or mention of Ukrainian nationality."[113] Wächter protested: to refuse the division the name "Ukraine," he wrote to Himmler on 30 July, would be tantamount to a German attempt to de-nationalise the Ukrainians; this was not in the German interest; it would predispose the Ukrainians to listen to Bolshevist blandishments.[114] Himmler re-affirmed his order, though he did agree not to punish anyone who used the title "Ukraine." When Wächter continued to object, Himmler refused to discuss the matter further.[115] In 1945, however, he gave ground once more, agreeing that the Galician Division be entitled "First Division of the Ukrainian National Army";[116] the Ukrainian General Schandruk was the first "sub-human" to wear the uniform of an SS-Gruppenführer.[117]

An increasing number of Eastern races were now found to be "SS-worthy." After the Ukrainians came a brigade under the Russian adventurer Kaminski,[118] then a White Russian SS Division,[119] then the Cossack formations commanded by Lieutenant-General von Pannwitz;[120] finally even Soviet Moslems appeared in ranks of the Waffen-SS.[121] The dramatic demise of the "sub-human" doctrine finally attracted a group of officers who were experts on eastern affairs, Nazis but nevertheless friends of Russia; for two years they had been trying in vain to offer Germany's political and military leaders a secret weapon which they hoped would produce a decisive turn of events in the Eastern campaign.

At an early stage certain army officers both in the general staff and the Abwehr had proposed that Germany constitute a Russian Liberation Army from the mass of Soviet prisoners of war; its members were first to be given an assurance that the Russia of the future would be granted full sovereignty and then they could be employed to fight the common Soviet enemy, not as "volunteer auxiliaries" but as full-scale allies of Germany. Chance had provided the planners with a Commander for such a Russian Army—Lieutenant General Andrei Andreievich Vlassov, the defender of Moscow in the 1941 winter battle, C-in-C of 2 Soviet Shock Army at Volkov, taken pris-

oner in 1942; he had declared himself ready to join
forces with the Germans against Stalin. Supported by a
number of young German officers acting on their own
initiative, he began to recruit in the prisoner-of-war camps
and his very first speeches brought an unexpectedly large
number of applicants.[122]

Hitler's reaction to the idea of a Vlassov army, however, was one of rage and contempt. He refused to have
any truck with Russian nationalism; even discussion of
the subject ran counter to his colonial policy, whose only
object was exploitation. On 8 June 1943 he said: "I will
never build up a Russian army. That is fantasy of the first
order. Let no one imagine that we have any need to
form a Russian State, that everything would then be in
order, that we should get a million men. We should get
nothing, not one man. We should merely have committed
a monumental folly."[123]

Vlassov's military friends capitulated, leaving only a
small group of incorrigible Russian enthusiasts still believing in the possibility of a Vlassov movement. The
group included one or two Hitler Youth Leaders, certain National-Socialist intellectuals, a few officers and a
woman named Melitta Wiedemann who was determined
to introduce her hero Vlassov to some important personality in the Third Reich.[124] Melitta Wiedemann had
been born in Saint Petersburg; she had been a secretary in the editorial office of Goebbels' paper *Der Angriff*
and was now a leader-writer for the anti-Comintern
journal *Die Aktion*. She hit upon the desperate notion
that the Vlassov Movement could only be helped by its
bitterest enemy, the SS. With an unerring feel for National-Socialist realities, she selected the SS leader whom
she thought had the courage to promote the Vlassov
movement in spite of all resistance—Wächter, the Governor of Galicia. She arranged for Vlassov and Wächter
to meet in her parents' house; Wächter was attracted by
the Russian and promised to help her.[125]

But Himmler could not bring himself to abandon his
own dogma or deviate from the orders of his Führer.
"We must never swallow the idea of this Russian General,"
he said. "We would be creating a new Russian nation
organised with our own help."[126] Carefully though Vlassov's friends pleaded their case, Himmler remained deaf

to their entreaties. Melitta Wiedemann, however, persisted. With the mighty head of the SS clinging help-
lessly to his obsolete doctrines, she harried him with letters and memoranda. Letter to Himmler dated 26 May
1943: "The theory that the Eastern peoples and, above
all, the Russians are sub-humans has been disproved in
practice. They fight well. They sacrifice everything for
their country. Their weapons are at least as good as
ours . . . if we wish to have millions of men labouring
for the Reich in the East and vast armies of Eastern
forces at the front, it is absolutely essential that this sub-
human theory disappear from our propaganda."[127] 5
October 1943: "Our use of the word sub-human has
enabled Stalin to declare a national war. Hatred of us is
frightful . . . As against this it is absolutely certain that
the entire Russian peasantry, the greater part of the intelligentsia and all middle- and senior-level commanders of
the Red Army are enemies of Bolshevism and in particular
of Stalin. By our policy we have faced these men with a
tragic dilemma: either to fight for Stalin or to see their
people and therefore themselves condemned to form part
of a colonial empire, where the inhabitants are murdered,
robbed, labelled as sub-humans and reduced to the status
of serfs for generations to come, whereas in fact they are
one of the most gifted peoples of the white race." The
only solution was a change of German policy in the East,
constitution of nation-states and of a Russian Liberation
Army. She concluded: "The only real danger lies in obdurate persistence in the present policy and failure to realise the causes of our present sinking fortunes of war."[128]

When Melitta Wiedemann asked for an interview with
Himmler he evaded the issue, taking refuge, as so often
when embarrassed, behind the Führer's orders. Rudolf
Brandt, his personal assistant, had to write to the lady:
"In particular I would not wish to go into this matter
further since I can tell you that, in the matter of Vlassov,
the Führer has already given clear instructions."[129]

As far as the SS was concerned the Vlassov movement would have been condemned to total failure had it
not been sponsored by Standartenführer Gunter d'Alquen,
the head SS war reporter. He used a mixture of shock
therapy and native cunning to wean Himmler slowly
away from his Führer's anti-Russian dream-world. On a

flight to the front in September 1943, Himmler showed
d'Alquen the "sub-human" brochure. D'Alquen thought
for a moment and then acted the disgruntled SS trooper.
The document was "a flop," he growled and then, in the
argot of the private soldier: "Our men out there don't
know where they're going to leave their arses and believe
you me if our men saw this brochure, they would ask
loud and clear: these people who are attacking us and
have better tanks than ours, are good at tactics and red
hot at strategy, are they just simple sub-humans? What
sort of super-men are we, then? Look what these sub-
humans are doing for their country and the sacrifices
they're making! Look at the beating they take."

Himmler retorted: "What's this rubbish you're talking?", and d'Alquen told him: "Reichsführer, that's the
sort of thing I hear from our men wherever I go
nowadays. After two years of war against our present
enemy, we can't go on any longer with such theories."[130]
Himmler broke off the conversation in a fury. Nevertheless the outburst had shaken him, for a few days later
he summoned d'Alquen and authorised him to take members of the Vlassov movement to the front and initiate
psychological warfare against the Soviet army—but only
within Hitler's prescribed limits—a promise to Soviet deserters of entry into a Russian Liberation Army which
did not exist and, if Hitler had his way, never would.[131]

D'Alquen kept any doubts about this order to himself
and went to work. His first venture was "Operation Winter Fairy-Tale," launched in the corps area of another
critic of the "sub-human" doctrine, Obergruppenführer
Steiner; it was the first of many propaganda operations
which ultimately succeeded in luring numbers of Soviet
deserters to the German side.[132] "Winter Fairy-Tale" also
opened a breach in Himmler's ideological defensive front
and gradually he withdrew his objections in face of
d'Alquen's arguments. D'Alquen was permitted to include
in his propaganda army increasingly prominent figures
from Vlassov's camp and eventually he succeeded in persuading Himmler to recognise Vlassov himself.[133] Only
in October 1943 Himmler had shouted: "This butcher's
apprentice is a dangerous Bolshevist,"[134] but a year later
he thought differently. Vlassov was permitted to form
two Russian divisions and Himmler wrote to the ex-

"sub-human": "I wish you all success in the interests of our common cause."[135]

Himmler was still on tenterhooks lest he get another bad mark from his Führer for this flirtation with Vlassov; but as the Nazi fortunes sank, all those who still laboured under the delusion that there might still be a change in German Eastern policy began to see in this alliance between the ex-Soviet General and the SS an indication that the SS might be their last sheet-anchor. Memorandum after memorandum in the files of Himmler's staff prove that the National-Socialist critics of Hitler's policy of conquest saw the SS as the only possible instrument of reform. At the same time these memoranda present a deplorable picture of both the situation and efficiency of the Nazi regime.

Melitta Wiedcmann renewed her pressure: "The tempo at which developments regarding Vlassov are proceeding bears no relation to the methods of an authoritarian state; it is a tempo of indecision and missed opportunities."[136] SS-Gruppenführer von Gottberg, Governor of White Ruthenia, struck a more resigned note: "I would point out that ever since the winter of 1941–42 I have continued to advocate both verbally and in writing the necessity of a change in our basic attitude. In view of the mentality of the Eastern peoples, who think only of the present, no nation has ever had a more favourable opportunity to bring the war in the East to a rapid conclusion than that now existing."[137]

The severest critic of German occupation policy was Alfred E. Frauenfeld, the ex-Gauleiter, now Commissar-General in the Crimea. (He used such strong language that even so harsh a critic of the Nazi regime as Robert Kempner, the Nuremberg prosecutor, exclaimed in astonishment: "But that's a staggering thing you've written there!"[138] Frauenfeld described German occupation policy as "a masterpiece of ineptitude; within a year it has achieved the considerable and astonishing feat of turning a completely pro-German people, who welcomed us as liberators, into partisans roaming the forests and marshes; its influence upon the course of events in the East has been wholly negative . . . policy of ruthless brutality . . . methods used centuries ago against black slaves . . . makes a mockery of any sensible policy . . . Proof of total lack of instinct in handling foreign people . . . the acme of stupidity . . . proof that those who parade their brutality and give themselves master-race airs are at heart uneducated louts."[139]

Bormann, the head of the Party Chancellery, forwarded Frauenfeld's memorandum to Himmler—it was, after all, primarily a criticism of the SS anti-Slav doctrine. On 26 March 1944 Himmler noted on it: "Frauenfeld is not far wrong."[140] Gradually, even the most fervent National-Socialist in the SS came round to the bitter realisation that the totalitarian state was not even in a position to apply the most elementary rules of psychological warfare. Incapable of reform, entangled in the struggle of the regime's warring power groups and exposed to the growing superiority of the allies both in the East and in the West, Hitler's Germany was tottering to its doom.

For the SS leaders, however, the question whether any future for the SS was conceivable in the post-Hitler period became increasingly insistent as the Reich's position deteriorated. The SD's "Reports from the Reich" left no doubt that the Germans were longing for peace and quiet and the end of Hitler's senseless war.

"Report from the Reich" 10 February 1944: "In spite of all his stupidity and obtuseness, the enemy is getting his claws upon us and no one can imagine how we can shake him off again, however often he has been or may be 'cracked over the head'."[141]

"Report from the Reich" 6 April 1944: "In this uneasy period of waiting for invasion and retribution and also for a change of fortunes in the East, many are wondering what would happen if we could no longer hold out. People are asking themselves whether the many severe sacrifices and hardships which the war demands and will continue to demand are worth it . . . people are gradually beginning to long for peace."[142]

"Report from the Reich" 20 April 1944: "The continual pressure, alarm at developments in the East and the continually deferred hope of 'a saving miracle' are gradually producing signs of weariness among the people. In general people are 'fed to the back teeth' with the war. Desire for a rapid end to the war is everywhere very great."[143]

Those of the SS leaders who read these secret SD reports must inevitably have wondered what would become of the SS on the day when everything in which they had believed collapsed. The SS leaders had long since begun to think about the unthinkable. To many the thought of Germany without Hitler no longer seemed revolutionary. The war had demolished many of their illusions; the daily grind of the regime and above all the Eastern campaign had destroyed the old identity of view between Adolf Hitler and his SS. Even the SS leaders could no longer evade the question with which every person in authority found himself confronted in 1944—whether to allow the country to be completely wrecked for the sake of a criminal regime.

But the SS would not have been the SS had its answer to this question been unanimous. The reactions of authoritative SS leaders ranged from a demand for the removal of Hitler to berserk defence of the regime. They fell into five groups: first a small circle centred around Arthur Nebe of the RKPA—for years he and his associates had been in touch with the internal German resistance, including the actual conspirators of 20 July 1944; secondly, the senior Waffen-SS Generals—they were opposed to the murder of Hitler, but wished to work with the Wehrmacht in removing Hitler from military command and concluding an armistice with the Western Allies; thirdly a circle grouped around Walter Schellenberg, the head of the SD—they wished (for a time with Himmler's approval) to conclude peace with the Allies, handing over Hitler if necessary; fourthly, a larger circle of SS leaders, ranging from Werner Best to Otto Ohlendorf—they were opposed to any violent change of regime in wartime but nevertheless believed in the possibility of reform after the war. Finally the "to-the-bitter-end" fanatics led by Ernst Kaltenbrunner, Heydrich's successor, and Heinrich Müller, head of the Gestapo—they stood for savage suppression of even the smallest criticism of the regime.

The Nebe circle had been anti-Hitler ever since 1938, the high-tension period of the Sudeten crisis. For the first time certain anti-Nazi Generals had then given serious consideration to a project for halting the march to catastrophe by a military putsch and the removal of Hitler.[144]

At that time Hans-Bernd Gisevius, an anti-Nazi civil servant, had introduced his friend Nebe into a circle of the resistance which included Colonel-General Beck, since retired, and Hans Oster, later of the Abwehr.[145] Nebe was then head of the Kripo (he later became an SS-Gruppenführer and head of a division in the RSHA); he viewed the resistance with suspicion and scepticism for, as an experienced criminal police officer, what he saw in his secret meetings with Oster and Beck gave him the impression that the conspirators were dilettantes.

Nebe, who was used to covering his tracks, was appalled by the levity with which the conspirators, apparently almost in public, were planning the removal of Hitler. He never drove to a conspirators' meeting in an official car; he would leave his car in a sidestreet, observe the vicinity of the meeting points with care and then suddenly appear in the midst of the conspirators.[146] Goerdeler, the over-garrulous head of the resistance, never even knew the name of the SS leader to whom the opposition owed its information from the RSHA. If Goerdeler threatened to appear at a conference when Nebe was present, the cautious police officer disappeared in good time.[147]

Whatever Nebe's reasons for joining the resistance— fear for his own future or anxiety for the country—he remained loyal to the conspiracy. In late 1941, when commanding an Einsatzgruppe, he could see no escape from the Nazi regime and his own guilt other than in the murder of Hitler.[148] From this time on he was continuously urging the plotters to carry out their attack on Hitler; each time the coup was planned and as often called off, he had a squad of police officers ready to open the Berlin ministries to the conspirators' army units on D-Day.[149] Such measures could not of course be taken without the complicity of other SS members of the police. Nebe recruited his friend Hans Lobbes, an SS-Sturm-bannführer and executive director in the RKPA;[150] the Gestapo furnished another anti-Nazi, SS-Brigadeführer Paul Kanstein. In 1937 Kanstein had taken over the Gestapo Leitstelle Berlin and had immediately become a key figure in all plans for an anti-Nazi putsch. He (an SS man, be it noted) had mended the broken fences between two prominent conspirators, Graf von Helldorf, the Berlin Police President and his Deputy, Fritz-Dietlof Graf von der Schulenburg,[151] thereby ensuring that the Berlin police would at least not be found in the anti-conspiracy camp. The putschists gave him his reward—had the 20 July 1944 coup succeeded, Kanstein, the ex-Gestapo official, would have become head of the new Sicherheitspolizei in post-Hitler Germany.[152]

Loosely connected to this circle in Berlin were a number of other SS officers working on their own. Sturm-bannführer Hartmut Plaas, for instance, an official in Göring's telephone-tapping organisation known as the "Air Research Office," warned the conspirators that they were under increasingly strict Gestapo observation;[153] Sturm-bannführer Hans-Viktor Graf von Salviati, head of the remount office in the SS-Hauptamt and, from 1941, ADC to Field-Marshal von Rundstedt, was another sym-pathiser;[154] so was Max Frauendorfer, an SS officer and old Party member who was president of the "Labour Division" in the Government-General of Poland—a sort of Ministry of Labour.[155] The common denominator between all these men distinguishing them from the other SS critics of Hitler, was moral indignation with a regime characterised by contempt for human rights and by self-destructive megalomania; on ethical grounds they re-volted against the irresponsibility of the men in charge of Germany. Von Hassell noted in his diary that Frauen-dorfer impressed him "because of his boundless despair about all he had lived through in Poland; it was so ter-rible that he could not endure it."[156]

Since undercover assistance appeared to be forthcom-ing from within Heinrich Himmler's empire, some of the resisters felt that, risky though it was, they must try to recruit more SS men; when the putsch took place, after all, the attitude of the SS might well decide the success or failure of the *coup d'état*. Canaris had already voiced the opinion that as so many attempts on Hitler's life had failed, there was now no alternative but to try to involve Himmler in action against the dictator and have a "frank discussion" with him.[157] Field Marshal von Bock had also declared that he would only collaborate if Himm-ler took part in the putsch.[158]

Goerdeler thereupon asked the advice of his friend, Jakob Wallenberg, the Swedish banker. Wallenberg asked:

"Does Himmler know what you're doing?" Goerdeler replied: "I don't know." (On hearing subsequently that a favourable opportunity for the attack upon Hitler had been missed because Himmler, who was also to be liquidated, was not present on that day, Wallenberg advised Goerdeler: "But leave Himmler out of your assassination plans. If you act against Hitler alone, Himmler won't stop you."[159])

In autumn 1943 von der Schulenburg took soundings in the SS-Hauptamt, asking Obersturmbannführer Riedweg of the Germanische Leitstelle for the names of SS officers with whom he could discuss the political situation frankly. Riedweg referred him to Hildebrandt, one of the HSSPF, and to two Waffen-SS generals, Hausser and Steiner.[160] Schulenburg had already contacted Steiner who had been his company commander in No. 1 Infantry Regiment. Meeting in a Berlin café, he had told the SS General that Hitler must be eliminated by force if the total collapse of the Reich was to be prevented, but Steiner did not agree; he pointed out to Schulenburg that the eastern front was already cracking at every joint, that the Western Allies' invasion might come at any moment and that a change of regime was therefore only possible if the entire Wehrmacht was behind the putsch —an unlikely contingency.[161] Certain of the conspirators, however, were not prepared to take this as the last word from the SS Generals. Marie-Louise ("Puppi") Sarre, for instance, who worked with von Hassell, was convinced that "the National-Socialist spirit of the Waffen-SS was becoming increasingly doubtful. They feel themselves at one with the fighting troops of the Wehrmacht."[162] She was right. Only a few weeks later Steiner and his Chief of Staff, SS-Oberführer Joachim Ziegler, held a three-day meeting with Melitta Wiedemann when they discussed how Hitler could be got rid of. They had even evolved a vague plan: during its move to the eastern front, Steiner's III "Germanic" Panzer Corps was to kidnap Hitler in his headquarters, "Wolfsschanze," and "declare him mentally deranged, publicising his crimes" (Melitta Wiedemann's description). A year later the Waffen-SS Commanders were prepared to tell the resistance what they really thought; then they gave Field Marshal Rommel their word that they would support him in a revolt against Hitler. But they had not reached that stage in 1943 and Schulenburg met with no success.

Equally fruitless were the efforts of Dr Jens Peter Jessen, the Professor of Political Science, to win over his former pupil and friend, Otto Ohlendorf, now an SS-Gruppenführer and head of Amt III in the RSHA. Jessen and Ohlendorf had once worked together for National-Socialism but Hitler's war and the drift into constitutional and political crime had driven the two apart. Basically both were still National-Socialists according to their lights, but they differed on the central issue: whether a regime which issued orders for murders in millions, and was now sacrificing the fatherland for one man's fanatical determination to survive, should continue to exist.

Ohlendorf, who after all had commanded an Einsatzgruppe, would have answered this question in the affirmative, although he found many aspects of the Third Reich as distasteful as did Jessen. He was the author of the "Reports from the Reich" and was regarded in National-Socialist circles as "the mouthpiece of an opposition which would otherwise remain dumb," as Fritzsche, the propaganda spokesman, described him with some justification.[163] He persisted in supporting the proscribed theosophist movement and was therefore an object of continual suspicion to Gestapo Müller;[164] he was friendly with Wilhelm Ahlmann, the anti-Nazi banker who later committed suicide when proved to have been in contact with Stauffenberg, Hitler's would-be assassin;[165] he had his own private plan for a future National-Socialist Germany in which the NSDAP was to be no more than a cypher. He collected letters from disillusioned youngsters at the front and contacted their authors; he envisioned the post-war regime taking its cue from the Hitler Youth Leaders and front-line soldiers with an NSDAP purged, freed from power politics and administrative responsibilities, and acting solely as a "temple of wisdom"—a political brains trust.[166]

Though these were the directions in which his mind was turning, Ohlendorf still could not conceive that Germany could be anything other than the realm of the NSDAP and the Reich of Adolf Hitler. He regarded any doubts on the subject as mortal sins against the fatherland and the "community." Even in his death-cell in Nuremberg in 1948, he was still fulminating against "the many people who had renounced their heritage and veiled the oath they had sworn to the Führer in a tissue of treachery and mendacity."[167] Even his one-time collaborator, Jessen, incurred his wrath for such supposed treachery. When the Gestapo later arrested the professor, Ohlendorf did not move a finger. But the sleepless night he spent when Jessen was hanged—that Ohlendorf would not forget. (Nor did he forget his conscience-stricken promise henceforth to share his salary with the Jessen family.[168])

Men such as Höhn and Best, Stuckart and Streckenbach reacted in the same way as Ohlendorf. None of them was capable of breaking loose from the still-compelling magic of Hitler and of acting to stave off catastrophe and ruin. Dimly they may have realised what the popular Führer State of their dreams had become, but they could not bring themselves to turn their backs on a lifetime of illusion, error and guilt.

But there was one SS leader who was both sufficiently unscrupulous and sufficiently clear-sighted to cast overboard all that he and his fellows had once worshipped— Brigadeführer Walter Schellenberg. He watched every move by the anti-Nazi conspirators and knitted them into his own plans—plans designed to ensure that when catastrophe came, he, Schellenberg, would be on the right side.

Ever since June 1941, when he was appointed to a senior post in the SD Foreign Intelligence Service (initially as Deputy Head), Schellenberg had regarded the prospects of outright German victory with scepticism. The SD reports provided far too realistic a picture of the enemy's growing war effort to permit any wishful thinking. As early as autumn 1941 he had begun cautiously and tentatively to probe the possibilities of a separate peace with the Western Allies and for this purpose he used a circle of anti-Nazi resisters, who, using international channels, had been carrying on confidential discussions with the Allies or with pro-Allied foreigners ever since the outbreak of war. There were many curiously fortuitous connections between these anti-Nazis and SS headquarters. Dr Carl Langbehn, for instance, a Berlin attorney and a member of the Beck-Goerdeler opposition group, was in contact with Himmler via his daughter who was a school friend of Himmler's daughter, Gudrun;[169] Jessen, one of the advocates of a *coup d'état*, was still friendly with Höhn, to whom he had once recommended his pupil Olhendorf;[170] even von Hassel could claim some connection with Himmler—Schuhknecht his ex-chauffeur was now in Himmler's service.[171]

Schellenberg thought it wise to listen in to these secret discussions between the anti-Nazis and their foreign friends. In late summer 1941 Stallforth, an American banker, arrived in Berlin and informed von Hassell that Roosevelt would only make a gesture to the Germans if they first removed Hitler. Calmly the SD listened;[172] Group B of the Ausland-SD in the RSHA dutifully noted down all the secret agreements between Hassell and his American opposite number. On 11 October 1941 they heard Stallforth telling Miss Boensel, his secretary, over the telephone to "inform Herr von Hassell [referred to as Howe] that his proposals had been very favourably received. Would von Hassell please let him know whether he could come to Lisbon with some authoritative personality and there discuss matters with leading Americans."[173] The code names and abbreviations used in the letters between Hassell and Stallforth, which the SD intercepted, caused Schellenberg's office no trouble. Group D noted: " 'The man in the South' must be Mussolini. 'Ph' refers to Phillips, the American Ambassador in Rome."[174]

The SD were so well informed about these secret negotiations that they began talking to the Americans themselves. Von Hassell was taken aback when an SD man named Danfeld brought him warm greetings from Stallforth. Hassell noted: "This particular SS man, still very young, showed himself remarkably well-informed in foreign political matters, sober in judgment and astonishingly free in his comments. He remained an hour and a half and broached certain subjects which I thought it more discreet not to discuss. My general impression was that people in Himmler's entourage are very worried and are searching around for some loophole."[175]

Schellenberg did not yet think the time ripe to reveal his far-reaching plans to Himmler. The German armies in Russia were still winning victory after victory and the

Russian campaign would decide whether Hitler would succeed in bringing about an early end to the war. On a trip through Spain and Portugal in April 1942 Schellenberg told the two police attachés, Winzer in Madrid and Schroeder in Lisbon, that the die would be cast in the forthcoming summer; if the German armies broke through in Southern Russia and in Egypt, then the war was decided; if they did not, the Reich had lost the gamble.[176]

When the midsummer reports on both operations painted an increasingly gloomy picture, Schellenberg had his answer. In his memoirs he says that as early as August 1942 he sought out Himmler in his command post at Vinnitsa in the Ukraine and put to him the question: "Reichsführer, in which drawer of your desk do you keep your alternative solution for ending the war?"

Himmler retorted: "Have you gone mad? Are you losing your nerve?"

Schellenberg said: "Reichsführer, I knew you'd go on like this. In fact I thought it might be even worse."

Himmler then calmed down, Schellenberg says, and asked him to work out a plan. Schellenberg proposed that, profiting from the tension between Russia and the Western Powers, secret peace discussions be opened with the Western Allies; a prior condition, however, was that Ribbentrop, the Foreign Minister, must disappear, for he, as Stallforth had confirmed, was regarded in the West as "primarily responsible for the war." Himmler apparently agreed to Schellenberg's plan—"he even grasped my hand and promised that by Christmas (1942) Ribbentrop would have been relieved of his post."[177]

Whether or not this conversation actually took place, the fact remains that from late summer 1942 Schellenberg and Himmler, assisted by Felix Kersten, Himmler's masseur, and Obergruppenführer Karl Wolff, head of his Personal Staff, seriously attempted to bring about a separate peace with the West, at the price, if necessary, of the deposition of Hitler. Himmler had for some time been toying with the alluring thought that, should the war situation worsen, his mission might be to replace Hitler and bring peace to Germany and the world. The idea had flashed through his mind and he had, as quickly, put it behind him—the Reichsführer-SS could never be unfaithful to the "greatest brain of all time." But the insidious thought returned again and again. In May 1942, Burckhardt, the Swiss, told Ilse von Hassell, the wife of the ex-Ambassador and daughter of von Tirpitz, that "an agent of Himmler's had come to him to find out whether England would perhaps make peace with Himmler instead of Hitler";[178] on 9 April 1942 Count Ciano, the Italian Foreign Minister, noted in his diary: "Himmler, who was an extremist in the past but now feels the real pulse of the people, wants a compromise peace."[179]

That Himmler, the agent of the most gruesome crimes of the century, should seriously have believed that the world would be prepared to regard him as a peace negotiator, today seems a fantastic idea. At the time, however, things looked different; people wished to see Himmler at the conference table precisely because they believed he had the power. Many statesmen secretly thought like José Maria Doussinague, the Director General of the Spanish Foreign Ministry; he included Himmler "among those who seek a peaceful accommodation with the Allies in order to forestall a Soviet Russian invasion. They are entirely agreed that the disappearance of Hitler and his immediate entourage is an essential condition. Himmler could bring this about. Consequently the key to peace negotiations lies in his hands."[180]

Although Himmler shrank from the horrifying prospect of falling out of step with his Führer, nevertheless in summer 1942 he provided himself with a weapon capable of eliminating the dictator if necessary; this was a 26-page medical report showing that Hitler was suffering from the after-effects of syphilis and was threatened with creeping paralysis.[181] When walking one evening with the head of the Criminal Biological Institute of the RKPA, Nebe had asked: "Tell me, doctor, can one justifiably say that the Führer is mentally ill?"[182] Himmler now put a similar question to Kersten and the answer came back pat: Adolf Hitler's place was in a hospital for nervous diseases, not in the Führer's Headquarters.[183] But Himmler could not bring himself to take a definite decision, replying: "I can't make a move against the Führer—I who am Reichsführer of the SS whose motto is 'my honour is loyalty'."[184]

Schellenberg, however, had no such scruples. Using numerous channels he initiated an operation aiming at two things: discussions with the Americans and the jettisoning of Ribbentrop. A variegated cross-section of society was included in his plans. For his battle against Ribbentrop he used Martin Luther, a corrupt Under-Secretary in the Foreign Ministry; he dispatched Langbehn to neutral countries to contact the Allies;[185] via SS-Oberführer Fritz Kranefuss, the ambitious secretary of the "Friends of the Reichsführer-SS," he used the international connections of the businessmen belonging to the "Friends";[186] last but not least he listened to a member of the most illustrious European aristocracy—Prince Max-Egon Hohenlohe-Langenburg, who figured on his list of agents as No. 144/7957.[187]

The Prince, born in 1897, had retired from the army as a 2nd Lieutenant, married the Spanish Marquesa de Belvis de las Navas and had been living in Spain for years.[188] His reason for keeping in contact with the SD was to preserve his family possessions—the Hohenlohes owned vast estates in the Sudetenland and the Prince was determined to preserve them in face of all upheavals and changing personalities. As a result, during the Sudeten crisis of 1938 he had opted for Hitler and made his not inconsiderable diplomatic abilities available to the SD. Now in wartime he was quick to seize any chance of a compromise peace which would preserve the Hohenlohe fortunes in the Sudetenland.[189]

His proprietary instincts, however, were not the Prince's only motives for taking a hand in Schellenberg's game. He was a member of the European aristocracy and his background was one of traditional diplomacy—in the nineteenth century, after all, the Hohenlohes had provided a German Chancellor, a French Marshal, a Roman Catholic Cardinal, a number of Austro-Hungarian Field Marshals, Generals of Prussia and Baden, hereditary Marshals of Württemberg and ADCs General to the Russian Czar, so Prince Max-Egon Hohenlohe was a believer in the old European concert of powers and he was quite prepared to use senior National-Socialist functionaries to tell the potentates of the Third Reich a few home truths.

In a memorandum of September 1939, submitted to Göring, he said: "In initiating World War II Germany has started from false premises and has miscalculated in every way. She did not calculate that England and France would fight for Poland, overlooking the fact that Poland is not the point—it is something quite different— the maintenance and assurance of peace in Europe." Quite unabashed he continued: "Even at this late stage the possibility of an overall solution must be borne in mind. It must include: re-establishment of confidence, a guarantee for the respect of treaties, disarmament under mutual control and possibly withdrawal from Czecho-slovakia and its reconstitution as a demilitarised state." He ended with a warning: "Roosevelt might still be prepared to mediate, but it will soon be too late."[190]

Working with SS-Oberführer Höhn, the Prince prepared a memorandum urging influential Nazi leaders and others to initiate some peace move; Ambassador Hewel, a long-standing Nazi and now the Foreign Ministry representative in Hitler's headquarters, was also working with Hohenlohe and Höhn; he even had certain of the memoranda re-typed on the Führer's special machine and submitted to the Dictator. But Hitler threw them out indignantly as "defeatist scribblings" and warned Höhn off.[191] Nevertheless the Prince continued to work for a separate peace with the Western Allies. He journeyed to Switzerland where Allied diplomats evinced interest in his proposals; he also gained the sympathy of the Vatican, which frequently used him as a channel of communication for warning messages to the Third Reich.[192]

Urged by the Vatican, Prince Hohenlohe now prepared a memorandum which he handed to Hewel when the latter visited Spain at the end of 1941. He said: "It is now quite clear that Adolf Hitler is under the thumb of the Prussian Generals and Prussian methods are being used in the treatment of the subject peoples. Each month that goes by will show the people that Europe is ruled by Prussian generals; they will have personal experience of the brutal methods of force used by Prussian generals and they will become ripe for rebellion. Every time men are shot, the word will go round and ultimately all Europe will form a single great moral defensive front. Germany . . . can only retreat step by step. Then the

great moment will come when the peoples will rise for
their war of liberation."[193] The Reich, he continued,
would lose this war unless it moderated its policy and
sought an accommodation with the peoples and powers
of Europe.

Göring read the Prince's memorandum but had not
the courage to go against his Führer's policy. So Hohenlohe looked around for some better ally—and found him
in Schellenberg. Hohenlohe made Schellenberg's acquaintance in 1942 and immediately realised that he was
determined to do away with Hitler if need be. Although
the Prince will not today admit to having played any
important role in Schellenberg's plan, he remembers his
line of argument very well: "Schellenberg went so far as
to tell me that he knew that the West would never
make peace with Hitler and therefore some internal
changes in Germany were necessary. Later in the conversation he told me that he hoped Hitler would be
patriotic enough to subordinate his own interests to those
of the German people. If he did not, he must be removed
by force."[194]

Hohenlohe had little difficulty in putting Schellenberg
in touch with American negotiators. One of his business friends, an SS man referred to in the SD files as
"Alfonso," had connections with Americans in Lisbon and
after a few preliminary questions, the latter showed interest in Schellenberg's proposals.[195] In December 1942
"Alfonso" met the American negotiators in Lisbon and
told them that his principals were ready for a separate
peace with the West provided Germany was allowed to
pursue the war in the East and drive Russia out of Europe.
The Americans considered the SD proposal worth discussing, provided Alfonso's masters could guarantee an internal political change in Germany such as would allow
the Western Governments to pacify public opinion. During the discussions the Americans' demands became increasingly centred upon the person of Hitler. The essential condition, they said, was that he must be handed
over alive to the Allies; only thus could the growth of a
posthumous Hitler myth be avoided and lasting peace
ensured.[196]

Even Schellenberg was taken aback by this demand but
having put his hand to the plough, he had no alternative.

The Reich's situation was deteriorating month by month; in November 1942 British and American troops had landed in North Africa, producing a dangerous threat to the Afrika Korps; in the East the Stalingrad disaster was looming. Schellenberg's reply must have sounded so forthcoming to the Americans in Lisbon that they were prepared to continue negotiations. They referred him to the man Hohenlohe called "the most influential White House man in Europe"—Allen W. Dulles, the US special representative in Berne, later head of the US Secret Service.[197] Hohenlohe told Schellenberg: "He is a tall, burly, sporting type of about 45, healthy-looking with good teeth and a fresh simple open-hearted manner";[198] another SD report stated: "It may be assumed with certainty, and has been confirmed by investigation, that if faced with serious negotiators, Mr Bull [the SD code name for Dulles] would never do anything underhand."[199]

Before Schellenberg could dispatch his emissaries to Berne, however, a time bomb which he himself had primed, exploded and jeopardized all his carefully laid intrigue. Luther, his accomplice in the Foreign Ministry, together with a group of young diplomats, loosed their attack on Ribbentrop.

SA-Brigadeführer Martin Luther was one of the most ill-bred and most hated figures in the Foreign Ministry; he owed his career to his friendship with Ribbentrop, which had brought him promotion to the rank of Under-Secretary of State and the post of head of the section dealing with relations between the Foreign Ministry, the Party and the SS; at the same time he had a hand in the annihilation of the Jews.[200] Though initially on bad terms with the RSHA, Luther had swung over into the anti-Ribbentrop camp primarily under pressure from a group of young Foreign Ministry bureaucrats who had persuaded him that Ribbentrop must go in order to prepare the way for peace negotiations. One of the anti-Ribbentrop conspirators, Counsellor Walther Kieser, who had known Schellenberg at university, told Schellenberg what was afoot and the latter immediately encouraged him to go all out in his criticism of Ribbentrop. The next day Luther called Schellenberg for confirmation of this conversation. Speaking to Luther in January 1943

Schellenberg was even more explicit; Walther Gödde, one of Luther's staff, noted that Schellenberg had already made an initial, but still tenuous, contact with the American secret service and it was "now essential to bring down Ribbentrop if progress was to be made with the Americans." Walter Büttner, the leader of the anti-Ribbentrop conspiracy in the Foreign Ministry, then contacted Schellenberg and made preparations for the coup.[201] At this point, however, Schröder, the Head of the Foreign Ministry Personnel Office, heard of Luther's plans and informed von Weizsäcker, the Secretary of State.[202]

Büttner recalls that "On 8 February 1943 Schellenberg again asked his opposite number to call and assured him that Himmler was prepared to urge upon Hitler the dismissal of Ribbentrop. He would, however, like a statement in writing of the Luther group's arguments. These had, in fact, been explained verbally early in February and were now dictated in Schellenberg's presence." The primary point made was that Ribbentrop was mentally ill and incapable of fulfilling the functions of his office. But Himmler once more relapsed into indecision and before he could make up his mind to act, Ribbentrop, who was well informed, struck back, summoning Luther and accusing him of treachery. Shortly thereafter Luther and his fellow-conspirators in the Foreign Ministry were arrested; Luther was sent to a concentration camp, Büttner and the others to the front. Just before his arrest on 10 February 1943 Luther, still the typical Berliner, called Büttner on the telephone and said: "It is all over for us; order two wreaths from Grieneisen" (the Berlin undertaker).[203]

In vain Schellenberg appealed to Himmler to save Luther from the concentration camp and to make use of the incident to bring down Ribbentrop. Himmler wavered. Wolff, the Head of his Personal Staff, hit upon a face-saving formula good enough to justify Himmler's inactivity in the eyes of any SS man: "But Reichsführer, you cannot let SS-Obergruppenführer Joachim von Ribbentrop, one of the highest-ranking members of our Order, be kicked out by this scoundrel Luther."[204] Schellenberg now had to try and keep conversations going with the Americans, even though Ribbentrop was still in the saddle. On 15 January 1943 Hohenlohe (known as Paul) and an SD officer (code name Bauer) had started negotiations with Dulles.[205] Like the other Americans, Dulles stressed that the elimination of Hitler was essential. He was obviously hinting to Schellenberg's man that with Hitler still there Germany was lost. Reporting Dulles' statements, Hohenlohe recorded that "acceptance of Hitler as undisputed ruler of Greater Germany was hardly conceivable in view of the inflamed state of public opinion in the Anglo-Saxon countries. They would have no confidence in the permanency or reliability of agreements made with him."[206] If, however, Dulles' argument continued, Hitler were to be deposed, a peace settlement recognising neither victor nor vanquished might be arranged. Dulles was quite prepared to hold out to his opposite numbers the hope that a powerful German state should remain as a factor in the orderly reconstruction of Europe; there was no question of its division nor of its separation from Austria. On the other hand the power of Prussia within the German state must be reduced to an acceptable level. "Mr Bull did not seem to attach much importance to the Czech question; on the other hand he favoured enlargement of Poland eastwards and the maintenance both of Rumania and a strong Hungary as a *cordon sanitaire* against Bolshevism and Panslavism . . . He regarded a Greater Germany, federated on American lines and allied to a Danube confederation, as the best guarantee for the orderly reconstruction of central and eastern Europe."[207]

The fact remained that Dulles was prepared to continue talking to Schellenberg's representatives. He told Prince Hohenlohe that he had instructed the American Embassy in Madrid to make itself available to him at all times, the contact being Butterworth, the Counsellor. "Alfonso," the SS Lisbon contact, was also authorised to call Dulles at any time, using an agreed code word.[208]

It soon became clear, however, that the British Government did not approve of the American discussions with the SD. Numerous reports confirm that the Americans were still willing to negotiate and the SD was later convinced that Schellenberg's game had failed primarily owing to British resistance. On 10 June 1943 SS-Ober-

sturmführer Ernst Kienast reported from American sources
in Hungary:

1. The US desires an agreement with the Reich on the
   following basis:

   (a) Germany to retain the Germanic North and
       East
   (b) The US to occupy Italy, approximately as far
       north as Florence
   (c) Thereafter the US would take no further in-
       terest in a war in Europe.

2. This plan was . . . ventilated in Spain.
3. This plan collapsed before it was ever put to the
   Reich owing to British disapproval.[209]

Schellenberg's people now set about using the neutrals
to overcome British resistance. Hohenlohe let senior officials of the Spanish Foreign Ministry into the secret
and was assured of their support for a plan to replace
Hitler by Himmler. Doussinague, the Permanent Secretary, noted: "We were told that the US Government was
well aware that it lay in Himmler's power to bring about
a radical political change in Germany, provided that this
was not synonymous with total military defeat. The
Americans were confident that he was both willing and
able to eliminate the leading personalities in the German Government."[120] But England said "no" to the
Spanish mediators too. When Doussinague attempted to
sell the plan to Yencken, First Secretary in the British
Embassy in Madrid, the latter brushed him off with: "I
am most astonished that Catholic Spain should be prepared to sit down to peace discussions with the SS, the
champion of German atheism."[211]

As a result of his setbacks in Spain, Schellenberg, with
Himmler trailing hesitantly behind him, peddled his peace
proposals in a wider forum. His emissaries appeared in a
number of neutral countries, holding out prospects of
Hitler's downfall and his replacement by his faithful SS
Chief. In May and June 1943 Himmler agreed that contact should be made with Jakob Wallenberg, the Swedish
banker, to examine the possibilities of a separate peace
under SS auspices.[212] That summer Schellenberg dis-

patched Langbehn, a member of the resistance, to Stockholm for talks with Soviet diplomats (he had already been negotiating in Stockholm with British and American representatives).[213] In late summer, Langbehn conferred in Berne with Gero von Gaevernitz, a German-American member of Dulles' staff.[214] In October Kersten went to Stockholm and discussed a seven-point American peace plan with Hewitt, the American special envoy, but could not persuade Himmler to see Hewitt personally; by 9 December, when Himmler did finally make up his mind to meet the American, Hewitt had already left.[215] On 25 December 1943 the British Ambassador in Moscow told Harriman, his American colleague, that via Sweden the British Government had been "informed of Himmler's desire to gain contact"; Himmler had apparently declared his readiness to send a representative to Great Britain to find out how England interpreted the phrase "unconditional surrender." The British replied that the words required no interpretation.[216]

The continual stumbling block was the question of how the SS could get rid of Hitler in order to clear the way for peace. The division of opinion was clear: Schellenberg was prepared to take the consequences, whatever they might be; Himmler, on the other hand, recoiled from the thought that he or the SS should take the life of his beloved Führer. Once more Wolff produced the face-saver. He proposed to wait and find out what those who were clearly working for the downfall of the regime proposed to do with Hitler. Possibly—it cannot be proved —this was cover for a sophisticated plan to allow Hitler to be eliminated by the anti-Nazis, who could then themselves be neutralised.

Contact was quickly established with the internal German resistance. Langbehn, who was both a friend of Himmler and a member of the anti-regime conspiracy, had access to the Berlin "Wednesday Club," the meeting-place of the most active opponents of the regime, Jessen, von Hassell and Colonel-General Beck, the most senior military officer in the resistance.[217] Another member of this circle was the Prussian Finance Minister, Dr Johannes Popitz, an energetic, intelligent but at times highly controversial advocate of a *coup d'état*. On Wolff's instruction he was asked by Langbehn whether it would not be worthwhile to explain the opposition's ideas quite openly to Himmler. Popitz found Langbehn's SS contacts somewhat sinister. He ruminated: "He can do anything with these people and yet he's their bitterest enemy; sometimes I believe they know it."[218] Nevertheless he accepted Langbehn's proposal.

As chance would have it, at exactly this time (summer 1943) the thoughts of the dissidents were running parallel to those of Himmler's entourage but in the opposite direction. In spite of the resistance pressure upon them to take the decisive step, the Wehrmacht Generals were still evading the issue; the conspirators therefore turned to the idea of using the other great power factor, the SS, to strike against Hitler and the Party. Von Hassell noted that "people are discussing more frequently the possibility of using the SS to overthrow the regime if all other means fail. They argue that this might not only put this organisation into our hands but would also prevent domestic disorders. They say that afterwards the SS will of course be dissolved too. The first question is whether Himmler and company would dare to play such a game and co-operate in the friendly manner desired; secondly what effect this procedure would have abroad, for every foreigner justly regards the SS as the very incarnation of the devil."[219] Even among the resistance leaders the "Himmler solution" was not without its opponents, but Beck, many of the soldiers (Olbricht, Witzleben and Tresckow), and temporarily even Goerdeler, subscribed to it.[220] Popitz was therefore deputed to enlist Himmler in the plan for a *coup d'état*.

On 26 August 1943 Popitz, accompanied by Langbehn, presented himself at the Reich Ministry of the Interior; Langbehn remained in the ante-room with Wolff, while Popitz in a long interview with Himmler explained that the war could no longer be won, that Hitler must be relieved of his position and a strong personality (meaning Himmler) must assume the duty of making peace with the West. Adroitly he appealed to Himmler's sense of mission. According to the subsequent case for the prosecution against Popitz he said that the people "were wondering: what does Himmler want, does he want to start a campaign of terror or does he really want to establish order? If he wants to do the latter quietly and reasonably, the State would be on firm foundations."[221] While Hitler was still there, Popitz continued, the Reich could not be saved. The "essential condition was that the Führer should go; he should be more or less pensioned off as honorary president"—this at least was the way Himmler put it in a later speech (after 20 July 1944) when he was trying to gloss over his part in the affair.[222]

Meanwhile in the ante-room Langbehn was working on Wolff using similar arguments. It was time, he said, that Germany once more became a State based on the rule of law and directed by intelligent, honest and far-sighted men—giving it to be understood, of course, that among such men were the SS leaders.[223] After the failure of the 20 July putsch, Himmler thought it wise to give an assemblage of Gauleiter and Reichsleiter his own version of these remarkable discussions with the resistance—remarkable at least for a Hitler supporter; he had immediately gone to the Führer, he told them, and reported everything; Hitler had, however, instructed him not to strike yet but to continue to watch the Popitz circle.[224]

In fact, Himmler's reaction bore little relation to his subsequent version of the affair. On 26 August he agreed to meet Popitz again;[225] the latter for his part went off to Field-Marshal von Witzleben and asked him (again according to the case for the prosecution against Popitz) "whether he [Popitz] might give his [Witzleben's] name as the future military Commander-in-Chief, should the plan for collaboration with the Reichsführer-SS prove feasible."[226]

On 27 August Wolff summoned Langbehn once more and discussed with him details of further meetings with leading members of the resistance.[227] The discussions progressed so favourably that a few days later Langbehn departed for Switzerland with instructions from Wolff.[228]

In Switzerland Langbehn met Gero von Gaevernitz of Dulles' office and told him that a senior SS leader on Himmler's staff (he was of course referring to Wolff) was party to a plan which aimed to reduce Hitler's still unlimited power; it was hoped thereby to create conditions which would facilitate discussions with the Western Powers.[229] At this moment, however, all the plans—both of the conspirators and of Himmler—were upset. In early

September 1943 the Gestapo, the most fanatical protector of the regime in the whole of Himmler's empire, deciphered a radio message which, according to Dulles, originated "from some Allied agency neither American nor British"—and it revealed the secret of Langbehn's discussions in Switzerland. The Gestapo forwarded the message to the Führer's headquarters without first showing it to Himmler;[230] whether this was chance or intrigue against the vacillating Reichsführer, Himmler was compelled to break off all relations with the resistance for fear Hitler should react. He had Langbehn arrested and sent to a concentration camp; he never received Popitz again.[231]

Schellenberg, however, continued to pursue his plans for the complete elimination of Hitler. He had contacted certain American military circles in Spain and had discussed with them a fantastic project referred to by the Madrid newspaper *Pueblo* as "Operation KN" (Kidnapping)—a plan in fact to kidnap Hitler and hand him over to the Allies. According to the Spanish paper the SS leaders and the American military had "reached full agreement to carry out the kidnapping plan. Technical and organisational details had been worked out and a complete organisation prepared with bases in Madrid, Lisbon and on the Mediterranean coast near Valencia."[232] But the plan never progressed beyond the discussion stage. The talks with the Allies were conducted by Paul Winzer, the Police Attaché in Madrid, who even attempted to recruit the Catholic Church to help. The Church was not unforthcoming; Father Conrado Simonsen, a liaison officer for the highest Vatican circles, placed himself at Winzer's disposal together with helpers, couriers and money from Spain, Portugal and South America.[233] The plan was only pigeon-holed in May 1944 when Winzer's head courier, a Frenchman named Letellier, stole the secret papers connected with Operation KN from Winzer's safe and sold them to an Allied Secret Service; meanwhile the SD had undoubtedly realised that in view of the close guard kept on Hitler, the kidnapping plan was not technically feasible.[234]

Nevertheless Schellenberg's negotiations in Spain did achieve one thing; they reinforced the feeling in allied circles that only Himmler and the SS could bring the

Hitler system down. Even the British authorities now began to show interest in the so-called "Himmler Solution." On 3 April 1944 SS-Brigadeführer Kranefuss noted that "in English circles the Reichsführer-SS and the SS are apparently the subjects of numerous rumours and schemings."[235] An SD informer (name unknown) located in Lisbon reported that the British now considered that a change of regime in Germany could be brought about only by the SS, not by the Wehrmacht. The report read: "During the last year, the attention of these [British] circles has been increasingly focused upon the SS and the Waffen-SS in particular. Reports that there is a possible or potential or even acute difference of opinion between the Führer and the SS or Waffen-SS can clearly be traced back to English sources." The informer continued that according to his British sources, the Waffen-SS Generals were becoming noticeably more critical of Hitler; "this stems from their estimate of the war situation." Early in January 1944, he continued, a rumour had been current in Lisbon that "Waffen-SS Generals, including a General who was decorated with the Oak Leaves to the Knights Cross in late autumn," had been in negotiation with the British.[236]

The author can hardly have realised that his report was to prove prophetic. Three months later the commanders of the SS formations in the West formed themselves into the first formal group of SS officers prepared to disobey Adolf Hitler. And their motive was exactly that which the Lisbon SD man had ascribed to the SS Generals—their estimate of the war situation.

Ever since 6 June 1944 the Normandy battle had been in the process of destroying the Waffen-SS commanders' last illusion concerning Hitler and the real situation of the Reich. SS regiment after SS regiment wasted away, sacrificed by a Führer immured in his eerie dream-world in Wolfsschanze and impervious to demands for withdrawal or reports of the enemy's material superiority and the exhaustion of the German troops. The SS Imperial Guard was in danger of total destruction, for the greater part of the Waffen-SS was fighting in the West—six divisions in all including the Leibstandarte, forming I SS Panzer Corps under Sepp Dietrich, and II SS Panzer Corps under Paul Hausser.[237]

The prospect of losing their troops altogether made even the SS Generals ripe for participation in the anti-Hitler conspiracy. Even so they might have hesitated, had they not met in Field-Marshal Erwin Rommel, now Commander-in-Chief of Army Group B, a soldier who like them had scaled the heights and plumbed the depths of Hitler discipleship. Early in 1944 Rommel had still been impervious to the arguments of the opposition but by May he knew that it was now a struggle for existence.

Time was pressing. Rommel estimated that the German defensive front in Normandy might hold for three weeks, but that then a breakthrough by the American forces and the loss of France must be reckoned with.[238] Realisation of this bitter conclusion led him to give support to a plan worked out by anti-Nazi officers on the staff of Army Group B even before the invasion had begun. Led by Lieutenant-General Hans Speidel, Rommel's Chief of Staff, a "mobilisation timetable" had been drafted envisaging evacuation of the occupied territories in the West without a fight, withdrawal of the German army behind the Siegfried line and the transfer to the Allies of administrative authority in the occupied territories. The central point of the plan was "the arrest of Adolf Hitler and his arraignment before a German court."[239]

By early July Rommel had made up his mind to carry out the programme. On the 9th he ordered Lieutenant Colonel Caesar von Hofacker, the head planner of the military opposition in the West and a cousin of Stauffenberg, to draft a missive to the allies in his, Rommel's, name, informing them that the German army in the West would cease hostilities on its own initiative and withdraw to the Reich.[240] But what would be the attitude of the Waffen-SS, those six divisions which formed the backbone of Army Group B? Rommel wished to be quite sure. Tirelessly he toured the front, questioning Commanding Generals and senior commanders. One after the other they declared themselves ready to break with Hitler. Moreover the Waffen-SS Generals were no exception. Even Party veterans such as Sepp Dietrich could no longer hide their heads in the sand; according to Speidel, Dietrich manifested his discontent with the high command and demanded "independent action if the front is broken."[241] SS-Obergruppenführer Hausser, who had mean-

while assumed command of 7th Army, joined in the
criticism of Hitler and his senseless "hang-on-at-all-costs"
strategy.[242]

The most outspoken was Obergruppenführer Wilhelm
Bittrich who had assumed command of II SS Panzer
Corps in succession to Hausser. As he returned to his
command post during the night of 15–16 July 1944, Field
Marshal Rommel was announced. Bittrich, who was re-
nowned in the Waffen-SS for his sharp tongue, did not
mince his words: "My knowledge is not restricted to
Normandy, Field-Marshal. I know how bad things are on
the Eastern front too. There is no more objective leadership there. All that's happening is the crudest gimmickry."
He growled on: "Up there they don't realise the danger
because they're not in touch and therefore can't estimate
the situation correctly. Every day I see young men being
killed unnecessarily because they're badly led from above,
so in future I'm not going to carry out senseless orders
and shall act as the situation demands." Rommel in-
terrupted him and told Bittrich of his own plans. "I too
know that it can't go on like this. But soundings have
been taken with the enemy and they lead me to hope
that we can make a planned withdrawal from occupied
France back to the Siegfried line." Without hesitation
Bittrich subscribed to the anti-Hitler pact: "Field-Marshal,"
he said, "if this is so, I am with you and so is II SS
Panzer Corps. My commanders think exactly as I do."[243]

Unfortunately the anti-Hitler alliance between the Waffen-SS commanders and the Army in the West collapsed as
soon as it had been formed. On 17 July, while on the
road behind the German front in Normandy, Rommel
was severely wounded by a British ground-attack aircraft;
the military opposition in the West had lost its leading
figure.[244] Three days later the unity of purpose achieved
between the SS Generals and the anti-Nazi Army Generals
in the West was destroyed by the action of Colonel Claus
Graf Schenk von Stauffenberg, Chief of Staff to Commander-in-Chief Replacement Army, when he set off the
bomb under Hitler's conference table. Rommel and the
SS Generals had agreed on one condition for their rebellion in the West—that Hitler should not be murdered; the whole basis of that agreement was now gone.
The assassination attempt in the Führer's Headquarters

took the SS political leaders by surprise no less than it did the rebellious Generals. Himmler and Schellenberg seemed semi-paralysed by the military putsch; hours passed before they recovered themselves sufficiently to take counter-measures—which they then did ruthlessly although the *coup d'état* had long since miscarried. Seeing that for months the SS leaders had been negotiating with the resistance and knew most of the secrets of the anti-Nazi opposition, their evident bewilderment sets the historian a pretty puzzle. How was it possible that the accessories of the 20 July movement could be so completely taken by surprise by Stauffenberg's action? Many have subscribed to the facile theory that the SS leaders' surprise was merely a piece of play-acting—in fact, they say, Himmler and his closest collaborators were merely awaiting the success of Stauffenberg's action to join the rebels.[245] The theory is based upon supposition only; there is no concrete proof.

Study of SS headquarters' files shows that neither Himmler's Personal Staff nor the RSHA had ever suspected the circle of conspirators centred around Stauffenberg. The 20 July movement fell into three groups; a circle of conservative officials and retired officers (the Beck-Goerdeler group); a circle of right-wing Christian intellectuals and socialist politicians (the Kreisau circle); and a circle of young regular officers grouped around Stauffenberg and formed early in autumn 1943. The Gestapo knew of only the first two groups. Detailed information on the Beck-Goerdeler group is to be found in the Gestapo files; men such as Beck, Goerdeler, Langbehn and Oster were well known to Gestapo Müller. As early as 1943 Himmler had warned Canaris, the head of the Abwehr, that he now knew who was behind the anti-regime opposition in the army and that he would "run people like Beck and Goerdeler out of business quick enough."[246] The Kreisau circle too held no secrets for the Gestapo since its leader, Helmuth James Graf von Moltke, and other members had been arrested in 1944.

Only Stauffenberg's group of officers remained unknown to the RSHA, for they worked under Wehrmacht cover and were therefore protected from the Gestapo investigators. So little did Himmler suspect Stauffenberg that during a visit to the Führer's Headquarters in mid-June 1944 he helped the severely handicapped Stauffenberg off with his coat and carried his heavy briefcase—the same case in which Stauffenberg later put the bomb with which he intended to murder Hitler.[247] Himmler had known Stauffenberg since early June 1944 and regarded him as a capable staff officer who merited promotion. In mid-July when Colonel-General Guderian told Himmler that the general staff must be manned by officers with fighting experience and that Stauffenberg should be Chief of Staff, Himmler at once volunteered to recommend him to Hitler.[248]

There can be no doubt that Himmler knew nothing of Stauffenberg's plans. He did not even suspect when, at about 1 p.m. his driver, Sturmbannführer Lukas, stormed into the sleeping-quarters of the Reichsführer's field headquarters, shouting: "Attempt on the Führer! Attempt on the Führer!"[249] Stauffenberg's bomb had exploded in Hitler's briefing hut at 12.42 p.m., but Stauffenberg himself had left shortly before. Just after the explosion he was stopped by a suspicious guard at the outer checkpoint of the Führer's headquarters but a telephone call had sufficed to send him on his way to carry out his putsch.[250]

Himmler was still in total ignorance. Even when, a few moments later, he rushed over to the Führer's Headquarters to congratulate Hitler on his escape, he was still on a false trail; he suspected a Todt Organisation construction group working in the headquarters of having built the bomb into the floor of the briefing hut.[251] Only considerably later did he take notice of a statement by a sergeant-major working in the camp telephone exchange who had observed that Colonel von Stauffenberg had left in a hurry. Even when the suspected criminal landed in Berlin, Himmler failed to have him arrested.[252]

Eventually someone from the Führer's Headquarters called Kaltenbrunner and hinted that it might be worth finding out from Colonel von Stauffenberg in the Bendlerstrasse (OKW Headquarters) why he had left Wolfsschanze so hurriedly. Kaltenbrunner despatched to the conspirators' headquarters, which was bristling with armed men, a lone body, Oberführer Dr Piffrader; the only result of this manoeuvre was to deprive Kaltenbrunner of Piffrader's services for some time—Stauffenberg simply waved his unsuspecting visitor away and had him locked up.[253]

This incident shows something of the bewilderment reigning in the SS camp. For years the SS had been girding its loins to deal with a *coup d'état;* for years the Sicherheitspolizei and SD had been battling against the so-called enemies of the State. But now a few hours were enough to destroy, at least temporarily, the myth of the alert, vigilant, all-powerful SS. The RSHA wildly overestimated the strength of the putschists in the Bendlerstrasse and during the afternoon of 20 July Berlin SS Headquarters was as if paralysed. Nebe's criminal police squads swarmed out to assist Stauffenberg's army units to cordon off the government quarter,[254] but the Leibstandarte companies remained prudently in their barracks at Lichterfeld.[255] No unit of the Waffen-SS or Ordnungspolizei hurried to the Prinz-Albrecht-Strasse to assist their RSHA masters, who were reduced to standing at the windows biting their nails and watching the Wehrmacht battalions, alerted by the conspirators' code word "Valkyrie," as they marched by. In the provinces and the German-occupied territories the SS Police formations were even more ineffective.

At 6.20 p.m. Colonel Heinrich Kodré, Chief of Staff to Wehrkreis XVII (Vienna) received a teleprinter message from the Bendlerstrasse telling him to arrest all senior Party and police officials in Austria because "an unscrupulous clique of chairborne Party leaders has attempted to use this situation [the attack on Hitler] to stab the fighting front in the back and seize power for their own selfish purposes."[256] Shortly thereafter the teleprinter produced another order from the putschists: "The following are immediately to be relieved of their offices and placed in strict solitary confinement: all Gauleiter, Reichsstatthalter, Ministers, Oberpräsidenten, Police Presidents, HSSPF, Heads of Gestapo and SS offices." The message continued: "Should there be doubt regarding the willingness of Commanders of Waffen-SS formations to obey or should they appear undesirable, they are to be taken into protective custody and replaced by army officers. Waffen-SS formations whose unconditional acceptance of orders is in doubt are to be ruthlessly disarmed."[257]

Kodré read these orders with some embarrassment; his was the entire responsibility, for his Commanding General was on a journey and the latter's deputy away. By the use of a little cunning combined with Viennese charm, however, he succeeded in persuading the mighty SS and Police functionaries to bow to the inevitable. He summoned them to an urgent conference in the General's room at 8 p.m.[258] and arrested them all—but with every military courtesy. And they came, every one—Querner the HSSPF, Schumann the General of Police, the Deputy Inspector of the Sicherheitspolizei and SD, the Waffen-SS Garrison Commander.[259]

These worthies soon recovered from their surprise. Obergruppenführer Querner and Gotzmann, the Police President, forthwith placed themselves at the disposal of the new regime;[260] Querner was almost indignant when Kodré assured him that he was only acting as instructed by a teleprinter message from the Bendlerstrasse which the Obergruppenführer might see if he liked; Querner waved the idea away, saying: "If you tell me so, of course I believe you."[261] In short the mighty policemen made no difficulties. They remained as prisoners in their respective rooms passing the time in small talk. Even when, at about 9.30 p.m., a final telephone conversation with Berlin proved that the putsch had failed, the SS leaders made no fuss of any sort.[262]

The military asked their prisoners' pardon, referred to the unfortunate orders from Berlin and bowed the SS dignitaries out. Kodré later recalled that "none of those present, even subsequently, complained in any way nor have they ever expressed a feeling that they were in the right and had been wrongly arrested."[263]

In Paris the SS and Police were similarly stampeded by the putschists. At about the time that Colonel Kodré was taking leave of his prisoners in Vienna, detachments of Security Regiment No. 1 under Lieutenant-Colonel von Kraewel were preparing to strike against the Sicherheitspolizei posts in Paris.[264] Major General Brehmer, Deputy Garrison Commander, Paris, a long-standing Nazi and wearer of the "Blood Order," personally carried out the arrests of the senior SS leaders in France—Carl-Albrecht Oberg, the HSSPF, and Standartenführer Helmut Knochen, Head of the Sicherheitspolizei. A few minutes sufficed for the change of regime. By 11 p.m. Oberg and Knochen were in a locked room of the Continental Hotel drinking brandy and listening to the radio;[265] 1,200 men of the Sicherheitspolizei had been incarcerated in the Wehrmacht prison at Fresnes and in the casemates of the old Fort de l'Est.[266]

In the Raphael Hotel the officers of the Paris garrison were just celebrating their victory over the SS when a broadcast speech by Hitler and orders from Field Marshal von Kluge, Commander-in-Chief West, put an end to all hopes of a *coup d'état*. Kluge had at one time been in close contact with the opposition but had then fallen under the spell of Hitler once more. When he heard of the arrest of the Sicherheitspolizei personnel in Paris, he dismissed General von Stülpnagel, the anti-Nazi Military Governor in France, and ordered the immediate release of Oberg's people.[267]

At 1.30 a.m. on 21 July Lieutenant General Freiherr von Boineburg-Lengsfeld, the Garrison Commander, Paris, set off to release the two SS leaders. Meanwhile in their hotel room Oberg and Knochen had also heard Hitler's speech. When the General told them that they were free again, Oberg jumped up shouting: "What damned game is this you're playing at, Boineburg?" Boineburg replied that von Stülpnagel would explain everything in the Raphael Hotel.[268] Oberg stumped indignantly through the bar of the Raphael and, as General von Stülpnagel rose, was about to fly at him when Ambassador Otto Abetz, who was also present, intervened saying: "What happens in Berlin is one thing. Here what matters is that the Normandy battle is raging and so here we Germans must show a united front."[269]

Oberg looked sulky but gradually calmed down. That night there occurred what Ritter von Schramm, the military historian, describes as one of the miracles of 20 July 1944—SS and Wehrmacht secretly joined forces against the SS persecutors. "To save what could still be saved, they built up a common front against Himmler's RSHA," Schramm says.[270] Knochen invented a face-saving story for Himmler and the outside world—the arrest of the Sicherheitspolizei men, so the story ran, had simply been an exercise, agreed beforehand between SS-Gruppenführer Oberg and General von Stülpnagel.[271]

For a few hours longer Oberg and the army were able to protect the Paris putschists from the RSHA. Even when orders began to arrive from Himmler, Oberg attempted to help; he selected with care the military members of the commission of enquiry to examine the conduct of officers; he listened to General Blumentritt, Chief of Staff to C-in-C West and an accomplice of the conspirators, and so limited the scope of the inquisition from the outset.[272] Oberg did what he could for Stülpnagel, whom Field Marshal von Kluge had reported to the Führer's Headquarters as one of the leading putschists; Stülpnagel was ordered to report to Berlin and tried to commit suicide on the journey; Oberg caught him up and promised to protect his family from reprisals.[273] Nevertheless Oberg was powerless to prevent the Gestapo from laying hands on the leaders of the putsch in France, Hofacker, Colonels Finckh and von Linstow, Dr Ernst Röchling, and Kreuter, a secret-service official. Thanks to Oberg, however, the majority of the conspirators and their accomplices were spared the journey to the Prinz-Albrecht-Strasse and thence to death. Von Schramm says: "The leaders of the surprise action against the Paris security services on 20 July all escaped with their lives. Not one hair fell from the head of any of the responsible officers."[274]

The Waffen-SS commanders also took part in the rescue operation. Three senior officers of the post-war German army (the Bundeswehr) owe their lives to the action of SS Generals; Sepp Dietrich intervened with the RSHA to obtain the release of Speidel;[275] Obergruppenführer Lombard saved Graf Kielmansegg, then a Colonel on the General Staff, from Gestapo arrest;[276] Major-General Heusinger also owed his freedom to SS intervention.[277]

When Obergruppenführer Bittrich, who had been in collusion with Rommel, heard on the radio that Colonel-General Erich Hoepner, his former commander in the Eastern campaign, had been condemned to death by hanging, he leapt from his chair in a great state of indignation, raging: "That is the end of the German army! Never in the history of the German army has an officer been hanged for treason—they have always been shot." Bittrich's Chief of Staff, an army officer seconded to the Waffen-SS, hissed to him: "General, I must ask you not to speak like this in public." But Bittrich waved him away with: "Oh, leave me alone!" The outburst was reported to Himmler who at once ordered Bittrich to relinquish his command. General Eberbach, however, Commander-in-

Chief of V Panzer Army and Bittrich's immediate superior, refused to release him, saying that the situation at the front was too critical; Himmler could do nothing since, when at the front, the Waffen-SS was under command of the army and his authority over his own troops was therefore limited. Nevertheless, he continued to try to rid himself of his refractory SS General. During the Arnhem battle a few weeks later, he saw a new opportunity. He dispatched his old friend Karl Gebhardt, the SS/Police Medical Officer-in-Chief and a Lieutenant-General in the Waffen-SS, to Bittrich with orders for him to report forthwith to the Reichsführer-SS. Once more, however, the army refused to accept Himmler's authority. Field-Marshal Model, the new Commander-in-Chief West, declared himself opposed to Bittrich's recall and even retained him after the withdrawal from France. Himmler never succeeded in disciplining his insubordinate General.[278]

The Bittrich setback, however, was one of the few suffered by Himmler in his extermination campaign against the conspirators of 20 July 1944 and their accomplices. Pitilessly he struck against suspected traitors and their families; the bloodiest purge in German military history began.

As early as 1.0 p.m. on 20 July Kersten realised to his despair that Himmler had once more become the fanatical disciple of his Führer—the same Führer whom he had so lately planned to depose with the help of the dissidents. Now all his doubts and hesitations were gone; he said to Kersten: "Now my hour has come. I will round up all the reactionary gang and have already given orders for the traitors' arrest."[279] When Kersten wondered whether Hitler's escape was really beneficial to Germany, Himmler retorted: "What's that you're saying, Kersten? Is that your real opinion? You oughtn't even to think that still less say so. By preserving the Führer Providence has given us a sign. The Führer lives, invulnerable—Providence has spared him to us so that we may bring the war to a triumphant conclusion under his leadership."[280]

In a sort of religious frenzy he rushed over to the Führer's headquarters and set the Gestapo death machine going in top gear. He sensed that fortune was smiling on him. He never left the side of his idol for a moment; yet, spellbound though he was, he kept his wits about him sufficiently to submit for Hitler's approval decrees making him, Heinrich Himmler, the second most powerful man in the Reich.

On the afternoon of 20 July Hitler was in a high state of excitement; reports indicated the spread of the revolutionary movement. This was the moment seized upon by Himmler to submit to him a document nominating the Reichsführer-SS as Commander-in-Chief of the Replacement Army. Hitler signed—he was in a state to sign anything which would ensure the annihilation of the conspirators. He screamed: "Shoot anyone who resists, no matter who he is. The fate of the nation is at stake. Be merciless." Himmler clicked his heels, saying: "My Führer, you can rely on me."[281] His master's faithful watchdog rushed out; and at 4.30 p.m. Himmler landed in Berlin.[282] The Führer's inquisitor was clever enough to give the conspirators enough rope to hang themselves but no sooner had Keitel, the Head of OKW, countermanded their orders by telephone, than Himmler let loose the terror of a counter-putsch. He moved the remaining units of the Leibstandarte and the SS-Standarte Saarow into the Government quarter; he set up a special "20 July Commission" and gathered up the reins of the Replacement Army, of which he was now in charge.[283] The Gestapo bloodhounds combed every corner; the slightest suspicion was enough for any German to find himself in the Prinz-Albrecht-Strasse interrogation cells. Savage and arbitrary police action was the order of the day; the iron curtain descended even upon innocent families. Hardly one of the resistance leaders escaped the regime's vengeance. By the evening of 20 July Stauffenberg and his group had already been shot in the Bendlerstrasse by officers loyal to Hitler but the remaining members of the resistance trod the martyr's road—Gestapo prison, concentration camp, fake trial under the lash of Roland Freisler's tongue, and finally the gallows.

The death-mills of the RSHA also swept up the SS leaders who had been in contact with the Beck-Goerdeler group. On 24 July Nebe, the Head of the Kripo, fled in the (erroneous) belief that the Gestapo had discovered his secret;[284] for months he was hunted by his own criminal police until eventually he was betrayed by a jealous woman friend and arrested in November 1944.[285] Colonels

Hansen and von Freytag-Loringhoven, ex-Abwehr and now in Schellenberg's "Amt Mil," were also victims;[286] SS-Sturmbannführer Plaas had been arrested even before the putsch and was executed on 19 July.[287] Von Salviati, the SS cavalry leader, was betrayed by his diary. He was a special target for Himmler's thirst for revenge. The Reichsführer instituted special investigation proceedings against Salviati conducted by the senior judge advocate; in the words of von Herff, Head of the SS Personnel Department, he was "an incorrigible enemy of National-Socialism and of the Führer";[288] Himmler added: "If the Peoples' Court had not condemned him, I would have had Salviati shot as a disloyal SS man."[289]

Among the anti-Nazi SS conspirators, however, Brigadeführer Kanstein escaped. He, it will be remembered, was the conspirators' Sicherheitspolizei Chief-designate; he was interrogated for hours in the RSHA, but was eventually released on an order from Stuckart, the Permanent Secretary of the Ministry of the Interior and an SS Obergruppenführer. Kaltenbrunner was furious and never forgave Stuckart for his interference.[290]

Yet the more savagely Himmler's thugs acted against the resistance leaders, the more reticent did he himself become. His renewed confidence in Adolf Hitler was short-lived. The old doubts which had affected his loyalty to his Führer raised their heads once more. A crazy notion took possession of him; might it not be possible, even now, to bring about peace via the men condemned to death for the assassination attempt—in fact to use the international contacts of the Beck–Goerdeler group? Himmler continually postponed the executions and initiated an eerie sequence of discussions with the victims. Goerdeler, Popitz and Graf von der Schulenburg were permitted to write learned theses setting out their reasons for opposing Hitler.[291]

Callously the victims' lives were prolonged while the SS considered whether to assume the mantle of the opposition. In October 1944 Himmler allowed Schellenberg to contact the Swedish banker, Jakob Wallenberg.[292] Himmler was now ready to use Goerdeler's contact with Wallenberg, hitherto considered a mortal crime, if he could thereby resume discussions with the Allies. But Wallenberg was not to be wooed by Schellenberg. Himmler persisted nevertheless. He summoned Goerdeler and urged him to render one last service to his country.[293]

Wilhelm Brandenburg, Goerdeler's guard, tells the story: "One day Goerdeler received an offer from the highest quarters [Himmler]; one might almost call it a mission. He was invited to use his close personal and political contacts and friendship with the Swedish financier Wallenberg in Stockholm and the Zionist leader, Dr Weizmann, and via them to the King of Sweden. In other words he was to do what he and his circle would most probably have done had the *coup d'état* succeeded—pave the way for contact with Churchill and so bring about a rapid end to the war on acceptable terms."[294] Goerdeler was ready, if Himmler would allow him to go to Sweden, but Himmler would not risk that. He and Goerdeler met once more but could not reach agreement.[295]

So Himmler broke off his discussions with Goerderler. On 2 February 1945 the German resistance martyr went to the gallows.[296] Heinrich Himmler, however, could now no longer escape from the regime which he wished both to defend and to remove. He and his SS order remained prisoners of their wishful thinking and of their fanaticism —to the bitter end.

18

The End

IN autumn 1944 Gebhard Himmler, the civil servant, met his brother Heinrich. Heinrich had a bad cold, but was nevertheless preparing to go to a conference of senior Nazi leaders. "You should take care of yourself," his brother said, "Why not postpone the Conference?" In a somewhat offended tone the Reichsführer replied: "Have you ever heard of Easter being postponed because the Pope had a cold?"[1]

The answer shows how Heinrich Himmler was living in a dream world, obsessed by a sort of missionary fervour. He had been the principal beneficiary of the failure of the 20 July putsch and now occupied an unparalleled position of power. To many it seemed that he was merely waiting for the death of Adolf Hitler to place himself at the head of the State. A mere list of his officers is enough to show the power he now wielded: he was lord of the SS—next to the Party the most important organisation in the Third Reich; he controlled the Police and the Secret Service; he was in charge of the Ministry of the Interior; as the "Reich Commissar for the Strengthening of Germanism" he was reponsible for the regime's racial policy; he supervised relations between the Reich and Nazi movements in the so-called Germanic countries; 38 Waffen-SS divisions owed allegiance to him, even if only on paper; as head of the armaments industry and Commander-in-Chief of the Replacement Army he commanded all armed forces in the home country; one of his Obergruppenführer, Gottlob Berger, administered the Wehrmacht's prisoner-of-war camps.[2]

Himmler's power was in fact such that even at the time many succumbed to the belief that, behind the ageing and decaying Hitler, he alone was responsible for holding the disintegrating regime together. Late in 1944 the world press from Stockholm to San Francisco carried the headline "Himmler—Dictator of Germany."[3] Anyone who did not have personal experience of the gruesome and grotesque realities of National-Socialism's final phase may be forgiven for thinking that, in its last months, Hitler Germany was ruled from the SS barracks. Even a decade later Karl O. Paetel considered that: "Ten months before the end, the SS finally held Germany in its grip. In 1944-45 no agency of the economy, the State or the Party could stand in the way of the SS. The Order had taken possession, sometimes openly, sometimes more discreetly, of all power. All that was not part of it was, in its view, no more than an instrument. At the end of 1944 there were only two men who mattered in Germany: Adolf Hitler and Heinrich Himmler."[4]

One man at least believed in this specious story of SS omnipotence—its own Grand Master. To him it seemed that the hour had come when he could purge National-Socialist Germany of all "treachery" and all doubts, of those satanic powers which, in his distorted view, had so far prevented Germany's final victory. In a sort of ecstasy he proclaimed in August 1944: "What we are waging now is a sacred war of the people."[5]

With threats, mobile courts martial and strident "rifle-in-hand" propaganda, Himmler mobilised the last levies —copying the Soviet system. He even publicly acknowledged his debt to his Bolshevist mentors, recommending to the Generals an SD study entitled *Soviet measures for the successful defence of Leningrad* as an indication of the lines on which the German defensive battle should be fought.[6] To the officers of a "Grenadier Division" he thundered: "I give you the authority to seize every man who turns back, if necessary to tie him up and throw him on a supply wagon . . . put the best, the most energetic and the most brutal officers of the Division in charge. They will soon round up such a rabble. They will put anyone who answers back up against a wall."[7]

In his mobilisation measures for his fanatical "last man, last round" strategy, Himmler was influenced by his long-standing hatred of the professional officer. Immediately after 20 July Hitler ordered him to form 15 new divisions and Himmler saw here a unique chance to create a new Wehrmacht, the "National-Socialist People's Army."[8] The men of these new formations were scraped together from factories and school classrooms and Himmler deliberately organised them on non-army lines; fervent young Nazis with only the sketchiest of training were appointed to officer the units; the authority of the "National-Socialist Leadership Officers," the Nazi version of the political commissars, was increased; even unit nomenclature demonstrated that Himmler's "revolutionary army" was something different. Formations were entitled "People's Grenadier Divisions" and "People's Artillery Corps."[9]

"True marriage between Party and Wehrmacht has today become a living reality" the *Völkischer Beobachter* proclaimed.[10] Himmler was determined to shield his people's army from any infiltration by regular officers. No "People's Officer" might be transferred to another unit; the new formations were invariably to remain under the jurisdiction of the Commander-in-Chief of the Replacement Army (Himmler). "The army which must win this war is the National-Socialist People's Army," he said.[11]

Simultaneously he infiltrated spies and informers into the remainder of the Replacement Army to report to him even the slightest deviation from the "last man, last round" policy. Speaking to Gauleiter in Poznan on 3 August 1944 he announced that he would be ruthless in bringing to justice any doubters in ultimate victory. And he knew where to begin: "There is a greater or smaller proportion, five, ten, fifteen per cent perhaps, who are real swine, people who belong to the officers' clique. These we should seek out and, if they are against us, bring them to justice sooner or later."[12] Throughout the Wehrmacht the SD spies kept their ears to the ground for any defeatist murmurs. The HSSPF were ordered to maintain regularly checked lists, showing whether the senior Wehrmacht officers in any particular locality were reliable and were applying the spur to their men to hold on until "final victory."[13]

Report from Obergruppenführer Gutenberger, HSSPF West: "Colonel Feind, Düren—lax in his attitude to duty and should be dismissed . . . Lieut-Colonel Bührmann,

Krefeld 60J—unwilling to take responsibility, no power of decision. Dismissal urgently necessary . . . Colonel Kaehler, Neuss—politically colourless, no power of decision, dismissal necessary."[14] From Obergruppenführer Hofmann, HSSPF South West: "Lieut-Colonel Graf, Schlettstadt—politically unreliable, dismissal urgently requested . . . Lieut-Colonel von Hornstein, Rastatt—should be dismissed, said to have a Jewish grandmother."[15] The all-seeing eye of the RSHA even watched unit officers. SD informers, mostly NCOs and men from the Allgemeine SS, sent in detailed reports describing "lack of planning in the higher military echelons . . . valuable troops and resources lying idle . . . disastrous irresponsibility in high places."[16]

On 14 November 1944 the SD-Hauptaussenstelle Mannheim reported to the SD commander Strasbourg: "Reference the situation in 205 Tank Battalion now at Dossenwald camp near Schwetzingen and in particular the unsuitable personality of the commander, Hirschberger—aged 29: further information best obtained from junior officers of the battalion."[17] The informer in this battalion missed nothing. Regarding the "National Socialist Leadership Officer" he reported: "Even today this officer is given insufficient scope. Many simply do not possess the necessary backbone. Officers, NCOs and even the men are wondering about this situation. They think that we should quite simply take our tune from the example of the Bolshevist army."[18] Regarding the officers: "Wasting their time in the mess is still their main occupation today. After being stationed in France, all they think of is drink and women. Many have no political education whatsoever."[19] Concerning the attitude to the National-Socialist officer: "With this officer clique, social standing is still the most important criterion for promotion of an NCO to officer rank. So far precautions have been taken to exclude avowed National-Socialists."[20]

Informers were employed to report whether court-martial sentences on so-called "saboteurs of the war effort" measured up to Himmler's severe standards and the reports were collated in Group A2 Amt III of the RSHA; when the RSHA began demanding to see the records of court martial proceedings in doubtful cases, however, the army jibbed, causing Kaltenbrunner to write to Himmler on 17 October 1944 "I therefore propose that henceforth all records and sentences of courts martial be forwarded to the RSHA on demand; further that SD Abschnitte or Leitabschnitte be entitled to see the proceedings of divisional courts held in their area."[21] Such interference with the prerogatives of the Wehrmacht, however, was too much even for Himmler; even the military yes-men such as Keitel of OKW were still insisting on the Wehrmacht's rights, tattered though they had now become. In the margin of Kaltenbrunner's letter, Himmler scribbled: "No, unwise."[22]

Himmler felt that time was on his side. Like a drowning man Hitler clung desperately to the belief that the pugnacity of the SS would save him from catastrophe and that only Himmler could achieve what the Wehrmacht generals had failed to do. The extent of Hitler's empire was growing ominously smaller; the 1944 summer offensive had brought the Red Army to the Vistula and East Prussia; in September British and American forces appeared on the original Western frontier of Germany. The Dictator was sustained only by his faith in the magic and terror of his SS.

And initially Himmler in fact accomplished what his Führer expected of him. During September and October, with his peculiar brand of organisational talent, he collected 500,000 fresh soldiers and dispatched them to the front, hurriedly and miserably trained though they were.[23] Even before this he had produced from the Repacement Army six brigades hitherto reserved for internal security duties.[24] He drew up fantastic plans for the defence of every German house; he even worked out a scheme, known as "Werewolf," for an organisation of fanatical Nazi partisans; he dreamed of an alpine fortress in Southern Germany as the last impregnable refuge of the National-Socialist elite. On 10 September he plastered the country with posters: "Every deserter . . . will find his just punishment. Furthermore his ignominious behaviour will entail the most severe consequences for his family."[25] Soon his summary courts were on the move to write the fulfilment of the Reichsführer's gruesome prophecy in letters of blood. The more desperate the battle both in East and West became, the more bestially did the death mills of Himmler's Sonderkommandos grind, the more frequently were victims of the summary courts to be seen hanging from trees with a placard: "I am a deserter" or "I am hanging here because I left my unit without permission."[26]

Wherever Hitler saw a new catastrophe looming at the front, the Reichsführer-SS moved his cohorts in to the counter-attack. Three times the dictator summoned his Imperial Guard and three times they brought the enemy to a halt.

By 1 August 1944 the Soviet armies had reached the Vistula on a broad front and their reconnaissance detachments were already in the Warsaw suburb of Praga west of the river. Thus encouraged, General Bor-Komorowski, the Polish insurgent leader, called his 35,000 partisans on to the Warsaw streets to fight the Germans. The revolt in Warsaw was a major threat since it cut communications to 9th Army, still fighting further east.[27] The city had not been declared part of the army operations zone and so Colonel-General Guderian, the Army Chief of Staff, applied to Hitler to have Warsaw placed under the Wehrmacht so that the army might put down the revolt. Hitler refused; the task was allotted to Himmler as Commander-in-Chief of the replacement army.[28]

Himmler ordered to the Warsaw front the head of his anti-partisan formations, SS Obergruppenführer von dem Bach-Zelewski, who put down the Polish revolt with his usual brutality. Bach-Zelewski mobilised the most notorious formations in the SS—twelve police companies under SS-Gruppenführer Heinz Reinefahrt, the regiment commanded by SS-Oberführer Dr Oskar Dirlewanger (composed of poachers and convicted criminals) and a force of Russian ex-prisoners-of-war under the White Russian, SS-Brigadeführer Bronislav Kaminski.[29] The story of the horrors perpetrated by Dirlewanger's and Kaminski's men even reached the Führer's headquarters. In his memoirs Guderian says; "What I learnt . . . was so appalling that I felt myself bound to inform Hitler about it that same evening and to demand the removal of the two brigades from the Eastern front." Even Gruppenführer Fegelein, Himmler's chief representative, confirmed the story, saying: "It is true, *mein Führer*, those men are real scoundrels."[30]

Grudgingly Hitler gave way to Guderian but not before giving Bach-Zelewski the opportunity of shooting the freebooter Kaminski as "a possibly dangerous witness" (Guderian's words).[31] The exploit confirmed the Dictator in his opinion that "this Bach-Zelewski is one of the cleverest of men."[32]

The ashes of the Warsaw rising were still smouldering when a new crisis in rear of the Eastern front brought another order to the SS from Hitler. Encouraged by the Russians, the Slovak politicians and some units of the Slovak army revolted, threatening to bar the way to German formations withdrawing from Galicia.[33] Before the revolt had spread throughout the country, however, and before the hesitant Bratislava Government had made up its mind, the SS struck once more. The SD arrested the leading revolutionaries and the SS training school in Bohemia and Moravia formed itself into an armoured regiment and marched.[34]

The training-school regiment captured Neusohl, the centre of the revolt; meanwhile 18 SS-Panzer-Grenadier division, known as "Horst Wessel," together with the newly-formed SS division "Galicia," moved in from the East; army units and the Dirlewanger regiment arrived later. From Berlin Himmler summoned the most faithful of all his followers, Gottlob Berger, the head of the SS-Hauptamt, and he took over as the new Wehrmacht Commander-in-Chief Slovakia.[35] Assisted by Einsatzgruppe H under SS-Obersturmbannführer Dr Josef Witiska, Berger took only four weeks to re-establish behind the front the perfect peace characteristic of German rule.[36] The Slovak Government "dwindled from a puppet regime to a shadow."[37] Together with the Wehrmacht the SS was now in effect the ruler of the satellite states.

When Berger reported back from his mission in Slovakia, he found in the Führer's headquarters a giant SS officer awaiting a new mission from Hitler. The Dictator had summoned to Wolfsschanze the man who had become a legend in the SS—Sturmbannführer Otto Skorzeny, destined to lead the SD's last international coup.

Skorzeny had been born in Vienna in 1908. He trained as an engineer and became manager of a scaffolding business; in 1939 he joined the Luftwaffe and later transferred to the Leibstandarte;[38] he then moved to the Ausland-SD where he was put in charge of sabotage operations[39] and became a sort of father-figure for all those Germans who hoped that some secret-service gimmick would produce a change in the fortunes of war. His almost mythical reputation dated from Sunday 12 September 1943 when, at the head of German parachute troops, he had rescued Mussolini from his Carabinieri guards in a mountain hotel in the Gran Sasso, one of the most inhospitable parts of Italy, where the ex-Dictator had been incarcerated by the Badoglio Government. Skorzeny had greeted the Duce with the words: "The Führer has sent me."[40] Now a year later Hitler proposed to despatch his guerrilla leader to another ally, but with a very different mission—to arrest him and remove him from the scene.

Hitler's orders to Skorzeny ran: "We have received secret reports that the Head of the Hungarian State, Admiral Horthy, is attempting to get in touch with our enemies with a view to a separate peace . . . You, Skorzeny, must be prepared to seize the Citadel of Budapest [the Burgberg—Horthy's residence] if he betrays his alliance with us."[41]

Skorzeny changed into mufti and set off for Hungary with a passport in the name of Dr Wolff.[42] On the way he thought up a code name for the operation; he had forgotten to tell the commanders of his paratroop units to take bazookas with them and so he christened the operation "Panzerfaust" [Bazooka].[43] On reporting to Obergruppenführer Dr Otto Winkelmann, the HSSPF Hungary, however, Skorzeny learnt that the situation had taken a dramatic turn; on 30 August 1944 Horthy had dismissed Hungary's pro-German Government and replaced it by a Cabinet, under Field-Marshal Geza Lakatos, clearly intended to prepare for Hungary's withdrawal from the war. Barely a month later Field-Marshal Farago was on the way to Moscow to arrange an armistice with the Russians.[44]

Farago signed his agreement with the Russians on 11 October,[45] but Winkelmann was forearmed. Ever since the installation of the Lakatos Government, which he regarded as a "sign of treachery,"[46] he had taken precautions to ensure that, should Hungary try to change sides, a Nazi-run Government would suddenly take the place of the Horthy regime.[47] Since late August Ferenc Szalasi, the Hungarian Nazi leader, had been prepared to take over;[48] the SD was holding ready 3 million leaflets proclaiming the new Nazi Government;[49] SS-Untersturmführer Erich Kernmayr with a special squad was waiting to seize Budapest radio station.[50]

Winkelmann was unwilling to wait further and decided to forestall the Hungarians. He reported: "On Friday 6 October 1944, knowing that treachery was round the corner but also that no major action could take place for military reasons, I took the decision to clarify the situation."[51] The decision was—"arrest Horthy's entourage as soon as possible."[52] Winkelmann, SS-Oberführer Hans Geschke (the Sicherheitspolizei Commander for Hungary) and Skorzeny drew up a plan of campaign and on the morning of 10 October they struck.

As Field-Marshal Bakay, commander of I Hungarian Army Corps stationed in Budapest and Horthy's principal military adviser, returned to his apartment he was kidnapped by Geschke's thugs.[53] Horthy thereupon nominated Field-Marshal Aggteleki to succeed Bakay but he too disappeared without trace.[54] The German plan also included the kidnapping of Nikolaus (Nikki) Horthy, the Regent's son whom the SD had been shadowing for some time on suspicion of attempts to negotiate an armistice with representatives of Tito, the leader of the Yugoslav partisans. The SD in Budapest had drawn up a typically SD plan. They proposed to capture Horthy *in flagrante delicto*, while actually negotiating with Tito's representatives, carry him off and then blackmail his father into agreement to continue to fight at Germany's side and install a pro-German Government.[55] The kidnapping operation was given the code name "Operation Mouse"—young Horthy's nickname "Nikki" had been misheard as "Mickey" and so the wags of the Budapest SD christened the operation "Mickey Mouse."[56]

Two SD men were disguised as officers of Tito's army and quickly gained contact with Nikolaus Horthy. They agreed on a secret meeting on 13 October but the premature appearance in Budapest of an SD Commander known to Nikki made him suspicious and he called the meeting off.[57] He did, however, agree to a further meeting to take place on 15 October in the office of the Director of the Hungarian "Danube Ports Association". Nikolaus took his precautions: he was accompanied by five Honved [Hungarian National Guard] officers to watch the door of the building; a Honved company was posted a couple of streets away.[58]

But the Germans had made their preparations too. The

previous day an SD commando had taken up residence in a *pension* one floor above the Ports Association's offices and in a side street Skorzeny had posted a company of his men in closed trucks.[59] The kidnapping of Horthy was planned for 10.10 a.m. Just after 10.0 Skorzeny, again in mufti, drove up to the building which young Horthy had just entered. Horthy's car was parked in front of the entrance and behind it was a jeep in which sat three Hungarian officers invisible to passers-by.[60]

Two SD men then approached the building. As they did so the three Honved officers realised the danger and fired. One of the SD men collapsed, dead.[61] At this moment the muzzles of Hungarian rifles and sub-machineguns appeared through the windows of the building, and Skorzeny's car came under heavy fire. Skorzeny drew his revolver and summoned his men. They occupied the opposite side of the square and, as the Hungarians moved forward, drove them back into the neighbouring houses. The alarm had hardly reached the Honved troops nearby, however, when the SD men already located in the building ran out with Horthy and the Director of the Ports Association both handcuffed. The two prisoners were hustled into a truck and a few minutes later were in the air heading for Mauthausen concentration camp.[62]

"Operation Bazooka" now got under way. At mid-day Dr Veesenmayer, the German Minister and also an SS officer, announced himself to Admiral Horthy with the demand that he forthwith declare himself for or against the Reich.[63] SS-Brigadeführer Veesenmayer did not feel very comfortable in his role of blackmailer; he had already been critical of Winkelmann's crude methods and Kaltenbrunner, the head of the RSHA, had once denounced him for "defeatism."[64] He did not, as Winkelmann later complained, "fire the biggest gun, which he should have done according to the plan; he did not tell the old man that at the slightest sign of treachery his son would be put against the wall."[65] The conscience-stricken Minister held his tongue, thereby jeopardising the entire operation—at 2 p.m. Radio Budapest announced that Hungary had signed an armistice with the Soviet Union.[66]

Meanwhile, however, Winkelmann had taken control of Budapest. To the threatening rumble of 40 German tanks[67] Untersturmführer Kernmayr occupied the Budapest radio station and proclaimed the new Nazi regime;[68] German troops occupied all key points in the city and Skorzeny now prepared to deal the Horthy regime its death-blow. He alerted 22 SS Cavalry Division which cordoned off all approaches to the Burgberg, Horthy's fortress;[69] he then deployed his parachute troops and early on 16 October they moved into the attack. Sharp at 6 a.m. Skorzeny and his men scaled the escarpment and were soon in control of the situation. Skorzeny reported: "We reached the Burgberg without firing a shot. The whole operation had not taken more than half an hour."[70] In fact he could have spared himself the trouble, for shortly before 4 a.m. Veesenmayer had reported to Winklemann that Horthy was prepared to hand over power to the Nazi leader, Szalasi.[71] Hungary was to continue to bleed for Hitler.

Once more the SS had shown that it could still snatch Pyrrhic victories to feed Hitler's "last man, last round" mania. And the more spectacular these SS successes, the higher Himmler rose in that extraordinary and melancholy court at the Führer's headquarters—a nest of intrigue increasingly reminiscent of some oriental fable.

October 1944 was the month in which Himmler's power reached its zenith. The Dictator showed his gratitude for his imperial guard's victories in Poland, Slovakia and Hungary: on 8 November 1944 Himmler was granted the privilege of taking Hitler's place for the delivery of the traditional speech commemorating the Munich beer-cellar putsch.[72] Himmler was entranced by his own power; the sense of being the principal and apparently indispensable assistant of his Führer intoxicated him. Trevor-Roper says sarcastically that the decline of the Reich had "brought Himmler to God"—that God was Hitler, whose removal in the interests of peace Himmler had been considering only a few months before but for whom he was now ready to demand the most horrifying offerings of blood.

"In the course of the last year," he confided to Schwerin von Krosigk, the Finance Minister, "I have learned to believe in miracles again. The Führer's escape on 20 July was a miracle."[73] With a ghastly, grotesque show of optimism he suppressed any doubts he might have had in the Dictator. To Kersten, who was notoriously sceptical, he proclaimed: "All Hitler's calculations will prove themselves correct. He is, after all, still the greatest genius of all time. He knows exactly the day when we shall be victorious. On 26 January next year we shall once more stand on the shores of the Atlantic."[74] When Guderian, the Army Chief of Staff, objected that he did not know where to find the troops to contain the next Russian offensive, Himmler simply laughed at so much unnecessary anxiety and lack of faith saying: "You know, my dear Colonel-General, I don't really believe the Russians will attack at all. It's all an enormous bluff."[75]

For a moment it seemed as if the Reich really was ruled by only two men—Hitler and Himmler, but the picture of Himmler's power was deceptive. Trevor-Roper says: "Nevertheless in spite of these apparent accessions of power, Himmler was in fact in decline."[76] Those who believe in the Hitler-Himmler theory have forgotten another man who was watching with burning jealousy every step taken by his rival Himmler. Martin Bormann, Head of the Party Chancellery, managing director of the Nazi Party, the Dictator's *éminence grise* and doorkeeper of his private office, blocked the rise of "Uncle Heinrich," as he liked to call Himmler.

The quarrel over the powers of the Inland SD had already shown that Bormann's influence in the Führer's headquarters was growing apace. The more the Reich shrank under its enemies' hammer blows, the more strident became the orders issued in rear of the front by Bormann's "birds of paradise" brigade. Bormann watched jealously to ensure that Himmler and his HSSPF did not infringe the Party's prerogatives. He intervened whenever some Gauleiter complained that SS interference was a challenge to his authority. Speer, the Armaments Minister, recalls that "Bormann immediately reported such cases to Hitler and exploited them to fortify his own position."[77] Hitler shared Bormann's view that as the war moved onto German territory political leadership was increasingly the prerogative of the Party and so Bormann began to dispatch his emissaries to the more important military headquarters. In the Führer's Headquarters the Wehrmacht was now discredited—and its place was taken, not by the SS but by the Gauleiter.

Among the most rabid of these was Erich Koch, who had been driven out of the Ukraine into his native East Prussia; he was the first to show what the Party leaders

understood by home defence, Bormann style. As Reich
Defence Commissar in his Gau, he made himself literally
the overlord of East Prussia,[78] disregarding both the Wehrmacht and the SS, whom he treated with equal contempt.
Without informing the responsible Army Group under
Colonel General Reinhardt, he constructed defensive positions; using invalids, old-age pensioners and teenagers, he
formed a private army which he called the "Volkssturm"
[Home Guard]; he requisitioned the armaments factories
in East Prussia and refused any expert military advice for
his Volkssturm.[79] Koch even extracted from the Führer's
Headquarters an agreement that he should carry out the
functions to which Himmler and the SS laid claim—he
reported on officers and men and took charge of the search
for deserters.[80]

Dilettante and megalomaniac though he was, Koch's
success inspired Hitler and Bormann to give the Party
nation-wide charge of this final levy. Guderian had proposed that a static Home Guard be formed in the East
under the army, but Hitler's version of this was a Volkssturm on the Koch model under the Party—and at its
head, of course, Martin Bormann.[81] On 26 September Bormann instructed the Gauleiter to start immediate preparations for the formation of a Volkssturm.[82] Three weeks
later, on the anniversary of the Battle of Leipzig (18
October 1813), it was officially constituted by Hitler
decree[83]—and a by-product of this last desperate measure
by the Nazi regime was a reduction in the power of Himmler; as Commander-in-Chief of the Replacement Army
he was responsible only for the organisation, training and
equipment of the Volkssturm; recruiting and political
leadership were Bormann's preserve.[84]

Bormann now brought another of Himmler's rivals into
the game—Goebbels. Before 20 July Goebbels had ruminated: "The Army for Himmler, and for me the civilian
direction of the war. That is a combination which could
re-kindle the power of our war leadership."[85] After the
attack on Hitler, however, Goebbels realised that Bormann was the stronger of the two and therefore threw in
his lot with him. Bormann succeeded in getting Goebbels
nominated Reich Plenipotentiary for Total War.[86] In
December he was commissioned to investigate the Wehrmacht's manpower position and recommend unit moves

to the Führer's Headquarters—another clear interference with Himmler's prerogatives as Commander-in-Chief of the Replacement Army.[87]

Nevertheless, so long as Himmler was still frequenting the Führer's Headquarters and therefore available to counter Bormann's backstairs influence, the power of the Reichsführer was inevitably a source of disquiet to the Party Chancellery. There was only one solution—Himmler must be removed from the Dictator's immediate entourage. Bormann had an idea. He knew that Himmler, once an army cadet, had always secretly longed to be at the head of a fighting formation; ever since World War I had denied the Landshut student his war experience, a warlord's career had been his dream. Martin Bormann gave it him —and it formed the prelude to Himmler's downfall.

By late November British and American forces had driven into Alsace and the German 19th Army was confined to a bridgehead on the left bank of the Rhine. The problem therefore was to create a fall-back position on the right bank through which the remnants of 19th Army might withdraw if necessary and which would hold any further enemy offensive. The Führer's Headquarters decided to form a new Army Group in the area between Karlsruhe and the Swiss frontier[88]—and Bormann proposed Himmler as its Commander-in-Chief. The horrified soldiers were forced to swallow the appointment since Hitler and Bormann pointed out that only Himmler, in his capacity as C-in-C of the Replacement Army, could provide the necessary forces for the new Army Group: since the problem was primarily to form a stop line, as Head of the Police Himmler was ideally suited for the post.[89]

Himmler was appointed early in December. The "Commander-in-Chief Upper Rhine" was radiant and entirely oblivious of the fact that Bormann was holding a knife to his throat. Now at last Himmler could fulfil the dream of his youth; now Himmler, the warlord, would bring about the great turning point in the Second World War. Initially he contrived by his industry and organising ability to deceive many even among the soldiers. He quickly formed a defensive front, mobilised units from his Replacement Army to reinforce Army Group Upper Rhine and soon assembled a heterogeneous force of stragglers, home guard men, customs officials, anti-aircraft auxiliaries and battalions of non-Germans from the East.[90] He did indeed seem to have a superstitious aversion to leaving his head-quarters in the Black Forest, but nevertheless he was clear-ly preparing himself for the great battle. Meanwhile he contented himself with more trivial victories over the ene-my within his own ranks: he dismissed Army and Corps commanders on pretexts of inefficiency and refused to recognise that Commander-in-Chief West, who was re-sponsible for the entire Western Front, had any authority over his Army Group.[91] (See Appendix 9.)

So busy was he fighting the great decisive battle in the West—though only on paper—from his headquarters, that the collapse of his authority both in the SS and in Ger-many passed him by. The Reichsführer's disappearance in-to the Black Forest was the signal for many SS leaders to try their luck with his rival Bormann, who was obviously more powerful. Highly influential SS men were among the deserters—SS-Gruppenführer Hermann Fegelein, for in-stance (Himmler's personal representative in the Führer's Headquarters, who was married to Gretel Braun, Eva's sister), and Obergruppenführer Kaltenbrunner, the Head of the RSHA.

Kaltenbrunner's defection was not without irony, for he was a second-rater selected by Himmler to head the Prinz-Albrecht-Strasse solely in order to ensure that there should not be another Heydrich.[92] He was an attorney from Linz, tall, scar-faced and a chain smoker; when he was appointed in January 1943 after Heydrich's death, hardly anyone knew him; he had been in charge of SS-Oberabschnitt Danube and gossip had it that he owed his career to the fact that by 1938 the semi-Fascist Austrian police had eliminated all his predecessors.[93] In addition Himmler en-sured that Kaltenbrunner did not possess the power of his predecessor, Heydrich. He removed from the RSHA re-sponsibility for personnel and economic questions and transferred them to two of its rivals—the SS Personnel Hauptamt and the WVHA.[94]

When Kaltenbrunner took over the RSHA he found that his Heads of Division had more authority than their new master. To his old class-mate, Skorzeny, he com-plained that he was "often by-passed" by his independent Heads of Division and "learnt many things only when they were over"; Skorzeny remarked: "It struck me that this

man . . . was not feeling quite at his ease."[95] Kaltenbrunner
made blatant attempts to turn on his Austrian charm, but
this could not conceal the fact that he was striving feverishly to recover his predecessor's power. By 1944 he was
considered the second most powerful man in the SS: even
Himmler sometimes shuddered, as had Canaris the Head
of the Abwehr, at the sight of Kaltenbrunner's coarse, un-
manicured hands.[96]

His alliance with Bormann, however, gave Kaltenbrunner a privilege which even Heydrich had not enjoyed. He
became a constant visitor to the Führer's Headquarters and
Hitler gave him orders direct—not through Himmler. This
was something entirely new—Kaltenbrunner acted as if he
was responsible to his Führer alone in matters of RSHA
policy.[97]

The Himmler loyalists realised the implications of Kaltenbrunner's defection. They warned the Reichsführer
against the machinations of the Bormann clique and attempted to rouse Himmler from his warlord daydreams.
On 21 December 1944 Gottlob Berger wrote to him: "I
request you to cut short your time as Commander-in-Chief
Upper Rhine and return to the Führer's headquarters. I
am actuated in this request not only by the knowledge
that rumours are being assiduously cultivated in certain
quarters—that the Reichsführer SS is in disfavour and that,
via Keitel, the Wehrmacht is calling the tune—but also
because I sense that when the Reichsführer-SS is not in the
headquarters, our political work . . . suffers badly."[98] The
loyalists in the "Kurt Eggers" Standarte, the Waffen-SS
propaganda squad, were also restless. Standartenführer
Gunter d'Alquen's staff was ordered to prepare a memorandum for Himmler demanding that the SS put an end
to the "Bormann monopoly."[99]

But Himmler, frozen in his martial pose, disregarded
these warnings. He was sure of his role as crown prince;
he believed firmly in his right to the succession. Only
later did he realise that Bormann and the OKW had out-
manoeuvred him; they had given him a military command
only to ensure that he would fail.[100] But in late 1944 he
would not believe it; a military future seemed to lie before him. When, in early January 1945, an opportunity
offered to display his military qualities, he pushed himself
forward as if possessed.

In a limited counter-offensive two moblie divisions of the neighbouring Army Group had succeeded in penetrating the French Maginot Line near Hagenau and breaking into northern Alsace. Spurred on by this success, Himmler worked out an ambitious plan: he requested the Führer's headquarters to allot him the two divisions and with them he proposed to recapture Strasbourg. He stressed that his 19th Army still retained a bridgehead in central Alsace; if this was reinforced with the two divisions now near Hagenau, he said, there would be little difficulty in re-taking Strasbourg. Contrary to the advice of Commander-in-Chief West, the Führer's headquarters approved the plan and General Himmler's orders went out.[101]

In an intricate move the two divisions at Hagenau were moved south along the Rhine, but before they could occupy their new positions the Allies had recovered from their setback in northern Alsace.[102] Even so, the Americans were so surprised by Himmler's attack (he penetrated to within a few miles of Strasbourg) that General Eisenhower, the Allied Commander-in-Chief, toyed with the idea of evacuating the city and withdrawing his right flank behind the Vosges. Frey, the Mayor of Strasbourg, however, protested and the Allies held the city.[103] The German attack bogged down. On 20 January the Allies moved in to counter-attack, rolled up Himmler's bridgehead west of the Rhine and a month later had driven the last German soldier across the river.[104]

Himmler's failure as a military commander was obvious, but Bormann had another command in store for his rival: it was to involve Himmler even more irrevocably in the military catastrophe of the sinking regime and expose him to outbursts of rage from the mistrustful Dictator. He was given another shadow army, this time on the eastern front—Army Group Vistula.

On 12 January 1945 the Soviets launched the attack at which Himmler had so lately scoffed, and it proved to be the greatest offensive in military history. Three million Russians over-ran 750,000 poorly armed German soldiers and in a few days the entire German front lay in ribbons. The Army Groups of Marshals Chernyakovsky and Rokossovsky drove forward to Königsberg and Marshal Koniev reached Sagan.[105] Panic seized the German defenders; apart from a coastal strip, East Prussia went

down in a welter of refugee columns, the screams of
women being raped, and the murderous sentences of
German summary courts; Army Group North had almost
ceased to exist.[106]

In the north-east the Soviet armies had opened a yawning gap between the German Army Groups North and
Centre. The area between the Oder and the Vistula, barely defended by a few scattered formations, reserve units
and home guard detachments and with no co-ordinating
headquarters,[107] lay wide open to the Russians. On 23
January, therefore, Guderian, the Chief of Staff, proposed
that a new Army Group staff be formed in Pomerania
to co-ordinate the forces located between the vistula and
the Oder and form a new defensive front. He suggested
that this "Army Group Vistula" be entrusted to Field-
Marshal Freiherr von Weichs, whose staff had been thrown
up by the shrinkage of the Balkan theatre of war.[108]

Hitler agreed but thought Guderian's candidate for
the command gave a "tired impression." He knew someone better—Himmler. No one could defend the area better than the Head of the SS. Guderian protested. "This
preposterous suggestion appalled me," he says, "and I
used such argumentative powers as I possessed in an attempt to stop such an idiocy being perpetrated on the
unfortunate eastern front. It was all in vain."[109] Hitler
insisted that Himmler had run his affairs very well on the
Upper Rhine; being in charge of the Replacement Army,
moreover, he could call direct on its resources. When
Guderian attempted to provide Himmler, who knew nothing of strategy, with minimal experienced general staff
assistance, Hitler scotched this idea too. As Chief of Staff
Himmler chose SS-Brigadeführer Heinz Lammerding, a
courageous but inexperienced tank general of the Waffen-
SS; he surrounded himself with SS officers and only later
accepted army officers on his staff.[110]

Nevertheless, as he left on 24 January to set up his
headquarters in Deutsch-Krone, Himmler had lost that
megalomaniac confidence which had governed his warlord
daydreams on the Upper Rhine.[111] He went eastwards in
fear—fear of the Dictator's ungovernable rages and of
his vindictiveness. Himmler knew only too well that he
could not afford another defeat if he was not to risk all
that he had so carefully built up over the years. He had

no time to lose; immediately and continuously, he must be able to report victories. So he departed on his new mission in a mixture of fear and fanatical determination.

He assembled the last forces from the Replacement Army; he had the lines of communication combed for fit soldiers by squads of SS and police; he formed new Waffen-SS formations although the existing divisions were already down to brigade strength; he summoned proven SS generals such as Obergruppenführer Steiner to his Army Group.[112] To offset his lack of troops he relied on the meaningless pathos of "last man, last round" appeals and martial announcements giving the civil population an impression of strength in which not even he himself believed. "The task now before us," he told the commanding generals and divisional commanders of his Army Group, "is one our ancestors have faced a hundred times in battle against Avars, Mongols and, in the south-east, Turks and Tartars. Even in those days, the only reliable allies were our own strength and our stout hearts."[113] Through the *Pommersche Zeitung*, the local Party newspaper, he announced: "Miracles are being worked as a result of full use of all available resources in men and weapons and the employment of all our strength in the rearward area. The population of South Pomerania has recognised the task of the hour; the front is holding and becoming stronger daily."[114]

Even the sound and fury of his own propaganda, however, could not conceal from Himmler the fact that he was headed for a catastrophe. He was a superstitious being who, more than any other Nazi potentate, believed in the stars and the prophesies of astrologers, and now he saw himself under an unlucky star. He dispatched X SS Army Corps to the Oder-Warthe bend to hold the Soviet drive towards the Oder but the operation was doomed to failure. On 29 January Zhukov's men appeared in front of the Oder position and quickly overran it.[115] Desperately Himmler attempted a counterattack to offset his reverse on the Oder. He launched his best SS units in a flanking attack against Zhukov's army in the Schneidemühl area—a hopeless operation from the outset.[116] The Germans were driven back once more. Haunted by defeat and no longer sure of his Führer's favour, warlord Himmler took refuge in his sickbed. His visits to

the SS hospital at Hohenlychen, run by his old friend Karl
Gebhardt, became more frequent; the C-in-C of the Army
Group now only appeared in his headquarters for a few
hours a day and by 10 p.m. the war was over as far as he
was concerned—he slept long and no officer dared wake
him.[117]

Now that Himmler had more or less eliminated himself, Guderian decided to attempt one last stroke with
Army Group Vistula. His plan was to launch a surprise
attack against the Soviet armies in the Arnswalde area,
defeat them north of the Warthe, clear Pomerania of
Russians and so secure the lines of communication to
West Prussia. To carry out this plan, Guderian proposed
to attach to Himmler's staff a new chief of operations,
General Walter Wenck, presumably hoping in practice
to remove the command from Himmler. On 13 February
he submitted his plan to Hitler in the Reich Chancellery[118] but the Dictator was quick to see through his
game. Himmler was present and, pale and embarrassed,
was forced to listen to the Dictator and the chief of
staff discussing his military qualities. The argument became heated and harsh words were used.

Guderian: "General Wenck must be attached to the
Reichsführer's staff since otherwise there can be no prospect of the attack succeeding."

Hitler: "The Reichsführer is man enough to carry out
the attack on his own."

Guderian: "The Reichsführer has neither the requisite
experience nor a sufficiently competent staff to control
the attack single-handed. The presence of General Wenck
is therefore essential."

Hitler: "I don't permit you to tell me that the Reichsführer is incapable of performing his duties."

Guderian: "I must insist on the attachment of General
Wenck to the Army Group staff so that he may ensure
that the operations are competently carried out."

For two hours Hitler and Guderian shouted at each
other, neither willing to give way. Furiously Hitler paced
up and down and then suddenly he stopped in front of
Himmler and said: "Well, Himmler, General Wenck will
arrive at your headquarters tonight and take charge of
the attack." He looked at Guderian with a dry laugh;

"Now please continue with the conference. The General Staff has won a battle this day."[119]

The end of Himmler's power was in sight, though Guderian's plan failed, for four days later Wenck was involved in a car crash and the attack miscarried.[120] Nevertheless Guderian continued his efforts to get rid of Himmler from the Army of the East; twice he asked Hitler to relieve the Commander-in-Chief Vistula and twice the Dictator refused.[121] In desperation Guderian decided to propose to Himmler himself that he should resign. When he reached the headquarters, however (which had meanwhile moved to Prenzlau), and asked to see the Commander-in-Chief of the Army Group he was told that Himmler had been in his friend Gebhardt's clinic for weeks suffering from "severe influenza." Brigadeführer Lammerding asked: "Can't you rid us of our Commander?"[122]

Guderian could. On 18 March he presented himself to Himmler who, when he recognised his visitor, shrank beneath the bedclothes, coughing. But Guderian comforted him, assuring him that he fully understood that with all his other responsible posts the Reichsführer could hardly attend to the little job of commanding an Army Group, particularly when his health was so bad. The fallen warlord took note, but recoiled again immediately. What would the Führer say, he mumbled, looking expectantly at Guderian. Guderian offered to help: if the Reichsführer had no objection, he, Guderian, on his own initiative would ask the Führer to release the Reichsführer from command of the Army Group.[123] On 20 March 1945 the thing was done. Almost without a murmur Hitler agreed to the proposal that Colonel-General Gotthard Heinrici, Commander-in-Chief I Panzer Army, should assume command of Army Group Vistula in place of the Reichsführer SS.[124] Himmler's vision of himself as warlord was extinguished.

Hardly a soul realised, however, that 20 March 1945 was a moment of leave-taking: Heinrich Himmler's departure from his lifelong idol, the renunciation of the demigod to whom he had been prepared to offer the most grisly blood sacrifices, the awakening from a life of self-deception unparalleled in history. From that day onwards Himmler was determined to save what he thought still might be saved—his own skin, his SS Order and the il-

lusions of his murky career. Himmler would not have
been Himmler had he not withdrawn into a new world
of illusion and it told him that he was the man whose
mission it was to bring peace to the world and guide post-
war Germany, liberated from Hitler, into a new era.

The first to learn of this change of heart was Colonel-
General Heinrici when he arrived at the Prenzlau headquarters on 22 March to take over. In some embarrassment Himmler explained what he was leaving behind
him, but when Heinrici asked for a "general political
orientation" all Himmler's old confidence returned. He
was a changed man. The head of the SS seized Heinrici
by the arm and led him conspiratorially to a sofa in the
corner of his office. Then he whispered: "The moment
has now come to initiate negotiations with our Western
enemies. I have already taken the first steps; my negotiators have already established contact."[125]

For the first time Himmler had revealed to an outsider
the secret which he had hitherto guarded so carefully:
through contacts in Sweden and Switzerland he had been
trying for months to gain contact with the Allies and
arrange a separate peace with the Western powers. Hitherto the Germans had seen only one of the two faces presented by the SS. Now, to the initiated at least, the
other face revealed itself and what the initiated saw was
bitter and grotesque. The SS had brutally punished any
who expressed doubt in ultimate victory; with their pathetic appeals and suicidal operations they had spurred
the Germans on to resist to the end. Now these same
SS were seeking to save their own skins by secret trafficking with the enemy because they themselves no longer
believed in victory. This grotesque change of heart, moreover, had its macabre side, for in their haste to capitulate
the SS leaders looked for salvation to the very people
whom they had set out to exterminate to the last man.
Their Jewish hostages, they calculated, could be both their
intermediaries and their guarantors, their lever for the
initiation of discussions with the West.

The fact that many SS leaders, including Himmler,
harboured such illusions was due in no small measure to
a fat, busy and somewhat boastful Balt who never tired of
urging the SS and its Reichsführer to break with Adolf
Hitler—Felix Kersten, Himmler's masseur. Born in Dorpat

in 1898 of a Brandenburg family, Kersten was both a *bon viveur* and a philanthropist; for years he had exerted on Himmler an influence comparable only to that of the astrologer Seni on Wallenstein; just as the Italian could exorcise the seventeenth-century Emperor's nightmares of the powers of evil, so "the man with the miraculous hands," as Joseph Kessel called him, could relieve Himmler of his almost intolerably painful stomach cramps.

With the sensitive pressure of his hands Kersten could relieve men of pain. As a young man in Finland he had studied manual therapy, whose theory, according to its supporters, is that many maladies result from nervous tension and can be cured by relaxation of the nerves. Having qualified as a masseur in Finland, Kersten had moved to Berlin where he had become a fashionable practitioner. When Dr Ko, the Chinese master masseur, once allowed Kersten to practise upon him, he exclaimed: "My young friend, you understand nothing as yet, but I have waited thirty years for you. You have the gift."[126]

Kersten's miraculous hands worked wonders and brought him the most profitable posts ever captured by any Berlin medical practitioner during the 1920s. His reputation spread rapidly across Europe, assisted by the fact that his undoubted ability, and insistence upon an adequate financial return for his labours, was allied to a courtly, aristocratic manner. The role of personal physician to illustrious potentates came naturally to him—Alexander Westberg, personal physician to the Czar of Russia, was one of his patrons.[127] In 1928 he was appointed personal physician to the Dutch royal family[128] and eleven years later he assumed responsibility for the most dangerous patient imaginable for any medical man in the Third Reich—the Reichsführer-SS, Heinrich Himmler.

Kersten had been introduced to Himmler by one of his patients, August Rosterg, a potash manufacturer and member of the "Friends of the Reichsführer-SS." According to Achim Besgen, Kersten's biographer, in March 1939 Kersten "established that Himmler was suffering from a most painful disturbance of the nervous system; he was in great pain but Kersten was able to relieve him in a few minutes." Himmler found this instantaneous cure almost incomprehensible saying: "I have consulted many German professors and none of them could help me.

Please help me, Professor." Kersten explained to his new patient that he was neither a professor nor a doctor; nevertheless he allowed himself to be engaged as the ogre's personal physician.[129]

Kersten now hardly left Himmler's side. He had soon realised that his pain-killing hands gave him a power over Himmler which ended only where the magic of Adolf Hitler began. Himmler was open to any proposal from Kersten; no sooner had the masseur's fingers sunk into the Reichsführer's tortured body than even Himmler showed that he was still a human being. With every soothing movement of his hand Kersten could extract some unusual concession from his patient—in one case the release of some individual from a concentration camp, in another permission for some fugitive to leave Germany, in yet another the rescue of thousands of Jews from the "final solution" machine. Kersten was always on hand to help, and frequently achieved the impossible. The list of those who owed their lives to him grew continually. For instance he saved Theodor Steltzer, later Minister-President of Schleswig-Holstein, from execution;[130] he stopped the annihilation of Finland's Jews; he prevented the theft of the Dutch art treasures;[131] he channelled the Scandinavian concentration-camp prisoners to neutral Sweden.

Eventually Himmler had such confidence in his cosmopolitan personal physician that by 1943 Kersten could act entirely on his own. He was allowed to leave his country house, Hartzwalde, north of Berlin, and move to Stockholm; using the code number 145 he was authorised to call Himmler at any moment.[132] The post-war world found Felix Kersten's story so fantastic and improbable that in 1947 the Dutch Government set up an historical commission under Professor Nicolaas Wilhelmus Posthumus, Director of the War History Institute, to enquire into the activities of the ex-Dutch Royal Physician. For three years the Commission interrogated both friends and enemies of Kersten; they examined the archives of many countries and Kersten's 800-page diary. In 1950 Posthumus pronounced judgment: Felix Kersten had rendered such outstanding service to mankind and to peace that he, Professor Posthumus, would make bold to say that history knew no comparable example of courageous philanthropy.[133] A major contributory factor to the Professor's conclusion was the adroitness with which Kersten contrived to instil into Himmler from early 1944 the erroneous belief that only by halting his murder programme could he gain the sympathy and the ear of the Western Allies. With Himmler vacillating between subservience to Hitler and his own determination to survive, Kersten gradually weaned him away from the extreme "final solution" policy, eventually persuading him that on the day when the Jewish annihilation programme halted, the door to negotiations with the Western powers would open automatically. Himmler was only too ready to believe Kersten's story.

Professor Posthumus was told by an SS-Obergruppenführer whose name he does not divulge: "At dinner in Hegewaldheim [East Prussia] in early summer 1944 Kersten brought up the Jewish question. He did so without any preamble. The conversation was extremely lively and sharp words were used. Kersten was dogmatic. I was there myself. Kersten worried away like a terrier until Himmler finally agreed to make a fundamental change in the whole Jewish business—in favour of the Jews. 'You will be pleased, Kersten,' Himmler said at the end."[134]

One of the first to see that something had changed was Adolf Eichmann, the "final solution" expert. With his henchmen Krumey, Dannecker, Wisliceny, Nowak, Hunsche and Abromeit he had moved to Hungary in March 1944 to stage the final act in the genocide drama, the annihilation of Hungarian Jewry.[135] Since the Soviet armies were approaching, Eichmann urged his German and Hungarian executioners to hurry. Hungary's 900,000 Jews were driven into ghettos and the country was divided into six deportation zones; the indefatigable Eichmann had already ordered up his death trains from the Reichsbahn. The funeral procession to Auschwitz was ready to start.[136] Eichmann was preparing to move the Jews in the first two zones when he came into collision with another SS authority.

SS-Hauptsturmführer Otto Clages, head of the SD in Hungary, sensing that the end of the Thousand-Year Reich was approaching, was searching in some trepidation for a method of insuring his own future after the catastrophe. His staff in Budapest included certain ex-members of Admiral Canaris' Abwehr. From them Clages learnt that they possessed contacts to a Zionist organisation prepared to pay vast sums of money if Germany would put a stop to its extermination programme.[137]

In January 1943 three Zionists, Otto Komoly, an engineer, Rezso Kastner, a journalist, and Joel Brand, a dealer in knitwear, had formed a group which they called "Waadat Ezra Vö-Hazzalah Bo-Budapest" (Waadah for short) meaning "Jewish Rescue Committee, Budapest." Their object was to assist the Jews of Germany, Poland and Slovakia to escape to Hungary, and from there to send them on their way to Palestine.[138] It occurred to them that they might be able to save the Jews by bribing the SS executioners and Kastner and Brand soon realised that behind the monolithic façade of the SS were men only too ready to be bought. The head executioner in Slovakia was SS-Hauptsturmführer Wisliceny who had already brought corruption in the SS to a fine art. In 1942 he had proposed that as part of the "Europe Plan" the surviving European Jews (Poland excepted) should be spared from the "final solution" if "world Jewry" would pay a ransom of 2 to 3 million dollars.[139] When Waadah now heard that this same Wisliceny was a member of Eichmann's Special Einsatzkommando for Budapest, Kastner and Brand were full of hope that a little bribery might ease the lot of the Hungarian Jews. Early in April 1944 Kastner sought out Wisliceny and put to him a deal which he accepted at once.[140] Against payment of 4 million marks Wisliceny promised to allow 600 Jews to emigrate to Palestine. Kastner's committee paid the ransom, whereupon Wisliceny revoked, contemptuously rejecting all Kastner's pleas.[141]

Nevertheless Waadah pursued its ransom plan and looked for some more reliable opposite number in the army of murderers. In doing so Brand contacted, among others, members of the German Abwehr and it was by this means that early in April 1944 Clages of the SD heard of Waadah's proposal. He passed on the offer to Himmler, recommending the Reichsführer to negotiate with the Jewish Rescue Committee deliveries of war material for the Waffen-SS. This clearly roused Himmler's acquisitive instincts, for a few days later Eichmannn received an order from the highest quarters to contact Joel Brand.[142]

Was avarice Himmler's only motive? Initially undoubtedly it was. It seems, however, that other considerations soon began to weigh and he began to wonder whether he might not be able to contact the allies via Brand the Zionist and Waadah; Kastner and Brand after all had proclaimed that behind them stood the money and power of what the superstitious SS called "World Jewry." Brand's cousin, Andreas Biss, a Hungarian businessman and an active supporter of Waadah, who later became the most knowledgeable historian of the "final solution" in Hungary, saw "ever more clearly the picture of a Heinrich Himmler who initially hoped that his contact with us would bring him weapons and equipment to reinforce and expand his SS, but who then—not much later—was aiming at re-insurance via Washington. Moreover, as I noted later, this re-insurance was confined to himself alone and entirely excluded his Führer, Adolf Hitler."[143]

As he read Himmler's order telling him to hold out to Waadah the prospect of an end to the murder programme, Eichmann must have been assailed by a small feeling of unease. On 25 April he summoned Brand and proposed to him that the Hungarian Jews be struck out of the programme if World Jewry paid a price—and not in money but in kind. Eichmann's bill amounted to 10,000 trucks, 2 million cases of soap, 200 tons of tea and 200 tons of coffee.[144] Brand, Eichmann stipulated, was to go to Istanbul and there negotiate the deliveries with the representatives of the Jewish World Organisation. At the same time, however, deportation of the Hungarian Jews would begin and would only be halted when Brand could produce World Jewry's agreement.[145] With many misgivings Waadah agreed but demanded that as a token of goodwill Eichmann should despatch "a sample train." Brand's arrival in Istanbul, they said, must coincide with the arrival in some neutral country of 600 to 1,200 Hungarian Jews. Eichmann agreed and on 17 May 1944 Brand left for Istanbul.[146]

Hardly had Brand packed his bags than Eichmann began to hunt the Jews of Hungary into his trains to Auschwitz. Brand was due back in Budapest in a fortnight at the latest and by that time, so Eichmann swore to himself, the majority of Hungarian Jewry must have been liquidated.[147] With the morbid persistence of a man who sees

himself cheated of his ambition in life, Eichmann despatched train after train to Auschwitz. His little mind had
grasped the fact that the days of the "final solution"
were numbered; Kaltenbrunner and Gestapo Müller, his
immediate superiors, were still firmly behind the murder
programme, but a new tone was detectable in Himmler's
instructions. So his deportation orders became more urgent and the Hungarian ghettos were emptied with increasing rapidity. By 7 June Zones 1 and 2 had been
cleared and 289,357 Jews murdered in the gas chambers
of Upper Silesia; by 17 June Zone 3 was clear and 50,805
Jews had been murdered in Auschwitz; by 30 June Zone 4
was free, with another 41,499 Jews murdered.[148]

Meanwhile Brand had apparently disappeared without
trace (he had been cold-shouldered by the Jewish representatives in Istanbul and arrested by the British on
his way through Syria).[149] And now there was no holding
Eichmann. He used every method to sabotage the agreed
transport of Jews abroad. He refused to assemble in
Budapest the Jews selected for the "sample train." He
was continually trying to reduce the number of Jews
selected. He refused to allow Jews to leave for Portugal as
previously agreed.[150] No subterfuge was too devious for
him if it would deny a few Jews their liberty. In vain
Kastner appealed to the agreements already concluded; in
vain he called for assistance from Clages. At last in desperation he turned to another of Himmler's Budapest
representatives whom Eichmann regarded as his bitterest
rival.

SS-Obersturmbannführer Kurt Becher was in charge of
an armaments commission of the SS-Führungshauptamt
whose job it was to obtain equipment for the Waffen-
SS.[151] By a quirk of fate he was to put a spoke in the
wheel of Eichmann's murder programme. While looking
for 20,000 horses for the Waffen-SS, Becher made the
acquaintance of a banker, Dr Franz Chorin, one of the
shareholders of the largest industrial concern in Hungary,
the Jewish-controlled Manfred Weiss works. Chorin was
a connoisseur of horses and Becher a dedicated horseman; on receiving a couple of useful tips on sources of
good horseflesh, Becher was only too willing to repay the
good turn.[152]

The horse business brought the two so close together

that Chorin eventually confided to Becher the troubles
of the late Manfred Weiss family. Most of the Jewish
members of the family wished to leave Hungary before
they were caught by Eichmann's death machine and
Chorin proposed that Becher might help—and do the SS
a good turn in the process. Becher and the Weiss firm
reached an agreement in which humanity and blackmail
both played their parts: the SS took over the stock (55
per cent of the share capital) held by the "Aryan" members of the Weiss family and allowed 48 (including 35
Jewish) members of the family to leave for Portugal,
paying them compensation of 3,000,000 marks and retaining nine members of the family as hostages.[153] On 17
May 1944 the agreement was signed and the Jewish
industrial dynasty travelled to freedom.[154]

The agreement sparked off a deadly enmity between
Becher and Eichmann, who now saw his "final solution"
programme being jeopardised by a fellow representative
of Himmler. The Hungarian puppet government was already protesting against Becher's interference with the
Hungarian economy and Eichmann was enraged by
Becher's coup, for behind it he sensed a principle which
to him was anathema—rescue of the Jews by ransom.
In Becher's action Eichmann saw confirmation of his
suspicion that, as the Nazi regime went down, even the
Reichsführer was becoming "soft" on the Jewish problem. Moreover Becher personified all that Eichmann hated
—he was the "SS Officer in kid gloves." Even his smart
uniform and his important position could not conceal the
fact that Eichmann, the petit bourgeois, was still only on
the fringe of society and he could not stand the sight of
Becher, the businessman's son, the product of established
Hamburg society, the SS cavalryman, the welcome guest
in feudal mansions. To cap it all, by his agreement with
Weiss this man had now become the last hope of the
Jews.[155]

To Waadah Becher was exactly the man for whom they
had been waiting to switch off Eichmann's death machine.
He had a direct line to Himmler (he signed his letters
"the Reichsführer's most obedient Becher") and his negotiations over the Weiss family were precisely on the
lines of Waadah's original programme. Kastner contrived
to get in touch with him and sell him the idea of the

sample train. In late July Becher flew off to see Himmler
and returned with authority to negotiate with Waadah in
Eichmann's stead.[156] Becher took up the "sample train"
plan with energy. He demanded a deposit of a certain
sum in Hungary, the remainder to be paid when the train
reached its destination. The price per head was $1,000.
Kastner accepted.[157] On 30 June the train left Budapest
carrying 1,684 Jews. [158]

Nevertheless Eichmann was not to be defeated. On his
own authority he diverted the train to Belsen concentration camp[159] and meanwhile Himmler changed course
once more. Reports appearing in the British and American
Press on Joel Brand's mission and the "trucks-for-Jews"
deal showed clearly that neither the Jewish organisations
nor the Allied Governments were in a mood to do business.[160] Triumphantly Eichmann threatened Waadah that
"the inmates of the sample train now located in Belsen
would be moved to Auschwitz in a week's time and there
fed into the 'mill' as they arrived" unless by that time
Brand had returned to Budapest carrying the agreement
of the Jewish World Organisation.[161] Kastner and Biss
rushed to their friend Becher to ask for help; but Becher
cold-shouldered them; the "Reichsführer's most obedient
Becher" had sensed the wind of change from Himmler's
headquarters and refused to assist.[162] This time, however,
Clages of the SD came to the rescue. He asked Biss to
draft a memorandum setting out Waadah's new financial
proposals and forwarded it to Himmler.[163] On 26 July
1944 he told Biss that "my memorandum has been
favourably received in Berlin and Himmler has given instructions for deportations from Hungary to cease until
further notice"—at least this is what Biss says in his
memoirs.[164] So an initial success had been achieved; the
death march to Auschwitz was halted for a time.

At this point Becher plucked up his courage once
more and flew off to see Himmler again. The latter
agreed that 500 Jews from the sample train might go
abroad immediately; regarding the finance for the transfer of the remainder, Becher was to discuss matters with
representatives of the Jewish-American Aid Organisation,
the "American Joint Distribution Committee" in Switzerland.[165] At last Himmler could see the door to negotiations
with the Western powers opening a crack. Being con-

vinced that America was in the grip of world Jewry, Himmler genuinely believed that if an offer of negotiations was made by Waadah, the "American Joint Distribution Committee" could provide a direct line to the White House in Washington and that this would lead to a separate peace between Germany and the Western Allies. Waadah did its best to foster this crazy notion. Biss recalls: "We were continually referring to President Roosevelt as our benefactor." [166] The gullible Himmler swallowed Waadah's every word on their fictitious relationship with Washington.

The SS leaders now proceeded to bring pressure to bear on their Jewish partners to open the door to negotiations with the West. After all, Clages said to Biss, the rescue of a few hundred thousand Jews was not the point; the Swiss negotiations might lead to "a development of international and historic significance."[167] But Becher soon saw through Waadah's propaganda game. At his first meeting on 21 August 1944 with the Swiss Federal banker Saly Mayer in the frontier town of St Margarethe, Becher realised that the Jewish organisations were not to be persuaded to agree to the trucks-for-Jews deal. Mayer was only willing to talk if Himmler first announced the official end of the murder programme and had released all the inmates of the sample train.[168]

A single report from Becher to Himmler would have sufficed to bring the negotiations with the Distribution Committee to an end but Becher did not tell his Reichsführer the true situation. He glossed over Mayer's unforthcoming statements and so dragged the vacillating, hesitating and timorous Himmler ever deeper into the jungle of anti-Hitler intrigue.[169] Whether Becher was genuinely concerned for the fate of the Jews, or whether he himself believed in the possibility of a separate peace once Hitler had gone, the fact remains that he played Waadah's game. When Hauptsturmführer Max Grüson, Becher's aide, saw Mayer on 1 September, he begged the Swiss to make at least one or two concessions, even at the risk of being disowned by the Joint Distribution Committee.[170]

But Mayer and the Distribution Committee would give no concrete assurances and Becher would have had to admit the failure of his efforts, had not Roosevelt an-

nounced at the end of September that he was despatching
Roswell D. McClellan, the Quaker leader, to Switzerland
as his personal representative—with the specific purpose
of participating in the negotiations between the SS and
the Distribution Committee.[171] This was precisely the news
for which Himmler had been waiting for months. He
reacted at once; on 30 September he informed Waadah
that he had finally authorised suspension of the "actions"
in Auschwitz (which was anyway now threatened by advancing Soviet Forces); in mid-October he decided that
the remaining inmates of the sample train might leave for
Switzerland whether the ransom had been paid or not.

For a moment it looked as if the United States would
respond to Himmler's gesture. McClellan expressed a desire to meet Becher, and the US legation in Berne
busied itself obtaining Swiss entry visas for Himmler's
representatives.[172] On 5 November 1944 McClellan and
Becher met in the Savoy Hotel, Baur-en-Ville, Zurich.[173]
Biss reports: "That this meeting took place at all, when
the Allies had agreed that all negotiations with Germany
should be tripartite and based on unconditional surrender,
must have seemed to Himmler an important—if not the
most important—result of his contact with us. Technically, moreover, the meeting was a breach of the Teheran
Agreement whereby the Western Allies had agreed with
Stalin to maintain a complete boycott of the Third
Reich."[174] But the hopes which Himmler and Becher had
placed in these discussions did not materialise. Himmler recalled Eichmann from Hungary and, in December, the remaining members of the Budapest sample train arrived in
Switzerland; further negotiations foundered, however, on
the refusal of the Jewish organisations to repay Himmler's gesture either in money or in kind.[175] There was,
however, another SS leader who, as we have seen, had
long been trying to move his Reichsführer to take action
against Adolf Hitler and he found encouragement in these
Swiss negotiations.

For more than two years SS-Brigadeführer Walter
Schellenberg, Head of the Ausland-SD, had been urging
Himmler to do something to put an end to the war and
guarantee the SS some future in the post-Hitler world.
Like Himmler, he believed that the way to negotiations
with the Allies lay via the Jewish hostages and he therefore

sought the acquaintanceship of prominent Jews abroad. In Montreux he contacted the Sternbuch brothers, two orthodox Jews representing the American Rabbinate in Switzerland.[176] Like Becher, Schellenberg offered them the chance of rescuing Jews from the grip of Himmler. From the Sternbuchs Schellenberg's contacts led to Dr Jean-Marie Musy, President of the Swiss Altbund, who was disposed, for humanitarian reasons, to take a hand in Schellenberg's double-faced game.[177]

Early in October 1944 Musy declared himself ready to go to Germany and discuss the fate of the Jews with Himmler.[178] The two met near Vienna. After some initial hesitation, Himmler declared himself ready gradually to release all Jews in German custody and allow them to travel to Switzerland.[179] In his memoirs Schellenberg states that Himmler thereupon dictated in his presence an instruction to Kaltenbrunner, the Head of the RSHA, that the lives of all Jews in concentration camps were to be spared.[180] At the Nuremberg trial, however, Beecher, now a corn merchant in Bremen, claimed that he was responsible; he could even remember Himmler's exact words: "By this order, which becomes effective immediately, I forbid any extermination of Jews and order that on the contrary care should be given to weak and sick persons."[181]

Whoever was responsible, the fact remains that Himmler had issued an order liable to bring him into sharp conflict with Hitler. It amounted to nothing less than total disregard of Adolf Hitler's directive that the final solution of the Jewish question was to be pursued without regard to the war situation. Heinrich Himmler had taken the first step on the road away from his demigod. Schellenberg kept up the pressure. Now was the moment when he must finally cut the ties between the Dictator and his Chief of Police. The next move was made by Kersten, who was doing his utmost to bring about Schellenberg's dream of weaning Himmler away from his Führer. Kersten had just received an appeal for assistance from the Swedish Government, which was in a state of acute political embarrassment.

The Swedes were being subjected to increasing Allied pressure to enter the war against Hitler and, in the hope of postponing a decision, the Swedish Government had decided to undertake a spectacular rescue operation. Sweden declared herself ready to provide food for all inmates of concentration camps and accept any prisoners released.[182] The Swedish Foreign Ministry applied to Himmler but he rejected all Swedish offers of help. The Foreign Minister, von Günther, thereupon turned to Kersten, who was living in Stockholm, and asked him to assist. Kersten worked on his patient so persisently that Himmler eventually gave way.[183] On 8 December 1944, in Himmler's command post at Triberg in the Black Forest, Kersten and Himmler concluded an agreement. Its provisions were that all Scandinavian concentration-camp prisoners should be moved to an assembly camp at Neuengamme near Hamburg; the prisoners were to be fed by the Swedish Red Cross; 1,000 Dutch, 800 French, 500 Polish, 400 Belgian, 50 Danish and 50 Norwegian women were to be released; all transport was to be carried out in Swedish buses.[184]

Günther tendered his thanks to Kersten and passed the word to Himmler that Sweden would make the buses and transport personnel available. This was on 1 January 1945.[185] But the Swedes were in no hurry, obviously hoping that the rapidly developing war situation would save them the necessity of carrying out this burdensome rescue operation. Not until 5 February did Günther make his next move, informing Kersten that the transport operation would be under the direction of Count Folke Bernadotte, a nephew of the King of Sweden and Vice-President of the Swedish Red Cross.[186] Further weeks passed in inactivity with Schellenberg and Kersten impatiently awaiting the arrival of the man who, they intended, should finally prise Himmler loose from his Führer.

At last, on 16 February 1945, Count Bernadotte left Bromma Airport, Stockholm, and flew to besieged and burning Hitler Germany.[187] The first SS officer to greet him on his arrival at Tempelhof Airport was Walter Schellenberg and he accompanied the Count to Kaltenbrunner, whom protocol dictated should be the first port of call.[188]

Bernadotte recognised at once that Schellenberg had only one object—to leave the sinking ship. In his memoirs he says: "I am quite willing to admit that from the first I felt a certain confidence in Schellenberg."[189] Never-

theless, Schellenberg did not find it easy to win Bernadotte
over to his and Kersten's plan. Moreover Himmler was
still hesitant and regarded the arrival of the Swede with
a mixture of curiosity and fear—fear because he knew
that Kaltenbrunner was watching Schellenberg's every
move with suspicion. At Kaltenbrunner's instigation Fegelein had enquired of the Dictator how Bernadotte's visit
should be handled and had received the answer: "One
cannot accomplish anything with this sort of nonsense in
a total war."[190] Schellenberg had to argue with his master
at great length before Himmler could be persuaded to
receive Bernadotte but finally, on 19 February, the introduction was made in the SS Hospital at Hohenlychen.[191]

Himmler emphasised at the outset: "I have sworn
loyalty to Adolf Hitler and as a soldier and as a German
I cannot go back on my oath. Because of this, I cannot
do anything in opposition to the Führer's plans and
wishes."[192] After two and a half hours, however, he thought
somewhat differently. He allowed Bernadotte to move a
proportion of the Scandinavian concentration-camp prisoners to Norway and confirmed what he had already
agreed with Kersten, namely that the Swedish Red Cross
might provide food for the Nordic prisoners.[193]

No sooner had Bernadotte flown back to Sweden than
Schellenberg turned on his Reichsführer the full force of
his indefatigable argumentative powers. Ceaselessly he
hammered at Himmler, always with the same argument—
finish with Hitler, finish with the war. Trevor-Roper describes the process thus: "In the niche of Himmler's
private worship, from which the idol of Hitler was thus
gradually crumbling away, Schellenberg substituted slowly
and tentatively, and against stubborn and despairing resistance from the worshipper, a new and even more
appropriate image: the image of Himmler himself crowned
as the second Führer, the second incarnation of the
spirit of Aryan Germany."[194] Tirelessly Schellenberg urged
that use must now be made of Bernadotte and that he
should be despatched to General Eisenhower's headquarters with an offer of capitulation. Himmler recoiled in
horror. Nevertheless he was so shaken by Schellenberg's
arguments that he gave his tormentor permission to use

his own initiative in persuading Bernadotte to undertake
the mission to the Allies.

On 2 April Bernadotte visited Himmler once more.[195]
At a certain point Himmler was called to the telephone
in the next room and Schellenberg seized his moment to
ask "if I could not see Eisenhower to discuss with him
the possibilities of arranging a capitulation on the Western
Front."[196] Bernadotte refused, saying that the initiative
must come from Himmler. But Schellenberg now went to
work on Bernadotte; on the way back to Berlin he
"talked the whole way in a confidential but rather forced
manner."[197] Bernadotte was prepared to go to Eisenhower
only if Himmler would declare himself Hitler's successor,
dissolve the NSDAP and release all Scandinavian prisoners. He says: "Personally I never imagined that Himmler
would accept these conditions but Schellenberg did not
hesitate. He told me that he would try to induce his
Chief to accept them."[198] Schellenberg went to work
again; in his view Himmler's stock in the Führer's headquarters had now fallen so low that his master had no
other choice but to strike against Hitler to save his own
skin.

"So you are demanding that I depose the Führer?"
asked Himmler. "Yes," replied Schellenberg.[199] He knew,
however, that Himmler would never make up his mind
unless it could be proved to him that Adolf Hitler's life
was nearly at an end anyway, so he sent his friend Max
de Crinis, Professor of Medicine and Director of the
Neurological Clinic of the Berlin Charité, to tell the
Reichsführer that Hitler was a very sick man, almost
totally paralysed and suffering from Parkinson's disease.
Himmler's conclusion was: "Schellenberg, I believe nothing
more can be done with Hitler."[200]

But Himmler was still unable to make up his mind. He
dreamed of himself as the saviour of Germany but could
not break loose from his Nazi superstitions. He planned the
death of the Dictator but could not free himself from
Hitler's influence. He knew that the war was lost but
exhorted the Germans to hold on. As late as 1 April he
was telling the Hamburg Nazi City Council that disagreements among the Allies and the imminent entry into service of the German jet fighters would produce a decisive
breathing-space.[201] On 13 April, when he heard that

Obergruppenführer Karl Wolff, his HSSPF in Italy, had been negotiating with Allen Dulles in Switzerland, his immediate reaction was "disloyalty to the Führer."[202]

Wolff had been on close personal terms with Himmler, having served him for years, first as senior aide and then as Head of his Personal Staff; he knew all the murkiest secrets of SS Headquarters. Yet that same night Himmler called him peremptorily to account, ordering him to report in person forthwith. Wolff agreed, but then sent his master a letter informing him drily that he could not come.[203] On 14 April Himmler once more called Wolff at his headquarters on Lake Garda. Twice he ordered Wolff to report at once and twice Wolff ignored the order.[204] Then Wolff asked Dulles' advice and the American recommended him to place himself out of Himmler's reach and take refuge in Switzerland with his family.[205] Wolff, however, decided otherwise; trusting to his personal charm, he took the risk of meeting Himmler. He wished to find out how much Himmler knew of his negotiations with the Allies.[206]

Wolff's journey to Berlin might well have been a journey to death, for he had dared to do what no other of Adolf Hitler's Generals had done—he had agreed with the enemy on the capitulation of one million German soldiers.

Though Wolff was a Nazi "Believer in God," an audience of Pope Pius XII in April 1944 had marked a turning point in his life. SS-Standartenführer Dr Eugen Dollmann, a historian, interpreter and Wolff's liaison officer to Mussolini's republic, had used his contacts in Roman society to arrange an audience and the Pope was impressed by Wolff. "How much misery might have been avoided if God had led you to me earlier," he said.[207] Wolff could never forget the Pope's parting words: "You are steering a difficult course, General Wolff. Allow me to send you on your dangerous road with my blessing on you and your family." Even at that time Wolff had hinted that he had long since known that Germany was defeated and that, using his own special channels, he might be able to bring fighting in Italy to an end.[208]

Negotiations had in fact reached an advanced stage as early as February. Here again Dollmann, with his knowledge of Italy and his manifold connections, had been the intermediary. One of his contacts, Baron Luigi Parilli, a Milan businessman with numerous influential Swiss friends, had passed the word to Swiss secret-service officers and thence to Dulles in Berne, that the commanders of the German army in Italy would be interested in a cessation of hostilities.[209] Dulles demanded some gesture of good-will and Wolff immediately released two of his most prominent prisoners, leaders of the Italian partisan movement.[210] Dollmann then went to Switzerland and negotiated with the Americans. He was followed by Wolff.[211] The decision was taken on 8 March 1945—SS-Obergruppenführer Wolff agreed to a German capitulation in Italy.[212] Inhibited by a perverted sense of loyalty to their oaths as officers, however, the German army commanders postponed the actual signing from week to week. First Field-Marshal Kesselring and then Colonel-General von Vietinghoff, his successor as Commander-in-Chief in Italy, took fright[213] and meanwhile news of Wolff's visits to Switzerland reached Himmler.[214]

So on his flight to Berlin Wolff was wondering whether Hitler knew of his pact with Dulles and whether therefore he would be arrested when he arrived: he landed near Berlin on 16 April, the day on which Zhukov launched his last great attack on Berlin—and so opened the final chapter in the history of the Third Reich.[215]

A few hours later Wolff was in Himmler's presence. But Himmler could not bring himself openly to accuse his "little Wolff" of treachery and left it to his old friend Gebhardt to interrogate his HSSPF. The two withdrew to the Adlon Hotel in Berlin.[216] Wolff had thought up a convincing story. Yes, he had negotiated with Dulles but only on an exchange of prisoners-of-war; moreover he had only been following the Führer's instructions, given him in February, to seize every opportunity of playing the Allies off against each other. That was what he, Obergruppenführer Wolff, had been doing.[217]

Himmler accepted Wolff's story, relieved that his old friend had not been disloyal to the Führer. Suddenly, however, Kaltenbrunner, the Head of the RSHA, entered the room with an ominous request that he might speak with Himmler alone. Kaltenbrunner was the bearer of dangerous news for Wolff; an informer had just reported that Wolff had been negotiating with Cardinal Schuster of

Milan for the capitulation of the German army in Italy and that the entire German southern front might collapse at any moment. With Kaltenbrunner urging him on, Himmler turned furiously on Wolff but the latter assured them: "I have never personally negotiated with Cardinal Schuster concerning capitulation." Nevertheless Wolff's back was against the wall. He realised that only a bold move could save him.[218]

Wolff therefore acted the injured innocent, saying that he must now ask the Reichsführer and Comrade Kaltenbrunner to accompany him to the Führer and in his presence repeat their scandalous statements. There and only there would he justify himself. Himmler went white; he did not dare go to Hitler. He decided that it would suffice if Kaltenbrunner accompanied Wolff to the Führer's bunker.[219]

The two SS men entered the bunker at 3 a.m. on 18 April 1945. In the corridor they met Hitler shuffling along and he greeted Wolff: "Ah! You're here, Wolff. Good. Please wait until the briefing is over."[220]

At 4 a.m. the two were summoned to Hitler. Casually the Dictator asked what Wolff had been doing with Dulles. Wolff explained that on 6 February he, the Führer, had told him in the presence of the Foreign Minister that, should the introduction of the new secret weapons be delayed, the next step should be to negotiate with the Allies. "Now I am happy to be able to report to you, my Führer," he said, "that I have succeeded in opening doors through Mr Dulles to the President, Prime Minister Churchill and Field-Marshal Alexander. I request instructions for the future." Hitler accepted Wolff's story and ordered him to report again in the afternoon when he explained his plans for the future—incomprehensible ravings which clearly confirmed to Wolff that Adolf Hitler was near losing his reason.[221]

For a moment the tyrant gazed searchingly at his visitor and then held out his trembling hand. His final words were: "Go back to Italy. Keep up your relationship with the Americans but see that you get better terms. Stall a bit. Give my best wishes to my friend the Duce. To you my thanks and my appreciation."[222] Wolff was saved. Hurriedly he flew back to his Italian headquarters, there to sign the capitulation on 29 April. Dollmann now

found that he had "time to fulfil my vow; while Wolff
was away I had sworn that, should we be saved, I would
light a candle to my Madonna del Rosario who was ever
present in my thoughts."[223]

Himmler's "little Wolff" was not the only SS leader
to desert Adolf Hitler. Three SS Obergruppenführer, Felix Steiner, Curt von Gottberg and Richard Hildebrandt,
were considering a plan to murder him and so put an
end to the war.[224] Even Kaltenbrunner, the regime's watchdog, had sent SS-Sturmbannführer Dr Wilhelm Höttl to
Switzerland at the end of February to offer Dulles the
surrender of Austria.[225] The most striking proof that the
ties between Hitler and the SS were now cut, however,
was provided by the Waffen-SS.

At the end of March the last great attack (in Hungary)
by 6 SS Panzer Army under Sepp Dietrich had collapsed
in face of the enemy's overwhelming superiority and the
Dictator's contempt and rage had descended on the heads
of his beloved Waffen-SS. Field Marshal Keitel telegraphed
to Dietrich: "The Führer believes that the troops have not
fought as the situation demanded and orders that the SS
divisions 'Adolf Hitler,' 'Das Reich,' 'Totenkopf' and
'Hohenstaufen' be stripped of their armbands" (carrying
the name of the division).[226]

The Waffen-SS soldiers were so incensed that they im-
plicitly believed the current story—Dietrich was said to
have summoned his divisional commanders, slammed
Keitel's telegram on the table and shouted: "That's all
the thanks you get for all you've done in the last five
years." He proposed to return his decorations to Hitler
and tell the Führer that rather than carry out his order
he would shoot himself. The only known fact is that
Dietrich ignored his Führer's order. He did not go as far
as did a certain SS-Sturmbannführer commanding the assault group which had penetrated furthest into the enemy
positions during the Hungary offensive. When he heard
of Hitler's order he turned furiously to his officers saying:
"Let's take a chamber pot, put all our medals in it and
tie around it the ribbon of the 'Götz von Berlichingen'*
division."[227]

* Götz von Berlichingen was a choleric knight in Goethe's
play, who said to the Bishop of Bamberg "Kiss my arse."

This was a somewhat crude method of giving notice that the SS had renounced the tyrant still crouched in his bunker in Berlin, bent on self-destruction. For thousands upon thousands of SS men their whole world was collapsing. Small groups of fantics fought on, hounding themselves senselessly into death, the scourge and terror of the civil population to the very end; but the mass of the SS Order was not prepared to commit their officially ordered suicide. At the battle of Waterloo when Napoleon's Old Guard had fired its last cartridge and, surrounded by British cavalry, was summoned to lay down its arms, the French General Cambronne is supposed to have said: "The Guard dies, it does not surrender." Though the remark was never in fact made, it was and is the motto of every Imperial Guard; it is the essence and justification of a military elite. But Hitler's Guard did not fire its last cartridge; the SS surrendered before it was totally surrounded by the enemy. Little by little the SS commanders gave up the fight.

In blind self-torturing indecision, however, Himmler was still feeling his way through the moonscape of the Nazi regime, driven fearfully hither and thither between the urgings of his adviser Schellenberg and the ghostly figure in the Führer's bunker. Schellenberg would not let go: Himmler must make up his mind at last. Schellenberg had found a new ally in Graf Schwerin von Krosigk, the Finance Minister, who on 19 April implored Himmler to liberate Germany from the madman in the Reich Chancellery and make peace.[228] Meanwhile Schellenberg and Franz Seldte, the ex-Stahlhelm leader, drew up a Government programme for Himmler providing for the deposition of Hitler, the dissolution of the Party, the abolition of the People's Courts and negotiations for capitulation.[229] When even this appeal did not rouse Himmler to act, Schellenberg summoned yet another ally. Kersten arrived from Stockholm, bringing with him the most memorable visitor imaginable for the Reichsführer-SS—Norbert Masur, the official representative of the Jewish World Congress. On 19 April Schellenberg met Masur at Tempelhof Airfield and a few hours later they reached Kersten's estate, Hartzwalde.[230]

But Himmler could not be contacted. He was already on his way to the Führer's bunker, for it was 20 April

1945, Hitler's birthday. Himmler was determined to pay his last reverence to his Führer. The Head of the SS could not be absent from the eerie birthday court which the Dictator held in the courtyard of the Reich Chancellery.[231] On the return journey, however, Himmler once more adopted the pose of the determined saviour of Germany. "Have you contacts to General Eisenhower?" he asked Kersten when he arrived at Hartzwalde. Kersten had not. Himmler thereupon asked whether he was willing to go to Eisenhower and negotiate the capitulation. Kersten, obviously prompted by Schellenberg, suggested Count Bernadotte as the most suitable personality to make contact with Eisenhower.[232] A few hours later (on 21 April) Bernadotte arrived, hurriedly summoned by Schellenberg, but Himmler's courage had evaporated once more. "The military situation is grave, very grave," Himmler whispered, but he made no mention of the Eisenhower plan. Bernadotte departed in puzzlement.[233]

No one in the Führer's headquarters realised at this time how close the faithful Himmler was to deserting his Führer. On the contrary, immured in his Chancellery the dictator pinned his last deperate, crazy hopes upon the SS, now personified for him by one man—Steiner. "Steiner, Steiner," Hitler kept mumbling, searching across the map with his magnifying glass. His quivering finger came to rest at a point north-east of Berlin where Felix Steiner, SS-Obergruppenführer and General of the Waffen-SS, had made a stand with a handful of worn-out units.[234] "Army Group Steiner"—this was the force which Hitler believed would liberate Berlin from the Soviet armies, now almost entirely surrounding the city.

On 21 April Hitler ordered Steiner to move south to Eberswalde, break through the Soviet flank and re-establish the crumbling German defences south-east of Berlin. "You will see. The Russians will suffer their greatest defeat, the bloodiest defeat of their history, before the gates of Berlin."[235] Hitler warned him: "It is expressly forbidden to fall back to the West. Officers who do not comply unconditionally with this order are to be arrested and shot immediately. You, Steiner, are answerable with your head for execution of this order."[236]

Throughout 22 April Hitler waited for Steiner to launch his great offensive. Hour after hour went by but

Steiner failed to issue the order to attack. To send 10,000 men into battle against 100,000 seemed to him to be total lunacy.[237] Again and again Hitler enquired how far Steiner's attack had progressed. The soldiers of the staff knew only too well that Steiner would never attack but they kept their knowledge to themselves. Not until the afternoon did Hitler learn the truth.[238] Then he cracked. Screaming and raging, he accused his staff of treachery and cowardice. Everyone had let him down, first the Wehrmacht, now even the SS. The National-Socialist concept was lost; it had no further purpose. He would not leave Berlin but would die in his capital. Transfixed, the staff gazed at their Führer as, shaken by sobs and howling, he suddenly slumped back in his chair.[239]

But no one was prepared to suggest to the madman that he abdicate and surrender. Everyone attempted to uphold the broken Führer, everyone had a word of encouragement—and leading them was Heinrich Himmler who, when informed over the telephone of the Dictator's outburst of rage, begged Hitler to leave Berlin and continue the battle in southern Germany. Then, one after another, they turned on the unhappy Steiner, urging him to make the last sacrifice for his Führer. Keitel, Jodl, Krebs—all were only too ready to descend on Steiner's headquarters and drive him into the attack; they requested, they implored, they threatened.[240] Colonel-General Heinrici, whose only concern was that the front should hold, urged: "But Steiner, this is for your Führer; he is relying on you to save him!" Keitel threatened Steiner with his Marshal's baton but Steiner remained firm: "No, I won't do it. This attack is nonsense—murder. Do what you want to me."[241] Still Hitler waited for reports from Steiner but on 27 April he gave up hope. He ordered the dismissal of Obergruppenführer Steiner and his replacement by an army officer, Lieutenant-General Holste.[242] Yet once more Steiner sabotaged a Führer order: he persuaded Holste to leave him in command.[243]

Twenty-four hours later an officer of the Ministry of Propaganda arrived in the Führer's bunker with a report substantiating all Hitler's nightmares. Lorenz had intercepted a despatch from Paul Scott Rankine, Reuter's correspondent in San Francisco, to the effect that the Reichsführer-SS Heinrich Himmler had offered the Western

Allies the capitulation of Germany. Walter Schellenberg
had finally triumphed over his timourous idolatrous
master.[244]

The men in the Führer's bunker were paralysed by
the news. At this point Werner Naumann, State Secretary
in the Propaganda Ministry, was called to the telephone
and returned with an even more circumstantial, though
still unconfirmed, report. Radio Stockholm had just announced that Himmler was already negotiating with the
Anglo-American High Command.[245] The Dictator looked
up. A whimper escaped him—the full extent of SS vil-
lainy had been revealed. Now he knew why Steiner had
not attacked, why the SS offensive in Hungary had broken
down, why Himmler had failed on the Vistula. It was all
a gigantic conspiracy engineered by that evil intriguer
whom he had once called the "faithful Heinrich." But as
long as blood ran in his veins he still had the strength to
smash the traitors. "A traitor must never succeed me as
Führer," he screamed; he summoned Field-Marshal Ritter
von Greim and ordered him to fly out of beleaguered
Berlin and arrest Himmler at all costs.[246]

Hitler would no longer tolerate any SS officer in his
presence; every SS man was suspect as a member of the
vast gang of traitors. On hearing that his brother-in-
law Hermann Fegelein, an SS-Gruppenführer and Himmler's chief representative, had left the bunker on his own
and been seen in civilian clothes, he had him shot in the
courtyard of the Reich Chancellery.[247] In his last will and
testament he declaimed: "Before my death I expel from
the Party and all his offices of State the former Reichsführer-SS and Minister of the Interior Heinrich Himmler
. . . By secretly negotiating with the enemy without my
knowledge and against my will, as also by attempting
illegally to seize power in the State, Göring and Himmler
have done the country and the people immeasurable harm,
quite apart from their infidelity to me personally."[248]

Two days later Adolf Hitler was dead, but his faithless
servant still believed in a future in which he, Heinrich
Himmler, would direct the fate of Germany. The Allies
had long since rejected Himmler's unilateral offer of
capitulation, yet the Reichsführer continued to hope.

He imagined himself founding a new Nazi party to be
known as the "Party of National Union."[249] He planned a

654 THE ORDER OF THE DEATH'S HEAD

post-war Government in which one of the Ministers was to be Otto Ohlendorf, the head of the Inland SD, with whom he had so long been at loggerheads.[250] He drew up a new Government programme. But as the Great German Reich disintegrated under the Allies' armoured thrusts, so Himmler's hopes and hallucinations shrank to a more modest scale. He started determined to be the Führer of post-war Germany. Then he coveted the position of No. 2 to Karl Dönitz, Hitler's successor, and fled to his headquarters in Flensburg.[251] Then he was prepared to be content with the post of Chief of Police.[252] Finally the job of Minister-President in Schleswig-Holstein seemed adequate.[253]

When Admiral Dönitz's rump regime collapsed, Himmler realised that he was a lost man. Graf Schwerin von Krosigk knew what he must be feeling—he was keeping control of himself only with difficulty mumbling: "Discipline, gentlemen, discipline."[254] Von Krosigk told him: "It must not happen that the Reichsführer decks himself out with a false name and a false beard. There is no other way for you but to go to Montgomery and say 'Here I am.' It is then that you must assume the responsibility for your men."[255]

Himmler, however, was proposing to do exactly what von Krosigk had warned him against. On 20 May 1945 he put on an eye-patch and Field Security Police uniform, carrying in his pocket a pass in the name of Heinrich Hitzinger, a man not unlike Himmler who had been condemned to death by a People's Court.[256] Then the Reichsführer-SS set forth on his exit from history. With a few faithful followers including Ohlendorf, Brandt, his personal assistant, Karl Gebhardt and Grothmann, his aide, Himmler marched through Holstein, crossed the Elbe and attempted to slip through the British check points. But the British had their eyes open. On 23 May Himmler's little group was captured and at 2 p.m. British Military Police handed them over to interrogation camp No. 031 near Lüneburg.[257]

When the new arrivals were paraded in front of Captain Tom Selvester, the Camp Commandant, three of them caught his eye. Two were tall but the third was "a small miserable-looking and shabbily dressed man." He ordered the three to step forward. The two larger men he dispatched to solitary confinement then—in Selvester's own words—"the small man who was wearing a black patch over his left eye removed the patch and put on a pair of spectacles. His identity was at once obvious and he said 'Heinrich Himmler' in a very quiet voice."[258]

Selvester immediately alerted Military Intelligence. Two officers of the Intelligence Corps soon appeared. They were followed that evening by Colonel Michael Murphy, head of Secret Intelligence on Field-Marshal Montgomery's staff. Murphy immediately suspected that Himmler had poison concealed somewhere and that he would take it the moment he was left unguarded. The British had in fact already found a phial of poison in Himmler's clothing, but Murphy was still not satisfied. He summoned a doctor, who examined Himmler once more. Himmler opened his mouth and the doctor caught a glimpse of something black between his teeth. As the doctor began to twist his head towards the light Himmler turned and snapped his teeth together with a crunch. The hidden phial of cyanide burst and in a few seconds Himmler breathed his last.[259]

23 May 1945: Heinrich Himmler was dead: the history of the SS was at an end. In the smoke of National Socialism's funeral pyre the SS Order dissolved, that fearsome instrument, symbol of an epoch, for in the SS had been reflected all the crime to which men can be led by lust for power, glorification of the State, the cult of personality and undiscriminating servility.

Only a few SS leaders followed their Grand Master's example and committed suicide. Globocnik took poison;[260] Grawitz, the SS Medical Officer-in-Chief, blew himself and his family up with a couple of hand grenades;[261] Conti, the denouncer of Stennes, committed suicide in his cell in Nuremberg;[262] Friedrich-Wilhelm Krüger, the HSSPF, committed suicide[263] and Prützmann, another HSSPF, did the same, not far from Himmler's camp.[264] The Allied Military Tribunals and the European People's Courts laid hands on the most important of Himmler's minions and exacted due vengeance.

Many SS leaders were executed: Höss, the Commandant of Auschwitz,[265] Jeckeln and Rauter, the HSSPF;[266] Kaltenbrunner, Pohl and Daluege, the heads of the Hauptämter;[267] Ohlendorf and Naumann, Commanders of Einsatzgruppen;[268] Greiser, Forster and Seyss-Inquart, Honorary SS Commanders.[269] The majority of the SS leaders, however, were treated with remarkable leniency. There survived: 16 out of 30 HSSPF, 8 out of 12 Heads of Hauptämter, 3 out of 6 Heads of Division in the RSHA, 3 out of 8 Commanders of Einsatzgruppen in Russia. The majority of the survivors were sentenced to periods of imprisonment but later pardoned and released. Some of the murkiest figures of the SS underworld escaped completely, the most notable being Eichmann who, however, was tracked down by Israeli agents in 1960 and condemned to death in Jerusalem two years later. Many of his most important minions, however, managed to disappear—Alois Brunner, Günther, Dannecker and Röthke; Gestapo Müller and Glücks, the Inspector of Concentration Camps, also vanished.

The mass of SS men, however, went into captivity to meet a fate which could be alleviated neither by the sentence of a court nor by some pronouncement of innocence. In the wooden huts and on the parade grounds of the Allied prisoner-of-war camps a great debate began —and it is not finished yet—the debate of the disillusioned and the defeated, the defiant and the retrospective, the ashamed and the broken. They were tortured by a sense of guilt and sin. Many were unable to still the nagging question: how had it come to pass that with enthusiasm and self-surrender young men had turned into unthinking instruments of force, into slaves to a perverted notion of loyalty and honour which had made every member of the SS a morally defenceless executive functionary of the Führer's will?

They could, of course, excuse themselves personally and shrug off the burden of collective guilt by saying that of one million SS men at most 50,000 had actually taken part in the more gruesome crimes.[270] But such an answer did not satisfy many; they dug deeper. Something had happened to make them susceptible to the call of barbarism, to the lust for power of unscrupulous small-timers concealed behind a façade of patriotism and socialism. The history of the SS unrolled itself before their eyes like a film. It told of a lost generation, brought up in the black pessimism of the anti-bourgeois cultural reaction and therefore attracted to an Order which promised them action and adventure as members of a primitive community serving a supposed genius and an ideal.

They had entered the SS order because it satisfied two innate yearnings peculiar to the Germans: the yearning to belong to a military community promising fame, security and the glitter of martial exercises, and the yearning to form part of a secret elite, an all-powerful secret society. To many Germans, after all, the words "politics" and "government" meant simply the rule of occult forces, secret circles and *éminences grises*. The SS Order was the answer to such daydreams; anyone who joined the SS became overnight one of the lords of the nation, a member of a secret society of selected noblemen, the main prop of the National-Socialist State.

They had been devoted disciples because they believed in what was preached to them—"popular togetherness" [Volksgemeinschaft], service to their country and a new social order. And they did not perceive the gradual debasement of their elite order into a bodyguard of thugs serving no other purpose than to do the dirty work for an unscrupulous unbridled dictator and his clique. The mental anguish of the SS dated from the "Röhm putsch" of 30 June 1934, the day of the SA murders; that was the start of the journey into the abyss, of the slow destruction of everything—of freedom, decency, humanity, and finally of the word which was always on the lips of the SS knights, the Reich.

In one of these prison-camp discussions, the former SS-Untersturmführer Erich Kernmayr shouted: "When our troops marched into Czechoslovakia after Munich did we say 'no' in our heart of hearts? Did we then say 'no' even to ourselves? No, a thousand times no! We were intoxicated by a vision of world power. It gripped the people like a great frenzy. The frenzy of power."[271] This march of the devotees of power knew no limits and disregarded all norms; its effects were all the more disastrous in that these youthful standard-bearers of this supposedly new Germany were not simply under the spell of the dictator's magic; they were also swayed by that old German belief that Government can do no wrong and if it does, then, by differentiating between his private life and his official duty, a citizen can emerge unsullied from any task laid upon him by the State.

So the bloody history of the SS is but another page in that of the old German nation-state; the acts and deeds of the SS are but an illustration of the hypertrophy of nationalism and state omnipotence. Have the Germans, and have the ex-SS-men, learnt their lesson? The historian would not make so bold as to give an answer. But the questions remain and will continue to nag at us. For one thing is certain—the history of the SS will continue to stalk the Germans, a record of terrifying lust for power. So long as Germany has a future, that history will stand as a warning and a challenge.

Appendix 1

NOTES

ABBREVIATIONS

BDC Microfilm
Files of the Berlin Documentary Centre, on microfilm in the National Archives, Washington (Groups 580, 611).

Central Archives
Files of the Central Archives of the NSDAP, on microfilm in the Hoover Institution on War, Revolution and Peace, Stanford University.

IMT
Record of International Military Tribunal, Nuremberg.

RFSS Microfilm
Files of the Personal Staff of the "Reichsführer-SS and Chief of the German Police," on microfilm in the National Archives, Washington (Group T–175).

RSHA
Anschriftenverzeichnis des Reichssicherheitshauptamtes.

CHAPTER ONE

1 IMT Vol. XXI, pp. 500–501.
2 Himmler: *Die Schutzstaffel als antibolschewistische Kampforganisation*, p. 29.
3 *SS Liederbuch* [Song Book] p. 18.
4 IMT Vol. XXI p. 502. Also RSHA, 1 October 1941, RFSS Microfilm No. 463. Jacques Delarue: *The History of the Gestapo*, p. 197.
5 Dienstaltersliste der Schutzstaffel der NSDAP, 9 Nov. 1944, p. 61. Hilberg: *The Destruction of the European Jews*, p. 134.
6 Martin Broszat: *Anatomy of the SS State*, pp. 503–4.

7 Paul Hausser: *Waffen-SS im Einsatz*, p. 16.

8 Letter of 23 Sept. 1947 from Dr Heinrich Malz, ex-adviser in the RSHA.

9 Hauptsturmführer Kähne, for instance, was not allowed to defend himself against the cigarette manufacturer Theodor Schmiedeberg because the SS leaders were afraid that SS secrets might emerge in court. See letter of 6 Aug. 1941 from Chef der Sicherheitspolizei und des SD (hereafter referred to as CSSD) to RFSS Private Office, RFSS Microfilm No. 25.

10 Enno Georg: *Die Wirtschaftlichen Unternehmungen der SS*, p. 139.

11 Hannah Arendt: *The Origins of Totalitarianism*, p. 372, Note 80.

12 Werner Bross: *Gespräche mit Hermann Göring während des Nürnberger Prozesses*, pp. 265, 288.

13 Reinhard Henkys: *Die nationalsozialistischen Gewaltverbrechen*, pp. 173, 176.

14 IMT Vol. XXII, p. 516.

15 IMT Vol. XXII, p. 517.

16 Felix Steiner: *Die Armee der Geächteten*, Plesse Verlag, Göttingen 1963.

17 Erich Kern: *Der grosse Rausch, Russlandfeldzug 1941–45*, Verlag Lothar Leberecht, Waiblingen 1948.

18 IMT Vol. XX, p. 368.

19 IMT Vol. XX, p. 343–4.

20 Ibid.

21 Eugen Kogon: *Der SS Staat*, p. 32. The book has been translated into English under the title *The Theory and Practice of Hell* but not all the quotations given, which are from the 1965 edition, occur in the English version.

22 Kogon: *The Theory and Practice of Hell*, p. 18.

23 Kogon: Ibid, p. 29.

24 Kogon: *Der SS Staat*, pp. 23 and 26.

25 Letter of 24 October 1948 from Ohlendorf to Dr Heinrich Malz.

26 Gerald Reitlinger: *The Final Solution*, p. 5.

27 Comer Clarke: *Eichmann, the Man and his Crimes*, p. 25.

28 Joseph Kessel: *The Man with the Miraculous Hands*, p. 4.

29 *Deutsche Zeitung*, 15 Aug. 1956.

30 Kogon: *Theory and Practice of Hell*, p. 260.

31 Ibid, p. 25.

32 Ibid.

33 Elie Cohen: *Human Behaviour in the Concentration Camp*, p. 233.

34 Ibid, p. 236.

35 Karl O. Paetel: "Die SS," *Vierteljahrshefte für Zeitgeschichte*, Jan. 1954, p. 25.

36 Ermenhild Neusüss-Hunkel: *Die SS*, p. 118.

37 Hilberg: op cit, p. 134.

38 Neusüss-Hunkel: op cit, pp. 105 and 111.

39 Letter of 26 Feb. 1949 from Dr Aschenhauer, a lawyer, to Bishop Neuhäusler.

40 Hans Rothfels: *Die deutsche Opposition gegen Hitler*, pp. 112, 227.

41 Raul Hilberg: *The Destruction of the European Jews*, Quadrangle Books, Chicago; W. H. Allen, London 1961.

42 Alexander Dallin: *German Rule in Russia 1941–45*, Macmillan, New York 1957.

43 Jacques Delarue: *The His-*

tory of the Gestapo (translated by Mervyn Savill), Macdonald, London 1964.

44 Edward Crankshaw: *The Gestapo*, Putnam, London 1956.

45 Jacques Benoist - Méchin: *Histoire de l'Armée Allemande*, Albin Michel, Paris 1964–66.

46 Hannah Arendt: *Eichmann in Jerusalem*, Viking Press, New York 1963.

47 Enno Georg: *Die wirtschaftlichen Unternehmungen der SS*, Deutsche Verlagsanstalt, Stuttgart 1963.

48 Helmut Krausnick, Hans Buchheim, Martin Broszat, Hans-Adolf Jacobsen: *Anatomy of the SS State*, Collins, London 1968.

49 Buchheim and others: op cit, p. xv.

50 George H. Stein: *The Waffen-SS*, Cornell University Press, Ithaca, New York; Oxford University Press, London 1966.

51 Stein: op cit, p. vii. It should be mentioned here that Horst Pelckmann, defence counsel for the SS at Nuremberg, did try to present a less stylised picture of the SS.

52 Paetel: op cit, p. 20.

53 Kogon: *Der SS Staat*, p. 32.

54 Buchheim: *SS und Polizei im NS-Staat*, pp. 16–17.

55 Trevor-Roper: *The Last Days of Hitler*, p. 2.

56 Hannah Arendt: *The Origins of Totalitarianism*, p. 398, Note 29.

57 Arendt: *Elemente und Ursprünge totaler Herrschaft*, p. 646 (not in English translation).

58 Buchheim: *Totalitäre Herrschaft*, p. 115.

59 Statement by Otto Ohlendorf, 8 October 1947, in the official record of Case X, Nuremberg Trials 2nd series p. 486 (Reference: American Military Tribunal, M-IL-I-I-Caming (Int Lea) Court IIa Case X).

60 Ibid.

61 Trevor-Roper: op cit, p. 2.

62 Werner Best: *Die deutsche Abwehrpolizei bis 1945*, p. 19.

63 Paul Seabury: *The Wilhelmstrasse*, p. 127.

64 Dallin: op cit, pp. 168-172.

65 Letter of 17 April 1943 from Hildebrandt to Himmler, RFSS Microfilm 117.

66 Heinz Boberach: *Meldungen aus dem Reich*, Vol. XXVII.

67 Martin Broszat: *Nationalsozialistische Polenpolitik, 1939–45*, pp. 83, 84.

68 Viktor Lutze's diary, *Frankfurter Rundschau*, 16 May 1957.

69 Walter Schellenberg: *Memoirs*, p. 179.

70 Bullock: *Hitler, A Study in Tyranny*, p. 269.

71 Report by the Commander of the Sicherheitspolizei and SD in White Ruthenia, RFSS Microfilm 59.

72 Robert Kempner: *Eichmann und Komplizen*, pp. 373–380.

73 Achim Besgen: *Der stille Befehl*.

74 Ibid, pp. 28, 29.

75 IMT Vol. XX, p. 418.

76 Correspondence between Himmler and Reeder, RFSS Microfilm 56.

77 Quarterly report of the Nuremberg SD Sector, 10 October 1941, RFSS Microfilm 406.

78 Letter of 2 April 1943 from Berger to Rudolf Brandt, RFSS Microfilm 117.

79 Ibid.

80 Correspondence between Ohlendorf and Wolf, Brandt and

d'Alquen 1942/43, RFSS Microfilm, 275.
81 Rudolf Höss: *Kommandant
in Auschwitz*, p. 130.
82 Jürgen Thorwald: *Wen sie
verderben wollen*, p. 360. Reitlinger: *The House built on*

Sand, p. 355. Dallin: op cit, p.
605.
83 Dr Korherr's private papers.
84 Enno Georg: op cit pp. 51
et seq.
85 Ibid, pp. 37–8.

CHAPTER TWO

1 Ernst Deuerlein: *Der Hitler-
Putsch*, p. 30.
2 Deuerlein: "Hitler's Eintritt
in die Politik und die Reichswehr," *Vierteljahrshefte für Zeitgeschichte*, No. 2, Apr. 1959, p.
185.
3 Ibid, p. 184.
4 Ibid, p. 208. Heinrich Bennecke: *Hitler und die SA*, p. 15.
5 Bennecke: op cit, p. 19.
6 Ibid p. 19. Hans Volz: *Daten
der Geschichte der NSDAP*, p. 5.
7 Ernst Röhm: *Die Geschichte
eines Hochverräters*, p. 86.
8 Werner Maser: *Die Frühgeschichte der NSDAP*, pp. 189-
190. Deuerlein: op cit, p. 26.
9 Röhm: op cit, p. 114.
10 Bennecke: op cit, pp. 13–14.
11 Konrad Heiden: *Geschichte
des Nationalsozialismus*, p. 83.
12 Bennecke: op cit, p. 13.
13 Ibid, p. 16.
14 Heiden: op cit, p. 86.
15 Ibid, p. 98.
16 Röhm: op cit, p. 115.
17 Ibid, p. 125.
18 Bennecke: op cit, p. 27.
19 Ibid.
20 Ibid, p. 28.
21 Ibid, p. 27.
22 Ernst von Salomon: *Der
Fragebogen*, p. 398.
23 Heiden: op cit, p. 87.
Bennecke: op cit, p. 28.
24 Röhm: op cit, p. 173.

25 Heiden: op cit, p. 87.
26 Ibid, p. 99.
27 Bennecke: op cit, p. 31.
Heiden: op cit, p. 81.
28 Bennecke: op cit, pp. 54–55.
29 Ibid, pp. 54, 56, 68.
30 Ibid, p. 54.
31 Ibid, p. 66.
32 Volz: op cit, p. 11. Röhm:
op cit, p. 149.
33 Bennecke: op cit, pp. 86, 88.
34 Ibid, p. 236.
35 Volz: op cit, p. 120.
36 Ibid.
37 Ibid.
38 Ibid.
39 Ibid. Josef Wulf: *Die SS*,
p. 2.
40 Maser: op cit, p. 357.
41 Ibid, p. 303.
42 Letter of 14 October 1966
from Herr Otto Eichinger.
43 Maser: op cit, p. 308.
44 Reitlinger: *The SS*, p. 13.
45 Deuerlein: *Der Hitler-
Putsch*, p. 99.
46 Maser: op cit, p. 443.
47 Bennecke: op cit, p. 92.
48 Maser: op cit, p. 448.
49 Ibid, p. 445.
50 Ibid.
51 Ibid, p. 448. Volz: op cit,
p. 122.
52 Maser: op cit, p. 445. Bennecke: op cit, p. 52.
53 Maser: op cit, p. 445.
54 Ibid, p. 446.

55 Bennecke: op cit, p. 94.
56 Maser: op cit, pp. 448 and 456.
57 Bennecke: op cit, p. 94.
58 Maser: op cit, p. 458.
59 Ibid, p. 459.
60 Ibid.
61 Ibid, p. 461.
62 Ibid, p. 460.
63 Volz: op cit, pp. 10–11.
64 Röhm: op cit, p. 206.
65 Ibid, p. 275.
66 Bennecke: op cit, p. 110.
67 Ibid.
68 Ibid, p. 111.
69 Röhm: op cit, pp. 324, 327.
70 Ibid, p. 329.
71 Bennecke: op cit, p. 62.
72 Röhm: op cit, p. 338.
73 Ibid, p. 293.
74 Ibid, p. 336.
75 Volz: op cit, p. 12.
76 Bennecke: op cit, p. 117.
77 Ibid.
78 Röhm: op cit, p. 341.
79 Bennecke: op cit, p. 120.
80 Reitlinger: *The SS*, p. 13.
81 Volz: op cit, p. 122.
82 Bennecke: op cit, p. 127.
83 Buchheim: *SS und Polizei im NS-Staat*, p. 27.
84 "Uns ist der Kampf," Official SS Brochure, RFSS Microfilm 161.
85 Walter Görlitz and Herbert A. Quint: *Adolf Hitler*, p. 251.
86 Bennecke: op cit, p. 125.
87 Circular No. 1 of 21 September 1925 from SS Headquarters, BDC Microfilm No. 87. See also Edgar Erwin Knoebel: *Racial Illusion and Military Necessity*, p. 3.
88 Knoebel: op cit, p. 3, Gunter d'Alquen: *Die SS*, p. 7.
89 Guidelines for the formation of the National-Socialist "Schutz-staffel" issued by SS Headquarters (no date), BDC Microfilm 87.
90 Ibid.
91 *Völkischer Beobachter*, 27 November 1925.
92 Letter from Schreck to Party Headquarters, 27 Sept. 1925, BDC Microfilm 87.
93 Undated memorandum by Julius Schreck, Central Archives Microfilm 17.
94 Address by Rosenwink, Central Archives Microfilm 17.
95 Ibid.
96 Ibid.
97 Ibid.
98 Neusüss-Hunkel: op cit, p. 7.
99 NSK - Wahlsonderdienst, 5 April 1938, Sheet 5, BDC Microfilm 87. Buchheim: *SS und Polizei*, p. 28.
100 Volz: op cit, p. 122.
101 Bennecke: op cit, p. 128.
102 Ibid, pp. 128–9.
103 Volz: op cit, p. 122, Bennecke: op cit, pp. 130–1–2.
104 Bennecke: op cit, pp. 132, 239.
105 Letter of 20 May 1926 from Ernst Wagner to Hitler, BDC Microfilm 87.
106 Ibid.
107 Guidelines for the SS, BDC Microfilm 87.
108 Circular No. 1, dated 14 April 1926, BDC Microfilm 87.
109 Wagner to Hitler, 20 May 1926, BDC Microfilm 87.
110 NSK - Wahlsonderdienst, 5 April 1938, Sheet 5, BDC Microfilm 87.
111 Bennecke: op cit, pp. 239–40.
112 SA Order No. 1, 16 Jan. 1931, BDC Microfilm 87.

113 Gunther d'Alquen: op cit, p. 8.

114 Bennecke: op cit, p. 239.

115 SS HQ memorandum, BDC Microfilm 87.

116 Heiden: op cit, p. 28.

117 Ibid.

118 Order No. 1 from SS Headquarters, 13 September 1927, BDC Microfilm 87.

119 Ibid.

120 Situation report of 7 May 1929 from Police Headquarters Munich, BDC Microfilm 87.

121 Ibid.

122 Heiden: op cit, p. 28.

123 SS Song-book, p. 4.

124 Heiden: op cit, p. 27.

125 Roger Manvell and Heinrich Fraenkel: Heinrich Himmler, p. 17.

CHAPTER THREE

1 Albert Krebs: Tendenzen und Gestalten der NSDAP, p. 209.

2 Ibid, p. 210.

3 Ibid, p. 209.

4 Hossbach: Zwischen Wehrmacht und Hitler 1934–38, p. 33.

5 Guderian: Panzer Leader, p. 446.

6 Carl J. Burckhardt: Meine Danziger Mission 1937–39, p. 123.

7 Alfred Rosenberg: Letzte Aufzeichnungen, p. 102.

8 Walter Dornberger: V2—der Schuss ins Weltall, pp. 196, 202.

9 Count Folke Bernadotte: The Fall of the Curtain, p. 20.

10 Trevor-Roper: The Last Days of Hitler, p. 20.

11 As an example see Willi Frischauer: Himmler, p. 20.

12 Manvell and Fraenkel: Heinrich Himmler, pp. 1–2.

13 Letter from Margarete Himmler to Heinrich Himmler, 11 April 1928, Central Archives, Microfilm 98.

14 Ernst Himmler qualified as an engineer and became a senior technician in the Berlin Radio; he died in 1945. Gebhard Himmler was a civil servant in the Reich Ministry of Education and is now working in the Europe/

Afghanistan Cultural Institute, Munich.

15 Verbal information 29 Jan. 1966 from a close relative of Himmler who wishes to remain anonymous.

16 Himmler to his mother, 2 June 1921, Central Archives, Microfilm 98.

17 Heinrich Himmler to Ernst Himmler, 14 November 1920, Central Archives, Microfilm 98.

18 Himmler to Paula Stölzle, 18 April 1923, Central Archives, Microfilm 98.

19 Letter from Max Blüml to Himmler, 14 March 1924, Central Archives, Microfilm 98.

20 Ibid.

21 Letter from Himmler to Rössner, 12 March 1924, Central Archives, Microfilm 98.

22 Letter from Himmler to Paula Stölzle, 13 April 1923, Central Archives Microfilm 98.

23 Manvell and Fraenkel: op cit, p. 1.

24 Ibid.

25 Ibid, p. 255 Note 2.

26 Werner T. Angress and Bradley F. Smith: "Diaries of Heinrich Himmler's Early Years," Journal of Modern History, September 1959. This arti-

cle by two American historians gives some most informative sidelights on the character of the man who was later to be Reichsführer-SS.

27 Ibid, p. 214.

28 Verbal information, 29 Jan. 1966, from a close relative who wishes to remain anonymous.

29 Questionnaire regarding Heinrich Himmler completed by his father, 26 June 1917, Central Archives, Microfilm 98.

30 Manvell and Fraenkel: op cit, p. 4.

31 Angress and Smith: op cit, p. 207.

32 Manvell and Fraenkel: op cit, p. 4.

33 Letter of 11 June 1917 to Gebhard Himmler from the Keeper of the Purse to the Dowager Princess Arnulf of Bavaria, Central Archives, Microfilm 98.

34 Letter of 17 June 1919 from Heinrich Himmler to the depot of 11 Bavarian Infantry Regiment, Central Archives, Microfilm 98.

35 Manvell and Fraenkel: op cit, p. 255, Note 4.

36 Josef Wulf: *Heinrich Himmler*, p. 8.

37 See letter of 17 June 1919 (Note 34 above).

38 Ibid.

39 Ernst Deuerlein: *Der Hitler Putsch*, pp. 19-20.

40 Ibid, p. 20.

41 Cuno Horkenbach: *Das deutsche Reich von 1918 bis heute*, Vol. 1, p. 65.

42 Deuerlein: op cit, p. 22.

43 Angress and Smith: op cit, p. 208.

44 Ibid.

45 Letter of 17 June 1919 from Himmler (Note 34 above).

46 Manvell and Fraenkel: op cit, p. 5.

47 Wulf: op cit, p. 8.

48 Wulf: *Die SS*, p. 9.

49 Angress and Smith: op cit, p. 208.

50 Ibid.

51 Ibid.

52 Ibid, p. 209.

53 Receipt dated 16 May 1920 from No. 14 "Alarm" Company, Central Archives, Microfilm 98.

54 Angress and Smith: op cit, p. 208.

55 Ibid, p. 210.

56 Ibid.

57 Ibid, p. 217.

58 Ibid.

59 Ibid, p. 211.

60 Verbal information, 29 Jan. 1966, from a relative who wishes to remain anonymous.

61 Angress and Smith: op cit, p. 217.

62 Ibid.

63 Ibid.

64 Ibid.

65 Besgen: *Der stille Befehl*, p. 77.

66 Letter of 14 Dec. 1966 from Herr Theodor Rosenfeld.

67 Letter of 15 Aug. 1950 from Herr Hans Knipp.

68 Letter from Robert Kistler to Himmler, 4 Jan. 1919, Central Archives, Microfilm 98.

69 Angress and Smith: op cit, p. 209.

70 Ibid.

71 Ibid.

72 General assembly of the NSDAP on 21 Jan. 1921. See Volz: op cit, p. 4.

73 Angress and Smith: op cit, p. 213.

74 Ibid.

75 Himmler's membership

cards in Central Archives, Microfilm 98.

76 Angress and Smith: op cit, p. 219.

77 Ibid, p. 220.

78 Ibid.

79 Ibid, p. 221.

80 Ibid, p. 216.

81 Ibid.

82 Ibid.

83 Ibid.

84 Letter from Himmler to his parents, 28 July 1922, Central Archives, Microfilm 98.

85 Röhm: *Die Geschichte eines Hochverräters*, p. 86.

86 Ibid, p. 115.

87 Angress and Smith: op cit, p. 211.

88 Ibid.

89 Certificate for Heinrich Himmler, dated 30 Aug. 1923, from the Stickstoff-Land-GmbH, Landwirtschaftlicher Betrieb, Schleissheim, Central Archives, Microfilm 98.

90 Angress and Smith: op cit, p. 211.

91 See note 89 above.

92 Röhm: op cit, p. 221.

93 Angress and Smith: op cit, p. 211.

94 Röhm: op cit, p. 233.

95 Ibid, p. 234.

96 Ibid.

97 Ibid.

98 Ibid, pp. 237-9.

99 Ibid, p. 240.

100 Ibid, p. 243.

101 Ibid. p. 242.

102. See Chapter 5.

103 Röhm: op cit, p. 242.

104 Ibid, p. 244.

105 Ibid.

106 Letter of 18 Nov. 1923 to Himmler from "L.M.", Central Archives, Microfilm 98.

107 Ibid.

108 The other group called itself "Grossdeutsche Volksgemeinschaft" [Greater Germany Peoples Community]; Alfred Rosenberg and Julius Streicher were among its more prominent members.

109 Volz: op cit, p. 16.

110 Ibid. Also Krebs: op cit, p. 183.

111 Angress and Smith: op cit, p. 222.

112 Ibid, pp. 221-2.

113 Letter of 22 Aug. 1924 from Himmler to Robert Kistler, Central Archives, Microfilm 98.

114 Volz: op cit, p. 17.

115 Letter of 22 Aug. 1924, see Note 113 above.

116 Angress and Smith: pp. 223-4.

117 Ibid, p. 215.

118 Ibid.

119 Ibid, p. 210.

120 Letter of 30 Dec. 1927 from Margarete Himmler to Heinrich Himmler, Central Archives, Microfilm 98.

121 Ibid, letter of 3 Jan. 1928.

122 Volz: op cit, p. 12.

123 Ibid, p. 122.

124 Manvell and Fraenkel: op cit, p. 14.

125 Frischauer: *Himmler*, p. 23.

126 Manvell and Fraenkel: op cit, p. 16.

127 Verbal information, 29 Jan. 1966, from relative who wishes to remain anonymous.

128 Frischauer: op cit, p. 24.

129 Besgen: op cit, p. 72.

130 Bernadotte: op cit, p. 28.

131 Letter of 2 Nov. 1927 from Frau M. Sieguth to Himmler, Central Archives, Microfilm 98.

132 Ibid, letter from Margarete Himmler, 26 Feb. 1928.

133 *Reichsführer-SS und Chef*

der Deutschen Polizei, SS official abridged biography of Himmler, undated, Central Archives, Microfilm 229.

134 Heinrich Himmler: *Völkische Bauernpolitik,* undated, Central Archives, Microfilm 98.

135 Joachim C. Fest: *Das Gesicht des Dritten Reiches,* p. 163.

136 Ibid.

137 Heinrich Himmler: *Das Zusammenleben,* undated, Central Archives, Microfilm 98.

138 Ibid.

139 Kersten: op cit, p. 299.

140 Himmler: *Völkische Bauernpolitik,* Central Archives, Microfilm 98.

141 Ibid.

142 Walter Z. Laqueur: *Young Germany,* p. 158.

143 Ibid.

144 Ibid.

145 Ibid, p. 31 (Note).

146 Ibid, p. 158. Degener: *Wer ist wer [Who's Who]* 1935 edition.

147 *Blut und Boden,* documentary film issued by the Head of the Rasse- und Siedlungshauptamt [Race and Resettlement Department], undated, Part II, p. 5, RFSS Microfilm 161.

148 Ibid, p. 25.

149 Ibid, Part I, p. 17.

150 Laqueur: op cit, p. 75.

151 Volz: op cit, p. 29.

152 Verbal information, 29 Jan. 1966, from relative who wishes to remain anonymous.

153 Ibid.

154 Ibid.

155 Ibid.

156 Ibid.

157 Certified copy of Heinrich and Margarete Himmler's marriage certificate provided by the Registrar's office, Berlin-Schöneberg, 7 Jan. 1960.

158 Information from anonymous relative 29 Jan. 1966. See Note 152 above.

159 Letter of 26 Feb. 1928 from Margarete Himmler to Heinrich Himmler, Central Archives, Microfilm 98.

160 Manvell and Fraenkel: op cit, p. 17.

161 Ibid.

162 Letter of 6 May 1929 from Margarete to Heinrich Himmler, Central Archives, Microfilm 98.

163 Ibid, undated letter.

164 Manvell and Fraenkel: op cit, p. 17.

165 Letter of 26 Feb. 1928 from Margarete to Heinrich Himmler, Central Archives, Microfilm 98.

166 Ibid, letter of 2 Feb. 1928.

167 Ibid, letter of 16 Feb. 1928.

168 Ibid, undated letter.

169 Ibid, letter of 20 March (year not given).

170 SS Seniority List, 1 July 1935, p. 2.

CHAPTER FOUR

1 Haase: *Der Nationalsozialistische Orden,* undated, Central Archives, Microfilm 98.

2 Knoebel: *Racial Illusion and Military Necessity,* University of Colorado thesis 1965, p. 8.

3 "Die Schutzstaffel", address of 18 Jan. 1943, RFSS Microfilm 155.

4 Knoebel: op cit, p. 9.

5 IMT Vol. XXIX, p. 208.

6 Ibid.

7 Ibid.

8 Ibid.

9 Röhm: op cit, p. 88.

10 IMT Vol. XXIX, p. 209.

11 Ernst Jünger: *Krieg und Krieger*, p. 106.

12 Arendt: op cit, p. 327.

13 Ernst Jünger: *Der Kampf als inneres Erlebnis*, p. 2.

14 Jünger: *Krieg und Krieger*, p. 119.

15 *Das Schwarze Korps*, 26 Nov. 1942.

16 Jünger: *Krieg und Krieger*, pp. 120–1.

17 Emphasised particularly by Paetel: op cit, p. 29.

18 Reitlinger: *The SS*, p. 76. Also Interpress, Biographical Service No. 86 of 1951.

19 IMT Vol. XX, pp. 283–285.

20 *Wer ist wer*, 1935 edition.

21 Josef Wulf: *Das Dritte Reich und seine Vollstrecker*, p. 227.

22 *Frankfurter Allgemeine Zeitung*, 14 July 1964.

23 Delarue: op cit, p. 235.

24 Krebs: *Tendenzen und Gestalten der NSDAP*, p. 209.

25 Letter from Himmler to Röhm, 29 Jan. 1930, RFSS Microfilm 199.

26 Ibid.

27 Knoebel: op cit, p. 17.

28 Bennecke: *Hitler und die SA*, p. 239.

29 Ibid.

30 Ibid, pp. 239–40.

31 Letter from Stennes to Röhm, 28 Feb. 1931, Central Archives, Microfilm 17.

32 Anonymous SA leaflet, 25 Feb. 1931, Central Archives, Microfilm 17.

33 Volz: op cit, p. 124. Bennecke: op cit, p. 153.

34 Notice to all SS men of No. 3

Sturm, No. III Sturmbann, No. 5 Standarte, undated (probably late 1930) RFSS Microfilm 15.

35 "National-Socialist Self-defence Formations" report from Munich Police Headquarters to the Bavarian Ministry of the Interior, 22 Dec. 1931, Central Archives, Microfilm 17.

36 Notice to all SS men (see Note 34 above), p. 5.

37 Supplement issued by OSAF Deputy South to Party and SA Supreme Headquarters Order of 7 Nov. 1930, Central Archives, Microfilm 17.

38 Order from Party and SA Supreme HQ. See Note 37 above.

39 Heiden: *Geschichte des Nazionalsozialismus*, p. 189.

40 Görlitz and Quint: *Adolf Hitler*, p. 256.

41 Paetel: op cit, p. 5.

42 Heiden: op cit, p. 282.

43 Ibid, p. 203.

44 Ibid, p. 204.

45 Görlitz and Quint: op cit, p. 260. *Führerlexikon*, p. 77.

46 Rosenberg: op cit, p. 35.

47 Heiden: op cit, pp. 202–3.

48 Görlitz and Quint: op cit, p. 258.

49 Ibid, p. 258–9.

50 Görlitz and Quint: op cit, p. 258.

51 Hans - Joachim Neufeldt, Jürgen Huck and Georg Tessin: *Zur Geschichte der Ordnungspolizei 1936–1945*, p. 107.

52 Martin Broszat: "Die Anfänge der Berliner NSDAP 1926–27," *Vierteljahrshefte für Zeitgeschichte*, Folio 1 Jan. 1960, p. 89.

53 Ibid.

54 Broszat: op cit, p. 90.

55 Ibid.

56 Ibid. Volz: op cit, p. 33.

57 Görlitz and Quint: op cit, p. 423.

58 Karl-Dietrich Bracher, Wolfgang Sauer and Gerhard Schulz: *Die nationalsozialistische Machtergreifung*, p. 843.

59 Ibid, p. 840.

60 Ibid.

61 Volz: op cit, pp. 123, 263.

62 Ibid, pp. 192, 123.

63 Görlitz and Quint: op cit, p. 263.

64 Bennecke: op cit, p. 154. Bracher, Sauer and Schulz: op cit, p. 848.

65 Heiden: op cit, p. 279.

66 Ibid, pp. 279–283.

67 Manvell and Fraenkel: *Heinrich Himmler*, p. 19.

68 Ibid.

69 Undated and unsigned report on the early history of the Berlin SS, clearly originating from Berlin SS circles, BDC Microfilm 87.

70 Packebusch's SS register in Tobias' papers. Letters from Daluege dated 20 Aug. 1938 and 9 Jan. 1939, also in Tobias' archives.

71 Bennecke: op cit, p. 148.

72 Letter of 28 Feb. 1931 from Stennes to Röhm, Central Archives, Microfilm 17.

73 See Bennecke: op cit, pp. 169 *et seq.* on the close connection between the rising unemployment and the increase in Nazi votes.

74 Bracher, Sauer and Schulz: op cit, p. 47.

75 Ibid, pp. 847–8.

76 See numerous anonymous leaflets by revolutionary Berlin SA men in Central Archives, Microfilm 17.

77 Leaflet drafted by unknown Party members and SA men, 31 May 1931, Central Archives, Microfilm 17.

78 Bennecke: op cit, p. 146.

79 OSAF Deputy South, Memorandum on proposed reorganisation of SA Command, 19 Sept. 1930, BDC Microfilm 85.

80 Report by Munich Police Headquarters, 24 Oct. 1930, BDC Microfilm 85. *Münchner Post*, 4 Sept. 1930.

81 Ibid.

82 Leaflet by Dresden SA men, 20 March 1931, Central Archives, Microfilm 17.

83 *Münchner Post*, 4 Sept. 1930.

84 Report from Munich Police Headquarters, 24 Oct. 1930, BDC Microfilm.

85 Ibid.

85 Ibid.

86 Ibid.

87 Ibid. Krebs: op cit, p. 167.

88 Heiden: op cit, p. 284; *Wahrheiten der Woche* (Stennes' supporters' paper) 10 Oct. 1931, Central Archives Microfilm.

89 *Völkischer Beobachter*, 4 Sept. 1930.

90 Letter from Conti to Pfeffer, 8 Sept. 1930, Central Archives Microfilm 17.

91 Ibid.

92 Heiden: op cit, p. 198.

93 Ibid.

94 Bracher, Sauer and Schulz: op cit, p. 349.

95 Ibid.

96 Bennecke: op cit, p. 164.

97 Letter from Daluege dated 9 Jan. 1939, Tobias' papers.

98 Letter from Daluege to Röhm, 1 April 1931, Central Archives, Microfilm 17.

99 Görlitz and Quint: op cit,

p. 312.

100 *Hamburger Fremdenblatt,*
2 April 1931.

101 *Hamburger Echo,* 3, 4, 5
April 1931.

102 Ibid, 3, 4 April.

103 Ibid, 3 April.

104 Special announcement
issued by Stennes, undated, Central Archives Microfilm 17. *Hamburger Echo* 2, 3, 4, 10 April
1931. *Hamburger Nachrichten,* 4
April 1931.

105 Bracher, Sauer and Schulz:
op cit, p. 852. Horkenbach: *Das
deutsche Reich von 1918 bis
heute,* Vol. III, p. 125.

106 Horkenbach: op cit, Vol.
III, p. 128.

107 Wulf: *Das Dritte Reich
und seine Vollstrecker,* pp. 225
and 228.

108 Buchheim: *Anatomy of the
SS State,* p. 142.

109 Leaders' Conference 13–14
June 1931, SS Headquarters Report, BDC Microfilm 87.

110 Provisional SS duty regulations, June 1931, BDC Microfilm
87.

111 Ibid.

112 Ibid.

113 SS Sector order No. 4, 21
March 1931, BDC Microfilm 87.

114 Letter from Wagener to
OSAF Deputies, 3 Oct. 1930,
BDC Microfilm 85.

115 Letter from Schreck to
Party Headquarters, 24 Sept.
1925, BDC Microfilm 87.

116 Provisional SS duty regulations, June 1931, BDC Microfilm
87.

117 Ibid.

118 Shlomo Aronson: *Heydrich
und die Anfänge des SD und der
Gestapo (1931–1935),* p. 87.

119 SS Order A 53, 10 Oct. 1931,

BDC Microfilm 87.

120 See Chapter 8.

121 Order 114/32a from SA
Supreme Commander, 25 Jan.
1932, Central Archives, Microfilm 17.

122 Ibid.

123 Ibid.

124 Röhm: op cit, p. 261.

125 Letter from Röhm to
Heimsoth, 3 Dec. 1928, Central
Archives Microfilm 85.

126 *Münchner Post,* 30 June
1931.

127 Ibid.

128 Bennecke: op cit, pp. 165–6.

129 Judgement of the Criminal
Division of the Munich Civil
Court in November 1934, case
against Peter Granninger and
others, Central Archives, Microfilm 17.

130 Ibid, p. 4.

131 Ibid, p. 9.

132 Ibid, p. 5.

133 Görlitz and Quint: op cit,
p. 313.

134 Ibid. *Münchner Post,* 24
and 27 June 1931.

135 Open letter from Dr Helmut Klotz, ex-NSDAP Reichstag
deputy, March 1932, Central Archives Microfilm 85.

136 Ibid. Also letter of 4 July
1934 from SA-Oberführer Hans
Kallenbach to Reichsleiter Fiehler, Central Archives, Microfilm
17.

137 Friedrich Stampfer: "Er-
fahrungen und Erkenntnisse"
quoted from *Die andere Zeitung*
No. 50 Dec. 1959.

138 Copy of an article in
Flammenzeichen of 5 Nov. 1932,
Central Archives, Microfilm 17.

139 Ibid.

140 *Glück und Ende des Nationalsozialisten Bell,* pp. 21–2.

141 Press report on the Danzeisen case, July 1932, RFSS Microfilm 476.

142 Supplement to Danzeisen case, statement by Karl Horn, 18 May 1932, RFSS Microfilm 467.

143 Press report, July 1932, RFSS Microfilm 467.

144 Murder letter, 14 March 1932, RFSS Microfilm 467.

145 Ibid.

146 Ibid.

147 In the Granninger case the Munich court certified that there was no proof of homosexual acts on the part of du Moulin-Eckart and released him. Judgment on Granninger and others, RFSS Microfilm 17.

148 Statement by Karl Horn, pp. 7, 8, RFSS Microfilm 467.

149 Ibid, p. 9.

150 Ibid, p. 10.

151 Ibid, p. 11.

152 Ibid, p. 12.

153 Ibid, p. 14.

154 Wilhelm Högener: *Die verratene Republik*, p. 325.

155 *Die andere Zeitung*, No. 12 of 1950.

156 Ibid.

157 See Horn files, RFSS Microfilm 467.

158 *Münchner Post*, 18 Nov. 1932.

159 Letter of 5 Oct. 1932 from Martin Bormann to Rudolf Hess, Central Archives, Microfilm 17.

160 Ibid.

161 Knoebel: op cit, p. 17.

162 Führer Conference 13–14 June 1931, Report by SS Headquarters, BDC Microfilm 87.

CHAPTER FIVE

1 Görlitz and Quint: *Adolf Hitler*, pp. 382, 389.

2 Ibid.

3 Buchheim: *SS und Polizei im NS-Staat*, p. 35.

4 Horkenbach: *Das deutsche Reich von 1918 bis heute*, Vol. IV, p. 929.

5 Rudolf Diels: *Lucifer ante Portas*, p. 179.

6 *Der Spiegel*, "Das Spiel ist aus —Arthur Nebe" (hereafter referred to as "Nebe series") 9 Feb. 1950.

7 Ibid.

8 Ibid.

9 Ibid. Also issue of 23 Feb. 1950.

10 Ibid.

11 Franz Neumann: *Behemoth*, p. 47.

12 Ibid.

13 Ibid.

14 Robert L. Koehl: *RKFVD, German Resettlement and Population Policy 1939–45*, p. 14.

15 Ibid, pp. 13–19.

16 Görlitz and Quint: op cit, p. 387.

17 Ibid.

18 Ibid.

19 Bracher, Sauer and Schulz: *Die nationalsozialistische Machtergreifung*, p. 925.

20 Ibid.

21 Görlitz and Quint: op cit, p. 276.

22 Diels: op cit, p. 229.

23 For Goebbels' increasing power see Bullock: op cit, p. 312.

24 Görlitz and Quint: op cit, p. 399.

25 Kersten: *Totenkopf und Treue*, p. 245.

26 Görlitz and Quint: op cit, p. 399.

27 Ibid.

28 Bracher, Sauer and Schulz: op cit, p. 588.

29 Ibid, p. 589.

30 Trevor-Roper: op cit, p. 1.

31 Fritz Tobias: *Der Reichstagsbrand*, p. 135 (not in English translation).

32 Ibid, pp. 135–6.

33 Ibid, p. 136.

34 Ibid, p. 135.

35 Ibid.

36 Diels: op cit, p. 71.

37 Bullock: *Hitler, a Study in Tyranny*, p. 256.

38 Stein: *The Waffen-SS*, p. 4.

39 Ibid: p. 5.

40 Ibid.

41 Buchheim: *SS und Polizei im NS-Staat*, p. 30.

42 K-G. Klietman: *Die Waffen-SS*, p. 54.

43 Ibid.

44 Ibid, p. 53.

45 Konrad Himmler's registration card, Record (Vol. I) of Infanterie-Leib-Regiment, Munich War Ministry Archives, Central Archives, Microfilm 98.

46 Buchheim: *Anatomy of the SS State*, p. 148.

47 Ibid (Broszat), p. 414.

48 Ibid, p. 405.

49 IMT Vol. XXIX, p. 226.

50 Ibid.

51 Best: *Heinrich Himmler*, p. 2.

52 Ibid.

53 Aronson: *Heydrich und die Anfänge des SD und der Gestapo 1931–1935*, pp. 177 et seq.

54 Tobias: *The Reichstag Fire*, p. 260.

55 Bracher, Sauer and Schulz: op cit, p. 865.

56 Buchheim: *Anatomy of the SS State*, p. 145.

57 Diels: op cit, p. 217.

58 Ibid, pp. 166, 228.

59 Delarue: op cit, p. 34.

60 Buchheim: *Anatomy of the SS State*, pp. 145–6.

61 Ibid.

62 Ibid (Broszat), p. 402–3.

63 Ibid (Buchheim), p. 146.

64 Ibid. Diels: op cit, p. 228.

65 Buchheim: *Anatomy of the SS State*, pp. 145–6.

66 Delarue: op cit, p. 38. Crankshaw: *Gestapo*, p. 15.

67 Horkenbach: op cit, Vol. IV, p. 66.

68 Bracher, Sauer and Schulz: op cit, p. 868.

69 Ibid, p. 872.

70 Ibid, p. 868.

71 Diels: op cit, p. 224.

72 Bracher, Sauer and Schulz: op cit, p. 873.

73 Diels: op cit, pp. 255–6.

74 Bracher, Sauer and Schulz: op cit, p. 865.

75 Ibid.

76 Diels: op cit, p. 253.

77 Ibid.

78 Ibid.

79 Ibid, p. 257.

80 Ibid, p. 311.

81 Ibid, p. 327.

82 Ibid, p. 249.

83 Ibid.

84 Manvell and Fraenkel: *Göring*, p. 50.

85 *Wahrheiten der Woche*, 10 Oct. 1931, Central Archives, Microfilm 17.

86 Ibid.

87 Diels: op cit, p. 250.

88 Ibid.

89 Wheeler-Bennett: *The Nemesis of Power*, p. 227 footnote.

90 Diels: op cit, p. 257.

91 Ibid, p. 262.

92 "Nebe series," 17 Nov. 1949, p. 24.

93 Ibid.

94 Ibid, p. 23.

95 Ibid, pp. 23–4.

96 *Völkischer Beobachter*, 10 June 1933.

97 Martin H. Sommerfeldt: *Ich war dabei*, p. 57.

98 H. B. Gisevius: *To the Bitter End*, p. 145.

99 "Nebe Series," 17 Nov. 1949, p. 25.

100 Ibid.

101 Charles Wighton: *Heydrich*, p. 61.

102 Diels: op cit, p. 328.

103 Ibid.

104 Ibid, p. 330.

105 Ibid.

106 Ibid.

107 Wighton: op cit, p. 61.

108 Ibid, p. 62.

109 Diels: op cit, p. 328.

110 Günter Plum: "Staatspolizei und innere Verwaltung",

Vierteljahrshefte für Zeitgeschichte, Issue 2 of 1965, p. 205.

111 Bracher, Sauer and Schulz: op cit, p. 600.

112 Ibid, p. 601.

113 Neufeldt, op cit, p. 5.

114 Bracher, Sauer and Schulz: op cit, p. 601.

115 Buchheim: *Anatomy of the SS State*, p. 146.

116 Plum: op cit, pp. 193–195.

117 Buchheim: *SS und Polizei im NS-Staat*, pp. 36–40.

118 Bracher, Sauer and Schulz: op cit, p. 598.

119 Ibid, p. 601.

120 Ibid.

121 Ibid, p. 602.

122 Ibid, p. 603.

123 Buchheim: *Anatomy of the SS State*, p. 151.

124 Diels: op cit, p. 412.

125 Ibid.

CHAPTER SIX

1 Hermann Rauschning: *Gespräche mit Hitler*, p. 144 (not in English translation).

2 Hossbach: *Zwischen Wehrmacht und Hitler 1934–1938*, p. 57.

3 Rauschning: *Hitler speaks*, p. 155.

4 Bracher, Sauer and Schulz: *Die nationalsozialistische Machtergreifung*, p. 853.

5 "National - Sozialistische Selbstschutzverbände," Report from Munich Police Headquarters to the Bavarian Ministry of the Interior, Central Archives, Microfilm 17.

6 Ibid.

7 Bennecke: *Die Reichswehr und der "Röhm-Putsch"*, p. 27. Bracher, Sauer and Schulz: op cit, p. 888.

8 Görlitz and Quint: *Adolf Hitler*, pp. 318–9.

9 Bracher, Sauer and Schulz: op cit, p. 940.

10 Ibid, p. 939.

11 Ibid, p. 886.

12 Ibid, p. 880.

13 Ibid, p. 886.

14 Ibid, p. 891.

15 Ibid, p. 939.

16 Ibid, pp. 890, 893.

17 Ibid, p. 893.

18 Ibid, p. 894.

19 Ibid, p. 941.

20 Announcement of 1 Dec. 1933 signed by Hitler, Central Archives, Microfilm 17.

21 Helmut Krausnick: "Der 30 Juni 1934", in *Das Parlament* 30 June, 1954, p. 320.

22 Bracher, Sauer and Schulz: op cit, p. 904.

23 Krausnick: op cit, p. 318.

24 Bracher, Sauer and Schulz: op cit, p. 924.

25 Krausnick: op cit, p. 319.

26 Bracher, Sauer and Schulz: op cit, p. 943. Krausnick: op cit, p. 319.

27 Bracher, Sauer and Schulz: op cit, p. 943.

28 Edgar Röhricht: *Pflicht und Gewissen*, p. 63.

29 Krausnick: op cit, p. 319.

30 *Der Spiegel*, 15 May 1957, p. 22, "Der Furcht so fern, dem Tod so nahe".

31 Krausnick: op cit, p. 319.

32 Ibid.

33 Hermann Foertsch: *Schuld und Verhängnis*, p. 48.

34 *Der Spiegel*, 15 May 1957, p. 23.

35 Reitlinger: *The SS*, p. 55.

36 See Lutze's allusions in Aug. 1935—end of this chapter.

37 Case for the prosecution against Josef Dietrich and Michael Lippert, Munich Provincial Court I, 4 July 1956, p. 35.

38 Bracher, Sauer and Schulz: op cit, p. 928.

39 Wighton: *Heydrich*, p. 46.

40 Bracher, Sauer and Schulz: op cit, p. 929.

41 See Chapter 10.

42 Anonymous: *Glück und Ende des Nationalsozialisten Bell*, p. 22.

43 Krausnick: op cit, p. 321.

44 Case against Dietrich, p. 46.

45 Ibid, p. 45. Bennecke: *Die Reichswehr und der "Röhm-Putsch"*, pp. 46–47.

46 Case against Dietrich, p. 45.

47 Ibid, p. 47.

48 Ibid, p. 41.

49 Bracher, Sauer and Schulz: op cit, p. 951.

50 Case against Dietrich, p. 51.

51 Record of interrogation of Max Jüttner 8 April 1949, Proceedings of Provincial Court I, Munich, p. 4.

52 Ernst von Salomon: *Der Fragebogen*, p. 438.

53 Ibid.

54 Case against Dietrich, p. 41.

55 Statement by Patzig in *Der Tagesspiegel*, 10 May 1957.

56 Bracher, Sauer and Schulz: op cit, p. 951.

57 Ibid.

58 Felix Steiner: *Die Armee der Geächteten*, p. 48.

59 Case against Dietrich, p. 49.

60 Ibid.

61 Ibid.

62 Bracher, Sauer and Schulz: op cit, p. 954.

63 Case against Dietrich, p. 50.

64 Ibid. Also Bracher, Sauer and Schulz: op cit, p. 954.

65 Ibid. Also *Der Spiegel*, 15 May 1957, p. 22.

66 Krausnick: op cit, p. 321.

67 Bennecke in *Die Reichswehr und der "Röhm-Putsch"*, p. 57, emphasises the importance of the role played by Gauleiter Wagner.

68 Bracher, Sauer and Schulz: op cit, p. 954.

69 Sommerfeldt: *Ich war dabei*, p. 76.

70 Bracher, Sauer and Schultz: op cit, p. 952. Krausnick: op cit, p. 320.

71 Bennecke: *Röhm - Putsch*, pp. 43–4.

72 Letter of 12 June 1934 from Höfle to Röhm, Central Archives, Microfilm 17.

73 Bennecke: *Röhm-Putsch*, p. 54.

74 Bracher, Sauer and Schulz: op cit, p. 952.

75 Krausnick: op cit, p. 320.

76 Ibid.

77 Wheeler-Bennett: *The Nemesis of Power*, p. 311.

78 Papen: *Der Wahrheit eine Gasse*, p. 346 (not in English translation). *Süddeutsche Zeitung* 30 June 1964.

79 Keesing's Contemporary Archives No. 34/1486.

80 Papen: *Memoirs*, p. 310.

81 Ibid.

82 Sommerfeldt: *Ich war dabei*, p. 58.

83 See Papen: op cit, pp. 247-8.

84 *Völkischer Beobachter*, 1 June 1934.

85 Sommerfeldt: op cit, p. 69.

86 Wheeler-Bennett: op cit, p. 319.

87 Ibid, pp. 319-20.

88 Ibid, p. 320.

89 Ibid.

90 Lutze's diary, published in *Frankfurter Rundschau*, 14 May 1957.

91 Ibid.

92 Case against Dietrich, p. 54.

93 Ibid.

94 Ibid, pp. 54, 61.

95 Ibid, p. 61.

96 Krausnick: op cit, p. 321; case against Dietrich, p. 52.

97 Bracher, Sauer and Schulz: op cit, p. 956.

98 Ibid.

99 Krausnick: op cit, p. 321. Case against Dietrich, p. 52.

100 Bracher, Sauer and Schulz: op cit, p. 959.

101 Westphal: *The German Army in the West*, p. 9.

102 *Die Welt* 30/31 May 1957.

103 Peter Bor: *Gespräche mit Halder*, p. 125.

104 Statement by Heinrici, *Abendpost*, 7 May 1957.

105 Foertsch: op cit, p. 52.

106 Bennecke: *Röhm-Putsch*, p. 52. Case against Dietrich, p. 53.

107 Case against Dietrich, p. 55.

108 Bracher, Sauer and Schulz: op cit, p. 958.

109 Bennecke: *Röhm-Putsch*, p. 49.

110 Bracher, Sauer and Schulz: op cit, p. 958. Foertsch: op cit, p. 49. Krausnick: op cit, p. 321.

111 Bracher, Sauer and Schulz: op cit, p. 958.

112 Ibid, p. 959.

113 Letter of 27 May 1949 from Karl Schreyer to Munich Police Headquarters, p. 5; Proceedings of Provincial Court I, Munich.

114 Bracher, Sauer and Schulz: op cit, p. 959.

115 *Blick in die Zeit*, 7 July 1934.

116 Even the latest German historians seem to accept this (see Bracher, Sauer and Schulz: op cit, p. 959).

117 *Völkischer Beobachter*, 26 June 1934.

118 *Der Spiegel*, 15 May 1957, p. 23.

119 Wheeler-Bennett: op cit, p. 321.

120 *Völkischer Beobachter*, 27 June 1934.

121 Lutze's diary, published in *Frankfurter Rundschau*, 14 May 1957.

122 Case against Dietrich, p. 59.

123 *Der Spiegel*, 15 May 1957, p. 24.

124 Lutze's Diary—*Frankfurter Rundschau*, 14 May 1957.

125 Ibid.

126 Ibid.

127 Case against Dietrich, p. 59.

128 Ibid, p. 52.

129 Ibid.

130 Ibid, pp. 54, 56. Lutze's Diary.

131 Bracher, Sauer and Schulz: op cit, p. 945.

132 Ibid, p. 960.

133 Case against Dietrich, pp. 61 et seq.

134 Ibid, p. 60. Lutze's diary.

135 Ibid, p. 57.

136 Statement by Dietrich, Abendpost, 7 May 1957.

137 Case against Dietrich, p. 60.

138 Ibid.

139 Ibid.

140 Judgement of the Assize Court, State Court I Munich on Josef Dietrich and Michael Lippert, 14 May 1957, p. 20.

141 Ibid.

142 Case against Dietrich, p. 60.

143 Bennecke: Röhm-Putsch, p. 53.

144 Ibid, p. 54.

145 Ibid.

146 Ibid.

147 Völkischer Beobachter, 1 July 1934. Case against Dietrich p. 58. Statement by Martina Schmid, Abendpost, 7 May 1957.

148 Bracher, Sauer and Schulz: op cit, p. 960.

149 Abendpost, 7 May 1957.

150 Case against Dietrich, p. 80.

151 Abendpost, 7 May 1957.

152 Interrogation of Brückner, Traunstein Court, 30 May 1949, p. 2.

153 Hannoversche Anzeiger, 30 June 1934.

154 Lutze's diary.

155 Case against Dietrich, p. 77; Süddeutsche Zeitung, 8 May 1957.

156 Statement by Martina Schmid, Abendpost, 7 May 1957.

157 Ibid.

158 Der Spiegel, 15 May 1957,

159 p. 25. Krausnick: op cit, p. 323. Lutze's diary in Frankfurter Rundschau, 14 May 1957.

159 Bennecke: Röhm-Putsch, p. 57.

160 Der Spiegel, 15 May 1957, p. 25.

161 Lutze's diary in Frankfurter Rundschau, 14 May 1957.

162 Ibid.

163 Ibid.

164 Völkischer Beobachter, 3 July 1934.

165 Lutze's diary in Frankfurter Rundschau, 14 May 1957.

166 Ibid.

167 Interrogation of Brückner, p. 3.

168 Ibid.

169 Ibid.

170 Ibid.

171 Written submission by Dr Robert Koch, 25 Jan. 1949, proceedings of State Court I Munich, p. 1.

172 Ibid.

173 Written submission by Max Jüttner, p. 3.

174 Ibid.

175 List of entrants to Munich prison, Proceedings of State Court I, Munich.

176 Submission by Max Jüttner, p. 3.

177 Ibid.

178 Der Spiegel, 15 May 1957, p. 27.

179 Bullock: op cit, p. 305.

180 Ibid.

181 Der Spiegel, 15 May 1957, p. 27.

182 Ibid. Also Bullock: op cit, p. 306.

183 Judgment on Dietrich, p. 60.

184 Letter from Schreyer to Munich Police Headquarters, p. 3.

185 Ibid, p. 4.
186 Judgment on Dietrich, p. 11.
187 Ibid.
188 Ibid, p. 12.
189 Ibid.
190 Bracher, Sauer and Schulz: op cit, p. 961. *Der Spiegel* 15 May 1957, p. 27.
191 Lutze's diary in *Frankfurter Rundschau*, 15 May 1957.
192 Judgment on Dietrich, pp. 12–13.
193 Ibid, p. 13.
194 List of entrants to Munich prison, Proceedings of State Court I, Munich.
195 Judgment on Dietrich, p. 61.
196 Ibid, p. 64.
197 Statement by Dietrich, *Die Welt*, 7 May 1957.
198 Case against Dietrich, p. 65.
199 Ibid.
200 Ibid, pp. 3, 72.
201 Ibid, p. 67.
202 Ibid.
203 Ibid, p. 68.
204 Ibid.
205 Judgment on Dietrich, p. 15.
206 Case against Dietrich, p. 69.
207 Judgment on Dietrich, p. 16.
208 Case against Dietrich, pp. 70, 72. Statement by Dietrich, *Frankfurter Allgemeine Zeitung*, 7 May 1957.
209 Case against Dietrich, pp. 72-3-4.
210 Papen: op cit, p. 315.
211 Gisevius: *To the Bitter End*, pp. 276 et seq.
212 Papen: op cit, p. 316.
213 Robert Kempner: *SS im Kreuzverhör*, p. 257.
214 Ibid, p. 256.
215 Ibid, p. 257.
216 Ibid.
217 Ibid, pp. 257–8.
218 Ibid, p. 255.
219 Ibid, pp. 258–9.
220 Ibid, p. 259.
221 Wheeler-Bennett: op cit, p. 232.
222 Salomon: op cit, p. 440.
223 Wheeler-Bennett: op cit, p. 324.
224 *Süddeutsche Zeitung*, 19 June 1961. Prosecution of Bach-Zelewski, pp. 3 et seq.
225 *Der Spiegel*, 15 May 1957, p. 29.
226 Statement by Dr Schaeffer, *Frankfurter Rundschau*, 23 May 1957.
227 Report by Dr Walter Schaeffer, an ex-State Attorney [Generalstaatsanwalt], 29 Nov. 1945, in Schaeffer's private collection. Affidavit (also in Schaeffer's collection) by Dr Werner von Haacke, another State Attorney [Oberstaatsanwalt] 15 Feb. 1957.
228 Verbal information from Dr Werner von Haacke, 9 Sept. 1965.
229 G. M. Gilbert: *The Psychology of Dictatorship*, p. 69.
230 Ibid, p. 95.
231 Bracher, Sauer and Schulz: op cit, p. 921. Krebs: *Tendenzen und Gestalten*, pp. 192-3.
232 *Der Spiegel*, 15 May 1957, p. 27.
233 Bullock: op cit, p. 303. Schreyer's statement, p. 7.
234 *Der Spiegel*, 15 May 1957, pp. 27–8.
235 François-Poncet: *The Fateful Years*, p. 139.
236 Krausnick, op cit, p. 320.
237 Ibid, p. 323; *Völkischer Beobachter*, 3 July 1934.

238 Bracher, Sauer and Schulz: op cit, p. 960. Papen: *Die Wahrheit eine Gasse*, p. 355 (not in English translation).

239 Papen: op cit, p. 316.

240 Bennecke: *Röhm - Putsch*, p. 61.

241 *Die Welt*, 4 May 1957.

242 Sommerfeldt: op cit, pp. 72, 73, 76.

243 Gisevius: *Bis zum bitteren Ende*, p. 155 (not in English translation). Case against Dietrich, p. 61.

244 Von Ribbentrop: *Memoirs*, p. 34 (Note).

245 Record of ministerial discussion, 3 July 1934, p. 7—in Tobias papers.

246 Deposition by Max Jüttner, p. 5.

247 Lutze's diary in *Frankfurter Rundschau*, 15 May 1957.

248 Bennecke: *Röhm - Putsch*, p. 89.

249 Paul Schulz: *Meine Erschiessung am 30 Juni 1934*, pp. 13 et seq.

250 Ibid, p. 9.

251 Ibid, p. 12.

252 Ibid, p. 14.

253 Ibid, p. 22.

254 Ibid. Also report by Otto Grub on events of 30 June to 4 July 1934, p. 2—in Tobias papers.

255 Ibid, p. 25. Grub report, p. 4.

256 Ibid, p. 35.

257 Case against Dietrich, p. 4.

258 Ibid.

259 Deposition by Koch, p. 3.

260 Ibid, p. 4.

261 Statement by Lippert, *Stuttgarter Zeitung*, 7 May 1957.

262 *Völkischer Beobachter*, 1 July 1934.

263 *Süddeutsche Zeitung*, 30/31 March, 11 May and 14 May 1947. *Frankfurter Rundschau*, 8 May 1957.

264 Letter from Schreyer, p. 6.

265 Ibid.

266 Ibid.

267 See Bennecke: *Röhm-Putsch*, pp. 87–8.

268 *Schulthess' calendar of European history 1934*, p. 184.

269 Record of meeting of Ministers, 3 July 1934, p. 8.

270 *Frankfurter Allgemeine Zeitung*, 10 May, 1957.

271 *Der Spiegel*, 15 May 1957, p. 29.

272 Bennecke: *Röhm - Putsch*, p. 65.

273 *Der Spiegel*, 15 May 1957, p. 29.

274 Kramarz: *Stauffenberg, The Life and Death of an Officer*, p. 49.

275 Foertsch, op cit, pp. 57–8.

276 Buchheim: *SS und Polizei im NS-Staat*, pp. 62–3.

277 *Völkischer Beobachter*, 26 July 1934.

278 Klietmann: op cit, p. 15.

279 Koehl: op cit, p. 21.

280 Order from SA Supreme Commander 2 July 1934, BDC Microfilm 85.

281 Ibid, 14 July 1934.

282 Ibid, 9 Aug. 1934.

283 Report by SA-Sturmführer Hermann Baecke, No. 3116/34, Central Archives, Microfilm 17.

284 "Die Vorgänge anlässlich der Röhm-revolte," Supplementary report by commander of Standarte 168, 27 July 1934, Central Archives, Microfilm 17.

285 Report to Sturm 3/R 168, 2 July 1934, Central Archives, Microfilm 17.

286 Report by SS-Standartenführer Schulz, 21 Aug. 1935,

RFSS Microfilm 33.
287 Ibid, pp. 6–7.

CHAPTER SEVEN

1 Kersten: *Totenkopf und
Treue*, pp. 245–6.
2 Schellenberg: *Memoirs*, p. 21.
3 IMT Document, 45–55.
4 Konrad Heiden: *Geburt des
Dritten Reiches*, p. 29.
5 Quoted from the *Stuttgarter
Zeitung*, 30 June 1964.
6 Quoted from the *Frankfurter
Allgemeine Zeitung*, 30 June
1964.
7 *NSDAP Organisation Hand-
book*, Tables 43 and 32.
8 Ibid, pp. 435, 52. (See also
Table of Ranks, p. 744, this
volume.)
9 Himmler: *Die Schutzstaffel*,
p. 24.
10 Robert Koehl: "The Character of the Nazi SS", *Journal of
Modern History*, Sept. 1960, p.
282.
11 SS Seniority List, 1945.
12 Ibid, 1944.
13 German State Archives: Der
Adel im deutschen Offizierkorps,
Statistische Übersicht, p. 12.
14 Georg: *Die wirtschaftlichen
Unternehmungen der SS*, p. 55.
15 Paul Hausser: *Wie andere
Soldaten auch*.
16 Verbal information from
Felix Steiner, 29 Jan. 1966.
17 Klietmann: op cit, p. 421.
Stein: *Die Waffen-SS*, p. 13.
18 Josef Wulf, for instance, in
Die SS, pp. 93 et seq.
19 SS Seniority List, 1944.
20 Ibid.
21 Letter of 2 Sept. 1943 from
Edda Ciano to Himmler, RFSS
Microfilm 33.

22 See Plum: *Staatspolizei und
innere Verwaltung, 1934–1936*,
pp. 198–206.
23 Correspondence between
Himmler and Reeder, RFSS Microfilm 56.
24 Walter Hagen (alias Wilhelm Höttl): *Die geheime Front*,
pp. 141–158. SS Seniority List,
1944.
25 Boberach: *Meldungen aus
dem Reich*, pp. xxvii et seq.
26 Undated statement before
the International Military Tribunal by the rider von Woykosky-Buedau—in Tobias' papers.
27 Undated submission by
Woykosky-Buedau entitled "Entwicklung der SS-Reiterei"—in
Tobias' papers.
28 Ibid.
29 *Das Schwarze Korps*
6 March 1935.
30 *Süddeutsche Zeitung*
19 June 1961.
31 Case against Bach-Zelewski,
p. 10; *Die Welt* 24 Dec. 1958.
32 Hassell: op cit, p. 359.
33 Written information from
Frida Fätkenheuer, 13 Nov. 1966.
34 SS Seniority List, 1944.
35 *Das Schwarze Korps*, Series
16 1935.
36 Wheeler-Bennett: *The Nemesis of Power*, pp. 77 et seq.
37 Letter of 2 July 1941 from
Berger to Himmler, describing
a discussion with Schwarz—in
Wulf's papers.
38 SS Order A 53 from Reichsführer-SS dated 10 Oct. 1931,
BDC Microfilm 97.

39 Salomon: *Der Fragebogen*, p. 477.
40 Emil Helfferich: *Ein Leben*, Vol. IV, pp. 26–7.
41 Ibid, p. 15.
42 Ibid, p. 26.
43 Ibid, p. 25.
44 Ibid, p. 27. Bernt Engelmann: *Deutschland-Report*, pp. 91–93.
45 Engelmann: op cit, p. 69. Michael H. Kater: *Der "Freundeskreis Himmler"*, p. 2.
46 Helfferich: op cit, p. 28.
47 Kater: op cit, p. 7.
48 Helfferich: op cit, p. 28. Kater, op cit, p. 8.
49 Engelmann: op cit, p. 92.
50 Buchheim: *Anatomy of the SS State*, p. 255.
51 Ibid.
52 Order from Wittje to SS Abschnitte IX and XVIII, 1 March 1933, Central Archives, Microfilm 17.
53 Wilhelm Ehrmann, Declaration of entry 1 Jan. 1934. Letter of 15 Nov. 1933 from Himmler, forbidding canvassing in writing —both from BDC Microfilm 10. Neusüss-Hunkel: *Die SS*, p. 17.
54 Letter of 7 Aug. 1933 from Himmler on the subject of Sponsoring Members' badges. Letter of 7 April 1934 from Wittje to all Oberabschnitt Press Officers. Undated FM Membership Book. Copy of FM Periodical—all in BDC Microfilm 10. See also Knoebel: *Racial Illusion and Military Necessity*, p. 4.
55 Letter from Pohl to Schwarz, undated—approx. end 1936, RFFS Microfilm 131.
56 Letter of 2 July 1941 from Berger to Himmler describing a discussion with Schwarz — in Wulf's papers.

57 Political report of 4 Jan. 1937 by Gauleitung Munich/Upper Bavaria on Kriminaloberinspektor Heinrich Müller—Wulf's papers.
58 Ibid.
59 Letter of 11 Jan. 1943 from RSHA to Reichsführer SS Private Office, RFSS Microfilm 56.
60 Ibid, 19 Jan. 1943. Wulf: *Die SS*, p. 79.
61 IMT Vol. XXIX, p. 210.
62 Ibid.
63 Ibid.
64 Ibid, p. 212.
65 Report of 21 Aug. 1935 by SS-Standartenführer Schulz, RFSS Microfilm 33.
66 *Das Schwarze Korps*, 22 May 1935.
67 Report by SS-Standartenführer Schulz: see Note 65 above.
68 Knoebel: op cit, p. 38.
69 Ibid, p. 23.
70 IMT Vol. XXIX, p. 210.
71 Knoebel: op cit, p. 19.
72 Ibid, p. 23.
73 Letters from Himmler to Berger, 2 Oct. 1943, and Berger to Himmler, 22 Oct. 1943, RFSS Microfilm 128.
74 Reitlinger: *The SS*, pp. 14–15.
75 Schellenberg: op cit, p. 32.
76 Paetel: "Die SS," in *Vierteljahrshefte für Zeitgeschichte* 1, 1954, p. 16.
77 *Brockhaus' Conversations-Lexikon*, Leipzig 1885.
78 OMGUS (Office of US Military Government) Public Safety Branch, Survey of Nazi Criminal Organisation.
79 Buchheim: *Anatomy of the SS State*, p. 256.
80 See Chapter 16.
81 OMGUS Survey (see Note 78 above).

82 Points noted during official inspection trips, address by Gruppenführer Zech at a Gruppenführer conference in Berlin, 23–25 Jan. 1939, RFSS Microfilm 17.

83 Ibid.

84 Ibid.

85 Knoebel: op cit, p. 15.

86 Ibid.

87 Ibid, pp. 15–17.

88 Besgen: *Der stille Befehl*, p. 75.

89 IMT Vol. XXIX, p. 211.

90 Ibid.

91 Knoebel: op cit, p. 15.

92 "Der Weg des SS-Mannes," directives drafted by Himmler, undated (approx. 1935), pp. 13–27, RFSS Microfilm 155.

93 Helfferich: op cit, p. 36.

94 "Der Weg des SS-Mannes" (see Note 92 above), pp. 13–27.

95 Ibid, pp. 16, 19, 23.

96 Ibid, p. 5.

97 Order dealing with engagements and marriages in "Uns ist der Kampf," undated (approx. 1942), RFSS Microfilm 161.

98 "Thoughts on SS jurisdiction," address by Scharfe at Gruppenführer Conference, Berlin 23–25 Jan. 1939, RFSS Microfilm 17.

99 Ibid, pp. 7–8.

100 "Das Ehrengesetz der SS" in "Uns ist der Kampf" (see Note 97 above).

101 Letter from Himmler to the SS-Gericht [SS Legal Service], 26 July 1938, RFSS Microfilm 161.

102 Record of proceedings in the Buchhold case by Hauptsturmführer Günther Bleyl, 22 June 1943; note by Bleyl, 22 June 1943, RFSS Microfilm 131.

103 This point is emphasised in Neusüss-Hunkel: op cit, p. 21.

104 Cover note to rules for the grant of the SS Death's Head ring, 1 Aug. 1939, RFSS Microfilm 15. SS seniority List, 1944.

105 Neusüss-Hunkel: op cit, p. 22.

106 SS Seniority List, 1944.

107 Besgen: op cit, p. 75.

108 Knoebel: op cit, p. 30.

109 Letter to Pohl of 17 July 1937—in Wulf's papers.

110 Ibid.

111 Ibid.

112 Verbal information from Rupprecht, the castle warden.

113 Ibid.

114 Trevor-Roper: op cit, p. 23.

115 Verbal information from Rupprecht.

116 Ibid.

117 W. Segin: *Geschichte der Wewelsburg*, p. 14.

118 Ibid, p. 10.

119 Frischauer: *Himmler*, pp. 67–8.

120 Heiner Lichtenstein, "Wo Himmler residieren wollte," West German Radio 30 Jan. 1965, script pp. 15–16.

121 Ibid, pp. 3, 6.

122 Enno Georg: op cit, p. 22. (Taubert should not be confused with Sigfred Taubert, head of the German Booksellers Association's Exhibition and Book Fair Organisation).

123 Ibid.

124 Inhabitants of Wewelsburg village can still remember this rumour.

125 Georg: op cit, p. 22.

126 IMT Vol. XXIX, p. 225.

127 Georg: op cit, p. 21.

128 IMT Vol. XXIX, p. 225. Georg: op cit, p. 21.

129 IMT Vol. XXIX, p. 225.

130 Georg: op cit, p. 23.

131 Wulf: *Die SS*, p. 18.

132 *Das Schwarze Korps*, July 1937.

133 Georg: op cit, p. 23.

134 Helfferich: op cit, p. 31.

135 Besgen: op cit, p. 76.

136 Ibid, p. 74.

137 Neusüss-Hunkel: op cit, p. 119.

138 Ibid, p. 71.

139 Address by Zechs, pp. 7–8, RFSS Microfilm 17.

140 Address by Standarten-führer Dr Cäsar "Education Experiences," Gruppenführer Conference, Berlin, 25 Jan. 1939, RFSS Microfilm 17.

141 Ibid.

142 "Der Weg des SS Mannes," pp. 6–7.

143 Knoebel: op cit, p. 21.

144 Speech by Himmler, 8 Nov. 1936.

145 Knoebel: op cit, p. 31.

146 Ibid, pp. 30–31.

147 Himmler: *Die Schutzstaffel als antibolschewistische Kampforganisation*, p. 22.

148 Speech by Himmler, 8 Nov. 1936, RFSS Microfilm 89.

149 Knoebel: op cit, p. 22.

150 Ibid.

151 Ibid.

152 Ibid.

153 Ibid, p. 35.

154 Ibid, p. 36.

155 Ibid.

156 Verbal information from ex-Obergruppenführer Wilhelm Bittrich, 29 Jan. 1966.

157 Numbers of married SS men and total numbers of children, return as at 1 Jan. 1939 franked by Himmler's Personal Staff, RFSS Microfilm 25.

158 "Two Years Work in Lebensborn," address by Standartenführer Dr Ebener, Berlin Gruppenführer Conference, 25 Jan. 1939, RFSS Microfilm 17.

159 Ibid.

160 Knoebel: op cit, p. 41.

161 See Bundesarchiv statistical review "Der Adel im Deutschen Offizierkorps," p. 12.

162 "Administrative and Economic Situation, end 1936"—Report by Brigadeführer Pohl, p. 2, RFSS Microfilm 131.

163 Ibid.

164 Annual Report of SS Personnel Chancellery, 31 Dec. 1938, p. 2 RFSS Microfilm 17.

165 Ibid, p. 3.

166 Report on the SS Leaders School, Munich-Dachau, Appendix to SS Personnel Chancellery Annual Report (see Note 164 above), p. 4.

167 Lutz Graf Schwerin von Krosigk: *Es geschah in Deutschland*, p. 250.

168 Ernst Jünger: *Der Kampf als inneres Erlebnis*, p. 78.

169 Werner Best: "Der Krieg und das Recht" in Jünger, *Krieg und Krieger*, 1930.

170 Ibid, p. 152.

171 Buchheim: *Anatomy of the SS State*, p. 329.

172 Ibid, p. 328.

173 Ibid.

CHAPTER EIGHT

1 Wulf: *Die SS*, 45–6.

2 Buchheim: *Anatomy of the SS State*, p. 166.

3 The document is in Wulf's papers.

4 Gercke's memorandum, p. 1.

5 Burckhardt: *Meiner Danziger Mission 1937–1939*, p. 57.

6 Reitlinger: *The Final Solution*, p. 13.

7 Michael Freund, quoted from Ulrich Popplow's "Reinhard Heydrich oder die Aufnordung durch den Sport" in *Olympisches Feuer*, Aug. 1963, p. 14.

8 Reitlinger: *The SS*, p. 35.

9 H. G. Adler: *Theresienstadt 1941–45*, p. 645.

10 Kersten: *Totenkopf und Treue*, pp. 97–8.

11 Burckhardt: op cit, p. 55.

12 Ibid, p. 57.

13 Michael Freund: *Deutschland unterm Hakenkreuz*, p. 336.

14 Kersten: op cit, p. 98.

15 Verbal information from Bruno Streckenbach, 21 Jan. 1966.

16 Popplow: op cit, p. 15.

17 Ibid.

18 Ibid, p. 18.

19 "Nebe Series", 9 Feb. 1950.

20 Ibid.

21 Verbal information from Streckenbach, 21 Jan. 1966.

22 Kersten: op cit. pp. 90–91. "Nebe Series", 9 Jan. 1950.

23 Kersten: op cit, p. 90.

24 Ibid.

25 Fest: *Das Gesicht des dritten Reiches,* p. 141. Wighton: *Heydrich,* p. 81.

26 Popplow: op cit, p. 16.

27 Fest: op cit, p. 139.

28 Statement by Rudolf Diels, *Frankfurter Allgemeine Zeitung,* 9 May 1957.

29 Wighton: op cit, pp. 93–4.

30 Burckhardt: op cit, p. 56.

31 "Nebe Series", 9 Feb. 1950, p. 23.

32 Aronson: *Heydrich und die Anfänge des SD und der Gestapo,* p. 1.

33 Wighton: op cit, p. 27.

34 Ibid, p. 29.

35 Abshagen: *Canaris, Patriot und Weltburger,* p. 77.

36 Ibid, pp. 146–7.

37 Ibid, p. 58.

38 Aronson: op cit, pp. 23, 42.

39 Abshagen: op cit, p. 80.

40 Aronson: op cit, p. 38.

41 Wighton: op cit, p. 33.

42 Aronson: op cit, p. 31.

43 Ibid, p. 43. "Nebe Series", 9 Feb. 1950.

44 Aronson: op cit, p. 46. Manvell and Fraenkel: *Himmler,* p. 26.

45 Aronson: op cit, p. 47. "Nebe Series", 9 Feb. 1950, p. 23.

46 Ibid. Wighton, op cit, p. 34.

47 Aronson: op cit, p. 48.

48 *Der Spiegel,* No. 9 of 1950, p. 42.

49 Ibid, p. 61.

50 Ibid, p. 42.

51 Wighton: op cit, p. 34.

52 Aronson: op cit, p. 51.

53 Verbal information from Streckenbach, 21 Jan. 1966.

54 Wighton: op cit, p. 35.

55 Hagen: *Die geheime Front,* p. 41.

56 Aronson: op cit, p. 51.

57 "Nebe Series", 9 Feb. 1950, p. 23.

58 Ibid.

59 Wulf: *Die SS,* p. 44.

60 Ibid.

61 Aronson: op cit, pp. 86–7.

62 Ibid, p. 87.

63 Ibid, p. 86.

64 Ibid, p. 87.

65 Ibid, p. 89. "Nebe Series", 9 Feb. 1950, p. 23.

66 Ibid, p. 98.

67 Ibid, p. 92.
68 Buchheim: *Anatomy of the SS State*, p. 142.
69 Aronson: op cit, p. 89.
70 Ibid.
71 Ibid, p. 98.
72 SS Seniority List.
73 Kersten: op cit, p. 99.
74 Schellenberg: *Memoirs*, p. 30.
75 Kersten: op cit, p. 99.
76 Ibid, p. 98.
77 Hagen: op cit, p. 86.
78 Alfred Schweder: *Politische Polizei*, p. 145.
79 Werner Best: *Die Deutsche Polizei*, p. 29.
80 Ibid, p. 44.
81 Wulf: *Die SS*, p. 55.
82 Ibid.
83 Buchheim: *Anatomy of the SS State*, p. 147.
84 Ibid, p. 148.
85 Ibid.
86 Ibid, pp. 147–8.
87 Ibid, p. 148.
88 Broszat: *Anatomy of the SS State*, p. 404–5.
89 Ibid, p. 401–2.
90 IMT Vol. XXIX, p. 217.
91 Broszat: op cit, p. 416.
92 Ibid, p. 424.
93 Buchheim: *Anatomy of the SS State*, p. 151.
94 Ibid, p. 170.
95 Aronson: op cit, p. 175.
96 Ibid.
97 Buchheim: *Anatomy of the SS State*, p. 167.
98 Aronson: op cit, p. 176.
99 Ibid, p. 177.
100 Ibid, pp. 154 et seq. SS Seniority List, 1935.
101 Ibid, pp. 154–5. Verbal information from Streckenbach, 21 Jan. 1966.
102 Ibid, p. 155.
103 Political appreciation on Senior Criminal Inspector Heinrich Müller, Headquarters of Munich-Upper Bavaria Gau, 4 Jan. 1934—in Wulf's papers.
104 Ibid.
105 Ibid.
106 Political appreciation on Müller by the local Nazi Group office in Pasing, 28 Dec. 1936—in Wulf's papers.
107 Aronson: op cit, p. 117.
108 Ibid, pp. ix and x.
109 SS Seniority List, 1934.
110 Kaltenbrunner Report. *Spiegelbild einer Verschwörung*, p. 245.
111 Ibid, p. 244. "Nebe Series", 17 Nov. 1949, p. 23.
112 Ibid, p. 244.
113 Ibid, p. 240. "Nebe Series", 17 Nov. 1949, p. 23.
114 "Nebe Series", 17 Nov. 1949, p. 24.
115 Ibid, p. 25.
116 Aronson: op cit, pp. 236–236c.
117 Jünger: *Krieg und Krieger*, p. 152.
118 Ibid, p. 157.
119 Ibid, pp. 153, 158.
120 Horkenbach: *Das deutsche Reich von 1918 bis Heute*, Vol. II, p. 364.
121 Ibid, p. 346.
122 Aronson: op cit, pp. 249–50.
123 Ibid, pp. ixx c, 253. Verbal information from Werner Best, 5 Feb. 1966.
124 Verbal information from Best.
125 IMT Vol. XXI, p. 501.
126 Buchheim: *SS und Polizei im NS-Staat*, pp. 32–34.
127 Aronson: op cit, p. 137.
128 Buchheim: *Anatomy of the SS State*, p. 146. Helmut Schlierbach: *Die Politische Polizei in*

Preussen, p. 48. Aronson: op cit, p. 294.

129 Buchheim: op cit, pp. 146–7.

130 Schlierbach: op cit, p. 53.

131 Ibid, pp. 41–2.

132 Reinhard Heydrich: *Wandlungen unseres Kampfes*, pp. 4, 5, 14.

133 Schweder: op cit, p. 14.

134 "Politische Polizei", Memorandum by Kriminalkommissar Wendzio, p. 7, RFSS Microfilm 432.

135 Letter of 7 July 1938 from Heydrich to all Gestapoleitstellen and Stellen, RFSS Microfilm 491.

136 Ibid.

137 Diels: op cit, pp. 160, 167. Aronson (op cit) gives a figure of approx. 35 men for 1933.

138 Buchheim: *SS und Polizei im NS-Staat*, p. 79. Schlierbach: op cit, p. 61.

139 Buchheim: *Anatomy of the SS State*, p. 244.

140 Best: *Die deutsche Abwehrpolizei*, p. 44.

141 "Wesen der Geheimen Staatspolizei"—author and date unknown, RFSS Microfilm 432.

142 Ibid.

143 Letter of 26 July 1937 from Best to Regierungspräsidenten and Police Presidents, RFSS Microfilm 403.

144 "Wesen der Geheimen Staatspolizei" (see Note 141 above).

145 Broszat: *Anatomy of the SS State*, p. 425.

146 Ibid, p. 427.

147 Verbal information from Werner von Haacke.

148 IMT Vol. XX, p. 471.

149 Ibid, pp. 455–6.

150 Broszat: op cit, p. 430.

151 Ibid.

152 IMT Vol. XX, p. 456.

153 Ibid, p. 458.

154 Ibid.

155 Ibid.

156 Aronson: op cit, pp. 257 and 272.

157 Diels: op cit, p. 310. Verbal information from Werner von Haacke.

158 Diels: op cit, p. 396.

159 Ibid, p. 400. Hubert Schorn; *Der Richter im Dritten Reich*, pp. 672–3.

160 Verbal information from Dr Walter Schaeffer, 24 Jan. 1966.

161 Diels: op cit, p. 399.

162 Schorn: op cit, pp. 107 and 642. Broszat: op cit, pp. 422–3.

163 Martin Broszat: "Zur Perversion der Strafjustiz im Dritten Reich" *Vierteljahrshefte für Zeitgeschichte*, Oct. 1958, p. 390.

164 Schorn: op cit, p. 11.

165 Broszat: "Perversion der Strafjustiz", p. 392, Schorn: op cit, p. 193.

166 Hans Frank: *Im Angesicht des Galgens*, p. 160.

167 Ibid, p. 161.

168 Broszat: *Anatomy of the SS State*, p. 424.

169 Schorn: op cit, p. 80.

170 Ibid, p. 91.

171 Plum: *Staatspolizei und innere Verwaltung 1934–1936*, pp. 200–1.

172 Ibid, p. 202.

173 Letter of 5 Aug. 1935 from Best to all Gestapo offices, RFSS Microfilm 139.

174 Werner Best: *Die Deutsche Polizei*, p. 26.

175 Helmut Krausnick: "Wehrmacht und Nationalsozialismus" *Das Parlament*, 9 Nov. 1955, p. 672.

176 Plum: op cit, pp. 198 and 206.
177 Ibid, p. 200.
178 Ibid, p. 198.
179 Aronson: op cit. p. 372. Plum: op cit, p. 221.
180 Plum: op cit, p. 221.
181 Ibid, p. 198.
182 Ibid, pp. 213-4.
183 Buchheim: *Anatomy of the SS State*, p. 154.
184 Ibid. Schlierbach: op cit, p. 55.

185 Plum: op cit, p. 203.
186 Neufeldt: *Zur Geschichte der Ordnungspolizei 1936-1945*, p. 9.
187 Ibid, p. 17.
188 Ibid, p. 14.
189 Ibid, p. 15.
190 Ibid, p. 16.
191 Ibid, p. 17. Schlierbach: op cit, p. 82.
192 Buchheim: *SS und Polizei im NS-Staat*, p. 55.

CHAPTER NINE

1 Broszat: *Anatomy of the SS State*, p. 448.
2 Ibid.
3 Ibid. Broszat: *Perversion der Strafjustiz*, p. 395.
4 "Nebe Series", 24 Nov. 1949, p. 28.
5 Best: *Die Deutsche Polizei*, p. 37.
6 Ibid.
7 Ibid, p. 38.
8 Even Best admits as much—*Die Deutsche Polizei*, p. 37.
9 Ibid, p. 38.
10 Broszat: *Perversion der Strafjustiz*, p. 395.
11 Ibid.
12 Ibid.
13 Neufeldt: *Zur Geschichte der Ordnungspolizei 1936-1945*, p. 25.
14 Ibid, p. 21.
15 Best: *Die Deutsche Abwehrpolizei*, pp. 29-30. Buchheim: *Anatomy of the SS State*, pp. 163-4.
16 Best: op cit, p. 29.
17 Address instructions for encoded correspondence, Issue of 10 May 1941, RFSS Microfilm 463. Friedrich Zipfel: *Kirchen-*

kampf in Deutschland 1933-34, p. 148.
18 Buchheim:*SS und Polizei im NS-Staat*, pp. 52-3.
19 Best: *Die Deutsche Polizei*, p. 21.
20 Schweder: *Politische Polizei*, p. 156.
21 Schlierbach: *Die politische Polizie in Preussen*, pp. 88-93.
22 "Wesen der Geheimen Staatspolizei", undated, RFSS Microfilm 432.
23 Broszat: *Anatomy of the SS State*, p. 418.
24 Ibid, pp. 446-7.
25 Broszat: *Perversion der Strafjustiz*, p. 391.
26 Ibid, p. 395.
27 Broszat: *Anatomy of the SS State*, pp. 443-50. Best: *Die Deutsche Polizei*, pp. 39-40.
28 Kogon: *The Theory and Practice of Hell*, p. 30.
29 Henkys: *Die nationalsozialistische Gewaltverbrechen*, p. 47.
30 Ibid, pp. 47, 48, 50.
31 IMT Vol. XX, pp. 132-3.
32 Schlierbach: op cit, p. 61.
33 Kogon (op cit, p. 40) wrongly assumes that the post of Con-

centration Camp Inspector was created by Heydrich and that Eicke's office was at No. 7 Prinz-Albrecht-Strasse. In fact Eiche's office was in Block, F, No. 129 Friedrichstrasse, Berlin NW7 (see also Broszat: *Anatomy of the SS State*, p. 443).

34 IMT Vol. XX, p. 133.

35 Broszat: *Anatomy of the SS State*, p. 405.

36 Aronson: *Heydrich und die Anfänge des SD und der Gestapo*, pp. 171–2.

37 Ibid, p. 171.

38 Broszat: *Anatomy of the SS State*, p. 431.

39 Benedikt Kautsky: *Teufel und Verdammte*, pp. 91–2.

40 Broszat: *Anatomy of the SS State*, p. 437.

41 Ibid, pp. 432–3.

42 Rudolf Höss: *Kommandant in Auschwitz*, p. 58.

43 Buchheim: *Anatomy of the SS State*, pp. 228, 256.

44 Ibid, p. 256.

45 Broszat: *Anatomy of the SS State*, pp. 444–5.

46 Ibid, p. 436.

47 Ibid.

48 Ibid, p. 433.

49 Kautsky: op cit, p. 87.

50 Buchheim: op cit, p. 260.

51 Ibid.

52 Ibid, p. 261.

53 Ibid.

54 Neufeldt: op cit, p. 8.

55 Ibid, p. 5.

56 Ibid, p. 36.

57 Buchheim: *SS und Polizei im NS-Staat*, p. 91.

58 Neufeldt: op cit, p. 76.

59 Ibid, p. 42.

60 Buchheim: *Anatomy of the SS State*, pp. 186–7. Letter from Pflomm to Bracht, 18 Feb. 1943;

letter from Pflomm to Wolff 3 April 1943, RFSS Microfilm 31.

61 Buchheim: *Anatomy of the SS State*, p. 194.

62 Ibid, p. 185.

63 Letter of 18 Feb. 1943 from Pflomm to Bracht. Buchheim: *Anatomy of the SS State*, p. 186.

64 "Nebe Series", 1 Dec. 1949, p. 22.

65 Ibid.

66 "Wesen der Geheimen Staatspolizei", p. 5.

67 IMT Vol. XX, p. 128.

68 See Chapter 4, this volume.

69 "Illegal information organisation", Report of 31 Mar. 1937 (probably from Munich Police Headquarters), pp. 9–10, RFSS Microfilm 467.

70 Ibid, pp. 5–6.

71 Ibid, p. 6.

72 Ibid, p. 3.

73 Ibid, p. 6.

74 Ibid, p. 7.

75 Wulf: *Die SS*, p. 118.

76 Adolf Eichmann: Record of interrogation, Vol. 1 Folio 44.

77 "How I came to be employed in Russia"; deposition (undated) by Otto Ohlendorf at his trial (in the private papers of Frau Käthe Ohlendorf).

78 Aronson: op cit, p. 250.

79 Ibid, pp. 279–80.

80 Ibid, pp. 281–2.

81 Kogon: op cit, p. 21.

82 Aronson: op cit, pp. 280–1.

83 Ibid, p. 382.

84 On the psychology of the SD elite see Zipfel: *Kirchenkampf in Deutschland 1933–1945*, pp. 165 et seq.

85 Schorn: *Der Richter im Dritten Reich*, p. 29.

86 Laqueur: *Young Germany*, p. 199.

87 Statement by Ohlendorf, 8 Oct. 1947, American Military Tribunal No. II A, Case IX. (Reference M-IL-I-I Caming (In Lea) Court IIa, Case IX.)

88 Ibid, p. 488.

89 Ohlendorf to his wife, Frau Käthe Ohlendorf, 6 Feb. 1934, Ohlendorf documents, Book 1a, Ohlendorf trial.

90 Statement by Ohlendorf (see Note 87 above), p. 490.

91 Aronson: op cit, p. 343.

92 Ibid, p. 269.

93 Ibid, p. 232.

94 Ibid, p. 271.

95 Verbal information from Prof. Reinhard Höhn, 15 Nov. 1966.

96 Aronson: op cit, p. 355.

97 Delarue: *History of the Gestapo*, p. 208.

98 Aronson: op cit, p. 360. Schellenberg: *Memoirs*, pp. 19–20.

99 Verbal information from Dr Werner Best, 5 Feb. 1966.

100 Werner Best: *Reinhard Heydrich*, p. 3.

101 Schorn: op cit, p. 11.

102 IMT Vol. XX, p. 194.

103 Ibid, pp. 141–2.

104 Aronson: op cit, p. 360.

105 Ibid, p. 275.

106 Ibid, pp. 96–7. Wulf: *Die SS*, p. 43.

107 Ibid, p. 344.

108 Ibid, p. 94.

109 Ibid.

110 Ibid, p. 93.

111 Ibid, p. 355.

112 Boberach: *Meldungen aus dem Reich*, p. xiii.

113 Aronson: op cit, p. 346.

114 Ibid, p. 75.

115 Zipfel: op cit, p. 379.

116 Ibid, pp. 383–4.

117 Ibid, p. 384.

118 Ibid, p. 383.

119 IMT Vol. XX, pp. 194.

120 Boberach: op cit, p. xxiv.

121 Schlierbach: op cit, p. 25.

122 Wendzio: "Politische Polizei", RFSS Microfilm 432.

123 Eichmann: Record of interrogations Vol. 1, p. 76.

124 Evaluation system used by Amt VI of the RSHA, worked out by Schellenberg 10 Aug. 1942, RFSS Microfilm 463.

125 Wulf: *Die SS*, p. 123.

126 Aronson: op cit, p. 332.

127 Ibid, p. 333.

128 IMT Vol. XXIX, p. 223.

129 Letter from Grillenberger to Amt I, SD-Hauptamt, 26 Jan. 1938, RFSS Microfilm 411.

130 Wulf: *Die SS*, pp. 124–5.

131 Office minute by Deck II 112, 29 Dec. 1937, RFSS Microfilm 411.

132 Office minute by Hagen, undated (approx. 1937–38), RFSS Microfilm 411.

133 Office minute by Hagen, 8 Jan. 1938, RFSS Microfilm 411.

134 Verbal information from Gunther d'Alquen, 30 June–1 July 1966.

135 Ibid.

136 Ibid.

137 Ibid.

138 Wulf: *Die SS*, pp. 108–9.

139 *Das Schwarze Korps*, 21 Jan. 1937.

140 Ibid, 27 Aug. 1935.

141 Ibid, 28 May, 1936.

142 Ibid, 5 June 1935 and 22 Apr. 1937.

143 Ibid, 27 Aug. 1936.

144 Ibid, 18 Feb. 1937.

145 Letter from editor's office *Schwarze Korps*, 21 June 1938, RFSS Microfilm 509.

146 Letter from Paul Koch to editor *Schwarze Korps*, 7 June

938. Letter *Schwarze Korps* to
ix 21 June 1938. Letter Desk II
12 to SD Führer East, 8 July
938. Letter Desk II 112 to
chwarze Korps.

47 Minute from aus den
..uthen to SD Hauptamt, 14 Apr.
938. Letter from Deck II 112 to
us den Ruthen, 21 Apr. 1938,
.FSS Microfilm 509.

48 Note by Hagen, 17 June
938, RFSS Microfilm 509.

49 *Das Schwarze Korps*, 16
uly 1936.

50 Ibid, 7 Aug. 1935.

51 Ibid, 5 Jan. 1939.

152 Ibid, 13 Feb. 1941.

153 Ibid, 11 July 1940.

154 Letter from d'Alquen to
Ohlendorf, 25 Sept. 1942, RFSS
Microfilm 275.

155 Comment by RSHA Amt
III on d'Alquen's letter of 25
Sept. 1942, RFSS Microfilm 275.

156 Ibid, p. 7.

157 Letter from d'Alquen to
Ohlendorf, 22 July 1942, RFSS
Microfilm 275.

158 Letter from Ohlendorf to
d'Alquen, 14 Aug. 1942, RFSS
Microfilm 275.

159 Ibid.

CHAPTER TEN

"Grundsätzliche Gedanken
ur Neugliederung" drafted by
chellenberg, undated (approx.
.mmer 1939), RFSS Microfilm
32.

Boberach: *Meldungen aus
em Reich*, pp. xiii, xiv.

Ibid, p. xiv.

"Die Eigenständigkeit des
ichcrhcitsdienstes," undated,
.FSS Microfilm 239.

Wighton: *Heydrich*, p. 115.

Ibid. *Hamburger Morgen-
ost*, 3 Feb. 1965.

Wighton: op cit, p. 116.

Ibid.

Ibid, p. 117.

) Ibid. *Hamburger Morgen-
ost*, 3 Feb. 1965.

◄ Werner Best: *Wilhelm Ca-
aris*, p. 6.

◄ Letters from Hagen and
ichmann, 4 Nov. 1937, RFSS
lcrofilm 411.

3 Ibid.

4 Ibid.

5 Abshagen: *Canaris, Patriot
nd Weltburger*, p. 94.

5 Ibid, pp. 19, 51, 68, 139.

17 Karl Bartz: *Die Tragödie
der deutschen Abwehr*, p. 80.

18 Abshagen: op cit, p. 147.

19 Werner Best: *Die deutsche
Abwehrpolizei bis 1945*, pp. 19,
19a, 19b.

20 Best: *Wilhelm Canaris*, p. 6.
Gerd Buchheit: *Der deutsche
Geheimdienst*, pp. 158 et seq.

21 Hagen: *Die geheime Front*,
p. 57.

22 See Delarue: *History of the
Gestapo*, p. 187.

23 Schellenberg: *Memoirs*, p.
46.

24 Ibid, p. 47.

25 Ibid, p. 49.

26 Hagen: op cit, p. 54;
"Braver, dummer Klim," *Der
Spiegel*, 8 Nov. 1961, p. 68.

27 B. H. Liddell Hart: *The
Red Army*, p. 69.

28 "Die Politische Lage in der
Roten Armee," issued by Head
of SD Hauptamt 1938, RFSS
Microfilm 467.

29 *Die Welt*, 4 Jan. 1962.

30 Karl Spalcke: "Der Fall

Tuchatschewski" in *Die Gegenwart*, 25 Jan. 1958.

31 *Der Spiegel*, 8 Nov. 1961, p. 70.

32 Ibid, p. 71.

33 Ibid.

34 Ibid.

35 Ibid.

36 Ibid.

37 Hagen (Höttl): op cit, p. 62.

38 Schellenberg: op cit, p. 49.

39 *Der Spiegel*, 8 Nov. 1961, p. 68.

40 Hagen: op cit, p. 62.

41 Spalcke: op cit, p. 47.

42 Abshagen: op cit, p. 169.

43 Buchheim: *SS und Polizei im NS-Staat*, pp. 62–3.

44 Buchheim: *Anatomy of the SS State*, p. 171.

45 Ibid.

46 Boberach: op cit, p. xiii. Ohlendorf's statement, 8 Oct. 1967, pp. 496 et seq.

47 Ohlendorf's statement, p. 490.

48 Verbal statement by Gunter d'Alquen, Nov. 1966.

49 Ohlendorf's statement, pp. 484 et seq.

50 Boberach: op cit, p. xiii.

51 Ohlendorf's statement, p. 490.

52 Ibid, p. 491.

53 Ibid.

54 "Die Wirtschaft im nationalsozialistischen Staat," undated memorandum by Ohlendorf, in Frau Käthe Ohlendorf's private papers.

55 Ohlendorf's statement, p. 491.

56 Boberach: op cit, p. xiii.

57 Ohlendorf's plea in mitigation, July 1950, p. 40 (Frau Ohlendorf's private papers).

58 Helmut Heiber: *Walter Frank*, pp. 430 et seq.

59 Ibid, pp. 441, 444.

60 Verbal information from Professor Höhn, Nov. 1966.

61 Affidavit by Karl Wolff, 1 Sept. 1947, Ohlendorf documents Book IV.

62 Ibid. Kersten: op cit, p. 209

63 Sworn statement by Luitpol Schallermeier, 21 Aug. 1947 Ohlendorf documents, Book IV

64 Ohlendorf's statement, Oct. 1947, p. 492.

65 Boberach, op cit, p. xiv.

66 Ohlendorf's statement, 8 Oc 1947, p. 493.

67 Ibid.

68 Verbal information from Frau Käthe Ohlendorf 26 Jar 1966.

69 Memorandum drafted b Schellenberg "Reorganisation c the SD with a view to its fusio with the Sicherheitspolizei," 2 Feb. 1939, RFSS Microfilm 239.

70 Judgment of court set up b Supreme Commander of th Wehrmacht in the case of Fre herr von Fritsch, 18 March 193 p. 3 (in the private papers c Fabian von Schlabrendorf).

71 Ibid, pp. 9–10.

72 Ibid, p. 3.

73 Ibid. Adolf Graf von Kie mansegg; *Der Fritschproze. 1938*, pp. 53 and 56.

74 Ibid, p. 3.

75 Ibid.

76 Verbal information from D Werner Best, 5 Feb. 1966.

77 Judgment of court (see No 70 above), pp. 4–9.

78 Ibid.

79 Ibid.

80 Ibid, p. 11.

81 *Der Spiegel*, No. 36 of 196 p. 46.

82 Hossbach: *Zwischen Weh*

nacht und Hitler 1934–1938, . 126.

3 Ibid, p. 103.

4 Krausnick: *Wehrmacht und Nationalsozialismus*, p. 666.

5 Foertsch: *Schuld und Verängnis*, p. 90. Krausnick: op cit, . 677.

6 Foertsch: op cit, p. 76.

7 Ibid. Hossbach: op cit, p. 88.

8 Hossbach: op cit, p. 190.

9 Ibid, p. 218.

o Foertsch: op cit, pp. 91, 138.

1 Kielmansegg: op cit, pp. 4–5.

2 Graf von der Goltz: "Die Entlassung des Generalobersten Freiherr von Fritsch."

3 Foertsch: op cit, p. 128.

4 Walter Görlitz: *Generalfeldmarschall Keitel, Verbrecher der Offizier?*, pp. 86, 88.

5 Ibid, p. 102.

6 Letter from Curt Hellmuth Müller, 9 Dec. 1949.

7 Ibid.

8 Ibid.

9 Ibid.

00 Gorlitz: *Keitel*, p. 103.

01 Ibid.

02 Hossbach: op cit, p. 123.

03 Ibid, p. 124.

04 Ibid, p. 123.

05 Ibid.

06 Krausnick: *Wehrmacht und Nationalsozialmus*, p. 679.

07 Hossbach: op cit, p. 123.

08 Foertsch: op cit, p. 141.

09 Ibid, p. 102.

10 Ibid, pp. 90–1.

11 Hossbach, op cit, pp. 126–7.

12 Quoted from Werner Picht: *om Wesen des Krieges und om Kriegswesen der Deutschen*, . 225.

13 Wilhelm Treue: script of radio talk "The Fritsch Affair," p. 35.

114 Hossbach: op cit, p. 129.

115 Ibid.

116 Ibid.

117 Foertsch: op cit, p. 138.

118 Ibid, p. 128.

119 Görlitz: *Keitel*, p. 106.

120 Foertsch: op cit, p. 88.

121 Ibid, p. 138.

122 Görlitz: *Keitel*, p. 107.

123 Kielmansegg: op cit, p. 38.

124 Foertsch: op cit, p. 88.

125 Ibid, pp. 88–9.

126 Gorlitz: *Keitel*, p. 109.

127 Foertsch: op cit, p. 106.

128 Ibid, p. 105.

129 Ibid, p. 118.

130 Ibid.

131 Heinrich Rosenberger: "Die Entlassung des Generalobersten Freiherrn von Fritsch" in *Deutsche Rundschau*, Nov. 1946, pp. 91–2.

132 Ibid.

133 Kielmansegg: op cit, pp. 48–9.

134 Judgment of Court (see Note 70), p. 28.

135 Ibid, p. 29.

136 Ibid, p. 1.

137 Kielmansegg: op cit, p. 50.

138 Foertsch: op cit, p. 100.

139 Ibid.

140 Verbal information from Dr Werner Best, 5 Feb. 1966.

141 Ibid.

142 Gisevius: *To the Bitter End*, p. 243.

143 Schellenberg: op cit, p. 32.

144 Foertsch: op cit, p. 120.

145 Judgment of Court, p. 23.

146 Gisevius: *Bis zum bittern Ende*, p. 274 (not in English translation).

147 Foertsch: op cit, p. 105.

148 Abshagen: op cit, p. 178.

149 Schellenberg: op cit, p. 33.

150 Krausnick: *Wehrmacht und Nationalsozialismus*, p. 678.
151 Gisevius: *Bis zum bitteren Ende*, p. 280 (not in English translation).
152 Krausnick: op cit, p. 681.
153 Judgment of Court, pp. 31–34.
154 Kielmansegg: op cit, p. 80.
155 Judgment of Court, p. 18.
156 Foertsch: op cit, p. 121. Kielmansegg: op cit, p. 82.
157 Foertsch: op cit, p. 122.
158 Ibid.
159 Kielmansegg: op cit, pp. 87–8.
160 Foertsch: op cit, p. 125.
161 Kielmansegg: op cit, p. 90.
162 Foertsch: op cit, p. 124.
163 Judgment of Court, p. 1.
164 Wolfgang Foerster: *Generaloberst Ludwig Beck*, p. 92.
165 Ibid, p. 169.
166 Foertsch: op cit, p. 129.
167 Wheeler-Bennett: *Nemesis of Power*, p. 381.
168 Foertsch: op cit, p. 129.
169 Ibid.
170 "Nebe Series," 29 Dec. 1949, p. 404.
171 Schellenberg: op cit, p. 34.
172 Verbal information from Bruno Streckenbach, 21 Jan. 1966.
173 Verbal information from Paul Hausser, 31 Jan. 1966.
174 Draft of an address by Brigadeführer Petri headed "General experiences of the call-up of reinforcements for the SS-Totenkopfverbände in September 1933 and of the mass employment of the Allgemeine SS"— initialled by Himmler 22 Jan. 1939, RFSS Microfilm 17.
175 Wighton: op cit, p. 150.
176 Abshagen: op cit, pp. 185–6.
177 Görlitz: *Keitel*, p. 407.
178 Comment by Schellenberg on Heydrich's proposals for re organisation of the SD an Sicherheitspolizei, 4 Apr. 193 RFSS Microfilm 239.
179 Buchheim: *Anatomy of th SS State*, p. 209.
180 Ibid, pp. 209–210.
181 Ibid, p. 185.
182 Ibid, pp. 213–4.
183 Best: *Die Deutsche Polize* pp. 85, 87.
184 Zipfel: op cit, pp. 159, 16
185 "Reorganisation of th Sicherheitsdienst Reichsführe SS with a view to organisation and personnel assimilation the Sicherheitspolizei"; meme randum drafted by Schellenber 24 Feb. 1939, RFSS Microfil 239.
186 Letter from Pohl Schwarz, undated (approx. en 1936), RFSS Microfilm 131.
187 Ibid.
188 Zipfel: op cit, p. 146.
189 Letter from Schellenberg Heydrich, 27 Feb. 1939, RF Microfilm 239.
190 Note by Schellenber dated 4 Apr. 1939, recommen ing formation of a working pa to discuss SD problems, RF Microfilm 239.
191 Buchheim: *SS und Poli im NS-Staat*, p. 61.
192 See Note 185 above.
193 "Comment on SS-Brigad führer Best's latest draft career structure," note Schellenberg dated 28 Aug. 19 RFSS Microfilm 239.
194 As evidence of Schelle berg's campaign against Best, s his note on SD careers, 28 Fe 1939, RFSS Microfilm 239.

5 *Deutsches Recht,* Folio 8–9, Apr. 1939.

6 Ibid, p. 198 (Best's article Kritik und Apologie des Jur- ten").

7 Letter from Schellenberg Heydrich, 25 Apr. 1939, RFSS icrofilm 239.

8 Ibid.

9 Verbal information from r Werner Best, 5 Feb. 1966.

0 Schellenberg: *Memoiren,* p. (not in English translation).

1 Ohlendorf's statement, 8 ct. 1947, p. 496.

2 The Reich Ministry of the terior, for instance, initially, ok no official cognisance of the rmation of the RSHA (see eufeldt, op cit, p. 21).

3 Buchheim: *Anatomy of the*

SS State, pp. 173–40.

204 Ibid.

205 Ibid.

206 Ibid.

207 Ibid.

208 Ibid.

209 Ohlendorf's statement, 8 Oct. 1947, pp. 495–6.

210 Ibid, p. 496.

211 Ibid.

212 Verbal information from Dr Werner Best, 5 Feb. 1966.

213 Ibid.

214 Letter from Best to Heyd- rich, 15 Apr. 1942 (in Wulf's papers).

215 Verbal information from Dr Werner Best, 5 Feb. 1966.

216 Buchheim: *Anatomy of the SS State,* p. 194.

CHAPTER ELEVEN

Hans-Adolf Jacobsen: *1939– , Der Zweite Weltkrieg in hronik und Documenten,* p. 5.

Ibid, p. 116.

Shirer: *The Rise and Fall of e Third Reich,* p. 532.

Ibid.

Ibid.

Halder's Diary, Vol. 1, p. 19.

Helmut Arntz: "Die Men- henverluste im Zweiten Welt- ieg," in *Bilanz des Zweiten eltkrieges,* p. 446.

Jürgen Runzheimer: "Der berfall auf den Sender Glei- itz" in *Vierteljahrshefte für itgeschichte,* No. 4 of 1962, 419.

Jürgen Thorwald: "Der ann, der den Krieg auslöste" *Der Stern,* 7 June 1953.

Ibid.

Ibid.

12 *Der Spiegel,* 13 Nov. 1963.

13 Ibid, p. 73.

14 Raimund Schnabel: *Macht ohne Moral,* p. 384.

15 Thorwald: op cit, p. 14.

16 *Der Spiegel,* 13 Nov. 1963; p. 71.

17 Ibid.

18 Runzheimer: op cit, p. 420.

19 Ibid.

20 Ibid, pp. 411, 413.

21 Thorwald: op cit, pp. 14 et seq.

22 Ibid.

23 Schnabel, op cit, p. 386.

24 Ibid.

25 Ibid.

26 Ibid.

27 Shirer: op cit, p. 547.

28 Rudi Strauch: *Sir Neville Henderson,* p. 278.

29 Ludwig Denne: *Das Danzig- Problem in der deutschen Aussenpolitik 1934–39,* p. 278.

30 Runzheimer: op cit, p. 425.

31 Shirer: op cit, p. 557.

32 Helmuth Greiner: *Die oberste Wehrmachtführung*, pp. 46–7.

33 "Nebe Series," 29 Dec. 1949, p. 27. Letter of 6 Feb. 1967 from Herr Jürgen Runzheimer.

34 Letter of 6 Feb. 1967 from Herr Jürgen Runzheimer. (I should like to take this opportunity of thanking Herr Runzheimer for his assistance and recommending to the reader his study "Die Grenzzwischenfälle am 30 Aug. 1939" in *Vierteljahrshefte für Zeitgeschichte*.)

35 Shirer: op cit, p. 569.

36 *Der Spiegel*, 13 Nov. 1963, p. 74.

37 Ibid. Runzheimer: op cit, p. 425.

38 *Der Spiegel*, 13 Nov. 1963, pp. 74–5.

39 Runzheimer: op cit, p. 415.

40 *Der Spiegel*, 13 Nov. 1963, p. 74.

41 Ibid, pp. 74–5. Runzheimer: op cit, p. 415.

42 Ibid, p. 75.

43 Schnabel: op cit, p. 390.

44 *Völkischer Beobachter*, 1 Sept. 1939.

45 Quoted from Thorwald: op cit, p. 14.

46 Runzheimer: op cit, p. 409.

47 Ibid.

48 Ibid.

49 "Nebe Series" 29 Dec. 1949, p. 27.

50 Ibid.

51 Knoebel: *Racial Illusion and Military Necessity*, p. 226.

52 Buchheim: *SS und Polizei im NS-Staat*, p. 168.

53 "Die Erhebung der österreichischen Nationalsozialisten im Juli 1934," Report by th[e] Reichsführer-SS Historical Com[m]ission, p. 68.

54 Adolf Eichmann: Record [of] proceedings, Vol. 1, Col. 36.

55 "Die Erhebung" (see No[te] 53), p. 68.

56 Ibid.

57 Ibid.

58 Ibid, p. 69.

59 Ibid, p. 67.

60 Ibid, p. 71.

61 Ibid, p. 70.

62 Ibid.

63 Ibid.

64 Ibid.

65 Ibid.

66 Ibid.

67 Ibid, p. 77. Gordon She[p]herd: *Dollfuss*, p. 235.

68 Shepherd: op cit, 213, 233.

69 Letter from Wächter to th[e] Supreme Party Court of th[e] NSDAP, 31 May 1938, RFS[S] Microfilm 32.

70 Shepherd: op cit, p. 237.

71 Ibid.

72 Ibid.

73 Letter from Wächter to Su[p]preme Party Court, p. 8, RFS[S] Microfilm 32.

74 Ibid, pp. 7–8.

75 Submission by Wächter [at] the Hamburg trial Jan. 1937, p[p.] 4–5, RFSS Microfilm 32.

76 Ibid, p. 4.

77 Ibid, p. 7.

78 Ibid, p. 5.

79 Ibid.

80 Ibid.

81 Hellmuth Auerbach: "Ein[e] nationalsozialistische Stimm[e] zum Wiener Putsch vom 25 Ju[li] 1934." in *Vierteljahrshefte fü[r] Zeitgeschichte*, Apr. 1964, p. 20[?]

82 Wächter's submission (se[e] Note 75), p. 8.

3 Shepherd: op cit, p. 243.
4 "Die Erhebung" (see Note 3), p. 81.
5 Shepherd: op cit, p. 243.
6 "Die Erhebung," p. 84.
7 Ibid, pp. 81–2.
8 Ibid, p. 81.
9 Wächter's letter to Supreme Party Court, p. 10.
0 "Die Erhebung," p. 82.
1 Ibid, p. 84.
2 Ibid, p. 85.
3 Ibid.
4 Shepherd; op cit, p. 249–50.
5 "Die Erhebung," p. 85.
6 Ibid, p. 88.
7 Ibid.
8 Ibid, p. 89.
9 Ibid, pp. 89, 94, 96.
00 Ibid, pp. 94, 96.
01 Ibid, p. 92.
02 Shepherd: op cit, p. 309.
03 Ibid, p. 310. "Die Erhebung," p. 102.
04 Ibid, p. 311.
05 "Die Erhebung," p. 128.
06 Ibid, p. 132. Wächter's submission (see Note 75) p. 10.
07 Ibid, p. 132.
08 Wächter's submission, p. 9.
09 "Die Erhebung," p. 140.
10 Papen: Memoirs, pp. 337–8.
11 Bullock: op cit, p. 328.
12 Wächter's submission, pp. 9–11.
13 Volz: Daten der Geschichte der NSDAP, p. 34. Louis de Jong: Die deutsche Fünfte Kolonne im Zweiten Weltkrieg, 260.
14 Ibid, p. 263.
15 Ibid.
16 MacAlister Brown: "The Third Reich's mobilisation of the German Fifth Column in Eastern Europe" in Journal of Central European Affairs, July 1959, p. 129.
117 de Jong: op cit, p. 264. Koehl: op cit, pp. 36–7.
118 Buchheim: Anatomy of the SS State, p. 284. Robert Koehl: "Towards an SS Typology: Social Engineers" in American Journal of Economics and Sociology, No. 18, Jan. 1959, p. 117.
119 Koehl: RKFVD, p. 39.
120 Ibid, p. 27.
121 de Jong: op cit, p. 264.
122 Ibid.
123 Ibid.
124 Ibid.
125 Neusüss-Hunkel: Die SS, pp. 81–2.
126 Organisationsbuch der NSDAP, p. 151.
127 Heinrich Orb: National-sozialismus, p. 389.
128 Wulf: Die SS, p. 96.
129 Ribbentrop: Memoirs, p. 22. Von Papen: Memoirs, p. 235.
130 Ribbentrop: op cit, p. 22 (Note).
131 Ribbentrop: Zwischen London und Moskau, p. 37 (not in English translation).
132 Neusüss-Hunkel: op cit, p. 82.
133 Seabury: The Wilhelm-strasse, p. 108.
134 Ibid.
135 Ibid, p. 106.
136 Ernst-Günther Krätsch-mer: Die Ritterkreuzträger der Waffen-SS, p. 208.
137 Erich Kordt: Nicht aus den Akten, p. 188.
138 Ibid. Weizsäcker was made SS-Brigadeführer in 1942 (see SS Seniority List, 1944).
139 Kordt: op cit, p. 188. Woermann was promoted SS-

Oberführer in 1942 (see SS seniority list 1944).

140 Kordt: op cit, p. 188.

141 Ibid.

142 Kempner: SS im Kreuzverhör, pp. 244–5.

143 Verbal information from Dr Werner Best, 5 Feb. 1966.

144 Hagen (alias Höttl): Die geheime Front, p. 142.

145 Ibid.

146 Ibid, pp. 123, 131.

147 Kurt Glaser: Die Tschechoslowakei, p. 52.

148 Hagen: op cit, p. 126.

149 Ibid, p. 138.

150 Ibid, pp. 144, 146.

151 Ibid, p. 156.

152 SS seniority List 1944.

153 Brown: op cit, p. 133.

154 Hagen: op cit, p. 174.

155 Ibid.

156 Ibid, p. 175.

157 Ibid.

158 Ibid, p. 541.

159 Ibid.

160 Letter from Keppler to Himmler, 11 July 1939, RFSS Microfilm 32.

161 Bullock: Hitler, a Study in Tyranny, p. 483.

162 Hagen: op cit, p. 76.

163 Ibid, p. 177.

164 Letter from Keppler to Himmler, 11 July 1939, RFSS Microfilm 32.

165 de Jong: op cit, p. 148.

166 Ribbentrop: op cit, p. 82.

167 Seabury: The Wilhelmstrasse, p. 194.

168 de Jong: op cit, p. 168

169 "Wenn ihr einmarschiert, schiessen wir," Der Spiegel No. 18, 1963, pp. 77 et seq.

170 Hagen: op cit, pp. 280 et seq.

171 Letter from Heydrich to the Foreign Ministry, 20 June 1941, RFSS Microfilm 199.

172 Seabury: op cit, p. 129. Ribbentrop op cit, p. 82.

173 Führer order, 3 Sept. 1939, RFSS Microfilm 199.

174 Schellenberg: Memoirs, p. 82.

175 S. Payne Best: The Venlo Incident, pp. 7–8. Schellenberg op cit, pp. 82–3.

176 Schellenberg: op cit, p. 85.

177 Ibid, p. 85.

178 Ibid.

179 Ibid.

180 Ibid, p. 86.

181 Ibid, p. 88.

182 Ibid, p. 91.

183 Ibid, p. 94.

184 Dr Werner Best: Joachim von Ribbentrop, p. 2.

185 Manuscript for discussion "Das bestellte Attentat," 2 July 1965, Channel 1 German TV, p. 5.

186 Schellenberg: op cit, p. 94.

187 Ibid, p. 95.

188 Ibid, p. 96.

189 Ibid, p. 97.

190 Ibid, pp. 101, 103

191 Ibid, p. 104.

192 Ibid.

193 Ibid.

194 "Nebe Series," 5 Jan. 1950, p. 24. Dr Albrecht Böhme: "Das Bürgerbräu-attentat" (MS), p. See also, by the same author, "Das Attentat auf Hitler im Bürgerbräukeller, kein Werk des englischen Geheimdienstes," in D Kriminalistik, No. 10, 1966.

195 Böhme: MS pp. 6–7 (see Note 194 above).

196 Record of interrogation Elser, Der Stern, 10 May 196

197 "Nebe Series," 5 Jan. 1950, p. 24. Böhme MS, p. 11.

198 Schellenberg: op cit, p. 110.

199 *Der Stern,* 17 May 1964, p. 34.

200 Böhme: MS, pp. 9–10 (see Note 194 above).

201 Statement by Haber in *Bild am Sonntag,* 6 Dec. 1959.

202 Schellenberg: op cit, p. 91 (German original—not in English translation).

203 "Das bestellte Attentat," p. 26 (see Note 185 above).

204 Schellenberg: op cit, p. 179.

205 Hagen: op cit, p. 283.

206 Ibid, p. 206.

207 Martin Broszat: "Das Dritte Reich und die rumänische Judenpolitik" in *Gutachten des Instituts für Zeitgeschichte,* p. 21.

208 Hagen: op cit, pp. 288–9.

209 Broszat: op cit, p. 124.

210 Hagen: op cit, p. 290.

211 Ibid. Broszat: op cit, p. 126.

212 Letter from Andreas Schmidt to Berger, 24 Sept 1943, RFSS Microfilm 128.

213 Hagen: op cit, p. 282

214 Letter from Heydrich to Foreign Ministry, 20 June 1941, RFSS Microfilm 199.

215 Seabury: op cit, p. 128.

216 Ibid.

217 Letter from Ribbentrop to Himmler 6 Sept. 1942, RFSS Microfilm 117.

218 Seabury: op cit, pp. 127, 194.

219 Verbal information from Dr Werner Best, 5 Feb. 1966.

CHAPTER TWELVE

Helmut Krausnick and others: "Denkschrift Himmlers über die Behandlung der Fremdvölkischen im Osten" in *Vierteljahrshefte für Zeitgeschichte,* Apr. 1957, p. 194.

Ibid, p. 196.

Ibid, p. 198.

Ibid, p. 197.

Ibid.

Helmut Heiber: "Der Generalplan Ost" in *Vierteljahrshefte für Zeitgeschichte,* Issue 3 of 1958, p. 284.

Kersten: *Totenkopf und Treue,* p. 132.

Neusüss-Hunkel: *Die SS,* p. 2.

Ibid, p. 71.

10 Ibid, p. 72.

11 Koehl: *RKFVD,* p. 27.

12 Ibid, p. 43. *Gutachten des Institut für Zeitgeschichte,* p. 46.

13 Ibid, p. 42.

14 Ibid, p. 43.

15 *Mein Kampf* (James Murphy's translation, Hurst & Blackett, 1939), p. 533.

16 Martin Broszat: *Nationalsozialistische Polenpolitik 1939–45,* p. 21.

17 Case for the prosecution against Karl Wolff for participation in mass murder, Public Prosecutor's Office, Provincial Court Munich II, Ref. 10aJS 39/60, p. 86.

18 Buchheim: *Anatomy of the SS State,* pp. 176–7.

19 Ibid.

20 Ibid.

21 Ibid.

22 Wulf: *Die SS,* pp. 242–3.

23 Ibid, p. 239.

24 Ibid.

25 Ibid, p. 240.

26 Ibid.

27 Ibid.
28 Helmut Krausnick: "Hitler und die Morde in Polen" in *Vierteljahrshefte für Zeitgeschichte,* April 1963, p. 198.
29 Ibid.
30 Ibid.
31 Ibid, p. 205.
32 Ibid, p. 207.
33 Case against Wolff (see Note 17 above), p. 87.
34 Ibid, pp. 87–8. Wulf: *Die SS,* p. 246.
35 Krausnick: op cit, p. 203.
36 Broszat: *Nationalsozialistische Polenpolitik,* p. 28.
37 Ibid, p. 45.
38 Ibid, p. 39.
39 Ibid, p. 45.
40 Ibid.
41 Ibid, p. 44.
42 Note by Schellenberg following a Heads of Section conference on 27 Sept. 1940, RFSS Microfilm 239.
43 de Jong: *Die deutsche Fünfte Kolonne im Zweiten Weltkrieg,* p. 54.
44 Ibid, pp. 55–6.
45 Ibid, p. 57.
46 Ibid.
47 Broszat: op cit, p. 47.
48 Ibid, p. 60.
49 Ibid, p. 28.
50 Ibid, pp. 29, 45, 46.
51 Ibid, p. 61.
52 Ibid.
53 Ibid.
54 Henkys: *Die nationalsozialistischen Gewaltverbrechen,* p. 82.
55 Krausnick: "Hitler und die Morde in Polen", p. 203.
56 Ibid, p. 198.
57 Reitlinger: *The Final Solution,* p. 37.
58 Hilberg: *The Destruction of the European Jews,* pp. 127–8.

59 Case against Wolff, p. 90.
60 Broszat: *Nationalsozialistische Polenpolitik,* p. 27.
61 Krausnick: op cit, p. 203.
62 Broszat: op cit, p. 28.
63 Case against Wolff, p. 94.
64 Ibid.
65 Broszat: op cit, p. 29.
66 Hilberg: op cit, pp. 129–31.
67 Krausnick: op cit, p. 202. Broszat: op cit, p. 22.
68 Broszat: op cit, p. 29.
69 Ibid.
70 Ibid, p. 58.
71 Ibid.
72 Buchheim: *Anatomy of the SS State,* pp. 213–4.
73 Broszat: op cit, p. 58.
74 Ibid, pp. 28, 58.
75 Ibid, p. 58.
76 Ibid.
77 Ibid.
78 Krausnick: op cit, p. 203.
79 Broszat: op cit, p. 78.
80 Ibid, pp. 74–5–6.
81 Krausnick: op cit, p. 204.
82 Broszat: op cit, p. 41.
83 Ibid.
84 Ibid.
85 Schnabel: *Macht ohne Moral,* p. 395.
86 Ibid, p. 396.
87 Wulf: *Das Dritte Reich und seine Diener,* p. 518.
88 Hilberg: op cit, p. 127. Broszat: op cit, p. 40.
89 Broszat: op cit, p. 204.
90 Krausnick: op cit, p. 205.
91 Broszat: op cit, p. 76.
92 Krausnick: op cit, p. 204.
93 Koehl: *RKFVD,* pp. 100, 101, 72.
94 Hans Buchheim: "Rechtsstellung und Organisation des Reichskommissars für die Festigung deutschen Volkstums" in *Gutachten des Instituts für Zeitgeschichte,* p. 275.

95 Ibid.
96 Koehl: "SS Typology", p. 115; *RKFVD*, p. 48.
97 Buchheim: *Rechtstellung RKF*, p. 276.
98 Ibid.
99 Ibid, p. 245.
100 Ibid.
101 Ibid.
102 Koehl: *RKFVD*, p. 49.
103 Ibid.
104 Ibid, p. 50.
105 Buchheim: *Anatomy of the SS State*, pp. 274–6. Decree of the Führer and Reich Chancellor for the Strengthening of Germanism, 7 Oct. 1939, RFSS Microfilm 239.
106 Ibid.
107 Buchheim: *Rechtsstellung RKF*, p. 245.
108 Ibid, p. 247.
109 Ibid, pp. 245–7.
110 Ibid, p. 261.
111 Ibid, p. 267.
112 Ibid, p. 265.
113 Koehl: *RKFVD*, p. 62.
114 Buchheim: *Rechtsstellung RKF*, pp. 248–9.
115 Koehl: *RKFVD*, pp. 62–3.
116 Ibid, p. 63.
117 Ibid.
118 Wulf: *Die SS*, p. 186.
119 Koehl: *RKFVD*, pp. 56, 73.
120 Buchheim: *Rechtsstellung RKF*, p. 270.
121 Ibid.
122 Koehl: *RKFVD*, p. 59.
123 Ibid.
124 Wulf: *Die SS*, p. 182.
125 Broszat: *Nationalsozialistische Polenpolitik*, pp. 63–4.
126 Koehl: *RKFVD*, p. 121.
127 Ibid, p. 130.
128 Ibid, p. 86.
129 Ibid, pp. 216–7.
130 Buchheim: *Rechtsstellung RKF*, p. 271. Koehl: op cit, pp. 120–1.
131 Wulf: *Die SS*, p. 195.
132 Ibid, p. 197.
133 Ibid, p. 200.
134 Ibid.
135 Ibid, pp. 101–2. Koehl: *RKFVD*, p. 144.
136 Ibid, pp. 205–6.
137 Koehl: *RKFVD*, pp. 212–3.
138 Broszat: *Nationalsozialistische Polenpolitik*, p. 93.
139 Ibid.
140 Letter from Willich to Kaltenbrunner, 16 Apr. 1943, RFSS Microfilm 117.
141 Broszat: op cit, p. 93.
142 Koehl: *RKFVD*, p. 146.
143 Heiber: *Generalplan Ost*, p. 285.
144 Ibid, pp. 298–9.
145 Ibid, p. 291.
146 Ibid, pp. 291–2.
147 Ibid, p. 297.
148 Ibid, p. 246.
149 Kersten: op cit, p. 133.
150 Ibid.
151 Wulf: *Das Dritte Reich und seine Vollstrecker*, p. 262.
152 Ibid, p. 271.
153 Koehl: *RKFVD*, p. 133.
154 Ibid, pp. 226–7.
155 Ibid, p. 227.
156 Ibid, p. 134.
157 Ibid, p. 152.
158 Gilbert: *The Psychology of Dictatorship*, p. 143.
159 IMT Vol. XXIX, p. 443.
160 Ibid, p. 444.
161 Ibid.
162 Ibid, p. 455.
163 Ibid.
164 Koehl: *RKFVD*, p. 130.
165 Broszat: *Nationalsozialistische Polenpolitik*, p. 183.
166 Verbal information from Gottlob Berger, 1 Feb. 1966.
167 Broszat, op cit, p. 81.
168 IMT Vol. XXIX, p. 507.
169 Ibid, p. 379.

170 Broszat: op cit, p. 82.
171 Letter from Reinecke to Himmler, 1 Dec. 1941, RFSS Microfilm 125.
172 Ibid.
173 Ibid.
174 Ibid.
175 Ibid.
176 Ibid.
177 Ibid.
178 Broszat: op cit, p. 82.
179 Office minute by Himmler dated 5 Mar. 1942, RFSS Microfilm 125.
180 Ibid.
181 Letter from Frank to Lammers, 10 Mar. 1942, RFSS Microfilm 125.
182 Lammers to Himmler 7 Mar. 1942. Führer decree on prerogatives of the Reichsführer-

SS and Chief of the German Police in the Government General, RFSS Microfilm 125. Broszat: *Nationalsozialistische Polenpolitik*, p. 83. Hilberg: op cit, p. 132.
183 IMT Vol. XXIX, p. 514.
184 Gilbert: op cit, p. 147.
185 IMT Vol. XXIX, p. 520.
186 Ibid, pp. 527, 519.
187 Ibid, p. 533.
188 Ibid, p. 537.
189 Ibid, p. 534.
190 Ibid, p. 555.
191 Ibid, p. 559.
192 Wulf: *Das Dritte Reich und seine Vollstrecker*, pp. 171–2.
193 Broszat: *Nationalsozialistische Polenpolitik*, p. 84.

CHAPTER THIRTEEN

1 Kersten: *Totenkopf und Treue*, p. 119.
2 Ibid.
3 Ibid, p. 120.
4 Ibid, p. 161.
5 Ibid, pp. 161–2.
6 Hans Lamm: *Über die innere und äussere Entwicklung des deutschen Judentums im Dritten Reich*, p. 94.
7 Ibid, p. 95.
8 See Wighton: *Heydrich*, p. 162.
9 Henry A. Zeiger: *The Case against Adolf Eichmann*, p. 100.
10 Case against Wolff, p. 108. Krausnick: *Denkschrift Himmlers*, pp. 194 et seq.
11 "Des nationalsozialistichen Menschen Ehre und Ehrenschutz", in *Deutsche Justiz* of 1938, p. 1660.
12 Krausnick: *Anatomy of the SS State*, pp. 11–12.

13 Buchheim: *Das Dritte Reich*, p. 41.
14 Wilhelm Schallmayer: *Vererbung und Auslese im Lebenslauf der Völker*.
15 Krausnick: op cit, p. 14.
16 Himmler: *Die Schutzstaffel als antibolschewistische Kampforganisation*, p. 3.
17 "Judentum, Freimaurerei, Bolschewismus" Part 1, issued by Head of RuSHA, undated (approx. 1936) pp. 10 et seq and 39, RFSS Microfilm 161.
18 *Das Schwarze Korps*, 5 June 1935.
19 Ibid.
20 Gestapo memorandum, 2 Oct. 1935, RFSS Microfilm 402.
21 Eichmann: Record of interrogation, Vol. 1, Col. 328.
22 Office minute by Hagen, 21 July 1938, RFSS Microfilm 509.

23 Office minute by Hagen, undated, RFSS Microfilm 509.
24 Office minute by Hagen, undated (approx. summer 1938), RFSS Microfilm 415.
25 Ibid.
26 Verbal information from Leopold von Mildenstein, 20 Nov. 1966.
27 Reinhard Höhn: *Artur Mahraun*, p. 61.
28 Lamm: op cit, p. 72.
29 Ibid, p. 53.
30 Ibid, p. 42.
31 Ibid, pp. 37–40.
32 Ibid, p. 45.
33 *Völkischer Beobachter*, 9 May 1935.
34 *Jüdischer Rundschau*, 2 July 1935.
35 Lamm: op cit, p. 48.
36 Ibid, p. 215.
37 Ibid, p. 144.
38 *Jüdischer Rundschau*, 28 April 1933.
39 Lamm: op cit, p. 161.
40 Ibid, p. 156.
41 Ibid, p. 149. Eichmann: Record of interrogation Vol. 1, Col. 67.
42 *Das Schwarze Korps*, 15 May 1935.
43 Lamm: op cit, p. 233.
44 Eichmann: Record of interrogation, Vol. 1, Cols. 61 et seq.
45 "Die Organisation der Judenheit, ihre Verbindungen und politische Bedeutung"—notes for an address by Hagen, 23 Sept. 1938, p. 2, RFSS Microfilm, 411.
46 Ibid.
47 Ibid, pp. 9–10.
48 Eichmann: Record of interrogation, Vol. 1, Cols. 6, 11, 61, 62.
49 Ibid, Col. 63.
50 Ibid, Col. 26. Ahrendt: *Eich-*

mann in Jerusalem, pp. 57–8. Reitlinger: *The Final Solution*, pp. 23–27.
51 Verbal information from von Mildenstein, 20 Nov. 1966.
52 Eichmann: Record of interrogation, Vol. 1, Col. 68.
53 Bracha Habas: *The Gatebreakers*, p. 49.
54 Arendt: *Eichmann in Jerusalem, p.* 36–7. Kempner: *Eichmann und Komplizen*, p. 39.
55 "Die Zionistische Weltorganization", Report prepared by Eichmann and Hagen, 20 Oct. 1936, RFSS Microfilm 411.
56 Ibid, Part II, p. 1.
57 Hagen's notes (see Note 45 above), Part B, p. 36.
58 Statement on oath by Dr H. Ehlich, Ohlendorf trial, Document volume, p. 2 (in Frau Käthe Ohlendorff's private papers).
59 "Die Zionistische Weltorganisation" (see Note 55 above), Part II, p. 3.
60 Eichmann: Record of Hearings, Vol. 1, Col. 69. Report on trip to Egypt and Palestine by Eichmann and Hagen 4 Nov. 1937 Part I, pp. 1–2, Part IV, p. 2.
61 "Die Zionistische Weltorganisation" Part I, p. 7.
62 Hagen's report, 17 June 1937, RFSS Microfilm 411.
63 Ibid.
64 Eichmann: Record of Hearings, Vol. 1, Col. 90. Hagen report 17 June 1937.
65 Hagen report, p. 4.
66 Ibid.
67 Ibid.
68 Ibid.
69 Eichmann: Record of interrogation, Vol. 1, Col. 90. Report on trip to Egypt and Palestine.

70 Ibid (Eichmann).

71 Ibid.

72 Report on Egypt and Palestine, p. 1.

73 Ibid, p. 33.

74 Ibid, p. 32.

75 Eichmann: Record of interrogation, Vol. 1, Col. 94.

76 Ibid, Cols. 94, 96, 108.

77 Ibid, Col. 101.

78 Ibid, Cols. 103, 107, 108. Kempner: *Eichmann und Komplizen*, p. 218.

79 Arendt: *Eichmann in Jerusalem*, pp. 39–40.

80 Ibid, p. 40. Kempner: op cit, p. 45.

81 Letter from Hagen, 24 June 1938, RFSS Microfilm 411.

82 Arendt: *Eichmann in Jerusalem*, p. 39. "Das Judentum in Deutschland", Memorandum by Desk II 112, 15 June 1939, RFSS Microfilm 411.

83 Note by Eichmann, 7 June 1938, RFSS Microfilm 415.

84 Ibid. Letter from Hiemer to Eichmann, 30 May 1938, RFSS Microfilm 415.

85 Letter from Hagen to Eichmann, 28 June 1938, RFSS Microfilm 415.

86 Ibid.

87 Letter from Six to Desk II 112, 23 June 1938, RFSS Microfilm 415.

88 Lionel Kochan: *Pogrom*, pp. 36 et seq.

89 German Foreign Policy Documents, Series D 1937–45, Vol. V, pp. 98, 115, 141.

90 Kochan: op cit, p. 38.

91 Hermann Graml: "Der 9 November 1938" in *Das Parlament*, 11 Nov. 1953, p. 7.

92 Ibid.

93 Hilberg: *The Destruction of the European Jews*, p. 23.

94 Kochan: op cit, p. 51.

95 IMT Vol. XX, p. 292.

96 IMT Vol. XIV, p. 422.

97 Kochan: op cit, pp. 52–3.

98 "Urkunden zur Judenpolitik des Dritten Reiches" in *Das Parlament*, 10 Nov. 1954, p. 582.

99 Ibid.

100 Kochan: op cit, p. 106.

101 Ibid, p. 55. Graml: op cit, p. 9.

102 Ibid.

103 IMT Vol. XX, p. 133.

104 IMT Vol. XLII, pp. 511–3, Vol. XXI, p. 354. Kochan: op cit, p. 55.

105 Graml: op cit, p. 9.

106 IMT Vol. XLII, p. 512.

107 Ibid.

108 Ibid, p. 511.

109 IMT Vol. XXXI, p. 516.

110 IMT Vol. XXI, p. 392.

111 Statement on oath by Fritz Schulz, 30 Sept. 1947, Ohlendorf trial, document book (in Frau Käthe Ohlendorf's private papers).

112 Statement by Hafiz Khan, *Frankfurter Allgemeine Zeitung*, 15 Sept. 1964.

113 IMT Vol. XX, p. 294.

114 Hassell: *Vom anderen Deutschland*, p. 34.

115 Ibid, p. 27.

116 Graml: op cit, p. 15.

117 IMT Vol. IX, p. 277. Kochan: op cit, p. 107.

118 "Urkunden zur Judenpolitik des Dritten Reiches", p. 585.

119 IMT Vol. IX, p. 277.

120 IMT Vol. XXI, p. 392.

121 Burckhardt: op cit, p. 227.

122 Ibid, p. 228.

123 Ibid.

124 Ibid, p. 230.

125 Schellenberg: *Memoiren*, p. 59 (not in English translation).

126 Burckhardt: *Meine Danziger Mission 1937–1939*, p. 230.

127 Ibid, p. 124.

128 "Urkunden zur Judenpolitik", p. 585.

129 IMT Vol. XXVI, p. 266.

130 Krausnick: *Anatomy of the SS State*, p. 46.

131 Ibid, p. 43.

132 Lamm: op cit, pp. 81, 217.

133 Ibid, p. 223.

134 Ibid. Poliakov and Wulf: *Das Dritte Reich und die Juden*, p. 120.

135 Ibid. *Keesing's Contemporary Archives 1937*, p. 3240B.

136 Habas: op cit, p. 71; *Schulthess' Europäische Geschichtskalender 1938*, p. 541, and 1939, p. 354. Jon and David Kimche: *The Secret Roads*, p. 40.

137 Habas: op cit, p. 23. Kimche: op cit, p. 40.

138 Kimche: op cit, p. 15. Habas: op cit, p. 48.

139 "Das Judentum in Deutschland", Memorandum by Desk II 112, 15 June 1939, RFSS Microfilm 411.

140 *German Foreign Policy Documents*, Series D, Vol. V, pp. 780, 784.

141 Kimche: op cit, p. 31.

142 Ibid, p. 32.

143 Ibid.

144 Ibid, p. 39.

145 Ibid, pp. 33, 34, 35. Habas: op cit, pp. 61, 63.

146 Ibid, pp. 35, 39.

147 Ibid, p. 41.

148 Ibid.

149 Ibid, pp. 41–2. *Schulthess 1939*, p. 362.

150 Ibid, p. 43.

151 Krausnick: *Anatomy of the SS State*, p. 48.

152 Eichmann: Record of Interrogation, Vol. 1, Cols. 126–7.

153 Krausnick: op cit, p. 48.

154 Eichmann: Record of Interrogation, Vol. 1, Cols. 127, 128, 132.

155 Ibid, Col. 128.

156 Ibid, Col. 121.

157 Ibid, Col. 124.

158 Office note on conference of heads of Ämter and Einsatzgruppen, 27 Sept. 1939, RFSS Microfilm 239.

159 Ibid.

160 Case against Wolff, pp. 90–1.

161 Eichmann: Record of Interrogation, Vol. 1, Col. 125. Reitlinger: *The Final Solution*, pp. 43 et seq.

162 Krausnick: *Anatomy of the SS State*, p. 54. Reitlinger: op cit, p. 42. Hilberg: op cit, p. 138.

163 Eichmann: Record of Interrogation, Vol. 1, Col. 121.

164 Hilberg: op cit, pp. 138–9.

165 Reitlinger: op cit, p. 45.

166 Krausnick: op cit, pp. 56–7. Reitlinger: op cit, pp. 76 et seq.

167 Eichmann: Record of Interrogation, Vol. 1, Col. 137.

168 Reitlinger: op cit, p. 77.

169 Ibid, p. 76. *German Foreign Policy Documents*, Series D, Vol. IV, pp. 420–1.

170 Bernhard Lösener: "Als Rassereferent im Reichsministerium des Innern" in *Vierteljahrshefte für Zeitgeschichte*, 1961, Issue 3, pp. 296 et seq.

171 Paul Schmidt: *Hitler's Interpreter*, p. 178.

172 Eichmann: Record of Interrogation, Vol. 1, Col. 140.

CHAPTER FOURTEEN

1 *German Foreign Policy Documents*, Series D, Vol. IV, p. 170.

2 Domarus: *Hitler Reden und Proklamationen 1932–45*, Vol. II, p. 1058.

3 Krausnick: *Anatomy of the SS State*, p. 63.

4 Ibid, p. 60.

5 Warlimont: *Inside Hitler's Headquarters*, pp. 150–1. Jacobsen: *Anatomy of the SS State*, pp. 512–4. Uhlig: "Der verbrecherische Befehl" in *Das Parlament*, 17 July 1957, p. 431.

6 Warlimont: op cit, pp. 157–9.

7 Schellenberg: *Memoirs*, p. 210.

8 Uhlig: op cit, p. 432. Warlimont: op cit, p. 161.

9 Jacobsen: *Anatomy of the SS State*, p. 532. Warlimont: op cit, p. 162.

10 Warlimont: op cit, pp. 158–160. Uhlig: op cit, p. 432. Schellenberg: op cit, pp. 213–4. Hilberg: op cit, p. 183.

11 Warlimont: op cit, pp. 158–9. Uhlig: op cit, p. 432.

12 Warlimont: op cit, pp. 158–9.

13 Jacobsen: *Anatomie des SS Staates*, Vol. 2, p. 206 (not in English translation).

14 "Nebe Series", 2 Feb. 1950, p. 24.

15 Ibid.

16 Hans-Bernd Gisevius: *Wo ist Nebe?*, p. 240.

17 Ibid, p. 244.

18 Krausnick: *Anatomy of the SS State*, p. 64.

19 "Nebe Series", 2 Feb. 1950, p. 25.

20 Verbal information from Frau Käthe Ohlendorf, 26 Jan. 1966.

21 Hilberg: *The Destruction of the European Jews*, p. 189. Statement by Ohlendorf, IMT Vol. XLII, p. 446.

22 Reitlinger: *The Final Solution*, p. 186.

23 Ibid, p. 192. Kempner: *SS im Kreuzverhör*, p. 281.

24 Ibid, pp. 192 et seq.

25 Wulf: *Die SS*, pp. 273 et seq.

26 Kempner: *SS im Kreuzverhör*, pp. 284 et seq.

27 Bomhard: IMT Vol. XLII, pp. 636, 644.

28 "Nebe Series", 2 Feb. 1950, p. 24.

29 Case against Wolff, p. 128. Reitlinger: op cit, p. 189.

30 Hilberg: op cit, p. 189.

31 Ibid.

32 Ohlendorf's statement, IMT Vol. IV, p. 313. C. Aubrey Dixon and Otto Heilbrunn: *Communist Guerilla Warfare*, p. 99. Kempner: *SS im Kreuzverhör*, p. 19.

33 "Nebe Series", 2 Feb. 1950, p. 24.

34 Ibid.

35 Krausnick: *Anatomy of the SS State*, p. 63.

36 Ohlendorf's plea in mitigation, p. 28.

37 Ibid, pp. 29–30.

38 Wulf: *Die SS*, p. 252. Hilberg: op cit, p. 188.

39 Wulf: *Die SS*, p. 261.

40 Hilberg: op cit, pp. 189–90.

41 Ibid, p. 207.

42 Ibid, p. 190.

43 Ibid, p. 191.

44 Kempner: *SS im Kreuzverhör*, p. 28.

45 Case against Wolff, p. 143.

46 Kempner: op cit, p. 25.

47 Ibid, p. 22.
48 Ibid.
49 Ibid, p. 23.
50 Ibid.
51 Ibid, p. 28.
52 Ibid, p. 29.
53 Ibid.
54 IMT Vol. VII, p. 535. Henkys: *Die nationalsozialistischen Gewaltverbrechen*, p. 117.
55 Henkys: op cit, p. 117.
56 Ibid, p. 118.
57 Ibid, p. 120.
58 Krausnick: *Anatomy of the SS State*, p. 64. Henkys: op cit, pp. 114–16.
59 Ibid, p. 66. Case against Wolff, p. 122.
60 Ibid, p. 62. Hilberg: op cit, pp. 193, 243.
61 Hilberg: op cit, p. 196.
62 Ibid, pp. 196, 225.
63 Reitlinger: op cit, p. 192.
64 Ibid, p. 187.
65 "Nebe Series", 2 Feb. 1950, p. 26. Gisevius: *Wo ist Nebe?*, p. 244.
66 "Nebe Series", 2 Feb. 1950, p. 26.
67 Case against Wolff, p. 161.
68 Quoted from *Süddeutsche Zeitung*, 25 July 1964.
69 Quoted from *Frankfurter Rundschau*, 10 July 1958. *Abendpost*, 14 July 1961.
70 Letter from Herf to Maximilian von Herff, 29 July 1943, RFSS Microfilm 38.
71 Hilberg: op cit, p. 440.
72 Wulf: *Die SS*, p. 269.
73 Poliakov and Wulf: *Das Dritte Reich und seine Diener*, p. 383.
74 IMT Vol. XXIX, p. 145.
75 Case against Wolff, p. 317.
76 Ibid, pp. 317–8.
77 Kersten: op cit, p. 151.
78 Buchheim: *Anatomy of the SS State*, p. 338.
79 Case against Wolff, p. 365.
80 Hilberg: op cit, pp. 218–9.
81 Crankshaw: *Gestapo*, pp. 128–9.
82 Hilberg: op cit, pp. 209–210. Reitlinger: op cit, pp. 207–8. Crankshaw, op cit, p. 129.
83 Hilberg: op cit, p. 215.
84 Ibid.
85 Ibid.
86 Ibid, p. 217.
87 Ibid, p. 216.
88 Ibid, p. 217.
89 Ibid. Reitlinger: op cit, p. 232.
90 "Niederschrift über Beobachtungen während meines Besuches in Italien vom 11 bis 14 Oktober 1942", memorandum by Himmler dated 22 Oct. 1942, RFSS Microfilm 69.
91 Hilberg: op cit, p. 196.
92 Ibid, p. 197.
93 Ibid.
94 Ibid, p. 198.
95 IMT Vol. XXXV, p. 85.
96 Hilberg: op cit, p. 198.
97 Ibid.
98 Dixon and Heilbrunn: op cit, pp. 143–4.
99 Hilberg: op cit, p. 199.
100 Ibid, p. 224.
101 Bor: *Gespräche mit Halder*, p. 197.
102 Reitlinger: *The House built on Sand*, p. 233; *The Final Solution*, p. 189.
103 Reitlinger: *The House built on Sand*, p. 232.
104 Hilberg: op cit, pp. 242–3.
105 Ibid, p. 243.
106 Ibid, p. 244.
107 Ibid, p. 251.
108 See detailed accounts of individual operations in Hilberg (op cit) and Reitlinger (*The House built on Sand*).

109 Hilberg: op cit, p. 250.

110 Case against Wolff, p. 137.
IMT Vol. XXXVII, p. 670.

111 IMT Vol. XXVII, p. 4.

112 Ibid, p. 6.

113 Ibid, p. 3.

114 Ibid.

115 Helmut Heiber: "Aus den Akten des Gauleiters Kube" in *Vierteljahrshefte für Zeitgeschichte*, Issue 1, 1956, p. 68.

116 Ibid.

117 Ibid, p. 67.

118 Letter from Strauch to Bach-Zelewski, 25 July 1943, RFSS Microfilm 59.

119 Office minute by Strauch, 20 July 1943, RFSS Microfilm 59.

120 Ibid.

121 Heiber: "Aus den Akten des Gauleiters Kube", p. 84.

122 Ibid.

123 Hilberg: op cit, p. 254.

124 Letter from Strauch to Bach-Zelewski, 25 July 1943.

125 Heiber: op cit, p. 76.

126 IMT Vol. XXXVIII, p. 373.

127 Ibid, p. 371.

128 Heiber: op cit, p. 77. Reitlinger: op cit, pp. 288–9.

129 Hilberg: op cit, p. 254.

130 Ibid, pp. 256, 767.

131 Henkys: op cit, p. 124.

132 Hilberg: op cit, p. 309. Henkys: op cit, p. 95. Poliakov and Wulf: op cit, p. 197. Case against Wolff, p. 221.

133 Henkys: op cit, p. 97. Reitlinger: op cit, p. 137.

134 Reitlinger: op cit, p. 137.

135 Ibid, p. 139.

136 Eichmann: Record of Interrogation, Vol. 1, Cols. 175–7.

137 Henkys: op cit, p. 86.

138 Case against Wolff, p. 198. IMT Vol. XXIX, pp. 502 et seq.

139 Henkys: op cit, p. 65. Reitlinger: op cit, pp. 129 et seq.

140 Buchheim: *Anatomy of the SS State*, pp. 223–4.

141 Hilberg: op cit, p. 562.

142 Ibid.

143 Gerstein Report (quoted in Poliakov and Wulf: op cit, p. 106).

144 Poliakov and Wulf: op cit, p. 104.

145 Ibid.

146 Ibid, p. 108. Henkys: op cit, p. 109.

147 Henkys: op cit, p. 110.

148 Case against Wolff, p. 210.

149 IMT Vol. XXVII, pp. 341 et seq. Höss: op cit, p. 159.

150 Hilberg: op cit, p. 567.

151 Poliakov and Wulf: op cit, p. 106.

152 Ibid, pp. 106–7.

153 Höss: *Kommandant in Auschwitz*, pp. 176–7.

154 Letter from Himmler to Krüger, 19 July 1942, RFSS Microfilm 122.

155 Case against Wolff, p. 226.

156 Poliakov and Wulf: op cit, p. 104.

157 Wolff trial, Hassler's statement, 20 Aug. 1964, quoted from *Süddeutsche Zeitung*, 21 Aug. 64.

158 Krausnick: *Anatomy of the SS State*, p. 105.

159 Ibid.

160 Ibid, p. 108.

161 Ibid, p. 108–9. Case against Wolff, pp. 230, 233.

162 Case against Wolff, p. 234.

163 Ibid, p. 235.

164 Krausnick: op cit, p. 110.

165 Ibid, p. 111.

166 From *Süddeutsche Zeitung*, 3 Sept. 1964.

167 Case against Wolff, p. 206. Henkys: op cit, pp. 95, 103, 106,

o8, 111. Krausnick: op cit, pp. o3–4.

68 Henkys: op cit, p. 107.

69 Ibid, p. 110.

70 Statement in evidence during the Auschwitz trial, 15 Oct. 964, quoted from *Frankfurter Allgemeine Zeitung*, 16 Oct. 1964.

71 Henkys: op cit, p. 92.

72 *Frankfurter Allgemeine Zeitung*, 25 May 1964.

73 *Frankfurter Rundschau*, 6 Nov. 1964.

74 *Frankfurter Allgemeine Zeitung*, 1 Dec. 1964. Henkys: op cit, p. 208.

75 From *Die Zeit*, 27 Aug. 965.

76 Statement in evidence by Dr Lingens-Reiner during the Auschwitz trial, quoted from *Frankfurter Allgemeine Zeitung*, Mar. 1964.

77 Hannah Arendt: "Organisierte Schuld" in *Die Wandlung*, No. 4, 1945/6, p. 341.

78 From *Die Zeit*, 25 June 965.

79 Buchheim: *Anatomy of the SS State*, p. 351.

80 Ibid, p. 353.

81 Ibid, p. 365.

82 Ibid, p. 352.

83 Verbal information from Dr Konrad Morgen, 3 Feb. 1966.

84 "Nebe Series", 23 Feb. 1950, p. 24.

85 "Lady mit Lampenschirm", *Der Spiegel*, 16 Feb. 1950, p. 12.

86 Testimony by Günter Reinecke, IMT Vol. XX, pp. 419 et seq, 436–7, 496 et seq. Statement by Dr Konrad Morgen, IMT Vol. XLII, pp. 551 et seq. 563 et seq. Statement by Dr Werner Paulmann, IMT Vol. XLII, pp. 543 et seq.

187 Reinecke: IMT Vol. XX, p. 505.

188 *Der Spiegel*, 16 Feb. 1950, p. 12.

189 Ibid.

190 Ibid. Verbal information from Dr Konrad Morgen, 3 Feb. 1966. IMT Vol. XX, pp. 510 et seq.

191 Ibid.

192 *Der Spiegel*, 16 Feb. 1950, pp. 13–14. IMT Vol. XX, pp. 506 et seq.

193 "Nebe Series", 23 Feb. 1950, p. 24.

194 Hilberg: op cit, p. 579.

195 Statement by Dr Konrad Morgen, *Süddeutsche Zeitung*, 11 Mar. 1964, p. 3.

196 Ibid.

197 IMT Vol. XLII, p. 552.

198 IMT Vol. XX, pp. 439–440.

199 Ibid.

200 Ibid, p. 508.

201 IMT Vol. XLII, p. 556. IMT Vol. XX, pp. 489, 438.

202 Hilberg: op cit, p. 579.

203 IMT Vol. XLII, p. 556.

204 IMT Vol. XLII, p. 548. Hilberg: op cit, p. 579.

205 IMT Vol. XLII, p. 556. IMT Vol. XX, p. 489.

206 IMT Vol. XX, p. 378. Verbal information from "Central Office for investigation of National-Socialist crimes", Ludwigsburg, 15 Dec. 1966.

207 Hilberg: op cit, p. 579.

208 Ibid.

209 Statement by Dr Morgen, *Frankfurter Allgemeine Zeitung*, 16 Mar. 1965.

210 IMT Vol. XX, p. 507. Verbal information from Dr Konrad Morgen, 3 Feb. 1966.

211 IMT Vol. XX, p. 442.

212 IMT Vol. XXIX, p. 146.

213 Höss: op cit, p. 17.

214 Hannah Arendt: "Organisierte Schuld", pp. 340, 342.

215 Höss: op cit, p. 129.

216 Ibid, p. 111.

217 Ibid, p. 133.

218 Ibid.

219 Statement by Schultz, Süddeutsche Zeitung, 28 Aug. 1964.

220 Hilberg: op cit, p. 332.

221 Höss: op cit, p. 124.

222 Gilbert: op cit, p. 255.

223 Georg: Die wirtschaftlichen Unternehmungen der SS, pp. 38–9.

224 Ibid, p. 32.

225 IMT Vol. XXXVIII, pp. 363–4.

226 Georg: op cit, p. 114.

227 Ibid, p. 111.

228 Ibid, p. 110.

229 Ibid, p. 114.

230 Jan Triska: "Work redeems" in Journal of Central European Affairs, April 1959, p. 15.

231 Georg: op cit, pp. 58, 61.

232 Henkys: op cit, p. 88.

233 Georg: op cit, p. 93.

234 Hilberg: op cit, p. 340.

235 Georg: op cit, p. 97.

236 Ibid.

237 Höss: op cit, pp. 138–9.

238 Hilberg: op cit, p. 264.

239 Henkys: op cit, p. 136.

240 Ibid. Reitlinger: op cit, p. 329.

241 Kempner: Eichmann und Komplizen, p. 293. Hilberg: op cit, p. 441.

242 Reitlinger: op cit, p. 360.

243 Hilberg: op cit, p. 437.

244 Ibid.

245 Ibid, p. 441.

246 Ibid.

247 Henkys: op cit, p. 144.

248 Hilberg: op cit, pp. 442–3. Henkys: op cit, p. 147.

249 Ibid, p. 443. Reitlinger op cit, p. 371.

250 Ibid, pp. 446 et seq.

251 Ibid, p. 446.

252 Ibid, p. 451.

253 Reitlinger: op cit, p. 342

254 Hilberg: op cit, p. 384. Henkys: op cit, p. 138. Reitlinger: op cit, pp. 342 et seq. Hannah Arendt: Eichmann in Jerusalem, p. 150.

255 Reitlinger: op cit, p. 309.

256 Henkys: op cit, p. 139.

257 Kempner: Eichmann und Komplizen, p. 208.

258 Henkys: op cit, p. 140.

259 Kempner: op cit, p. 208.

260 Ibid, p. 209.

261 Renzo de Felice: Storia degli ebrei italiani sotto fascismo, p. 460.

262 Ibid, p. 459.

263 Ibid.

264 Ibid, p. 460.

265 Hilberg: op cit, p. 414.

266 Ibid, p. 415.

267 Ibid.

268 Kempner: Eichmann und Komplizen, p. 321.

269 Ibid.

270 Ibid. p. 323.

271 Felice: op cit, p. 462. Hilberg: op cit, pp. 415–6.

272 Kempner: op cit, p. 329 Felice: op cit, p. 462. Reitlinger op cit, p. 324.

273 Hilberg: op cit, p. 416.

274 Ibid.

275 Reitlinger: op cit, p. 328

276 Ibid, p. 390. Henkys: op cit, p. 144. Hilberg: op cit, p. 470

277 Ibid, p. 404. Henkys: op cit p. 149.

278 Hilberg: op cit, p. 485 Henkys: op cit, p. 148.

279 Hilberg: op cit, p. 429. Case against Wolff, p. 285.

280 Case against Wolff, p

5–6. Henkys: op cit, p. 143.
1 Besgen: op cit, p. 28.
rsten: op cit, p. 144.
2 Besgen: op cit, pp. 28–9.
3 Reitlinger: op cit, pp. 342–
. Hilberg: op cit, p. 384.
4 Reitlinger: op cit, pp.
2–45.
5 Lösener: "Als Rassereferent
n Reichsministerium des Inn-
n" in Vierteljahrshefte für
eitgeschichte, No. 4 1963. Hil-
rg: op cit, pp. 268, 277.
6 Hilberg: op cit, pp. 269,
0, 273.
7 Lösener: op cit, p. 298.
8 Ibid, pp. 299–300.
9 Ibid, pp. 300, 302, Hilberg:
p cit, p. 270.
0 Henkys: op cit, p. 142. Hil-
rg: op cit, p. 357. Werner Best:

Die deutsche Politik in Dänemark, p. 47. Kempner: Eichmann und Komplizen, pp. 372–3.
291 Best: op cit, p. 48.
292 Ibid.
293 Ibid, p. 50.
294 Ibid, p. 49. Kempner: op
cit, p. 374.
295 Ibid, p. 51. Kempner: op
cit, p. 377.
296 Henkys: op cit, p. 142.
297 Kempner: op cit, p. 379.
Reitlinger: op cit, pp. 347–8
(footnote).
298 Kempner: op cit, p. 375.
Reitlinger: op cit, pp. 349–50.
Henkys: op cit, p. 142.
299 Kempner: op cit, p. 376.
300 Ibid, pp. 378–80.
301 Eichmann: Record of Interrogation, Vol. 1, Col. 251.

CHAPTER FIFTEEN

Knoebel: Racial Illusion and
Military Necessity, p. 226.
Broszat: Zur Perversion der
trafjustiz im Dritten Reich, p.
8.
Helmut Heiber: "Zur Justiz
n Dritten Reich — Der Fall
lias", Vierteljahrshefte fur Zeit-
eschichte, No. 4 of 1955, pp.
5–7, 279.
Ibid, p. 279.
Ibid, pp. 231–2.
Ibid, p. 282.
Ibid.
Ibid, pp. 287, 290.
Broszat: Perversion der Straf-
ustiz, p. 403.
Ibid, p. 404.
Ibid.
Broszat: Anatomy of the SS
tate, p. 413.
Neufeldt and others: Zur
eschichte der Ordnungspolizei,
31.

14 Ibid, pp. 31–2.
15 Ibid, p. 31.
16 Ibid.
17 Ibid, pp. 43, 109.
18 Ibid, p. 32.
19 Ibid.
20 Georg: Die Wirtschaftlichen
Unternehmungen der SS, p. 25.
21 Buchheim: Anatomy of the
SS State, p. 298. Georg: op cit,
p. 29.
22 Buchheim: op cit, p. 298.
23 Ibid, p. 299.
24 Georg: op cit, p. 41.
25 Ibid, p. 37.
26 Ibid, pp. 42, 44, 56.
27 Ibid, pp. 58, 62.
28 Ibid, pp. 62, 64.
29 Ibid, pp. 66, 69.
30 Ibid, p. 70.
31 Ibid, p. 71.
32 Ibid, pp. 30–31 (WVHA organisation table).
33 Ibid, p. 131.

34 Ibid, pp. 72–74.

35 Ibid, p. 74.

36 Ibid, pp. 75–6.

37 Ibid, pp. 79–81.

38 Ibid, pp. 80, 82.

39 Ibid, pp. 80–81.

40 Ibid, p. 87.

41 Ibid, p. 88.

42 Ibid, pp. 92–3.

43 Ibid, p. 97.

44 Ibid, p. 130.

45 Ibid, p. 37.

46 Ibid.

47 David Irving: *The Mare's Nest*, p. 123.

48 Georg: op cit, p. 38.

49 Ibid.

50 Ibid.

51 Irving: op cit, p. 283.

52 Ibid, p. 294 (footnote).

53 Ibid, pp. 260, 295.

54 Paetel, for instance, in *Die SS*, p. 20.

55 Arendt: *The Origins of Totalitarianism*, p. 395.

56 Ibid, p. 405.

57 Arendt: *Elementer und Ursprünge totalitärer Herrschaft*, p. 642 (not in English version).

58 Krausnick: *Hitler und die Morde in Polen*, p. 197.

59 Ibid, p. 198.

60 Ibid, p. 200.

61 Ibid.

62 Ibid, p. 201. Delarue: op cit, p. 219.

63 Delarue: op cit, pp. 219–20.

64 Krausnick: op cit, p. 201.

65 Ibid.

66 Ibid.

67 Hilberg: op cit, pp. 434–5.

68 See correspondence between Himmler and Reeder referred to below, RFSS Microfilm 56.

69 Letter from Himmler to Reeder, 16 Feb. 1943, RFSS Microfilm 56.

70 Letter from Berger to Ru-

dolf Brandt, 25 Feb. 1943, RFS Microfilm 56.

71 Letter from Reeder t Himmler, 20 Feb. 1943, RFS Microfilm 56.

72 Letter from Himmler t Reeder, 16 Feb. 1943.

73 Werner Best: *Erinnerunge aus dem besetzten Frankreic 1940–1942*, p. 27. Verbal inform: tion from Dr Best, 5 Feb. 196

74 Letter from Kiesel, 31 Ma 1942, RFSS Microfilm 72.

75 Ibid.

76 Ibid.

77 Letter from Foertsch t Turner, 29 Dec. 1941, RFSS M crofilm 72.

78 Letter from Foertsch t Turner, 2 Feb. 1942, RFSS M crofilm 72.

79 Letter from Turner t Meyszner, 29 Aug. 1942, RFS Microfilm 140.

80 Ibid.

81 Ibid.

82 *Bild-Zeitung*, 1 July 1964.

83 Fabian von Schlabrendorf *The Secret War against Hitle* p. 187.

84 Eberhard Jäckel: *Fran\
reich in Hitlers Europa*, p. 34

85 Letter from Korsemann t von Kleist, 30 June 1943 (i Wulf's papers).

86 Ibid.

87 Letter from Berger to vc Herff, 6 July 1943 (in Wul\
papers).

88 Letter from Himmler t Korsemann, 5 July 1943 (i Wulf's papers).

89 Krausnick: *Wehrmacht un Nationalsozialismus*, p. 681.

90 Ibid.

91 Ibid.

92 *The Goebbels Diaries*, ɪ 284.

APPENDIX 1

711

3 Ibid, pp. 284, 102.

4 Letter from Berger to Rudolf Brandt, 12 Mar. 1940, RFSS Microfilm 33.

5 Ibid.

6 Letter from Berger to Himmler, 24 Nov. 1941, RFSS Microfilm 117.

7 Letter from Himmler to Bormann, Feb. 1940, RFSS Microfilm 33.

8 Letter from Weitzel to Himmler, 17 April 1938, RFSS Microfilm 33.

9 Broszat: "Der Sonderdienst in General Gouvernement" in *Gutachten des Instituts für Zeitgeschichte*, pp. 408–10.

100 Letter from Krüger to Himmler, 10 Oct. 1942, RFSS Microfilm 128.

101 Ibid.

102 Ibid.

103 Letter from Berger to Himmler, 21 Nov. 1942, RFSS Microfilm 128.

104 Letter from Himmler to Bormann, 26 Feb. 1943, RFSS Microfilm 33.

105 Ibid.

106 *Archiv für Publizistische Arbeit*, 26 Aug. 1943.

107 Letter from Berger to Himmler, 10 Oct. 1942, RFSS Microfilm 22.

108 Hilberg: op cit, p. 230.

109 Albert Krebs: *Fritz-Dietlof Graf von der Schulenburg*, pp. 30–31.

110 Letter from Berger to Himmler, 20 Nov. 1943, RFSS Microfilm 22.

111 Letter from Berger to Himmler, 30 Oct. 1943, RFSS Microfilm 22.

112 Letter from Lohse to SSPF Ostland, 13 Apr. 1942, RFSS Microfilm 155.

113 Letter from Himmler to Koch, 9 Oct. 1942, RFSS Microfilm 56.

114 Dallin: *German Rule in Russia*, p. 174.

115 Statement by Hans Ehlich at the Ohlendorf trial, 20 Sept. 1947 (in Frau Käthe Ohlendorf's private papers).

116 Ibid.

117 Trevor-Roper: *The Last Days of Hitler*, p. 42.

118 "Nebe Series", 19 Jan. 1950, p. 22.

119 Boberach: op cit, p. xvii.

120 Ortsgruppenleiter Löcken to Frau Scholtz-Klink, 27 June 1938, RFSS Microfilm 69.

121 Office minute, 4 July 1938, RFSS Microfilm 69.

122 Letter from Karl Fiehler to Frick, 19 Apr. 1941, RFSS Microfilm 69.

123 Letter from Bormann to Himmler, 28 Apr. 1941, RFSS Microfilm 69.

124 Letter from Himmler to editor *Schwarze Korps*, 2 May 1941, RFSS Microfilm 69.

125 Information, 29 Jan. 1966, from a close relative of Himmler who wishes to remain anonymous.

126 Certificate dated 27 July 1937 and identity card dated 23 May 1933 from Industrial College, Mannheim. Telegram from Himmler to Hedwig Potthast, 5 Dec. 1937—all in Central Archives Microfilm 99.

127 Information from close relative of Himmler (see Note 125 above).

128 Certificate of guardianship for Helge and Nanette Dorothea Potthast, 12 Sept. 1944 from Berlin-Charlottenburg District

Court, Central Archives Microfilm 99.

129 Certificate from District Court acknowledging Hedwig Potthast's renunciation of the Church, 2 June 1939, Central Archives, Microfilm 99.

130 See correspondence quoted below between Hedwig Potthast and Hilde Potthast, Central Archives Microfilm 99.

131 Letter from Hilde Potthast to Hedwig Potthast, 26 Mar. 1942, Central Archives, Microfilm 99.

132 Hilde Potthast to Hedwig Potthast, 8 May 1942, Central Archives, Microfilm 99.

133 Ibid.

134 Schellenberg: Memoirs, p. 358.

135 See certificate of guardianship (Note 128 above).

136 See letter from Gerda Bormann to her husband, 21 Sept. 1944 in Trevor-Roper: The Bormann Letters, p. 119.

137 Trevor-Roper: op cit, p. 126.

138 Ibid, p. 2.

139 Hilberg: op cit, p. 256.

140 Statement by Dr Justus Beyer at the Ohlendorf trial, 22 Oct. 1947 (in Frau Käthe Ohlendorf's private papers).

141 Boberach: op cit, p. xviii.

142 Ibid, p. xxii.

143 Peter Schneider: "Rechtssicherheit und richterliche Unabhängigkeit aus der Sicht des SD" in Vierteljahrshefte für Zeitgeschichte, No. 4, 1956, p. 416.

144 Kersten: op cit, p. 215.

145 Memorandum from SD Aussenstelle Bünde to SD Abschnitt Bielefeld, 13 May 1941, RFSS Microfilm 269.

146 Memorandum from SD Aussenstelle Minden to SD Abschnitt Bielefeld, 24 June 194 RFSS Microfilm 269.

147 Memorandum from SD Aussenstelle Erfurt to SD Hauptaussenstelle Weimar, 12 Jan 1942, RFSS Microfilm 269.

148 Ibid.

149 Memorandum SD Aussenstelle Erfurt to SD Hauptaussenstelle Weimar, 5 Jan. 1942, RFSS Microfilm 269.

150 IMT Vol. XXIX, p. 514.

151 Letter from Florian to Bormann, 30 Nov. 1942, RFSS Microfilm 59.

152 Letter from Weinrich to Party Chancellery, 22 Jan. 194 RFSS Microfilm 59.

153 Letter from Hildebrandt to Himmler, 17 Apr. 1943, RFSS Microfilm 117.

154 Boberach: Meldungen au dem Reich, p. xviii.

155 Kersten: Totenkopf und Treue, p. 215.

156 Ibid, p. 209.

157 Ohlendorf's statement, Oct. 1947, p. 508 (in Frau Käthe Ohlendorf's private papers).

158 Kersten: op cit, p. 216.

159 Boberach: op cit, p. xxv

160 Statement by Hans Fritzsche at the Ohlendorf trial, Aug. 1947, p. 510 (in Frau Käthe Ohlendorf's private papers).

161 Goebbels Diaries, p. 293.

162 Boberach: op cit, p. xxvi.

163 Ibid, p. xxviii.

164 Ohlendorf's statement, Oct. 1947, p. 510 (in Frau Käthe Ohlendorf's private papers).

165 Boberach: op cit, p. xvii.

166 Ibid.

167 IMT Vol. XXIX, p. 107.

68 Buchheim: *Anatomy of the S State*, pp. 227–8.

69 Letter from Andreas chmidt to Gottlob Berger, 24 ept. 1943, RFSS Microfilm 128.

70 Buchheim: *Anatomy of the S State*, pp. 213–4.

71 Buchheim: "Die Höhere S-und Polizeiführer" in *Viertel- jhrshefte für Zeitgeschichte*, No. , 1963 pp. 362–4.

72 Ibid, p. 387.

73 Ibid.

74 Buchheim: *Anatomy of the S State*, p. 231.

75 Ibid.

76 Ibid, p. 232.

77 Ibid, p. 235.

78 Ibid, p. 219.

79 Draft on prerogatives of the SSPF, 8 Jan. 1943, RFSS Micro- lm 119.

80 Ibid.

81 Ibid.

82 Buchheim: *Anatomy of the S State*, pp. 237–8.

83 Ibid, p. 228.

84 Letter from Himmler to lintze, 11 May 1944, RFSS ficrofilm 56.

85 Teleprinter message from limmler to Hintze, undated, FSS Microfilm 56.

86 Letter from Himmler to aldschmidt, 20 Apr. 1944, RFSS ficrofilm 33.

87 Letter from Himmler to ofmann, 29 Nov. 1944, RFSS ficrofilm 56.

88 Letter from Himmler to aluege, 4 Feb. 1943, RFSS ficrofilm 60.

89 Letter from Himmler to ancke, 16 May 1944, RFSS ficrofilm 56.

190 Letter from Wolff to Kal- tenbrunner, 23 Nov. 1942; anon- ymous letter to editor *Schwarze Korps* (both in Wulf's papers).

191 Letter from Ohlendorf to Wolff, 6 Aug. 1942, RFSS Micro- film 122.

192 Verbal information from Dr Richard Korherr, 8 Mar. 1966.

193 Questionnaire on Korherr, District HQ Würzburg, Person- nel Office, dated 30 Sept. 1940 (in Korherr's private papers).

194 Verbal information from Dr Richard Korherr, 8 Mar. 1966.

195 Ibid.

196 Ibid.

197 Ibid.

198 Letter from Korherr to Himmler, 13 Aug. 1943 (in Dr Korherr's papers).

199 Letter from Hildebrandt to Himmler, undated (in Dr. Kor- herr's papers).

200 Verbal information from Dr Korherr, 8 Mar. 1966.

201 IMT Vol. XX, p. 426.

202 Höss: op cit, p. 138.

203 Reitlinger: *The House built on Sand*, pp. 355, 358.

204 Letter from Müller to Sicherheitspolizei and SD Com- manders, 28 Aug. 1941, RFSS Microfilm 491. Letter from SD Leitabschnitt Munich, 8 Mar. 1943, RFSS Microfilm 269.

205 See statement by Dr Hans Hohberg, 11 July 1947. Files of U.S. Military Court II, Case IV.

206 See correspondence be- ween Berger and his son-in-law Andreas Schmidt, RFSS Micro- film 128.

CHAPTER SIXTEEN

1 Memorandum from Strecken-bach to Himmler, approx. 9 Mar. 1942, RFSS Microfilm 140.

2 Kesselring: *Gedanken zum Zweiten Weltkrieg*, p. 164.

3 Westphal: *The German Army in the West*, p. 54.

4 von Manstein: *Lost Victories*, p. 188.

5 Stein: *The Waffen-SS*, p. 215. OKW Reports 1943, Vol. II, p. 1010.

6 *Wiking-Ruf* No. 6 of 1955, pp. 13 et seq; No. 7 of 1955, pp. 10 et seq.

7 Hausser: *Soldaten wie andere auch* (uncorrected MS), p. 2. Buchheim: SS und Polizei im NS-Staat, pp. 29–30.

8 Hausser: op cit, p. 2.

9 Hausser: *Waffen-SS im Einsatz*, p. 10. Klietmann: *Die Waffen-SS*, pp. 53-4.

10 Judgment on Dietrich, p. 4.

11 Stein: op cit, p. 4.

12 Judgment on Dietrich, p. 4.

13 Klictmann: op cit, p. 71. Hausser: *Soldaten*, p. 2.

14 Klietmann: op cit, pp. 71, 51.

15 Hausser: *Soldaten*, p. 2.

16 Verbal information from Wilhelm Bittrich, 29 Jan. 1966.

17 Stein: op cit, p. 5.

18 Ibid.

19 Ibid.

20 Görlitz: *Die Waffen-SS*, p. 9.

21 See Chapter 6, this volume.

22 See Chapter 6, this volume.

23 Klietmann: op cit, p. 53.

24 Ibid, p. 15.

25 Hausser: *Soldaten*, p. 107.

26 Verbal information from Paul Hausser, 31 Jan. 1966.

27 Hausser: *Soldaten*, p. 1. Ver-bal information from Paul Hausser, 31 Jan. 1966.

28 Letter from Paul Hausser, 10 Feb. 1966.

29 Verbal information from Paul Hausser, 31 Jan. 1966.

30 Ibid.

31 Klietmann: op cit, p. 18.

32 Ibid, p. 421. Hausser: *Soldaten*, p. 33.

33 Verbal information from Paul Hausser, 31 Jan. 1966.

34 Klietmann: op cit, p. 21 Buchheim: SS und Polizei in NS-Staat, p. 167-8.

35 Hausser: *Soldaten*, p. 10.

36 Stein: op cit, p. 10.

37 Letter from Himmler to al SS-Oberabschnitte, 17 Sept. 1936 RFSS Microfilm 155.

38 Ibid.

39 Letter from Himmler t Dietrich, undated, RFSS Micro film 33.

40 Verbal information from Felix Steiner, 28 Jan. 1966.

41 Ibid.

42 Letter from Heissmeyer t Himmler, 18 July 1938, RFS Microfilm 33.

43 Ibid.

44 Letter from Himmler t Dietrich, 2 July 1938, RFS Microfilm 33.

45 Steiner: *Armee der Geächte ten*, p. 70.

46 Verbal information from Wilhelm Bittrich, 29 Jan. 1966.

47 Verbal information from Felix Steiner, 28 Jan. 1966.

48 Ibid.

49 Steiner: op cit, p. 351.

50 Verbal information from Paul Hausser, 31 Jan. 1966.

51 Steiner: op cit, p. 351.

52 Ibid, p. 39.

53 Verbal information from Felix Steiner and Paul Hausser, Jan./Feb. 1966.

54 Steiner: *Von Clausewitz bis Bulganin*, p. 69.

55 Verbal information from Felix Steiner, 28 Jan. 1966.

56 Stein: op cit, p. 13.

57 Hausser: *Soldaten*, p. 22.

58 Verbal information from Felix Steiner, 28 Jan. 1966.

59 Stein: op cit, p. 13.

60 Article entitled "Die reformerischen Leistungen der ehemaligen Waffen-SS", probably written by Steiner, *Wiking-Ruf* No. 4 of 1955, p. 12.

61 Ibid.

62 Steiner: *Von Clausewitz bis Bulganin*, p. 234.

63 Steiner: *Die Armee der Geächteten*, p. 92.

64 Verbal information from Paul Hausser, 31 Jan. 1966.

65 Verbal information from Felix Steiner, 28 Jan. 1966.

66 Karl Demeter: *The German Officer Corps*, p. pp. 54–6 and 268. Steiner: *Die Armee der Geächteten*, pp. 96–7.

67 *Wiking-Ruf* article (see Note 60 above), p. 12.

68 See Krausnick: *Wehrmacht und Nationalsozialismus*, pp. 669 et seq.

69 Ibid.

70 Foertsch: op cit, p. 148.

71 Krausnick: *Wehrmacht und Nationalsozialismus*, p. 669.

72 Ibid.

73 Buchheim: *Anatomy of the SS State*, p. 259.

74 Ibid.

75 Hossbach: op cit, p. 32.

76 Klietmann: op cit, pp. 26–7.

77 Address by Gruppenführer Petri, Jan. 1939, entitled "Experiences of the initiation of expansion of the SS-Totenkopfverbände in September 1938 and of large-scale employment of the Allgemeine SS."

78 SS pamphlet "Uns ist der Kampf", undated (approx. 1942), RFSS Microfilm 161.

79 Knoebel: op cit, p. 35.

80 Letter from OKW to Himmler, 7 Dec. 1942. Letter from Archbishop of Freiburg's Chancellery to OKW, 25 Nov. 1942.

81 Letter from Archbishop of Freiburg to OKW, 25 Nov. 1942.

82 Ibid.

83 Draft (dated 16 Jan. 1939) of an address for Gruppenführer conference, 23–25 Jan. 1939, RFSS Microfilm 17. Half-yearly report on advanced education of VT officers graduating from SS Cadet Colleges, 5 Apr. 1938, RFSS Microfilm 69.

84 Ideological instruction for the month of Oct. 1943, syllabus of SS Panzer-grenadier Division "Hohenstaufen", 18 Sept. 1943, RFSS Microfilm 161.

85 IMT Vol. XXX, p. 516.

86 Eichmann: Record of Interrogation, Vol. II, Col. 1683.

87 Hausser: *Soldaten*, p. 21.

88 Ibid, p. 50.

89 Ibid, p. 20.

90 Ibid.

91 Ibid, p. 49.

92 Ibid, p. 50.

93 Ibid.

94 Stein: op cit, p. 28.

95 Ibid.

96 Ibid, p. 35.

97 Ibid, p. 40.

98 Verbally from Felix Steiner, 28 Jan. 1966.

99 Verbally from Wilhelm Bittrich, 29 Jan. 1966.

100 Verbally from Felix Steiner, 28 Jan. 1966.
101 Gottlob Berger's autobiography, undated, in Wulf's papers.
102 Ibid.
103 Letter from Berger to Himmler, 28 July 1943, RFSS Microfilm 56.
104 Letter from Berger to Himmler, 9 Mar. 1943, RFSS Microfilm 117.
105 Berger's autobiography.
106 Letter from Berger to Hanns Ludin, 13 Nov. 1934 (in Wulf's papers).
107 Berger's autobiography.
108 Letter from Ludin to SA Supreme Headquarters Special Court, 7 Dec. 1934 (in Wulf's papers).
109 Ibid.
110 Personal file, "SS Brigadeführer Berger, Gottlob" undated (approx. 1940) in Wulf's papers.
111 Buchheim: *Anatomy of the SS State*, pp. 260-62.
112 Stein: op cit, p. 33.
113 Ibid, pp. 38 et seq.
114 Klietmann: op cit, p. 37.
115 Buchheim: *SS und Polizei im NS–Staat*, 165–7.
116 Ibid.
117 Aronson: op cit, p. 171.
118 Buchheim: *Anatomy of the SS State*, p. 228.
119 Ibid, p. 258.
120 Ibid.
121 Ibid, pp. 331, 333.
122 Ibid, p. 331.
123 Speech by Himmler, 19 June 1942, RFSS Microfilm 89.
124 Klietmann: op cit, pp. 131, 123.
125 Ibid, pp. 104, 87.
126 Ibid, pp. 107, 108, 121.
127 Ibid, p. 72.
128 Neusüss-Hunkel: op cit, pp. 72, 499.
129 Hausser: *Soldaten*, p. 76. Stein: op cit, p. 36.
130 Stein: op cit, p. 40.
131 Ibid, p. 46.
132 OKW Secret Order, 8 Mar. 1940, "Wehrdienstverhältnis und Wehrüberwachung der Angehörigen der Waffen-SS während des Krieges", RFSS Microfilm 119.
133 Hausser: *Waffen-SS im Einsatz*, p. 16.
134 Seraphim: "SS Verfügungstruppe und Wehrmacht", in *Wehrwissenschaftliche Rundschau*, No. 12, 1955.
135 Klietmann: op cit, p. 44.
136 Ibid, p. 45.
137 Ibid, p. 46.
138 Stein: op cit, p. 169.
139 Ibid.
140 Robert Herzog: *Die Volksdeutschen in der Waffen-SS*, p. 4.
141 Ibid.
142 Ibid, p. 5.
143 Ibid, p. 6.
144 Stein: op cit, p. 153. Klietmann: op cit, p. 506.
145 Stein: op cit, p. 138.
146 Ibid, p. 146.
147 Klietmann: op cit, p. 133.
148 Hausser: *Soldaten*, p. 62.
149 Ibid.
150 Stein: op cit, p. 63.
151 Guderian: op cit, p. 117.
152 Klietmann: op cit, p. 76.
153 Hausser: *Waffen-SS im Einsatz*, pp. 33, 39, 40.
154 Picht: *Vom Wesen des Krieges und vom Kriegswesen der Deutschen*, p. 248.
155 Görlitz: *Die Waffen-SS*, p. 19.
156 *Das Schwarze Korps*, 26 Nov. 1942.
157 Stein: op cit, p. 81.
158 Ibid, p. 90.
159 Letter from Jüttner to

Eicke, 24 Oct. 1940, RFSS Microfilm 107.

160 Letter from Eicke to Wolff, 9 Oct. 1940, RFSS Microfilm 107.

161 Cyril Jolly: *The Vengeance of Private Pooley.*

162 See correspondence between Eicke and Jüttner, Autumn 1940.

163 Verbal information from Gunter d'Alquen, Nov. 1966.

164 Letter from Jüttner to Eicke, 24 Oct. 1940.

165 Ibid.

166 Letter from Eicke to Wolff, 22 Oct. 1940, RFSS Microfilm 107.

167 Ibid.

168 Letter from Himmler to Eicke, 30 Jan. 1941, RFSS Microfilm 108.

169 Klietmann: op cit, pp. 76, 70, 90.

170 Ibid, p. 501.

171 Ibid, pp. 184, 90, 110, 130.

172 Hausser: *Soldaten,* Documents 19 and 20.

173 Buchheim: *SS und Polizei im NS-Staat,* pp. 182–3.

174 Stein: op cit, p. 111.

175 Buchheim: *Anatomy of the SS State,* p. 273.

176 Stein: op cit, p. 258.

177 Ibid, p. 259.

178 Görlitz: *Die Waffen-SS,* p. 18.

179 Stein: op cit, p. 261.

180 Ibid.

181 Ibid, p. 264.

182 Görlitz: op cit, p. 18.

183 Stein: op cit, pp. 266–8.

184 Ibid, p. 103.

185 Hausser: *Soldaten,* p. 55. Buchheim: *Anatomy of the SS State,* pp. 270–1.

186 Stein: op cit, p. 103.

187 Ibid, p. 109.

188 Klietmann: op cit, p. 393.

189 Ibid, p. 395.

190 Ibid, p. 78. Hausser: *Waffen-SS im Einsatz,* p. 46.

191 Ibid, p. 90.

192 Steiner: *Armee der Geächteten,* pp. 162, 164.

193 Verbal information from Gunter d'Alquen, Nov. 1966.

194 Steiner: op cit, pp. 164 et seq.

195 Letter from Busch to Himmler, 4 May 1942, RFSS Microfilm 108. Steiner: op cit, p. 165.

196 Teleprinter message from Heydrich to Himmler, 6 Nov. 1941, RFSS Microfilm 108. Steiner: *Die Freiwilligen,* pp. 377 et seq.

197 Stein: op cit, p. 216.

198 Letter from Mackensen to Himmler, 26 Dec. 1941, RFSS Microfilm 108.

199 Letter from Eicke to Jüttner, 5 Aug. 1942, RFSS Microfilm 107.

200 "T.E.": "Die Rede Himmlers vor den Gauleitern am 3 Aug. 1944" in *Vierteljahrshefte für Zeitgeschichte,* No. 4, 1953, p. 372.

201 Letter from Simon to Eicke, 2 Aug. 1942, RFSS Microfilm 108.

202 Letter from Eicke to Jüttner, 5 Aug. 1942, RFSS Microfilm 107.

203 Dixon and Heilbrunn: *Communist Guerrilla Warfare,* p. 107.

204 Ibid.

205 Ibid.

206 Letter from War Graves Officer of the Leibstandarte to Divisional Headquarters, 29 Mar. 1942, RFSS Microfilm 108.

207 Letter to the author from Wilhelm Keilhaus, 4 Mar. 1967.

208 Stein, op cit, p. 272.

209 Letter from von Reinholz to Einsatzgruppe E, 15 July 1943, RFSS Microfilm 140.

210 Görlitz: *Die Waffen-SS*, p. 27. Stein: op cit, p. 277.

211 See the latest account of historical investigation on this subject in Jäckel: *Frankreich in Hitlers Europa*, pp. 326–8.

212 Stein: op cit, p. 277.

213 Letter to Wolff from Allgemeines Wehrmachtsamt of OKW, 2 Aug. 1943, RFSS Microfilm 122.

214 Ibid.

215 Ibid.

216 Letter from Dr Plötz to Brandt, 17 Nov. 1942, RFSS Microfilm 140.

217 Letter from Reinholz to Einsatzgruppe E, 15 July 1943.

218 Note for the file by Kumm on conversation with Reichsführer-SS and Obergruppenführer Phleps on 28 July 1943, undated, RFSS Microfilm 140.

219 Klietmann: op cit, p. 151.

220 Ibid, p. 157.

221 Ibid, p. 165.

222 Ibid, p. 169.

223 Ibid, p. 178.

224 Ibid, p. 181.

225 Ibid, p. 187.

226 Stein: op cit, p. 206.

227 Steiner: *Armee der Geächteten*, p. 173.

228 Stein: op cit, p. 209.

229 Klietmann: op cit, pp. 59–61.

230 Ibid, pp. 49, 61 et seq.

231 Ibid, p. 60.

232 Stein, op cit, p. 218.

233 Ibid, p. 217.

234 Ibid, p. 213.

235 Steiner: *Armee der Geächteten*, p. 173.

236 Estimate by Steiner during interview with the author.

237 Stein: op cit, p. 134.

238 Ibid, p. 217.

239 Letter from Eicke to Führungshauptamt, 15 Nov. 1941, RFSS Microfilm 108.

240 Copy of summarised report forwarded to Himmler by SS-Führungshauptamt, 11 May 1943, RFSS Microfilm 131.

241 Stein: op cit, p. 204.

242 Summarised report (see Note 240 above).

243 Ibid.

244 Ibid.

245 Ibid.

246 Ibid.

247 Ibid.

248 Ibid.

249 Ibid.

250 Ibid.

251 Letter from Berger to Himmler, 18 Apr. 1943, RFSS Microfilm 131.

252 Letter from Himmler to Bormann, 14 May 1943, RFSS Microfilm 131.

253 Stein: op cit, p. 204.

254 Letter from Kallmeyer, a Labour Service Leader, to Simon, Head of the Labour Service, 26 Feb. 1943, RFSS Microfilm 70.

255 Ibid.

256 Letter to his father from some young man unknown, undated, registered in by Himmler's Personal Staff as No. 1319, RFSS Microfilm 70.

257 Letter from Bormann to Himmler, 24 Feb. 1943, RFSS Microfilm 70.

258 Letter from Acting Commander V Corps to OKW, 30 Mar. 1943, RFSS Microfilm 70.

259 Ibid.

260 Ibid.

261 Stein: op cit, p. 172.

262 Ibid, pp. 172–3.

263 Letter from Eicke to Füh-

rungshauptamt, 15 Nov. 1941, RFSS Microfilm 108.

264 Special instructions for ideological education issued by Section 1a/VI SS Cavalry Division HQ, 5 Apr. 1943, RFSS Microfilm 70.

265 Ibid.

266 Ibid.

267 Letter from Eicke to Führungshauptamt, 15 Nov. 1941.

268 Stein: op cit, p. 192.

269 See letter from Himmler to Berger and Jüttner, 13 Apr. 1942, RFSS Microfilm 66.

270 Ibid.

271 Ibid.

272 Letter from Berger to Himmler, 12 Oct. 1942, RFSS Microfilm 66.

273 Ibid.

274 Letter from Himmler to Bender, 22 Feb. 1944, RFSS Microfilm 22.

275 Knoebel: op cit, p. 177.

276 Letter from a Dutch SS man named Thoen to the Head of the Dutch SS, undated, forwarded to Himmler, 16 June 1942, RFSS Microfilm 122.

277 Letter from Rauter to Himmler, 6 June 1942, RFSS Microfilm 122.

278 Verbal information from Felix Steiner.

279 On morale among the European SS volunteers see extracts from the diary of an unknown SS man in *Christ und Welt*, 10 Aug. 1950.

280 Rolf Bigler: "Sie wollen ganz anders sein", *Frankfurter Allgemeine Zeitung*, 12 Feb. 1964.

281 Letter to the author from Paul Hausser, 5 Feb. 1967.

282 Letter from Berger to Himmler, 22 Jan. 1942, RFSS Microfilm 108.

283 Letter from Colonel-General Zeitzler to Himmler, 21 Mar. 1944, RFSS Microfilm 66.

284 Letter from von Herff to Wolff, 23 Nov. 1942, RFSS Microfilm 70.

285 Buchheim: *Anatomy of the SS State*, p. 231.

286 Teleprinter message from Himmler to Jüttner, 10 Feb. 1944, RFSS Microfilm 69.

287 Quarterly report SD Abschnitt Nuremberg, period to 10 Oct. 1941, undated, RFSS Microfilm 406.

288 Verbal information from Felix Steiner, 28 Jan. 1966.

289 Letter from Brandt to Berger, 21 June 1943, RFSS Microfilm 56.

290 Aide-mémoire on SS ranks issued by Press Office, Reichsführer's Personal Staff, 31 Dec. 1942.

291 SS Order, 24 Feb. 1943, RFSS Microfilm 225.

292 Letter from Berger to Brandt, 10 July 1944, RFSS Microfilm 64.

293 Memorandum "Attitude of Section VI of Div. HQ" from Section VI HQ 13 SS Division, 10 Apr. 1944, RFSS Microfilm 70.

294 Unsigned letter to "Dear Willi", 2 Oct. 1943, RFSS Microfilm 64.

295 Letter from Berger to Himmler, 30 Aug. 1944, RFSS Microfilm 64.

296 Letter from Himmler to Höfle, 30 Dec. 1944, RFSS Microfilm 59.

297 Verbal information from Wilhelm Bittrich, 29 Jan. 1966.

298 Verbal information from Felix Steiner, 28 Jan. 1966.

299 Letter from Himmler to Steiner, Aug. 1942, RFSS Microfilm 70.

300 Ibid.

301 Ibid.

302 Letter from Fick to Wolff, 27 Jan. 1942, RFSS Microfilm 38.

303 Letter from Himmler to Berger, 15 July 1943, RFSS Microfilm 56.

304 Ibid.

305 Ibid.

306 Letter from Berger to Brandt, 9 July 1943, RFSS Microfilm 56.

307 Letter from Berger to Himmler, 28 July 1943, RFSS Microfilm 56.

308 Verbal information from Gottlob Berger, 1 Feb. 1966.

309 Steiner: *Armee der Geächteten*, p. 271. Krebs: *Fritz-Dietlof Schulenburg*, p. 145.

CHAPTER SEVENTEEN

1 Bartz: *Die Tragödie der deutschen Abwehr*, pp. 129, 133.

2 Ibid, pp. 129, 145.

3 Buchheit: *Der deutsche Geheimdienst*, p. 419.

4 Bartz: op cit, p. 154.

5 Buchheit: op cit, p. 419.

6 Schellenberg: *Memoiren*, p. 322 (not in English translation).

7 Buchheit: op cit, p. 139. Abshagen: *Canaris*, p. 140. Hassell: *Von andern Deutschland*, pp. 32–3. (not in English translation).

8 Abshagen: op cit, p. 180.

9 Buchheit: op cit, pp. 303–4.

10 Bartz: op cit, pp. 151, 154.

11 Buchheit: op cit, p. 419.

12 Ibid.

13 Buchheit: op cit, p. 420.

14 Gisevius: *To the Bitter End*, p. 472. Buchheit: op cit, p. 420.

15 Buchheit: op cit, p. 420.

16 Ibid.

17 Gerhard Ritter: *Carl Goerdeler und die deutsche Widerstandsbewegung*, p. 372. Gisevius: op cit, pp. 472–3.

18 Buchheit: op cit, p. 428.

19 Abshagen: op cit, p. 368. Buchheit: op cit, p. 429.

20 Ibid.

21 Buchheit: op cit, pp. 421–2.

22 Schellenberg: *Memoiren*, p. 333 (not in English translation).

23 Note by Schellenberg, 30 Jan. 1941, RFSS Microfilm 463.

24 Abshagen: op cit, p. 375.

25 Buchheit: op cit, p. 438.

26 Verbal information from Bruno Streckenbach, 21 Jan. 1966.

27 Schellenberg: *Memoirs*, p. 30.

28 Verbal information from Bruno Streckenbach, 21 Jan. 1966.

29 Schellenberg: *Memoiren*, p. 52 (not in English translation).

30 Ibid, p. 18.

31 Ibid, p. 137.

32 Schellenberg: *Memoirs*, p. 222.

33 Buchheit: op cit, pp. 429–31.

34 Ibid, pp. 430-2. Abshagen: op cit, p. 369.

35 Ibid, p. 431.

36 Ibid, pp. 429, 433. Schellenberg: *Memoiren*, p. 333 (not in English translation).

37 Ibid, p. 432.

38 See Chapter 15, this volume.

39 Buchheit: op cit, p. 415.

40 Besgen: *Der stille Befehl*, p. 72.

41 Verbal information from Professor Reinhard Höhn, 15 Jan. 1967.

42 Denne: *Das Danzig-Problem in der deutschen Aussenpolitik*, p. 182.

43 Ibid.

44 Burckhardt: op cit, p. 334.

45 Ibid.

46 Seabury: op cit, p. 135.

47 Hassell: *The von Hassell Diaries*, p. 78.

48 Ibid, p. 242.

49 IMT Vol. XXXVIII, p. 88.

50 Goebbels: *Diaries*, p. 322.

51 Dallin: *German Rule in Russia*, p. 57.

52 Buchheim: *Anatomy of the SS State*, p. 369.

53 Heiber: *Zur Justiz im Dritten Reich—Der Fall Elias*, pp. 275 et seq.

54 Wighton: *Heydrich*, pp. 238–41.

55 Ibid, pp. 253 et seq.

56 Ibid. pp. 257–8.

57 Ibid, p. 259.

58 Ibid.

59 Ibid.

60 Ibid, p. 260.

61 Ibid, p. 268.

62 Ibid, p. 270.

63 Ibid, p. 271.

64 Ibid, p. 272.

65 Ibid.

66 Ibid.

67 Ibid, p. 275.

68 "Nebe Series", 9 Feb. 1950, p. 28.

69 Wighton: op cit, pp. 275, 278.

70 Ibid, p. 270.

71 Best: *Die deutsche Politik in Dänemark*, pp. 10 et seq.

72 Hassell: op cit, pp. 245-6. Joergen Haestrup: *Til Landets bedste*, p. 25. Best: op cit, pp. 8, 11.

73 Hassell: op cit, p. 278. Haestrup: op cit, p. 25. Best: op cit, p. 18.

74 Best: op cit, p. 23. Haestrup: op cit, p. 25.

75 Best: op cit, pp. 30, 74. Haestrup: op cit, p. 26.

76 Best: op cit, pp. 37–8. Haestrup: op cit, pp. 22–3.

77 Best: op cit, pp. 40, 42. Haestrup: op cit, pp. 23, 533.

78 Best: op cit, p. 42. Haestrup: op cit, pp. 22, 35, 44, 45.

79 Best: op cit, p. 67. Haestrup: op cit, p. 288, 320, 321.

80 Best: op cit, p. 67. Haestrup: op cit, p. 320.

81 Best: op cit, p. 83.

82 Ibid, p. 84.

83 Ibid.

84 Verbal information from Felix Steiner, 28 Jan. 1966.

85 Paul Kluke: "Nationalsozialistische Europa-Ideologie" in *Vierteljahrshefte für Zeitgeschichte*, No. 3, 1955, p. 265.

86 Ibid, p. 267.

87 Hans-Dietrich Loock: "Zur grossgermanischen Politik des Dritten Reiches" in *Vierteljahrshefte für Zeitgeschichte*, No. 1, 1960, pp. 59–60.

88 Buchheim: *Anatomy of the SS State*, p. 234.

89 Loock: op cit, p. 61.

90 Record of conference in the SS-Hauptamt held on 10 Oct. 1942, date illegible, RFSS Microfilm 70.

91 Ibid.

92 Letter from Berger to Himmler 25 June 1943, RFSS Microfilm 125.

93 Letter from Berger to Himmler 25 Sept. 1943, RFSS Microfilm 125.

94 Report on effect of declarations made in Norway by Reichskommissar Terboven on behalf of the Führer, undated, registered under No. 60–17 in the files of the Reichs führer-SS Personal Staff, RFSSMicrofilm 125.
95 Letter from Jeckeln to Lohse, 30 July 1942, RFSS Microfilm 122.
96 Letter from Meyer to Lohse, 14 Aug. 1942, RFSS Microfilm 122.
97 Basil Dmytryshyn: "The Nazis and the SS Volunteer Division 'Galicia'" in *The American Slavic and East European Review*, July 1956.
98 Dallin: *German Rule in Russia*, p. 221.
99 Wulf: *Die SS*, p. 162.
100 Dallin: op cit, pp. 119-122.
101 Ibid, pp. 217–220. Letter from Strauch to von dem Bach-Zelewski 25 July 1943, RFSS Microfilm 59.
102 Letter from Himmler to d'Alquen, July 1943, RFSS Microfilm 267.
103 Boberach: op cit, p. 287.
104 Steiner: *Armee de Geächteten*, p. 179.
105 Letter from Himmler to d'Alquen, July 1943, RFSS Microfilm 267.
106 Dallin: op cit, pp. 193-4.
107 Ibid, p. 194.
108 Ibid, p. 195.
109 Ibid.
110 Ibid, p. 194 (footnote).
111 Ibid, p. 598. Dmytryshyn: op cit, p. 3.
112 Ibid, pp. 598-9; Klietmann: op cit, p. 194; Dmytryshyn: op cit, p. 6.
113 Letter from Himmler to all Heads of Hauptämter, 14 July 1963, RFSS Microfilm 267.

114 Dmytryshyn: op cit, p. 7.
115 Ibid, p. 8.
116 Klietmann: op cit, p. 193.
117 Reitlinger: *The House built on Sand*, p. 365.
118 Dallin: op cit, p. 599.
119 Ibid. Klietmann: op cit, p. 319.
120 Ibid.
121 Ibid, p. 600.
122 Ibid, pp. 553–556.
123 Thorwald: *Wen sie verderben wollen*, p. 236.
124 Ibid, pp. 260 et seq.
125 Ibid, pp. 266–7.
126 Letter from Himmler to Bach-Zelewski, Jan. 1943, RFSS Microfilm 128.
127 Letter from Melitta Wiedemann to Himmler, 26 May 1943, RFSS Microfilm 38.
128 Extract taken by Himmler's Personal Staff from letter of 5 Oct. 1943 from Melitta Wiedemann (in Wulf's papers).
129 Letter from Brandt to Melitta Wiedemann, 30 June 1943, RFSS Microfilm 38.
130 Thorwald: op cit, pp. 351-2.
131 Ibid.
132 Ibid, p. 355.
133 Ibid, pp. 355-380.
134 Dallin: op cit, p. 606.
135 Thorwald: op cit, p. 433.
136 Letter from Melitta Wiedemann to Brandt, 10 Oct. 1944, RFSS Microfilm 38.
137 Letter from Gottberg to Rosenberg, 31 Aug. 1944, RFSS Microfilm 59.
138 Kempner: *SS im Kreuzverhör*, p. 286.
139 Letter from Frauenfeld, 10 Feb. 1944, RFSS Microfilm 125.
140 Letter from Bormann to Himmler, 18 Feb. 1944 and manuscript note thereon by

Himmler, 26 Mar. 1944, RFSS
Microfilm 56.

141 Boberach: op cit, p. 487.

142 Ibid, p. 491.

143 Ibid, p. 503.

144 Gisevius: *Wo ist Nebe?*, pp. 109 et seq.

145 Ibid, pp. 110–113.

146 "Nebe Series," 16 Mar. 1950, p. 31.

147 Ibid.

148 Ibid.

149 Ibid.

150 Ibid.

151 Krebs: *Fritz-Dietlof Schulenburg*, p. 156.

152 Ibid, p. 320.

153 Ibid, p. 262.

154 Hassell: *Vom anderen Deutschland*, p. 185 (not in English translation).

155 Hassell: op cit, p. 152.

156 Ibid, p. 250.

157 Ritter: op cit, p. 355.

158 Allen Dulles: *Germany's Underground*, p. 149.

159 Ritter: op cit, p. 429.

160 Krebs: *Fritz-Dietlof Schulenburg*, p. 262.

161 Ibid, p. 145. Steiner: *Armee der Geächteten*, p. 271.

162 Dulles: op cit, p. 149.

163 Statement by Hans Fritzsche at the Ohlendorf trial, 18 Aug. 1947 (in Frau Käthe Ohlendorf's papers).

164 Verbal information from Frau Käthe Ohlendorf, 26 Jan. 1966.

165 Statement by Karl Hedrich at the Ohlendorf trial, undated, Document No. 4 (in Frau Käthe Ohlendorf's papers).

166 Statement by Dr Hans Rössner at the Ohlendorf trial, Document No. 27 (in Frau Käthe Ohlendorf's papers).

167 Letter written by Ohlen-

dorf from Nuremberg, 8 June 1948 (in Frau Käthe Ohlendorf's papers).

168 Verbal information from Frau Käthe Ohlendorf and Frau Käthe Jessen, Jan. 1966.

169 Dulles: op cit, pp. 147–8.

170 Ritter: op cit, p. 547.

171 Hassell: op cit, p. 43.

172 Ibid, p. 193.

173 Letter from Heydrich to Ribbentrop, 6 Nov. 1941, RFSS Microfilm 125.

174 Ibid.

175 Hassell: op cit, p. 194.

176 Heinrich Brackelmann: *Die SS und die geplante Entführung Hitlers*, p. 1.

177 Schellenberg: op cit, pp. 351–7.

178 Hassell: op cit, p. 177.

179 Ciano: *Diary*, p. 455.

180 José M. Doussinague: *España Tenia Razon*, p. 295.

181 Kersten: op cit, pp. 165–6.

182 "Nebe Series," 16 Mar. 1950, p. 28.

183 Kersten: op cit, p. 166.

184 Ibid, p. 169.

185 Schellenberg: op cit, pp. 365 et seq, 428.

186 See letter from Kranefuss to Brandt, 23 Sept. 1942, RFSS Microfilm 60. Kranefuss was later the channel for reports from Himmler's contact men in Lisbon and Stockholm (see RFSS Microfilm 22).

187 Letter from SS-Hauptsturmführer Ahrens to Amt VID (Western Group Ausland-SD) of the RSHA, 30 Apr. 1943, in Bezimenski's papers.

188 *Genealogisches Handbuch des Adels*, p. 235.

189 Heinrich Brackelmann: *Prinz Hohenlohe*, p. 2.

190 Report by Hohenlohe to

Hewel, Sept. 1939 (in Hohen-lohe's papers).

191 Verbal information from Professor Höhn, Feb. 1967.

192 Hohenlohe's report, Dec. 1941 (in Hohenlohe's papers).

193 Ibid.

194 Letter from Prince Hohenlohe, Feb. 1967.

195 Brackelmann: *Die SS und die geplante Entführung Hitlers*, p. 2. Letter from Hohenlohe on his meeting with Dulles, mid-Feb. 1943 (in Bezimenski's papers).

196 Brackelmann: op cit, pp. 2–3.

197 Ibid, p. 2.

198 Letter from Hohenlohe to an unnamed SS authority, mid-Feb. 1943 (in Bezimenski's papers).

199 Undated SD report on negotiations with Dulles, approx. spring 1943 (in Bezimenski's papers).

200 Schellenberg: op cit, p. 277. Seabury: op cit, p. 132.

201 Letter to the author from Walter Büttner, Feb. 1967. Note by Gödde of Luther's staff, undated (in Büttner's papers).

202 Seabury: op cit, p. 196.

203 Note by Gödde. Letter to the author from Walter Büttner, Feb. 1967. Hassell: op cit, p. 263.

204 Schellenberg: op cit, p. 368.

205 SD report on negotiations with Dulles, undated and unsigned.

206 Memorandum by Prince Hohenlohe, mid-Feb. 1943.

207 Ibid.

208 Ibid.

209 Letter from Kienast to SS-Hauptamt, 10 June 1943, RFSS Microfilm 45.

210 Doussinague: op cit, p. 296.

211 Ibid, p. 299.

212 Dieter Ehlers: *Technik und Moral einer Verschwörung*, p. 220.

213 Schellenberg: op cit, p. 428.

214 Verbal information from Gero von Gaevernitz, 3 Feb. 1947.

215 Schellenberg: op cit, p. 432. Besgen: op cit, pp. 33–4.

216 Ehlers: op cit, p. 220.

217 Dulles: op cit, p. 27.

218 Ibid.

219 Hassell: op cit, 275.

220 Ehlers: op cit, p. 220.

221 Dulles: op cit, p. 159.

222 "T.E.": *Die Rede Himmlers vor den Gauleitern am 3 Aug. 1944*, p. 376.

223 Dulles: op cit, p. 160.

224 "T.E.": op cit, p. 376.

225 Dulles: op cit, p. 160.

226 Ibid.

227 Ibid.

228 Ibid, p. 162.

229 Verbal information from Gero von Gaevernitz, 3 Feb. 1967.

230 Dulles: op cit, p. 162.

231 Ibid, p. 161.

232 Mario Rodriguez Aragon: "Operacion KN" in *Pueblo*, 21 Aug. 1958.

233 Brackelmann: *Die SS und die Entführung Hitlers*, p. 5.

234 Diary of German Embassy Madrid 1941–45, Vol. II, Chapter 7.

235 Letter from von Kranefuss to Brandt, 3 Apr. 1944, RFSS Microfilm 22.

236 Ibid.

237 Schramm: *Conspiracy among Generals*, pp. 31–2.

238 Speidel: *We defended Normandy*, pp. 123, 126.

239 Ibid, pp. 90–1.

240 Schramm: op cit, p. 34.

241 Speidel: op cit, p. 125.
242 Schramm: op cit, pp. 14, 31.
243 Steiner: *Armee der Ge-ächteten*, pp. 188–9.
244 Schramm: *Der 20 Juli in Paris*, p. 84 (not in English translation).
245 See Ehlers: op cit, pp. 158–9.
246 Schlabrendorff: *The Secret War against Hitler*, p. 273.
247 Zeller: *Geist der Freiheit*, p. 271.
248 Ibid, p. 339.
249 Kersten: op cit, p. 201.
250 Zeller: op cit, p. 381.
251 Ibid, p. 247.
252 Ibid, p. 246.
253 Ibid, p. 387.
254 Kaltenbrunner Report, pp. 27–8.
255 Ehlers: op cit, p. 220.
256 Ludwig Jedlicka: *Der 20 Juli in Österreich*, pp. 54, 117.
257 Ibid, p. 55.
258 Ibid, p. 119.
259 Ibid, p. 58.
260 Ibid, p. 60.
261 Ibid, p. 59.
262 Ibid, p. 121.
263 Ibid.
264 Schramm: op cit, pp. 57, 66.
265 Ibid, p. 68–9.
266 Ibid, p. 68.
267 Ibid, pp. 71, 95–6.
268 Ibid, p. 100.
269 Ibid, p. 105.

270 Ibid, p. 109.
271 Ibid, pp. 109–110.
272 Ibid, pp. 144–5.
273 Ibid, pp. 120 et seq, 170.
274 Ibid, pp. 169 et seq.
275 Steiner: *Armee der Ge-ächteten*, p. 191.
276 Ibid.
277 Ibid.
278 Ibid, p. 190. Verbally from Wilhelm Bittrich, 29 Jan. 1966.
279 Kersten: op cit, p. 201.
280 Ibid, p. 202.
281 Zeller: op cit, p. 251.
282 Ibid, p. 249.
283 Ibid, p. 251. SS Report on 20 July in *Nordwestdeutsche Hefte*, Feb. 1947, p. 3.
284 "Nebe Series," 30 Mar. 1950, p. 20.
285 "Nebe Series," 6 Apr. 1950, pp. 22 et seq.
286 Abshagen: op cit, p. 345. Buchheit: op cit, p. 426.
287 Krebs: *Fritz-Dietlof Schulenburg*, p. 262.
288 Letter from von Herff to Himmler, 9 Oct. 1944, RFSS Microfilm 155.
289 Letter from Himmler to Kaltenbrunner, 14 Oct. 1944, RFSS Microfilm 155.
290 Kreb: op cit, pp. 304, 326.
291 Ritter: op cit, p. 547.
292 Ibid, p. 422.
293 Ibid.
294 Ibid, p. 427.
295 Ibid, p. 428.
296 Ibid, p. 435.

CHAPTER EIGHTEEN

1 Frischauer: op cit, p. 225.
2 Paetel: "Die SS" in *Viertel-jahrshefte für Zeitgeschichte*, No. 1, 1954, p. 13.
3 Frischauer: op cit, p. 225.
4 Paetel in *The Third Reich*, Weidenfeld & Nicolson, 1955, p. 661.
5 "T.E.": *Die Rede Himmlers vor den Gauleitern am 3 Aug. 1944*, p. 392.
6 Letter from Himmler to

Commanding Generals and Divisional Commanders of Army Group Vistula, 19 Feb. 1945, RFSS Microfilm 59.

7 Reitlinger: *The SS*, p. 385.

8 "T.E.": op cit, p. 388.

9 Ibid, p. 392. Guderian: *Panzer Leader*, p. 364.

10 *Völkischer Beobachter*, 3 Aug. 1944.

11 "T.E.": op cit, p. 392.

12 Ibid, p. 389.

13 Reports by SS-Obergruppenführer Gutenberger, HSSPF West, on senior officers in Wehrkreis VI, RFSS Microfilm 59.

14 Ibid.

15 Report by SS-Obergruppenführer Hofmann, HSSPF Southwest, on senior officers in Wehrkreis V, RFSS Microfilm 59.

16 Report from SD-Hauptaussenstelle Mannheim to SD Commander Strasbourg, 14 Nov. 1944, RFSS Microfilm 269.

17 Ibid.

18 Ibid.

19 Ibid.

20 Ibid.

21 Letter from Kaltenbrunner to Himmler, 17 Oct. 1944, RFSS Microfilm 131.

22 Ibid.

23 Reitlinger: *The SS*, p. 387.

24 "T.E.": op cit, p. 389.

25 Manvell and Fraenkel: *Himmler*, pp. 201–2.

26 I saw them myself (author).

27 Guderian: op cit, p. 355.

28 Ibid.

29 Hanns von Krannhals: *Der Warschauer Aufstand*, 1944, pp. 125–6.

30 Guderian: op cit, p. 356.

31 Ibid.

32 *Frankfurter Allgemeine Zeitung*, 22 Dec. 1958.

33 Hagen: op cit, p. 189. Reitlinger: *The SS*, pp. 377–8.

34 Ibid.

35 Hilberg: *The Destruction of the European Jews*, p. 472. Klietmann: *Die Waffen-SS*, p. 195.

36 Hilberg: op cit, p. 472.

37 Ibid.

38 Skorzeny: *Skorzeny's Special Missions*, pp. 7, 8, 12.

39 Ibid, pp. 26–7.

40 Ibid, pp. 78 et seq, 80.

41 Ibid, p. 130.

42 Ibid, p. 133.

43 Ibid, p. 132.

44 Hagen: op cit, p. 369.

45 Nikolaus von Horthy: *Ein Leben für Ungarn*, p. 282.

46 Letter from Winkelmann to Himmler, 25 Oct. 1944, RFSS Microfilm 59.

47 Ibid.

48 Ibid.

49 Ibid. Kern: *Der grosse Rausch*, p. 156.

50 Kern: op cit, p. 156.

51 Letter from Winkelmann to Himmler, 25 Oct. 1944.

52 Ibid.

53 Hagen: op cit, p. 374. Horthy: op cit, p. 282.

54 Horthy: op cit, p. 282.

55 Skorzeny: op cit, pp. 134–5.

56 Ibid, p. 135. Hagen: op cit, p. 375.

57 Hagen: op cit, p. 375.

58 Ibid, p. 376. Skorzeny: op cit, pp. 135–6. Letter from Winkelmann to Himmler, 25 Oct. 1944.

59 Skorzeny: op cit, pp. 135–6.

60 Ibid, p. 136.

61 Ibid.

62 Ibid, p. 137. Letter from Winkelmann to Himmler, 25 Oct. 1944.

63 Letter from Winkelmann to Himmler, 25 Oct. 1944.

64 Seabury: *The Wilhelm-strasse*, p. 195.

65 Letter from Winkelmann to Himmler, 25 Oct. 1944.

66 Hagen: op cit, p. 376.

67 von Senger und Etterlin: *24 Panzerdivision*, p. 266.

68 Letter from Winkelmann to Himmler, 25 Oct. 1944.

69 Skorzeny: op cit, p. 138.

70 Ibid, p. 143.

71 Letter from Winkelmann to Himmler, 25 Oct. 1944.

72 *Völkischer Beobachter*, 9 Nov. 1944.

73 Trevor-Roper: *The Last Days of Hitler*, pp. 37–8.

74 Kessel: *The Man with the Miraculous Hands*, p. 202.

75 Guderian: op cit, p. 383.

76 Trevor-Roper: op cit, p. 40.

77 Ibid, p. 42.

78 Jürgen Thorwald: *Es begann an der Weichsel*, p. 17.

79 Thorwald: *Das Ende an der Elbe*, p. 17.

80 Ibid.

81 *Keesing's Contemporary Archives.*

82 Reitlinger: *The SS*, p. 386.

83 *Keesing's Contemporary Archives.*

84 Reitlinger: *The SS*, p. 386.

85 Ibid, p. 381.

86 Ibid.

87 Ibid, p. 382.

88 Kurt von Tippelskirch: *Geschichte des Zweiten Weltkriegs*, p. 521. Westphal: *The German Army in the West*, p. 187.

89 Westphal: op cit, pp. 187–8.

90 Hausser: *Waffen-SS im Einsatz*, p. 185.

91 Westphal: op cit, p. 188.

92 Delarue: *History of the Ge-stapo*, p. 286; Reitlinger: *The SS,* pp. 236 et seq.

93 Delarue: op cit, pp. 283–4, 287.

94 Ohlendorf's statement, 8 Oct. 1947, p. 502.

95 Skorzeny: op cit, p. 31.

96 Abshagen: op cit, p. 356.

97 Delarue: op cit, p. 363.

98 Letter from Berger to Himmler, 21 Dec. 1944, RFSS Microfilm 122.

99 Verbal information from Gunter d'Alquen.

100 Best: *Himmler*, p. 13.

101 Westphal: op cit, p. 189.

102 Ibid.

103 Reitlinger: *The SS*, p. 398.

104 Ibid, p. 399.

105 Toland: *The Last 100 Days*, pp. 4–5.

106 Tippelskirch: op cit, pp. 536–7.

107 Ibid, p. 539.

108 Guderian: op cit, p. 403.

109 Ibid.

110 Ibid, pp. 403–4.

111 Reitlinger: *The SS*, p. 401.

112 Verbal information from Felix Steiner.

113 Letter from Himmler to Commanding Generals and Divisional Commanders of Army Group Vistula, 19 Feb. 1945.

114 Thorwald: *Es begann an der Weichsel*, p. 221.

115 Ibid, p. 218.

116 Ibid, p. 219.

117 Ibid, p. 220.

118 Guderian: op cit, p. 413.

119 Ibid, pp. 414–5.

120 Ibid, p. 415.

121 Thorwald: *Das Ende an der Elbe*, p. 10.

122 Guderian: op cit, p. 421. Thorwald: op cit, p. 11.

123 Guderian: op cit, pp. 421–

2; Reitlinger: *The SS*, p. 412.

124 Thorwald: *Das Ende an der Elbe*, p. 7. Toland: op cit, pp. 259 et seq.

125 Thorwald: *Das Ende an der Elbe*, pp. 18, 21.

126 Kersten: *Totenkopf und Treue*, p. 15 (not in English translation). Besgen: op cit, pp. 17–8.

127 Besgen: *Der stille Befehl*, p. 15.

128 Ibid, p. 20.

129 Ibid, pp. 21–22. Engelmann: *Deutschland Report*, p. 93.

130 Ibid, pp. 38–9.

131 Ibid, p. 36.

132 Ibid, pp. 20, 37.

133 Ibid, pp. 14, 65.

134 Ibid, p. 53.

135 Arendt: *Eichmann in Jerusalem*, pp. 176 et seq.

136 Andreas Biss: *Der Stopp der Endlösung*, p. 24.

137 Ibid, pp. 48, 24.

138 Ibid, p. 25. Hilberg: op cit, p. 542.

139 Ibid, pp. 34–5.

140 Arendt: *Eichmann in Jerusalem*, p. 179.

141 Hilberg: op cit, p. 543.

142 Biss: op cit, p. 37.

143 Ibid.

144 Ibid, pp. 37, 50. Hilberg: op cit, p. 544.

145 Ibid, p. 51.

146 Ibid, p. 53.

147 Ibid, p. 59.

148 Hilberg: op cit, p. 547.

149 Biss: op cit, p. 302.

150 Ibid, p. 60.

151 Ibid, p. 69.

152 Hilberg: op cit, p. 532. *Süddeutsche Zeitung*, 27 Aug. 1966.

153 Hilberg: op cit, p. 532.

154 Ibid.

155 Kurt Emmenegger: "Reichsführers gehorsamster Becher" in *Sie und Er*, Jan./Feb. 1963, Serial 7.

156 Biss: op cit, pp. 106 et seq.

157 Ibid, p. 107.

158 Ibid, pp. 110, 349.

159 Ibid, p. 110.

160 Ibid, p. 141.

161 Ibid, p. 129.

162 Ibid.

163 Ibid, p. 135.

164 Ibid, p. 145.

165 Ibid, p. 148.

166 Ibid, p. 157.

167 Ibid, pp. 156–7.

168 Ibid, pp. 150–3.

169 Ibid, p. 153.

170 Ibid, pp. 166–7.

171 Ibid, pp. 167, 178, 180.

172 Ibid, pp. 178, 180, 201.

173 Ibid, pp. 202, 205.

174 Ibid, pp. 205–6.

175 Ibid, pp. 351 et seq.

176 Schellenberg: *Memoirs*, p. 428. Biss: op cit, p. 250.

177 Schellenberg: op cit, p. 428.

178 Ibid, pp. 428–9.

179 Ibid, p. 429.

180 Ibid, p. 430.

181 IMT Vol. XI, p. 334.

182 Besgen: op cit, p. 43.

183 Ibid.

184 Ibid. Schellenberg: op cit, pp. 441–444.

185 Ibid.

186 Ibid.

187 Bernadotte: *The Fall of the Curtain*, p. 8.

188 Ibid, p. 10.

189 Ibid, pp. 12–3.

190 Schellenberg: op cit, p. 434.

191 Ibid, p. 435.

192 Bernadotte: op cit, p. 22.

193 Ibid, pp. 23, 26, 29.

194 Trevor-Roper: *The Last Days of Hitler*, pp. 96–7.

195 Bernadotte: op cit, p. 44.

196 Ibid, p. 45.

197 Ibid, p. 47.

198 Ibid, p. 48.

199 Trevor-Roper: op cit, p. 99.

200 Ibid, pp. 99–100.

201 Kurt Detlev Möller: *Das letzte Kapital*, pp. 55–6.

202 Toland: op cit, p. 478.

203 Ibid.

204 Allen Dulles: *The Secret Surrender*, pp. 155–6.

205 Toland: op cit, p. 478.

206 Verbal information from Gero von Gaevernitz.

207 Eugen Dollmann: *Wie Italien vor dem Bolschewismus gerettet wurde*, pp. 4 ct seq.

208 Ibid, p. 6.

209 Toland: op cit, p. 239.

210 Dollmann: *Die Kapitulation von Caserta*, p. 19.

211 Ibid, p. 24.

212 Ibid.

213 Dulles: op cit, p. 165.

214 Toland: op cit, p. 478.

215 Ibid.

216 Ibid.

217 Ibid.

218 Ibid, p. 479.

219 Ibid.

220 Ibid.

221 Ibid, p. 480.

222 Ibid, p. 481. Dollmann: *Die Kapitulation von Caserta*, p. 40.

223 Dollmann: op cit, p. 40.

224 Trevor-Roper: op cit, p. 188, footnote.

225 Hagen: op cit, pp. 460–1.

226 Toland: op cit, p. 338.

227 Ibid.

228 Trevor-Roper: op cit, pp. 102, 115 et seq.

229 Ibid, p. 117.

230 Besgen: op cit, p. 51.

231 Trevor-Roper: op cit, p. 123.

232 Besgen: op cit, p. 51.

233 Bernadotte: op cit, p. 53.

234 Thorwald: *Das Ende an der Elbe*, p. 76. Cornelius Ryan: *The Last Battle*, pp. 334–5.

235 Thorwald: op cit, p. 76. Ryan: op cit, p. 335.

236 Klietmann: op cit, pp. 56–7. Ryan: op cit, p. 335.

237 Toland: op cit, p. 420. Thorwald: op cit, p. 87.

238 Thorwald: op cit, p. 89.

239 Ibid.

240 Ryan: op cit, pp. 373–4; Toland: op cit, pp. 436–7.

241 Ryan: op cit, p. 374. Letter from Gotthard Heinrici, 1 Mar. 1967. Toland: op cit, p. 437.

242 Thorwald: op cit, p. 143.

243 Felix Steiner: *Die Freiwilligen*, pp. 328–9.

244 Trevor-Roper: op cit, p. 186. Ryan: op cit, p. 392.

245 Ryan: op cit, p. 392.

246 Trevor-Roper: op cit, p. 189.

247 Toland: op cit, p. 520.

248 Hans-Adolf Jacobsen: *1939–1945*, p. 532.

249 Trevor-Roper: op cit, p. 184.

250 Reitlinger: *The SS*, p. 435.

251 Ibid, p. 441.

252 Ibid, p. 445.

253 Ibid, p. 446.

254 Ibid, p. 443.

255 Ibid, p. 446.

256 Manvell and Fraenkel: *Himmler*, pp. 244, 246.

257 Ibid, p. 245.

258 Ibid.

259 Ibid, p. 248.

260 Hilberg: op cit, p. 706.

Reitlinger: *Final Solution*, p. 357.

261 Ryan: op cit, p. 319.

262 Hilberg: op cit, p. 694.

263 Reitlinger: *Die Endlösung*, p. 586 (German edition only).

264 Reitlinger: *Die Endlösung*, p. 589 (German edition only).

265 Hilberg: op cit, p. 707.

266 Ibid, pp. 708, 712.

267 Reitlinger: *Final Solution*, pp. 510, 513, 507.

268 Hilberg: op cit, p. 711.

269 Ibid, pp. 707, 706, 713.

270 See data passim in Hilberg, op cit, and Reitlinger, *Final Solution*.

271 Kern: op cit, p. 187.

Appendix 2

GLOSSARY

Abschnitt
: A regional sub-division of the SS territorial organisation, subordinate to an Oberabschnitt. Also a regional HQ of the SD.

Abteilung
: A branch, section or sub-division of a main department or office (Amt, Amtsgruppe or Hauptamt). Alternatively a military unit or detachment up to battalion strength.

Abwehr
: The Intelligence and Clandestine Warfare Service of the German High Command— Amt Ausland/Abwehr.

Abwehrpolizei
: Counter-espionage police. A function of the Frontier Police—controlled by the Gestapo.

Ahnenerbe
: "Ancestral heritage." An organisation, created by Himmler, the primary object of which was to search for early German relics and research into early German history.

Allgemeine SS
: The general body of the SS consisting of part-time, full-time and inactive or honorary members, as distinct from the Waffen-SS.

Allgemeine Wehrmachtsamt
: The General Armed Forces Office (in OKW) concerned principally with personnel, training and equipment.

Amt (pl. Ämter)
: An office, branch or directorate of a Ministry; in certain cases an independent ministry, e.g. Auswärtiges Amt [Foreign Ministry].

Amtsgruppe
: A branch of a Hauptamt.

Anwärter
: A cadet or candidate.

AO
: Auslandsorganisation (q.v.).

AOK
: Armee-Oberkommando (q.v.).

Armee-Oberkommando
: An Army Headquarters.

731

Ausland/Abwehr	See Abwehr.
Auslandsorganisation	The Nazi Party agency concerned with the care and supervision of Germans abroad. Ranked as a Gau (q.v.).
Ausland-SD	The branch of the SD dealing with foreign intelligence.
Aussendienststelle	An out-station of a Ministry or agency.
Aussenstelle	Alternative form of Aussendienststelle (q.v.).
Auswärtiges Amt	The Foreign Ministry.
AWA	Allgemeine Wehrmachtsamt (q.v.).
Barbarossa	Code word for the German attack on Russia, 22 June 1941.
Bauinspektion	Building Inspectorate—part of Amtsgruppe C of the WVHA.
BdO	Befehlshaber der Ordnungspolizei (q.v.).
BdS	Befehlshaber der Sicherheitspolizei (q.v.).
Beamter	Official or functionary.
Befehl	An order or command.
Befehlshaber	A senior military commander.
Befehlshaber der Ordnungspolizei	Commander of the uniformed police at regional and Wehrkreis level and in occupied territories—subordinate to the HSSPF—previously entitled Inspekteur der Ordnungspolizei.
Befehlshaber der Sicherheitspolizei und des Sicherheitsdienstes	Commander of the Security Police and Security Service in occupied territories—subordinate to the HSSPF for particular tasks but under direct RSHA control. Latterly the title of the IdS in certain areas of the Reich.
Bereitschaft	An emergency or alarm detachment of the Party or police (see also under Politische).
Bereitschaftspolizei	Mobile barrack police units of the Landespolizei administered by the Länder until the centralisation of the police in 1935–36.
Bezirk	A district or administrative unit.
Brigadeführer	See Appendix 3.
Burgomeister	Mayor of a town or city.
Bürgerwehr	Citizens defence force (of the early post-1918 period).
Chef des Generalstabes des Heeres	Chief of Staff of the Army.
Chef der Sicherheitspolizei und des SD	Chief of the Security Police and Security Service—Heydrich until 1942, then Kaltenbrunner.
Chef der Zivilverwaltung	Head of the Civilian Administration in an occupied territory.

CSSD	Chef der Sicherheitspolizei und des SD (q.v.).
DAG	Deutsche Ansiedlungsgesellschaft (q.v.).
DAW	Deutsche Ausrüstungswerke (q.v.).
DEST	Deutsche Erd- und Steinwerke (q.v.).
Deutsche Ansiedlungs-gesellschaft	The German Settlement Company, affiliated to the RKF in 1940.
Deutsche Ausrüstungs-werke	The German Armaments Works. An SS enterprise established in 1939.
Deutsche Erd- und Steinwerke GmbH	German Excavation and Quarrying Company Ltd. An SS enterprise formed in 1938. Used concentration-camp labour.
Deutsche Umsiedlungs-Treuhand GmbH	German Resettlement Trust Ltd—affiliated to the RKF.
Deutsche Wirtschafts-betriebe	German Economic Enterprises. A holding company formed to cover all SS economic enterprises.
Dienststelle	A headquarters, administrative office or station.
DUT	Deutsche Umsiedlungs-Treuhand GmbH (q.v.).
DWB	Deutsche Wirtschaftsbetriebe (q.v.).
Ehrenführer	Honorary SS officers, usually of senior rank. A distinction granted by Himmler to leading Party and State personalities, e.g. Bormann, Ribbentrop.
Einsatzgruppe	An operational group or task force of the Sipo and SD for special missions (usually liquidations) in occupied territory. Consisted of up to six Einsatzkommandos.
Einsatzkommando	A detachment of the Sipo. Part of an Einsatzgruppe.
Einsatzstab	An operational staff of the Sipo and SD employed in occupied territory; also used for an RSHA operational staff dealing with the appropriation of real estate in the Eastern territories.
Einwandererzentralstelle	Central Immigration Office controlled by the RSHA; also part of the RKF.
Einwohnerwehr	Citizens Defence Force (of the early post-1918 period).
Ersatzheer	The Replacement Army.
EWZ	Einwandererzentralstelle (q.v.).
Fachreferat	A specialist sub-section or "desk" in an office or headquarters.
Feldjägerkorps	A shock formation of the SA, disbanded in 1935 and incorporated in the police.

Feuerschutzpolizei | Fire Fighting Police—a branch of the Orpo.

Feuerwehr | Fire Brigade; these were controlled by the Orpo.

FHA | Führungshauptamt (q.v.).

FHQ | Führerhauptquartier (q.v.).

Fördernde Mitglied (of the SS) | Patron or sponsoring member of the SS; administered by the WVHA; paid a monthly contribution.

Führer | Leader, commander or chief. "Der Führer" [The Leader] was used only in relation to Hitler.

Führerhauptquartier | Hitler's Field Headquarters.

Führungshauptamt | Operational headquarters of the whole SS, responsible for training, organisation and employment with the exception of tactical employment of the Waffen-SS divisions in the field. Its head was Obergruppenführer Hans Jüttner.

Gau | The main territorial division of the Nazi Party. Germany was divided into 42 Gaue.

Gauleiter | The highest ranking Party official in a Gau, responsible for all political and economic activity, mobilisation of labour and civil defence.

Geheime Feldpolizei | Secret Field Police. The executive arm of the Abwehr. Largely taken over by the Sipo and SD in 1942.

Geheime Staatspolizei | Secret State Police. Became Amt IV of the RSHA. Its head was Obergruppenführer Heinrich Müller.

Geheimes Staatspolizeiamt | The national headquarters of the Secret State Police. Absorbed into the RSHA in 1939.

Gemeinde | A municipality or community.

Gemeindepolizei | Municipal police.

Gendarmerie | The rural police, including motorised traffic-control units.

Generalgouvernement | The Government General—German-occupied Poland and its administration.

Generalkommando | An Army Corps Headquarters.

Generaloberst | Colonel-General. An army rank senior to General but below Field Marshal—no precise equivalent in the British or U.S. armies.

Generalquartiermeister (of the Army) | Quartermaster-General of the Army or Deputy Chief of Staff.

Gericht | A court of law or tribunal.

Germanische Leitstelle	The "Germanic" Liaison Office in the SS Hauptamt responsible for the supervision of the "Germanic" SS.
Germanische SS	The "Germanic" formations in the Waffen-SS; also the indigenous "Germanic" organisations in the occupied territories.
Gesamt SS	Lit. overall SS, a term used to cover all SS branches.
Gestapa	Geheimes Staatspolizeiamt (q.v.).
Gestapo	Geheime Staatspolizei (q.v.).
Grenzpolizei	Frontier or Border Control Police—controlled by the Gestapo.
Grenzpolizei-kommissariat	A territorial division of the Grenzpolizei.
Gruppe	An elastic term used for a territorial HQ of the SA, an *ad hoc* military formation, or a section in a ministry.
Gruppenführer	See Appendix 3.
Hauptabteilung	A main division of a department or office.
Hauptamt SS	The Central Office of the SS responsible for recruitment, training, education, welfare etc of the entire SS. Its head was Obergruppenführer Gottlob Berger.
Hauptamt SS-Gericht	The SS Legal Department administering the special disciplinary and penal code governing all SS and police personnel. Its head was Obergruppenführer Franz Breithaupt.
Hauptamt Haushalt und Bauten	SS Department of Budget and Buildings. Controlled construction work and the allocation of concentration camp labour, later part of the WVHA. Its head was Obergruppenführer Oswald Pohl, later head of the WVHA.
Hauptamt Sicherheits-polizei	The Headquarters of the Security Police (Gestapo and Kripo), integrated into the RSHA in 1939.
Hauptamt Verwaltung und Wirtschaft	See WVHA.
Hauptaussenstelle	A main outstation of the SD.
Hauptscharführer	See Appendix 3.
Hauptsturmführer	See Appendix 3.
Haupttreuhandstelle Ost	Main Trust Office for the East. A public corporation created by Göring for the seizure and administration of Polish and Jewish property.

HIAG	Hilfsgemeinschaft auf Gegenseitigkeit— Mutual Help Association. The present welfare organisation for former Waffen-SS personnel. Located in Lüdenscheid, West phalia.
Höhere SS- und Polizeiführer	Senior SS and Police commander. Himmler's personal representative in each Wehrkreis and liaison officer with the military and senior regional authorities. Also established in occupied territories. Nominally the commander of all SS and police units in his area.
HSSPF	Höhere SS- und Polizeiführer (q.v.).
HTO	Haupttreuhandstelle Ost (q.v.).
IA Abteilung	The section of the former Berlin Police Presidency responsible for the collection of political police intelligence. Taken over by the Gestapa in 1933–34.
Ic	The intelligence officer in a military HQ or formation. Used to designate an intelligence service, e.g. that set up by Heydrich as the forerunner of the SD.
IdO	Inspekteur der Ordnungspolizei (q.v.).
IdS	Inspekteur der Sicherheitspolizei (q.v.).
Inspekteur der Ordnungspolizei	The original title of the BdO.
Inspekteur der Sicherheitspolizei und des Sicherheitsdienstes	Inspector of the Security Police and Security Service at regional and Wehrkreis level. Under direct RSHA control but subordinate to the HSSPF for particular tasks. See also BdS.
Jagdverbände	SS sabotage and subversive units. Their chief was Otto Skorzeny.
Junkerschule	An SS officer-cadet training school.
Kasernierte Polizei	Militarised barrack police organised in motorised units. Extensively employed in the eastern occupied territories.
KdO	Kommandeur der Ordnungspolizei (q.v.).
KdS	Kommandeur der Sicherheitspolizei (q.v.).
Kommandeur	Officer commanding a unit.
Kommandeur der Ordnungspolizei	Commander of the uniformed police in a General Kommissariat—subordinate to the BdO.
Kommandeur der Sicherheitspolizei und des Sicherdienstes	Commander of the Security Police and Security Service in a sub-district (General Kommissariat) of a Reichskommissariat in occupied territory. Also the commander of an Einsatzkommando.

Kommandoamt	The department within the Führungshauptamt responsible for the general operational control of the Waffen-SS.
Kommissariat	A regional HQ of the Frontier Police (See also Reichskommissariat).
Kreis	A district or county. The principal subdivision of a Gau.
Kreishauptmann	The principal district official in the Government-General.
Kreisleiter	The lowest salaried official of the Nazi Party. Responsible for a Kreis.
Kriminalkommissar	The lowest rank in the upper officer class of the Criminal Police.
Kriminaloberkommissar	The next senior rank in the Criminal Police above Kriminalkommissar.
Kriminalpolizei	The Criminal Police which, together with the Gestapo, formed the Security Police (Sipo). In 1939 became Amt V of the RSHA. Its head was Gruppenführer Arthur Nebe.
Kriminalrat	Kriminalrat. A senior rank in the Kriminalpolizei, below Kriminaldirektor.
Kripo	Kriminalpolizei (q.v.).
Land (pl. Länder)	One of the fifteen territorial divisions of Republican Germany, each with its own government. From 1933 the Central Government controlled the Länder through Reichsstatthalter.
Landeskriminalpolizeiamt	Criminal Police HQ in a Land prior to the centralisation of the police in 1936.
Landeskriminalpolizeistelle	A local office of the Criminal Police in a Land.
Landkreis	Rural sub-division of a Regierungsbezirk in Prussia.
Landrat	The chief authority in the administration of a Landkreis. Frequently the same man as the Party Kreisleiter.
Landtag	Chamber of Deputies or diet in a Land—abolished by the Nazis.
Lebensborn	Lit. "Spring of Life"—the SS maternity organisation.
Legationsrat	Embassy or Legation Counsellor. A Foreign Service rank.
Leibstandarte SS Adolf Hitler	The Adolf Hitler Bodyguard Regiment. The oldest of the SS militarised formations, formed in 1933. Reached divisional status in 1941. Commanded from 1933 to 1943 by Oberstgruppenführer Sepp Dietrich.

Leitabschnitt	A regional HQ of the SD, coinciding approximately with a Wehrkreis.
Leitstelle	A regional HQ of the Gestapo or Kripo established at the HQ of a Wehrkreis or capital of a Land.
LKPA	Landeskriminalpolizeiamt (q.v.).
Ministerialdirektor	A senior official in the civil service. Head of a department in a ministry.
Ministerialrat	Senior counsellor in the civil service. Usually head of a section in a ministry.
Ministerpräsident	Minister-President. The Prime Minister of a Land government.
Nationalsozialistische Deutsche Arbeiter Partei	National-Socialist German Workers' Party —the official title of the Nazi Party.
Nationalsozialistische Kraftfahr-Korps	National-Socialist Motor Corps. One of the para-military formations of the Nazi Party.
Nationalsozialistische Volkswohlfahrt	National-Socialist People's Welfare Organisation, responsible largely for the care of mothers and juveniles.
NSDAP	Nationalsozialistische Deutsche Arbeiter Partei (q.v.).
NSKK	Nationalsozialistische Kraftfahr-Korps (q.v.).
NSV	Nationalsozialistische Volkswohlfahrt (q.v.).
ObdH	Oberbefehlshaber des Heeres (q.v.).
Oberabschnitt	The main territorial division of the SS, approximately equivalent to a Wehrkreis.
Oberbefehlshaber des Heeres	The Commander-in-Chief of the Army (von Brauchitsch 1938–41 *vice* von Fritsch, then Hitler).
Oberführer	See Appendix 3.
Obergruppe	A main territorial division of the SA.
Obergruppenführer	See Appendix 3.
Oberkommando des Heeres	The High Command of the Army.
Oberkommando der Wehrmacht	The High Command of the Armed Forces (Hitler was supreme commander with Keitel as Chief of OKW).
Oberkriegsverwaltungs-rat	A senior administrative counsellor in occupied territory.
Oberpräsident	The senior administrative official in a Prussian province.
Oberregierungsrat	Government counsellor—a senior civil service rank.
Oberscharführer	See Appendix 3.

Oberste SA Führer	Supreme Commander of the SA (Hitler from 1930).
Oberstes Parteigericht	The Supreme Court of the Nazi Party under Reichsleiter Walter Buch.
Oberstgruppenführer	See Appendix 3.
Obersturmbannführer	See Appendix 3.
Obersturmführer	See Appendix 3.
Oberverwaltungsrat	A senior administrative counsellor.
OKH	Oberkommando des Heeres (q.v.).
OKW	Oberkommando der Wehrmacht (q.v.).
Ordnungspolizei	Lit. "Order police". The regular uniformed police comprising the Schutzpolizei, Gendarmerie and Feuerschutzpolizei together with certain technical and auxiliary services.
Organisation Todt	A semi-military government agency established in 1933 and used mainly for the construction of strategic highways and military installations.
Orpo	Ordnungspolizei (q.v.).
Ortsgruppenleiter	A Nazi Party official in charge of one or more parts of a town, subordinate to a Kreisleiter.
Ortspolizei	Local police.
OSAF	Oberste SA Führer (q.v.).
Ostindustrie GmbH	Eastern Industries Ltd—an SS concern formed with the primary purpose of exploiting Jewish labour in Poland.
Ostministerium	Ministry for the East—see Reichsministerium für die besetzten Ostgebiete.
OT	Organisation Todt (q.v.).
Personalhauptamt	The main SS personnel department responsible for the records of all SS officers. Its head was Gruppenführer Maximilian von Herff.
Politische Bereitschaft	Political alarm squad. The precursor of the SS-Verfügungstruppe.
Polizeipräsident	Police President. The head of the regular police in a large city.
Rasse- und Siedlungshauptamt	SS department for Race and Re-settlement. The office responsible for the racial purity of the SS and the settlement of SS colonists in the conquered eastern territories.
Referat	A sub-section or "desk" within a Gruppe.
Referent	The official in charge of a referat.
Regierungsbezirk	Sub-division of a Prussian province. Also a Bavarian administrative district.

Regierungspräsident	The senior government official in a Regierungsbezirk.
Regierungsrat	Government counsellor. The lowest rank in the higher civil service.
Reichsführer-SS und Chef der Deutschen Polizei	"Reich SS Leader and Chief of the German Police"; Himmler's full title from June 1936.
Reichsführung-SS	The High Command of the SS, comprising Himmler's Personal Staff and the Hauptämter (including the RSHA).
Reichsgau	One of eleven regions formed from territories annexed after 1939. Administered by a Reichsstatthalter.
Reichskommissar für die Festigung Deutschen Volkstums	Reich Commissar for the Strengthening of Germanism. An office created in 1939 under Himmler for the repatriation of "racial Germans" and settlement of German colonies in eastern occupied territories.
Reichskommissariat für das Ostland	The German Civil Administration in occupied Soviet territories (except the Ukraine) and ex-Russian-occupied Poland. Divided into "General Kommissariats."
Reichskriminalpolizeiamt	The headquarters of the Criminal Police. Became Amt V of the RSHA.
Reichsleiter	The highest-ranking Nazi Party official.
Reichsministerium für die besetzten Ostgebiete	Reich Ministry for the Occupied Eastern (Soviet) Territories. Created in 1941 under Rosenberg.
Reichssicherheitshauptamt	Reich Central Security Department. Formed in 1939. Combined the Security Police (Gestapo and Kripo) and the SS Security Service (SD). It was both an SS Hauptamt and a branch of the Ministry of the Interior.
Reichsstatthalter	The Governor of a Land or Reichsgau. Frequently identical with the Party Gauleiter.
Reichswehr	The 100,000 army to which Germany was restricted under the Treaty of Versailles.
RFSS	Reichsführer-SS.
RKF	Reichskommissar für die Festigung Deutschen Volkstums.
RMO	Reichsministerium für die besetzten Ostgebiet.
Rottenführer	See Appendix 3.
RSHA	Reichssicherheitshauptamt (q.v.).
RuSHA	Rasse- und Siedlungshauptamt (q.v.).

SA	Sturmabteilung (q.v.).
Scharführer	See Appendix 3.
Schupo	Schutzpolizei (q.v.).
Schutzpolizei	Lit. "Protection Police." The regular uniformed municipal and country constabulary, forming the bulk of the Ordnungspolizei.
Schutzstaffel	Lit. "Protection" or "Guard Detachment" —the SS.
SD	Sicherheitsdienst RFSS (q.v.).
Selbstschutz	A self-defence militia recruited from the German minority in Poland.
Sicherheitsdienst RFSS	The SS Security Service formed in 1932 under Heydrich. Intended to be the sole Party intelligence organisation. The HQ's of the Sipo and SD formed the core of the RSHA in 1939.
Sicherheitshauptamt	The SS Security Department under Heydrich. Also known as the SD Hauptamt.
Sicherheitspolizei	The Security Police consisting of the Gestapo and the Kripo—under Heydrich.
Sipo	Sicherheitspolizei.
Sonderkommando	A special detachment of the SS employed for police and political tasks in occupied territory.
SS	Schutzstaffel.
SSPF	SS- und Polizeiführer (q.v.).
SS- und Polizeiführer	District SS and Police Commanders in Eastern occupied territories—subordinate to the HSSPF.
Staatsanwalt	Public Prosecutor.
Staatsschutzkorps	State Protection Corps—an unofficial term used to describe the combined functions of the Gestapo, Kripo and SD.
Staatspolizei	Initially the Prussian Political Police. Later the Nazi Political Police i.e. the Gestapo.
Staatspolizeileitstelle	The regional HQ of the Gestapo in a Wehrkreis, Prussian province, Land or Reichsgau, controlling a number of Aussendienststellen.
Staatspolizeistelle	The regional HQ of the Gestapo in a Regierungsbezirk, smaller Land or Reichsgau. Co-ordinated by but not subordinate to a Leitstelle.
Staatssekretär	State Secretary. The permanent head of a ministry—Permanent Under-Secretary.
Stabshauptamt	The Staff Office of the RKF.

Stabswache	"Headquarters Guard". The original Party guard detachment formed from the SA in 1923. Forerunner of the Leibstandarte.
Stahlhelm	The Nationalist ex-servicemen's organisation founded by Franz Seldte in 1918. Compulsorily absorbed into the SA in 1933.
Standarte	An SS (and SA) formation approximately equivalent to a regiment.
Standartenführer	See Appendix 3.
Standgericht	Court martial.
Standrecht	Martial law.
Stapo	Staatspolizei (q.v.).
Stapostelle	Staatspolizeistelle (q.v.).
Stelle	Place, position, appointment, establishment.
Stellvertreter	Deputy or representative.
StHA	Stabshauptamt (q.v.).
Stosstrupp	Assault or shock troop, battle group.
Streifendienst	Patrol Service manned by the Hitler Youth, trained and officered by the SS.
Sturm	An SS (or SA) unit equivalent to a company.
Sturmabteilung	Lit. "Storm Detachment". The SA (the "Brown-shirts"). The original Nazi paramilitary organisation founded in 1921.
Sturmbann	An SS (or SA) unit approximately equivalent to a battalion.
Sturmmann	See Appendix 3.
Technische Nothilfe	Technical Emergency Corps. An auxiliary police force of the Orpo consisting of engineers, technicians and specialists for construction work, public utilities, communications, salvage etc.
Teno	Technische Nothilfe.
TN	Technische Nothilfe.
Totenkopfverbände	"Death's Head Formations". The concentration-camp guard units. In 1939 formed the nucleus of the SS Totenkopf Division, one of the first field formations of the Waffen-SS.
Truppführer	See Appendix 3.
TV	Totenkopfverbände.
Umwandererzentralstelle	Central Re-settlement Office concerned with the re-settlement of Polish deportees from the Wartheland. Part of the RKF organisation controlled by the RSHA.

Unterscharführer	See Appendix 3.
Untersturmführer	See Appendix 3.
UWZ	Umwandererzentralstelle (q.v.).
VDA	Volksbund für das Deutschtum im Ausland (q.v.).
Verfügungstruppe	The militarised formations of the SS renamed Waffen-SS in the winter of 1939/40.
Verwaltung	Administration.
Volksbund für das Deutschtum im Ausland	League for Germans Abroad. A pre-Nazi organisation dealing with the Volksdeutsche. Taken over by the Party in 1930. Its head was Obergruppenführer Lorenz who was also head of VOMI (q.v.).
Volksdeutsche	"Racial Germans". German minorities in foreign countries.
Volksdeutsche Mittelstelle	Racial German Assistance Office. One of the organisations through which contact was maintained with Germans abroad. Largely run by the SS. Head—Obergruppenführer Lorenz.
Volkssturm	Home Guard.
VOMI	Volksdeutsche Mittelstelle (q.v.).
VT	Verfügungstruppe (q.v.).
Waffen-SS	Fully militarised SS formations, initially composed of the Verfügungstruppe and the Totenkopfverbände, later including non-German units. Provided nearly 40 divisions during the second World War.
Wehrbezirkskommando	Military District—subordinate to a Wehrkreis—concerned primarily with recruiting.
Wehrkreis	Military region, indicated by roman numeral. The main military territorial organisation in Germany. In peacetime each Wehrkreis contained an active infantry corps.
Wehrmacht	The armed forces (Army, Navy, Air Force).
Wehrmachtführungsstab	The armed forces operations staff. Part of OKW under Colonel-General Alfred Jodl.
Wirtschafts- und Verwaltungshauptamt	SS Economic and Administrative Department formed from the SS Hauptamt in 1940. Controlled the SS economic enterprises and administered the concentration camps. Its head was Obergruppenführer Oswald Pohl.
WVHA	Wirtschafts- und Verwaltungshauptamt.
Zentralabteilung	Co-ordinating section of an office or agency.

Appendix 3

TABLE OF SS RANKS

SS	Approximate Equivalent	
	British Army	*U.S. Army*
Reichsführer-SS	Field Marshall	General of the Army
SS-Oberstgruppenführer	General	General
SS-Obergruppenführer	Lieutenant-General	Lieutenant-General
SS-Gruppenführer	Major-General	Major-General
SS-Brigadeführer	Brigadier	Brigadier-General
SS-Oberführer	Senior Colonel	Senior Colonel
SS-Standartenführer	Colonel	Colonel
SS-Obersturmbannführer	Lieutenant-Colonel	Lieutenant-Colonel
SS-Sturmbannführer	Major	Major
SS-Hauptsturmführer	Captain	Captain
SS-Obersturmführer	Lieutenant	1st Lieutenant
SS-Untersturmführer	2nd Lieutenant	2nd Lieutenant
SS-Sturmscharführer	Regimental Sergeant-Major	Sergeant-Major
SS-Hauptscharführer	Sergeant-Major	Master-Sergeant
SS-Oberscharführer	Quartermaster-Sergeant	Technical Sergeant
SS-Scharführer	Staff Sergeant	Staff Sergeant
SS-Unterscharführer	Sergeant	Sergeant
SS-Rottenführer	Corporal	Corporal
SS-Sturmmann	Lance-Corporal	Corporal
SS-Oberschütze	Senior Private	Private 1st Class
SS-Schütze	Private	Private

Appendix 4

PARTITION OF POLAND 1939–42

PARTITION OF POLAND 1939-1942

BALTIC

REICHS-KOMMISSARIAT

Danzig

Königsberg

OSTLAND

REICH

Stettin

Danzig/West Prussian Gau

Upper Silesian Gau

Bydgoszcz

Bialystok

administered by East Prussian Gau

Poznan

Gau Wartheland

Warsaw

REICHS-KOMMISSARIAT UKRANE

Radom

Lublin

East Prussian Gaus

Zamosc

Hrubieszow
Tomaszow

Kattowitz

Cracow

Lwow

SLOVAKIA

HUNGARY

RUMANIA

Frontiers of Poland and Danzig, August 1939

Soviet- occupied area 1939-1941

National frontiers 1942

German administrative boundaries 1942

Government General

Attached to East Prussian Gau

SS/Police Headquarters

HSSPF   SSPF

745

Appendix 5

THE FATE OF GERMAN JEWRY

Jewish population 1933	**503,000**

Emigrants 1933-1945	**207,000**
to U.S.A.	90,000
to Palestine	50,000
Murdered	**170,000**
(including emigrants to countries occupied by Germany during the war)	
Excess of deaths over births 1933-1945	**72,000**
(excluding those murdered)	

Jewish population in 1945	**23,000**

All figures refer to the Jewish population within the 1933 Reich frontiers

Appendix 6

EINSATZGRUPPEN IN OCCUPIED RUSSIA (NOVEMBER 1941)

Appendix 7

THE DESTRUCTION OF EUROPEAN JEWRY

THE DESTRUCTION OF EUROPEAN JEWRY

Jews murdered as a percentage of the 1939 Jewish population (actual numbers in brackets)

Norway (750) 38%

Denmark (70) 1%

Holland, Belgium and Luxembourg (130,000) 56%

Germany, Austria and Czechoslovakia (310,000) 50%

Poland (3,000,000) 90%

Soviet Union (900,000) 28%

Hungary (300,000) 75%

Rumania (270,000) 34%

France and Italy (70,000) 22%

Yugoslavia (60,000) 80%

Bulgaria 0%

Greece (60,000) 81%

Maximum penetration of the Axis Powers during World War II

Appendix 8

THE VICTIMS OF THE "FINAL SOLUTION"

Jews murdered in areas under SS control

Germany		250,000
(including Austria and the "Reich Protectorate of Bohemia and Moravia")		
Slovakia		60,000
Denmark and Norway	under	1,000
Holland, Belgium and Luxembourg		130,000
France and Italy		70,000
Soviet Union		900,000
(including Latvia, Estonia and Lithuania)		
Poland		3,000,000
Yugoslavia		60,000
Greece		60,000
Rumania		270,000
Hungary		300,000
Total		5,100,000

These figures are based on those of the American historian, Raul Hilberg, who has extracted them, almost without exception, from SS and Reich Foreign Ministry documents.

Appendix 9

THE MILITARY SITUATION AT THE END OF JANUARY 1945

Appendix 10

BIBLIOGRAPHY

. *Unpublished Sources*

ach-Zelewski, Erich von dem—Public Prosecutor's case for the prosecution, Provincial Court Nuremberg-Fürth—reference AZ. la Js 228/60 dated 11 March 1960.

:st, Werner: Wilhelm Canaris—monograph dated 10 April 1949.

:st, Werner: Joachim von Ribbentrop—monograph dated 6 March 1949.

:st, Werner: Reinhard Heydrich—monograph dated 18 September 1949.

:st, Werner: Reinhard Heydrich—monograph dated 1 October 1949.

:st, Werner: Die deutsche Politik in Dänemark während der letzten 2½ Kriegsjahre—monograph completed on 8 June 1960.

:st, Werner: Die deutsche Abwehrpolizei bis 1945.

:st, Werner: Erinnerungen aus dem besetzten Frankreich 1940–1942—monograph of summer 1951.

ackelmann, Heinrich: Prinz Hohenlohe.

ackelmann, Heinrich: Die SS und die geplante Entführung Hitlers.

:r Adel im deutschen Offizierkorps—statistical survey compiled by the Bundesarchiv, Zentralnachweisstelle, Kornelimünster, April 1966.

ary of the German Embassy Madrid 1941–1945.

illmann, Eugen: Die Kapitulation von Caserta 29 April 1945—supplement by General Hans Röttiger, Frankfurt 1953.

illmann, Eugen: Die Kapitulation der deutschen Italien-Armee im Frühjahr 1945, Parts I and II, undated.

illmann, Eugen: Wie Italien vor dem Bolschewismus gerettet wurde, undated.

Files of the Personal Staff of the "Reichsführer-SS and Chief
the German Police," on microfilm in the National Archive
Washington (Group T-175)—referred to as "RFSS Microfilm."

Files of the Central Archives of the NSDAP, on microfilm in th
Hoover Institution on War, Revolution and Peace, Stanford Un
versity—referred to as "Central Archives."

Files of the Berlin Document Centre, on microfilm in the Nation
Archives, Washington (Groups 580, 611)—referred to as "BD
Microfilm."

Files of the cases against Josef Dietrich and Michael Lippert befo
Provincial Court I Munich 1956/57.

Files of Amt VI of the RSHA—in the papers of the Soviet historia
Lev A. Bezymenski, Moscow.

Hohenlohe, Prince Max-Egon—private papers.

Interim judgement in case of Gunter d'Alquen 25 July 1955. D
Nazification Board, Berlin.

Kater, Michael P: Der "Freundeskreis Himmler" 1933–1945—submi
sion, Heidelberg 1964.

Memorandum (anonymous) from SS Prisoner of War Camp su
mitted to Nuremberg Tribunal, dated 16 December 1945.

von Mildenstein, Leopold: Memorandum 24 April 1961.

Schaeffer, Dr Walter—private papers.

Wulf, Josef: Die SS.

II. Published Sources

Absolon, Rudolf: Wehrgesetz und Wehrdienst 1935–1945. Das Pe
sonalwesen in der Wehrmacht, Harald Boldt Verlag, Boppard a
Rhein, 1960.

Boberach, Heinz: Meldungen aus dem Reich (Excerpts from th
SD's secret situation reports 1939–44), Hermann Luchterha
Verlag, Neuwied & Berlin 1965.

Degener, Herrmann A L: Degener's Wer ist's? Verlag Herrma
Degener, Berlin 1935.

Das Deutsche Führerlexikon 1934/35, Verlagsanstalt Otto Stollber
Berlin 1934.

Die Verfolgung nationalsozialistischer Straftaten im Gebiet d
Bundesrepublik Deutschland seit 1945—issued by the Federal Ge
man Ministry of Justice, July 1964.

Dienstaltersliste der Schutzstaffel der NSDAP (SS Seniority List)
at 1 October 1934, Buchdruckerei Birkner sponsored by Herm
Munich 1934.

Dienstaltersliste der SS—as at 1 July 1935, Reichsdruckerei, Ber
1935.

Dienstaltersliste der SS—as at 9 November 1944, Reichsdrucker
Berlin 1944.

ienstalersliste der Waffen-SS, SS-Obergruppenführer to SS-Hauptsturmführer—as at 1 July 1944.

ichmann, Adolf: Record of interrogation by the Israeli police,
six Vols.

enealogisches Handbuch des Adels, C. A. Starke Verlag, Limburg
a.d. Lahn.

istorische Kommission des Reichsführers-SS: Die Erhebung der
österreichischen Nationalsozialisten im Juli 1934, Europa Verlag,
Vienna, Frankfurt, Zurich 1965.

Iorkenbach, Cuno: Das Deutsche Reich von 1918 bis heute, Vols 1–3
Verlag für Presse, Wirtschaft und Politik, Berlin 1930–33; Vol 4,
Presse- und Wirtschaftsverlag, Berlin 1935.

eiber, Helmut: Hitlers Lagebesprechungen. Die Protokollfragmente
seiner militärischen Konferenzen 1942–45, Deutsche Verlags-Anstalt
Stuttgart 1962.

nstitut für Zeitgeschichte—submissions, Selbstverlag des Instituts
für Zeitgeschichte, Munich 1958.

nternational Military Tribunal (referred to as IMT) Record of the
Nuremberg Trials 14 November 1945–1 October 1946, 42 Vols,
H.M.S.O. 1947–1949.

acobsen, Hans-Adolf: 1939–1945. Der Zweite Weltkrieg in Chronik
und Dokumenten, Wehr und Wissen Verlagsgesellschaft, Darmstadt 1961.

ietmann, K-G: Die Waffen-SS. Eine Dokumentation, Verlag "Der
Freiwillige," Osnabrück 1965.

altenbrunner, Ernst: Spiegelbild einer Verschwörung—the Kaltenbrunner reports to Bormann and Hitler on the coup of 20 July
1944. Secret documents from the former RSHA, edited by Archiv
Peter für historische und zeitgeschichtliche Dokumentation, Seewald Verlag, Stuttgart 1961.

eesing's Contemporary Archives 1931–1945.

eilig, Wolf: Das deutsche Heer 1939–1945. Gliederung, Einsatz,
Stellenbesetzung. 3 Vols, Verlag Hans-Henning Podzun, Bad
Nauheim (year not given).

rätschmer, Ernst-Günther: Die Ritterkreuzträger der Waffen-SS,
Plesse-Verlag, Göttingen 1957.

urawski, Erich: Der deutsche Wehrmachtbericht 1939–1945. Ein
Beitrag zur Untersuchung der geistigen Kriegführung. 2nd edition.
Harald Boldt Verlag, Boppard am Rhein 1962.

berkommando der Wehrmacht. Die Berichte des Oberkommandos
der Wehrmacht 1 September 1939–31 December 1940, Wiking
Verlag, Berlin 1941.

KW (as above) Reports 1 January–31 December 1941, Wiking
Verlag Berlin 1942.

rganisationsbuch der NSDAP issued by the Reichsorganisations-
leiter of the NSDAP, 5th impression, Zentralverlag der NSDAP,
Franz Eher II, Munich 1938.

Picker H: *Hitlers Tischgespräche im Führerhauptquartier 1941*
1942, Seewald Verlag, Stuttgart 1963; *Hitler's Table Talks*, Introduction by Professor H. R. Trevor-Roper, translated by Norman
Cameron and R. H. Stevens, Weidenfeld & Nicolson, London
1953.

Reichsführer-SS: *Dich ruft die SS*, Verlag Hermann Hillger, Berlin
Grünewald & Leipzig 1943.

Schnabel, Reimund: *Macht ohne Moral. Eine Dokumentation über*
die SS, Röderbergverlag, Frankfurt 1957.

Schulthess' *Europäischer Geschichtskalender*, issued by Ulrich
Thürauf Vol 75 1934, C. H. Beck'sche Verlagsbuchhandlung
Munich 1935.

SS im Einsatz. Eine Dokumentation über die Verbrechen der SS
Kongress-Verlag, East Berlin 1957.

Allgemeines Liederbuch der SS (SS Song Book), Ostenddruckerei
Frankfurt (year not given).

Unsere Ehre heisst Treue. War diary of Reichsführer-SS Operational
staff. Activity reports of 1 and 2 SS Infantry Brigades, 1 SS Cavalry
Brigade and SS Sonderkommandos, Europa Verlag, Vienna, Frankfurt, Zurich 1965.

Volz, Hans: *Daten der Geschichte der NSDAP*, Verlag A. G. Ploetz
Berlin & Leipzig 1935.

Wer leitet? Die Männer der Wirtschaft und der einschlägigen Ver-
waltung einschliesslich Adressbuch der Direktoren und Aufsichts-
räte 1941/42, Spezialarchiv der deutschen Wirtschaft, Verlag
Hoppenstedt & Co, Berlin 1942.

"Urkunden zur Judenpolitik des Dritten Reiches, Dokumente zur
Reichskristallnacht,"—in *Das Parlament* No 54, 1954.

Wolff, Karl: Case for the prosecution against—Provincial Court
Munich II—reference 10a Js 39/60.

III. *Theses*

Aronson, Shlomo: "Heydrich und die Anfänge des SD und der
Gestapo 1931–1935." Inaugural Dissertation of Faculty of Philosophy in the Free University of Berlin, Berlin 1966.

Knoebel, Edgar Erwin: "Racial Illusion and Military Necessity:
Study of SS Political Objectives in occupied Belgium." Thesis
submitted to the Faculty of the Graduate School of the University
of Colorado 1965.

Lamm, Hans: "Uber die innere und äussere Entwicklung des deut-
schen Judentums im Dritten Reich." Inaugural Dissertation
Faculty of Philosophy in the Friedrich-Alexander University
Erlangen 1951.

Schweder, Alfred: "Politische Polizei—Wesen und Begriff der
politischen Polizei im Metternichschen System, in der Weimarer
Republik und im nationalsozialistischen Staat." Inaugural disser-

tion for the Doctorate of Law in the Faculty of Law and Economics, University of Rostock, Carl Heymanns Verlag, Berlin 1937.

IV. Books

Abshagen, Karl Heinz: *Canaris, Patriot und Weltbürger*, Union
Deutsche Verlagsanstalt, Stuttgart 1950.

Adler, H. G.: *Theresienstadt 1941–1945*, J. C. B. Mohr (Paul Siebeck),
Tübingen 1955.

d'Alquen, Gunter: *Auf Hieb und Stich*, Zentralverlag der NSDAP,
Franz Eher II GmbH, Berlin & Munich 1937.

d'Alquen, Gunter: *Die SS. Geschichte, Aufgabe und Organisation
der Schutzstaffel der NSDAP*, Junker & Dünnhaupt Verlag, Berlin
1939.

Andreas-Friedrich, Ruth: *Berlin Underground 1939–1945*, Latimer
House, London 1948.

Anonymous: *Glück und Ende des Nationalsozialisten Bell*, Verlags-
genossenschaft Ausländischer Arbeiter in der USSR, Moscow &
Leningrad 1933.

Arendt, Hannah: *Eichmann in Jerusalem. A report on the Banality
of Evil*, Viking Press, New York 1963.

Arendt, Hannah: *The Origins of Totalitarianism*, Allen & Unwin,
London 1958; *Elemente und Ursprünge totaler Herrschaft*,
Europäische Verlagsanstalt, Frankfurt 1955.

Armstrong, John: *Ukrainian Nationalism 1939–1945*, Columbia University Press, New York 1955.

Aretin, Erwein Freiherr von: *Fritz Michael Gerlich. Ein Märtyrer
unserer Tage*, Verlag Schnell & Steiner, Munich 1949.

Aretin, Erwein Freiherr von: *Krone und Ketten*, Süddeutscher
Verlag, Munich 1955.

Bartz, Karl: *Die Tragödie der deutschen Abwehr*, Pilgram Verlag,
Salzburg 1955.

Bennecke, Heinrich: *Hitler und die SA*, Günter Olzog Verlag,
Munich & Vienna 1962.

Bennecke, Heinrich: *Die Reichswehr und der "Röhm-Putsch,"*
Günter Olzog Verlag, Munich & Vienna 1964.

Benoist-Méchin, Jacques: *Histoire de l'armée allemande*, Albin
Michel Paris 1964–66.

Bernadotte, Count Folke: *The Fall of the Curtain*, Cassell & Co,
London, Toronto, Melbourne & Sydney 1945.

Besgen, Achim: *Der stille Befehl. Medizinalrat Kersten und das
Dritte Reich*, Nymphenburger Verlagshandlung, Munich 1960.

Bezymenski, Lev: *Martin Bormann*, Aurora Verlag, Zurich 1965.

Best, S. Payne: *The Venlo Incident*, Hutchinson & Co, London, New
York, Melbourne, Sydney & Cape Town 1950.

Best, Werner: *Die Deutsche Polizei*, L. C. Wittich Verlag, Darmstadt
1941.

Biss, Andreas: *Der Stopp der Endlösung. Kampfgegen Himmler und Eichmann in Budapest*, Seewald Verlag, Stuttgart 1966.

Bor, Peter: *Gespräche mit Halder*, Limes Verlag, Wiesbaden 1950.

Bouhler, Philipp: *Kampf um Deutschland*, Zentralverlag der NSDAP, Berlin 1939.

Bracher, Karl Dietrich: *Die Auflösung der Weimarer Republik*, 1st edition, Ring-Verlag, Stuttgart & Düsseldorf 1955, 3rd edition Ring-Verlag, Villingen/Schwarzwald 1960.

Bracher, Karl Dietrich; Sauer, Wolfgang; Schulz, Gerhard: *Die nationalsozialistische Machtergreifung*, Westdeutscher Verlag, Köln & Oppladen 1960.

Bross, Werner: *Gespräche mit Hermann Göring während des Nürnberger Prozesses*, Wolff Verlag, Flensburg & Hamburg 1950.

Broszat, Martin: *Nationalsozialistische Polenpolitik 1939-45*, Deutsche Verlagsanstalt, Stuttgart 1961.

Buchheim, Hans; Broszat, Martin; Krausnick, Helmut; Jacobsen, Hans-Adolf: *Anatomie des SS-Staates*, Walter Verlag, Olten & Freiburg im Breisgau 1965; *The Anatomy of the SS State*, translated R. H. Barry, Marian Jackson & Dorothy Long, Collins, London 1968.

Buchheim, Hans: *Glaubenkrise im Dritten Reich*, Deutsche Verlagsanstalt Stuttgart 1953.

Buchheim, Hans: *SS und Polizei im NS-Staat*, Selbstverlag der Studiengesellschaft für Zeitprobleme, Duisdorf nr Bonn 1964.

Buchheim, Hans: *Totalitäre Herrschaft*, Kösel Verlag, Munich 1962

Buchheit, Gert: *Der deutsche Geheimdienst*, List Verlag, Munich 1966.

Bullock, Alan: *Hitler. A Study in Tyranny*, Odhams Press, London 1964.

Burckhardt, Carl J.: *Meine Danziger Mission 1937-1939*, Verlag Georg D. W. Callwey, Munich 1960.

Carell, Paul: *Unternehmen Barbarossa*, Verlag Ullstein, Frankfurt, Berlin & Vienna 1963; *Hitler's War on Russia*, translated by Ewald Osers, Harrap, London, 1940.

Carell, Paul: *Verbrannte Erde*, Verlag Ullstein, Frankfurt, Berlin & Vienna 1966.

Ciano, Count Galeazzo: *Ciano's Diary*, Wm Heinemann, London & Toronto 1947.

Clarke, Comer: *Eichmann. The Man and his Crimes*, Ballantine Books, New York 1960.

Cohen, E: *Human Behaviour in the Concentration Camps*, translated from the Dutch by M. H. Braaksma, W. W. Norton & Co, New York 1953.

Cole, Hubert: *Laval*, Wm Heinemann, London, Melbourne & Toronto 1963.

Colvin, Ian: *Chief of Intelligence*, Victor Gollancz, London 1951.

Crankshaw, Edward: *The Gestapo*, Putnam, London 1956.

Craig, Gordon A: *The Politics of the Prussian Army 1640–1945,* OUP, New York 1964.

Dallin, Alexander: *German Rule in Russia 1941–1945,* Macmillan & Co, New York 1957.

De Felice, Renzo: *Storia degli ebrei italiani sotto il fascismo,* Giulio Einaudi, Turin 1961.

Degrelle, Leon: *Die verlorene Legion,* Veritas Verlag, Stuttgart 1952.

Delarue, Jacques: *Histoire de la Gestapo,* Fayard, Paris 1962; *The History of the Gestapo,* translated Mervyn Savill, Macdonald, London 1964.

Demeter, Karl: *Das deutsche Offizierkorps in Gesellschaft und Staat 1650–1945,* Bernard & Graefe Verlag für Wehrwesen, Frankfurt 1962; *The German Officer Corps,* translated by Angus Malcolm, Weidenfeld & Nicolson, London 1965.

Denne, Ludwig: *Das Danzig-Problem in der deutschen Aussenpolitik 1934–1939,* Ludwig Röhrscheid Verlag, Bonn 1959.

Diels, Rudolf: *Lucifer ante portas,* Deutsche Verlagsanstalt, Stuttgart 1950.

Dixon, C. Aubrey; Heilbrunn, Otto: *Communist Guerrilla Warfare,* Allen & Unwin, London 1954.

Domarus, Max: *Hitler. Reden und Proklamationen 1932–1945,* 4 Vols, Süddeutscher Verlag, Munich 1965.

Dönitz, Karl: *Zehn Jahre und Zwanzig Tage,* Athenäum Verlag, Bonn 1958; *Memoirs, Ten Years and Twenty Days,* translated R. H. Stevens, Weidenfeld & Nicolson, London 1959.

Dornberger, Walter: *V2—Der Schuss ins Weltall,* Bechtle Verlag, Esslingen 1952.

Doussinague, José M.: *España tenia Razon 1939-1945,* Espasa-Calpe S.A., Madrid 1950.

Dulles, Allen: *The Secret Surrender,* Weidenfeld & Nicolson, London 1946.

Dulles, Allen: *Germany's Underground,* Macmillan, New York 1947.

Ehlers, Dieter: *Technik und Moral einer Verschwörung, 20 Juli 1944,* Athenäum Verlag, Frankfurt & Bonn 1964.

Engelmann, Bernt: *Deutschland Report,* Ex-libris Buchhandlung GmbH-Verlag, Berlin 1965.

Fest, Joachim C.: *Das Gesicht des Dritten Reiches,* R. Piper & Co Verlag, Munich 1963.

Foerster, Wolfgang: *Generaloberst Ludwig Beck,* Isar Verlag, Munich 1953.

Foertsch, Hermann: *Schuld und Verhängnis. Die Fritsch-Krise im Frühjahr 1938,* Deutsche Verlagsanstalt, Stuttgart 1951.

Francois-Poncet, André: *The Fateful Years,* translated Jacques Le Clercq, Victor Gollancz, London 1948.

Georg, Enno: *Die wirtschaftlichen Unternehmungen der SS,* Deutsche Verlagsanstalt, Stuttgart 1963.

Gilbert, G. M.: *Nuremberg Diary*, New American Library, New York 1947.

Gilbert, G. M.: *The Psychology of Dictatorship*, Ronald Press Co New York 1950.

Gisevius, Hans-Bernd: *Bis zum bitteren Ende*, Fretz & Wasmuth Verlag, Zurich 1946; *To the Bitter End*, translated Richard & Clara Winstone, Jonathan Cape, London 1948.

Gisevius, Hans-Bernd: *Wo ist Nebe?*, Droemersche Verlagsanstal AG, Zurich 1966.

Glaser, Kurt: *Die Tschechoslowakei*, Athenäum Verlag, Bonn & Frankfurt 1964.

Goebbels, Joseph: *Tagebücher aus den Jahren 1942–43*, Atlantis Verlag, Zurich 1948; *The Goebbels Diaries*, edited and translated Louis P. Lochner, Hamish Hamilton, London 1948.

Gordon, Harold J.: *The Reichswehr and the German Republic*, OUP, London 1947.

Görlitz, Walter, and Quint, Herbert A.: *Adolf Hitler. Eine Biographie*, Steingruben Verlag GmbH, Stuttgart 1952.

Görlitz, Walter: *Generalfeldmarschall Keitel. Verbrecher oder Offizier?* Musterschmidt Verlag, Göttingen, Berlin, Frankfurt 1961

Görlitz, Walter: *Die Waffen-SS*, Arani Verlag GmbH Berlin-Grünewald 1960.

Greiner, Helmuth: *Die Oberste Wehrmachtführung 1939–1943* Limes Verlag, Wiesbaden 1951.

Groppe, Theodor: *Ein Kampf um Recht und Sitte*, Paulinus Verlag Trier 1947.

Guderian, Heinz: *Erinnerungen eines Soldaten*, Kurt Vowinckel Heidelberg 1951; *Panzer Leader*, foreword Sir Basil Liddell Hart translated Constantine Fitzgibbon, Michael Joseph, London 1952

Habas, Bracha: *The Gate Breakers*, Thomas Yoseloff, New York London 1963.

Hagen, Walter: *Die geheime Front*, Nibelungen Verlag, Linz & Vienna 1950.

Haestrup, Jørgen: *Til Landets Bedste*, Gyldendal, Copenhagen 1966.

Hassell, Ulrich von: *Vom anderen Deutschland*, Fischer Bücherei Frankfurt & Hamburg 1964; *The von Hassell Diaries*, Hamish Hamilton, London 1948.

Hausser, Paul: *Soldaten wie andere auch*, Munin Verlag, Osnabrück 1966.

Hausser, Paul: *Waffen-SS im Einsatz*, Plesse Verlag K. W. Schütz Göttingen 1953.

Heiber, Helmut: *Adolf Hitler. Eine Biographie*, Colloquium Verlag Berlin 1960.

Heiber, Helmut: *Walter Frank und sein Reichsinstitut für Geschichte des neuen Deutschlands*, Deutsche Verlagsanstalt, Stuttgart 1967.

Heiden, Konrad: *Geburt des Dritten Reiches,* Europa Verlag AG, Zurich 1934.

Heiden, Konrad: *Geschichte des Nationalsozialismus,* Rowohlt, Berlin 1932.

Helfferich, Emil: *Ein Leben,* Vol 4. Printed as facsimile manuscript by C. L. Mettcker & Sons, Jever 1964.

Henkys, Richard: *Die nationalsozialistischen Gewaltverbrechen,* Kreuz Verlag, Stuttgart & Berlin 1964.

Herzog, Robert: *Die Volksdeutschen in der Waffen-SS,* Institut für Besatzungsfragen, Tübingen, May 1955.

Heusinger, Adolf: *Befehl im Widerstreit,* Rainer Wunderlich Hermann Leinz, Tübingen & Stuttgart 1950.

Hewins, Ralph: *Quisling. Prophet without Honour,* W. H. Allen, London 1965.

Heydrich, Reinhard: *Wandlungen unseres Kampfes,* Verlag Franz Eher II, Munich & Berlin 1935.

Hilberg, Raul: *The Destruction of the European Jews,* Quadrangle Books, Chicago, W. H. Allen, London 1961.

Himmler, Heinrich: *Die Schutzstaffel als antibolschewistische Kampforganisation,* Zentralverlag der NSDAP, Franz Eher II, Munich 1936.

Hirsch, Kurt: *SS, Gestern, heute und . . . ,* Progress Verlag Johann Fladung, Darmstadt 1960.

Hitler, Adolf: *Mein Kampf,* Zentralverlag der NSDAP, Franz Eher II, Munich 1942; translated James Murphy, Hurst & Blackett, London 1939; translated Ralph Manheim, Houghton Mifflin, Boston 1943.

Hoegner, Wilhelm: *Die verratene Republik,* Isar Verlag, Munich 1958.

Höhn, Reinhard: *Arthur Mahraun, der Wegweiser zur Nation,* Schleswig-Holsteinische Verlagsanstalt, Rendsburg 1929.

Hofer, Walther: *Der Nationalsozialismus. Dokumente 1933–1945,* Fischer Bücherei No 172.

Hofmann, Hans Hubert: *Der Hitlerputsch,* Nymphenburger Verlagshandlung, Munich 1961.

Horthy, Nikolaus von: *Ein Leben für Ungarn,* Athenäum Verlag, Bonn 1953.

Hossbach, Friedrich: *Zwischen Wehrmacht und Hitler 1934–1938,* Wolfenbütteler Verlagsanstalt, Wolfenbüttel & Hannover 1949.

Höss, Rudolf: *Kommandant in Auschwitz,* edited Martin Broszat, Deutscher Taschenbuch Verlag, Munich 1965.

Irving, David: *The Mare's Nest,* Wm Kimber, London 1964.

Jäckel, Eberhard: *Frankreich in Hitlers Europa,* Deutsche Verlagsanstalt, Stuttgart 1958.

Jaksch, Wenzel: *Europas Weg nach Potsdam,* Deutsche Verlagsanstalt, Stuttgart 1958.

Jedlicka, Ludwig: *Der 20 Juli 1944 in Österreich,* Verlag Herold, Vienna & Munich 1965.

Jolly, Cyril: *The Vengeance of Private Pooley*, Wm Heinemann London 1956.

de Jong, Louis: *Die deutsche Fünfte Kolonne im Zweiten Weltkrieg* Deutsche Verlagsanstalt, Stuttgart 1959.

Jünger, Ernst: *Der Kampf als inneres Erlebnis*, E. S. Mittler & Son Berlin 1922.

Jünger, Ernst: *Krieg und Krieger*, Junker & Dünnhaupt Verlag Berlin 1930.

"Kameraden bis zum Ende"—History of 4 "DF" SS-Panzergrenadier Regiment 1939-1945, Plesse Verlag, Göttingen 1962.

Kautsky, Benedikt: *Teufel und Verdammte*, Büchergilde Gutenberg, Zurich 1946.

Kempner, Robert M. W.: *Eichmann und Komplizen*, Europa-Verlag AG, Zurich, Stuttgart & Vienna 1961.

Kempner, Robert M. W.: *SS im Kreuzverhör*, Rütten & Loening Verlag, Munich 1964.

Kern, Erich: *Der grosse Rausch*, Verlag Lothar Leberecht, Waiblingen/Württemberg 1948.

Kersten, Felix: *Totenkopf und Treue*, Robert Mölich Verlag, Hamburg 1952; *The Kersten Memoirs 1940–1945*, introduction Professor Trevor-Roper, translated Constantine Fitzgibbon & James Oliver, Hutchinsons, London 1956.

Kessel, Joseph: *The Man with Miraculous Hands*, introduction Professor Trevor-Roper, translated from the French Helen Weaver & Leo Raditsa, Farrar, Straus & Cudahy, New York 1961.

Kesselring, Albert: *Gedanken zum Zweiten Weltkrieg*, Athenäum Verlag, Bonn 1955.

Kesselring, Albert: *Soldat bis zum letzten Tag*, Athenäum Verlag Bonn 1953; *Memoirs*, translated Lynton Hudson, Wm Kimber London 1953.

Kielmansegg, Adolf Graf von: *Der Fritschprozess 1938*, Hoffmann & Campe Verlag, Hamburg 1949.

Kimche, Jon: *General Guisans Zweifrontenkreig*, Verlag Ullstein Berlin, Frankfurt, Vienna 1962.

Kimche, Jon & David: *The Secret Roads*, Secker & Warburg, London 1955.

Kleist, Peter: *Zwischen Hitler und Stalin 1939–1945*, Athenäum Verlag, Bonn 1950.

Kochan, Lionel: *Pogrom. 10 November 1938*, André Deutsch, London 1957.

Koehl, Robert L.: *RKFVD: German Resettlement and Population Policy 1939–1945*, Harvard University Press, Cambridge, USA 1957.

Kogon, Eugen: *Der SS-Staat*, 1st 100,000 Verlag des Druckhauses Tempelhof, Berlin 1947; 211,000—224,000 Europäische Verlagsanstalt, Frankfurt 1965; *The Theory and Practice of Hell*, translated Heinz Norden, Secker & Warburg, London 1950.

Kordt, Erich: *Nicht aus den Akcen*, Union Deutsche Verlagsgesellschaft, Stuttgart 1950.

Kramarz, Joachim: *Claus Graf Stauffenberg*, Bernard & Graefe Verlag für Wehrwesen, Frankfurt 1965; *Stauffenberg, The Life and Death of an Officer*, introduction Professor Trevor-Roper, translated R. H. Barry, André Deutsch, London 1967.

Krannhals, Hanns von: *Der Warschauer Aufstand 1944*, Bernard & Graefe Verlag für Wehrwesen, Frankfurt 1962.

Krebs, Albert: *Fritz-Dietlof Graf von der Schulenburg*, Leibnitz Verlag, Hamburg 1964.

Krebs, Albert: *Tendenzen und Gestalten der NSDAP*, Deutsche Verlagsanstalt, Stuttgart 1959.

Langbein, Hermann: *Im Namen des deutschen Volkes*, Europa Verlag AG, Vienna, Köln, Stuttgart, Zurich 1963.

Langemann, Hans: *Das Attentat*, Kriminalistik, Verlag für kriminalistische Literatur, Hamburg 1956.

Laqueur, Walter Z.: *Young Germany*, introduction R. H. S. Crossman, Routledge & Paul Kegan, London 1962.

Leverkuehn, Paul: *Der geheime Nachrichtendienst der Wehrmacht im Kriege*, Athenäum Verlag, Frankfurt, Bonn 1964.

Liddell Hart, Sir Basil: (editor): *The Red Army*, Weidenfeld & Nicolson, London 1956.

Macdonald, Bruce J. S.: *The Trial of Kurt Meyer*, Clarke Irwin Co, Toronto 1954.

Manvell, Roger, and Fraenkel, Heinrich: *Heinrich Himmler*, Wm Heinemann, London, Melbourne, Toronto, Cape Town, Auckland 1965.

Manstein, Erich von: *Verlorene Siege*, Athenäum Verlag, Bonn 1958; *Lost Victories*, translated A. G. Powell, Methuen, London 1958.

Maser, Werner: *Die Frühgeschichte der NSDAP*, Athenäum Verlag, Frankfurt & Bonn 1965.

Meyer, Kurt: *Grenadiere*, 4th edition, Schild Verlag, Munich-Lochhausen 1965.

Mitscherlich, Alexander; Mielke, Fred: *Das Diktat der Menschenverachtung*, Verlag Lambert Schneider, Heidelberg 1947.

Mitscherlich, Alexander; Mielke, Fred: *Medizin ohne Menschlichkeit*, Fischer Bücherei, Frankfurt & Hamburg 1960.

Möller, Kurt Detlev: *Das letzte Kapitel. Geschichte der Kapitulation Hamburgs*, Hoffmann & Campe Verlag, Hamburg 1947.

Müller-Hillebrand, Burkhart: *Das Heer 1933–1945*, 2 Vols, Verlag E. S. Mittler & Son, Frankfurt 1954–56.

Neufeldt, Hans-Joachim; Huck, Jürgen; Tessin, Georg: *Zur Geschichte der Ordnungspolizei 1936–1945*, printed as manuscript, Koblenz 1957.

Neumann, Franz: *Behemoth. The Structure and Practice of National-Socialism*, Victor Gollancz, London 1943.

Neusüss-Hunkel, Ermenhild: *Die SS*, Norddeutsche Verlagsanstalt, Hannover & Frankfurt 1956.

Orb, Heinrich: *Nationalsozialismus, 13 Jahre Machtrausch*, Verlag Otto Walter, Olten 1945.

Paetel, Karl O.: "The SS" in *The Third Reich* (composite authorship), Weidenfeld & Nicolson, London 1955.

Papen, Franz von: *Der Wahrheit eine Gasse*, Paul List Verlag, Munich 1952; *Memoirs*, translated Brian Connell, André Deutsch, London 1952.

Pechel, Rudolf: *Deutscher Widerstand*, Eugen Rentsch Verlag, Erlenbach Zurich 1947.

Picht, Werner: *Vom Wesen des Krieges und vom Kriegswesen der Deutschen*, Friedrich Vorwerk Verlag, Stuttgart 1952.

Piotrowski, Stanislav: *Hans Franks Tagebuch*, Polnischer Verlag der Wissenschaften, Warsaw 1963.

Poliakov, Leon; Wulf, Josef: *Das Dritte Reich und seine Diener*, Arani Verlags-GmbH, Berlin-Grünewald 1956.

Poliakov, Leon; Wulf, Josef: *Das Dritte Reich und seine Denker*, Arani Verlags-GmbH, Berlin-Grünewald 1959.

Poliakov, Leon; Wulf, Josef: *Das Dritte Reich und die Juden*, Arani Verlags-GmbH, Berlin-Grünewald 1955.

Quinton, René: *Die Stimme des Krieges*, Der graue Verlag, Berlin & Zurich 1936.

Raeder, Erich: *Mein Leben*, 2 Vols, Verlag Fritz Schlichtenmayer, Tübingen 1957; *Struggle for the Sea*, translated E. Fitzgerald, Wm Kimber, London 1959.

Rahn, Rudolf: *Ruheloses Leben*, Diederichs Verlag, Düsseldorf 1949.

Rauschning, Hermann: *Gespräche mit Hitler*, Europa Verlag AG, Zurich, Vienna, New York 1940; *Hitler speaks*, Thornton Butterworth, London 1939.

Reitlinger, Gerald: *The House built on Sand*, Weidenfeld & Nicolson, London 1960.

Reitlinger, Gerald: *The Final Solution*, Valentine Mitchell, London 1953.

Reitlinger, Gerald: *The SS. Alibi of a Nation*, Wm Heinemann, London, Melbourne, Toronto 1956.

Reynolds, Quentin: *Minister of Death. The Eichmann Story*, Viking Press, New York 1960.

Ribbentrop, Joachim von: *Zwischen London und Moskau*, Druffel-Verlag, Leoni am Starnberger See 1961; *The Ribbentrop Memoirs*, introduction Alan Bullock, translated Oliver Watson, Weidenfeld & Nicolson, London 1954.

Ritter, Gerhard: *Carl Goerdeler und die deutsche Widerstandsbewegung*, Deutsche Verlagsanstalt, Stuttgart 1956.

Röhm, Ernst: *Die Geschichte eines Hochverräters*, 3rd edition, Verlag Franz Eher II, Munich 1933.

Röhricht, Edgar; *Pflicht und Gewissen*, W. Kohlhammer Verlag, Stuttgart 1965.

Rosenberg, Alfred: *Letzte Aufzeichnungen*, Plesse Verlag, Göttingen 1955.

Rothfels, Hans: *Die deutsche Opposition gegen Hitler*, Scherpe-Verlag, Krefeld 1949.

Ryan, Cornelius: *The Last Battle*, Simon & Schuster, New York, Collins, London 1966.

Salomon, Ernst von: *Der Fragebogen*, Rohwolt Verlag, Hamburg 1951.

Schallmayer, Wilhelm: *Verrbung und Auslese im Lebenslauf der Völker*, Gustav Fischer Verlag, Jena 1903.

Schellenberg, Walter: *Memoiren*, Verlag für Politik und Wirtschaft, Köln 1956; *The Schellenberg Memoirs*, introduction Alan Bullock, translated Louis Hagen, André Deutsch, London 1961.

Schlabrendorff, Fabian von: *Offiziere gegen Hitler*, edited by Gero von Gaevernitz, Europa Verlag, Zurich 1946; *The Secret War against Hitler*, translated Hilda Simon, Hodder & Stoughton, London 1961.

Schlierbach, Helmut: *Die politische Polizei in Preussen*, Verlag Heinrich & J. Lechte, Emsdetten 1938.

Schmidt, Paul: *Statist auf diplomatische Bühne 1923-45*, Athenäum Verlag, Bonn 1949; *Hitler's Interpreter*, edited R. H. C. Steed, Wm. Heinemann, London, Melbourne, Toronto 1951.

Schorn, Hubert: *Der Richter im Dritten Reich*, Vittorio Klostermann, Frankfurt 1959.

Schramm, Wilhelm von: *Der 20 Juli in Paris*, Kindler & Schiermeyer Verlag, Bad Wörishofen 1953; *Conspiracy among Generals*, translated and edited R. T. Clark, Allen & Unwin, London 1956.

Schulz, Paul: *Meine Erschiessung am 30 Juni 1934*. Private publication 1948.

Schwerin von Krosigk, Lutz Graf: *Es geschah in Deutschland*, Rainer Wunderlich Verlag Hermann Leins, Tübingen & Stuttgart 1951.

Seabury, Paul: *The Wilhelmstrasse*, University of California Press, Berkeley & Los Angeles, Cambridge University Press, London, 1954.

Segin, W.: *Geschichte der Wewelsburg*, Druck u. Verlag P. N. Esser, Büren, Westphalia 1925.

Shepherd, Gordon: *Dollfuss*, Macmillan & Co, London & New York 1961.

Shirer, William L.: *The Rise and Fall of the Third Reich*, Secker & Warburg, London 1961.

Skorzeny, Otto: *Geheimkommando Skorzeny*, Hansa Verlag Josef Toth, Hamburg 1950; *Skorzeny's Special Missions*, Robert Hale, London 1957.

Sommerfeldt, Martin H.: *Ich war dabei*, Drei Quellen Verlag, Darmstadt 1949.

Speidel, Hans: *Invasion 1944*, Rainer Wunderlich Verlag Hermann Leins, Tübingen & Stuttgart 1951; *We defended Normandy*, translated Ian Colvin, Herbert Jenkins, London 1951.

Staff, Ilse: *Justiz im Dritten Reich*, Fischer Bücherei, Feb 1964.

Stein, George H.: *The Waffen-SS*, Cornell University Press, Ithaca, N.Y. 1966.

Steiner, Felix: *Die Armee der Geächteten*, Plesse Verlag, Göttingen 1963.

Steiner, Felix: *von Clausewitz bis Bulganin*, Deutsche Heimat Verlag, Bielefeld 1956.

Steiner, Felix: *Die Freiwilligen*, Plesse Verlag, Göttingen 1958.

Strasser, Otto: *Hitler und ich*, Johannes Asmus Verlag, Constance 1948.

Strauch, Rudi: *Sir Neville Henderson*, Ludwig Röhrscheid Verlag Bonn 1959.

Taylor, Telford: *Final Report to Secretary of the Army*, U.S. Department of Army 1949.

Thorwald, Jürgen: *Das Ende an der Elbe*, Droemersche Verlagsanstalt Th. Knaur II, Munich & Zurich 1965.

Thorwald, Jürgen: *Es begann an der Weichsel*, Steingruben-Verlag Stuttgart 1953.

Thorwald, Jürgen: *Wen sie verderben wollen*, Steingrüben-Verlag Stuttgart 1952.

Tippelskirch, Kurt von: *Geschichte des Zweiten Weltkriegs*, 2nd edition, Athenäum Verlag, Bonn 1956.

Tobias, Fritz: *Der Reichstagsbrand*, G. Groete'sche Verlags-buchhandlung, Rastatt 1962.

Toland, John: *The Last 100 Days*, Random House, New York, Arthur Barker, London 1965.

Trevor-Roper, Prof. H. R.: *The Bormann Letters*, Weidenfeld & Nicolson, London 1954.

Trevor-Roper, Prof. H. R.: *The Last Days of Hitler*, Macmillan & Co, London & New York, 3rd edition 1956.

Vogelsang, Thilo: *Reichswehr, Staat und NSDAP*, Deutsche Verlagsanstalt, Stuttgart 1962.

Vollmer, Bernhard: *Volksopposition im Polizeistaat*, Deutsche Verlagsanstalt, Stuttgart 1957.

Warlimont, Walter: *Im Hauptquartier der deutschen Wehrmacht 1939-1945*, Bernard & Graefe Verlag, Frankfurt 1962; *Inside Hitler's Headquarters*, translated R. H. Barry, Weidenfeld & Nicolson London 1964.

Weizsäcker, Ernst von: *Erinnerungen*, Paul List Verlag, Munich Leipzig & Freiburg 1950.

Westphal, Siegfried: *Heer in Fesseln*, 2nd edition, Athenäum Verlag Bonn 1952; *The German Army in the West*, Cassell & Co, London 1951.

Wheeler-Bennett, Sir John W.: *The Nemesis of Power*, Macmillan London, St. Martin's Press, New York 1953.

Wiesenthal S.: *Grossmufti—Grossagent der Achse*, Ried-Verlag, Salzburg & Vienna 1947.

Wighton, Charles: *Heydrich*, Odhams Press, London 1962.

Wilmot, Chester: *The Struggle for Europe*, Collins, London, Harper Bros, New York 1952.

Wulf, Josef: *Das Dritte Reich und seine Vollstrecker*, Arani Verlags-GmbH, Berlin-Grünewald 1961.

Wulf, Josef: *Heinrich Himmler*, Arani Verlags-GmbH, Berlin-Grünewald, 1960.

Henry A.: *The Case against Adolf Eichmann*: New American Library, New York 1960.

Zeller, Eberhard: *Geist der Freiheit*, Verlag Hermann Rinn, Gotthold Müller Verlag, Munich 1963.

Zipfel, Friedrich: *Gestapo und Sicherheitsdienst*, Arani Verlags-GmbH, Berlin-Grünewald 1960.

Zipfel, Friedrich: *Kirchenkampf in Deutschland 1933–1945*, Walter de Gruyter & Co, Berlin 1965.

V. *Periodicals*

Adler, H. G.: "Selbstverwaltung und Widerstand in den Konzentrationslager der SS"—*Vierteljahrshefte für Zeitgeschichte*, No 3 1960.

Angress, Werner T.; Smith, Bradley F.: "Diaries of Heinrich Himmler's Early Years"—*Journal of Modern History*, No 3 1959.

Auerbach, Helmuth: "Die Einheit Dirlewanger"—*Vierteljahrshefte für Zeitgeschichte*, No 3 1962.

Auerbach, Helmuth: "Eine nationalsozialistische Stimme zum Wiener Putsch vom 25 Juli 1934"—*Vierteljahrshefte für Zeitgeschichte* No 2 1964.

Berger, Gottlob: "Zum Ausbau der Waffen-SS"—*Nation Europa*, No 4 1953.

Best, Werner: "Kritik und Apologie des Juristen"—*Deutsches Recht*, 8/15 April 1939.

Bihl, K.: "Kommandobehörden, Verbände und selbständige Truppenteile der Waffen-SS"—*Feldgrau* Nos 1, 2 & 3 1961, Nos 3 & 4 1963, Nos 1 & 2 1965.

Bihl, K.: "Die Waffen-SS, Allgemeines zur Entstehung und Stellung" —*Feldgrau* Nos 5 & 6 1964.

Bihl, Wolfdieter: "Zur Rechtsstellung der Waffen-SS"—*Wahrwissenschaftliche Rundschau*, No 7 1966.

Broszat, Martin: "Die Anfänge der Berliner NSDAP 1926/27"—*Vierteljahrshefte für Zeitgeschichte*, No 1 1960.

Broszat, Martin: "Zur Perversion der Strafjustiz im Dritten Reich" —*Vierteljahrshefte für Zeitgeschichte*, No 4 1958.

Brown, MacAlister: "The Third Reich's Mobilisation of the German Fifth Column in Eastern Europe"—*Journal of Central European Affairs*, No 2 1959.

Buchheim, Hans: "Die Höheren SS- und Polizeiführer"—*Vierteljahrshefte für Zeitgeschichte,* No 4 1963.

"Das Ende einer Illusion"—*Christ und Welt* 10/17 August 1950.

Davis, Forrest: "The Secret History of a Surrender"—*Saturday Evening Post,* 22/29 September 1945.

Deuerlein, Ernst: "Hitlers Eintritt in die Politik und die Reichswehr"—*Vierteljahrshefte für Zeitgeschichte,* No 2 1959.

Dmytryshyn, Basil: "The Nazis and the SS Volunteer Division 'Galicia,'"—*The American Slavic and East European Review,* No 1 1956.

"T.E.": "Die Rede Himmlers vor den Gauleitern am 3 August 1944" —*Vierteljahrshefte für Zeitgeschichte,* No 4 1953.

Franz, Georg: "Munich; Birthplace and Center of the National-Socialist German Workers Party"—*Journal of Modern History,* No 4 1957.

Goltz, Graf von der: "Die Entlassung des Generalobersten Freiherr von Fritsch"—*Deutsche Rundschau,* No 3 1947.

Graml, Hermann: "Der 9 November 1938"—*Das Parlament* 11 November 1953.

Günther, Joachim: "Die Stufe zum Satanismus"—*Deutsche Rundschau* 1948.

Heiber, Helmut: "Zur Justiz im Dritten Reich. Der Fall Elias"—*Vierteljahrshefte für Zeitgeschichte,* No 4 1955.

Heiber, Helmut: "Aus den Akten des Gauleiters Kube"—*Vierteljahrshefte für Zeitgeschichte,* No 1 1956.

Heiber, Helmut: "Der Generalplan Ost"—*Vierteljahrshefte für Zeitgeschichte,* No 3 1958.

Koehl, Robert: "Toward an SS Typology: Social Engineers"—*American Journal of Economics and Sociology,* No 18, Jan 1959.

Krausnick, Helmut: "Denkschrift über die Behandlung der Fremdvölkischen im Osten"—*Vierteljahrshefte für Zeitgeschichte,* No 4 1957.

Krausnick, Helmut: *Hitler und die Morde in Polen*—Vierteljahrshefte für Zeitgeschichte, No 4 1963.

Krausnick, Helmut: "Wehrmacht und Nationalsozialismus"—*Das Parlament* 9 November 1955.

Lösener, Bernhard: "Als Rassereferent im Reichsministerium des Innern"—*Vierteljahrshefte für Zeitgeschichte,* No 3 1961.

Maier, Hedwig: "Die SS und der 20 Juli"—*Vierteljahrshefte für Zeitgeschichte,* No 3 1966.

Mau, Hermann: "Die 'Zweite Revolution'—der 30 Juni 1934"—*Vierteljahrshefte für Zeitgeschichte,* No 2 1958.

Noack, W. D.: "Sind Führer der Waffen-SS berechtigt Dienstgrade der Wehrmacht zu verwenden?"—*Militärarchiv,* No 7 1965.

Paetel, Karl O.: "Die SS (Geschichte und Soziologie)"—*Vierteljahrshefte für Zeitgeschichte,* No 1 1954.

Plum, Günter: "Staatspolizei und Innere Verwaltung 1934–1936" —*Vierteljahrshefte für Zeitgeschichte,* No 2 1905.

Popplow, Ulrich: "Reinhard Heydrich oder die Aufnordnung durch die Sport"—*Olympisches Feuer*, No 8 1963.

'Prememoria eines bayerischen Richters zu den Juni-Morden 1934"—*Vierteljahrshefte für Zeitgeschichte*, No 1 1957.

Pruck, Erich F.: "Die Rehabilitierung von Kommandeuren der Roten Armee"—*Osteuropa*, No 3 1964.

Reitlinger, Gerald: "The Doubts of Wilhelm Kube"—*Wiener Library Bulletin*, No 5/6 1950.

Rosenberger, Heinrich: "Die Entlassung des Generalobersten Freiherr von Fritsch"—*Deutsche Rundschau*, No 8 1946.

Runzheimer, Jürgen: "Der Uberfall auf den Sender Gleiwitz im Jahre 1939"—*Vierteljahrshefte für Zeitgeschichte*, No 4 1962.

Schneider, Peter: "Rechtssicherheit und richterliche Unabhängigkeit aus der Sicht des SD"—*Vierteljahrshefte für Zeitgeschichte*, No 6 1956.

Seraphim, Hans-Günther: "SS-Verfügungstruppe und Wehrmacht"—*Wehrwissenschaftliche Rundschau*, No 12 1955.

Spalcke, Karl: "Der Fall Tuchatschewski"—*Die Gegenwart*, 25 Jan 1958.

Der Spiegel: "Das Spiel ist aus—Arthur Nebe" 29 September 1949—20 April 1950.

Der Spiegel: "Lady mit Lampenschirm"—16 February 1950.

Der Spiegel: "Der Furcht so fern, dem Tod so nahe"—15 May 1957.

Der Spiegel: "Braver, dummer Klim"—8 November 1961.

Der Spiegel: "Wenn ihr einmarschiert, schiessen wir"—1 May 1963.

Der Spiegel: " 'Grossmutter gestorben.' Interview mit dem ehemaligen SS-Sturmbannführer Alfred Naujocks"—13 November 1963.

'SS-Bericht über den 20 Juli"—*Nordwestdeutsche Hefte*, February 1947.

Thorwald, Jürgen: "Der Mann der den Krieg auslöste"—*Der Stern*, No 23 1953.

Triska, Jan F.: "Work redeems": Concentration-camp Labor and Nazi German Economy"—*Journal of Central European Affairs*, No 1 1959.

Uhlig, Heinrich: "9 November 1938"—*Das Parlament*, 6 November 1963.

Urrisk, Otto R.: "Uber den Begriff der 'Garde' und die Schaffung militärischer 'Eliten' "—*Osterreichische Militärische Zeitschrift*, Nos 2-3 1964.

Wolff, Richard: "Der Reichstagsbrand 1933"—*Das Parlament* 18 January 1956.

VI. Radio and Television Scripts

Lichtenstein, Heiner: "Wo Himmler residieren wollte," West German Radio, Programme 2, 30 January 1965.

Zipfel, Friedrich: "Ein Volk in Waffen. Die SA der NSDAP," Radio Bremen, 6 June 1966.
Kipphardt, Heinar: "Die Geschichte von Joel Brand," German TV, Channel 2.
Panorama: "Das bestellte Attentat," German TV Channel 1, 26 July 1965.

VII: *Standard Newspapers and Periodicals*

Frankfurter Rundschau 1957.
Hamburger Echo 1934.
Münchner Post 1931, 1932.
Das Schwarze Korps 1935–1945.
Völkischer Beobachter 1933–1945.
Die Welt 1955–1967.
Süddeutsche Zeitung 1955–1967.

Index

Abetz, Ambassador Otto, 604
Abwehr, 296–7
  and Gestapo, 547–50
  and SD, 258–60, 551–3
Adam, Lt. General Wilhelm, 112
Adenauer, Konrad, 161
Adler, H.G., 184
Ahlmann, Wilhelm, 581
Albert, Wilhelm, 243
Al Difah, 258
Alexander, Leo, 6
Alvensleben, Ludolf von, 341
Alvensleben, Werner von, 341
Amann, Max, 133, 249, 372
"American Joint Distribution
  Committee", 639–40
American military circles in
  Spain, peace plan discussions,
  591–2, 593, 596
Ampletzer, Albert, 235
Angress, Werner, 41
Anti-criminal campaign, 221–6
Antonescu, General, 327, 328
"Apollo" (students' association),
  40
Arco-Valley, Count, 40, 92
Arendt, Hannah, 9, 432–3, 439,
  464
Armaments, construction of,
  462–3
"Army Group Steiner", 651
"Army Group Vistula", 626–30
Aronson, Shlomo, 189, 199, 243
"Artamans", 53–4
Assault Squad, 22, 27
Auerbach, Hellmuth, 307

Auerbach, Moshe, 392–3, 394
August Wilhelm of Prussia,
  Prince, 117
Auschwitz, 229, 426, 428, 430,
  431, 432, 437, 438, 443, 445,
  636
Austria, 282
  Arrest of Party and Police
  officials in, 602
  German policy re, 302–11
  Hitler's plans for, 278
  Jews in, 383

Bach-Zelewski, Erich von dem,
  64, 138, 357, 411, 418, 615
Baecke, Hermann, 147
Baltic States, autonomy ques-
  tions, 569–70
Bangerskis, Rudolf, 570
Barco, Inge, 42
Bartels, Hermann, 173
Bassewitz-Behr und von Pfeil-
  Burghauss, Count, 153
Bavaria —
  Police policy in, 196–7
  Politics, 17–19, 23–5, 38
Becher, Kurt, 637–42
Beck, Ludwig, 122, 548, 578,
  573–4, 600
Beckerle, Adolf-Heinz, 330
Behrends, Dr. Hermann, 101,
  241, 260, 314
Belgium, Jews of, 445
Bell, Georg, 82–3, 85, 111, 112
Belzec Camp, 425, 426, 430
Beneš, Eduard, 558

Benoist-Méchin, 8
Berchtold, Joseph, 22, 23, 28–9, 61
Berger, Gottlob, 12, 14, 161, 165, 329, 341, 361, 466, 469, 471, 472, 473, 474, 485, 511–14, 515–20, 535–9, 542–5, 565–7, 610, 616
Bergk, Schwarz van, 247
Berliner Arbeiter Zeitung, 69
Bernadotte, Count Folke, 35, 38, 643–4, 651
Bernau, SD school at, 296
Besgen, Achim, 632
Best, Captain S. Payne, 322–4
Best, Dr. Werner, 13–14, 95, 102, 115, 180, 181, 195, 203–4, 215–6, 222, 224, 231, 240–1, 242, 263, 279, 288–90, 291, 330, 451–3, 467, 551, 553, 557, 561–4, 577, 582
Beuthel, Lothar, 337
Bigler, Rolf, 540
Biss, Andreas, 636, 639, 640
Bittrich, Wilhelm, 155, 497, 511, 540, 543, 599, 605–6
Blaskowitz, Colonel-General Johannes, 346–7
Blobel, Paul, 412, 422
Blomberg, Werner von, 107, 109, 119–20, 123–4, 141, 146, 271, 273–4, 276–7, 470, 506, 565
Blume, Dr. Walter, 406
Bluml, May, 36
Bock, Field Marshal von, 336, 579
Boden, Margarete (wife of Himmler), 55–6
Boger, Wilhelm, 431–2
Bohle, Wilhelm, 302, 312
Bohme, Franz, 445, 532
Boineburg-Lengsfeld, General Freiherr von, 604
Bolschwingh, Otto von, 380
Bonhoeffer, Pastor Dietrich, 548–9
Bormann, Gerda, 477–8
Bormann, Martin, 85–6, 133, 156, 237, 472, 474, 475–8, 481, 482–4, 621–5
Bouhler, Philip, 29
Bracht, Werner, 232, 457
Brand, Joel, 635–7, 639
Brand, Walter, 317

Brandenburg, Wilhelm, 609
Brandt, Rudolf, 267, 482, 573, 654
Brauchitsch, Walter Von, 281, 298, 465, 470
Bredow, Ferdinand von, 137
British Government and Jewish Question, 392, 394
Broad, Perry, 432
Broszat, Martin, 230, 339, 344, 439
Brunner, Anton, 445
Buch, Walter, 68, 83–4, 85, 133
Buchenwald, 7, 227, 230, 434–7
Buchheim, Hans, 9, 181
Buchhold, Johannes, 170
Burckel, Josef, 319, 320
Burckhardt, Carl, 34, 184, 188, 390, 555, 585
Butefisch, Dr. Heinrich, 157, 161
Buttner, Walter, 590

Canaris, Erika, 189, 259
Canaris, Wilhelm, 189, 259, 263, 280, 281, 283, 284, 294, 296, 338, 546, 548, 550, 552, 579, 600
Carol of Rumania, King, 328
Cäsar, Dr., 176
Chanti, Ibrahim, 258
Chorin, Dr. Franz, 637–8
Christof, Prince, 153
Cinano, Signora, 155
Cinano, Count, 585
Clages, Otto, 634, 637, 639, 640
Clausen, Fritz, 561
Cohen, Elie, 6
Communist Party, 79
Concentration camps, 225–31, 425, 514, 524
Conti, Dr. Leonardo, 75, 76, 373, 451, 655
Courts martial, 614
Crankshaw, Edward, 8
Crinis, Max de, 645
Czechoslovakia, 335, 554
    General Alois Elias, 455–6
    Heydrich and SS in, 557–60
    Hitler's plans for, 271–2
    Revolt, 616
    Sudeten crisis, 316–7

Dachau, 94, 114, 120, 132, 210, 211, 227–30, 237

Dahlerus, Birger, 301
Dallin, Alexander, 8
d'Alquen, Gunter, 238, 241, 248–53, 569, 573–4, 625
d'Alquen, Rolf, 252
Daluege, Kurt, 69, 72, 76, 77, 78, 88, 100–1, 104, 122, 147, 218, 219, 220, 223, 231–3, 291, 457, 489, 655
Damzog, Ernst, 337
Dannecker, Theodor, 398, 446, 656
Danzeisen, Emil Traugott, 83, 84, 85, 235–6
Darre, Richard Walther, 53–4, 56, 58, 164, 176, 334–5, 353
Das Schwarze Korps, 156–7, 162, 248–53, 371, 476
Degrelle, Leon, 539
Delarue, Jacques, 8
Denk, Dr. Wolfgang, 252
Denmark —
  Danish resistance to SS, 561–3
  Jews in, 451–3
Der Angriff, 77, 249, 373, 572
Der Judenspeigel (The Jewish Mirror), 372
Der Judenstaat, 379
Der Sturmer, 369, 371, 372, 383, 384
Detten, Georg von, 116, 131, 144
Die Aktion, 572
Diebitsch, Karl, 172
Diels, Dr. Rudolf, 96–102, 104, 115, 155, 202, 212, 216, 368
Dietrich, Josef (Sepp), 93, 120, 122, 126–7, 132, 133, 134, 135, 154, 188, 496–7, 499, 501, 520, 530, 540, 541, 597, 598, 605, 649
Dincklage, Major Paul, 71
Dingler, Captain, 296
Dirlewanger, Doctor Oskar, 526, 615
Dobler, Johann, 308
Doerr, Hans, 128
Dohnanyi, Dr. Hans von, 546, 547, 548–9
Dollfuss, 302, 304–9
Dollmann, Dr. Eugen, 646–9
Dornberger, Walter, 35
Doussinague, Jose Maria, 585, 592
Duckwitz, Georg Ferdinand, 452

Duesterberg, Theodor, 108
Dulles, Allen W., 589, 591, 596, 646, 647

East, racial policy in the, 332–366
Eberstein, Friedrich Karl Freiherr von, 64, 120, 191, 386, 388
Ebner, Dr. Gregor, 179, 490
Eden, Anthony, 117
Eher, Franz, 249, 496
"Ehrhardt Brigade", 20, 25, 157–8
Ehrhardt, Captain, 20–2, 26, 79–80, 137
Eichmann, Adolf, 14, 237, 245, 373, 378–84, 391, 392, 396–8, 423, 443, 444, 446, 448, 450, 453, 634, 636–9, 641
Eicke, Theodor, 114, 115, 120, 143–4, 228–31, 440, 514–5, 521, 522, 527–8, 429, 537
Einsatzgruppen, 464, 465, 655–6
  and "Final Solution", 402–18
  and Polish campaign, 336–45
  Structure of, 405–6
  Russian murders, 568
Eirenschmalz, Franz, 459
Eisenlohr, Ernst, 316
Eisner, Kurt, 38, 40, 92
Elias, General Alois, 455–6, 557
Elser, Georg, 325–7
Epp, Ritter von, 18, 25, 45, 87, 132, 141, 197
Equestrian Associations, SS members, 156–7
Ernst, Karl, 82, 116, 122, 127, 137, 248, 268, 269
Esser, Hermann, 67, 79

Falkenhausen, General Alexander von, 445, 466
Falkenhausen, Hans Joachim von, 131, 144
Fegelein, Hermann, 615, 624, 644, 653
Fey, Emil, 308
Fiehler, Karl, 476
"Final Solution", see under Jewish Question
Finland, Jews of, 449–50
Fischer, Dr. Herbert, 337
Flesch, Reinhard, 200–1

Flick, Friedrich, 158
Florian, Albert, 481
Florstedt, Hermann, 437
Foertsch, Hermann, 468
Foreign policy, 301–30
Formis, Rudolf, 257
Forster, Albert, 155, 340–1, 343,
    352, 357, 555, 656
"Four-Year Plan", 349, 375
Franz, Wilhelm, 210
France —
    German discussions with, 109
    Jews of, 444–7
Frank, August, 457
Frank, Carl Hermann, 317
Frank, Dr. Hans, 134, 144, 211,
    213, 214, 343, 344, 348, 359,
    360–6, 374, 397, 471–2, 479,
    481
Frank, Lorenz, 17
Frank, Professor Walther, 266
Frankfurter Zeitung, 151, 247
Franz, Kurt, 431
Frauendorfer, Max, 579
Frauenfeld, Alfred E., 575
Free Corps, The, 16, 19, 25, 38,
    61–5, 69, 72, 153, 180
Freisler, Roland, 212, 479
Freter, Colonel, 428, 429
Frick, Dr. Wilhelm, 87, 91, 93,
    102, 103, 104, 122, 198, 216,
    217, 218, 219, 220, 224, 457
"Friends of the Reichsfuhrer—
    SS", 158–9
Frischauer, Willi, 49
Fritsch, General Freiherr von,
    120, 121, 141, 145, 470, 406
    Scandal, 268–83
Fritzsche, Hans, 483
Frontbann, 25, 65, 69
"Frontier Protection Service
    East", 108–9

Gabcik, Josef, 558–9
Gaevernitz, Gero von, 593, 595
Gas Vans, use of, in extermina-
    tion of Jews, 423–6
Gebhardt, Karl, 606, 654
Geneva Disarmament Confer-
    ence, 109
Gercke, Dr. Achim, 182–3, 373
German Settlement Policy, 335
Germanism, strengthening of,
    349–61

Gerstein, Kurt, 426, 427
Gerstel, Emil, 460
Geschke, Dr. Hans, 456, 618
Gestapo, 103, 104, 110–11, 115,
    136, 137–40, 142, 198–9, 202,
    220, 223–4, 228, 230, 231–2,
    233–5, 241–2
    Abwehr, relations with, 547–50
    Birth of, 95–6
    Card indexes and lists, 207–8
    Concentration camps, 209–14
    and Enemies of the State,
        206–7, 209–18
    Foundations of, 204–6
    Fritsch affair, 279–83
    Functions, 279
    Law, 217–20
    Preventive arrest warrants, 209
    Responsibilities, 259
    and SD, friction between, 255–6
    Stellen (local offices), 208, 215,
        216, 217
    Struggle with military authori-
        ties, 279–92
    Tracking system, 208
Geyr, Freiherr von, 153
Gienanth, Curt Freiherr von,
    428, 429, 430
Gildisch, Kurt, 136, 137
Ginzburg, Pino, 392–3
Gisevius, Hans-Bernd, 100, 280,
    403, 411, 578
Glass, Fridolin, 302–4, 306–8
Gleichen-Russwurm, von, 118
Gleiwitz Radio Station, 294–300,
    301
Globocnik, Odilo, 359–60, 364,
    366, 425, 440, 655
Glucks, Richard, 441, 656
Godde, Walther, 590
Goebbels, Joseph, 28, 36, 67, 68,
    69, 70, 74–5, 87, 89, 91, 126,
    130, 131, 135, 374, 622
    Dismissed by Stennes, 77
    and Jewish Question, 367, 374,
        384–91
    Propaganda methods, 555
    and SD reports, 480–1, 483
    and Viktor Lutze, 471
Goerdeler, Carl, 548, 578, 579,
    594, 600, 609
Goetsch, Werner, 257
Golomb, Eliahu, 392, 393

Goltz, Rudiger Graf von der, 153, 157, 269, 281

Goring, Hermann, 21, 77, 87, 88, 91, 113, 115, 124, 125, 126, 135, 138, 139, 140, 198, 212, 216, 217, 271, 272, 300, 554, 555

Escape after November putsch, 24

"Final Solution", 400

"Four-Year Plan", 349, 353, 375

Fritsch affair, 274–5, 276–7

and Gestapo, 205–6

and Himmler, 111

Jewish question, 368, 387, 389, 391, 397

Police empire, 95–105

and Prince Max-Egon Hohenlohe, 586, 587–8

and Reichswehr/SA affair, 141

Russian campaign, 357

and SA, 111

and State of Emergency, 126

Goring, Ilse, 96

Gottberg, Curt von, 335, 567, 649

Grabner, Maximilian, 438

Graf, Mathias, 405

Graf, Ulrich, 22, 24, 61

Granninger, Peter, 82

Grawitz, Dr. Ernst, 411, 425, 655

Greece, Jews in, 445

Greifelt, Ulrich, 349–50, 351, 353, 354, 356

Greiser, Arthur, 343, 355, 422, 424, 555, 656

Grober, Dr., 151

Gross, Dr. Walther, 374

Gruhl, Erich, 235

Gruhn, Erna, 273

Grund, Werner, 252

Grunewald, Adam, 438

Grzimek, Josef, 296–7, 300

Guderian, General, 34, 601, 615, 621, 622, 627–30

Guntel, Marie, 139

Gunther, Rolf, 426–7

Gunther, von, 642–3

Gurtner, Dr. Franz, 213–6, 278, 455

Haacke, Werner von, 98, 212

Haase, Ludorf, 58, 59, 67

Habicht, Theo, 302, 303–6, 310

Hackmann, Hermann, 437

Hagana, The, 380–1, 392

Hagan, Herbert, 372, 379–82, 384, 392, 393

Hagenau, German divisions at, 626

Halder, Franz, 121, 122, 284, 294

Hallgarten, Wolfgang, 42

Hamburger, Friedrich, 306–7

Handschuch, Hugo, 210

Hassell, Ilse von, 585

Hassell, Ulrich von, 389, 555, 579, 580, 583, 594

Hassler, Friedrich Wilhelm, 429

Hauptamt Orpo, 232–3, 345, 457, 486

Hausser, Paul, 4, 154, 269, 494, 499–502, 503, 507, 510, 515, 533, 540, 580, 597, 598–9

Hayn, Hans, 131, 132, 133

Headquarters Guard, 93, 496

"Headquarters Staff Reichsfuhrer-SS", 526

Heiden, Erhard, 30

Heiden, Konrad, 19, 151

Heines, Edmund, 25, 82, 113, 130, 132, 133–4

Heinrich of Wittelsbach, Prince, 37, 38

Heinrici, Gotthard, 121, 122, 146, 630, 631, 652

Heinsoth, Dr., 81

Heissmeyer, August, 164–5, 196

Held, Dr. Heinrich, 87

Helfferich, Emil, 168

Helldorf, Graf, 25, 64, 273, 274, 578

Hellwig, Ottfried, 296, 298, 299

Henlein, Konrad, 156, 317–8

Herbst, Heinrich, 364

Herf, Eberhard, 411

Herff, Maximilian von, 165, 541

Herzl, Theodor, 379

Hess, Rudolf, 86, 110, 124, 133, 134, 238, 263, 289, 311, 312

Heydebreck, Hans Peter von, 25, 113, 131, 132, 133

Heydrich, Bruno, 182

Heydrich, Ernestine Wilhelmina, 183

Heydrich, Lina, 88, 186–7, 190–1, 199, 558

Heydrich, Reinhard, 1, 88, 95, 101-2
  Assassination and death of, 559-60
  and Bavarian Police Force, 196-8
  Becomes Minister of the Interior, 457-8
  and Canaris, 259, 260, 263
  Character, 183-4, 187
  Childhood, 189
  and Concentration camps, 226, 228, 230-1
  and Das Schwarze Corps, 248-9, 250, 251, 252-3
  Dismissal from Navy, 191
  Driving force of, 193
  and Einsatzgruppen in Poland, 336-7, 338, 341-3
  and "Final Solution", 401-7, 420, 422, 428
  and Fritsch affair, 271, 280, 284
  Genealogy of, 182-3
  and General Alois Elias, 455-6
  and Gestapo, 104, 204-6, 217-8, 220, 255
  Himmler, relations with, 185-8, 193-4
  and Jewish Question, 368, 382, 383, 384, 387-9, 391-4
  Naval career, 189-91
  and Otto Ohlendorf, 267
  and Otto Strasser's "black radio", 257
  Poland, plan for faked incident in, 294-300
  Police, policy re, 194-6, 223-7
  Preventive arrest warrants, 225
  Rohm and Reichswehr/SA problem, 110-1, 112-24
  Rumours, false reports etc., 122-3
  and SD, 193-5, 199-200, 241-3, 257, 258, 286, 287, 322
  and Sicherheitspolizei, 223
  Sport, interest in, 185, 194
  and SS, 80, 164, 192-3, 284-5, 557-60
  Sudeten crisis, 317
  Technologist of government by brute force, 185
  and Tukachevsky affair, 260-3
  and Werner Best, 288-9, 291-2
Hiemer, Ernst, 372, 383

Hierl, Konstantin, 90
Hilberg, Raul, 8
Hildebrandt, Richard, 345-6, 482, 491, 580, 649
Himmler, Ernst, 35
Himmler, Gebhard (brother of Heinrich), 35, 36, 37, 55, 610
Himmler, Gebhard (father of Heinrich), 37
Himmler, Gudrun, 56, 583
Himmler, Heinrich, 2, 3, 32, 92
  Abwehr and SD, 549, 551
  Adulation for Hitler, 49
  Anti-Ribbentrop campaign, 590
  Anti-Slav policy, 52
  Appearance, 34-5
  Army career, 38
  Army Group Vistula, 628-30
  Army Missile Units, 463
  "Artamans", 53-4
  and Attempt to assassinate Hitler, 600, 601
  Background, 35-7
  and Baltic States, 569-70
  and Bavarian Police Force, 195-8
  and Beer drinking, 40
  and Berger, 513
  and Bittrich, 606
  and Blaskowitz, 348
  "Blood and Soil" philosophy, 50-1, 53-4, 60
  and Bormann, 476-8
  and Capitulation of Germany, 651-3
  Career ambitions, 38
  and the Catholic Church, 40-1
  Character, 33-4, 37, 47-8
  Chicken farming, 55-6
  Childhood, 37-8
  and Concentration camps, 214-5, 226-31
  and Count Arco-Valley, 92
  Courts martial, 613-4
  Cult of ancestors and Germanic tribes, 175
  and Czechoslovakia, 335
  Dachau, 94
  Dancing lessons, 41
  Death of, 655
  and Dietrich, 501-2
  and Duelling, 40
  Eccentricities, 59
  Ehrhardt's Brigade, 157-8

Himmler, Heinrich, (contd)
and Eicke, 523
Enrolls as student of agriculture, 39
and Equestrian Associations, 156–7
and Erich Koch, 474
Extermination campaign against conspirators, 606–9
Family background, 36–7
Farming interests, 39
and Felix Steiner, 502–5, 543–5
and "Final Solution", 401, 410–6, 418, 422, 424–5, 428, 432–4, 436, 438, 441, 449–51
Foreign policy, 301–2, 313, 314, 315
Free Corps, 38
Fritsch scandal, 271, 280, 281, 282, 283
and Georg Elser, 326, 327
German occupation policy, 576
Gestapo law, 217–20
Gottlob Berger, 512
and Gunter d'Alquen, 249
Hagenau, German divisions at, 626
Health, 39
and Hedwig Potthast, 476–8
Heydrich, relations with, 186–8, 193–4
Hitler, relations with, 294, 554–5
HSSPF, 345–6, 486
Interest in history, legend and paganism, 174–5
and Japanese ambassador, Berlin, 320
and Jewish Question, 42, 52, 367–8, 378, 382, 387–8, 389, 390–1, 634–43
Joins "Apollo", 40
and King Heinrich I Memorial Foundation, 174
and Kurt Daluege, 88
Kyffhauser leaders, 157
Lack of self-confidence, 47–8
Learns Russian, 48
Lebensborn, 179, 355
Loss of power, 630–1
and Lutze, 471, 472
and Maja Loritz, 39, 41, 42, 45
Marriage, 55; breakdown, 56

Meets and marries Margarete Boden, 55
Member of National-Socialist Freedom Movement, 46–7
Member of NSDAP, 48
Military career, 38–9, 42
"National Socialist People's Army", 612–5
National Socialist police work, 94
Nordic-Germanic policy, 564
November putsch, 44–6
Objects to brother's engagement to Paula Stolze, 36
Occultism, 175
and Otto Ohlendorf, 267–8, 478
Passes agricultural exams, 43
Peace plan proposals, 583–5, 592–5, 596, 631
Peasant policy, 50–4, 334, 349
Police policy, 217–20
Political ideas, 42
Posts held —
  Acting Police President of Munich, 88–9
  C-in-C, Upper Rhine, 623
  Head of Security in the Brown House, 80
  Head of SS, 56
Promotion in Party Hierarchy, 50
Racial policy in the East, 332–5, 336–8, 345–6
and "Reichskriegsflagge", 43–5
and Reichstag elections, 47
Reports to Hitler, 80
and Richard Korherr, 490–1
and Rohm, 43–5
Rohm and Reichswehr/SA problem, 110, 111
Russian campaign, 357
Russian Liberation Army proposal, 572–4
and Schellenberg, 551
and SD, 264, 291, 482–5
  functions, 329–30
  in Holland, 324
  terms of reference, 246–7
and SS, 78–80, 150, 151, 466, 467, 469–70, 475, 579
  Anti-Church programme, 178–9
  Financial support from the business world, 158–9
  Head of SS, 59–60

Himmler, Heinrich, (contd)
and SS,
  Homosexuality within ranks
    of, 162
  Honorary members, 155–6
  Insignia, 171
  Marriage rules for members,
    177
  Members and Jewish blood,
    162–3
  "Nordic" types, 166–7
  Order reminiscent of Jesuits,
    164
  Policy of neo-paganism, 176–8
  Recruitment, 152–3, 155–6
  "Sponsoring members", 159–
    60
  Temporary halt to recruitment,
    161
  Units, 94
State Protection Corps, 285
Strengthening of Germanism,
  350–61
Third Reich, 87, 88, 90, 91
Ukrainians and Russians,
  568–71
Verfugungstruppe, 510
Waffen-SS, 516, 519, 524–6,
  538–9, 541–5
Warns Hitler of assassination
  plot, 92
Warsaw revolt, 615–6
Wewelsburg Castle, 172–3
and WVHA, 458–60
Youth of, 41–2
Himmler, Konrad, 94
Himmler, Margarete, 35, 55–6,
  186
Hindenburg, Field Marshal von,
  117, 118, 141, 145
Hirszfeld, Professor Ludwik, 431
Hitler, Adolf —
  Assassination plots, 92, 599–601
  Attends Josef Terboven's wed-
    ding, 124–5
  Austria, policy re, 282, 303,
    304–5, 310
  Concentration camps, 214
  Czechoslovakia, 318, 319, 335
  and Danish Jews, 451–2
  Death of, 653
  Decision to go to war, 293–5
  Disbands War Ministry, 277
  "Final Solution", 400, 401, 449

Foreign policy, 316–7
Forms body guard, 22, 23
Fritsch affair, 270–1, 275–9,
  282
and Goebbels, 70
and Gottlob Berger, 513
and Guderian, 629–30
Health, 585
Himmler, relations with, 49–50,
  554, 607
and Hindenburg, 118
Imprisonment in Landsberg, 24
and Jewish Question, 368–9,
  387, 389
and Josef (Sepp) Dietrich,
  496–7, 649
and Karl Wolff, 648
Kidnap plan, 596
and Leibstandarte, 497–8
Military plans, 271–2
Norway, 566
November putsch, 23–4, 44–6
and NSDAP, 20, 48
and Otto Skorzeny, 616–7
Polish Question, 335–8, 339,
  340
Political position, 67–70
Relations with his military advisers, 272, 274–7
Release from Landsberg prison,
  48
and von Ribbentrop, 314–5
Rise of, 16–7
and Röhm, 20, 25, 80–1,
  109–10, 113–4, 115–20,
  123–34, 141, 144
and Rumania, 327–8, 329
and Russia, 357, 572
and SA, 21, 28–9, 70, 71–7
and SS, 26, 28, 65–6, 77–8,
  553–6, 577, 649
and Steiner, 651–2
Totalitarian State, 89–92
and Verfungstruppe, 506–7
and Waffen–SS, 516–7
Hochlinden Customs Post, 294,
  295, 298, 300
Hoepner, Erich, 521, 605
Hoffmann, Joachim, 212
Höfle, Hermann, 45, 116, 440,
  543
Hohberg, Dr. Hans, 14, 462
Hohberg und Buchwald, Anton
  Freiherr von, 138, 156

Hohenlohe-Langenburg, Prince Max-Egon, 586–9
Hohenzollern-Emden, Prinz von, 153
Höhere SS-und Polizeifuhrer-Senior SS and Police Commanders (HSSPF), 2, 332, 345–6, 354, 361, 362, 366, 410, 418, 419, 428, 429, 465, 467, 468, 469, 471, 473, 486–9, 539, 566, 580, 602, 612, 613, 617, 621, 655, 656
Höhn, Professor Reinhard, 154, 224, 240–1, 243, 264–7, 373, 554, 555, 582, 587
Holland —
 Jews of, 444
 SD work in, 322–4
Holtschmidt, Emil, 434–5
Höppner, Heinz, 248
Horn, Karl, 83, 84, 85
Horn, Dr. Max, 443
Horthy, Admiral Nikolaus, 617–20
Höss, Rudolf, 53, 229, 428, 437, 438, 439, 440, 443, 655
Hossbach, Friedrich, 34, 271, 274–6, 281, 283
HSSPF see Hoehere SS—und Polizeifuhrer
Hoven, Dr. Waldemar, 436
Huber, Franz Josef, 95, 200, 201, 234, 242, 279, 327
Humann-Heinhofen, Rolf von, 315
Hungary, operation in, 617–20

Illustrierte Beobachter, 30
Italian Army and Jewish Question, 446–8

Jacob, Fritz, 413
Jager, Karl, 405
Jagow, Dietrich von, 330
Jahnke, Erich, 260
Jeckeln, Friedrich, 410, 418, 489, 566–7, 655
Jena, Leo von, 487, 541
Jessen, Jens Peter, 240, 581, 593
Jewish Question, 3–4, 67–8, 367–99
 "Final Solution", 367, 368, 396, 400–453
 Himmler's policy, 51–2, 163

Jewish Rescue Operation, 633–44
 Madagascar, question of shipping Jews to, 398
 Palestine, emigration to, 375–82, 392–4
 Upper Silesia, Jews, deportation to Poland, 342
Jodl, General Alfred, 227, 280, 400, 652
Joel, Gunther, 98, 212
Jordan, Rudolf, 182
Jost, Heinz, 101, 244, 258, 290, 296, 404, 551
Judische Rundschau, 375, 376
Jungblut, Lily, 341
Junger, Ernst, 62, 180, 203
Juristische Wochenschrift, 215
Juttner, Hans, 165, 22–3, 537, 541
Juttner, Max, 113, 130, 141

Kaduk, Oswald, 431
Kahr, Gustav Ritter von, 23, 24, 25, 44, 45, 131
Kallenbach, Hans, 236
Kaltenbrunner, Ernst, 202, 490, 577, 601, 608, 613–4, 619, 624–5, 637, 642, 643, 647–8, 649, 655
Kaminski, Bronislav, 615
Kammler, Hans, 461–3
Kanstein, Paul, 578–9, 608
Kappler, Herbert, 449
Kasbach, Edith, 257
Kasche, Siegfried, 140, 330
Kasner, Max, 431
Kastner, Rezso, 635–7, 639
Katz, Dr. Delwin, 211
Kautsky, Benedikt, 229
Keitel, General Wilhelm, 273, 276, 277, 278, 284, 298, 338, 344, 346, 429, 430, 552, 614, 625, 649
Kempf, Werner, 510
Kempner, Robert, 575
Kenstler, Georg, 53
Keppler, Wilhelm, 158, 318, 319, 320
Kernmayr, Eric, 4, 617, 620, 657
Kersten, Felix, 13, 49, 51, 150, 175, 186, 194, 358, 367–8, 414, 449–50, 482–3, 584, 585,

593, 606, 620, 631–4, 642, 643–4, 650, 651
Kesselring, Field Marshal, 494, 647
Khan, Hafiz, 388
Kiesel, Dr. Georg, 467
Kieser, Walther, 589
Killinger, Manfred Freiherr von, 20, 71, 77, 131, 330
King Heinrich I Memorial Foundation, 174
Kircher, Rudolf, 247
Kistler, Robert, 41, 47
Klausener, Dr. Erich, 136
Kleikamp, Gustav, 190–1
Kleist, Ewald von, 121, 122, 469, 520, 541
Klintzsch, Johann Ulrich, 20
Klotz, Dr. Helmut, 82
Kluke, Paul, 564
Knipp, Hans, 41
Knochen, Dr. Helmut, 241, 446, 447, 450, 465, 603
Koch, Erich, 217, 344, 353, 357, 473–4, 621–2
Koch, Karl, 435–8
Koch, Paul, 251
Koch, Dr. Robert, 130, 133, 134, 135, 143–4
Kodré, Heinrich, 602–3
Koehl, Robert L., 89–90, 360
Kogon, Eugen, 5–6, 227
Kohler, Hans, 305
Koppe, Wilhelm, 346
Kordt, Erich, 315
Korherr, Dr. Richard, 14, 490–1
Körner, Paul, 125
Korsemann, Gerret, 410, 469
Kranefuss, Fritz, 158–9, 586
Krannhals, Hanns von, 430
Krausnich, Helmut, 347, 400
Krausser, Ritter von, 123, 130–1, 134, 144
Krebs, Albert, 33–4, 64, 652
Kriminalpolizei (KRIPO), 221, 222, 223–4, 230, 232, 233, 234, 325, 326, 405
Krosigk, Schwerin von, 116, 180, 620, 650, 654
Kruger, Friedrich-Wilhelm, 12, 64, 77, 108, 112, 346, 361–2, 364, 366, 428, 429, 434, 471–2, 487, 512, 655

Kube, Wilhelm, 13, 419–22
Kubis, Jan, 558–9
Kulmhof Camp, 423–5, 430
Kumm, Otto, 527
Kunstler, Karl, 438
Kursell, Otto von, 312
Kyhausser leaders, SS members, 157

Lamm, Hans, 376, 377
Lammerding, Heinz, 627, 630
Langbehn, Dr. Carl, 582, 586, 593–6, 600
Lange, Commander, 423, 424, 425
Lasch, Dr. Karl, 363
Latvia, 567
Lautz, Ernst, 455
Laval, Pierre, 446
Lawrence, T.E., 61
Lawyers and Bureaucrats, work against Gestapo, 210–7
Lebensborn, 179, 355, 490
Leibstandarte, 94, 120, 125, 127, 136, 163, 496–7, 510, 515, 516, 520, 523, 527, 528
Lettow, Paul, 500
Ley, Robert, 91, 264
Likus, Rudolf, 315
Lingens-Reiner, Dr. Ella, 432
Lippert, Michael, 143, 144
Lobbes, Hans, 234, 325, 578
Lochner, Louis, 297
Lohse, Hinrich, 33, 421, 473
Lorenz, Werner, 312–3, 317–8, 329, 350, 352
Loritz, Anna, 41
Loritz, Hans, 438
Loritz, Maja(Maria), 39, 41, 42, 45
Lörner, Georg, 459, 460
Lörner, Hans, 459
Lösener, Dr. Bernhard, 374, 398, 450–1
Lospinoso, Guido, 448
Lossow, Otto Herman, 23, 24, 44
Lov, Lorenz, 362
Lublin Camp, 425, 426, 437
Ludendorff, Ex-Quarter-Master General, 23, 24, 25, 46
Ludin, Hans, 330, 512
Luther, Martin, 441, 586, 589–90
Lutze, Viktor, 71, 110, 119, 125, 126, 128, 129, 131, 133, 141,

147, 148, 149, 162, 311, 372, 469–72

Maas, Hermann, 297
Madagascar, question of shipping Jews to, 398–9
Maidanek, 430
Massow, Ewald von, 314
Mattoni, Grun, 460
Mattoni, Heinrich, 460
Maurice, Emil, 22
Mauthausen, 228
May, Dr. Kurt, 460
Mayer, Saly, 640
Mayr, Karl, 16–17, 18, 83, 85
McClellan, Rosewell D., 641
Mecklenburg, Grand Duke of, 153
Mehlhorn, Dr. Herbert, 240, 243, 296, 297, 298–9
Mein Kampf, 373
Meisinger, Josef, 95, 200, 234, 269, 270, 272, 274, 283
Meyer-Heterling, Professor Konrad, 353, 357–8
Meyszner, August, 468
Mildenstein, Edler von, 373, 375, 377, 378, 380
"Mischlinge", the, (Half-Jews), 450–1
Model, Field-Marshal, 527, 543, 606
Moltke, Helmuth James Graf von, 549, 600
Morgen, Dr. Konrad, 434–8
Mossad le Aliyah Bet, 392, 394
Moulin-Eckardt, Leonhardt Graf du, 45, 83, 84, 85
Muller, Curt Hellmuth, 273
Muller, Ernst, 126
Muller, Heinrich, 95, 161, 200–2, 204, 224, 234, 242, 290, 296, 297, 298, 299, 300, 301, 325, 327, 388, 391, 395, 401, 404, 423–4, 436, 546–8, 551, 577, 581, 600, 637, 656
Muller, Josef, 547–8, 549
Muller, Karl Alexander von, 16
Muller, Max, 114
Mumm, Michel, 476
Munchner Post, 74, 82, 85
Munich *Condottieri* 1919, 18

Musy, Dr. Jean-Marie, 642
Muszynski, Brunhilde, 356

"National Revolution" 1933, 87
National-Socialist German Workers Party (NSDAP), 17, 20, 21, 22, 24, 31, 44, 46, 48, 53, 56, 58, 59, 67, 69, 70, 74, 80, 83, 90, 112, 146, 157, 302, 312, 581, 645
National-Socialist Intellectuals and SD, 238–41
National-Socialist Movement, 16–17, 46, 67–9, 89–92
National-Socialist People's Army, 612–5
National-Socialist Shadow Organizations, 90
National-Socialistische Korrespondenz, 124
Nationalsozialist, The, 30
Nationalsozialistische Deutsche Arbeiter Partei, see National Socialist German Workers Party
Nauck, Gerhard, 234, 273
Naujocks, Alfred, 257, 260, 295, 297, 299–300, 324
Naumann, Dr. Werner, 158, 655
Nebe, Arthur, 100–1, 104, 202, 224, 233, 234, 273, 280, 290, 301, 325, 326, 403, 404, 405, 411, 414, 436, 468, 548, 577–8, 585, 602, 607
Neufeldt, Hans-Joachim, 219
Neurath, Freiherr von, 271, 277, 302, 305, 312, 455
Neususs-Hunkel, Dr. Ermenhild, 6
Nordic-Germanic Policy, 564–5
Norway, SS in, 465, 566
Notbann, 25
November Putsch, 23–4, 44–6, 58
NSDAP see National-Socialist German Workers Party

Oberg, Dr. Carl-Albrecht, 64, 467, 468–9, 603, 604
Oberkamp, Ritter von, 532
Oberkommando des Heenis (OKH), 402, 465, 541
Oberkommando der Wehrmacht (OKW), 277, 284, 322, 356,

402, 429, 430, 508, 509, 510, 511, 516, 517, 524, 526, 531, 541, 552, 562, 601, 614
"Official Criminal Law Commission", 214
Ohlendorf, Otto, 5, 11, 14, 154, 237, 240, 253, 264–8, 290, 388, 404, 405, 406, 414–5, 478–81, 490, 492, 577, 581, 582
OKH, see Oberkommando des Heenis
OKW, see Oberkommando der Wehrmacht
Orainienburg, 437
Organizational structure of Nazi regime, 463–4
Oster, Hans, 284, 546, 547, 548, 578, 600

Packebusch, Herbert, 76, 101
Paetel, Karl O., 6, 9, 611
Paget, R. T., 560
Palestine, Jewish emigration to, 375–82, 392–4
Papen, Franz von, 117, 119, 135, 140, 310, 314
Parilli, Baron Luigi, 647
Paris, arrest of SS and Police leaders, 603–4
Patin, August Wilhelm, 40
Patzig, Conrad, 114, 123, 259
Peace, moves for, 582–609
Peasant policy of Heinrich Himmler, 50–4
Pechel, Rudolf, 6
Petri, Leo, 284, 507, 541
Pfeffer von Salomon, Franz, 28, 29, 59, 65, 66, 70, 71, 74, 75
Pfeffer-Wildenbruch, Karl, 515
Pflomm, Karl, 233
Phleps, Arthur, 533, 543
Picht, Werner, 521
Picot, Werner, 315
Piorkowski, Alex, 438
Pitschen Forestry Station, 294, 296
Plaas, Hartmuth, 158, 579
Planck, Erwin, 145–6
Planetta, Otto, 309, 310
Planning Committee for Economic Problems, 158
Pohl, Oswald, 165, 172, 286, 435, 437, 440–1, 442–3, 458–60, 461

Pöhner, Ernst, 18
Poison Pill, The, 372
Poland —
Einsatzgruppen in, 336–45
Industry taken over by SS, 461
Massacre of Jews in, 338–44, 345–8, 423–30, 442
Plan for attack on, 293–300
Racial policy in, 332–3, 335–9
Wehrmacht in, 464
Poliakov, Leon, 368
Politische Bereitschaften, 495, 496, 498, 500, 501, 514
Polkes, Feivel, 258, 380–1, 392
Popitz, Johannes, 593–6, 608
Posthumus, Professor Nicholaas Wilhelmus, 633–4
Post-war period in Germany, 62
Potthast, Hedwig, 476–7
Preventive arrest warrants, 225–6
Prinz, Dr. Joachim, 376
Prisoners of war, barbaric treatment, 529–30
Protocols of Zion, 372
Prussia, police force, 95–105, 198–9, 218, 221, 223–4
Prutzmann, Hans, 410, 473, 655
Putna, Vitaliy, 262

Racial policy in the East, 332–66
Radek, Karl, 262
Rademacher, Franz, 398
Raeder, Admiral Erich, 185, 190, 191, 271
Rasch, Dr. Otto, 296, 404, 405, 411, 414–5
Rasse und Siedlungshauptampt (RuSHA), 164, 166, 169, 176, 177, 333, 354, 356, 357, 491
Rath, Ernest von, 385
Rathenau, 42, 61
Rauschmeier, Mariele, 46
Ravensbruck, 459
Rechenbach, Dr. Horst, 335
Reeder, Eggert, 155, 216–7, 450, 466–7
Reich Police Force, 218–20
Reichenau, Walter von, 107, 108, 110, 114, 121, 123, 124, 140, 145, 348, 417
Reichert, Dr., 258, 380
Reichskommissar fur die Festigung Deutschen Volkstums (RKF), 351–5, 487

"Reichsflagge", 43–6
Reichskriminalpolizeiamt (RKPA), 224, 233, 234, 434–8
Reichssicherheitshauptamt (RSHA), 161, 289–91, 321–5, 329, 337, 351, 395, 402–8, 420, 423, 443, 445, 450, 453, 454–8, 463, 465, 467–8, 491, 493, 494, 532, 546–52, 557, 566, 568, 578, 581, 583, 589, 600, 602, 604, 605, 607, 613, 614, 619, 624–5, 656
Reichstag elections, 47, 74, 102
Reichswehr, 16, 18, 21, 38, 39, 43, 44, 45, 93, 498–9, 500
  and SA, 106–149
  Strength and equipment, 18
Reinecke, Dr. Gunther, 14, 362
Reinefahrt, Heinz, 615
Reinhard, Wilhelm, 157, 622
Reitlinger, Gerald, 5, 183–4
Reitzenstein, Freiherr von, 153
Reschny, Hermann, 71, 305, 306, 310
Ribbentrop Bureau, 90
Ribbentrop, Joachim von, 12, 277, 300, 302, 314–6, 318, 320–3, 327, 328–30, 390, 393, 448, 451, 554, 555, 561, 563, 586, 589–90
Riedweg, Dr. Franz, 565
Riemanns, Hugo, 182
Rintelen, Dr. Anton, 304, 307
RKF, see Reichskommissar fur die Festigung Deutschen Volkstums
RKPA, see Reichskriminalpolizeiamt
Rochling, Dr. Ernst, 605
Rodenbucher, Alfred, 302
Rodërn, Count von, 153
Roeder, Dr. Manfred, 339, 548
Röhm, Captain Ernst, 17, 18, 19, 20, 21, 22, 60
  Anti-Hitler remarks, 110–1
  Arms and equipment, collecting, 19
  Arrest of, 130
  Execution of, 143–4
  Expelled from German Officers Association, 124
  and Frontbann, 25
  Health, 115–6
  and Himmler, 43–5
  and Hitler, 20, 25–6, 64–5
  Homosexual learnings, 81–6
  Imprisonment in Stadelheim, 45
  and November putsch, 24, 25
  Putsch against, 106–49
  Recalled from Bolivia by Hitler, 75
  Reich Minister without Portfolio, 109
  and "Reichskriegsflagge", 44–6
  and SA, 20, 21, 25, 76, 106–7
  and Third Reich, 91
Rommel, Erwin, 580, 598–9
Rosenberg, Alfred, 12, 34, 36, 68, 81, 91, 302, 312, 352, 373, 374, 410, 421, 452, 472, 570
Rosenberg, Dr. Heinrich, 278
Rosenwink, Alois, 28
Rothfels, Hans, 8
Röthke, Heinz, 446, 448, 656
RSHA, see Reichssicherheit-schauptamt
Rumania —
  SD in, 327–8
  SS in, 492, 517–8
Runstedt, General Gerd von, 275, 281, 342–3, 344, 346, 579
RuSHA, see Rasse und Siedlungshauptamt
Russia —
  Hitler decides to attack, 524, 527–8, 540–1
  Jews in, 406–10, 412–20
  Soviet armies' offensive, 626–9
  SD, 260–3
  SS, 357, 567–8, 571
Russian Liberation Army, 571–5
Rust, Bernhard, 91
Rutha, Heinrich, 317

SA, see Sturmableitung
Sack, Dr. Carl, 279, 281
Sahm, Dr., 216
Salomon, Ernst von, 61, 63, 113
Salpeter, Dr. Walter, 154
Salviati, Hans-Viktor Graf von, 156, 579, 608
Sandberger, Martin, 406
Sarre, Marie-Louise ("Puppi"), 580
Sauer, Wolfgang, 70
Schaefer, Dr. Emanuel, 337
Schaeffer, Dr. Walther, 212, 215

Schallermeier, Luitpold, 388
Schallmayer, Wilhelm, 370
Scharfe, Paul, 164, 169, 499
Schellenberg, Walter, 150, 154,
    194, 204, 241, 242, 245, 261,
    262, 280, 287–8, 322–6, 404,
    550–2, 577, 582–6, 588–93,
    596, 600, 608, 641–5, 650, 653
Schiele, Eberhard, 283
Schirach, Baldur von, 90, 386
Schlange, Ernst, 69
Schlegelberger, Franz, 455
Schleicher, Kurt von, 113, 118,
    131, 139–40
Schlierbach, Helmut, 228, 245
Schmid, Wilhelm, 127, 128, 129,
    131, 133
Schmidhuber, Wilhelm, 546–7
Schmidt, Andreas, 328, 329, 485,
    517, 543
Schmidt, Otto, scandal re,
    268–70, 272, 275, 276,
    279, 281, 282, 470
Schmidt, Paul, 368, 371–2
Schmitt, Carl, 215, 265
Schmitt, Gunther, 389
Schmitt, Ludwig, 131
Schneidhuber, August, 66–7, 71,
    127, 129, 132, 133, 134, 135
Scholtz-Klink, Gertrud, 476
Schramm, Ritter von, 604, 605
Schreck, Julius, 22, 26–9, 79,
    126
Schreyer, Karl, 123, 132, 144
Schroder, Kurt Freiherr von,
    158, 159, 161, 590
Schulenburg, Friedrich Graf von
    der, 112
Schulenburg, Fritz-Dietlof Graf
    von der, 545, 579, 580, 608
Schultz, Professor Bruno K.,
    166, 167
Schulz, Erwin, 405, 411
Schulz, Paul, 77, 85, 142–3
Schulz, Robert, 148, 149
Schutzstaffel (SS), 70, 87, 99,
    100, 101, 104, 110, 164, 165,
    244–5
    Action against SA, 75–8,
    131–49
    "Austrian Legion", 302
    Berchtold and command of, 29,
    30
    Birth of, 26, 48

Blue blood in, 153
Catechism, 168
Coats of arms, 172
Code of honour suicide, 170
Corps spirit, 169
Dagger of, 169, 171
Danish resistance, 561–3
Death lists, 115
Death's head signet ring, 171
Departments of, 164–5
Discipline within, 30–1
Education within, 176
Ehrhardt's Brigade, 157–8
Elite of National-Socialist
    Germany, 151, 152
Equestrian Association mem-
    bers, 156–7
Farming community members,
    155
Financial support from industry
    and the business world, 158–9
Firms owned by, 459
Formation of, 16–32
ex-Free Corps men, 63–4, 153
Functions, 31–2, 76, 79–80
Germ of, 22
German resistance, 577–608
Headquarters Guard, 93
Himmler —
    Anti-Church programme,
    177–8
    Becomes Head of, 56
    Extermination campaign
    against conspirators,
    606–9
and Hitler, 553–6, 649
Homosexuality, 161–2
Honorary Commanders, 155–6
Idealogy, 168, 175–6, 178
Independence, 146–7, 169
Insignia, 168, 171
Kurt Daluege as head of, 72
Kyffhauser leaders, 157
Labour Service, candidates'
    term in, 168
Members —
    Duelling, 170
    Jewish blood, 162–3
    Rules re marriage, 177–9
and Military authorities, 464–72
Military exploits, 520–1, 526–7,
    540–1, 597–9
New organisation, 66
"Nordic" types, 166–7

Schutzstaffel (SS), (contd)
in Norway, 465, 566
Novitiates, phases, 167–9
Oath-taking ceremony, 168
Occupation policy, 556–63, 575
Order reminiscent of the
Jesuits, 163–4
Organisation, 78–9, 485–6
and Party leaders, 29–30, 474–5
Police, merger with, 285–6
Policy of neo-paganism, 176–8
Ranks and units, 66
Recruitment, 27–8, 30, 59–61,
152–8, 180–1, 566
Reich Sport Badge, 168
Reichswehr officer corps men,
154
Reichswehr/SA affair, 111–5,
119, 120, 121
Reports, 79–80, 576–7
in Russia, 567–9
Russians and Ukrainians, re-
cruitment of, 570–2
ex-SA men, 65, 66
Sadists in, 432–4
Secret intelligence sections,
79–80
Sponsoring members, 159–60,
179
Status of, 464
Strength, 30, 59
Task of, 67
Temporary halt to recruitment,
161
Uniform, 27, 65–6, 151–2, 316
Units of, 94
Vienna Putsch, 303–10
Wehrmacht, candidates' term
in, 168
Schwarz, Franz Xaver, 29, 157,
161, 286
Schweder, Alfred, 195, 207
Schweitzer-Mjölnir, Hans, 249
SD, see Sicherheitsdienst
Sebekowski, Wilhelm, 317
Selchow, Bogislaw von, 19
Seraphim, Professor Heinrich,
248
Serbia —
Jews of, 444
SS in, 467–8
Seyss-Inquart, Arthur, 444, 465,
656
Shepherd, Gordon, 309

Sicherheitsdienst (SD), 3, 6, 7,
80, 101, 120, 146, 152, 154,
156, 164, 193, 194, 195, 199–
200, 201–2, 224, 235–54, 284–
91, 582–3
Arab-Jew conflict in Palestine,
collection of information, 258
in Budapest, 618–9
Czechoslovakia, 317–20
"Danzeisen", 235–6
Das Schwarze Korps, 251–4
and Elections, 247
Espionage work, 258–63
Economic situation, 286–7
Foreign policy, 314, 320–3, 329
Gestapo, relations with, 255–6
and Heydrich, 194–5
Intellectuals and Jewish Ques-
tion, 371–2
Intelligence, machine of, 244–6
and Jewish Question, 377–83,
393–5
Members of, 237
National-Socialist intellectuals,
238–41
Otto Ohlendorf's work in,
264–8
Otto Strasser's "black radio",
257
and the Party, 479–84
Poland, attack on, 294–300
"Reports from the Reich",
576–7
Responsibilities, 255–6
and Rumania, 328–9
and Sicherheitspolizei, 287–9
and Soviet Union affairs, 260–3
Status and functions, 242, 246–
7, 264–5, 268, 285–6, 290–1
Structure, 242–6
Sudeten crisis, 316–7
Terms of reference, 246–7
Upper middle class members,
154
Sicherheitspolizei, 7, 220, 222–6,
232–3, 285–7, 289, 290, 291,
295, 300, 352, 354, 356, 361,
363, 382, 397, 398, 401, 403,
406, 420, 421, 444, 446, 447,
452, 457, 465, 474, 487, 562,
563, 579, 602, 603, 604
Sidor, Dr. Karel, 319
Siegesmund, Hermann, 81

Silesia, SS, murders in, 138; see also Upper Silesia
Sima, Horia, 328–9
Simonsen, Father Conrado, 596
Six, Franz, 154, 241, 243, 248, 290, 404
Skorzeny, Otto, 616–20, 624–5
Slavs, Himmler's policy, 52
Smith, Bradley, 41
Sobibor Camp, 426, 430
Society for the Promotion and Preservation of German Cultural Monuments, 174
Solf, Hanna, 549
Sommer, Paul, 185
Sommerfeldt, Martin, 118
Sonnenberg, Liebermann von, 100
Soviet Union, see Russia
Spalcke, Karl, 261, 262, 263
Speer, Albert, 172
Speidel, Hans, 598, 605
Spreti, Count, 83, 84, 85
SS, see Schutzstaffel
Stadelheim Prison, 129, 130–1, 134, 141, 143, 498
Stahlecker, Walter, 396, 404, 405, 414, 418, 419
Stallforth, Mr. (American banker), 583
Stapel, Wilhelm, 252
State Protection Corps, 195, 285, 287
Stauffenberg, Schenk Graf von, 146, 550, 599–602, 607
Stein, George, 9, 504, 533
Steinacher, Dr., 313
Steiner, Felix, 4, 114, 155, 494, 502–6, 507, 510, 511, 533, 540, 542, 543–4, 545, 569, 580, 649, 651–2
Stempfle, Father Bernhard, 131
Stennes, Walther, 65, 71, 73, 74, 75, 76, 77, 99
Steppe, Dr. Walther, 211–2
Stetzer, Theodor, 633
Stevens, Major, 323, 324, 325
Stölzle, Paula, 36
Strasser, Gregor, 46, 49, 56, 68, 70, 72, 77, 103, 138, 142, 182
Strasser, Otto, 68, 69, 71, 72, 131, 326; "black radio", 256, 257
Strauch, Dr. Eduard, 419–21

Streckenbach, Bruno, 337, 404, 582
Streicher, Julius, 67, 369, 371, 372, 374, 383, 384
Stuckart, Wilhelm, 450, 451, 453, 555, 582, 608
Stulpnagel, Carl-Heinrich von, 338, 445–6, 465, 468, 604, 605
Sturmableitung (SA), 20, 21, 22, 31, 48, 65, 66, 67, 87, 107, 330
  Action against enemies of the State 1933, 97–8
  Arrests and murder of members of, 127–49
  and Austria, 302, 303, 305, 306, 310
  Becomes illegal organisation, 24
  Berlin Unit, 69, 72–4
  Conspiracy, 71–7
  Criminal elements, 73
  Formation of, 20–1
  ex-Free Corps men, 63
  Goring as head of, 21
  and Hitler, 28–9, 116–7
  Hitler and Röhm, clash over reconstitution, 25–6
  Homosexual element, 80–6
  Independence, 65–6, 71
  Marching columns, 70–1
  New defence organisation (Frontbann) formed from, 25–6
  Oberfuhrer Commands, 71
  Organisation of, 21–2
  as People's Army, 106–7
  Relations with political leadership, 22
  SS, relations with, 469–73
  Strength, 30, 71
  Uniform, 27, 65–6
Sturmer, the, 30
Sudetenland, 316–7, 460
Sudwestdeutscher Beobachter, 30
Suss, Gustav Robert, 183
Swedish Government, Jewish rescue operation, 642–4
Szalasi, Ferenc, 617, 620

Tass, 261
Taubert, Albert, 173
Taubert, Siegfried, 243
Terboven, Josef, 124, 465
Thedieck, Franz, 467
Thierach, Dr. Otto, 455–6

Third Reich, 87–8
Thomas, Dr. Max, 466
Tiso, Josef, 318, 319
Totenkopfverbände, 3, 513–6, 524
Tournelle, Baron Guy de la, 555
Treblinka, 426, 430, 431
Treviranus, Gottfried, 137
Trevor-Roper, Professor, 10, 35, 92, 479, 620, 621, 644
Trummler, Dr. Hans, 296
Tschirschky, Fritz-Gunther von, 135
Tukachevsky, Marshal, 260–3
Tungen, Reichsfreiherr von, 153
Turner, Dr. Harald, 444, 467–8

Uhl, Julius, 83, 111, 130
Ukrainians, recruitment into SS, 570–1
Ulex, General, 348, 470
Ulrich, Curt von, 71
Upper Silesia —
  Heydrich's plans for faked incident in, 294–300
  Jews in, deportation to Poland, 342

Veesenmayer, Edmund, 318, 619, 620
Verfugungstruppe (VT), 154, 159, 495, 498, 499, 500, 501–14
Versailles Treaty, 18
Villain, Dr. Erwin, 137
Vlassov, Andrei Andreivich, 571–5
Vogel, Erich, 213
Vögler, Albert, 158
Volkdeutsche Mittelstelle (VOMI), 312–4, 316, 317, 318, 329, 350, 351, 352, 492
Völkisch Socialism, 67–9, 374–5
Völkischer Beobachter, 27, 28, 30, 115, 118, 144, 241, 248, 300, 374, 385, 612
VOMI, see Volkdeutsche Mittelstelle
Vorwärts, 85
VT, see Verfugungstruppe

"Waadah" (Jewish Rescue Committee, Budapest), 635–42
Waag, Carl Friedrich, 189

Wächter, Dr. Otto Gustav, 304–10, 570–1, 572
Waffen-SS, 3, 487, 493–545, 564, 565, 566, 569, 649
  Armour deficiencies, 533
  Brutalities committed by, 530–2
  Divisions of, 533–4
  Manpower losses, 534
  Military exploits, 533–4
  Picture of, 493–4
  Recruitment, 518–20, 535–8
  Training of recruits, 538–9
  Verfugungstruppe, 495, 498, 499, 500, 501–14
  and Wehrmacht, 541–2
Wagner, Adolf, 127, 134, 211
Wagner, Eduard, 342, 401, 402
Wagner, Ernst, 29, 76
Wagner, Josef, 344, 356, 357
Wagner, Richard, 81
Wahrheiten der Woche, 99
Wäkkerle, Hilmar, 211
Waldecke und Pyrmont, Prince zu, 134, 153
Waldmann, Franz, 508
Waldschmidt, Arnold, 489
Wallenberg, Jakob, 579–80, 592, 608
Walz, Hans, 158
Wannsee Conference, 443–4
Warsaw, revolt in, 615–6
Weber, Christian, 22–3
Wehner, Dr. Bernhard, 560
Wehrmacht, The, 19, 168, 179, 464, 465–6
  and SD, 263–4
  and Verfugungstruppe, 505–7
  and Waffen-SS, 541–2
Weingärtner, Martin, 269–70
Weinrich, Carl, 481
Weizsäcker, Ernst Freiherr von, 155, 315
Wenck, Walter, 629–30
Westdeutscher Beobachter, 30
Westphal, Siegfried, 121, 494
West Prussia, 340–1, 343
Wewelsburg Castle, Himmler's use of, 172–4
Weydenhammer, Dr. Rudolf, 304, 307
Wheeler Bennett, Sir John, 119, 124
White Ruthenia, 567
  Jewish extermination, 419–22

WHVA, see Wirtschafts-und
    Verwaltungshauptamt
Wiedemann, Fritz, 272, 274, 276
Wiedemann, Melitta, 572–3, 575,
    580
Wighton, Charles, 558
Wilhelm of Hesse, Prince, 153
Winkelmann, Dr. Otto, 617–19,
    620
Winkler, Max, 353
Winzer, Paul, 596
Wirth, Christian, 425–8
Wirtschafts-und Verwaltung-
    shauptamt (WVHA), 14,
    435, 440–3, 458–63,
    491–2, 525, 624

Wisliceny, Dieter, 1, 445, 634–5
Witiska, Dr. Josef, 616
Wittje, Kurt, 160, 162, 249
Woermann, Ernst, 315
Wolff, Karl, 64, 159, 164, 327,
    387, 388, 390, 468, 490, 522,
    584, 590, 593, 594–5, 646-9
Woyrsch, Udo von, 64, 126, 138,
    342–3

Ysenburg, Prince zu, 132, 134

Zehnter, Karl, 82
Zeiger, Henry A., 368
Ziegler, Joachim, 580
Zionism, 375–81, 392–3